CENTER FOR HELLENIC STUDIES COLLOQUIA 3

War and Society in the Ancient and Medieval Worlds

War and Society in the Ancient and Medieval Worlds

Asia, The Mediterranean, Europe, and Mesoamerica

EDITED BY

Kurt Raaflaub
&
Nathan Rosenstein

Center for Hellenic Studies
Trustees for Harvard University
WASHINGTON, D.C.

Distributed by Harvard University Press
Cambridge, Massachusetts, and London, England
1999

Photo credits: Cover, Greek vase—Chalkidic amphora, early 6th century BCE, formerly collections Pembroke and Hope (1843-1849), now lost; reproduced from *Monumenti dell'Instituto* 1:51; see Andreas Rumpf (ed.), *Chalkidische Vasen* (Berlin 1927): 9 and Table XII. Cover and p. 61, Samurai-The image of the samurai is in the possession of San No Moru Shō Zō Kan of the Imperial Household Agency; see Moko Shurai Eko-toba in Nihon no Emaki 13, page 34 (Chuokoron-Shinsha, Inc.).

Library of Congress Cataloging-in-Publication Data

War and society in the ancient and medieval worlds: Asia, the Mediterranean, Europe, and Mesoamerica / [Kurt Raaflaub and Nathan Rosenstein, editors].
    p. cm. — (Center for Hellenic Studies colloquia; 3)
    Based on papers presented at a colloquium held June 1996, Center for Hellenic Studies, Washington, D.C.
    Includes bibliographical references (p.) and index.
    ISBN 0–674–00659–3
    1. Military history, Ancient Congresses. 2. Military history, Medieval Congresses. 3. War and society Congresses. 4. War—Social aspects Congresses.
I. Raaflaub, Kurt A. II. Rosenstein, Nathan Stewart. III. Series.
D104.W37 1999
355'.0093—dc21

99–16656
CIP

CONTENTS

◲◲◳◳

Center for Hellenic Studies Colloquia

The Center for Hellenic Studies (CHS), located on a wooded campus in Washington, D.C., is a privately endowed residential research institute affiliated with Harvard University. At its core is a specialized library devoted to ancient Greek literature, history, philosophy, and related fields. Each academic year the Center offers Fellowships to an international group of Hellenists in the earlier stages of their careers, and sponsors, in addition to the annual Colloquium, a summer session for scholars who need ready access to a strong research library.

The CHS colloquia are devoted to examining significant topics that will profit from extended interaction of experts in various fields within and outside of Ancient Greek studies. These projects have a distinctly collaborative character. The organizers first formulate their proposed topic in consultation with the Center's Directors and its academic advisory board of Senior Fellows. They then invite participants to prepare original papers that will address designated aspects of the topic. In addition to those who are writing papers, several experts are invited to contribute to the process as discussants. At the colloquium itself, in the relaxed and intimate atmosphere of the Center, participants present and discuss the papers over the course of five or six days. Each chapter is then rewritten in light of the discussion, again in collaboration with the organizers. The goal is to achieve, at the end of this long process, an integrated volume that will be of interest to specialists and nonspecialists alike.

This volume contains the revised papers of the third CHS colloquium, which was organized by Kurt Raaflaub and Nathan Rosenstein in June 1996. With its broadly comparative approach, it brought together specialists from a wide range of fields, many of whom do not usually interact with one another.

We thank all who have contributed to the process: Nathan Rosenstein for his thoughtful initiatives, generosity in collaboration, energy, and persistence, the Center's Senior Fellows for their support and constructive advice, all participants for their cooperative spirit and intellectual energy, the staff of nSight (in particular Jane Judge Bonassar) for their patience and commitment to realizing this difficult book project, and not least the entire CHS staff, whose support and dedication made the colloquium a practical reality, and who assisted in many ways in the production of this volume. Special thanks are due to our Research Assistant, Heath Martin, whose help was crucial in the final stages of production. We hope that this book will convey to its readers some of the sense of excitement, mutual illumination, and truly interdisciplinary discourse that was experienced by all who participated in our meeting of 1996.

The first volume in the series, *Written Voices, Spoken Signs: Tradition, Peformance, and the Epic Text,* edited by former CHS Fellows Egbert Bakker and Ahuvia Kahane, was published in 1997. The second volume, *Democracy, Empire, and the Arts in Fifth-Century Athens,* edited by ourselves, appeared in December 1998. Subsequent colloquium topics in the series include "Matrices of Genre: Authors, Canons, and Society," organized by Mary Depew and Dirk Obbink; "Ancient Perceptions of Greek Ethnicity," organized by Irad Malkin; and "Plato and Socrates," organized by Julia Annas and Christopher Rowe.

Deborah Boedeker and Kurt Raaflaub
Directors, Center for Hellenic Studies

ONE

Introduction

KURT RAAFLAUB AND NATHAN ROSENSTEIN

The origins of this book lie in a casual conversation between the two editors-to-be at the meeting of the Association of Ancient Historians in Dayton, Ohio, in May 1994: talking about recent courses we had taught, we wondered whether there was a good, modern book on war and society in the ancient world. As discussion ensued, the answer proved to be no. The interaction between military developments in Greece and Rome and their social, cultural, political, and economic contexts so far had not been studied systematically and comparatively, a deficiency we both found puzzling. War pervaded the ancient world, from the clash of the great Bronze Age chariot armies in the Near East at its beginning to the battles that marked the dissolution of the western Empire at its end. Even at times of peace the specter of war haunted men—as Plato makes one of the speakers in his *Laws* say, "What most men call peace is merely an appearance; in reality all cities are by nature in a permanent state of undeclared war against all other cities" (626A). Yet while military narratives and the struggles for power among individuals, cities, and states had long been the stock-in-trade of ancient historians—a practice stretching back to the founders of Western historical tradition, Herodotus and Thucydides—scholars of antiquity had focused rarely and then only selectively on how the experience of war and the needs of military organization affected and were affected by their broader social milieux[1]—a surprising omission in our view, since an understanding of their conjunction also goes back to the roots of Western political theory.[2]

This lack was all the more surprising because the connection is axiomatic in contemporary studies of the history of warfare. No serious scholar in the field today would deny, for example, the critical importance of war's social bases to an

1

analysis of military developments in the West since the Middle Ages. As one has recently written, "Because the Western military style rested upon certain political, social, economic, and cultural foundations, . . . Western states produced particular kinds of military institutions."[3] Indeed, much of the long-standing debate over the "military revolution" in early modern Europe turns on questions of the impact of the changes then taking place in government, commerce, manufacture, science, and technology upon the practice of war, and how alterations in the latter in turn affected them.[4] Most analyses of twentieth-century military history likewise take the connection for granted.[5] Students of the relationship between war and society in the non-Western world can turn to a large and theoretically sophisticated literature on the topic, the work of anthropologists who have long examined the role of war in cultures at comparatively simple levels of institutional organization—tribes, bands, or large villages—or, to a lesser extent, in the states and empires of the New World.[6]

We had every reason to expect, therefore, that such models would have led some ancient historian to produce comprehensive general work on the subject. Yet when we turned to broad studies of warfare in the ancient Mediterranean world, we found that these works all but entirely neglect its social dimensions. Their authors, often writing popular works for a wide readership interested in military history, restrict themselves in the main to such oft-discussed topics as army organization, weapons and armor, strategies, tactics, and battles.[7] While a number of specialized works by scholars in the field have considered particular aspects of the problem,[8] general consideration of the nexus between how wars were fought and their larger social contexts has remained mainly the province of sociologists and political scientists who all too often betray a regrettable lack of familiarity with the specific nature of ancient societies.[9] We concluded that there is a need for a serious, systematic, and comprehensive study of the relationship between war and society in antiquity, and we resolved to meet this need by writing one ourselves.

Unlike many resolutions arising out of casual conversations at conferences, lightly made and quickly forgotten, this one took root later that summer and grew steadily over the next year and a half, evolving from a simple, jointly authored survey to a multiauthored social history of war from the third millennium B.C.E. to the tenth century C.E. in Europe and the Near East, with parallel studies of Mesoamerica and East Asia. We soon became convinced that the themes we were proposing to examine—war and the military in relation to contemporary social, political, and economic structures as well as cultural practices—would require a broadly based and comparative perspective. Social and economic changes often are visible only over the *longue durée;* specific patterns frequently emerge only through a wide-ranging process of collation and juxtaposition. In order to appreciate fully the interaction between the military and nonmilitary spheres and to get a clear sense of both recurring patterns and unique phenomena, we felt it essential to extend the time frame of the work beyond the traditional boundaries of Greco-

Roman antiquity. Consequently, we sought to include developments at the beginning of the period in ancient Egypt and Mesopotamia, as well as to encompass events at its end in Byzantium, the emergent world of Islam, and western Europe in the early Middle Ages. We decided to include pre-Columbian Mesoamerica and ancient and medieval East Asia as well to enhance the comparative dimension by providing analogies and contrasts. Finally, we wanted to set our project in the broader context of theoretical work on war and society in preindustrial society.

We asked specialists in each of these fields to contribute to a collaborative work on the topic geared to an academic readership but written to be accessible to nonspecialists—both scholars in fields other than ancient or medieval history and general readers—and with the potential for classroom use. Each chapter was to meet two requirements: it should offer a broad and informative survey of pertinent developments and constellations in the field and period involved, and it should analyze a few key problems in more depth. In every case, the focus was to be on elucidating the complex reciprocal interactions between war (including military technology, structures, and organization) and social, economic, political, and cultural developments. Actual wars and battles in and of themselves were to receive only limited consideration. We wanted readers to be able to understand in each case how the military sphere was organized, to what extent it was embedded in other structures of society, and what the origins of that system were. Contributors were to identify the key historical events or developments that triggered major social, political, economic, or other changes that in turn had important implications for military developments and vice versa, as well as discuss the most important problems and issues for an understanding of how war and society influenced one another. In addition, we invited Brian Ferguson to give an overview of the theoretical work anthropologists have done concerning war and society and to contribute a chapter on that topic.

In June 1996 the contributors convened for a colloquium at the Center for Hellenic Studies in Washington, D.C. They read and critiqued drafts of one another's chapters and developed through the ensuing discussions a sense of common themes and methodologies that, we hope, provide a greater measure of coherence to a multiauthored volume than might have been the case among authors working independently. We sought, too, the stimulation to reexamine and rethink conventional assumptions and approaches to problems within our own areas that direct contact with scholars grappling with similar problems in very different fields of study always brings. The present volume represents the fruits of the collaboration emerging from that colloquium. The contributor on Bronze Age Mesopotamia regrettably had to withdraw from the project at the last minute, but we were fortunate to secure the participation of Pierre Briant, then in Chicago for a year of study, who contributed a discussion of and ultimately a chapter on the Persian Empire during the Achaemenid era. Several "participants without portfolio" also enriched and enlivened the discussion: George Dennis, Jeffrey Quilter, Brent Shaw, Barry Strauss, and Victor Hanson. The latter two also generously agreed to write an epilogue to conclude the volume.

The structure and organization of each chapter have been left to its author's individual judgment, but central themes and concerns that emerged in the course of the colloquium have been integrated into the analysis where appropriate. The goal was to reach a compromise between establishing the necessary degree of commonality throughout the volume to make it useful to readers while leaving sufficient creative freedom to each author to address these themes in the ways appropriate to his or her own field. Certain basic questions, however, were to be addressed in each chapter: What types of evidence exist, and what are their limitations? Who serves in the military, and what are their motivations? What is their ethnic, legal, social, and/or economic status? How are the resources of a society used for war? What is the social and economic impact of war? How do people justify war and think about it? How does warfare affect and interact with political structures and behavior? Further important questions concern the economy, including land tenure and taxation; the ecology and seasonality of war; the antecedents and models for warfare available to each society; the technology of weapons and military equipment; religion, ideology, and/or theoretical thinking about war; the goals and results of war; the various categories of war and fighting recognized by each society (e.g., set-piece battles versus sieges or ambushes and raids, internal versus external wars, private warfare versus communal wars, ritualistic forms of combat or types of "pseudofighting"); the various categories of armed forces each society mobilized, as well as many others. While all these questions are important, each nevertheless cannot and need not be covered systematically or in the same way in every chapter. To repeat, the main focus throughout rests on the changing interaction between military organization and warfare on the one hand and, on the other, the social, economic, political, and cultural structures of the society under discussion.

It has been gratifying to us to see in the last few years the renewal of interest in the military history of antiquity and the early Middle Ages and the high quality of much of this work.[10] We are convinced that the present volume on the social history of warfare will fill an important need and in turn will stimulate further studies of the topic.

Notes

1. Notable exceptions include scholarship on the period of the late Roman Republic, archaic Greece, and the Athenian democracy.
2. For example, Aristotle, *Politics* 1289b, on which see, however, Raaflaub, this volume.
3. Lynn 1996.508; cf. 511. The whole of this work is an extended analysis of the ways in which these factors, what Lynn calls "state infrastructure," and warfare have influenced one another in the West since the Middle Ages. Cf. also Keegan 1993.3–60.
4. See esp. Roberts 1956, reprinted with minor revisions in Roberts 1967 and Rogers 1995, for the origins of the problem, and Rogers 1995 for the current state of the debate.
5. Note, e.g., Millett and Murray 1988.1–30; cf. Kennedy 1987.
6. Interest in the topic originates with Turney-High 1949. See in general Ferguson 1988, 1990, and in this volume; Keeley 1996; Hassig 1992.
7. E.g., Delbrück 1975; Connolly 1981; Ducrey 1986; Hackett 1989; Ferrill 1997. Even Garlan 1975, who endeavors to go beyond this narrow range of topics, barely scratches the surface.
8. Most notably Brunt 1962, republished with revisions in Brunt 1988.240–80, and Snodgrass 1965.
9. E.g., Andreski 1968.
10. E.g., Hanson 1989, 1991; Spence 1993; Elton 1996; Goldsworthy 1996.

Bibliography

Andreski, Stanislav. 1968. *Military Organization and Society.* 2d ed. Berkeley and Los Angeles: University of California Press.

Brunt, Peter. 1962. "The Army and the Land in the Roman Revolution." *Journal of Roman Studies* 52, 69–86.

———. 1988. *The Fall of the Roman Republic and Related Essays.* Oxford: Oxford University Press.

Connolly, Peter. 1981. *Greece and Rome at War.* London: Macdonald.

Delbrück, Hans. 1975. *Warfare in Antiquity.* Translated by Walter J. Renfroe. Westport, Conn.: Greenwood Press. A translation of vol. 1 of *Geschichte der Kriegskunst im Rahmen der politischen Geschichte,* first published in 1920.

Ducrey, Pierre. 1986. *Warfare in Ancient Greece.* Translated by Janet Lloyd. New York: Schocken Books.

Elton, Hugh. 1996. *Warfare in Roman Europe: AD 350–425.* Oxford: Oxford University Press.

Ferguson, R. Brian. 1988. *The Anthropology of War: A Bibliography.* New York: Harry Frank Guggenheim Foundation.

———. 1990. "Explaining War." In *The Anthropology of War,* edited by J. Haas, 199–227. Santa Fe, N.M.: School of American Research Press.

Ferrill, Arther. 1997. *The Origins of War: From the Stone Age to Alexander the Great.* Revised Edition. Boulder, Colo.: Westview Press.

Garlan, Yvon. 1975. *War in the Ancient World: A Social History.* Translated by Janet Lloyd. London: Chatto and Windus.

Goldsworthy, Adrian. 1996. *The Roman Army at War: 100 BC–AD 200.* Oxford: Oxford University Press.

Hackett, John, ed. 1989. *Warfare in the Ancient World.* London: Sidgwick and Jackson.

Hanson, Victor D. 1989. *The Western Way of War: Infantry Battle in Classical Greece.* New York: Oxford University Press.

———. 1991. *Hoplites: The Classical Greek Battle Experience.* London: Routledge.

Hassig, Ross. 1992. *War and Society in Ancient Mesoamerica.* Berkeley and Los Angeles: University of California Press.

Keegan, John. 1993. *A History of Warfare.* New York: Knopf.

Keeley, Lawrence H. 1996. *War before Civilization.* New York: Oxford University Press.

Kennedy, Paul M. 1987. *The Rise and Fall of the Great Powers: Economic Change and Military Conflict from 1500 to 2000.* New York: Random House.

Lynn, John A. 1996. "The Evolution of Army Style in the Modern West, 800–2000." *International History Review* 18, 505–545.

Millett, Allan R., and Williamson Murray, eds. 1988. *Military Effectiveness.* Vol. 1. Winchester, Mass.: Allen and Unwin.

Roberts, Michael. 1956. *The Military Revolution, 1560–1660.* Belfast: M. Boyd.

———. 1967. *Essays in Swedish History.* Minneapolis: University of Minnesota Press.

Rogers, Clifford, ed. 1995. *The Military Revolution Debate: Readings on the Military Transformation of Early Modern Europe.* Boulder, Colo.: Westview Press.

Snodgrass, Anthony. 1965. "The Hoplite Reform and History." *Journal of Hellenic Studies* 85, 110–122.

Spence, I. G. 1993. *The Cavalry of Classical Greece: A Social and Military History.* Oxford: Oxford University Press.

Turney-High, H. 1949. *Primitive War: Its Practice and Concepts.* Columbia: University of South Carolina Press.

Early China

ROBIN D. S. YATES

Xia	ca. 2000–1750 B.C.E.
Shang	ca. 1750–1045 B.C.E.
Western Zhou	ca. 1045–770 B.C.E.
Eastern Zhou	770–256 B.C.E.
Springs and Autumns	*722–481 B.C.E.*
Warring States	*453–221 B.C.E.*
Qin	221–206 B.C.E.
Western Han	206 B.C.E.–9 C.E.
Eastern Han	23 C.E.–220 C.E.

Introduction: War in Early China

The present chapter studies the role of warfare in society in the early period of Chinese history, roughly the first one and a half millennia before the common era, a period in which wars were frequent and during which many of the characteristic features of Chinese culture were created. It is a period that can, for the present purposes, be divided roughly into three stages: the first, the early

7

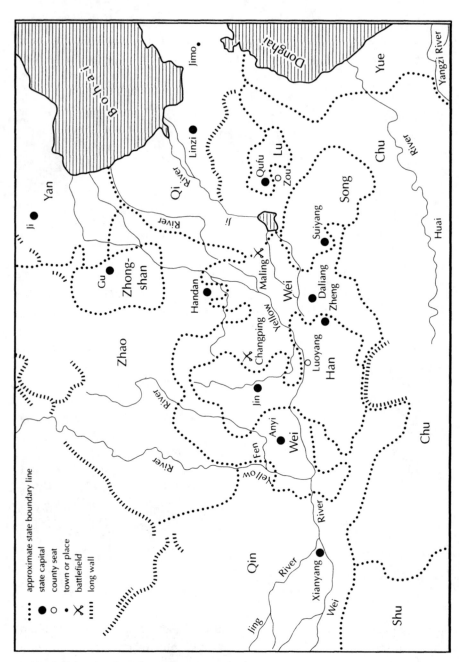

Map of China in the Warring States Period

Bronze Age from the Shang dynasty through the Western Zhou dynasty and the first half of the Eastern Zhou, called the Springs and Autumns period, roughly 1500 to 500 B.C.E. In this stage, warfare was an integral and essential part of the religious system. It could almost be claimed that the state and the social order were entirely dependent for their existence on warfare and sacrifice. The second stage is the latter part of the Eastern Zhou, aptly designated the Warring States, from roughly 500 to the foundation of the Chinese empire by King Zheng of the state of Qin in 221 B.C.E. In this period, warfare among the regional city-state systems was perpetual and increasingly fierce, and many technological and tactical inventions were adopted on the battlefields. The whole of society, including for the first time peasants, was organized to meet the needs of war, and major innovations in social organization resulted. War itself was theorized and integrated into an all-inclusive cosmological system.

In the third stage, the early empire, primarily the Han that replaced the Qin in 206 B.C.E. and survived, with a brief interregnum 9–23, to 220 C.E., warfare was concentrated at the periphery of the Chinese heartland, especially against nomadic tribesmen in the north, but, with the rise of Confucian literati at the imperial court and the fear that powerful generals might challenge for the throne, military values as key components in the ideology of the state were downgraded. Among the scholar-official elite, war would never again be recognized as the means of bringing order to the world as it had in the first two periods. However, skill in the military arts remained highly valued among the northern aristocracy that ruled north China from the end of Han to the Song (220–960 C.E.), many of whom were of either pure or mixed ethnic, non-Han, heritage, and among the populace as a whole. In this chapter I will concentrate my remarks on the first two of these periods and attempt to delineate the complex interrelationships between war, social formations, the economy, and religious beliefs. I will just sketch the changes that occurred in the third.

Warfare and Ritual Sacrifice: The Neolithic and Bronze Ages

The ancestors of the Chinese began to use long-range projectile weapons as long ago as 28,000 B.C.E., at least for hunting, and intrahuman conflict may have appeared much earlier.[1] Although Chinese scholars have a tendency to believe that war was not present at the earliest stages of the Neolithic period from about 5000 B.C.E., villages definitely began to be protected by deep ditches from about 4000 B.C.E. in the Yangshao stage in the Yellow River valley.[2] The economy of these peoples was mixed: in the north, the grains cultivated were forms of millet *(Setaria italica)*, vegetables included oil cabbage *(youcai)* and Chinese cabbage, and hemp was grown for fiber. Pigs, dogs, and chickens were domesticated. In addition, hunting, fishing, and gathering provided important sources of foods, and most settlements were constructed on terraces above tributaries of the Yellow River. In south China, where the climate was warmer and wetter, more reliance was placed on water products, such as rice, water chestnuts, and water caltrops. The most valuable of animals was the water buffalo, followed by the pig. Some villages were constructed on stilts in lakes or marshes, providing easy access to fish and crustaceans, as well as affording protection from potential enemies. At Hemudu in Zhejiang, the world's earliest lacquer bowl was discovered.[3] Pottery was hand thrown, and, in north China by the Yangshao stage, ritual vessels, such as large storage jars used for containing the bones of dead children, who were buried inside the village compound rather than outside it, as adults were, were distinguished from those of everyday use by their fineness, exquisite decorations, and the thinness of their walls. This interest in ritual objects was only to be intensified in the later centuries and millennia.

In the next stage, the Longshan interaction sphere (ca. 3000–2000 B.C.E.), which may have been one of agglomerated settlements and chiefdoms, some villages began to be walled, suggesting growing conflict between competing groups.[4] In the hills of the northern uplands, the steppe region that is now the border between the Chinese and the Mongolian peoples, these walls were constructed of rocks and boulders, but along the tributaries of the Yellow River and, farther south, in the Yangzi River valley, these were built out of stamped earth. This method of construction, in which successive layers of earth were poured between wooden frames and beaten down with mallets until they were as hard as concrete, became a typical feature of traditional Chinese architectural design. It required enormous amounts of labor input as well as considerable organizational capacity on the part of the chiefs and their administrative cadres, especially considering the tools employed to erect these walls were made out of stone, wood, and bone.

Although there is little evidence to support the contention, it seems likely that offensive capabilities were outweighed by the defensive potential of these thick and high pounded earthworks, and attacking forces may have had to try to starve out the defenders, or to resort to trickery and the subornation of the gate guards, to gain entry into the perimeter, although they certainly could have used fire arrows to try to burn down the wattle-and-daub houses and granaries inside.[5] Hand weapons consisted of short knives, spears, and the prototype of what became the typical long-handled weapon of the Bronze Age, the dagger-ax (ge). In addition, soldiers may have used implements normally used in agriculture; one later military treatise, the Liu Tao (Six Bowcases) lists the functions that plowshares, sickles, hoes, spades, saws, axes, and mallets could fulfill in both offensive and defensive warfare.[6] Finally, Chang finds evidence of institutional forms of violence and raids or wars in the discovery of skulls and skeletons at the bottom of a well at Jiankoucun, and the burial of victims of possible ritual murder associated with the entombment of chiefs and the foundations of important buildings.[7]

The first of China's traditional dynasties, the Xia, has been correlated with some sites that begin to show evidence of knowledge of bronze metalworking dating from about 2000 B.C.E., but the identifications are hotly disputed.[8] Unfortunately, there are no contemporary written documents from this period, although it is possible that writing had been invented by this time.[9] The last stage of the Shang dynasty is, however, much clearer because inscriptions on cattle scapulae and the carapaces of turtles, primarily the plastrons, recording the results of divinations made by the king, have been discovered at Anyang, Henan province, southwest of modern Beijing.[10] Hence I have identified for the purposes of this paper the first stage as beginning with the Xia's successor, the Shang, which began its rule sometime in the middle of the second millennium B.C.E.

The Shang sociopolitical order was based on a dominant, hierarchically organized, bronze-manufacturing aristocratic patrilineage (*zu*), led by a king who claimed to be the sole intermediary between the human and spiritual worlds, supported by and intermarried with other lineages, each apparently possessing its own eponymous walled settlement.[11] The Shang's last capital at Anyang, however, appears to have been protected only by a river on the north and east sides and a ditch on the west and south.[12] This may have been because the site was actually a mortuary and ritual center, where the dead kings and their consorts were buried and where sacrifices, including human sacrifices, were made to appease and seek the assistance of the powerful ancestral spirits, rather than the economic and political capital, or it may have been because the Shang felt sufficiently secure from their enemies that they did not need to expend resources on erecting a wall.[13] Eventually, the Shang were, in fact, destroyed by their former subordinate, possibly vassal, neighbors to the west, the Zhou, in approximately 1045 B.C.E.

Little textual evidence has survived that provides insights into the strategies and tactics of real combat in this early period, although we do know that armies of infantry and small numbers of chariots, probably introduced from Mesopotamia by way of central Asia, took part.[14] On the other hand, much rich ethnographic material, including the main reasons for fighting, can be discerned from quasi-historical works, such as the *Zuo Zhuan* (Master Zuo's Commentary on the Springs and Autumns Annals of the State of Lu, a work edited by Confucius [551–479 B.C.E.]), the *Shang Shu* (Book of Documents, a collection mostly of speeches claiming to derive from late Shang and Western Zhou), and literary compositions, such as the *Shi Jing* (Book of Odes or Songs, one of the Confucian Classics, some poems of which may date as early as the late Shang and early Western Zhou). All of these texts have probably undergone later editing in some form or another.

The role of warfare in contemporary social, religious, and personal life may be seen in the *Zuo Zhuan*, where a minor lord, Kang of Liu, is said to have declared on the occasion of a sacrifice at the *she* altar, the altar of soil that was the ritual center of any state or settlement, at which his colleague, the lord of Cheng, showed disrespect when he received the raw meat of sacrifice:

> I have heard it said that the people receive (the region) between heaven and earth to live in, and this is what is called their fate *(ming)*. From that they have the means to act and create—ritual and right behavior, and the rules of authority and deportment—so as to determine this fate. The able nurture these so as to secure good fortune, while those without ability contravene them and earn misfortune. For this reason superior men diligently observe ritual, and lesser men exhaust their physical strength. In diligently observing ritual, nothing is so essential as utmost respectfulness; in exhausting one's strength, nothing is so essential as genuine sincerity. That respectfulness consists in nourishing the spirits, that sincerity in attending to duty. The great affairs of the state are sacrifice and warfare. At sacrifices one presides over cooked meat, and in war one receives raw meat: these are the great ceremonies of the spirits.[15]

Although this is a late, possibly apocryphal, record, it illustrates well the overwhelming importance of sacrifice and war for the dominant Bronze Age elite, the leading members of the lineages that had supported the Zhou in their conquest of the Shang. Lewis is correct when he posits, "This passage states explicitly that sacrifice and warfare were the principal forms of state or public service, and it links them through the shared ritual consumption of meat. This consumption, in turn, presupposed the killing of sacrificial animals, so the ritualized taking of life constituted the defining feature of the political realm in Zhou China."[16] Contemporary texts from the early part of the period, the last 250 years of the Shang and the 300 or so years of the Western Zhou, confirm this vision. This evidence is supplemented by archaeological discoveries of bronze weapons, the imprints of chariots found in or associated with tombs, and the excavations of sites of towns, cities, and palatial compounds.[17]

Unfortunately, the internal organization of towns and cities from this period cannot be determined in any very precise way because Chinese archaeologists have not been able to provide sufficiently detailed analyses of the areas inside the walls. So we do not know how a population or besieged army might have defended itself. Nevertheless, some of the enceintes, such as that of the middle Shang city at Zhengzhou, Henan, were huge, a rough square 1,690 by 1,870 meters, and another city west of Yanshixian, Henan, on the banks of the Yellow River, was found to be approximately 1,710 meters long on the west side, 1,230 meters on the north, and 1,640 meters on the east, where the wall ranges from 16 to 25 meters wide at the base.[18] A mid-Shang outpost farther south on the shores of Lake Panlong was smaller, the walls being roughly 290 meters north-south and 260 meters east-west and protected by a moat 10 meters wide.[19]

As far as can be determined, the Shang forces were organized into three main units, left, right, and center armies, which in turn were based upon centuries, multiples of one hundred men. These may well have been drawn from the lineages, because the graph for the term for lineage, *zu,* shows men standing under a flag or standard: flags and pennants were attached to every sort of weapon and to the stands of drums, which were mounted horizontally.[20] The flags were carried into battle and designed to bring down the spirits of the ancestors to assist the participants. By Eastern Zhou times, flags, drums, and bells were employed to direct the movement of forces in the heat of battle, and, because white was the color of death in Chinese symbolism, those who wished to surrender waved a white flag and donned white clothing to indicate that they considered themselves to be already dead and at the disposal of their conquerors; they could be killed or enslaved as the victors saw fit.[21] The use of flags, and the symbolism of white for surrender, was subsequently in early medieval times transmitted to western Asia, and has since then been disseminated throughout the world.

Two groups of infantry were employed by the Shang king, the *zhong* ("masses") and the *ren* ("people"), who were mobilized for warfare, agriculture, and other forced labor projects.[22] The former were counted only in the hundreds and may have been more directly under the control of the king, whereas there are examples of the latter being numbered by the three thousand and the five thousand, three thousand being the more common number.[23] Probably the *ren* were, therefore, members of the general populace. In one famous case, an army was counted as being ten thousand strong, and, combined with another group of three thousand, was the largest force ever put into the field by the Shang. Remarkably, it was led by King Wuding's favorite consort, Fuhao. Together, this pair seem to have revived the fortunes of the Shang dynasty at the beginning of its last phase and to have expanded the realm quite considerably, engaging in conflicts with tribes or chiefdoms quite distant from the Anyang core.[24] In later times, consorts never took to the field of battle, although there were definitely situations when women took up arms.[25] The figures in the thousands, however, should perhaps be understood as indications of large size, rather than real numbers. Most conflicts reported in the oracle bones involved far smaller numbers. The terms used for mobilizing such forces were also used to present offerings to the spirits, thus revealing, as Keightley argues, "the quasi-religious nature of the mobilizations themselves, [and] the absence of any sharp distinctions between mobilizing the *ren* for warfare and mobilizing the spirits for support." [26]

In addition to the infantry, reference is made in the bone inscriptions to the "Many Horse" *(duo ma),* probably the title of a charioteer of some substance, an officer who controlled the *zhong* or *zhongren* (or, *zhong* and *ren*), as well as to the "Many Archers." The "Many Artisans" and "Many Dogs" may also be titles of officials of units employed by and dependent upon the ruling lineage. The artisans we know manufactured bronze dagger-ax and spear blades, arrowheads, chariot fittings, helmets, and shields.[27]

Warfare was closely connected to hunting and agriculture throughout the Bronze Age. In the Shang, all three were divined about, and in fact the word *tian* signified both hunting and agriculture. Hunting, especially the seasonal hunts in spring and autumn, provided training for soldiers and was part of certain important sacrifices that were offered as service to the ancestors.[28] The Shang king frequently sent out his *zhongren* to open up fields in the territory of his neighbors who were termed X-*fang* (X-place or direction). They would first burn the trees and undergrowth, and capture and kill the fleeing animals. Then the ashes were used to fertilize the fields. Sometimes the enemy would respond and enter and seize the crops, usually various grains, such as millet, and these incursions were also divined about by the king. Eventually, in a good number of cases, the *fang* in the name was dropped in the record, indicating that the Shang had achieved permanent control over the invaded territory.[29] Both the animals and the humans captured in the hunt were victims of Shang sacrifice and dedicated to particular ancestors, and, counting the numbers of victims mentioned in the oracle bones correlated with the number of skeletal remains, sometimes beheaded, buried in tombs and in house and palace foundations, historians and archaeologists reckon that more than thirteen thousand victims were killed at the Anyang complex in the 250 years or so of its occupation.[30]

The Shang engaged in raids as well as long wars of attrition against a large number of *fang* on their periphery, perhaps the most famous being the Gong-*fang* and the Yu-*fang*, but the exact location of the peoples recorded in the oracle bones is the subject of much dispute.[31] By late Shang, the kings were not able to maintain permanent, continuous control over a broad swathe of territory; rather, they had intermittent control of places along the trail where they could sacrifice in safety. The longest campaign surviving in the oracle bone records is that against the Ren-*fang*, probably to the east, where the entire campaign, going and returning, took 106 days.[32] Evidently, the Shang were able to maintain a relatively sophisticated long-distance trade network, because the main prestige items they bestowed as special gifts were cowry shells that came from the southern ocean, as well as turtle shells used in pyromancy; they also needed salt and the smelted raw materials of tin and copper in enormous quantities for the production of the ritual vessels and bronze weapons whereby they maintained connection with the unseen powers of deities and ancestors and dominance over their neighboring peoples.[33] But it is not at all clear whether the Shang actually controlled the trade routes themselves, guarding them by force of arms, or whether, in a redistributive economy, they exchanged items of value, such as vessels, silk cloth, and lacquerware, the fragmentary remains of which have been discovered, for the products they desired.

As indicated earlier, the Shang were destroyed by their neighbors to the west, the Zhou, led by King Wu, whose capital was near present-day Xi'an, in a famous battle at Muye in about 1045 B.C.E.[34] The Zhou challenged the overlordship of the Shang by mobilizing the support of a number of groups and legitimized their seizure of power by claiming that Heaven, the high god of the Zhou, which was not apparently worshiped by the Shang, had decided to confer on them the mandate to rule the all-under-heaven. They maintained that the Shang had lost their mandate to govern the world by being morally corrupt and dissolute, indulging in drunken orgies and feasts, and killing upright ministers of state. Most scholars have followed the lead of Chinese savants and interpreted the new order imposed by the Zhou on the Shang and their other subject peoples in the east as being a form of feudalism. Most have tried to interpret inscriptions on bronzes of gift exchanges that record the beneficence of the Zhou king to subordinates as feudal investitures, similar to those found in medieval Europe.[35] But this interpretation is now being challenged.[36]

Certainly, there are similarities, as can be seen from one such lengthy "investiture" inscription on the so-called *Yihou Ze gui* vessel:[37]

It was the fourth month, the *chen* was on *dingwei* (day 44), <the king> inspected the King Wu and King Cheng attack on Shang map, [then] went to inspect the eastern countries map. The king stood in the Yi ancestral temple, facing south. The king commanded Lord Ze of Yu, saying: "Move to be lord at Yi. [I] award *sao*-fragrant wine one *you*, one Shang wine vessel, . . . one red-lacquered bow and one hundred red-lacquered arrows, ten black bows and 1,000 black arrows; award land: its acreage 300 . . . , its . . . 100 and . . . , its towns 35, its . . . 140; award at Yi king's men . . . and seven clans, award seven earls of Zheng and their retainers 1,050 men, award at Yi common men 600 and . . . (and) six men." Lord Ze of Yi extols the king's beneficence, making (for) Father Ding, the Duke of Yu, (this) sacrificial vessel.[38]

Here we see that, as early as 1000 B.C.E., maps of military campaigns and of specific regions were drawn and kept by officials, although of course it is not now possible to determine the precise nature of Western Zhou cartography. A number of later maps have, however, been discovered, seven of Qin date (late third century B.C.E.) drawn on wooden boards and excavated from the tombs at Fangmatan, Gansu, in the northwest, and three others, drawn on silk, deposited in a Han tomb in 168 B.C.E. at Mawangdui, Changsha, Hunan province. Two of these latter maps are most interesting because they represent the southern region of China, the Han kingdom of Changsha. One of them marks the location of troop dispositions, as well as towns and forts, and geographic features, such as rivers and mountains.[39]

The importance of maps as a source of military knowledge can be seen from a late Warring States (fifth to third centuries B.C.E.) fragment preserved in the philosophical compendium Guanzi:[40]

> All military commanders must first examine and come to know maps. They must know thoroughly the location of winding, gate-like defiles, streams which may inundate their chariots, famous mountains, passable valleys, arterial rivers, highlands, and hills; where grow grasses, trees and rushes, the distances of the roads, the size of the city and suburban walls, famous and deserted towns, and barren and fertile land. They should thoroughly store up [in their minds] the relative location of the configurations of the terrain. Then afterwards they can march their armies and raid towns. In the disposition [of troops] they will know [what lies] ahead and behind, and will not lose the advantages of the terrain. This is the constant [value] of maps.

So presumably the Zhou maps mentioned in the bronze inscription must have been prototypes of these examples, although the extent to which they actually indicated the successive deployment of the Shang and Zhou forces during the course of this most important campaign regrettably cannot be determined.

The present author argues that the political system of Western and Eastern Zhou was composed of a large number of city-states, whose ruling aristocratic lineages were linked by real or fictive kin relations in the so-called *zongfa* system initially under the overlordship of the Zhou kings until they were defeated in battle in 770 B.C.E. and forced to move their capital from the western "Zhou yuan" (plains of Zhou) to the city of Chengzhou, the modern city of Luoyang, Henan province, just south of the Yellow River.[41] This city had been founded shortly after the Zhou conquest of Shang to house some lineages of the defeated Shang elite and their associated retainers, as well as to provide a ritual center and military strongpoint from which the Zhou could oversee the conquered territories.[42] After the defeat of the Western Zhou, in the Springs and Autumns period lasting to about 500 B.C.E., various regional powers were able to force their weaker neighbors into regional peer-polity systems, until, in the Warring States period, only a very few, finally only seven[43] city-state systems were left to fight it out for control of the entire subcontinent. It was the warlike state of Qin based in the northwest, like their Zhou ancestors, that was finally successful in destroying all its rivals, unifying China under a single authority and creating the empire in 221 B.C.E.

Cook, however, rejecting the feudal model, emphasizes the economic, specifically gift-exchange, nature of the Western Zhou, and argues that "investiture inscriptions," in which charges of service appear with donations of land, must be understood within the whole system of exchanges:

> An analysis of gifts and gift-giving in the inscriptions shows that all inscriptions can be seen as parts of a whole in the sense that they record various aspects of exchange cycles memorialized at different points in the Zhou ritual calendar. These points, mostly ceremonies involving ancestor worship, have more in common with the festivals of redistribution and competitive feasting in pre-colonial Pacific Rim cultures than with feudal investiture ceremonies. Western Zhou inscriptions can be understood as records of wealth and prestige made by lineage representatives for display and use during mortuary feasts. Feast participants included members of the lineage—past, present and future: the ancestral spirits who began the accumulation, the living representative who accumulates new merit and the future generations who must be impressed and pressed into the service of maintaining the wealth and prestige accumulated thus far.[44]

She notes that in Shang inscriptions cowry shells, which resemble the vulva, and thus probably were symbols of fertility, were the only objects of value recorded and circulated as gifts under that dynasty. By contrast, in the Western Zhou other items of value in bronze, stone, lacquer, leather, and cloth were transferred, together with cowries, varying, of course, with the particular circumstances, and these were used in sacrifice to the ancestors and in warfare. By the late Western Zhou, "cowrie presentations were rare, but military gear presentations common."[45] Thus warfare and the circulation, transferal, and transmission of military equipment, whether bows and arrows, flags and standards, greaves, shields, or chariot fittings, were at the very heart of the Western Zhou social, political, and economic system, a significant change from the cultural system of the earlier Shang. Small wonder, then, that the Lord of Liu stated in the *Zuo Zhuan* that the "great affairs of the state are sacrifice and warfare." But it is hard to tell if it was the Zhou's diffusion of military gear and military prestige to their subordinates throughout the country that encouraged the development at the regional and local levels of military values, techniques of warfare, and military hardware that ultimately were used to terminate the Zhou's administrative, though not ritual, dominance of the entire political system.

With respect to the organization of the Western Zhou armed forces, more information can be gathered from literary sources than what has survived in the oracle bone records of the Shang. It would appear that the Zhou were able to muster not only their own forces for the attack on Shang but also those of the Yong, Shu, Qiang, Mao, Peng, Pu, and other chiefdoms or tribes. They are said to have put on the field of battle three hundred war chariots, three thousand "tiger warriors" (huben), and forty-five thousand cuirassed soldiers.

After the conquest, they maintained six divisions in the west in their capital region "Within the Passes" of Shaanxi province in the Wei river valley, and organized the remaining forces of the Shang into eight divisions of the Yin (the Zhou name for the Shang) and eight of their own divisions, both of which were stationed at Chengzhou. The smallest unit in these forces, whose origins are unknown, although they probably were composed of junior members of the locally dominant lineages and their dependents, was the hundred-man century led by a centurion (baifu zhang), then a thousand-man brigade commanded by a millenarian (if I may coin the term) (qianfu zhang), and a five-thousand-man division commanded by a division commander (shishi); above him was a yalü in charge of fifteen thousand men, and the entire army was commanded by a master of horse (sima) in command of forty-five thousand men. In addition, as far as the chariot arm was concerned, they were divided into units of ten, and a yalü commanded a one-hundred-chariot brigade.[46] Whether or not these units held precisely these numbers of men and how they were actually supported (were they professional forces, or did they farm when not out on campaign?) is impossible to tell. Shaughnessy has demonstrated, however, that it took a long time before the Zhou were able to consolidate control even over the region close to their eastern capital.[47]

By the middle of the Western Zhou, King Zhao was campaigning in the southeast against the powerful Huai Yi peoples, and he is said to have drowned in the Changjiang (Yangtze) River while fighting the Chu. In his reign, too, the Huai Yi may have been able to launch a counterattack that penetrated deep into Zhou territory in the Yellow River valley, and apparently the northern Rong invaded from the other direction, causing grave difficulties to city-states allied with the Zhou. These latter peoples were probably nomadic warriors, the first of numerous steppe tribes that penetrated the Chinese lands to their south. In King Yi's reign the Zhou attacked the Rong in the region of modern Taiyuan, directly west of Beijing across the Taihang mountains in the Shansi uplands. From their enemies the Zhou were able to procure one thousand horses.[48] Throughout later history, the Chinese always needed to gain access to well-bred horses from the steppe-land, because environmental conditions in China proper—in the Yellow River valley and farther south—were not conducive to maintaining a strong stock, and the Chinese preferred to farm their lands using the techniques of intensive agriculture rather than turning them over to pasture for horses and cattle. Also, farther south, various types of insects infected the animals with debilitating diseases.[49]

Throughout the Western Zhou, the main weapons used by the elite in fighting remained the bow and arrow, and the curved dagger-ax *(ge)* with descending edge attached to a long wooden pole that they had inherited from the Shang. The ax *(yue)* appears to have become less common, being reserved for use as a symbol of high social and military status.[50] However, the Zhou seem to have adopted from the steppe peoples, particularly those in the northeast, a short bronze dagger. The blades of these weapons were from seventeen to eighteen centimeters up to twenty-seven centimeters long and shaped like a willow leaf.[51] Many examples have pommels in the shape of animals, such as the tiger, and sometimes these pommels are curved. These weapons were used in close hand-to-hand combat, presumably when the chariots became locked together, or when they had bogged down in marshy or muddy ground and the driver, the bowman, and the dagger-ax bearer had to defend themselves against enemy infantry. What those infantry were equipped with is unknown, but they may have had only stone, bone, and wooden implements, like their Neolithic forebears, or they may have wielded long pikes or spears *(mao):* the blades of these latter long-handled weapons look remarkably similar to the short daggers.[52]

As indicated previously, the Zhou were driven out of their original homeland in the Wei river valley and obliged to move east to what had been their secondary capital at Chengzhou in 770 B.C.E., thus initiating the period known as the Eastern Zhou. From 722 B.C.E., the Springs and Autumns period, the history of warfare is the history of the various city-states and state groups that fought each other for local and regional dominance, and ultimately for control of the whole East Asian subcontinent. Furthermore, the documentation for warfare becomes infinitely richer with records such as the *Zuo Zhuan,* which contains many battle narratives, 483 by Lan Yongwei's count. Most of such encounters were held in the open field, for the techniques necessary to mount a successful assault on the many cities were as yet rudimentary: forces tried either to gain entry to the gates by surprise, by suborning the defenders, starving them out, or by erecting ramps to match the height of the city walls. This latter operation was extremely time-consuming and labor-intensive, and the defenders could easily increase the height of their walls by erecting false walls made out of wooden boards, or could isolate the section where the enemy was building their ramp by constructing a secondary wall inside the first.[53]

The historical records that describe warfare in the early part of the Eastern Zhou were written by and for the aristocratic elite of the expanding city-states. As a consequence, the accounts dwell in loving detail on the actions of this elite and do not provide much information on the crowds of commoner foot soldiers who presumably accompanied the chariots. Certainly, as the larger, more powerful states increased the size of their territories by incorporating their smaller, weaker neighbors, they were able to put more chariots into the field. So by the end of the Springs and Autumns period and into the following Warring

States times, states were categorized by their number of chariots, ten thousand being considered a large state, one thousand a smaller. Nevertheless, it is likely that infantry drawn from the peasantry came to constitute the major fighting force of these states, and that these foot soldiers were equipped with dagger-axes, halberds, and swords, and protected with leather armor.

Kierman has examined in detail the phases of a typical Springs and Autumns battle, and it is clear that there was considerable continuity between war in this period and the preceding Western Zhou.[54] Yet it appears that populations were increasing and the size of cities was expanding. Further, the gift-exchange economy was gradually transformed into one that was market-based; merchants engaged in local, interstate, and interregional trade began to appear; first cloth and then metal coinage began to circulate, contributing to interregional economic activity; and, by the end of the period, cast iron tools began to be distributed among the peasant populace.[55] Further, as the territories expanded, new techniques of administration developed and bureaucracies became more complex.[56] Still, it is difficult to determine in this complex process of change, which increased in speed in the Warring States period, how the total ensemble of changes were related to each other and which factors were primarily responsible or the main factors causing the process and which were secondary.[57]

Kierman has determined that there were three main phases to a military engagement: before the battle, the battle itself, and after the battle; and the authors of the account were not so much interested in the details of the killing on the field itself as in the divination process and the attempt on the part of the combatants to establish their correct relationship to divine and cosmic processes that would affect the outcome.[58] Initial plans were made at the outset of a campaign in the ancestral temple; if success was achieved, the left ears of the defeated were presented to the altars of soil and grain as blood sacrifices at the termination of hostilities. Generally speaking, the day and place of battle were agreed on with the enemy before engaging in the combat itself, and hortatory speeches, prayers, and communications with the ancestors were made, and challenges issued. Songs sung by the soldiers on either side were interpreted as omens of the outcome. Strict rules of etiquette were followed in the course of battle, and combatants refused to engage or kill those who were not of the same social station as themselves. Although some attention was paid in the course of the battle to formations and improvisation, as well as to psychological warfare, these were by no means as important as they were in the Warring States, where they were raised to a high art and became the subject of study and theorizing by military specialists such as Sunzi and Wu Qi.[59] Acts of bravery and courtesy by individual aristocrats were of far more interest to the chroniclers than the activities of the foot soldiers, who probably, in fact, decided the outcome of many a battle. After the battle, the defeated could escape, commit suicide, or submit, and not infrequently suffer enslavement, and the winning army usually feasted on the provisions of their opponents. But in most cases the emphasis in the account was laid upon whether the combatants had followed correct ritual procedure, and there are many examples where campaigns were initiated on the grounds that the enemy had failed to conform to appropriate ritual behavior. A good example of such behavior is quoted by Kierman in the case of a three-man chariot belonging to the southern state of Chu before Bi (romanization changed):

> Xubo of Chu drove Yuebo, with Sheshu as [spearman on] the right to provoke the Jin army. Xubo said, "I have heard that in flouting armies, one drives, flaunting a standard, up to strike against the fortifications and then retires." Yuebo said, "I have heard in flouting armies, the man on the left shoots [so as to split] a reed, then takes the reins to control the pair [of horses], while the charioteer gets down to wipe the horses and adjust the harness and then they return." Sheshu said, "I have heard that, in flouting armies, the [spearman on the] right enters the fortifications, cuts off an ear, takes a prisoner, and returns." All did as they had heard [they should] and turned back; and the men of Jin pursued them [coming from] left and right like horns. But Yuebo shot horses on the left and men on the right, and the horns could not close [upon them]. He had but one arrow left, when a stag leaped up before [them] and he shot it in the spine. Bao Gui of Jin was just behind them, so Sheshu took the stag and presented it to him, saying, "It is not the proper time of the year and the presentation animals have not arrived, yet I presume to feast all the pursuers." Bao Gui stopped [the chase], saying, "The one on the left is good at shooting, the one on the right has [the art of correct ceremonial] speaking. They are superior men." And so they got away.[60]

Whether or not real battles were fought in this fashion is impossible to say. However, such concern with ritual performance from the initiation to the end of a campaign is consistent with the elite's interest in ritual that can be deduced from other sources, such as the magnificent ritual bronzes buried in their tombs that have been excavated in large numbers in recent years. The practice of making war in a ritual style is also paralleled in the hoplite warfare analyzed by Raaflaub and is recorded for the style of fighting between the Japanese samurai.[61]

Nevertheless, economic and political interests were also at stake in wars in this period, and they had serious consequences. Hsu has determined that in the course of the Springs and Autumns period (722–481 B.C.E.) the members of the upper aristocratic elite, members of ancient lineages that had dominated the city-states for many centuries, engaged in so much warfare that, by the end of the period, the lineages that provided the leading ministers of the various states were virtually eliminated and more than one hundred city-states were destroyed, being incorporated into increasingly complex hierarchies of regional systems. Further, no longer did rulers themselves or their immediate offspring participate in warfare. It began to be left to professional generals and soldiers who traveled from one state to another offering their services to the highest bidder. The rulers came to be more supervisors of complex administrations than active warriors themselves.

The organization of the armies in the various states is not entirely clear not only because there was evolution over time but also because the texts that describe the systems were written down only later. For example, the major source, the *Zuo Zhuan,* probably was put together in about 300 B.C.E., long after the events it records. These later texts, especially those that were consigned to writing after the unification of the empire by the Qin in 221 B.C.E., are often accused by scholars of being "systematizing" or "idealizing," giving the impression of order and rationalization where there was disorder, confusion, or ad hoc arrangements. The following is an example from the *Guanzi,* probably composed about 300 B.C.E., purporting to record the coordinated system of civil and military organization established by the famous legalist minister Guan Zhong for the first hegemon *(ba),* Duke Huan of Qi (685–643 B.C.E.), the powerful state in Shandong province on the Bohai bay, whose economy was based on cloth manufacturing and salt production:

> Guanzi replied, "In ancient times when the sage kings governed their people, they divided the country proper *(guo)* into three parts and the outer territories *(bi)* into five parts. They fixed the dwelling places of the people and arranged their work in order to bring about their proper regulation. They were careful in using the six handles [of power]. In such a way the nature of the people could be manipulated and the hundred surnames controlled."
>
> Duke Huan said, "What are the six handles?"
>
> "To kill, to nurture, to honor, to degrade, to impoverish, to enrich—these are the six handles," replied Guanzi.
>
> "What about dividing the country proper into three parts?" asked Duke Huan.
>
> Guanzi replied, "Organize the country proper into twenty-one districts *(xiang):* six districts for merchants and artisans and fifteen for the gentry and peasants. Of these districts, you should command eleven, Gaozi five, and Guozi five. Since [the operation of] the country proper is divided into three parts, they should form the three armies. Appoint ministers in charge of the three bureaus [administering the fifteen districts for

the gentry and peasants under the command of yourself, Gaozi, and Guozi], three district supervisors *(xiang)* in charge of the markets, three clan elders *(zu)* in charge of the artisans, three wardens *(yu)* in charge of the marshes, and three foresters *(heng)* in charge of the mountains.

"Organize [the country proper] so five households will constitute a neighborhood *(gui)*, with each neighborhood having a leader *(zhang)*; ten neighborhoods will constitute a village *(li)*, with each village having an officer *(si)*; four villages will constitute a community having a chief *(zhang)*; ten communities will constitute a district, with each district having a governor *(liangren)*. For every five districts there will be a commanding general *(shuai)*."

"What about dividing the outer territories into five parts?" asked Duke Huan.

Guanzi replied, "Organize [the outer territories] so five households will constitute a neighborhood with each neighborhood having a leader; six neighborhoods will constitute a camp *(yi)* with each camp having an officer in charge; ten camps will constitute a military colony *(shuai)* with each colony having a commandant *(zhang)*; ten military colonies will constitute a dependency *(shu)* with each dependency having a commanding general. For each of the dependencies there will be a great officer. A military government will administer the dependencies, a civil government the districts. Each will maintain its separate administration and so there will be no confusion or laxity."[62]

A number of features in this text bear commenting upon. The first is that the Chinese loved to organize their administration into elaborate hierarchies. In this, as I have said elsewhere, they were mirroring the mythological or cosmological ordering of space, civilizing their realm, and claiming legitimacy for their rule.[63] Second, by the Springs and Autumns time, generally speaking, states divided their armies into three: left, middle, and right. However, theoretically speaking, in the Western Zhou, it was only the Son of Heaven, the Zhou king, who had the right to establish such a military organization. The lesser lords beneath him, the earls, viscounts, and barons, did not have the right to raise armies. Only the king's immediate junior, the primal earl *(yuanhou)*, had the right to raise a Guard Army.[64] In fact, of course, the lords of the various states paid no attention to these ideal prescriptions, and they did indeed develop their own military organizations. Theoretically speaking, too, they were not supposed to go on an offensive campaign without permission of the Zhou king: they could only punish the refractory and those disobedient to the Zhou. All results were also to be reported to the throne. Again, this prescription was ignored in practice.

Third, the entire state of Qi was to be divided into two main regions, an inner and an outer, both of which were to be organized in such a way that the populace, especially the males, could be easily mobilized into military service. The outer region's organization was quite unambiguously intended to put the population in a state of permanent readiness to serve in defensive units. Even the inner region, although ostensibly run by civilian administrators, was also to provide soldiers for the three main armies. Each family, integrated into a system of five-family units, was to provide one soldier for the army, and these five soldiers formed the five-man squad. So those who ate together and probably were interrelated by marriage in ordinary life were also to fight together. Needless to say, this arrangement was intended to increase their mutual solidarity. It was a system that was continued and developed in Qin and the later empires.

The Qi ruler was to maintain control over the greater part of the military forces in his state, which may have been divided into armored soldiers (*jiashi*) and followers (*tu*), the usual situation at this time.[65] It seems a historical fact that the heads of the Gao and Guo lineages did indeed serve as hereditary commanders of their respective sections of the Qi armed forces well into the Warring States times. This was unusual: in most states, as Hsu has shown, hereditary aristocrats such as these lost their powers, if not also their lives, by the Springs and Autumns–Warring States divide.[66] Actually, Duke Huan's successors eventually lost the throne to another lineage in Qi, the Tians. They had been originally the Chens, possessors of their own small state on the borders of Chu until that great southern power, in its northern and eastern expansion, annexed their territories and one scion of the house of Chen fled into exile in Qi. There, he changed his name to Tian (Chen and Tian sounded the same in archaic Chinese, although the graphs were different) and proceeded to take charge of the Qi state armories, a minor bureaucratic position, but very important: his successors were able to take control of production and management of weapons. It is recorded that Qi also instituted a system of fines in their legal procedures in the form of shields and suits of armor. So criminals directly assisted the state in building up its military strength and preparedness. Later this system was adopted by Qin, although it is a little unclear whether the Qin required the guilty to provide the actual equipment or only a sum of money equivalent to one or two shields or sets of armor. Needless to say, this must have been quite a heavy fine.[67]

Finally, it should be noted that the nature of the land tenure system in Qi, or any other of the Western Zhou and Springs and Autumns states, is not clear and still very much in dispute among scholars. Chinese scholars, as a rule, argue that this and the succeeding period were characterized by the slave mode of production, and that the aristocrats and kings were members of the slave-owning class. There is little evidence to support this contention.[68] Others, such as

Cho-yun Hsu, argue for a manorial economy, with peasants tied to self-suffi-cient manors, much as in Europe in medieval times.[69] This manorial economy was integrated with a feudal system, they claim, as mentioned earlier. The evidence becomes much clearer in the following Warring States period, but is no less subject to different interpretations for all that. Whatever the situation in the state of Qi, evidently the text was written at a time when urbanization and commerce were relatively well developed, for the author mentions both artisans and merchants as well as peasants.

The Second Stage: The Warring States

A significant change in the techniques of warfare is signaled during the lifetime of Confucius (551–479 B.C.E.) in China's most famous treatise on warfare, *The Art of War* by Sunzi, or Master Sun (Sun Wu). Up to that time, battles were fought as much to demonstrate the individual aristocrat's comprehension and mastery of complex rituals *(li)* as they were to gain victory and destroy the ene-my. Such rituals were the foundation of Confucius's philosophical teachings and what he attempted to revitalize to re-create the utopia he thought had existed at the beginning of the Western Zhou dynasty.[70] Wars thereafter were to be fought without mercy and with the sole intention of achieving victory over the enemy and the preservation of the state.[71] As Sunzi introduces his *Art of War,* "War is a matter of vital importance to the state; a matter of life and death, the road either to survival or to ruin. Hence, it is imperative that it be thor-oughly studied."[72] Although in one sense this dictum is a continuation of the previous stage's view of warfare ("The great affairs of the state are sacrifice and warfare"), in others it is not.[73] Survival began to depend less on the perfor-mance of the culturally sanctioned correct sacrificial rituals to the ancestors and the spirits and more on economic, geographic, social, and political factors: the labor force of the population, its produce and territory, with the necessary means of controlling and exploiting them through the elaboration of a sophis-ticated administrative system.[74] Universal military conscription for adult males and annual corvée labor for both females and males was introduced in all the competing states, which necessitated the establishment of detailed population records held by local government offices.[75]

In the new mode of combat, the general was required to possess preternat-ural cognizance of the cosmic forces that impinged upon the outcome of the conflict, and it was still considered essential to undertake all the preliminary planning for a campaign in the ancestral temple of the state ruler's lineage under the watchful eyes of all the previous occupants of the throne.[76] Defeat on the battlefield could lead to the destruction of a state's altars of soil and grain and of the ancestral tablets in the temple. With no altar where the defeated ruler or his successors could provide blood, grain, and wine sacrifices to his fore-bears, his ancestors truly died and his state was completely obliterated. Its ter-ritory was integrated into the victor's administrative regional hierarchy, the most advanced form of which, the "commandery-county" system, was under the direct control of the central authorities.[77]

Other revolutionary changes in the techniques of warfare and in the nature of the state and society took place in this period. First, within two generations of Sunzi, in about the middle of the fourth century, as cities came to be larger and more numerous centers of production, population, and administration, they came to be prime targets of invading forces. As a consequence, techniques in siege warfare advanced to such a level of sophistication that it was no longer inconceivable or unwise for a general to mount an assault on their walls.[78]

Next, the armies of the Warring States, far fewer in number than their pre-decessors, grew much larger, and infantry came to be the primary fighting force, necessitating the development of sophisticated techniques of training, logistics, and weapons manufacturing facilities, and the art of command. Those who led armies were no longer the rulers or their immediate offspring, but rather the heads of the civil administration, who could indeed be related by blood or marriage to the rulers, but could equally well have belonged to less prestigious families that specialized in producing officers. In fact, with the demise of the aristocratic lineages dominant in the earlier period, armies began to be led by professional soldiers, such as the two Sunzis, Sun Wu and Sun Bin, Wu Qi, Mozi and his followers, and many other experts in the military arts. These individuals, just like their contemporaries, the philosophers, traveled from one state to another offering their services to the highest bidder. It appears that such men were appointed only for a particular campaign, rather than being given the permanent position of "general." The reason for this was that in the ritual of appointment the ruler conferred on the general the right to kill and the right to reward symbolized by the conferral of a bronze ax. Until the general returned the ax, no one, not even the ruler, could countermand his orders, a practice that was continued into the Han dynasty. As a result, in China empha-sis was laid on the brilliance of such men, and wars were believed to be won by skillful generals, not by skillful armies, as Rosenstein argues was the case in con-temporary Rome.[79] These generals deployed their troops in numerous forma-tions depending on the terrain and the disposition of the enemy's forces, in a constantly changing mixture of "regular" (zheng) and "irregular" (qi) forms: no one fixed method of fighting was used for all occasions.[80]

Many of these generals, on their return from successful combat, also initi-ated structural reforms in the administrative, economic, and legal systems of the states they served. The most renowned and effective of these itinerant war-riors was Wei Yang, later Lord Shang, who put the state of Qin on a permanent war footing using the legalist *(fajia)* philosophy. He thereby to a large extent destroyed the social and political power of Qin's hereditary aristocratic elite.[81] Lord Shang laid the foundations for Qin's ultimate conquest of its rivals and the institutional structures for the empire that was established one hundred years later in 221 B.C.E. The state of Qin promoted agriculture and war as the only acceptable occupations, and it reorganized its entire social system on a military basis. A hierarchical meritocratic ranking system was established for males, with seventeen ranks, later rising to twenty, based on success in battle: an ordinary soldier was awarded one rank for each enemy head he cut off, whereas officers were rewarded for the number of heads their subordinates seized.[82] Strict differentiation of function and discipline was also enforced: soldiers were not to engage in undisciplined acts of bravery if such acts went against orders, and they were rewarded if they could prove a head-chop, regardless of whether the battle had been a victory or a defeat. In other words, soldiers in an army were not indiscriminately rewarded for victory or punished for defeat. This rank was a negotiable commodity: it could be exchanged for an appointment as a low-level bureaucrat, or for the manumission of close relatives held in slavery or forced bondage. It entitled the holder to suffer less severe punishments for crimes committed and to receive land to till and slaves to help work the land. However, such a rank holder was also expected to help supervise corvée laborers in times of peace and to serve in the army when called upon by the state.

Yet, despite the importance and success of professional soldier-administrators like Lord Shang, the rulers of the various states were always able to keep the upper hand, for they were believed to have inherited by birth some measure of the charisma of the state's founding ancestors, and thus they held the legitimate right to worship the powerful spirits that controlled men's destiny. The soldier-administrators were never able to forge such close links with their men that they and their armies could threaten the political authority of the ruler or disrupt the social order, even though some of them kept bodies of personal dependents or slaves who were trained specifically in swordsmanship. In fact, it was rare for a general to be able to live out his days with rank and wealth intact. Most died at the hands of official executioners, like Lord Shang, or were forced to commit suicide. This situation lasted until the beginning of the Han dynasty, when Liu Bang, who began life as a commoner and petty Qin official, seized the imperial throne. But he was advised that although he had won the empire on horseback, he could not rule it from horseback: he had to institute religious ritual to make manifest that he was the legitimate emperor and had the right, as Son of Heaven, to perform the sacrifices to Heaven and Earth, and the other powerful celestial spirits.

Unfortunately, the exact relationship between the soldiers serving in the army and the ownership or exploitation of the land is nowhere near as clear in

China as it is in Greece and Rome. We do know that eventually, by about 250 B.C.E., the buying and selling of land had appeared in a number of states, including Qin, but the state still seems to have claimed ownership in most cases: land was either farmed by tenants who paid taxes to the state or worked by official state slave laborers.[83] The proportion of land cultivated by independent farmers, who were conscripted into the army, and that cultivated by state slaves or tenants is not known. As mentioned earlier, all members of the population, both male and female, owed corvée labor obligations to the state, in the case of Qin, perhaps of one month a year, and males owed military service from about the age of sixteen or seventeen until retirement at age sixty.[84] Laws were strictly enforced and crimes punished by mutilations and hard labor, whereas rewards of rank were given to men for outstanding service. Women who fought in times of siege were rewarded with donations of 5000 cash (*qian*), whereas those who did not fight and infirm males were given 1000 cash (*qian*) and granted remission of taxes for three years.[85]

By 221 B.C.E., when huge labor projects, such as the Great Wall and the First Emperor's mausoleum, were initiated, some scholars have reckoned that more than one-tenth of the total population of the country, ten million, were engaged in forced labor for the state. All members of this population were organized into groups of five families, as Guanzi recommended for the state of Qi quoted previously, and they were liable for one another's behavior.[86] If a family member committed a crime, it was the responsibility of the group to denounce him. If they failed to denounce him, all members were punished as though they had committed the crime themselves. Thus the heads of the five-family units and the village heads were essentially members of the state administrative system responsible for law and order, labor, and registration of their members.

To return to more specifically military matters, by the end of the fourth century B.C.E., cavalry had been adopted from the northern nomadic peoples who increasingly threatened the burgeoning commercial centers of Chinese civilization. These nomads, known to the Chinese by the collective name of *hu*, began developing their skills in fighting from horseback, although they did not, apparently, possess as yet the stirrup.[87] New weapons were invented or introduced. Among these was the lethal crossbow, whose bolts were more accurate and more highly penetrating than the arrows fired by the reflex bow, yet which required a much more advanced casting for its bronze trigger mechanism and better training for firing in formation.[88] Another was the long sword. This probably would have been used to the best advantage by cavalrymen, but the current evidence is that infantry were equipped with this weapon. Further, there developed considerable regional specialization in different weapons, shapes, and designs, perhaps reflecting different fighting techniques in the different ecological zones, although there is insufficient detail in the sources to verify this supposition.[89]

Finally, the technology for casting iron was invented in about the sixth century B.C.E., first for agricultural implements and then for weapons, such as swords and pikes, and armor.[90] Such states as Yan, near modern Beijing, and Han, in the central Yellow River valley, became particularly noted for their iron weapons, and the Japanese archaeologist Sekino Takeshi even suggested that the reason the Qin was able to unify China was because it had access to large numbers of cheap wrought iron swords.[91] Without a doubt, swords came to hold a special place in the social life of the Chinese at this time, for the ceremony of initiation into adulthood, or capping, of a young man consisted of his donning a sword for the first time. According to recently excavated Qin almanac texts, this ceremony had to take place on an auspicious day, otherwise it was thought that the recipient would suffer bad fortune. Surprisingly enough, through the Han dynasty, officials in the government bureaucracy, who were educated in civil Confucian learning, were also expected to wear ceremonial swords. The importance of these weapons can be judged from the fact that many individuals chose to have themselves buried with their swords at their side *inside* their coffins, keeping other weapons and grave goods in the outer coffins.

The discovery in 1975 of the pottery army of approximately six thousand life-size figurines of infantry, chariots, and cavalry to the east of the emperor's mausoleum at Mount Li, however, has given scholars a very clear idea of what the Qin army looked like, even though there are many disagreements about the precise nature of the forces represented in the pits: were the soldiers, every one different in facial features, modeled from real life (see Figure 2-1)?[92] Do the figurines represent the actual field army that conquered China, or is it the capital garrison force, or the emperor's personal bodyguard?[93] Whatever the answer, what is remarkable is that only one iron weapon was found; all the others were made of bronze.[94] This, with other evidence, suggests that the Qin was successful in conquering its rivals not because it had more advanced weapons technology but because it had created a better military organization and a better military training program, it applied military law and organization to its population, and it developed sophisticated logistical skills for the storage, transportation, and disbursement of grain and other necessities.[95]

Finally, the First Emperor and his advisers, such as his first prime minister Lü Buwei, believed strongly in the idea that it was the ruler's responsibility to bring harmony to the cosmos by unifying the entire known world, and that it was essential for all the ruler's actions to be in accord with the seasonal changes and the waxing and waning of the cosmic forces of *yin* and *yang* that alternated perpetually throughout the year, *yang* reaching its zenith at the summer solstice and *yin* at the winter solstice. The ruler had to embody the changes in the natural world by ingesting foods appropriate to each season, and he had to signify that he was a model or template for correct action by clothing his body

Figure 2-1   *An officer of the First Emperor's pottery army (courtesy Metropolitan Museum of Art)*

with appropriately colored vestments and making sacrifices to temporally appropriate deities. By these ritual performances, the ruler was conceived of as mediating between Heaven, Earth, and Man, maintaining the balance of the cosmic forces and ensuring the harmonious continuity of the natural cycle. The unification of the world was to be achieved by force of arms because the ruler and his advisers believed that Qin operated under the aegis of the phase "water" in the five-phase scheme, the phase that was dominant in winter, when *yin* was at its height, and when it was naturally appropriate to apply punishment.[96] It was these ideas applied by means of the military techniques outlined earlier in this chapter, I believe, above all else that enabled the First Emperor to defeat his rivals and found the empire in 221.[97]

The Han Dynasty

A few words should be said about the last period to be considered here, the last two hundred years before the turn of the millennium.[98] The Han dynasty continued much of the administrative and economic system of its predecessors, the Qin, adopting their bureaucratic titles and offices and extending the land system. The Qin social system was also continued, although the Han emperors made a habit of granting degrees of rank to the general male populace on occasions of ritual significance, like the establishment of the heir apparent, or when cosmic portents seemed to indicate that the emperor should renew the social fabric and improve his moral behavior rather than donating it solely on the basis of military success, as the Qin had done.[99]

Internal military affairs were dominated in the first few decades of the dynasty by the need to suppress those warlords who had helped Liu Bang win the throne and imperial princes who felt that they either should be elevated to the highest honor or should be allowed as much freedom to govern and exploit their territories as the lords of the independent states of the Warring States period had possessed. All these challengers and pretenders were eventually defeated and their kingdoms incorporated into the areas directly administered by the central authorities based in the capital. As a consequence, the Han dynasty enjoyed prolonged periods of peace, and the population and the economy boomed.

On the other hand, externally, the major threat to the Han empire came from the Xiongnu nomadic secondary empire on the northern frontier, and for close to seven decades the Han were obliged to adopt a defensive policy toward them, buying them off with enormous quantities of silk and foodstuffs, creating a marriage link between the royal house of Han and the khan, recognizing the equal status of the emperor and the khan, and recognizing the Great Wall as the official boundary between the two empires, all to discourage the Xiongnu from raiding close to the capital of Changan in the west and penetrating into the commanderies of Yanmen and Dai in the northeast.[100] Then, under Emperor Wu (r. 141–81 B.C.E.), the policy was reversed, and the Chinese sent out large expeditionary forces to push the Xiongnu away from the northern borders and to prevent them from threatening the routes leading west along the Gansu corridor and through the Taklamakan Desert in central Asia. The official Zhang Qian had undertaken an exploratory expedition to the far west and reported back to the throne on the diplomatic and trade possibilities that these routes offered. Emperor Wu was enticed, and, as he attempted to exert greater central control over the internal economy by instituting state monopolies over the production of cast iron and salt and the brewing of alcohol, he also sought to push the boundaries of the empire out to the northwest, the southwest, and

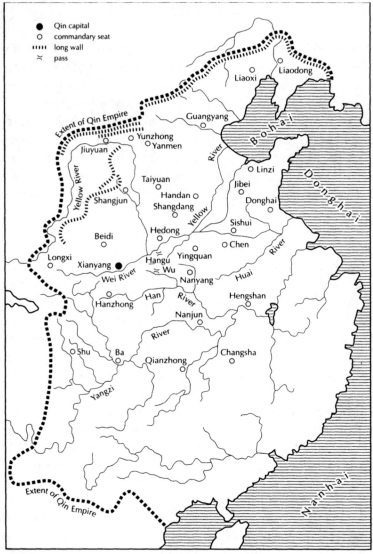

The Qin Empire

into what is now Korea. Despite enormous losses in men and matériel, eventually the Han were indeed able to establish a series of lookout stations and commanderies and counties in these forbidding regions, and were able to assert authority over many of the tribes and chiefdoms located there.

These policies, which had been promoted by officials with connections to rich merchant families and who supported the general approach of earlier legalist centralizers, such as Lord Shang, were bitterly criticized in an imperially sponsored review in 81 B.C.E. The critics were Confucian literati who advocated a return to policies that promoted retrenchment from foreign adventures and a removal of the government from active involvement in the economy.[101] Although it is likely that the critics did not force an immediate major shift in imperial direction, nevertheless, their strong objection to a forward military policy profoundly affected the Han attitude toward the military in general, and, by the end of the Han, it was the civil arts that were culturally favored.

Fortunately, the dryness of the climate in the regions where the forts and walls were constructed in the Gobi Desert is such that tens of thousands of wooden slips have been preserved, abandoned when the Han gave up their hold in about 140 C.E., and these provide scholars with a richness of detailed source material about the actual day-to-day life of the soldiers in the desert unparalleled in other ancient societies.[102] Regrettably, the historical sources for the situation inside the empire are nowhere near as comprehensive, and there is considerable dispute among scholars about the military obligations of the general populace. Loewe suggests that the servicemen of both static garrison forces and expeditionary armies were essentially derived from three main sources: they were either conscripts, volunteers, or convicts who were serving their time of hard labor under terms of an imperial remission of crimes or amnesty.[103] The conscripts probably constituted the largest portion of the forces, but it is not clear exactly what the compulsory obligation was. From the beginning of the dynasty in 206 to 156 B.C.E., the age of conscription was between twenty-three and fifty-six years, and from 155 to the reign of Zhaodi (87–74 B.C.E.), all men, except those specially exempted because they possessed degrees of high rank, were called up from the age of twenty. It is likely that service lasted two years, the first consisting of training in the man's home commandery; the second year was spent either at one of the frontiers or at the barracks at the capital or some other strategic site. However, some scholars believe that, in addition, a man had the obligation to serve three days annually, which was taken in longer, consecutive spells. Possibly also some men were trained as specialist cavalry on the northern frontier and as marines on the rivers, lakes, and seas of the southeast and south.[104]

Over time, however, ordinary individuals could pay cash to buy themselves out of service and to pay substitutes, possibly at the rate of three hundred cash (*qian*) per month, but there is much dispute about how this system operated. What is clear is that the universal military service was formally abolished just after the Han regained the throne from the usurper Wang Mang and after that Han forces were essentially professional.[105] As in other societies discussed in this volume, such as the Islamic, the Han paid men from particular tribes or regions to perform specialist services for them; for example, the southern Xiongnu, who had broken with their northern kinsmen and settled within the line of the Han Great Wall defenses, served as expert cavalry, and peoples from a county in

Sichuan served as crossbowmen.[106] Eventually, in the second century C.E., the power of the central authorities decreased, and the countryside came to be dominated by local magnates who controlled large estates and prevented the government from levying taxes and corvée labor on their dependents and tenants. In addition, political infighting among eunuchs loyal to the imperial family, including empresses and the empress-dowagers, and the bureaucracy staffed by Confucian literati reached savage proportions. With deteriorating conditions in the countryside and the shrinking of urbanization, two main millenarian rebellions erupted, one in east China, the Yellow Turbans, in 184 C.E. and the other in Sichuan, the Five Pecks of Rice, and the Han dynasty fell in confusion in 220 C.E., allowing the northern nomadic peoples to push south and occupy regions within the Chinese heartland for the next three hundred years.[107]

Conclusion

From what has been presented in this chapter, it can be seen that, from Bronze Age times on in China, warfare was considered an essential component of the sacrificial system on which the state based its existence and its legitimacy. Further, the personnel needs of the army were considered paramount in the social engineering that statesmen-philosophers of the Warring States instituted to strengthen their states in the competitive environment that culminated in the unification of China in 221 B.C.E. The army thus was the basis of traditional Chinese social organization. In other words, what some scholars have seen in China as a civil or civilian society in late imperial times was actually based on the military system of the ancient period. In addition, military values and practices were intimately connected with religious values and cosmological beliefs: China certainly could not have been unified without this emphasis on the military by the Qin.

In Han times, after internal peace had been achieved, Confucian literati, who were gaining greater dominance in the state bureaucracy and influencing the development of state ideology, downplayed the importance of warfare and advocated the idea that it was because of the Han's virtue (de), not because of its military prowess, that it was able to triumph and establish imperial institutions. In Han cosmology, which came to be the foundation of all later traditional ideology, war was deemed to be concerned with death, ghosts, and the spirit world; that is, it was deemed a highly inauspicious activity and categorized in the bipolar yin-yang correlative cosmology as yin. It was not concerned with those activities associated with life-giving and life-preserving, such as marriages, that were deemed auspicious and yang. Within the complex discourse of purity and pollution that I have analyzed elsewhere, war was reckoned to be a means of exorcising the polluted or impure, much as punishments and the legal system were.[108] Thus, war was not to be spoken about with pride, nor were military heroes and deeds of martial prowess to be glorified, although they were tolerated, or even considered necessary, in the broader scheme of things in the all-under-heaven.[109] Since it was the literati who wrote history, and since they considered warfare to be an inauspicious activity not to be praised or encouraged, the all-important interconnection between warfare and society in early China was forgotten and erased from memory. This prejudice against the military was accepted by twentieth-century Chinese scholars and Westerners who followed their lead in choosing subjects to study. It is only recently that the significance of war in Chinese history has begun to be appreciated. This chapter is a small contribution to this reevaluation, written in the light of the other chapters in this volume that analyze war in other ancient and medieval societies.

Notes

1. Needham and Yates 1994.
2. This is because Chinese scholars follow the Morgan paradigm (Morgan 1877) that was incorporated into Marxist periodization of history by Engels; they claim that this was the age of primitive communism and matriarchy. Earliest stages: Needham and Yates 1994; Yates 1997.
3. Ditches: Fung 1994.
4. Liu Li 1994; Underhill 1991, 1992; Yates 1997a.
5. Generally speaking, the later Chinese preferred a defense in depth, and most defenders were not prepared merely to wait out an attacking force; rather, they seized the initiative and took the fight to the enemy. This may have been the custom in the late Neolithic too, but unfortunately we do not have the archaeological evidence to make a final determination.
6. Chap. 3, section 30: 14b.
7. Chang 1986.287.
8. Allan 1991; Thorp 1991.
9. Boltz 1994; Yates 1997a.
10. These consist of brief and sometimes fragmentary divination charges and records called *oracle bones* used in the sacrifices to the ancestors. The Shang kings divined when and where they should go into combat, and they reported to their ancestors the outcome of conflicts in detail in the oracle bone inscriptions. These inscriptions have been deciphered and interpreted by several generations of scholars in the past ninety years or so since their discovery, but many graphs still remain unidentified and unexplained: Keightley 1978b. A few inscriptions on bronze vessels survive from the Shang. The succeeding Zhou, however, inscribed very long texts on their bronzes, and these are invaluable records for understanding the nature of their society (see below).
11. Chang 1980; Keightley 1978a, 1995; Zhu Fenghan 1990.

12. According to later historical records, the Shang are said to have had five successive capitals.

13. Keightley 1995.

14. Keightley 1996; Shaughnessy 1988; Barbieri-Low 1997.

15. Duke Cheng year 13, 576 B.C.E.; Kierman 1974.28 with emendations; Legge 1872. 379 (text), 381 (translation).

16. Lewis 1990.17.

17. Bronze weapons: Chen Fang-mei 1995; chariot imprints: Yang Hong 1985b; excavations: Chang 1977, 1980; Needham and Yates 1994.

18. Chang 1980.263–88; An Jinhuai 1961; Needham and Yates 1994.292, 295.

19. Needham and Yates 1994.293; Bagley 1977.

20. Cf. Hayashi Minao 1966; Yang Yingjie 1986. Drums were beaten to exorcise evil spirits, for example, those that were believed to be eating the sun and moon during eclipses. It is not unreasonable to assume that the beating of drums in battle had a similar function: the enemy were conceived of as being evil spirits that had to be exorcised.

21. See Gnirs, this volume, at n. 4, on the dehumanization of enemies in Egypt. In the ancient West, surrendering cities were known to have suspended incense burners over the walls to indicate their willingness to yield to their attackers: Classen, Howes, and Synnott 1994.39; cf. Nielsen 1986.13.

22. Keightley 1969. Military service was reckoned as part of corvée labor service in China until the beginning of the later Han dynasty, when universal military service was abolished by Guangwu di: see Lewis 1997; Hsing 1997. See also Gnirs, this volume, on the army as corvée labor force in Egypt.

23. Keightley 1969.68; 1995.124–25.

24. Keightley 1983.

25. Women fought in sieges (see below) and, not infrequently, in rebellions, the case of the women warriors of the Taiping Heavenly Army during the mid-nineteenth century being the most famous.

26. 1995.125. A typical example of an oracle bone record reads as follows: "Divination on the day gengzi. Bin asked: 'If we do not levy ren, 3,000, and order: "[Attack] Gong-fang," will we not receive divine assistance?'": Luo Zhenyu 1933.7.2.3; Chen Enlin 1991.27; emended trans. of Keightley 1969.67–68.

27. Hayashi Minao 1976; Zhou Wei 1957; Keightley 1995, 1996; Kolb 1991; Zhong Bosheng 1991.

28. Lewis 1990.21. These rituals continued to be important events in the ritual calendar in early imperial times: Bodde 1975.349–59.

29. Zhong Bosheng 1972; Zhang Zhenglang 1973.

30. Cf. Yates 1990; Lewis 1990.21; Cook 1997.

31. Chen Mengjia 1956; Li Xueqin 1959; Shima Kunio 1958; Chang 1980; Keightley 1983; Shaughnessy 1989; Zheng Jiexiang 1994.

32. Keightley 1996.

33. Cook 1997.260–69; Chang 1980.

34. Shaughnessy 1981.

35. Creel 1970b; Hsu 1965; Hsu and Linduff 1988; Shaughnessy 1989; Wheatley 1971;

cf. Le Goff 1980.

36. Cook 1997, esp. 284–90; Yates 1997a.

37. As indicated in n. 10 above, the Zhou inscribed their ritual vessels with much longer documents than the Shang did: most Shang vessels are either uninscribed or have only the mark of the lineage engraved on them: Allan 1991.89. The translation changes Shaughnessy's romanization system, makes one emendation, and incorporates two emendations from the published version supplied to me by Shaughnessy. For these I am most grateful to the author.

38. This vessel was cast in King Kang's reign (1005–978 B.C.E.) and discovered in a cache south of the Yangtze River east of Nanjing in Jiangsu province. The translation is by Shaughnessy 1989.14–15.

39. Cao Wanru et al. 1990; Bulling 1978. Traditionally, Chinese maps were drawn to be read in the opposite way to what we in the West are used to: south is at the top of the map and north to the bottom, as though they were being read by a ruler who was facing south. In addition, the relative heights of mountains in the Mawangdui maps are indicated by narrow concentric lines, a technique that was only adopted in the West more than a thousand years later.

40. Chap. X, section 27 "Ti T'u" (Ditu) (On Maps), translated by Rickett 1965.234. One must remember that the term *tu* also referred to cosmographic charts and pictures of gods and spirits. All these maps and charts were believed to contain esoteric spiritual knowledge that could reveal to the possessor or beholder the identity and disposition of unseen forces that might threaten or harm him.

41. Yates 1997a; *zongfa* system: Chun 1990.

42. Shaughnessy 1989; Hsu and Linduff 1988.123–26.

43. Qin, Chu, Qi, Yan, Han, Wei, and Zhao.

44. Cook 1997.254–55.

45. Cook 1997.260.

46. Ye Daxiong 1979.

47. Shaughnessy 1989.

48. Hsu and Linduff 1988.138.

49. Creel 1970a; cf. Goodrich 1984.

50. There are examples of halberds *(ji)*, combinations of spear and dagger-ax, in the Western Zhou, which were cast in one piece, but they too may have been used less for actual combat than to symbolize military authority: Chen Fang-mei 1995.

51. Yang Hong 1985a.

52. Hayashi Minao 1976.

53. Needham and Yates 1994; cf. Yates 1982.

54. Kierman 1974.

55. Hsu 1965; Wagner 1993.

56. Yates 1995.

57. Lewis 1990.5–6.

58. Kierman 1974.30–31.

59. Ames 1993; Sawyer 1993; Yates 1988.

60. Kierman 1974.36.

61. See Raaflaub and Farris, this volume; Farris 1995.270.
62. Translated by Rickett 1985.
63. Yates 1994.62–63.
64. Yan Zhu 1980.224–25.
65. Xiong Tieji 1981.
66. Hsu 1965.
67. Hulsewé 1985.
68. Yates 1997a.
69. Hsu 1965.
70. Eno 1990.
71. Ames 1993; Kierman 1974.
72. Wu Jiulong 1990.263.
73. Kierman 1974.28.
74. Yates 1995. The use of spies also became an essential component of war, a practice that was at complete variance with the code of honor in the previous period.
75. Du Zhengsheng 1990; Yates 1987.
76. Lewis 1990.
77. In some cases, conquered territory was given as a kind of fief to deserving officers. However, the "commandery-county" system was applied to the entire country by the Qin after the unification in 221 B.C.E. (cf. Yates 1995), when there were thirty-six commanderies instituted, and this form generally prevailed throughout later imperial history. Only when the central government was weak was territory given to powerful magnates, such as generals or imperial relatives, in the form of fiefs.
78. Yates 1982; Needham and Yates 1994. The size of many Warring States cities was considerable: the capital of Qi in the Warring States, Linzi, is recorded as containing seven hundred thousand people. Whether this is a truly accurate count is not clear. However, archaeologists have demonstrated that later Han dynasty cities were smaller than their predecessors. The *Mozi* describes twelve methods of attacking a city, from underground mining to flooding, and provides the defenders with the solutions to these assaults: Yates 1982; Needham and Yates 1994.
79. Rosenstein, this volume.
80. Yates 1988; Lau and Ames 1996. From the time when cavalry made its appearance in the mid-fourth century B.C.E., it was usually, but not invariably, characterized as the "irregular" force. But "regular" could also be what the enemy thought you were going to do. So if a general used the infantry in an unexpected fashion and the cavalry in an expected fashion, the infantry could be the "irregular" and the cavalry the "regular" force. Needless to say, the permutations could be endless.
81. His policies earned him their undying hatred. They took their revenge after his lord, Duke Xiao of Qin, died in 338 B.C.E.: he rebelled, and they had him ripped apart by four chariots, one of the punishments for high treason.
82. It appears that commoners were only permitted to reach the eighth rank; aristocrats could hold the upper ranks.
83. One of the reforms instituted by Lord Shang in Qin was the extension of the Qin acre from 100 square paces to 240 paces, which we now know he adopted from the

state of Zhao: Yates 1988; Ames 1993. At the same time, he broke down the old boundaries between the fields and had constructed pathways running north and south. This system was applied to the whole country in the Qin and Han dynasties. Han Confucian scholars heavily criticized Lord Shang for the commercialization of land and accused him of initiating the system that led to consolidation of land-holding in the hands of a small elite of local magnates and the despoliation of the ordinary peasant farmer.

84. Yates 1987; cf. Xiong Tieji and Wang Ruiming 1981; Yu Haoliang and Li Junming 1981. The retirement age was fifty-six if one possessed rank. There are some indications in the sources that slaves and convicts were recruited as soldiers, especially in times of emergency, but the exact nature and extent of the involvement of such persons in military activities is currently unknown.

85. Hulsewé 1985; Yates 1980. Fragment 86.

86. Different occupations were listed on different registers: Yates 1987.

87. By the end of the third century B.C.E., the most powerful group of tribesmen in the northern steppes were the Xiongnu. Regarding the absence of stirrups among the northern nomads, I have discovered evidence from tombs of one of the central Asian peoples that may challenge this idea. Stirrups may have appeared in the steppeland by the end of the Warring States and the beginning of the empire, roughly 200 B.C.E., a full five hundred years before the first appearance of the representation of a stirrup in a post-Han tomb dated 302 C.E.: Dien 1986; Yang Hong 1985b; cf. Goodrich 1984.

88. Needham and Yates 1994.

89. The southeastern states of Wu and Yue, later conquered by Chu, for example, were known for their high level of craftsmanship in making swords, the best of which displayed an exceptional sophistication in varying the metal composition of the different parts of the weapon, in inlay work, and in surface treatment of the blades to create exquisite designs. Because the southeast was a land of rivers and marshes, chariot warfare was never really significant there; rather, techniques of naval warfare were developed. The crossbow may well have been invented among indigenous tribes in south-central China: Needham and Yates 1994.135–40.

90. Wagner 1993.

91. Cf. Keightley 1976.

92. Wang Xueli 1994; Yuan Zhongyi 1988, 1990; Shaanxi sheng kaogu yanjiusuo and Shihuang ling Qinyongkeng kaogu fajue dui 1988.

93. It seems clear that the pottery warriors and horses were buried to protect the dead First Emperor from ghosts and other evil emanations that might disturb his tomb. That these warriors were equipped with real weapons, more than forty thousand of which have been excavated so far, suggests that the Qin saw little differentiation between such ghosts and the soldiers that the Qin forces encountered above ground.

94. The most impressive of the weapons found in the pits are the meter-long bronze swords, the surface of whose blades were treated with chrome to ensure permanent sharpness and brightness of color.

95. Yates 1995; cf. Hulsewé 1985.

96. The other phases are wood (spring), fire (summer), earth (late summer), and metal (autumn). Each of these phases was coordinated with a color and a number: water's color was black and its number six. This is why, on establishing the empire, the First Emperor changed all the imperial symbols and numbers to conform to this scheme; chariot axles, for example, were all made six feet wide, the commanderies were thirty-six in number, and the flags and palaces were painted black.

97. For example, general Bai Qi of Qin is said to have forced a Zhao army to surrender in 260 B.C.E. He decided to execute the prisoners to the number of four hundred thousand! This number was quite probably an exaggeration, but it certainly suggests that large armies were in the field on both sides. At least twelve of the pits into which the Qin threw their executed enemy have recently been identified, and one has been excavated: Shanxi sheng Kaogu yanjiusuo, Jincheng shi wenhuaju, and Gaoping shi bowuguan 1996.

98. For a comprehensive analysis of the political, economic, social, and philosophical history of the Han, see Twitchett and Loewe 1986.

99. Loewe 1960; cf. Loewe 1980. Han emperors also granted bolts of cloth, grain, and oxen on these ritual occasions, demonstrating that they were capable of providing the material needs of the population and were acting as "fathers and mothers" of the people.

100. Twitchett and Loewe 1986.

101. Loewe 1974.

102. Loewe 1967. There was a period at the turn of the millennium when the central authorities were weak and the throne was seized by a royal relative, Wang Mang, who reigned from 9 to 23 C.E. During this time, the Han forces retreated from central Asia, but after the Han regained the throne, they reoccupied their defenses.

103. Loewe 1967, vol. 1, 77.

104. It seems from the documentary evidence of the wooden slips that the Han government tried to feed its garrisons on the northwest frontier from the produce grown locally by volunteer agricultural colonists.

105. Hsing 1997; Lewis 1997.

106. See Crone, this volume.

107. The climate in East Asia reached its nadir shortly after the fall of the Han, and it may be that life on the marginal steppeland became increasingly difficult. Thus fewer people were able to be supported there. Enterprising warriors pushed south when the central power in north China weakened.

108. Yates 1997b.

109. As the natural cosmic cycle consisted of the alternation of *yang* and *yin*, both were considered indispensable, and thus punishment and war, the human manifestations of the *yin* phase, were also considered necessary human activity. Similarly, military ritual was one of the five official rituals performed by all Chinese emperors, or his substitutes, down to the twentieth century. Inauspicious portents, especially those manifesting themselves in the heavens, such as comets, were believed to presage military activity: Loewe 1980; 1994.61–84, 191–213.

Bibliography

Allan, Sarah. 1991. *The Shape of the Turtle: Myth, Art, and Cosmos in Early China.* Albany: State University of New York Press.

Ames, Roger T. 1993. *Sun-Tzu* The Art of Warfare: *The First English Translation Incorporating the Recently Discovered Yin-ch'üeh-shan Texts.* New York: Ballantine.

An Jinhuai. 1961. "Shi lun Zhengzhou Shang dai chengzhi Aodu," *Wenwu* 4–5, 73–80.

Bagley, Robert W. 1977. "P'an-Lung-Ch'eng: A Shang City in Hupei." *Artibus Asiae* 39, 3–4, 165–219.

Barbieri-Low, Anthony Jerome. 1997. "Wheeled Vehicles in the Chinese Bronze Age. (c. 2000–771 B.C.)" M.A. thesis, Harvard University.

Bodde, Derk. 1975. *Festivals in Classical China: New Year and Other Annual Observances during the Han Dynasty, 206 B.C.–A.D. 220.* Princeton, N.J.: Princeton University Press.

Boltz, William G. 1994. *The Origin and Early Development of the Chinese Writing System.* New Haven, Conn.: American Oriental Society.

Bulling, A. 1978. "Ancient Chinese Maps: Two Maps Discovered in a Han Dynasty Tomb from the 2nd Century." *Expedition* 20.2, 16.

Cao Wanru, Zheng Xihuang, Huang Shengzhang, Niu Zhongxun, Ren Jincheng, and Ju Deyuan. 1990. *Zhongguo gudai ditu ji (Zhanguo—Yuan) (An Atlas of Ancient Maps in China—From the Warring States Period to the Yuan Dynasty (476 B.C.–A.D. 1368).* Beijing: Cultural Relics Publishing House.

Chang, Kwang-chih. 1977. *The Archaeology of Ancient China.* 3d ed. New Haven, Conn.: Yale University Press.

———. 1980. *Shang Civilization.* New Haven, Conn.: Yale University Press.

———. 1986. *The Archaeology of Ancient China.* 4th ed. New Haven, Conn.: Yale University Press.

Chen Enlin. 1991. *XianQin junshi zhidu yanjiu.* Jilin: Jilin wenshi chuban she.

Chen Fang-mei. 1995. "Major Lines of Development in Shang and Chou Dynasty Bronze Weapons." In *Illustrated Catalogue of Ancient Bronze Weaponry in the National Palace Museum,* edited by Kuo-li Ku-kung Po-wu-yüan pien-chi wei-yüan hui, 80–125. Taipei: National Palace Museum.

Chen Mengjia. 1956. *Yinxu buci zongshu.* Beijing: Science Press.

Chun, Allen J. 1990. "Conceptions of Kinship and Kingship in Classical Chou China." *T'oung Pao* 76, 16–48.

Classen, Constance, David Howes, and Anthony Synnott. 1994. *Aroma: The Cultural History of Smell.* London: Routledge.

Cook, Constance A. 1997. "Wealth and the Western Zhou." *Bulletin of the School of Oriental and African Studies* 60.2, 253–94.

Creel, Herrlee G. 1970a. "The Horse in Chinese History." In *What Is Taoism? and Other Studies in Chinese Cultural History.* Chicago: University of Chicago Press.

———. 1970b. *The Origins of Chinese Statecraft.* Vol. 1, *The Western Chou Empire.* Chicago: University of Chicago Press.

Dien, Albert E. 1986. "The Stirrup and its Effect on Chinese Military History." *Ars Orientalis* 16, 33–56.

Du Zhengsheng. 1990. *Bianhu Qimin: Chuantong zhengzhi shehui jiegou zhi xingcheng.* Taipei: Lianjing chuban shiye gongsi.

Engels, Friedrich. 1972. *The Origin of the Family, Private Property and the State.* Edited with an introduction by Eleanor Burke Leacock. London: Lawrence and Wishart.

Eno, Robert. 1990. *The Confucian Creation of Heaven: Philosophy and the Defence of Ritual Mastery.* Albany: State University of New York Press.

Farris, William Wayne. 1995. *Heavenly Warriors: The Evolution of Japan's Military, 500–1300.* Cambridge, Mass.: Council on East Asian Studies, Harvard University.

Fung, Christopher. 1994. "The Beginnings of Settled Life." In Murowchick 1994.51–59.

Goodrich, Chauncey S. 1984. "Riding Astride and the Saddle in Ancient China." *Harvard Journal of Asiatic Studies* 44.2, 279–305.

Hayashi Minao. 1966. "Chūgoku Sen Shin jidai no hata." *Shirin* 49.2, 66–94 (234–62).

———. 1976. *Chūgoku YinShū jidai no Buki.* Kyoto: Jimbun Kagaku Kenkyūjo.

Hsing, I-tien. 1997. "Middle Rank Officers of the Han Army as Seen in Pictorial and Literary Sources." Paper prepared for the Conference on Military Thought and Practice in Chinese History. Cambridge, England, December 12–13.

Hsu, Cho-yun. 1965. *Ancient China in Transition: An Analysis of Social Mobility, 722–222 B.C.* Stanford, Calif.: Stanford University Press.

Hsu, Cho-yun, and Kathryn M. Linduff. 1988. *Western Zhou Civilization.* New Haven, Conn.: Yale University Press.

Hulsewé, A. F. P. 1985. *Remnants of Ch'in Law: An Annotated Translation of the Ch'in Legal and Administrative Rules of the 3rd Century B.C. Discovered in Yün-meng Prefecture, Hupei Province in 1975.* Leiden: E. J. Brill.

Keightley, David N. 1969. "Public Work in Ancient China: A Study of Forced Labor in the Shang and Western Chou." Ph.D. diss., Columbia University.

———. 1976. "Where Have All the Swords Gone? Reflections on the Unification of China." *Early China* 2, 31–34.

———. 1978a. "The Religious Commitment: Shang Theology and the Genesis of Chinese Political Culture." *History of Religions* 17, 211–24.

———. 1978b. *Sources of Shang History: The Oracle-Bone Inscriptions of Bronze Age China.* Berkeley and Los Angeles: University of California Press.

———. 1983. "The Late Shang State: When, Where, and What?" In *The Origins of Chinese Civilization,* edited by David N. Keightley, 523–64. Berkeley and Los Angeles: University of California Press.

———. 1995. "The Shang: China's First Historical Dynasty." Draft for the *Cambridge History of China.*

———. 1996. "Warfare and Its Representations in Ancient China: Preliminary Observations." Paper presented in the panel "Warfare in Ancient Societies," International Studies Association Annual Convention, San Diego, California, April 18, 1996.

Kierman, Frank A., Jr. 1974. "Phases and Modes of Combat in Early China." In Kierman and Fairbank 1974.27–66.

Kierman, Frank A., Jr., and John K. Fairbank, eds. 1974. *Chinese Ways in Warfare.* Cambridge, Mass.: Harvard University Press.

Kolb, Raimund Theodor. 1991. *Die Infanterie im alten China: ein Beitrag zur Militärgeschichte der vor-Zhan-Guo-Zeit.* Mainz: Philipp von Zabern.

Lan Yongwei. 1979. *Chunqiu shiqi de bubing.* Beijing: Zhonghua shuju.

Lau, D. C., and Roger T. Ames. 1996. *Sun Pin: The Art of Warfare.* New York: Ballantine Books.

Legge, James. 1872. *The Chinese Classics.* Vol. 5, *The Ch'un Ts'ew, with the Tso Chuen.* Reprint, Hong Kong: Hong Kong University, 1960.

Le Goff, Jacques. 1980. "The Symbolic Ritual of Vassalage." In *Time, Work, and Culture in the Middle Ages,* translated by Arthur Goldhammer, 237–87. Chicago: University of Chicago Press.

Lewis, Mark Edward. 1990. *Sanctioned Violence in Early China.* Albany: State University of New York Press.

———. 1997. "The Han Abolition of Universal Military Service." Paper prepared for the Conference on Military Thought and Practice in Chinese History. Cambridge, England, December 12–13.

Li Xueqin. 1959. *Yindai dili jianlun.* Beijing: Kexue chuban she.

———. 1985. *Eastern Zhou and Qin Civilizations.* New Haven, Conn.: Yale University Press.

Liu, Li. 1994. "Development of Chiefdom Societies in the Middle and Lower Yellow River Valley in Neolithic China: A Study of the Longshan Culture from the Perspective of Settlement Patterns." Ph.D. diss., Harvard University.

Liu Tao. 1990. *Siku bingjia lei congshu.* Vol. 1. Shanghai: Shanghai Guji chuban she.

Loewe, Michael. 1960. "The Orders of Aristocratic Rank of Han China." *T'oung Pao 48,* 1–3, 97–174.

———. 1967. *Records of Administration.* 2 vols. Cambridge: Cambridge University Press.

———. 1974. "The Grand Inquest—81 B.C." In *Crisis and Conflict in Han China,* 91–112. London: George Allen and Unwin.

———. 1980. "The Han View of Comets." *Bulletin of the Museum of Far Eastern Antiquities* 52, 1–31. Reprinted in Loewe 1994.61–84.

———. 1994. *Divination, Mythology and Monarchy in Han China.* Cambridge: Cambridge University Press.

Luo Zhenyu. 1933. *Yinxu shuqi qianbian.*

Morgan, Lewis H. 1877. *Ancient Society.* Cleveland: World Publishing Society.

Murowchick, Robert E., ed. 1994. *Cradles of Civilization: China.* Sydney: Weldon Russell.

Needham, Joseph, and Robin D. S. Yates. 1994. *Science and Civilisation in China.* Vol. 5, *Chemistry and Chemical Technology.* Part 6, *Military Technology: Missiles and Sieges.* Cambridge: Cambridge University Press.

Nielsen, K. 1986. *Incense in Ancient Israel.* Leiden: E. J. Brill.

Rickett, W. Allyn, trans. 1965. *Kuan-tzu, A Repository of Early Chinese Thought.* Hong Kong: Hong Kong University Press.

———, trans. 1985. *Guanzi: Political, Economic, and Philosophical Essays from Early China.* Vol. 1. Princeton, N. J.: Princeton University Press.

Sawyer, Ralph D., trans. 1993. *The Seven Military Classics of Ancient China.* Boulder, Colo.: Westview Press.

Shaanxi sheng kaogu yanjiusuo and Shihuang ling Qinyongkeng kaogu fajue dui. 1988. *Qin Shihuang ling bingma yongkeng yihao keng fajue baogao 1974–1984.* 2 vols. Beijing: Wenwu chuban she.

Shanxi sheng kaogu yanjiusuo, Jincheng shi wenhuaju, and Gaoping shi bowuguan. 1996. "Changping zhi zhan yizhi Yonglu yihao shigu keng fajue jianbao." *Wenwu* 6, 33–40.

Shaughnessy, Edward L. 1981. "New Evidence on the Zhou Conquest." *Early China* 6, 57–79.

———. 1988. "Historical Perspectives on the Introduction of the Chariot into China." Harvard Journal of Asiatic Studies 48.1, 189–237.

———. 1989. "Historical Kingdoms and the Extent of the Earliest Chinese Kingdoms." *Asia Major,* 3d ser., 2.2, 1–22.

Shima Kunio. 1958. *Inkyo Bokuji Kenkyū.* Hirosaki: Chūgokugaku kenkyūkai.

Thorp, Robert L. 1991. "Erlitou and the Search for the Xia." Early China 16, 1–38.

Twitchett, Denis, and Michael Loewe, eds. 1986. *The Cambridge History of China.* Vol. 1, *The Ch'in and Han Empires.* Cambridge: Cambridge University Press.

Underhill, Anne P. 1991. "Pottery Production in Chiefdoms: The Longshan Period in Northern China." *World Archaeology* 23.1, 12–27.

———. 1992. "Regional Growth of Cultural Complexity during the Longshan Period of Northern China." In *Pacific Northeast Asia in Prehistory: Hunter-Fisher-Gatherers, Farmers, and Sociopolitical Elites,* edited by C. Melvin Aikens and Song Nai Rhee, 173–77. Pullman: Washington State University Press.

Wagner, Donald B. 1993. *Iron and Steel in Ancient China.* Leiden: E. J. Brill.

Wang Xueli. 1994. *Qin yong zhuanti yanjiu* (Special Studies on Qin Terracotta Figures). Xian: San Qin chuban she.

Wheatley, Paul J. 1971. *The Pivot of the Four Quarters.* Edinburgh: Edinburgh University Press.

Wu Jiulong, ed. 1990. *Sunzi jiaoshi.* Beijing: Junshi kexue chuban she.

Xiong Tieji. 1981. "Lun Qindai junshi zhidu," In Zhongguo Qin Han shi yanjiu hui ed., *Qin Han shi luncong,* Vol. 1, 41–60. Xi'an: Shaanxi renmin chuban she.

Xiong Tieji and Wang Ruiming. 1981. "Qindai de fengjian tudi suo you zhi." In Zhonghua shuju bianji bu, ed., *Yunmeng Qin jian yanjiu,* 67–78. Beijing: Zhonghua shuju.

Xu Baolin. 1988. *Zhongguo bingshu zhijian lu.* Beijing: Jiefangjun chuban she.

Yan Zhu. 1980. "Chunqiu shidai de junshi zhidu (shang)." *Shehui kexue zhanxian* 3.2 (10), 224–28.

Yang Hong. 1985a. "Jian he dao." In Yang Hong 1985d.115–30.

———. 1985b. "Qibing he jiaqi juzhuang." In Yang Hong 1985d.94–104.

———. 1985c. "Zhanche yu chezhan." In Yang Hong 1985d.79–93.

———. 1985d. *Zhongguo gu bingqi luncong (zengding ben).* Beijing: Wenwu chuban she.

———. 1992. *Weapons in Ancient China.* New York: Science Press.

Yang Yingjie. 1986. "Xian Qin qizhi kaoshi." *Wenwu* 2, 52-56.

Yates, Robin D. S. 1980. *The City under Siege: Technology and Organization as seen in the Reconstructed Text of the Military Chapters of Mo Tzu.* Unpublished Ph.D. diss. Harvard University, Cambridge, Mass.

———. 1982. "Siege Engines and Late Zhou Military Technology." In *Explorations in the History of Science and Technology in China,* edited by Li Guohao, Zhang Mengwen, Cao Tianqin, and Hu Daojing, 409. Shanghai: Shanghai Guji chuban she.

———. 1987. "Social Status in the Ch'in: Evidence from the Yün-meng Legal Documents. Part One: Commoners." *Harvard Journal of Asiatic Studies* 47.1, 197–236.

———. 1988. "New Light on Ancient Chinese Military Texts: Notes on Their Nature and Evolution and the Development of Military Specialization in Warring States China." *T'oung Pao* 74.3–5, 212–48.

———. 1990. "War, Food Shortages, and Relief Measures in Early China." In *Hunger in History: Food Shortage, Poverty, and Deprivation,* edited by Lucile F. Newman, 147–177. Cambridge: Basil Blackwell.

———. 1994. "Body, Space, Time and Bureaucracy: Boundary Creation and Control Mechanisms in Early China." In *Boundaries in China,* edited by John Hay, 56–80. London: Reaktion.

———. 1995. "State Control of Bureaucrats under the Qin: Techniques and Procedures." *Early China* 20, 123–52.

———. 1997a. "The City State in Ancient China." In *The Archaeology of City-States: Cross-Cultural Approaches,* edited by Deborah L. Nichols and Thomas H. Charlton, 71–90. Washington, D.C.: Smithsonian Institution Press.

———. 1997b. "Purity and Pollution in Early China." *Zhongguo kaoguxue yu lishixue zhi zhenghe yanjiu* (Integrated Studies on Chinese Archaeology and Historiography), Symposium Series of the Institute of History and Philology, Academia Sinica, Number 4, 479–536. Taibei: Academia Sinica.

Ye Daxiong. 1979. "XiZhou bingzhi de tantao." *Guoli Taiwan daxue Lishi xuexi xuebao* 6, 1–16.

Yu Haoliang and Li Junming. 1981. "Qin jian suo fanying de junshi zhidu." In Zhonghua shuju bianji bu, ed., *Yunmeng Qin jian yanjiu,* 152–170. Beijing: Zhonghua shuju.

Yuan Zhongyi. 1990. *Qin Shihuang ling bingma yong yanjiu.* Beijing: Wenwu chuban she.

———, ed. 1988. *Qin Shihuang ling bingma yong.* Taipei: Luotuo chuban she.

Zhang Zhenglang. 1973. "Buci poutian ji qi xiangguan zhu wenti." *Kaogu xuebao* 1, 93–120.

Zheng Jiexiang. 1994. *Shangdai dili gailun.* Zhengzhou: Zhongzhou guji chuban she.

Zhong Bosheng. 1972. "Buci zhong suojian Yinwang tianyou diming kao—jianlun tianyou dimingyanjiu fangfa." M.A. thesis, National Taiwan University.

———. 1991. "Buci zhong suojian Yindai de junzheng zhi yi—Zhanzheng qidong de guocheng ji qi junbei gongzuo." *Zhongguo wenzi* 14, 95–156.

Zhou Wei. 1957. *Zhongguo Bingqi shi gao.* Beijing: Sanlian chuban she.

Zhu Fenghan. 1990. *Shang Zhou jiazu xingtai yanjiu.* Tianjin: Guji chuban she.

Japan to 1300

W. WAYNE FARRIS

Introduction and Previous Research

War has been known in Japan since about 300 B.C., and specialized fighters have been an important component of society from at least the late fourth century. This chapter will explore the place of war and the military in Japanese society from earliest times until the end of the thirteenth century. The year 1300 was chosen as the terminus for this study because it simultaneously marks the triumph of the warrior in the political arena and the beginning of a new era in population, the economy, social relations, and the technology and tactics of warfare.

Historians have focused their attention on the samurai, seeking the origins of this lightly armored mounted archer and explaining how he came to dominate politics.[1] Until 1965, scholars presented "the rise of the warrior" as a short-term phenomenon beginning after 900 and concluding in 1185. Usually, they portrayed the transition from the Chinese-style state (645–900) to the samurai government in Kamakura (1185–1333) as a fundamental transformation of society, politics, the economy, and culture. Scholars measured Japan against the yardstick of European history, applying such terms as *ancient* and *public* to the Chinese-style state, and *medieval, private,* and *feudal* to the Kamakura polity.[2]

Over the past thirty years, Japanese researchers have led the way in revising old interpretations. Increasingly, historians in both Japan and the United States have found pre-900 origins for the samurai, and few would argue that the samurai was supreme in politics by 1185.[3] Terms derived from European history,

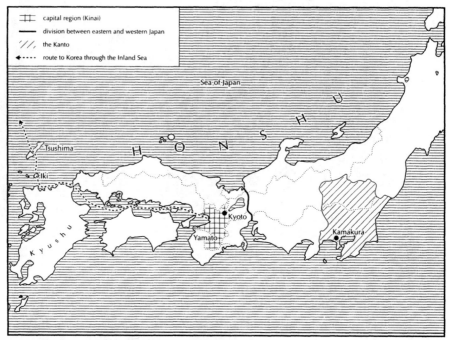

The Japanese Archipelago ca. 1300 B. C .E.

especially feudalism, have fallen into desuetude.[4] Scholars are beginning to recognize that the "rise of the warrior" constituted only one aspect of the complex interaction between war and society in early Japan.

Generalizations about Society and Economy to 1300

While researchers recognize a great deal of change over this period and regional variation throughout the archipelago, a few constants hold true over time and space. Atop the social hierarchy was the emperor and court aristocracy, a tiny elite that obtained its living through offices, salaries, lands, and other perquisites. This coterie was preeminent throughout the period under consideration due to its monopoly of literacy, wealth, and political acumen, religious and ideological sanctity, and connections to the advanced technologies of the continent. Every region had its own families of notables, not nearly as lofty in status as the capital aristocracy but all-important in local society. Beneath the court and local elites subsisted the mass of population—mostly peasants, with a few artisans and traders.

Despite the existence of these diverse classes, binding social ties tended to be vertical and not horizontal.[5] People of the same occupation or status were competitors and rarely banded together; instead, the most enduring relations were regional and factional. In particular, individual courtiers habitually formed patron-client bonds with local notables.

Kinship was bilateral, meaning that a family could trace its descent through either the paternal or the maternal line.[6] Each parent could hold property, and they frequently lived in separate dwellings. Children were often raised by maternal grandparents. The reason for such a system may have been economic, but the result was a flexible and enduring lineage. Especially for the court and local elites, the family line was sacred, and extraordinary steps were taken to guarantee continuity.

The rural economy was far from the "agrocentric" regime that it would become by the eighteenth century.[7] Courtiers preferred polished rice in their diets and to this end tried to encourage the planting of wet-rice. However, paddy farming is backbreaking work, and while yields per unit of land were much higher than for any other crop, most of the surplus went to support a large population (five to six million in 700). In other words, per capita yields were low. Frequently, peasants resorted to dry cropping, slash-and-burn agriculture, hunting, fishing, gathering, and other occupations.

Settlement patterns also suggest the rigors of peasant life.[8] Rural residents typically lived in isolated homesteads or dispersed settlements. There is no trace of the nucleated village that formed the basis for peasant community in later times. Blood ties also tended to be weak and ephemeral. People frequently migrated. Collecting taxes and raising labor gangs from this dispersed and mobile populace became a primary goal of each political administration.

Origins: From Prehistoric Times to A.D. 645

The main sources for this period are archaeology and *The Chronicles of Japan*, a court history compiled in 720. Despite the paucity of materials, this era witnessed the formation of many basic patterns in the technology and social organization of warfare that continued until 1300.

The only legacy of the Paleolithic (150,000?–10,500 B.C.) and Jōmon (10,500–300 B.C.) eras for warfare in later periods was the development of a meter-long, highly sophisticated hunting bow and arrow, especially common in eastern Honshu.[9] With the onset of the Yayoi period (300 B.C.–A.D. 300), wet-rice agriculture and bronze and iron metallurgy entered the archipelago via Korea, resulting in a demographic explosion to between one and four million by the third century, mostly in western Japan.[10] Evidence of war is plentiful for this period. Large settlements were frequently ringed with ditches and wooden spikes, with watchtowers overhead. In northern Kyushu, artisans cast ceremonial bronze spear and halberd blades, which villagers interred en masse with the dead. Of the more than one thousand skeletons recovered from this period, over one hundred bear graphic signs of violent death.[11]

By the late third century, a small state had formed in the Kinai, and chieftains began building gigantic tumuli, many larger than the pyramids of Egypt. Even the earliest tombs contained iron weapons. By the fifth century, tumuli revealed the strong militaristic bent of the Kinai's early rulers. At Nonaka tomb near Osaka, archaeologists have uncovered eleven suits of iron armor complete with helmets, 169 iron swords, three iron spear points, and three hundred arrowheads. It is little wonder that archaeologists call the 400s "the century of armor."[12]

The most common type of armor until 500 was the iron cuirass with helmet, worn by foot soldiers. The only other fighters in East Asia to utilize this armor were those of the southern Korean peninsula, suggesting the close tie between Japan and that region.[13] In addition to handheld shields, fighters also hid behind implanted shields of wood and leather measuring 1.5 meters high and 60 centimeters wide.[14]

After 500, lamellar armor came into vogue. Composed of about eight hundred iron slats, this armor was lighter and more flexible than the cuirass. Its dispersion went hand in hand with the spread of horse-riding skills. Popular among the light cavalry of China, Tibet, and central Asia, lamellar armor probably came to the attention of the Japanese from their neighbors in Korea. Lamellar armor was the direct ancestor of samurai battle gear.

Around 400, the Japanese encountered the horse in battle in Korea.[15] The horse was imported into the archipelago between 425 and 450, and by the sixth century was common throughout Japan, especially in the large Kanto plain. Soon fighters combined archery with horse riding, and the resulting fighting technology dominated war in Japan until 1300. Because Japanese horses were small (130 centimeters at the shoulder), covering both animal and rider in heavy iron armor was never popular.

The use of the horse defined warfare for almost a millennium. The animal was too expensive for the average peasant to own because of feeding, sheltering, and mating requirements. Learning to release the reins and aim and shoot a bow required hours of practice. Therefore, from the 500s mounted archery tended to be the preserve of local notables, who had the wealth to own horses and the leisure to practice the equestrian arts. Even during the sixth and early seventh centuries, mounted archery was a skill passed down through generations in the same privileged house.

By the 500s, ancestors of Japan's present-day rulers had come to sit upon the throne in Yamato. A bureaucracy evolved to serve the needs of the dynasty, and aristocratic houses came into being and formed a court. From the beginning, the monarch had a sacerdotal role, and he or she decided policy questions only after consulting other aristocrats at court. Some aristocrats, like the Saeki and Ōtomo, led the royal army. This court claimed suzerainty over numerous local notables throughout Japan, but it is doubtful that the monarch really exercised any coercive control over these families. The government is best characterized as a confederation of chieftains, with the Yamato monarch being the primus inter pares.

The fledgling court fought several battles in Korea before 645 and therefore needed a navy. Vessels seem to have been made of several hollow logs tied together end to end, with planks attached to the sides and tops of the logs to enhance seaworthiness. A typical boat measured 20 meters long, 1 to 2 meters wide, and 0.5 to 1 meter deep, and could carry twenty-five men and two horses. The captains of the king's navy were the Ki (or "Tree") family, local notables who lived along the Inland Sea and in northern Kyushu.[16]

Little is known about martial tactics in this early epoch. *The Chronicles* mentions gongs, bells, and drums, implying that soldiers moved in coordinated groups. Some envision Japanese armies as consisting of foot soldiers who shot arrows from behind large implanted shields, followed by horse riders who galloped from behind the lines and attacked the enemy with swords. Most battle descriptions in *The Chronicles* emphasize individual heroism, however.

A 602 expedition planned for Korea is described as being composed of Shinto priests, local notables, royal officers, and twenty-five thousand troops.[17] Shinto priests prayed for the army's success before battle, local notables supplied the lion's share of soldiers, and royal officers led the court's contingent. Yamato monarchs were not powerful enough to recruit and lead a large force by themselves; they required the cooperation of local notables, dispersed throughout the archipelago and supreme in their bailiwicks. Notables with ties to the court numbered about 120 houses around 600.

The presence of Shinto priests raises the question of the ideological justification for war. Of the two religions popular in Japan at this time, the native cult of Shinto was far more militaristic than Buddhism (imported in the first half of the sixth century). During the sixth and seventh centuries, Yamato rulers collected and edited myths connected with lineages of local notables and the aristocracy, especially those of the Yamato dynasty. War and the military figure prominently in these myths. The first "emperor" in the line of Yamato monarchs was descended from the sun goddess and called Jimmu, or "Divine Warrior." He installed the dynasty in Yamato after subjugating several "barbarian" peoples. His descendant Yamato Takeru was another valorous hero. The Consort Jingū supposedly led expeditions to Korea to make the peninsular peoples obey the Yamato court, and her son Ōjin was renowned for his martial virtues. Later samurai would claim descent from these various figures, and through them from the Shinto god of war, Hachiman. Thus Shinto mythology glorified and justified war through its militaristic heroes and stories.

Buddhism was another matter. The teachings of Buddhism were pacifistic, but more important for the Yamato kings was the protection Buddhism offered rulers who promoted its worship. In addition, Buddhism was one element of continental civilization, and the Yamato dynasty took seriously its duty of spreading its version of civilization, by force if necessary. While Buddhism could be used to justify war, it was far less intertwined with warriors and warfare than Shinto.

The Chinese-Style Military, 645–900

These two and one-half centuries are much more richly documented than the preceding period. In addition to archaeological data, the era of apprenticeship to Chinese models produced voluminous written materials. Legal codes and commentaries lay out the basic structure of the government and give valuable evidence on society and economy. Court annals relate the course of events from the center. Literary sources describe social relations and shed light on popular beliefs. Wooden tablets bearing writing and recovered in excavations provide fascinating detail about daily life, while nearly ten thousand documents of practice show how lower-level officials lived and worked.

Overview

Three events in the middle and late seventh century resulted in the Yamato kings trying to borrow and adapt continental, especially Chinese, institutions to enhance their rule.[18] The first incident, the palace coup of 645, brought to power vigorous leaders anxious to make the Yamato monarch into a Chinese-style emperor in direct control of the entire archipelago's land and people. The second event was the decisive defeat of Japanese forces at the battle of the Paekch'on River in Korea at the hands of the Koreans and the Chinese in 663. The Japanese court may have lost as many as 27,000 soldiers in the disaster. The third milestone was the civil war of 672, which enthroned the martial Temmu (r. 672–686), the "Heavenly Warrior" Emperor.

None of these events can be understood unless one grasps the international situation in East Asia. From A.D. 220 to 589, China was disunified and under constant attack by nomads of the central Asian steppe. The early Yamato kings thus enjoyed the luxury of ruling while the mighty Chinese were weak. In 589, the Sui dynasty (589–617) reunited China and immediately mounted campaigns to secure its borders. The Sui collapsed after failing to subdue warriors in northern Korea, but the Tang dynasty (617–906), one of China's most glorious ruling houses, followed in the Sui's footsteps. By the late seventh century, the Japanese court faced the aggressive Tang Empire and the Kingdom of Silla just across the Korean Straits.[19]

Utilizing this perception of foreign threat, the Yamato dynasty attempted to assert greater control over the court and local nobility. In military terms, this meant adopting a Chinese-style draft, described in the Taihō Code of 701. The essence of this institution was to conscript commoners, place them under strong centralized command, and mold them into highly disciplined infantry and cavalry units using coordinated tactics. Draftees were expected to provide many of their own supplies and weapons. Sun-tzu's *The Art of War* was required reading for commanders, while the crossbow became a central piece of equipment for foot soldiers, either as artillery or as a handheld weapon.

Little evidence survives to show how the Taihō military actually functioned. But between 774 and 812, the Chinese-style system was put to a stiff test in a war with the residents of northeastern Honshu, whom the court considered to be "barbarians" (*emishi*). Five times, the court mounted expeditions to subdue these people. Sources are fragmentary, but these campaigns may have involved as many as fifty thousand persons, including cooks and porters, making them the largest organized force until after 1300. Armies included both horsemen and foot soldiers, attempted to coordinate movements with bells, gongs, drums, and banners, and employed crossbows to great effect.[20]

The opposition fought as mounted archers in guerrilla style and caused the failure of the first two massive campaigns. Sources describe *emishi* fighters as follows:

> The barbarians' custom is battle as
> mounted archers; ten of our commoners
> can not rival one of the enemy.
> They swarm like bees and gather like
> ants. . . . But when we attack, they flee into
> mountains and forests. When we let them
> go, they assault our fortifications. . . . Each of
> their leaders is as good as 1,000 men.[21]

Finally, in 791 the court chose Sakanoue no Tamuramaro to help lead an army, and victory resulted. Eventually Sakanoue, who was the scion of a military family boasting Korean blood, oversaw the subjugation of the residents of northeastern Honshu.

The long campaigns had two major effects on Japanese society. First, the success of the *emishi*'s tactics led to technological innovations. In particular, court armies adopted lighter leather armor to replace iron pieces and began to swing the *emishi*'s short curved sword. Both would become important parts of the samurai's equipment.

Second, the five gigantic campaigns contributed to a fiscal crisis for the court. The sources of the crisis were manifold: epidemics entering the archipelago from China and Korea beginning around 690 reversed the demographic boom initiated in the Yayoi period, and taxpaying adults were the primary victims; poor agricultural technology hindered farming; construction projects, including six new capitals and numerous Buddhist temples, caused government expenditures to skyrocket; and the expeditions against the *emishi* cost money to raise and outfit. Social dislocation was especially rife in the Kanto, which had sent many fighters into battle.

Even as the expeditions were taking place, the Kinai court attempted to reduce the costs of enforcing the draft by abolishing the conscript army and navy in 792. The government replaced the draft with a new system based on military specialists called "Strong Fellows"—mounted archers who numbered about thirty-two hundred. A large proportion hailed from the Kanto, where most horse pastures were located and where horse riders had been stationed in the wars against the "barbarians." Not long after the Strong Fellows were established, similar units of mounted archers were formed in Kyushu and northeastern Honshu.

The Strong Fellows were meant to maintain domestic tranquillity. For foreign enemies, such as the Korean pirates of the ninth century, the court turned to a technological remedy: the crossbow. This weapon was fundamentally different from the bow used by mounted archers. The crossbow was expensive to produce because of the sophisticated trigger mechanism, while the long bow was simple to make. But the long bow required hours of practice to master, while the crossbow was easy to use, the antique analogue of the modern handgun.

In the second half of the ninth century, the government authorized the arming of provincial headquarters with crossbows to frighten off troublemakers. The crossbows were effective for a while, but the high cost of maintenance led to a decline in their use after 900. One report noted that crossbows were "either out of kilter, or the trigger was not aligned properly." Perhaps the crossbow was also a victim of government retrenchment. Because of its deadliness against horsemen, one can only wonder how the history of the samurai would have been different if the crossbow had remained in use.

The Taihō Military and the District Magistrate

To envision how the court could implement conscription, one needs to know more about local society. The key to understanding local society is the role of the notable. Unfortunately, detailed evidence showing one family in all its various military, political, social, and economic functions is unavailable. The description that follows is a composite from several sources.

Recall that before 645 the Japanese polity was a confederation of chieftains from throughout the islands. To institute the draft and all the other centralizing reforms of the late seventh and early eighth centuries, the Yamato monarch needed the cooperation of these chieftains. Therefore, when the Taihō Code was written, many local notables were given the powerful position of district magistrate to supervise the localities in which they resided. Above them in the bureaucratic chain of command was the provincial governor, but governors were drawn from the ranks of the court aristocracy and served for only four years. As outsiders, the governors, and by extension the emperor and the court, were forced to rely upon the district magistrate to carry out the laws.

To control these magistrates, the imperial court adopted a carrot-and-stick policy. On the one hand, the court made the position heritable and included a sizable parcel of land. Moreover, magistrates could appoint their relatives to be officers in the provincial militia and priests at the local Shinto shrine. On the other hand, magistrates received lowly court ranks, an expression of their subservience to the aristocratic elite in the capital. Since local notables hungered for the official preference indicated by the possession of rank, the court was able to play different local families off against each other by granting or withholding ranks. The notable could thus dominate his district politically as long as he worked with the imperial court.

Surviving evidence reveals the magistrate's strong social and economic base.[22] A household register from 702 records that the magistrate of Shima district in northern Kyushu was Hi no Kimi Ite, holding lowly civil and military ranks. But Hi no Kimi's family was composed of 124 members, including 4 spouses, 31 children and grandchildren, 30 brothers, sisters, and in-laws, 26 dependents, and 37 slaves. Moreover, the land system allowed Hi no Kimi to hold over twenty *chō* of rice paddies (about sixty acres), by far the largest parcel in his district. Furthermore, Hi no Kimi's family was involved in lucrative trade in salt and possibly hemp cloth.

Another well-known magistrate was Ikue no Omi Azumabito from central Honshu along the Sea of Japan. In 755–56, Azumabito's position and wealth proved useful in establishing farms in his Asuwa district for the state temple Tōdaiji. Azumabito invested 7,838 sheaves of rice toward clearing and converting land into rice paddies. These sheaves, which probably included both his personal fortune and rice he collected from neighboring peasants, went to pay laborers and provide seed. Then, Azumabito contributed one hundred *chō* of his own rice fields to the project, in hopes of receiving higher court rank and more prestigious offices. These farms produced yields for Tōdaiji for about 150 years, and sources suggest that the Ikue no Omi acted as Tōdaiji's foreman, organizing peasant workers and collecting and shipping a share of the harvest to the capital.

Altogether, there were about 550 magistrates in the mid–eighth century, and institutions established by the court further strengthened their control over the local peasantry. Magistrates were responsible for allocating land to farmers, and they oversaw a system of rice loans that kept many peasants indebted until the harvest. Loaned out in the spring, rice sheaves came due in the fall with 50 percent interest; proceeds were used to finance district and provincial government. Magistrates also raised labor gangs and collected taxes due the court.

Few peasants were in a position to challenge the magistrate. Agricultural technology was primitive, and yields were often poor. In particular, peasants had difficulty mastering the engineering techniques necessary for river-fed irrigation. The waterwheel was unknown. In the end, the peasantry's most effective form of resistance against the local notable was flight from the land, an act that magistrates desperately tried to prevent.

Undoubtedly notables supported the centralizing reforms of this period because they enhanced their own control over the local peasantry. This probably explains why the draft worked as well as it did. While information on the Chinese-style military in action in the eighth century is sparse, it seems to confirm the central role of the district magistrate and his relatives. The court called out an expedition of seventeen thousand men to suppress a revolt in northern Kyushu in 740. The turning point in the action came when four district magistrates who had sided with the rebels betrayed their leader and went over to the court with five hundred fine mounted archers. A poetry collection suggests that many soldiers traveling from their homes in eastern Honshu to northern Kyushu for guard duty were scions of families of local notables.[23]

The 792 order establishing the Strong Fellows also hints at the military power of the district magistrates. The law states that these thirty-two hundred mounted archers would all come from the ranks of district magistrates and their extended families. Therefore, although there is little direct evidence, it seems likely that the Chinese-style draft of the eighth century was based upon and reinforced the considerable political, social, and economic power of the local notable. In this sense, the "new" institution of the eighth century owed much to pre-645 arrangements.

Toward the Age of the Samurai, 900–1050

This crucial transitional era is poorly documented. Archaeology is just getting under way. Detailed court chronicles end before 900, and administrative records have not survived in great numbers. Furthermore, since the court was no longer strictly enforcing Chinese-style laws, such compendia are of limited value. Fortunately, court aristocrats kept diaries of political meetings, and authors wrote stories and war tales that provide data unavailable in earlier centuries.

Overview
By the late eighth century, foreign-borne plagues of smallpox, measles, influenza, and other diseases had been decimating a populace without immunities for four generations.[24] Peasant flight from fields and settlements increased as the demo-

graphic debacle deepened. Rural society became deeply divided between a few wealthy and a multitude of poor. The "rich," as the sources termed the new class, loaned rice sheaves and cash during subsistence crises and foreclosed on homes and lands when the unfortunate borrowers defaulted. Furthermore, since revenues were collected as head taxes, the loss of taxpayers due to famine, pestilence, and the maldistribution of wealth resulted in a fiscal crisis for the old elites.

The court, now located in the new capital of Heian (Kyoto), responded to the financial bind by becoming more aggressive about tax collection.[25] It tried various means to raise revenues, with district magistrates and provincial governors serving as the court's agents. Beginning in the second half of the ninth century, this new aggressiveness exploded into violence between taxpayers and collectors. The Kanto in particular became a lawless land.

The court took several steps to halt the mayhem. It formed new provincial police offices and granted governors more authority to raise troops. Because the Kanto was so hard-hit, the court took special precautions to deal with violence there. One step was to send Prince Takamochi, an imperial offspring trained in the martial arts, to settle down and keep law and order. Takamochi and his numerous descendants intermarried with local families, enhancing the stature of those elites.

These policies seemed to quiet the disorder for a few decades, but in 935 first the Kanto, then western Japan, and finally northeastern Honshu exploded into violence. The most serious upheaval was in the Kanto, where Taira no Masakado, one of Takamochi's grandsons, led a rebellion that nearly succeeded in creating an independent kingdom.[26] Masakado's revolt began as a family quarrel, but the court was forced to intervene when Masakado began protecting outlaws and tax evaders and capturing provincial headquarters. Finally in 940, as the court was outfitting an expedition, Masakado was killed in battle and his forces dispersed.

In the midst of Masakado's revolt, two other serious upheavals occurred. Almost nothing is known about the *emishi* disorder in northeastern Honshu, but there are more sources for the insurrection in western Japan. Led by the pirate Fujiwara no Sumitomo, the rebellion aimed to cut sea routes for tax shipments to the court. Unlike Masakado, Sumitomo had no vision for an independent kingdom, and his revolt ended when several of his henchmen revealed the harbors he used as hideouts.

After the revolts, a modified military system took shape in the capital and the provinces.[27] In Heian, there were two sources of soldiers: the police and aristocratic households. New police offices had been set up in the ninth century as violence in the capital increased, but these were generally small and not very effective. The real forces for law and (dis)order were the soldiers of aristocratic houses. No civil aristocrat worth his salt was without a few "hired assassins."

These bodyguards and enforcers demolished houses, kidnapped political foes, fought pitched archery battles in the streets, murdered policemen, and demonstrated their skills in archery tournaments organized by their patrons.

Civil-military distinctions among aristocratic families became sharper. To go along with a class of purely civil aristocrats, a new group of military aristocrats came to the fore. By the tenth century, certain houses (*tsuwamono no ie*) became renowned for their prowess in the "way of the horse and the bow" and obtained the exclusive right to practice the arts of violence. For example, in 1028 a certain civil aristocrat killed an underling. A diarist noted that this man "enjoyed the martial arts, but people do not approve. . . . He is not of warrior blood."[28]

By the tenth century, older families of military aristocrats gave way to new names. The Taira originated with Prince Takamochi, while the Minamoto also derived from the imperial family. In the early eleventh century, an important branch of the Taira settled in Ise (central Honshu), but the Minamoto preferred the Kanto. Other houses encompassed the Nagara Fujiwara, Montoku Genji, Ōkura, Tachibana, and Hidesato line of the Fujiwara.

Although these new warrior families were aristocrats, they were foreclosed from attaining the high court ranks of civil aristocrats. One reason may have been their ties to local society, which was scorned by Heian aristocrats. The violent craft of the military aristocrats was also an impediment to advancement, partly because killing ran counter to Shinto prohibitions against pollution. More important, by the tenth century court society was thoroughly Buddhist, and Buddhism abhorred the use of force.

The military in the countryside revolved around Japan's sixty-six provincial headquarters, which replaced the district magistracy as the critical office. Most governors hired warriors to serve on their personal staffs, collect taxes, and keep order. These servants were often rapacious. In one province, "while mounted on horses," they "had their followers and dependents wreck doorways and throw open shutters to look for and take various items" from peasants. These retainers were "essentially no different from barbarians." Such servants left the province as the governor's four-year term ended, but the headquarters also maintained a permanent staff of around six hundred persons, most of whom gained the right to bear arms in the ninth and tenth centuries.[29]

New offices were created to allow especially enterprising fighting men to help the governor. These offices were essentially constabulary, and a governor might attract good soldiers in his province by inviting them on an official hunt, enrolling them in guard duty, or having them perform Shinto rites, such as sumo bouts. Despite the resources at their disposal, most governors usually faced a few martial families who remained aloof from their headquarters, with whom they were required to work out mutually advantageous alliances.

Because the use of force was often necessary to collect taxes, military aristocrats sometimes made the best governors. Only they could truly command the respect of other fighting men in their jurisdictions. Throughout the period 900–1050, members of the Taira and Minamoto enjoyed such appointments, as they each gathered a small following and accumulated wealth from their tax-farming activities.

Masakado's Social and Economic Base

The Tale of Masakado, the major primary source describing the revolt, provides a fairly clear picture of rural society and the provincial military in the mid–tenth century.[30] To begin with, as a descendant of the imperial family on his father's side and local nobility on his mother's, Masakado's bloodline commanded great respect among Kanto residents. His economic base was similarly impressive: he owned numerous rice paddies, horse pastures, and an ironworks, holdings perhaps even more widespread and productive than those of the district magistrate of the eighth century. The focus of Masakado's life was a walled residential complex, which included his home-headquarters, storage bins for weapons and rice, corrals, sentry posts, forges, looms, and other functional areas. Entry or search of the premises by even government officials was not permitted.

The local populace related to Masakado in one of two ways. First there was a small group of dependents who fought as mounted archers. Masakado himself rode a horse, and other equestrian soldiers lived within his household compound, received rewards and supplies from their lord, and were relatively reliable in battle. Occasionally, an average commoner could rise to this status, as when Hasetsukabe no Koharumaru, a peasant charcoal maker, betrayed a secret entrance to Masakado's camp for a reward of silk cloth and a position as a horse rider dependent of Masakado's enemies.

Second, Masakado controlled peasants using many of the means first developed by district magistrates, including rice loans, provision of tools and seed, and even assistance in tax payments. Unlike dependents, these peasant allies served as foot soldiers and had no personal ties to Masakado. They usually fled at the first sign that the battle was turning against them. The composition of Masakado's infantry meant that fighting was limited to the summer months to avoid planting, harvesting, and the cold winter. Combatants on all sides employed scorched-earth tactics to ruin the homes and fields where their enemies' peasant–foot soldiers lived and worked.

By 950, warrior families such as Masakado's were scattered throughout the archipelago. They jockeyed for political preferment by forming ties with high-ranking court aristocrats, such as Masakado's allegiance to the all-powerful Fujiwara Regent. Ultimately, Masakado attempted to lead a Kanto independence movement using his status as an imperial offspring. His attempt failed, but later samurai would look back to his rebellion as an expression of political autonomy from the Kinai court.

The Age of the Samurai: Stage One, 1050–1185

Compared with the previous era, the late eleventh, twelfth, and thirteenth centuries are richly documented. Only the archaeological record is missing. Kyoto aristocrats kept detailed diaries on political events and in-fighting. Legal compendia and court chronicles are less copious than those from the eighth century but are valuable nonetheless. War tales (*gunki monogatari*) describe the exploits of the samurai in gory detail, but since they were not written down until long after the battles they portray, these tales are often not highly reliable. Most important, the twelfth and thirteenth centuries are rich in administrative documents that describe local society as never before.

Overview

The mid–eleventh century was another era of social and economic dislocation.[31] In the Kanto, Taira no Tadatsune killed a governor and resisted tax collection from 1028 to 1032. Both sides used scorched-earth tactics, and even though Tadatsune eventually surrendered, the Kanto was devastated. The peasant population fled the fighting, and land went out of cultivation. In one province with a recorded total of twenty-three thousand units of rice fields in 1027, only eighteen units were being farmed two years after the rebellion. In the rest of Japan, a severe cycle of epidemics killed cultivators and left land lying unfarmed.

Once again, the court faced a fiscal crisis. To encourage rejuvenation of the economy, the court allowed its members to form estates (*shōen*), farms in which courtiers invested and received a portion of the harvest. Every estate needed a foreman on-site to organize and prod the workforce. In several instances, warrior families took over these jobs and received a minimal income. By the twelfth century, about half the farmland in Japan had become estate land, with the other 50 percent remaining under the control of the provincial headquarters. Fighting men continued to play an important role in those offices, too.

From the late eleventh century until 1185, the central changes in Japan were not economic but political.[32] Specifically, there was a struggle among military aristocrats for the title "chief of warriors" (*bushi no tōryō*). During the eleventh century, the leaders in this struggle were the Kawachi branch of the Minamoto. They had been responsible for crushing Tadatsune's revolt and putting down tax evaders in northeastern Honshu from 1051 to 1062.

The latter conflict shows how samurai fought in their heyday. Battles turned on the actions of a handful of mounted archers. The chieftain Minamoto no Yoshiie was described as follows:

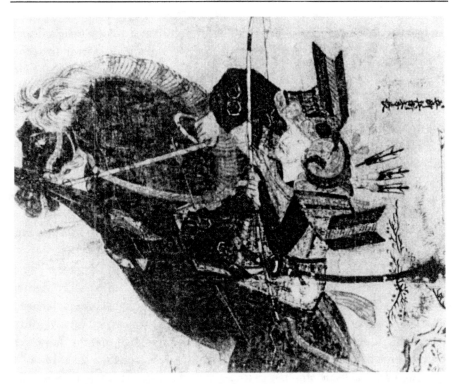

A samurai in full armor

> The great hero . . . shot arrows from horse-
> back like a god; undeterred by gleaming
> blades, he lunged through the rebels'
> encirclements to emerge on the left and right.
> With his great arrowheads he transfixed
> one enemy chieftain after another, never
> shooting at random but always inflicting a
> mortal wound. He galloped like the wind
> and fought with a skill that was more than
> human. The barbarians fled rather than
> face him, calling him the first born son of
> Hachiman, the god of war.[33]

By the late eleventh century, full-blown samurai combat was the order of the day. Battles began with a whistling arrow, and then mounted archers paired off. After announcing their pedigrees to each other, the beautifully clothed fighters engaged in combat until death. After the victor had become clear, the groom-cum-foot-soldiers of the winner took the head of the loser as proof of the triumph. This individualized, highly ritualized form of combat has been categorized as "intraspecific," after battles for dominance among male animals, such as bucks. The aim of this type of fighting was for the victor to secure dominance within a hierarchy of males, and to ensure continuation of the victor's line by securing females.

Even as Yoshiie attained the pinnacle of martial respect by being named "the chief of warriors" in the early twelfth century, the Minamoto began to suffer internal dissension. In the meantime, the Ise Taira gained the favor of the Retired Emperor, who was a new contender for political power at court.[34] The Taira commanded naval forces stationed along the Inland Sea and subdued pirates raiding tax shipments. Conflicts in Kyoto in 1156 and 1159–60 secured the place of the Ise Taira as the "teeth and claws" of the court and Kiyomori as their leader. Combat was typical samurai style: in the war of 1156, the total number of samurai on the victorious side was six hundred.

From 1160 to 1180, the Ise Taira commanded the court's military.[35] They battled pirates, subdued the protests of Buddhist monks, and enrolled fighters as their allies from Kyushu to the Kanto. They controlled most provincial headquarters, especially in western Honshu and Kyushu, and carried on a vigorous trade with Sung China. One Japanese historian has argued that the Taira were on the verge of establishing an independent kingdom along the Inland Sea.

Taira martial leadership began to destabilize before 1180, as galloping inflation resulted from a massive expansion of the money supply occurring when Chinese copper cash was imported. In the meantime, Yoritomo, a Minamoto offspring who had survived his family's defeats, managed to overwhelm his captors and throw his lot in with a disgruntled imperial prince plotting against the Taira. Japan descended into five years of devastating civil war from 1180 to 1185.

The conflict was Japan's version of the Peloponnesian War, matching the naval forces of the Taira against the superior mounted archers of the Minamoto. A famine occurring in 1180–82 slowed fighting to a standstill. Then in 1184, Yoritomo seized the initiative, invaded western Honshu, and destroyed the Taira at the naval battle of Dannoura. The Ise Taira ceased to exist, and Yoritomo became "the chief of warriors."

Samurai and Land

The treasure trove of administrative documents enables scholars to understand the functions of the samurai in the agricultural economy.[36] A major responsibility of local warriors was to assemble peasants to work the fields. Samurai were often brutal, as shown in this 1275 excerpt from documents associated with Ategawa Estate. In the words of peasant protesters, "When we refused to do things his way, the samurai chased down our wives and children, cut off their ears, shaved off their noses, clipped their hair, and said he was forcing them to take the tonsure." Reliable labor was scarce, and the samurai's methods obtained results.

Warriors played a crucial function in local society, but the land system of 1050–1185 did not grant them security of tenure, as seen at Sōma Estate in the Kanto. Sometime after Tadatsune's devastating revolt of 1028–32, a local samurai family named Chiba reopened fields at Sōma and took the position of foreman, overseeing the operation of the farm. By 1126, the Chiba gained exemption from levies by the provincial office, and to guarantee this advantage, in 1130 they commended the lands to the Ise Shrine, seeking the protection of the powerful Shinto institution at court. In return for its favor, the Chiba granted Ise a sizable portion of the harvest.

In 1143, the military aristocrat Minamoto no Yoshitomo rode into Sōma, forged land titles, pressured the Chiba with his horsemen, and took over the estate. Then Yoshitomo commended the land to Ise in his name. Faced with a rival, the Chiba signed on as Yoshitomo's fighters, in return for Yoshitomo's withdrawal of his claim to the land. However, just when the Chiba's hold over Sōma seemed secure, another samurai stepped in, commended the land to a different patron, and eventually succeeded in ousting the Chiba from land they had been clearing for several generations. This case shows not only the great attraction that productive fields held for samurai but also how insecure their tenure was.

One of the underlying themes of the 1180–85 civil war between the Minamoto and the Taira was the samurai drive for greater security. It was just too easy for aristocrats and religious institutions to dispossess samurai, even though the warriors had done most of the hard work of assembling the cultivators and overseeing the conversion of wasteland into productive paddies. With their victory in 1185, the Minamoto guaranteed that warriors would have more secure tenure by allotting them posts beyond the control of the Kyoto court. Still, however, revenues derived by samurai from the land did not equal rents allocated to nonsamurai members of the court until after 1300.

The Age of the Samurai: Stage Two, 1185–1300

After rebelling against the Taira and the court in 1180, Yoritomo followed Masakado's pattern of "hijacking" nearby provincial headquarters. Eventually, he established his own government in the small fishing village of Kamakura. This administration came to be called the "tent government" (*bakufu*), in contrast to the court of civil aristocrats in Kyoto, and in 1192 Yoritomo took the title of "Great Barbarian-subduing Generalissimo" (*sei-i tai shōgun*) once held by Sakanoue no Tamuramaro. Throughout the Kamakura period, the shogunate had responsibility for police and tax collection, especially in the Kanto.[37] At one time historians thought that Yoritomo had established a Japanese version of feudalism, and that 1185 marked the inception of the medieval era. This view is no longer tenable for many reasons, the most important of which is that the Kyoto court of civil aristocrats and religious institutions continued to function unimpaired until the end of the thirteenth century. Instead of being a feudal polity, Japan was a dyarchy: Kamakura ruled eastern Honshu, and Kyoto was supreme in the west.

Over the course of the thirteenth century, however, the balance shifted slowly and inexorably in Kamakura's favor. In 1189, Yoritomo conducted a campaign against the Fujiwara of northeastern Honshu, subduing the family and bringing the region under Minamoto control, with court authorization after the fact. In 1221, an ambitious Retired Emperor nearly destroyed Kamakura with the forces at his disposal, but he failed when warrior families remained loyal to Kamakura despite his bribes. The result of Kamakura's victory was some shogunate penetration into Kyoto's sphere of influence in western Japan. But for most of the rest of the century, Kamakura was supreme in eastern Honshu, while the Kyoto court oversaw the western archipelago.

The beginning of the end for the Kyoto court came in 1274 and 1281 when the Mongols invaded Japan.[38] Unable to respond militarily, the court left defense of the islands to Kamakura. The "tent government" used the emergency to take control of western Honshu and Kyushu, where the fighting took place. By 1300, Kamakura ruled the archipelago.

The Mongols were the greatest fighting force in premodern history, and Kamakura was fortunate to escape defeat. The Mongols assembled expeditions of one hundred thousand men and quickly overwhelmed defenses at Tsushima and Iki on the way to northern Kyushu from Korea. Kamakura tried to entice its men to battle the Mongols, but samurai were understandably reluctant. One recent figure for the total samurai force that met the Mongols numbered about fifteen hundred mounted archers, with another thirty-five hundred foot soldiers.[39]

The encounter between the samurai and the Mongols, who fought using coordinated mass tactics and bombs, was unusual:

> The Mongols disembarked, mounted their horses,
> raised their banners, and began to attack . . .[One
> Japanese] . . . shot a whistling arrow to open the
> exchange. All at once the Mongols down to the
> last man started laughing . . .
> Whereas we [Japanese] thought about reciting
> our pedigrees to each other and battling
> man-to-man in glory or defeat as was the custom
> of Japanese armies, in this battle the Mongols
> assembled at one point in a great force.[40]

Apparently, the Japanese had forgotten the lessons of mass tactics learned so painfully at the battle of the Paekch'on River. In the end, a typhoon spelled doom for the Mongols and reinforced the court's belief in the islands' divine protection.

Despite Kamakura's eventual hegemony, many factors militate against calling thirteenth-century Japan feudal.[41] First, the warrior class was small. Although no method of counting fighters is beyond reproach, there were probably never more than three thousand samurai, about the same as the total of Strong Fellows in 792. Thus the establishment of a warrior government was no revolution of numbers.

Second, in most of the archipelago, samurai incomes were significantly smaller than those of members of the great religious institutions and civil aristocratic houses. While again data are rare, they suggest that samurai serving as foremen on estates in western Honshu and Kyushu earned about half the income of their patrons. Because the agrarian economy did not begin a new cycle of growth until after 1300, samurai were forced to redistribute wealth to increase their incomes. In western Japan, warrior bands were just too small and weak to overcome entrenched interests.

Only in the Kanto plain near Kamakura did samurai garner the lion's share of produce. There the division of spoils was reversed, as samurai bands were larger and more distant from temples and civil aristocrats serving as estate patrons. It is improper to view the founding of Kamakura as a sweeping economic revolution; rather, it marks the culmination of the Kanto independence movement harking back to Masakado.

Ideological Justifications for War

As noted previously, Shinto mythology provided early legitimacy for war and warriors. During the eighth-century borrowing from China, the court elaborated an ideology that further sanctioned official violence.[42] According to the Taihō Code, the court considered itself ruler of Japan (*Nihon*), which it called the Middle Kingdom (*chūka*). The Chinese had originated the concept of the Middle Kingdom, a sinocentric view in which all other states could be considered civilized only to the extent that they recognized the superiority of the Chinese. The Japanese court adopted the same self-perception; to deal with China, which was obviously more advanced, the Japanese court utilized the term "the country next door" (*rinkoku*). Korea and the other peoples around the periphery of the archipelago became "barbarians" (*bankoku*). This ideology justified the campaigns against the *emishi* and hostility toward the Korean state of Silla.

From 900 on, the most common justification for war was nonpayment of taxes.[43] However widespread, violence among family members or ruffians was not enough to provoke the court to raise an army. For example, between 1083 and 1087, Minamoto no Yoshiie carried out a personal vendetta in northern

Honshu. He presented his struggle as an attempt to ensure the flow of taxes from that region, but when it became clear that his victims were in fact law-abiding, the court refused to grant Yoshiie the customary rewards for service. It even forced him to repay to the court the revenues his campaigns had disrupted.

The Mongol Invasions of 1274 and 1281 added a new dimension to the link between ideology and war.[44] The court branded the Mongols as a "strange country" (ikoku), in the spirit of the formulations in the eighth century. For their part, the Mongols sought merely to open relations with the Japanese court, a request that it rejected. When the Mongols decided to invade, the government in Kamakura made pragmatic preparations for defense, while the court encouraged Buddhist temples and Shinto shrines to offer prayers for the defeat of the Mongol fleet. The famous monk Nichiren advocated the chanting of the Lotus Sutra to ward off the Mongols and warned that prayers to any other sacred object would only enhance the invaders' chances. He saw the invasion as divine punishment for the failure of the Japanese to follow his sect of Buddhism. In the end, of course, the Mongols were thwarted not by the samurai but by a typhoon (kamikaze), an act of nature that encouraged some religious figures and courtiers to see Japan as a divinely protected land.

Conclusion

From the perspective of world history, the samurai style of combat prevailing between 1050 and 1300 was extraordinary. A few expert warriors dominated the battlefield, fighting in a colorful, highly ritualized way. Such a military system presupposed a general agreement regarding what war was all about. One may therefore ask: Why did no one develop effective countermeasures to challenge this unique way of fighting?

Within Japanese society, the peasantry might have been organized against the samurai, as it certainly had reasons to resent warriors. But the challenge to mounted warfare could not come until after 1300, when agricultural technology improved and the life of peasants became more prosperous and settled. Besides, Japan lacked the iron necessary for heavily armored infantry, and the manufacture of the handheld crossbow, a weapon that might have overthrown the samurai, was too difficult for even the government to master after 900.

A challenge to the samurai class might also have come from among their own numbers. Such a challenge was not forthcoming in these centuries because man-to-man, ritualized mounted combat was too heavily bound up with concepts of manly pride and honor. Samurai fighting was intraspecific, wherein the chief goal was to determine one's position in a hierarchy of males. Remember that the samurai class was small, and the shared values of the group appear prominently in war stories found in The Tale of Masakado or The Tale of the Heike.

A final—and crucial—factor was the dearth of external threats. The Koreans and Chinese were too absorbed in their own problems to invade. The Mongol Invasions presented the stiffest test for the samurai, and the mounted archers were just effective enough to limit the Mongols' gains until the typhoon struck in 1281. Without the hurricane, the giant Mongol force that had conquered much of Eurasia certainly had all the advantages. For many reasons, the destruction of the Mongol fleet marked a major turning point in Japanese history.

Notes

1. Technically, *samurai* is a term for "one who attends" the great noble houses of the Fifth Rank and higher. Samurai included all servants possessing the Sixth Court Rank, martial or not.
2. Reischauer 1956.26–48; Fairbank 1989.324–91.
3. Three recent English-language studies are Friday 1992; Varley 1994; and Farris 1992.
4. Hall 1982.251–67.
5. On the vertical structure of Japanese society, see Nakane 1970.
6. Yoshida 1975.156–61; Yoshie 1986.
7. On the agrarian economy, see Farris 1985.74–117.
8. Farris 1985.118–40.
9. Amino 1982.71.
10. Sahara and Kanaseki 1975.30 give population figures. For an example of a Yayoi settlement, see Barnes and Hudson 1991.211–35.
11. Sahara 1987.291–98.
12. Tanaka 1991.321.
13. Note Gina Barnes, Don Wagner, Albert Dien, Shin Kyong ch'ol, and Yoshimura Kazuaki, "Roundtable on Early Korean Armour" (paper presented at the Association for Asian Studies, Los Angeles, March 1993). Since Japan did not have facilities for smelting iron until about A.D. 500, material for the first armor, if not the finished suits themselves, was probably imported from iron-rich southern Korea. The iron trade was a major reason that the Japanese became embroiled in wars in Korea between A.D. 375 and 700.
14. Friday 1992.41.
15. Farris 1992.14–23.
16. Farris 1992.23.
17. Sakamoto 1967.2.178–79; Aston 1972.125–26.
18. Farris 1992.33–80.
19. Batten 1986.199–219.
20. Farris 1992.81–119.
21. Farris 1992.92.
22. Hara 1975.201–31.
23. Gomi, Ōno, and Takagi 1959.4.426–30; Nippon gakujutsu shinkokai 1965.250–55.

24. Farris 1985.69–73, 91–93; 1992.120–30.
25. Farris 1992.129–31.
26. Farris 1992.131–62; Rabinovitch 1986.
27. Friday 1988.153–85; Farris 1992.163–203.
28. Farris 1992.173.
29. Farris 1992.179.
30. Fukuda 1975.83–91; Ishii 1974.113–49, 226–36; Farris 1992.150–59.
31. See Farris 1992.204–51.
32. Mass 1974.59–92; Farris 1992.289–307; Shinoda 1960.
33. McCullough 1964–1965.65–191.
34. In the late eleventh century, the imperial family freed itself from the control of its marital line and established independent offices with the ex-emperor as head. See Hurst 1976.
35. Farris 1992.273–89 believes in a large role for the Ise Taira in the late Heian military, while Mass 1974.15–30 does not. Amino 1982.123–24 argues for a Taira maritime kingdom.
36. Amino 1974.177 (Ategawa); Mass 1974.31–56 (Sōma).
37. The leading American scholar on Kamakura institutions is Jeffrey Mass. See 1974, 1979, and 1989.
38. On the Mongols, see Hori 1974.184–98; Farris 1992.328–35.
39. Amazu 1994.88–97.
40. Farris 1992.331.
41. Farris 1992.371–79. Also see Hall 1968.15–51.
42. Kuroita 1966.2.774. Also note Hayakawa 1988.47–82.
43. Farris 1992.233–40.
44. Amino 1974.167–77.

Bibliography

Amazu, Ichirō. 1994. "Kassen no senryoku kazu—Kamakura bakufu no Koma shuppei keikaku o sozai toshite." *Nihon shi kenkyū* 388, 88–97.

Amino, Yoshihiko. 1974. *Nihon no rekishi 10 Mōko shūrai*. Tokyo: Shōgakkan.

——. 1982. *Higashi to nishi no kataru Nihon no rekishi*. Tokyo: Soshiete bunko.

Aston, William, trans. 1972. *Nihongi, Chronicles of Japan from the Earliest Times to 697*. Tokyo: Tuttle Books.

Barnes, Gina, and Mark Hudson. 1991. "Yoshinogari: A Yayoi Settlement in Northern Kyushu." *Monumenta Nipponica* 46, 211–35.

Batten, Bruce. 1986. "Foreign Threat and Domestic Reform." *Monumenta Nipponica* 41, 199–219.

Butler, Kenneth. 1969. "The *Heike Monogatari* and the Japanese Warrior Ethic." *Harvard Journal of Asiatic Studies* 29, 93–108.

DeBary, William, Ryusaku Tsunoda, and Donald Keene, eds. 1958. *Sources of the Japanese Tradition*. Vol. 1. New York: Columbia University Press.

Duus, Peter. 1969. *Feudalism in Japan*. New York: Knopf.

Fairbank, John, Edwin O. Reischauer, and Albert Craig. 1989. *East Asia: Tradition and Transformation*. Rev. ed. Boston: Houghton Mifflin.

Farris, William Wayne. 1985. *Population, Disease, and Land in Early Japan, 645–900*. Cambridge, Mass.: Harvard University Press.

———. 1992. *Heavenly Warriors: The Evolution of Japan's Military, 500–1300*. Cambridge, Mass.: Harvard University Press.

Friday, Karl. 1988. "Teeth and Claws: Provincial Warriors and the Heian Court." *Monumenta Nipponica* 43, 153–85.

———. 1992. *Hired Swords: The Rise of Private Warrior Power in Early Japan*. Palo Alto, Calif.: Stanford University Press.

Fukuda, Toyohiko. 1975. "Ōchō gunji kikō to nairan." In *Iwanami kōza Nihon rekishi*, vol. 4, 82–120. Tokyo: Iwanami shoten.

Gomi, Tomohide, Ōno Susumu, and Takagi Ichinosuke, eds. 1959. *Nihon koten bungaku taikei: Man'yōshū*. 4 vols. Tokyo: Iwanami shoten.

Hall, John W. 1966. *Government and Local Power in Japan, 500–1700*. Princeton, N.J.: Princeton University Press.

———. 1968. "Feudalism in Japan: A Reassessment." In *Studies in the Institutional History of Early Modern Japan*, edited by John W. Hall and Marius Jansen, 15–51. Princeton, N.J.: Princeton University Press.

———. 1982. "Epilogue." In Mass 1982.

Hall, John W., and Jeffrey Mass, eds. 1974. *Medieval Japan: Essays in Institutional History*. New Haven, Conn.: Yale University Press.

Hara, Hidesaburo. 1975. "Gunji to chihō gōzoku." In *Iwanami kōza Nihon rekishi*, Vol. 3, 202–31. Tokyo: Iwanami shoten.

Hayakawa, Shōhachi. 1988. "Higashi Ajia gaikō to Nihon ritsuryō sei no suii." In *Nihon no kodai 15 Kodai kokka to Nihon*, edited by Kishi Toshio, 47–82. Tokyo: Chūō koron.

Hori, Kyotsu. 1974. "The Economic and Political Effects of the Mongol Wars." In *Medieval Japan: Essays in Institutional History*, edited by John W. Hall and Jeffrey Mass, 184–98. New Haven, Conn.: Yale University Press.

Hurst, G. Cameron. 1976. *Insei: Abdicated Sovereigns in the Politics of Late Heian Japan, 1086–1185*. New York: Columbia University Press.

Ishii, Susumu. 1974. *Nihon no rekishi 12 Chūsei bushidan*. Tokyo: Shōgakkan.

Kidder, J. Edward. 1985. "The Archaeology of the Early Horse-riders in Japan." *Transactions of the Asiatic Society of Japan*, 3d ser., 20, 89–123.

Kuroita, Katsumi, ed. 1966. *Shintei zōho kokushi taikei: Ryō no shūge*. 2 vols. Tokyo: Yoshikawa kōbunkan.

Ledyard, Gari. 1975. "Galloping along with the Horseriders: Looking for the Founders of Japan." *Journal of Japanese Studies* 1, 217–54.

Lu, David, ed. 1974. *Sources of Japanese History*. Vol. 1. New York: McGraw-Hill.

Mass, Jeffrey. 1974. *Warrior Government in Early Medieval Japan*. Palo Alto, Calif.: Stanford University Press.

———. 1979. *The Development of Kamakura Rule, 1180–1250*. Palo Alto, Calif.: Stanford University Press.

———. 1989. *Lordship and Inheritance in Early Medieval Japan*. Palo Alto, Calif.: Stanford

University Press.

———, ed. 1982. *Court and Bakufu in Japan*. Palo Alto, Calif.: Stanford University Press.

McCullough, Helen, trans. 1964–1965. "A Tale of Mutsu." *Harvard Journal of Asiatic Studies* 25, 17–211.

———. 1988. *The Tale of Heike*. Palo Alto, Calif.: Stanford University Press.

McCullough, William, trans. 1964. "*Shōkyūki*: An Account of the Shōkyū War." *Monumenta Nipponica* 19, 163–215, 420–55.

Nakane, Chie. 1970. *Japanese Society*. Berkeley and Los Angeles: University of California Press.

Nippon gakujutsu shinkōkai, trans. 1965. *The Manyoshu*. New York: Columbia University Press.

Rabinovitch, Judith, trans. 1986. *Shōmonki: The Story of Masakado's Rebellion*. Tokyo: Monumenta Nipponica Monographs.

Reischauer, Edwin O. 1956. "Japanese Feudalism." In *Feudalism in History*, edited by Rushton Coulborn, 26–48. Princeton, N.J.: Princeton University Press.

Reischauer, Edwin O., and Joseph Yamagiwa, trans. 1951. "*Heiji monogatari*." In *Translations from Early Japanese Literature*, edited by Edwin Reischauer, 377–457. Cambridge, Mass.: Harvard University Press.

Sahara, Makoto. 1987. *Taikei Nihon no rekishi 1 Nihonjin no tanjō*. Tokyo: Shōgakkan.

Sahara, Makoto, and Kanaseki Hiroshi, eds. 1975. *Kodai shi hakkutsu 4 Inasaku no hajimari*. Tokyo: Kōdansha.

Sakamoto, Tarō, et al., eds. 1967. *Nihon koten bungaku taikei: Nihon shoki*. 2 vols. Tokyo: Iwanami shoten.

Sansom, George. 1958. *A History of Japan to 1334*. Palo Alto, Calif.: Stanford University Press.

Shinoda, Minoru. 1960. *The Founding of the Kamakura Shogunate, 1180–85*. New York: Columbia University Press.

Tanaka, Migaku. 1991. *Nihon no rekishi 2 Wajin no sōran*. Tokyo: Shūei sha.

Varley, Paul. 1994. *Warriors of Japan as Portrayed in the War Tales*. Honolulu: University of Hawaii Press.

Wilson, William, trans. 1971. *Hogen monogatari, Tale of the Disorder in Hogen*. Tokyo: Monumenta Nipponica monographs.

———. 1973. "The Way of the Bow and Arrow: The Japanese Warrior in *Konjaku monogatari*." *Monumenta Nipponica* 28, 177–234.

Yamamura, Kozo, ed. 1990. *The Cambridge History of Japan*. Vol. 3, *Medieval Japan*. Cambridge: Cambridge University Press.

Yoshida, Takashi. 1975. "Ritsuryō sei to sonraku." In *Iwanami kōza Nihon rekishi*, Vol. 3, 142–200. Tokyo: Iwanami shoten.

Yoshie, Akiko. 1986. *Nihon kodai no uji no kōzō*. Tokyo: Yoshikawa kōbunkan.

FOUR

⊡⊡⊡⊡

Ancient Egypt

ANDREA M. GNIRS

Predynastic Period	ca. 5000–3000 B.C.E.
Early Dynastic Period: Dyn. I–II	ca. 3000–2650
Old Kingdom: Dyn. III–VI	ca. 2650–2160
First Intermediate Period	ca. 2160–2040
Middle Kingdom: Dyn. XI–XII	ca. 2040–1785
Second Intermediate Period:	
Dyn. XIII–XVII	ca. 1785–1550
Dyn. XV–XVI (Hyksos)	1650–1550
New Kingdom: Dyn. XVII–XX	ca. 1640–1070
Dyn. XVII (Theban family)	1640–1550
Dyn. XVIII (Thutmoside Period)	1550–1307
Dyn. XIX–XX (Ramesside Period)	1307–1070
Third Intermediate Period:	
Dyn. XXI–XXV	ca. 1070–664
Dyn. XXII–XXIV (Libyans)	945–712
Dyn. XXV (Kushites)	712–664

(continued)

Late Period: Dyn. XXVI–XXX	ca. 664–343
Dyn. XXVII (Persians)	525–404
Dyn. XXVIII–XXX	404–343
Second Persian Period	343–332
Greek Period	332–30
Alexander the Great	332–323
Ptolemaic Period	323–30
Roman Period	30 B.C.E.–395 C.E.

The Ecological Environment and the Emergence of the Monarchy[1]

Among other ancient cultures of Africa and the Near East, Egypt holds a privileged position due to exceptional ecological and geographic conditions: protected by the first Nile Cataract in the south, the Mediterranean Sea in the north, and mountain deserts in the east and west, the naturally isolated land of the Nile took advantage of its environment and its climate: annual inundation favored agriculture, and an economic surplus could be easily obtained. Fast mobility on the Nile facilitated interregional contacts and, later on, political control, while early established trade routes favored exchange between the north and south of the country, with the oases in the western desert, the Red Sea, Nubia, Palestine, and even Mesopotamia.[2] This position fostered a political ideology that emphasized the superiority of Egyptian civilization, represented by its king, over all surrounding countries and peoples. The inhabitants of the outside world were perceived as evil, hostile, and cowardly by nature, a constant threat to Egypt and to the cosmic order.[3] The following characterization of Egypt's Asiatic enemies, contained in a fictional posthumous instruction left by a king to his son and successor, is paradigmatic.

> But this should be said to the Bowman: Lo, the miserable Asiatic, he is wretched because of the place he is in. Short of water, bare of wood, its paths are many and painful because of mountains. He does not dwell in one place, food propels his legs, he fights since the time of Horus, not conquering or being conquered, he does not announce the day of combat, like a thief who darts about a group. (*Instruction Addressed to Merikare*, Lichtheim 1975.103–4)

Egyptian propaganda never abandoned this negative image of the foreigner.[4] In the New Kingdom, however, a more cosmopolitan orientation occasionally allowed a revised picture of the interactions with the foreign world: enemies could now be represented in more human ways, by mentioning their personal names or addressing them in direct speech. While the traditional view of the foreigner reinforced the elite's collective cultural identity, a more personal attitude toward Egypt's enemies emerged from the grass roots of Egyptian society, based on the supposed testimony of historical persons.[5]

> Then there was fighting in Egypt to the south of this town, and I carried off a man as a living captive. I went down into the water—for he was captured on the city side—and crossed the water carrying him. When it was reported to the Royal Herald I was rewarded with gold once more. (*Autobiography of Ahmose Sa Ibana*, Lichtheim 1976.12–13)

Although changes occurred in the New Kingdom, the official justification of war and military aggression was never altered. War was conceived of as the inevitable answer to enemy provocation, giving reason to "expand Egypt's borders."[6] Here, the "revenge motif"—stressed by Ferguson[7]—can be reduced to the formula "violation of the frontier." Unauthorized crossing of the border and interference with trade had to be punished as inexorably as the failure to accept Egypt's dominion.

The border as symbol of Egypt's integrity, implying a dual model of the world as divided between inside and outside, left an imprint even on the lexicon of neighboring cultures. In Akkadian the word for *Egypt* is *miṣru(m)*,[8] "frontier, territory" (Arabic *miṣr*), the land of borders, inaccessible to the outside world. This idea probably originated in Egypt's exceptional geography, but also in the state's propaganda of superiority. While Egyptian sources do not speak explicitly of a collective experience of external threat or domination before the sixteenth century,[9] early official representation in images and texts already reduces foreign affairs to the ritualized suppression of the enemy, including the topos of the "smiting of the foes."[10]

Warfare, however, was not ritualized as was, for example, phalanx warfare in archaic Greece or the samurais' fighting in ancient Japan.[11] Initially, Egypt reacted with methods of "total warfare" against those who challenged it, applying the strategy of scorched earth, extinction, and large-scale deportation. This policy was never given up. Yet a form of ritualized warfare was developed during the New Kingdom when it was the king's obligation to undertake his first official campaign as a form of initiation rite in order to reestablish tradition and cosmic order. Usually these first-year campaigns were aimed at Nubia, which, long conquered and colonized, did not pose a real threat to Egypt; hence, victory and its ideological consequence, the removal of chaos, were a foregone conclusion.[12]

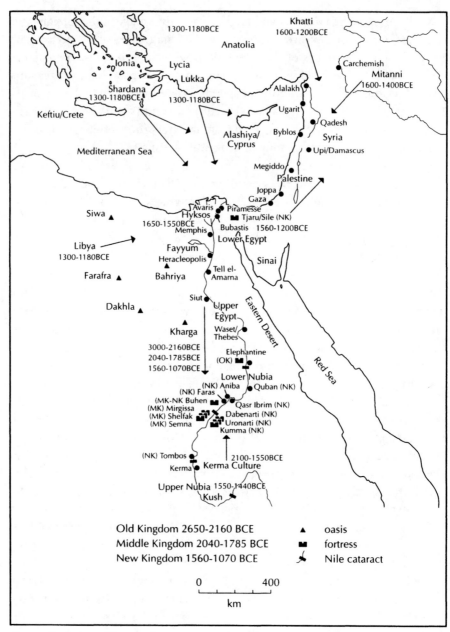

Egypt (3rd–1st mill. B.C.E.)

The foundations of a centralized state, corresponding to a hierarchically organized society, were laid in Egypt around 3000.[13] The unification is reflected in the spreading of a homogeneous material culture all over the country, starting from Upper Egypt.[14] Simultaneously, the beginning of writing and the development of official representational art, monumental architecture, both secular and funerary, and exclusive funerary practices indicate institutionalized political power.[15] Insight into the ideology of the emerging state comes from decorated "ceremonial" slate palettes, knife handles, mace heads, and carved tags, whose carvings represent a mixture of icons and incipient hieroglyphic writing. In their depiction of ritual and symbolic scenes (animal processions, animal fights, taming of fabulous creatures, hunting scenes, the attack of fortified places by zoomorphic symbols of power such as the lion or the falcon, the execution of prisoners, or the performance of rites), these artifacts allude to the impact political power supposedly had on the cosmos: the elimination of chaos and the establishment of order.[16]

The land's exceptional ecological and geographic conditions fostered rapid cultural progress, resulting in social stratification and the emergence of an elite. From the mid–fourth millennium, city-states probably developed throughout the country. By about 3000 Egypt was *culturally* unified. The question of whether this was achieved by force or through nonviolent developments (e.g., climatic change that required cooperation in food production and economic exchange) is a hotly debated issue.[17]

The warlike nature of this society is documented by a whole array of weapons, such as axes, mace heads, daggers, throwsticks, and arrowheads.[18] Even if used as prestige objects, arms point to martial orientation. Similarly, the earliest pictorial representations of power imply armed aggression: the "Narmer-palette" shows the king smiting an enemy—a motif of highest significance, since it remained central to royal representation throughout Egypt's history—and attending the execution of prisoners; the "Town-palette" displays symbols usually considered to stand for power or even kingship, such as the lion, the falcon, or the scorpion, each wielding a hoe, on top of fortified structures.[19] Although these pictures were long interpreted as early royal proclamations concerning specific historical events, such as the violent process of Egypt's unification, it is preferable, in accordance with later sources, to understand them as first attempts at ritualizing history and kingship.[20]

Submission and Entrepreneurship: The Old Kingdom

From the Fourth Dynasty, material evidence for a markedly hierarchical society increases explosively, showing great differences between king, elite, and broad population.[21] The absolute power of the king is reflected in the layout of cemeteries near royal residences, where social rank is clearly connected with the proximity to the king's funerary complex; textual evidence such as titulatures of courtiers and officials and, from the Fifth Dynasty, so-called autobiographies also reveals the administration's and the individual's almost total dependence on the king.[22] He was perceived as the living effigy of Horus, the mythical founder of kingship, who guaranteed the connections between gods and mankind.[23] Social success—promotion and rank—relied largely on the king; so did life after death through his provision of mortuary offerings.

While in terms of social stratification the early Egyptian state can be seen as an advanced form of clan chiefdom in which the king's family controlled the administration, economic progress fostered the expansion of administrative personnel and thus of a nonroyal elite, and the establishment of provinces, or "nomes," led by governors. Eventually, a country nobility emerged and became politically important by controlling the foundations of state economy.[24]

In the Old Kingdom, royal display did not break with the ideological conventions of Early Dynastic kingship, but its media changed, and representations became more eloquent. Rich elaboration of the Egyptian cosmos, in the decoration of royal funerary and solar temples, intended to demonstrate the king's sovereignty, included scenes of soldiers or combat between Egyptians and foreigners.[25] These represent Egypt's perpetual conflict with the outside world, the eternal fight against disorder and chaos, constantly reemphasizing the Egyptian dualistic concept of the world.[26] Similarly, figurines of bound foreign captives found in royal temples, cemeteries, and later also in the vicinity of Nubian forts served to reaffirm the monarchy's superiority and the anathematization of its enemies.[27] These often crudely shaped objects provide the first evidence of a personalization of political or social opponents: as inscriptions make clear, they were identified with individual human beings, personal rivals, or foreign enemies and their clans, and aimed at the persons' ritual annihilation.[28]

Although Egypt had numerous terms for combat and ranks and titles, including a technical terminology for weaponry and military equipment, unlike, for instance, ancient China or medieval Japan, it did not develop a literary genre that gave instruction in the art of warfare or established a strict set of behavioral rules in the martial sphere.[29] The Egyptian outlook on war is best reflected in sources whose primary intention was not to give exact historical information—although they are usually referred to as "historical" or "historiographical"—but to confirm the established conception of the world by using official topoi and patterns of representation, especially monumental records of kings, court officials, and provincial nobility. Apart from administrative documents, private letters, and some literary texts, written sources always reflect elite ideology: how the world *should* be rather than how the world *is*. Hence texts and depictions are markedly propagandistic; tradition and preservation of cultural identity were highly important to Egyptian society, whereas the individual rarely appeared as a historical actor.[30]

Apart from rock inscriptions in the surrounding deserts that sometimes also attest to early military activities,[31] almost all the other evidence for Egyptian foreign affairs and warfare during the Old Kingdom comes from nonroyal inscriptions and autobiographies of court officials and the provincial elite, who were the actual carriers of royal ideology and of an idealized concept of society. Especially at the end of the period, some expedition reports offer historical information about the state's foreign policy.[32] Apparently, trade expeditions and exploration missions involved large armies, both for transporting trade goods or building materials and for combat when necessary.[33] Raids against Nubian tribes were undertaken perpetually. They mainly aimed at supplying cheap manpower—one text speaks of the deportation of seventeen thousand Nubians to Egypt[34]—and safeguarding trade routes, mines, and quarries. In addition, textual and iconographic evidence—showing, for example, fighting soldiers and the siege of a Palestinian fortress—proves military campaigns against Asiatic peoples.[35] The variety of weaponry had not developed much since the Early Dynastic Period, but mobile ladders were now used for sieges.[36]

In the Old Kingdom, warfare was supposed to be aggressive and total, geared to demolishing the enemy's economic infrastructure and to killing or deporting its population. In typical exaggeration, one text claims,

> This army returned in safety, after it had flattened the sand-dwellers' land. This army returned in safety, after it had sacked its strongholds . . . after it had cut down its figs, its vines . . . after it had thrown fire in all its [mansions] . . . after it had slain its troops by many ten-thousands . . . after [it had carried] off many [troops] as captives. (*Autobiography of Uni*, Lichtheim 1975.20)

The army consisted of auxiliary Nubian and—to a lesser extent—Libyan troops, but Egyptian levies were drafted by conscription as well, depending on the dimension of the campaign.[37] One expedition inscription mentions twenty thousand soldiers,[38] but the reliability of numbers in Egyptian nonadministrative texts is questionable. Since the Egyptian lexicon displays several terms for Nubian mercenaries and their commanders, they presumably formed an essential part, if not the basis, of the army.[39] If so, Egypt's population—whatever its other obligations to the state—may have been largely exempted from campaigning.

Where mountains and the desert failed, Egypt relied on strongholds to defend its territory against potential aggressors. One such fortification, at the Nubian border where expeditions started and trade goods passed frequently, is also well documented archaeologically.[40]

On the whole, warfare had two principal stimuli: border defense and the exploitation of natural resources beyond the borders (especially building materials and manpower). Large-scale projects such as monumental construction and quarry and trade expeditions depended on state control, which guaranteed the supply and organization of manpower, an effective transportation system, and smooth communication among various departments of the administration.

Provincial governors, palace officials, and priests served as military commanders.[41] While governors were in general responsible for border control, military ranks held by palace officials probably imply the existence of a royal guard; the frequent occurrence of such ranks among the titulatures of leaders of expeditions suggests that military functions were an integral part of the "department of expedition and construction"—as was the navy, which mainly met transportation needs.[42] Since mobility and quick accessibility were indispensable for economic and political progress, in the early period the navy evolved more rapidly than the military; accordingly, we know many more naval than military titles.[43]

Given that royal aggression and the suppression of the foreign world were essential to Egyptian ideology, it is surprising that warfare played only a small role in the elite's self-presentation.[44] Three factors may explain this: (1) The king monopolized the art and practice of war—in fact, weaponry was stored under the royal seal[45]—and he alone was ideologically permitted to perform violent acts. (2) Since the state relied on mercenary troops, military service may have been considered "dirty work," which thus affected the population as a whole only exceptionally. (3) Although sufficient evidence confirms that wars were waged, war as a topic does not dominate historiography, which focuses on other important aspects of political or social life, such as social and moral obligations, the exploration and exploitation of natural resources and trade contacts, the construction of monumental tombs, or official careers beyond reproach. Due to Egypt's geographic isolation and highly developed political structure, its territorial integrity was not threatened.[46] Display of military power, certainly a constant factor in state affairs, was necessitated neither by competition nor by serious threats. Even border control, still manageable on the provincial level, probably mostly served the purpose of displaying Egyptian power. In general, outside aggression was rare and modest and had only a small impact on foreign policy that, during the Old Kingdom, did not result in a permanent political presence abroad.

Political Fragmentation and Cultural Provincialization: The First Intermediate Period

Around the turn from the third to the second millennium, Egypt experienced a phase of political fragmentation for sixty to ninety years, the First

Intermediate Period.[47] Its causes are difficult to identify. The traditional argument holds that under the pressure of a growing court aristocracy and administration on the one side and the excessive needs of the provincial elite on the other, Egypt's redistribution system eventually collapsed, thus depriving the palace of its main resources.[48] The ephemeral kings were unable to maintain central control. As a shadowy remnant, the monarchy lasted in the north until the centralized state was restored, but in all other parts of the country provincial magnates ("nomarchs") gained power and eventually independence.

Assuming the role of economic benefactors and military protectors of their nomes, these self-appointed lords programmatically turned away from the ideals of the Old Kingdom elite and developed a new image of rulership, based on individual effectiveness, support and defense of the population, martial qualification, and divine selection. Written sources are again propagandistic in their representation of events but now frequently refer to internal difficulties. Food supply and military aggression among the different principalities must have been a constant problem. Archaeology suggests, however, that these political and social changes mostly affected the upper classes, not the broader population. Material culture in the provinces was thoroughly transformed, reflecting not economic deficiencies but autonomy from the old court traditions and economic rise among the broad population.[49]

As the result of power struggles among rival potentates, warfare became endemic within the country, and the military changed substantially. Just as they now had to fend for themselves in terms of subsistence and political organization, the nomes or urban centers also took care of their own defense. They sustained troops consisting of Nubian mercenaries and the provinces' young men, who constituted the entourage of the local rulers.[50] This patron-client relationship between elite and common population affected all parts of society and triggered broad cultural changes.[51] Although the equipment and techniques of war had hardly changed since the Old Kingdom,[52] naval power and sieges became popular motifs in official display. War was now presented as a major issue in the autobiographies of provincial leaders and in inscriptions left by ordinary people.[53] In dismantling royal ideology, the new military model broke a taboo: what used to be a royal prerogative, the representation of war and martial achievement, was now the business of the self-made man.[54]

The process of the political reunification of Egypt and the foundation of the Middle Kingdom began in Upper Egypt, propelled by an aristocratic family from Thebes, later the Eleventh Dynasty. When centralized power was eventually reestablished, violence and warfare were once again de jure prerogatives of the king, but society had changed considerably, and so had its modes of self-expression.

The Birth of Imperialism: The Middle Kingdom

The Middle Kingdom was the heir of both the old and the recent past. While relying on the achievements of the Old Kingdom in terms of transportation and organization of mass labor, it adjusted its administration, economy, and military to the municipal model of the First Intermediate Period, which better matched the geopolitical structure of the country. Bureaucracy was reorganized and expanded.[55] The kings of the later Twelfth Dynasty launched large-scale projects, which became hallmarks of the high Middle Kingdom: a building program promoting the erection of temples in stone all over Egypt, the cultivation and colonization of the Fayyum Oasis, the conquest of Lower Nubia, and the establishment of an imperial military system.

Parallel to the bureaucratic evolution, there emerged a new class of officials and literati who self-consciously expressed their thoughts on kingship and society by propagating the image of the perfect bureaucrat, including also the patronage model promoted during the First Intermediate Period.[56] First traces of individualistic thinking appear in funerary and narrative literature, shaping the image of the high Middle Kingdom[57] and influencing the kingship. The king now shared his ability to become a god after death with every human being. At the same time, although the king's role as the sole performer of cult remained untouched, everybody was meant to partake of the interaction between the gods and the state.[58] Moreover, in literary sources the figure of the king became associated with human aspects: emotions, failure, the recognition of one's own mistakes.[59] Royal representation consciously seems to counterbalance such admissions of the king's vulnerability by stressing his qualifications: divine origin, performance and maintenance of cult, benefaction for his people, protection of territorial integrity, and aggressive oppression of chaos and evil, including the outside world.

Military and imperial success became a constant part of royal propaganda. Although political events were barely articulated, official representation expanded remarkably, displaying a variety of motifs in martial discourse. Especially in literary contexts, royal eulogy developed dramatic images of the king as the invincible warrior:

> Stouthearted when he [the king] sees the mass, he lets not slackness fill his heart. Eager at the sight of combat, joyful when he works his bow. Clasping his shield he treads under foot, no second blow needed to kill. None can escape his arrow, none turn aside his bow. (Eulogy in the *Story of Sinuhe*, Lichtheim 1975.225–26)

Royal wrath aimed equally at the "vile" enemies and internal opposition, which, according to a fictive posthumous royal autobiography, might even have cost one king his life.[60] The appearance of this topic in historical inscriptions of the early Middle Kingdom suggests that internal disturbances and resistance were not only a literary reminiscence of the First Intermediate Period but a political reality during the transition from the Eleventh to the Twelfth Dynasty.[61]

The most important information about military efforts and imperialism is based on archaeological evidence from Egyptian fortresses in Lower Nubia. In the late Twelfth Dynasty, Egypt pursued a radical policy of conquest and permanent occupation that required a great deal of expenditures, organization, and discipline. These efforts probably responded to a threat from the south, posed by the emerging kingdom of Kerma. Hence one purpose of building a dense network of forts beyond the Egyptian border was defense in depth. Another presumably was to protect the transportation and storage of trade goods, tributes, and raw materials at locations that did not allow quick and smooth traffic on the river.[62]

Military architecture was fairly sophisticated. The forts were built adjacent to the cliffs along the Nile; they were surrounded by massive enclosure walls and, if necessary, by additional ditches. Fortified gateways, watchtowers, and loopholed ramparts on the inside and covered glacis on the outside made them almost impregnable. Probably fifty to three hundred soldiers were stationed in one fort at a time, depending on its size, which implies that small military units were able to hold the position.[63] Although grain supply must have been a priority in the imperial system, apparently the soldiers' provisions were fairly low (six hundred grams of grain per day, according to bread-ration tokens found in one of the forts), but this might suggest that there was a dietary supplement to the grain rations.[64]

The Middle Kingdom's imperial ambitions relied, in principle, on the military structure of the First Intermediate Period, using Nubian mercenaries as well as Egyptian levies.[65] The conscription of young recruits and the discharge of veterans were, it seems, institutionalized at the beginning of the Middle Kingdom. Like officials, they probably were remunerated with goods, land endowments, and cattle.[66] The militias fulfilled paramilitary tasks, controlling forced labor and forming labor corvées themselves, or were stationed in Egypt's remote Nubian fortresses. Most of the soldiers posted there, however, were drafted in Upper Egypt, in the Theban area, where Nubians had already been acculturated.[67] This may imply that Nubian mercenaries too served in the southern territories. Life in a Nubian fort included military defense, the surveillance of caravans and naval transportation, control of the local population, and the exchange of goods that took place between local tradesmen and the Egyptian military bases.[68]

Much less is known about Egypt's foreign affairs in Asia. Apart from trade connections with Palestine and Syria, Egypt's most serious concern was the protection of its borders. Although official propaganda might refer to the attack and depletion of Asiatic towns, administrative information relating to the same events implies that these expeditions were not military clashes but Egyptian raids of poorly defended Asiatic places in order to extort tribute, weapons, and cheap manpower.[69]

Indirectly, the lack of professional specialization in the Middle Kingdom is documented by a literary text, the "Satire of Trades," which parodies common professions and extols the scribe's role. Interestingly, in the list of standard trades of the period that of the soldier is missing—in contrast to a later version from the New Kingdom in which the life of the soldier is pictured at length in all its misery and danger. This may indicate that soldiery was not considered a full-time profession before then.[70]

Still, the impact of warfare on the elite's self-representation and ideology was significant. Narrative autobiographies now place much more emphasis on the protagonist's military function than during the Old Kingdom. They may even contain detailed historical information, such as the amount of booty granted a soldier during a campaign.[71] Individual military heroism, downplayed in autobiographical discourse, is fully unfolded in literary narrative. In the fictional autobiography of an Egyptian dignitary who, during his exile in Palestine, faces a challenge by an Asiatic warrior, the protagonist's martial capabilities are amplified in a way unknown in private or royal display of the time:

> He came toward me while I waited, having placed myself near him. Every heart burned for me. The women jabbered. All hearts ached for me thinking: "Is there another champion who could fight him?" . . . When I had made his weapons attack me, I let his arrows pass me by without effect, one following the other. Then, when he charged me, I shot him, my arrow sticking in his neck. He screamed. He fell on his nose. I slew him with his axe. I raised my war cry over his back, while every Asiatic shouted. (*Story of Sinuhe,* Lichtheim 1975.228)

During the First Intermediate Period the iconography of warfare was limited to the depiction of soldiers holding their weapons or bringing in prisoners; in the early Middle Kingdom military scenes become more frequent and even integrate elements of a narrative structure: troops are shown engaged in combat on warships or in the siege of an Asiatic fort—a motif especially prominent in the tombs of provincial governors.[72] Although military ranking does not show dramatic changes from the Old Kingdom, the traditional weaponry was enhanced by new martial tools that would become the standard accoutrement in Late Bronze Age Egypt: javelins, short bronze swords, spears, differently shaped bronze arrowheads, and even parts of chariots entered Egypt as the equipment of Asiatic mercenaries settled in the Nile Delta or as the spoils of Egyptian raids in Syria and Palestine.[73]

The increased importance of warfare at the beginning of the period is also perceptible in miniature models of soldiers and weapons found in the tombs of provincial magnates. The wooden figures, Egyptian spearmen and Nubian archers, were meant to assist the tomb owner after death as real troops did in his lifetime.[74] All this implies that even after the reunification of the state it was still common practice to maintain armies in the provinces. In theory under the command of the king, these troops were actually still controlled by local governors and military leaders who *could* challenge the king's sovereignty. This perhaps explains why after the reorganization of bureaucracy during the Twelfth Dynasty the governors were gradually replaced by heads of a purely municipal administration.[75] Not accidentally, soon thereafter military scenes and models disappeared again from the repertoire of private tombs.[76]

Expansion and Cosmopolitanism: The New Kingdom

The transition from the Middle to the New Kingdom (the Second Intermediate Period) is characterized by the decline of central power, usurpations, rapid successions to the throne,[77] and the infiltration of West Semitic migrants into the Nile Delta. Archaeological evidence shows that Asiatic soldiers and laborers had already been settled in the Nile Delta in the Twelfth Dynasty. They gradually gained political authority as a result of the decentralization of the state and the increase of Semitic population in the north, where settlements and cemeteries indicate a reduction of cultural assimilation. Gradually, social stratification emerged within this community, fostering the formation of a small kingdom that extended into Palestine. Its rulers are known by the ancient name of Hyksos.[78]

The experience of foreign occupation, even if it did not affect the entire country, left its marks in the conception of the past promoted, for propagandistic reasons, by the first dynasty of the New Kingdom (the Eighteenth Dynasty). For generations to come, the expulsion of the foreign intruders and the reestablishment of central monarchy were memorialized as both a traumatic experience and a national moment of glory.

While royal ideology had hardly changed since the Middle Kingdom, there is strong evidence for a growing need for political justification. Even in official display, the king's role and actions could now be adjusted to episodic events, thus making him the prime agent of history.[79] Striking innovations in this context are the emergence of royal historiography, with strong links to nonroyal autobiography, and panoramic tableaux in temple decoration, frequently showing the major events of a specific campaign abroad.[80]

Royal representation focused on temple endowments and warfare. The temples now became the economic centers of the state, administering vast landed properties and industries,[81] and the places where kings asserted their legitimacy.[82] All the king's obligations and actions—maintenance of cults, construction and embellishment of temples, especially of the state god Amun-Re at Thebes, military campaigns, or trade expeditions to distant countries—were presented in harmony with the gods' sphere.

According to royal ideology, the king was the god's representative and chosen son. Nonetheless, depending on the circumstances of his accession, this status needed to be reaffirmed either by an oracle or by the claim to divine birth.[83] Since the gulf between kingship and the gods' sphere had apparently widened,[84] the king constantly needed to prove his responsibility vis-à-vis his office and to make efforts far surpassing those of his predecessors to demonstrate his legitimate claim to the throne.[85] This idea was conveyed especially through monumental building and in warfare.

The traditional image of the king as the eternal warrior was now expanded and humanized, showing him as the active and successful commander in chief and victorious war hero, leading his soldiers in battle and acting to the glory of Egypt. The mastery of the art of warfare was considered a paradigm of kingship and essential criterion for royal succession.[86]

> He [the king] also came to do the following. . . . Entering his northern garden, he found erected for him four targets of Asiatic copper, of one palm in thickness, with a distance of twenty cubits between one post and the next. Then his Majesty appeared on the chariot like Mont [the god of war] in his might. He drew his bow while holding four arrows together in his fist. Thus he rode northward shooting at them, like Mont in his panoply, each arrow coming out at the back of its target while he attacked the next post. It was a deed never yet done, never yet heard reported: shooting an arrow at a target of copper, so that it came out of it and dropped to the ground. (*Great Sphinx Stela* of Amenhotep II, Lichtheim 1976.41–42)

Military success also guaranteed Egypt's territorial integrity and well-being. The early New Kingdom was a period of political consolidation, economic growth, and social change. Lower Nubia, reconquered early in the Eighteenth Dynasty, had become an Egyptian province, headed by a governor, the "viceroy of Kush," often an accomplished military leader himself.[87] The state pursued an aggressive foreign policy in western Asia, establishing political control over Syria and Palestine[88] and increasing the country's prosperity. Precious raw materials and products from the deserts and Nubia, as well as agricultural and industrial surplus, were exported, while trade goods, tributes, and technological know-how from Africa, the Mediterranean world, and the Near East came to Egypt.[89] Economy and society flourished under a centralized administration. Political stability, wealth, the availability of cheap manpower from abroad, and the expansion of bureaucracy all contributed to social stratification and the evolution of a broad literate middle class.[90] Gradually, there developed specialized professional groups, such as the bureaucracy, the soldiery, and priests, often adopting hereditary succession.

The New Kingdom version of the "Satire of Trades," mentioned earlier, offers an example of how society, from the scribe's perspective, viewed the range of professions. By focusing on the peasant and soldier and thus on the lowest stratum of these professions, the text undermines the social status of the military and the landowning populace and exalts the bureaucratic career.[91] Accordingly, the military was probably considered a strong professional class. Confirmation comes from prosopography. In the army of the New Kingdom only a few of the traditionally ambiguous upper-level titles survived, for example "general," referring equally to leaders of labor corvées and commanders of an army. Otherwise, the old system of ranks was almost completely replaced by a new, sophisticated nomenclature and structure, including a completely new department, the chariotry.[92] This army was no longer split into units subordinated to provincial or municipal administrations but was placed, like all other state structures, under the direct control of the central government.

Yet trends toward increasing centralization of bureaucracy do not sufficiently explain the professionalization and technical development of the army. Warfare had considerable consequences for society as a whole. Purely military careers were possible and became increasingly frequent, especially in the chariotry; participation in war and possession of a chariot were tantamount to prestige and status; as a result, originally military attributes developed into upper-class symbols deprived of any real link to the military profession: now representatives of the bureaucracy also adopted military epithets emphasizing a close relationship with the king and drove chariots granted by the king.[93] A new military class emerged, founded on a new set of social values and a new model of common identity. Military functions and ranks were no longer valued against the background of the traditional bureaucracy; now being a soldier sufficed to elicit public respect. All this is reflected also in both royal and nonroyal military reports,[94] which are now clearly inspired by the desire to surpass established limits and prove individual exceptionality and efficacy, as in the following text:

> [His Majesty ordered to] tell the whole army: "[Your valiant lord will guide your steps on] this road which becomes narrow." [For his Majesty had taken] an oath, saying: "I shall not let [my valiant army] go before me from [this place!" Thus his Majesty resolved] that he himself should go before his army. [Every man] was informed of his order of march, horse follow-

ing horse, with his Majesty at the head of his army. (*Annals of Thutmosis III, The Battle of Megiddo,* Lichtheim 1976.31)

This text illustrates the close ties between the military elite and the commoners and exemplifies a growing tendency to humanize the king, who acted as the *primus inter pares* rather than as the stereotyped smiter of the enemies. The same tendency seems to have led to the recording of individual prowess at the cost of undermining the king's infallibility; in his autobiography a battle companion of Amenhotep II boasts of having saved not only the Egyptian army from harm—a topic principally reserved for the king—but also the king's life.[95]

The solidarity between king and military elite may have originated partly in a palatial practice introduced early in the Eighteenth Dynasty: the education of young men, sometimes of foreign origin or low birth, at court. These "Striplings of the Nursery" often started their career as war comrades of the king and ended up in high bureaucratic positions. Indeed, a kind of adoptive kinship might have played a role in that policy, since the children and spouses of royal wet nurses also bore that title.[96] On this basis, during the earlier Eighteenth Dynasty, the monarchy built a stable and dependable network of allies around the king. By appointing his companions to high positions, the king had direct access to administrative and economic structures, while excluding hereditary claims or the pressure of conservative forces.[97]

The study of contemporary international relations further elucidates the emergence of militarism in Egypt. Around the time when central power was reestablished in Egypt, a new system of empires and satellite states developed in western Asia. The impact of "superpowers" such as the kingdom of Khatti (Hittites) or Mitanni (Hurrians) on the Egyptian view of the outside world was fundamental.[98] After the expulsion of the Hyksos, Nubia was reconquered, while Palestine and Syria witnessed numerous encounters, first with the Hurrians, later with the Hittites. Apparently, the early kings of the Eighteenth Dynasty themselves developed an interest in expanding their sphere of influence.[99] The concept of supremacy over foreign countries had changed in substance. Previously, foreign policy aimed at exploiting less organized political systems and hence converged with the Egyptian idealization of war; now superiority was no longer a given fact, and Egypt had to accept its new role among other competing states and their vassals. To establish political influence and control in this arena required not only military parity but also diplomatic skills and economic strength.

Four factors contributed to the emergence of Egyptian imperialism: (1) the state's long experience in maintaining a complex bureaucratic system, (2) the centralization of the military, (3) its politicization and linkage to economic growth,[100] and (4) constant contact and interaction with rival states, which, among other things, prompted "military transculturation": the adaptation of foreign war practices and weapons.[101] Hence the military, following western Asiatic structures, was almost completely reorganized, and new titles and ranks were introduced; the army was expanded (in Ramesside times, up to thirty-seven thousand infantry) and employed a high number of Asiatic mercenaries.[102] New body armor and weapons such as the scimitar, special javelins and spears, the short sword, the composite bow, sophisticated projectiles, and shields were taken over from Asiatic neighbors and the Mediterranean world.[103] Egyptian soldiers were now distinguished by a military skirt, mercenaries by their ethnic dresses and sometimes also by helmets.[104] The most innovative weapon was the chariot, which became common in the entire Near East in the Late Bronze Age.[105] The large number of foreign technical terms connected with maintaining horses and vehicles suggests that the Egyptians adapted the chariot from the Hurrians. It is not clear, however, whether it actually served as a shock weapon or rather as a vehicle of prestige and speed.[106] Egyptians and their Asiatic adversaries used the light chariot—only the Hittites and later the Assyrians developed heavier versions; thus, chariotry was deployable only in plain areas. Yet according to battle scenes and reports it must have had a certain strategic importance. Moreover, the command of the chariotry required standardized military training, which seems to corroborate its crucial military role.[107]

According to iconographic evidence, during the early New Kingdom weapon production was administered by temples. Eventually, the main armories were attached to state and military departments, the Royal Treasury located in Memphis and the Royal Chariotry based at Piramesse, the Ramesside capital in the Delta.[108] Hence they were in the reach of the fort of Sile at the northeastern border, which functioned as arsenal and point of departure for campaigns in Asia. Archaeological evidence shows that foreign craftsmen, for example, Hittites, were employed in weapon industries.[109]

Although large portions of the army consisted of mercenaries, the old system of recruitment was still in use. Desertion was frequent, and perpetrators were punished harshly: they and their families were put in jail.[110] In contrast, military service paid well. Soldiers received a share of the booty, certainly one of the most important incentives of campaigning, enjoyed allocations or donations of land, or even profited from appointments to high positions at court or in the economic system.[111] This, in turn, was advantageous to the king, who could build a network of reliable officials and control more directly the flux of state resources.

The Militarization of Kingship, Political Conservatism, and Ethnic Pluralism: The Ramesside Period

After the vain attempts of the so-called Amarna Period to reshape the idea of kingship according to a monotheistic doctrine in which the king was the only intermediary to the divine,[112] the monarchy lost much of its former status. At the same time, Egypt's hegemonic interests collided with the expansionist ambitions of the Hittite Empire, a conflict that, in the long run, affected the state's economy. The military profited most from the weakness of post-Amarnian kingship. The inevitable consequence was usurpation. Haremhab, commander in chief of the army and general consultant of the king under Tutankhamun, facing the need to justify his assumption of power, made divine oracular choice responsible for his appointment; in practice, he based his legitimation on the reorganization of the bureaucracy and the preservation of Egypt's sphere of influence in western Asia, a political program he had promoted already before his assumption of power.[113]

The aftermath of Amarna and the usurper's accession made it necessary to redefine the monarchy, which now came to be understood as an office. Candidates for the throne had to prove their qualifications. Not accidentally, Haremhab's successor, Ramses I and his son, Seti I, had previously been politically powerful army officers. From its beginning, then, the new royal dynasty was founded on the model of elective succession, a model that paid closer attention to political reality and the needs of the state; accordingly, royal display emphasized rather than suppressed the king's human nature and the dynasty's "bourgeois" background—a strong contrast to the totalitarian tendency of the Amarna Period. The only attempt to counter the devaluation of kingship is visible in the self-deification of the king, inaugurated just before the Amarna Period and rediscovered by Ramses II after the consolidation of the Nineteenth Dynasty.[114]

The first Ramesside kings met the demand for political legitimation by again stressing dynastic lineage. Princes assumed a crucial role in royal representation as their fathers' assistants and occupied important positions, especially in cult and the military. The promotion of former military officers to high administrative offices helped improve control over the economy.

The dogmatic principle of striving to surpass previous achievements was a major feature of the new era, expressed in religion—Egypt and Lower Nubia were covered with temples, the monumental manifestations of royal piety—and warfare. Domestically, military success guaranteed political stability and the maintenance of the economic status quo.[115] Hence the rank of the commander in chief of the army became a legitimating attribute of the crown prince.[116] Externally, the Ramesside militaristic ideology aimed at recovering the predominance in Asia the preceding dynasty had achieved. This policy resulted in a period of intensive warfare between Egypt and the Hittite empire, focusing on former Egyptian territories in Syria. The high point of this long-lasting conflict was the battle of Qadesh in northern Syria, where about sixty-six thousand infantrymen and five thousand chariots clashed in the early thirteenth century.

This hard-fought victory, salvaged out of near defeat, became a centerpiece of royal ideology, represented in temple reliefs and inscriptions more frequently than any other.[117] The dramatic narrative of this accomplishment served as prelude to the king's self-representation: directed and protected by god, through his incomparable martial virtues, his destructive rage, and his deep concern for the Egyptian people, he has saved the state from disaster.

> "We stand alone in the midst of battle, abandoned by soldiers and chariotry." . . . His Majesty said to his shield-bearer: "Stand firm, steady your heart, my shield-bearer! I will charge them as a falcon pounces, I will slaughter, butcher, fling to the ground. Why do you fear these weaklings whose multitudes I disregard?" His Majesty then rushed forward. At a gallop he charged the midst of the foe. For the sixth time he charged them. I was after them like Baal in his moment of power, I slew them without pause. (*Qadesh-Poem* [dialogue between the royal shield-bearer and Ramses II], Lichtheim 1976.69)

The conflict with the Hittites lasted for about twenty years, punctuated by further clashes and periods of truce. Peace negotiations eventually succeeded, resulting in relations that were sanctioned by diplomatic marriages and a treaty of parity between the great powers.[118]

Peace, however, did not last long. Under Ramses's successor Egypt faced the first serious offensives of its Libyan neighbors and the so-called Sea Peoples, alliances of warrior tribes from the Ionian and Lycian coasts and later also from Libya, who attacked the country from sea and land.[119] Over the next thirty to forty years, the borders had to be defended against several massive invasions.[120] When Ramses III, the second king of the Twentieth Dynasty, succeeded in thwarting the final attack, the political landscape in western Asia and the Levant had changed dramatically.[121]

Ramses III was the last Egyptian monarch to meet the political prerequisites of his office as established by his predecessors. After his reign, the only remaining domain in which the king could still play his traditional role was the temples, which, however, were economically affected by Egypt's losses in Asia. Meanwhile, even much of this sphere of official representation—the building of sanctuaries, the performance of cults, and donations to the temples—had been appropriated by nonroyal people.[122]

In the long run, Egypt's reduced range of international contacts and economic exchanges had a massive effect on its infrastructure. There was no need anymore to maintain a large army and bureaucracy. During the following century down to the end of the New Kingdom, the well-organized bureaucratic system gradually became top-heavy and far too costly for a state that was losing its means of control. Unable to overcome internal problems such as economic losses, deficiencies in the supply network, corruption, theft, and even raids on public institutions, centralized power declined.[123] Moreover, the succession to the throne was increasingly contested, and the reigns were too short to fight political instability.[124]

At this point ethnic minorities emerged as a political factor. Already the kings of the early Ramesside Period had recognized the military potential of foreign warriors. In order to prevent defeated enemies from regaining control over their soldiers, they settled them and their families in garrisons where they could be controlled and enrolled in Egypt's own armies.

> He (Ramses III) has captured the land of the [Temehu], Libu, and Meshwesh (Libyan tribes), he made them cross the Nile, carried off into Egypt. They are settled into strongholds of the Victorious King. They hear the language of the (Egyptian) people, serving the King. He makes their language disappear, he changes (?) their tongues. They go on a way that they have not descended before. (Stela of Ramses III from Deir el-Medineh, Kitchen 1990.21)

While official sources claimed to have achieved a rigorous policy of cultural assimilation,[125] contemporary archaeological and literary evidence shows that in practice cultural adaptation was less successful because the settlement of foreigners in their own communities helped preserve ethnic identity and traditional customs.[126] The state apparently was not aware of any political danger that might emerge from these pockets of ethnic diversity, but by the end of the New Kingdom these same garrisons had become centers of a new elite out of which later arose the so-called Libyan dynasty (ca. 950).[127]

By this time the military system relied mainly on a network of forts and garrisons, which served as a defense against occasional intrusions of desert tribes and internal instability. As a result, the institutions essential to the maintenance of the state were gradually militarized: the fortified temples now sustained military personnel, many of whom were recruited from mercenary garrisons. A new military class increased its influence by invading other politically important institutions, the economy and priesthoods, gaining power first on the communal, then on the state level. By contrast, the traditional military branch shrank considerably because long-distance campaigns were no longer feasible. The old ranks of command, especially those of the chariotry, were mostly limited to the king's family and still associated with royal succession, indicating that the court with its own troops clung to the old system and still tried to fit the legitimation model of the early Ramesside state.[128]

At the end of the Twentieth Dynasty, the leaders of the new military class, apparently exploiting riots in the Upper Egyptian nome of Thebes, were able to take over the granaries and the local army, mainly consisting of Nubian mercenaries, and to occupy the highest positions in local cult and state bureaucracy, including the government of Nubia.[129] Within decades military commanders of foreign origin dominated the state and achieved virtual autonomy. While the last Ramesside king was still residing in the north, Egypt was split into two politically independent entities. Unlike after the collapse of the Old and the Middle Kingdoms, now, at the beginning of the Third Intermediate Period, no attempts were undertaken to reunify the country.[130] Fragmentation continued but did not have any impact on the peaceful coexistence of these principalities; despite occasional efforts at rebuilding central monarchy, the political landscape of the country remained pluralistic.[131]

Conclusion

From the formation of the Egyptian state, warfare was a constant and important factor in society and politics; the maintenance of troops, preparation of weapons, and campaigning in and submission of foreign countries all formed a royal monopoly. Ideologically, warfare was an integral part of the official worldview and representation, symbolizing royal sovereignty and the domination of the foreign world. Only in periods of political fragmentation and the collapse of monarchical power did warfare become an internal affair, and it was officially described as such to justify the ambitions of regional leaders.

In the early Egyptian state (the Old Kingdom), wars probably were fought only sporadically, when border territories were threatened or Egypt's economic interests abroad were jeopardized. In these cases, the state applied all its military might. Due to Egypt's isolated position between Africa and the Near East, however, constant preparedness for war was not necessary. The entire population seems to have been involved only in rare cases of armed conflict that required a large-scale deployment of manpower; normally, fighting was limited to standing contingents of Nubian auxiliary troops.

For several reasons, in the Middle Kingdom, warfare assumed a more central role. Apart from internal conflicts connected with the collapse of the Old Kingdom, the new rulers may have aspired to exploit systematically resources and trade relations outside Egypt, mainly in Nubia. This task required military occupation to safeguard trade and control against intruders and potential rivals. In the occupied territory this was achieved by a system of defense in depth, based on a chain of forts. Besides Nubian mercenaries, young men from Egyptian towns were drafted to serve in the army. Although apparently no large-scale campaigns were fought in that period and war did not affect society at large, Egyptian imperialism in Nubia sufficed to enhance the role and image of the warrior and thus change the society's perception of warfare.

These conditions changed at the beginning of the Late Bronze Age when Egypt broke out of its isolation and became part of a large-scale political network in western Asia. Transcultural contacts that had slowly developed from the Middle Bronze Age onward offered opportunities and challenges; the state needed to adapt its diplomatic and bureaucratic apparatus and its military policy, and to develop equal standards in military technology and organization. Warfare now went far beyond punitive expeditions in neighboring territories. International contacts, which were always accompanied by the display of military power, now brought wealth and cultural diversity to Egypt, but they also triggered the emergence of a military class.

This phase of Egyptian expansionism and international alliances was followed by a defensive phase. Losing allies also meant losing economic advantages and thus political power. Conquest, in turn, fostered the state's prosperity, which necessitated expansion of the bureaucracy managing economic flow and redistribution. There arose a broad literate "middle class" that loosened the hierarchical structure of Egyptian society. As long as a balance could be maintained between the multiple and diverse facets of the Egyptian system, state and society thrived and political power remained stable. The preservation of the status quo therefore was the highest political priority, which meant that the achievements of the past needed to be repeated, even surpassed. Thus, the defense of territories that traditionally were under Egyptian influence easily turned into expansion. This was the situation in the early Ramesside Period.

When in the later New Kingdom Egypt for the first time faced the danger of foreign invasion, its defensive system was so well developed that the invaders had to withdraw. The state was not equipped, however, to protect its vassal territories as well. The resulting deficiencies in the economic system immediately affected the bureaucracy, society, and monarchy. The change in Egypt's relations to the outside world transformed its militaristic concept of kingship and its methods of political legitimation. The kingship became vulnerable. Attempts to counterbalance these insufficiencies failed. Society had become too pluralistic and kingship and bureaucracy too lethargic to adjust and reorganize outdated structures. Police and military control now were enhanced domestically to support the economic administration and maintain public order. The time was ripe for innovation and change, which were eventually brought about by an empowered military class that emerged not from the old system but from groups of former prisoners of war who had been resettled and trained as Egyptian mercenaries. This new elite, bringing with it different cultural assumptions, may have perceived political fragmentation not negatively, as the result of necessity, but as a functional alternative to the traditional centralized monarchical model.

Notes

1. I thank Michael Cooperson and Antonio Loprieno for constructive criticisms and especially Kurt Raaflaub for a thorough revision of the first draft.
2. Butzer 1976; Krzyzaniak, Kobusiewicz, and Alexander 1993; Midant-Reynes 1992.
3. Loprieno 1988.
4. See Ferguson, this volume, for an anthropological perspective, and Farris, this volume, on Japanese martial ideology.
5. Gnirs 1996a.209–15, 228–30.
6. Hornung 1980; Galán 1995.
7. Ferguson, this volume.
8. Von Soden 1972.659.
9. All dates are B.C.E.
10. Swan Hall 1986.
11. Raaflaub and Farris, this volume.
12. Hornung 1971 and, for cultural comparison, Hassig, this volume.
13. Hoffman 1991; Kemp 1989.31–63; Baines 1995b.95–124.
14. See especially Kaiser 1957, 1961, 1964; cf. von der Way 1993.76–111; van den Brink 1992.
15. Kemp 1989.35–46; Baines 1995b.135–44.
16. Davis 1992.
17. E.g., Köhler forthcoming.
18. Cf. Emery 1987.112–18.
19. Davis 1992.162–63 fig. 38; 230 fig. 53.
20. Cf. Baines 1995b.95–99; Kemp 1989.46–53.
21. Seidlmayer 1990.398–430; 1988; for pyramid-building and royal tomb complexes, see Edwards 1985; Stadelmann 1985.
22. Strudwick 1985; Gnirs 1996a.220–23.
23. Baines 1995a.9–19; 1995b.128–35.
24. Martin-Pardey 1976.
25. See the résumé in Jaroš-Deckert 1984.44; cf. Leclant 1980.
26. For comparison, see Webster, this volume.
27. Eichler 1993.200–201.
28. Sethe 1926; Posener 1987.2–6; Koenig 1990.
29. See Yates and Farris, this volume. Egyptian sources do not provide specific information about strategies, combat techniques, logistics, or troop dispositions and numbers: Schulman 1995.291–92.
30. Eyre 1996; cf. Assmann 1985a.
31. Eichler, 1993.29–126.
32. Cf. Roccati 1982.
33. Eyre 1987.
34. Eichler 1993.155–56. Mass deportation could have been one of the causes of the abrupt disappearance of the so-called A-group culture in Nubia at the end of the Early Dynastic Period: Adams 1977.139.

35. Jaroš-Deckert 1984.44; Shaw 1996.242–46.
36. Shaw 1991.31–39.
37. Sheikh 'Ibada al-Nubi 1990.164–65; Redford 1992.51–55.
38. Helck 1974.
39. Bell 1976; Zibelius-Chen 1988.115–17.
40. The main sources are textual: titulatures of governors and border officers (Eichler 1993.198–268). The remains of a fort of the early Old Kingdom are known from Elephantine: Ziermann 1993.
41. Eichler 1993.198–268.
42. Bietak 1988.
43. Chevereau 1987, 1989.
44. Cf. Yates, this volume, for the loss of interest in military affairs and a plain disesteem of the soldiery in China during the Han dynasty.
45. Suggested by titles that refer to a "house of weapons": Eichler 1993.207–09.
46. Trigger 1976.40–48.
47. Barta 1981.
48. Müller-Wollermann 1986; Martin-Pardey 1976.202–33.
49. Seidlmayer 1987; 1990, with a comprehensive synthesis, 431–441.
50. Fischer 1961.
51. Seidlmayer 1987; Franke 1990.
52. Shaw 1991.31–39.
53. Gnirs 1996a.223–25.
54. See the translated texts in Schenkel 1965.
55. Gestermann 1987; Quirke 1986.
56. Gnirs forthcoming.
57. Parkinson 1996.
58. Baines 1991.147–61.
59. Blumenthal 1996.
60. The *Instruction of King Amenemhet I:* see Lichtheim 1975.135–39.
61. Willems 1985. In a royal historical text (Barbotin and Clère 1991), the perpetrators are categorized as "unpropertied" or "beggars." This might refer to people impoverished by the wars, including unemployed mercenaries who roamed the country marauding after the reorganization of the state.
62. Smith 1995.1–24; Gratien 1994. On defense in depth, see, for comparison, Hassig, Bachrach (this volume); Luttwak 1976.
63. Trigger 1976.68–77; Kemp 1989.166–78.
64. Kemp 1989.127–28.
65. For the military ranking associated with Egyptian administration in Nubia, see Leprohon 1994.
66. *Instruction Addressed to King Merikare* (a fictive *speculum regis*) lines 57–61: Quack 1992.36–39.
67. Berlev 1971; Vercoutter 1957; Fischer 1961.
68. Smither 1945; Kemp 1989.176–78.
69. Altenmüller and Moussa 1991; Goedicke 1991.

70. Texts (translated) in Lichtheim 1975.184–92; 1976.168–75. See below at n. 91.
71. Baines 1987.
72. Jaroš-Deckert 1984.44–47, 102–12; Schulman 1982.
73. Altenmüller and Moussa 1991.12–16, 35–36; Bietak 1996.10–19.
74. Bietak 1985.
75. Franke 1991; for comparison, see Haldon, this volume.
76. Contemporaneous changes in the repertoire of funerary pottery point to even broader cultural changes: Seidlmayer 1990.216–33, 436–37; Bourriau 1991.
77. Quirke 1991a; Franke 1990.
78. Bietak 1996.
79. Baines 1995a.22–31.
80. Assmann 1985b.314–17; Shaw 1996.247–53.
81. Janssen 1975, 1979.
82. Kemp 1989.183–217.
83. Römer 1994.478–87; Brunner 1964.
84. Baines 1995a.22–31; Redford 1995.173–75.
85. Hornung 1980.403–11.
86. Decker 1992.19–59.
87. Smith 1995.141–88. Military careers of Nubian governors: Gnirs 1996b.35–36, 134–41.
88. Redford 1992.125–237.
89. Davies and Schofield 1995; Smith 1995.143–83; Gordon 1983; Bleiberg 1988.
90. Kemp 1989.238–60; Baines 1983; Baines and Eyre 1983.
91. See above at n. 70 and also the *Satirical Letter* from Papyrus Anastasi I: Fischer-Elfert 1983; 1986.148–57.
92. Gnirs 1996b.1–34.
93. Guksch 1994.58–68; Decker and Herb 1994.191–263.
94. Spalinger 1982.
95. Text edited by Sethe 1961.893–94.
96. Feucht 1995.259–99; Roehrig 1990.
97. For explanation, see Murnane 1977.32–57. For comparison, see Crone, this volume.
98. Liverani 1988.449–576.
99. Redford 1992.125–91; cf. Kemp 1978; Frandsen 1979.
100. For comparison, see Rosenstein, this volume.
101. Cf. Ferguson, this volume.
102. Redford 1992.214–21.
103. Pusch 1996; Drews 1993.174–208; also, e.g., Müller 1987; Philip 1989.
104. Curto 1971.
105. Raulwing 1993; Littauer and Crouwel 1979.
106. Cf. Briant, this volume; Drews 1993.104–34, 209–25.
107. Cf. Schulman 1979.
108. Sauneron 1954; Drenkhahn 1976.131–32; Pusch 1996. 134–44.
109. Again Pusch 1996.140–44.

110. Sheikh 'Ibada al-Nubi 1990.187–88.
111. Katary 1983; Gnirs 1996b.37–39, 172–91.
112. Redford 1984; Assmann 1980.
113. Murnane 1995.186–97.
114. Habachi 1969; Wildung 1977.1–30.
115. Cf. Campbell, this volume.
116. Gnirs 1996b.34–35, 79–128.
117. Von der Way 1984; Redford 1992.177–91.
118. Murnane 1990; 1995.212–15.
119. Deger-Jalkotzy 1983; Sandars 1985.
120. Redford 1992.241–56.
121. Liverani 1988.629–42; Bietak 1991; Drews 1993.
122. Römer 1994.96–102; Meeks 1979.605–11; Vernus 1978.136–37.
123. E.g., Gutgesell 1983; Haring 1993; Helck 1955.
124. Kitchen 1982, 1984.
125. Sauneron and Yoyotte 1951; Kitchen 1990.
126. New forms of funerary customs developed, for example, in Bubastis, which at that time harbored Libyan garrisons: Bakr 1982.157–67; Habachi 1957.97–102. From a literary text we learn that foreign mercenaries spoke their mother tongues even when they were on duty: Fischer-Elfert 1986.148–57.
127. Kitchen 1986.243–347; Jansen-Winkeln 1994.
128. Gnirs 1996b.128–34.
129. Gnirs 1996b.193–211; Jansen-Winkeln 1992.
130. Yoyotte 1961; Kitchen 1986.348–77.
131. Leahy 1985.

Bibliography

Adams, William Y. 1977. *Nubia: Corridor to Africa.* London: Penguin.

Altenmüller, Hartwig, and Ahmed M. Moussa. 1991. "Die Inschrift Amenemhets II. aus dem Ptah-Tempel von Memphis. Ein Vorbericht." *Studien zur Altägyptischen Kultur* 18, 1–48.

Assmann, Jan. 1980. "Die 'Loyalistische Lehre' Echnatons." *Studien zur Altägyptischen Kultur* 8, 1–32.

——. 1984. *Ägypten. Theologie und Frömmigkeit einer frühen Hochkultur.* Stuttgart: W. Kohlhammer.

——. 1985a. "Die Entdeckung der Vergangenheit. Innovation und Restauration in der ägyptischen Literaturgeschichte." In Gumbrecht and Link-Heer 1985.484–99.

——. 1985b. "Flachbildkunst des Neuen Reiches." In Vandersleyen 1985.304–17.

Baines, John. 1983. "Literacy and Ancient Egyptian Society." *Man*, n.s., 18, 572–99.

——. 1987. "The Stela of Khusobek: Private and Royal Military Narrative and Values." In Osing and Dreyer 1987.41–61.

——. 1991. "Society, Morality, and Religious Practice." In Shafer 1991.123–200.

——. 1995a. "Kingship, Definition of Culture, and Legitimation." In O'Connor and Silverman 1995.9–48.

——. 1995b. "Origins of Egyptian Kingship." In O'Connor and Silverman 1995.95–156.

Baines, John, and Christopher J. Eyre. 1983. "Four Notes on Literacy." *Göttinger Miszellen* 62, 65–96.

Baines, John, T. G. H. James et al., eds. 1988. *Pyramid Studies and Other Essays Presented to I. E. S. Edwards.* London: Egypt Exploration Society.

Bakr, Mohammed. 1982. "New Excavations of Zagazig University." In *L'Egyptologie en 1979: Axes prioritaires de recherches,* vol. 1, 153–67. Paris: Editions du Centre National de la Recherche Scientifique.

Barbotin, C., and J.-J. Clère. 1991. "L'inscription de Sésostris Ier à Tôd." *Bulletin de l'Institut Français d'Archéologie Orientale* 91, 1–32.

Barta, Winfried. 1981. "Bemerkungen zur Chronologie der 6.–11. Dynastie." *Zeitschrift für Ägyptische Sprache und Altertumskunde* 108, 23–33.

Bell, L. D. 1976. "Interpreters and Egyptianized Nubians in Ancient Egyptian Foreign Policy: Aspects of the History of Egypt and Nubia." Ph.D. diss., University of Philadelphia.

Berlev, Oleg D. 1971. "Les prétendus 'citadins' au Moyen Empire." *Revue d'Egyptologie* 23, 23–48.

Bietak, Manfred. 1985. "Zu den nubischen Bogenschützen aus Assiut. Ein Beitrag zur Geschichte der Ersten Zwischenzeit." In *Mélanges Gamal Eddin Mokhtar,* edited by Paule Posener-Kriéger, vol. 1. Bibliothèque d'Etude, vol. 97.1, 87–97. Cairo: Institut Français d'Archéologie Orientale.

——. 1988. "Zur Marine des Alten Reiches." In Baines et al. 1988.35–40.

——. 1991. "Zur Landnahme Palästinas durch die Seevölker und zum Ende der ägyptischen Provinz Kana'an." In *Festschrift für Werner Kaiser, Mitteilungen des Deutschen Archäologischen Instituts, Abteilung Kairo* 47, 35–50.

——. 1996. *Avaris. The Capital of the Hyksos. Recent Excavations at Tell el-Dab'a.* London: British Museum Press.

Bleiberg, Edward. 1988. "The Redistributive Economy in New Kingdom Egypt: An Examination of B3kw(t)." *Journal of the American Research Center in Egypt* 25, 157–68.

Blumenthal, Elke. 1996. "Die literarische Verarbeitung der Übergangszeit zwischen Altem und Mittlerem Reich." In Loprieno 1996.105–35.

Bourriau, Janine. 1991. "Patterns of Change in Burial Customs during the Middle Kingdom." In Quirke 1991a.3–20.

Brink, Edwin C. M. van den, ed. 1992. *The Nile Delta in Transition: 4th to 3rd Millennium B.C.* Published by the editor.

Brunner, Hellmut. 1964. *Die Geburt des Gottkönigs: Studien zur Überlieferung eines altägyptischen Mythos,* Ägyptologische Abhandlungen, vol. 10. Wiesbaden: Otto Harrassowitz.

Butzer, Karl W. 1976. *Early Hydraulic Civilization in Egypt: A Study in Cultural Ecology.* Chicago: University of Chicago Press.

Chevereau, Pierre-Marie. 1987. "Contribution à la prosopographie des cadres militaires de l'Ancien Empire et de la Première Période Intermédiaire." *Revue d'Egyptologie* 38, 13–47.

———. 1989. "Contribution à la prosopographie des cadres militaires de l'Ancien Empire et de la Première Période Intermédiaire. B—Titres nautiques." *Revue d'Egyptologie* 40, 3–36.

Curto, Silvio. 1971. *The Military Art of the Ancient Egyptians*. Turin: Fratelli Pozzo.

Davies, W. Vivian, and Louise Schofield, eds. 1995. *Egypt, the Aegean, and the Levant: Interconnections in the Second Millennium BC*. London: British Museum Press.

Davis, Whitney. 1992. *Masking the Blow: The Scene of Representation in Late Prehistoric Egyptian Art*, California Studies in the History of Art, vol. 30. Berkeley and Los Angeles: University of California Press.

Decker, Wolfgang. 1992. *Sports and Games of Ancient Egypt*. New Haven, Conn.: Yale University Press.

Decker, Wolfgang, and Michael Herb. 1994. *Bildatlas zum Sport im Alten Ägypten. Corpus der bildlichen Quellen zu Leibesübungen, Spiel, Jagd, Tanz und verwandten Themen*, vol. 1. *Handbuch der Orientalistik*, 1st section, *Der Nahe und der Mittlere Osten*, vol. 14. Leyden: E. J. Brill.

Deger-Jalkotzy, Sigrid, ed. 1983. *Griechenland, die Ägäis und die Levante während der "Dark Ages" vom 12. bis zum 9. Jh. v. Chr.*, Sitzungsberichte der Österreichischen Akademie der Wissenschaften, Phil.–hist. Kl., vol. 418. Vienna: Österreichische Akademie der Wissenschaften.

Donadoni, Sergio, ed. 1990. *L'uomo egiziano*. Rome: Gius. Laterza & Figli.

Drenkhahn, Rosemarie. 1976. *Die Handwerker und ihre Tätigkeiten im Alten Ägypten*, Ägyptologische Abhandlungen, vol. 31. Wiesbaden: Otto Harrassowitz.

Drews, Robert. 1993. *The End of the Bronze Age: Changes in Warfare and the Catastrophe ca. 1200 B.C.* Princeton, N.J.: Princeton University Press.

Edwards, I. E. S. 1985. *The Pyramids of Egypt*. Rev. ed. Harmondsworth: Penguin.

Eichler, Eckhard. 1993. *Untersuchungen zum Expeditionswesen des ägyptischen Alten Reiches*, Göttinger Orientforschungen, 4th series, vol. 26. Wiesbaden: Otto Harrassowitz.

Emery, W. B. 1987. *Archaic Egypt. Culture and Civilization in Egypt Five Thousand Years Ago*. Reprint, Harmondsworth: Penguin.

Eyre, Christopher J. 1987. "Work and the Organisation of Work in the Old Kingdom." In Powell 1987.5–47.

———. 1996. "Is Egyptian Historical Literature 'Historical' or 'Literary'?" In Loprieno 1996.415–33.

Feucht, Erika. 1995. *Das Kind im Alten Ägypten*. Frankfurt: Campus Verlag.

Fischer, Henry George. 1961. "The Nubian Mercenaries of Gebelein during the First Intermediate Period." *Kush* 9, 44–80.

Fischer-Elfert, Hans-Werner. 1983. "Morphologie, Rhetorik und Genese der Soldatencharakteristik." *Göttinger Miszellen* 66, 45–65.

———. 1986. *Die Satirische Streitschrift des Papyrus Anastasi I. Übersetzung und Kommentar*, Ägyptologische Abhandlungen, vol. 44. Wiesbaden: Otto Harrassowitz.

Frandsen, P. J. 1979. "Egyptian Imperialism." In Larsen 1979.167–90.

Franke, Detlef. 1990. "Erste und Zweite Zwischenzeit—Ein Vergleich." *Zeitschrift für ägyptische Sprache und Altertumskunde* 117, 119–29.

——. 1991. "The Career of Khnumhotep III of Beni Hasan and the So-Called 'Decline of the Nomarchs.'" In Quirke 1991b.51–67.

Galán, José M. 1995. *Victory and Border: Terminology Related to Egyptian Imperialism in the XVIIIth Dynasty*, Hildesheimer Ägyptologische Beiträge, vol. 40. Hildesheim: Gerstenberg.

Garnsey, P. D. A., and C. R. Whittaker, eds. 1978. *Imperialism in the Ancient World.* Cambridge: Cambridge University Press.

Gestermann, Louise. 1987. *Kontinuität und Wandel in Politik und Verwaltung des frühen Mittleren Reiches in Ägypten*, Göttinger Orientforschungen, 4th series, vol. 18. Wiesbaden: Otto Harrassowitz.

Gnirs, Andrea M. 1996a. "Die ägyptische Autobiographie." In Loprieno 1996.191–242.

——. 1996b. *Militär und Gesellschaft. Ein Beitrag zur Sozialgeschichte des Neuen Reiches*, Studien zur Archäologie und Geschichte Altägyptens, vol. 17. Heidelberg: Heidelberger Orientverlag.

——. Forthcoming. "The Social Background of the Eloquent Peasant." *Lingua Aegyptia 8.*

Goedicke, Hans. 1991. "Egyptian Military Actions in 'Asia' in the Middle Kingdom." *Revue d'Egyptologie* 42, 89–94.

Gordon, A. H. 1983. "The Context and Meaning of the Ancient Egyptian Word *inw.*" Ph.D. diss., University of California–Berkeley.

Gratien, Brigitte. 1994. "Départements et institutions dans les forteresses nubiennes au Moyen Empire." In *Hommages à Jean Leclant*, vol. 2. *Nubie, Soudan, Ethiopie*, edited by Catherine Berger, Gisèle Clerc, and Nicolas Grimal. Bibliothèque d'Etude, vol.106/2, 185–98. Cairo: Institut Français d'Archéologie Orientale.

Guksch, Heike. 1994. *Königsdienst. Zur Selbstdarstellung der Beamten in der 18. Dynastie*, Studien zur Archäologie und Geschichte Altägyptens, vol. 11. Heidelberg: Heidelberger Orientverlag.

Gumbrecht, H. U., and U. Link-Heer, eds. 1985. *Epochenschwellen und Epochenstrukturen im Diskurs der Literatur- und Sprachhistorie.* Frankfurt: Suhrkamp.

Gutgesell, Manfred. 1983. *Die Datierung der Ostraka und Papyri aus Deir el–Medineh und ihre ökonomische Interpretation.* Teil I. *Die 20. Dynastie*, Hildesheimer Ägyptologische Beiträge, vol. 18–19. Hildesheim: Gerstenberg.

Habachi, Labib. 1957. *Tell Basta*, Supplément aux Annales du Service des Antiquités de l'Egypte, vol. 22. Cairo: Institut Français d'Archéologie Orientale.

——. 1969. *Features of the Deification of Ramses II*, Abhandlungen des Deutschen Archäologischen Instituts Kairo, vol. 5. Glückstadt: J. J. Augustin.

Haring, Ben. 1993. "Libyans in the Theban Region, 20th Dynasty." In Zaccone and di Netro 1993, vol. 2, 159–65.

Helck, Wolfgang. 1955. "Zur Geschichte der 19. und 20. Dynastie." *Zeitschrift der Deutschen Morgenländischen Gesellschaft* 105, 27–52.

——. 1974. "Die Bedeutung der Felsinschriften J. López, *Inscripcionas rupestras* Nr. 27 und 28." *Studien zur Altägyptischen Kultur* 1, 215–25.

Hoffman, Michael A. 1991. *Egypt before the Pharaohs. The Prehistoric Foundations of Egyptian Civilization.* Rev. ed. Austin: University of Texas Press.

Hornung, Erik. 1971. "Politische Planung und Realität im alten Ägypten." *Saeculum* 22, 48–58.

———. 1980. "Von zweierlei Grenzen im alten Ägypten." *Eranos Jahrbuch* 49, 393–427.

Jansen-Winkeln, Karl. 1992. "Das Ende des Neuen Reiches." *Zeitschrift für ägyptische Sprache und Altertumskunde* 119, 22–37.

———. 1994. "Der Beginn der libyschen Herrschaft in Ägypten." *Biblische Notizen* 71, 78–97.

Janssen, J. J. 1975. "Prolegomena to the Study of Egypt's Economic History during the New Kingdom." *Studien zur Altägyptischen Kultur* 3, 127–85.

———. 1979. "The Role of the Temple in the Egyptian Economy during the New Kingdom." In Lipinski 1979.505–15.

Jaroš-Deckert, Brigitte. 1984. *Das Grab des Jnj-jtj.f. Die Wandmalereien der XI. Dynastie, Grabung im Asasif 1963–1970,* vol. 5. Archäologische Veröffentlichungen, vol. 12. Mainz am Rhein: Philipp von Zabern.

Kaiser, Werner. 1957. "Zur inneren Chronologie der Naqadakultur." *Archeologia Geographica* 6, 69–77.

———. 1961. "Einige Bemerkungen zur ägyptischen Frühzeit, II. Zur Frage einer über Menes hinausreichenden ägyptischen Geschichtsüberlieferung." *Zeitschrift für Ägyptische Sprache und Altertumskunde* 86, 39–61.

———. 1964. "Einige Bemerkungen zur ägyptischen Frühzeit, III. Die Reichseinigung." *Zeitschrift für Ägyptische Sprache und Altertumskunde* 91, 86–125.

Katary, S. L. D. 1983. "Cultivator, Scribe, Stablemaster, Soldier: The Late Egyptian Miscellanies in Light of P. Wilbour." In *Egyptological Miscellanies, The Ancient World,* edited by James K. Hoffmeier, vol. 6, 1–4, 71–93.

Kemp, Barry J. 1978. "Imperialism and Empire in New Kingdom Egypt (c. 1575–1087 B.C.)." In Garnsey and Whittaker 1978.7–57.

———. 1989. *Ancient Egypt. Anatomy of a Civilization.* London: Routledge.

Kitchen, Kenneth A. 1982. "The Twentieth Dynasty Revisited." *Journal of Egyptian Archaeology* 68, 116–25.

———. 1984. "Family Relationships of Ramesses IX and the Late Twentieth Dynasty." *Studien zur Altägyptischen Kultur* 11, 127–34.

———. 1986. *The Third Intermediate Period in Egypt (1100–650 B.C.).* 2d rev. ed. Warminster: Aris and Phillips.

———. 1990. "The Arrival of the Libyans in Late New Kingdom Egypt." In Leahy 1990.15–27.

Koenig, Yvan. 1990. "Les textes d'envoûtement de Mirgissa." *Revue d'Egyptologie* 41, 101–25.

Köhler, Christiana. Forthcoming. "Evidence for Interregional Contacts between Late Prehistoric Lower and Upper Egypt: A View from Buto." In Krzyzaniak et al. forthcoming.

Krzyzaniak, Lech, et al., eds. Forthcoming. *Interregional Contacts in the Later Prehistory of Northeastern Africa.*

Krzyzaniak, Lech, Micha Kobusiewicz, and John Alexander, eds. 1993. *Environmental Change and Human Culture in the Nile Basin and Northern Africa until the Second Millennium B.C.* Studies in African Archaeology, vol. 4. Poznan: Poznan Archaeological Museum.

Larsen, Mogens T., ed. 1979. *Power and Propaganda. A Symposium on Ancient Empires*, Mesopotamia 7. Copenhagen: Akademiske Forlag.

Leahy, Anthony. 1985. "The Libyan Period in Egypt." *Libyan Studies* 16, 51–65.

———, ed. 1990. *Libya and Egypt c1300–750 B.C.* London: Centre of Near and Middle Eastern Studies.

Leclant, Jean. 1980. "La 'famille libyenne' au Temple Haut de Pépi I." In *Livre du Centenaire 1880–1980*, edited by Jean Vercoutter. Mémoires publiés par les membres de l'Institut Français d'Archéologie Orientale du Caire, vol. 104, 49–54. Cairo: Institut Français d'Archéologie Orientale.

Leprohon, Ronald J. 1994. "Les forces du maintien de l'ordre dans la Nubie au Moyen Empire." In *Hommages à Jean Leclant*, edited by Catherine Berger, Gisèle Clerc, and Nicolas Grimal, vol. 2. *Nubie, Soudan, Ethiopie*, Bibliothèque d'Etude, vol.106/2, 285–91. Cairo: Institut Français d'Archéologie Orientale.

Lichtheim, Miriam. 1975. *Ancient Egyptian Literature: A Book of Readings*, vol. 1. Berkeley and Los Angeles: University of California Press.

———. 1976. *Ancient Egyptian Literature: A Book of Readings*, vol. 2. Berkeley and Los Angeles: University of California Press.

Lipinski, Edward, ed. 1979. *State and Temple Economy in the Ancient Near East*, Orientalia Lovaniensia Analecta, vol. 6. Leuven: Departement Orientalistiek.

Littauer, Mary, and J. H. Crouwel. 1979. *Wheeled Vehicles and Ridden Animals in the Ancient Near East*. Leyden: E. J. Brill.

Liverani, Mario. 1988. *Antico Oriente. Storia società economia*. Rome: Gius. Laterza & Figli.

Lloyd, Alan B., ed. 1996. *Battle in Antiquity*. London: Duckworth and Swansea: Classical Press of Wales.

Loprieno, Antonio. 1988. *Topos und Mimesis. Zum Ausländer in der ägyptischen Literatur*, Ägyptologische Abhandlungen, vol. 48. Wiesbaden: Otto Harrassowitz.

———, ed. 1996. *Ancient Egyptian Literature. History and Forms*, Probleme der Ägyptologie, vol. 10. Leyden: E. J. Brill.

Luttwak, Edward N. 1976. *The Grand Strategy of the Roman Empire: From the First Century A.D. to the Third*. Baltimore, Md.: Johns Hopkins University Press.

Martin-Pardey, Eva. 1976. *Untersuchungen zur ägyptischen Provinzverwaltung bis zum Ende des Alten Reiches*, Hildesheimer Ägyptologische Beiträge, vol. 1. Hildesheim: Gerstenberg.

Meeks, Dimitri. 1979. "Les donations aux temples dans l'Egypte du Ier millénaire avant J.–C." In Lipinski 1979.605–87.

Midant-Reynes, Béatrix. 1992. *Préhistoire de l'Egypte des premiers hommes aux premiers pharaons*. Paris: Armand Colin.

Müller, Hans W. 1987. *Der Waffenfund von Balâta-Sichem und die Sichelschwerter*, Abhandlungen der bayerischen Akademie der Wissenschaften, phil.–hist. Kl., Neue Folge, vol. 97. Munich: Bayerische Akademie der Wissenschaften.

Müller-Wollermann, Renate. 1986. "Krisenfaktoren im ägyptischen Staat des ausgehenden Alten Reichs." Ph.D. diss., University of Tübingen.

Murnane, William J. 1977. *Ancient Egyptian Coregencies.* Studies in Ancient Oriental Civilizations, vol. 40. Chicago: Oriental Institute of the University of Chicago.

———. 1990. *The Road to Kadesh. A Historical Interpretation of the Battle Reliefs of King Sety I at Karnak.* 2d rev. ed. Studies in Ancient Oriental Civilizations, vol. 42. Chicago: Oriental Institute of the University of Chicago.

———. 1995. "The Kingship of the Nineteenth Dynasty: A Study in the Resilience of an Institution." In O'Connor and Silverman 1995.185–217.

O'Connor, David, and David P. Silverman, eds. 1995. *Ancient Egyptian Kingship,* Probleme der Ägyptologie, vol. 9. Leyden: E. J. Brill.

Osing, Jürgen, and Günter Dreyer, eds. 1987. *Form und Maß. Festschrift für Gerhard Fecht,* Ägypten und Altes Testament, vol. 12. Wiesbaden: Otto Harrassowitz.

Parkinson, Richard B. 1996. "Individual and Society in Middle Kingdom Literature." In Loprieno 1996.137–55.

Philip, Graham. 1989. *Metal Weapons of the Early and Middle Bronze Ages in Syria-Palestine.* 2 vols. Oxford: B.A.R. International Series.

Posener, Georges. 1987. *Cinq figurines d'envoûtement,* Bibliothèque d'Etude, vol. 101. Cairo: Institut Français d'Archéologie Orientale.

Powell, Marvin A., ed. 1987. *Labor in the Ancient Near East.* American Oriental Series, vol. 68. New Haven, Conn.: American Oriental Society.

Quack, Joachim F. 1992. *Studien zur Lehre des Merikare,* Göttinger Orientforschungen, 4th series, vol. 23. Wiesbaden: Otto Harrassowitz.

Quirke, Stephen. 1986. "The Regular Titles of the Late Middle Kingdom." *Revue d'Egyptologie* 37, 17–130.

———. 1991a. "Royal Power in the 13th Dynasty." In Quirke 1991b.123–39.

———, ed. 1991b. *Middle Kingdom Studies.* New Malden: Sia Publishing.

Pusch, Edgar B. 1996. "'Pi-Ramses-Beloved-of-Amun, Headquarters of thy Chariotry.' Egyptians and Hittites in the Delta Residence of the Ramessides." In *Pelizaeus Museum Hildesheim. The Egyptian Collection,* 126–144. Mainz am Rhein: Philip von Zabern.

Raulwing, Peter. 1993. "Pferd und Wagen im Alten Ägypten: Forschungsstand, Beziehungen zu Vorderasien, interdisziplinäre und methodenkritische Ansätze." *Göttinger Miszellen* 136, 71–83.

Redford, Donald B. 1984. *Akhenaten. The Heretic King.* Princeton, N.J.: Princeton University Press.

———. 1992. *Egypt, Canaan, and Israel in Ancient Times.* Princeton, N.J.: Princeton University Press.

———. 1995. "The Concept of Kingship during the Eighteenth Dynasty." In O'Connor and Silverman 1995.157–84.

Roccati, Alessandro. 1982. *La littérature historique sous l'Ancien Empire Egyptien.* Paris: Les Editions du CERF.

Roehrig, Catharine. 1990. "Eighteenth Dynasty Titles Royal Nurse (*mnˁt nzwt*), Royal Tutor (*mnˁ nzwt*), and Foster Brother/Sister of the Lord of the Two Lands (*zn znt mnˁ n nb t3wy*)." Ph.D. diss., University of California–Berkeley.

Römer, Malte. 1994. *Gottes- und Priesterherrschaft in Ägypten am Ende des Neuen Reiches,* Ägypten und Altes Testament, vol. 21. Wiesbaden: Otto Harrassowitz.

Sandars, Nancy K. 1985. *The Sea Peoples: Warriors of the Ancient Mediterranean, 1250–1150 B.C.* Rev. ed. London: Thames and Hudson.

Sauneron, Serge. 1954. "La manufacture d'armes de Memphis." *Bulletin de l'Institut Français d'Archéologie Orientale* 54, 7–12.

Sauneron, Serge, and Jean Yoyotte. 1951. "Traces d'établissements asiatiques en Moyenne–Egypte sous Ramsès II." *Revue d'Egyptologie* 7, 67–70.

Schenkel, Wolfgang. 1965. *Memphis–Herakleopolis–Theben. Die epigraphischen Zeugnisse der 7.–11. Dynastie Ägyptens,* Ägyptologische Abhandlungen, vol. 12. Wiesbaden: Otto Harrassowitz.

Schulman, Alan R. 1979. "Chariots, Chariotry and the Hyksos." *Journal of the Society for the Study of Egyptian Antiquities* 10, 105–53.

——. 1982. "The Battle Scenes of the Middle Kingdom." *Journal of the Society for the Study of Egyptian Antiquities* 12, 165–83.

——. 1995. "Military Organization in Pharaonic Egypt." In *Civilizations of the Ancient Near East,* edited by Jack M. Sasson et al., vol. 1, 289–301. New York: Scribner's.

Seidlmayer, Stephan J. 1987. "Wirtschaftliche und gesellschaftliche Entwicklung im Übergang vom Alten zum Mittleren Reich. Ein Beitrag zur Archäologie der Gräberfelder der Region Qau-Matmar in der Ersten Zwischenzeit." In *Problems and Priorities in Egyptian Archaeology,* edited by Jan Assmann, Günter Burhard, and Vivian Davies. Studies in Egyptology. London: Kegan Paul.

——. 1988. "Funerärer Aufwand und soziale Ungleichheit. Eine methodische Anmerkung zum Problem der Rekonstruktion der gesellschaftlichen Gliederung aus Friedhofsfunden." *Göttinger Miszellen* 104, 25–51.

——. 1990. *Gräberfelder aus dem Übergang vom Alten zum Mittleren Reich. Studien zur Archäologie der Ersten Zwischenzeit,* Studien zur Archäologie und Geschichte Altägyptens, vol. 1. Heidelberg: Heidelberger Orientverlag.

Sethe, Kurt. 1926. *Die Ächtung feindlicher Fürsten, Völker und Dinge auf altägyptischen Tongefäßscherben des Mittleren Reiches.* Berlin: Verlag der Akademie der Wissenschaften.

——. 1961. *Historisch-Biographische Urkunden,* vol. 4. Urkunden der 18. Dynastie, vol. 3. Reprint, Berlin: Akademie-Verlag.

Shafer, Byron E., ed. 1991. *Religion in Ancient Egypt: Gods, Myths, and Personal Practice.* Ithaca, N.Y.: Cornell University Press.

Shaw, Ian. 1991. *Egyptian Warfare and Weapons.* Buckinghamshire: Shire Publications.

——. 1996. "Battle in Ancient Egypt: The Triumph of Horus or the Cutting Edge of the Temple Economy?" In Lloyd 1996.239–69.

Sheikh 'Ibada al-Nubi. 1990. "Il soldato." In Donadoni 1990.161–95.

Smith, Stuart T. 1995. *Askut in Nubia: The Economics and Ideology of Egyptian Imperialism in the Second Millennium B.C.* Studies in Egyptology. London: Kegan Paul International.

Smither, Paul C. 1945. "The Semnah Despatches." *Journal of Egyptian Archaeology* 31, 3–10.

Soden, Wolfram von. 1972. *Akkadisches Handwörterbuch,* vol. 2. Wiesbaden: Otto Harrassowitz.

Spalinger, Anthony. 1982. *Aspects of the Military Documents of the Ancient Egyptians.* Yale Near Eastern Researches, vol. 9. New Haven, Conn.: Yale University Press.

Stadelmann, Rainer. 1985. *Die ägyptischen Pyramiden. Vom Ziegelbau zum Weltwunder,* Kulturgeschichte der Antiken Welt, vol. 30. Mainz am Rhein: Philipp von Zabern.

Strudwick, Nigel. 1985. *The Administration of Egypt in the Old Kingdom: The Highest Titles and Their Holders,* Studies in Egyptology. London: Routledge and Kegan Paul.

Swan Hall, Emma. 1986. *The Pharaoh Smites His Enemies: A Comparative Study.* Münchner Ägyptologische Studien, vol. 44. Munich: Deutscher Kunstverlag.

Trigger, Bruce. 1976. *Nubia under the Pharaohs,* Ancient Peoples and Places, vol. 85. London: Thames and Hudson.

Vandersleyen, Claude. 1985. *Das Alte Ägypten. Propyläen Kunstgeschichte,* vol. 17. Berlin: Propyläen Verlag.

Vercoutter, Jean. 1957. "Upper Egyptian Settlers in Middle Kingdom Nubia." *Kush* 7, 61–69.

Vernus, Pascal. 1978. "Littérature et autobiographie. Les inscriptions de Z3-Mwt surnomé Kyky." *Revue d'Egyptologie* 30, 115–92.

Way, Thomas von der. 1984. *Die Textüberlieferung Ramses' II. zur Qadeš-Schlacht: Analyse und Struktur,* Hildesheimer Ägyptologische Beiträge, vol. 22. Hildesheim: Gerstenberg.

———. 1993. *Untersuchungen zur Spätvor- und Frühgeschichte Unterägyptens,* Studien zur Archäologie und Geschichte Altägyptens, vol. 8. Heidelberg: Heidelberger Orientverlag.

Wildung, Dietrich. 1977. *Egyptian Saints: Deification in Pharaonic Egypt.* New York: New York University Press.

Willems, Harko O. 1985. "The Nomarchs of the Hare Nome and Early Middle Kingdom History." *Jaarbericht van het Vooraziatisch-Egyptisch Genootschap Ex Oriente Lux* 28, 80–102.

Yoyotte, Jean. 1961. "Les principautés du Delta au temps de l'anarchie libyenne (Etudes d'histoire politique)." In *Mélanges Maspero,* part 1. Orient Ancien, Mémoires de l'Institut Français d'Archéologie Orientale, vol. 66.4, 121–81. Cairo: Institut Français d'Archéologie Orientale.

Zaccone, Gian M., and Tomaso R. di Netro, eds. 1993. *Sesto Congresso Internazionale di Egittologia. Atti.* 2 vols. Turin: Società Italiana per il Gas p.A.

Zibelius-Chen, Karola. 1988. *Die ägyptische Expansion nach Nubien. Eine Darlegung der Grundfaktoren,* Beihefte zum Tübinger Atlas des Vorderen Orients, series B, vol. 78. Wiesbaden: Dr. Ludwig Reichert Verlag.

Ziermann, Martin. 1993. *Befestigungsanlagen und Stadtentwicklung in der Frühzeit und im frühen Alten Reich, Elephantine,* vol. 16. Archäologische Veröffentlichungen, vol. 87. Mainz am Rhein: Philipp von Zabern.

The Achaemenid Empire

PIERRE BRIANT

Introduction

Around 550[1] the countries of the Middle East and central Asia were still divided among several kingdoms that were competing with and hostile to each other. Most important among these were the Neo-Babylonian Kingdom (Babylon, containing Babylonia and the Fertile Crescent, including Judaea), the Kingdom of Media (extending from Ecbatana westward to the right bank of the Halys River in Anatolia), the Lydian Kingdom (with Sardes and western Anatolia), and the Pharaonic Kingdom of Egypt; possibly, eastern Iran constituted itself a kingdom around Bactra. With the arrival of Cyrus the Great (557–530), this equilibrium was destroyed: within a few decades, the Persian kings (called "Achaemenids" after the eponymous ancestor of the dynasty), Cyrus, Cambyses (530–522), and Darius (522–486) created the first unified empire reaching from the Indus to the Mediterranean, from Syr-Darya to Assuan. Despite the setbacks Xerxes suffered in Greece (480–479), this immense empire remained intact and flourished until the defeats of Darius III in 334–330. To a large measure, however, even Alexander the Great continued the imperial history of Achaemenid Persia. It was only the struggles caused by his premature death that resulted, within two decades (323–300), in the breakup of the imperial structures inherited from the Achaemenids and the reemergence of a Middle East disputed among competing dynasties. The Achaemenid period thus is a decisive phase in the development of the ancient Near East.

Scholars used to postulate a contrast between the forms of domination

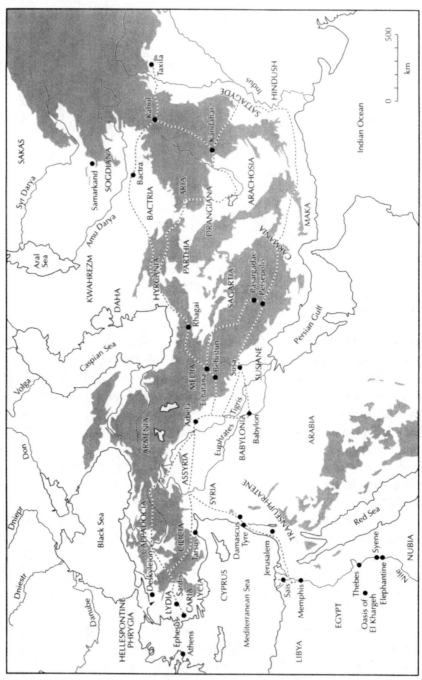

The Persian Empire (6th to 4th century) and its Main Roads

exercised by the Achaemenids over subjected countries and peoples and those of the Assyrians. According to this theory, the latter imposed their rule by armed force, never hesitating to massacre rebels, destroy cities and sanctuaries, and deport the survivors in the thousands; the Persians, on the contrary, were praised for their "religious tolerance" and the establishment of collaborative ties with the elites of the conquered countries. Essentially, though, this contrast is artificial: the Assyrians did not ignore, for example, the fact that imperial power is gained and preserved equally by means other than armed force, while the Persians did not hesitate, in turn, to destroy cities and sanctuaries of rebellious peoples and to deport the survivors. The postulated contrast between the two imperial systems is based partly on questionable ideological presuppositions and partly on an accurate but too general analysis of the decorations of the Assyrian and Persian palaces. The Assyrian kings, just as their Hittite or Egyptian counterparts, showed a marked preference for war and hunting scenes. Such scenes are absent on the walls of the Achaemenid palaces; instead, we find in Persepolis scenes that glorify the power of the Great King and his rule over peoples who bring him gifts and tribute—with no mention of war as the cause of such domination.

Yet, without question, in a state built by conquest, the armed forces were an indispensable instrument of domination—a fact of which the Achaemenid kings were no less aware than their Assyrian and Babylonian predecessors. Moreover, hunting and war scenes are frequent on small objects, especially seals, and royal declarations are not silent at all about the king's military virtues (see below, "The Leader in War"). The study of warfare and the army thus is as crucial to historians of the Achaemenid Empire as it is to those of other states. In fact, such studies are exceptionally helpful to understand the functioning of the state, not least by revealing the scope of the mobilization of human and material resources and technologies made necessary by military expeditions. It suffices to look at the chapters in which Herodotus (7.20–26) describes the logistical preparations ordered by Xerxes before launching his expedition against Greece, and many other documents provide useful information (such as texts on cuneiform tablets from Persepolis and Babylonia, and archaeological evidence).

Nevertheless, particularly in this area of research, Achaemenid studies are somewhat lagging behind. There exists at this point no comprehensive monograph on the Achaemenid armed forces, their composition, the methods of their recruitment, their financing, their command structure, or their fighting tactics.[2] The nature of the available sources has favored a traditional focus particularly on three events: first, what is called, from the Greek perspective, the "Persian Wars," described above all by Herodotus; second, the expedition of Cyrus the Younger to overthrow his brother, Artaxerxes II, in 401, an attempt that failed at Cunaxa but was immortalized in Xenophon's *Anabasis;* and third, the victories of Alexander the Great over Darius III in the late fourth century, recorded by Arrian, Quintus Curtius, Plutarch, and others. The results of this line of research are important but limited; for example, we still do not have entirely satisfactory answers to basic questions, such as why the Persians lost the battles of Salamis, Plataea, and Mycale (480–79), and why Alexander won all three pitched battles against the Persians.[3] There is, of course, an intrinsic difficulty in answering such questions, but it needs to be emphasized that the extant documentation hardly permits solutions that will be acceptable to all. To give another example, nobody believes that Herodotus's figures for Xerxes' army are authentic, but every alternative proposal runs into endless counterarguments based again on the nature of the evidence used (see below, "Parade Army and War Army"). The unfortunate fact is that all such inquiries are decisively hampered by the lack of Achaemenid sources; where these exist and are used rigorously, they permit us, for example, to contest the traditional thesis of the military decline of the Achaemenid Empire.

The study presented here naturally cannot aim at filling the gap described earlier. Rather, I intend to discuss some of the issues this volume is concerned with, especially the connection between war and society. There exists, however, no "Achaemenid society" as such; one can only speak of the Babylonian (or Egyptian, or Jewish, or Greek) societies under Achaemenid rule. I shall thus focus on the war practices of a particular society, that of Persia itself, that is, the people that conquered the empire and provided the kings with political and military leaders (satraps, generals). In the first part, I shall concentrate on the crucial question of "social reproduction," that is, on the practices by which the Persian monarchy and society succeeded in transmitting the ideals and training methods that turned young Persian aristocrats into highly acclaimed soldiers. In the second part, I shall broaden my perspective and analyze the relations between the Persians and the various ethnic contingents that formed the armies of kings and satraps. I suggest that institutions that initially were purely Persian (such as the so-called *kardakes*) were extended to other regions and populations to strengthen the Empire's military capacity—an aspect that in turn sheds important light on the much-debated question of traditional Achaemenid components in the policies of Alexander the Great.

The High Valuation of Warrior Qualities among the Persians

Military Activities and Aristocratic Mentality

In his description of Persian customs, Herodotus (1.131–40) refers to the education of the young Persians in a famous phrase: "The Persians teach their sons, between the ages of five and twenty, only three things: to ride, use a bow, and speak the truth" (136.2). This statement is part of and highlighted by more general remarks about the ethical and family values that determine the social and political behavior of the Persian elite: "The chief proof of manliness (*andragathiē*), after prowess in fighting, is to have many sons. Those who have the most sons receive an annual present from the king—on the principle that there is strength in numbers" (136.1, trans. de Sélincourt, modified).

The decisive importance of the warrior function is illustrated as well by the way in which classical authors introduce persons of high rank in the empire. For example, Mardonios, "a Persian by birth and brother-in-law of the king, was also among the first for his bravery in war and his wisdom in council" (Cornelius Nepos, *Pausanias* 1.2); or Tiribazos "showed exceptional courage in war and gave such judicious advice that the king always did well in following it" (Diodorus Siculus 15.10.3); or finally, Orontas, "a Persian by origin, related to the king by birth, was said to be among the best of the Persians in matters of war" (Xenophon, *Anabasis* 1.6.1). There are countless examples of soldiers honored by the king because of their military exploits,[4] and Herodotus famously describes how Xerxes, watching the battle of Salamis from the shore, has the names of the fighters who distinguish themselves before his eyes written down immediately; they thus earn the right to be listed in the Book of Benefactors (8.86–90). In his portrait of Cyrus the Younger, representing an idealized king, Xenophon emphasizes as "a well-known fact that he honored in extraordinary ways those who proved brave in war. . . . Those whom he saw voluntarily exposing themselves to danger, he put in charge of the lands he conquered, and he honored them with additional gifts" (1.9.14). All these texts agree that the social position of a Persian was determined not only by nobility of descent but also by qualities and deeds that attracted the king's attention.[5] Confirmation is found in the criteria used in selecting the elite troops, especially the "King's Kinsmen" (*syngeneis*): "They are chosen for their bravery and devotion" (Diodorus 17.59.2).

The explicit connection Herodotus makes between high birth rate and military function obviously is not fortuitous. We know in fact that the great Persian families were particularly prolific.[6] Strabo understood perfectly well that polygamy (whether or not the wives were legitimate), among other functions, had the purpose of making sure that numerous children ensued (15.3.17)—understandably, especially in view of a terribly high rate of infant mortality.[7] Nor is there any doubt that this high reproduction rate was strongly encouraged by the Great King, who must have been anxious to have at his disposal a constantly replenished reserve of political and military officials; he himself each year made the decision about gifts and awards for fathers of large families and of young men who distinguished themselves in physical and military exercises. This reproduction rate was not decisively affected by the losses of the second campaign against Greece, and the royal policy to encourage it continued throughout Achaemenid history, as is implied by the custom according to which each time he went to Persia the Great King gave a gold coin to the Persian women who were pregnant (Plutarch, *Alexander* 69.1; *Moralia* 264ab). Finally, a contemporary of the diadochs (Hieronymos of Kardia) perfectly sums up the favored demographic condition of Persia: "The population level (*polyanthrōpia*) is much higher there than in the other satrapies" (Diodorus 19.21.3).

Similar notions can be found in the inscriptions where the kings emphasize the intimate relationship between the dynasty and the native people (*dahyu*) of Persia, which is praised as a country "with good horses and good warriors" (*AmH; DPd*).[8] It is due to his Persian warriors that the Great King has accomplished his conquests: this is the message Darius intends for those seeing the representations of the peoples carrying his throne on the tomb in Naqšh i-Rustam: "If now thou shalt think that 'How many are the countries which Darius held?', look at the sculptures (of those) who bear the throne, then shalt you know, then shall it become known to thee: the spear of a Persian man/warrior (*martiyā*) has delivered battle far indeed from Persia" (*DNa*).[9] Similarly, the trilingual inscription on the left side of Darius's statue discovered in Susa announces: "This is the stone statue that Darius the King has ordered to be made in Egypt so that in the future whoever sees it will know that the Persian man (*Pārsa martiyā*) holds Egypt" (*DSab*). In this case, the "Persian man" is generally taken to point implicitly to the king himself. This is certainly correct, but at the same time the expression refers metonymically to all the Persian warriors who accompany the conquering king.

At any rate, apart from polemical statements on the alleged military weakness of the Persians,[10] numerous Greek texts emphasize their bravery in battle. Speaking of Plataea, Herodotus (9.62.3) notes, for example, that the Persians "were inferior neither in courage nor in strength," and he reports that they showed no less courage in their resistance at the battle of Mycale (9.102). Greek awareness of Persian bravery is equally visible in the juxtaposition of two texts.[11] In book 9 of his *Histories*, Herodotus gives a long account of the dispute between Mardonios and Artabazos, two Persian generals with different assessments of situations and strategies. The latter, wise and cautious, proposes to bribe the Greeks with gold and thus "not to risk a battle." Mardonios, by contrast, certain of his army's superiority, favors a military solution and thus, at least according to Herodotus, insists on the need to "follow the custom of the Persians and to fight" (9.41). The words and thoughts attributed here to Mardonios strangely recall the proposal ascribed by Diodorus to Arsites during the war council before the battle of Granicus. In opposition to Memnon, who recommends the scorched-earth policy, Arsites and other Persians respond that such delaying tactics "are unworthy of the great-hearted dignity (*megalopsychia*) of the Persians" and that one should rather fight (17.18.2). The two narratives, although separated by four centuries, are obviously related, even if

Diodorus is not necessarily aware of it. Does that mean that the Persians, led primarily by a "chivalrous spirit,"[12] were incapable of tactical and strategic thinking? Obviously not. The contrast between two generals, dramatized here by Herodotus and Diodorus, fits into a traditional scheme, based as it is on two typical literary characters: on one side the wise leader (Artabazos, Memnon) who declines a confrontation with a *Greek* army he claims to be superior and, on the other, a leader basking in his glory and sense of superiority (Mardonios, Arsites) who allows himself to be guided by an improbable Persian custom (Mardonios) and/or by an irresistible "generosity of body and mind (*megalopsychia*)" (Arsites), which Diodorus understands, pejoratively, as "mad temerity."[13] In reality, Mardonios in 479 and Arsites in 334 had different reasons for their decision: they had simply received binding orders from their kings (Xerxes and Darius III, respectively) to fight against the enemy.

Similarly, it is somewhat mad bravery that the troops of the "King's Kinsmen" and Spithrobates demonstrate at the Granicus (Diodorus 17.20.1) and Oxathres displays at Issos (17.34.3). Diodorus describes Spithrobates' action at the Granicus in the context of a duel (*monomachia*) with Alexander (17.20.3–4). The theme of monomachy, present in one version of the accession of Darius III (below at n. 17), is fully developed in the description of confrontations taking place in Aria in 330–329 between the generals of Alexander and the Iranian Satibarzanes, "a man distinguished by his military talents and his bravery" (Diodorus 17.83.4). At the end of an indecisive battle, Satibarzanes proposes a duel (*monomachia*), in which he is defeated and killed by the Macedonian Erigyios, as a result of which his troops submit to the victor (Diodorus 17.83.4–6; Quintus Curtius 7.4.32–38). Did this monomachy take place, as Curtius maintains, "in a space left free by the two armies"? Hardly! While confirming that Satibarzanes was killed personally by Erigyios, Arrian (3.28.3) indicates clearly that the confrontation between the two leaders took place in the course of the general melee. Again we should thus take with a grain of salt the interpretation of Greek authors who tend to describe the Persians as courageous but lacking discipline.

The Leader in War

The Persian king has the duty, assigned him by the gods, to protect land and people from the ravages of an enemy army (*hainā*), from a bad year (*dušiyārā*), that is, from bad harvest or famine, and from perjury and rebellion (*drauga: DPd*). If he is able to meet these expectations, it is because the royal ideology (reported as well in his own way by Xenophon in the *Oeconomicus* 4.4–25) attributes to him extraordinary qualities both in the palace and on the battlefield (*DNb* §8–9). Already Darius represents his actions in this way in the rock inscription of Behistun, in both writing and images: standing upright, the bow, symbol of sovereignty, resting on his left foot, he crushes his enemy Gaumata lying on the ground and looks straight at the approaching line of the "liar-kings" who have been defeated by his armies and his genius (*DBb–k*): "Saith Darius the King: This is what I did by the favor of Ahura-Mazda in one and the same year after I became King. Nineteen battles I fought; by the favor of Ahura-Mazda I smote them and took prisoner nine kings . . . These nine kings I took them prisoner within these battles" (*DB* IV. §52–53). Created by the same Darius, the royal coins carry the image of a warrior king who, armed with bow and spear, pursues the enemy. But it is on the facade of the royal tomb at Naqšh i-Rustam that the king expresses with the greatest force and conviction the idea of his absolute superiority in his domain:

> Of such sort is my understanding and my command: when what has been done by me thou shalt see or hear of, both in the palace and in the war-camp, this is my thinking power and my understanding. This indeed is my activity: inasmuch as my body has the strength, as battle-fighter I am a good battle-fighter. Once let there be seen with understanding in the place (of battle), what I see to be rebellious, what I see (to be) not (rebellious); both with understanding and with command then am I first to think with action, when I see a rebel as well as when I see a not-(rebel). Trained am I both with hands and with feet. As a horseman I am a good horseman. As a bowman I am a good bowman both afoot and on horseback. As a spear-man I am a good spearman both afoot and on horseback. And the (physical) skillfulnesses which Ahura-Mazda has bestowed upon me and I have had the strength to use them—by the favor of Ahura-Mazda what has been done by me, I have done with these skillfulnesses which Ahura-Mazda has bestowed upon me (*DNb*, §8f-g-h-i).[14]

Like all members of the Persian aristocracy, the king thus is an elite warrior, deftly handling bow and arrows, whether on foot or on horse. Thanks to the very special protection of the supreme god Ahura-Mazda, he has not only great physical strength but also the necessary intellectual qualities: on the battlefield he alone is able to resist panic and to make the appropriate tactical decisions that will secure victory.[15] Hence, despite a certain correspondence between the warrior virtues of the Persians and the fighting qualities of the Great King, only the latter has the proper qualities to make him a leader of men and truly supreme commander. As a logical consequence, to doubt the reality of an exploit of the king is considered treason. Two participants in the battle of Cunaxa learned that to their detriment. Both claimed to have killed Cyrus the Younger, while the official version asserted that he had died by the hand of Artaxerxes himself; the braggarts were simply put to death (Plutarch, *Artaxerxes*

14.1–10, 15–16). The same ideological assumptions are illustrated by anecdotes about courtiers doubting the king's qualities as a lion hunter.[16]

According to Strabo (11.13.11), "it is a Medic custom to choose as king the most courageous man." It is impossible to decide whether the term "Mede" here, as elsewhere, includes the Persians. At any rate, among the Persians as among many other peoples, martial valor is often adduced as justification for the seizure of royal power, particularly, of course, in periods of dynastic struggles. It is exactly into this ideological context that Xenophon fits his funeral eulogy for Cyrus the Younger: "He was also adjudged the most eager to learn, and the most diligent in practising, military accomplishments, alike the use of the bow and of the javelin. Then . . . he was the fondest of hunting and, more than that, the fondest of incurring danger in his pursuit of wild animals" (*Anabasis* 1.9.5–6, trans. C. L. Brownson). Clearly here, as elsewhere (e.g., Plutarch, *Artaxerxes* 6.5), the praise of Cyrus's physical and martial valor intends to cast doubts on the legitimacy of his brother, Artaxerxes II.

The court propaganda accompanying power struggles is especially interesting in the case of the future Darius III, called (we do not know why) Codomannus by Justin, but in reality Artashata.[17] According to the Persian version, preserved by Diodorus (17.6.1–3) and Justin (10.3), his accession to the throne was secured by an exceptional exploit. As Diodorus writes,

> Darius' selection for the throne was based on his known bravery, in which quality he far surpassed the other Persians. Once when King Artaxerxes [III] was campaigning against the Cadusians, one of them with a wide reputation for strength and courage challenged a volunteer among the Persians to fight with him in single combat. No other dared accept, but Darius entered the contest and slew the challenger, being honoured in consequence by the king with rich gifts, while among the Persians he was conceded the first place in prowess. It was because of this prowess that he was thought worthy to take over the kingship (trans. C. B. Welles, modified).

Here we find the theme of single combat and duel (*monomachia*), particularly frequent in the historians of Alexander, around which ultimately the personal confrontation between Alexander and Darius at Issos was constructed.

The School of Warriors

The Training of the Young Persians

Herodotus's information on the education of the young Persians—"to ride a horse, use the bow, and speak the truth" (1.136)—is echoed by Strabo in almost the same words but with many interesting details (15.3.18):

From five years of age to twenty-four they are trained to use the bow, to throw the javelin, to ride horseback, and to speak the truth; and they use as teachers of science the wisest men, who also interweave their teachings with the mythical element, thus reducing that element to a useful purpose, and rehearse both with song and without song the deeds both of the gods and of the noblest men. And these teachers wake up the boys before dawn by the sound of brazen instruments, and assemble them in one place, as though for arming themselves or for a hunt; and they divide the boys into companies of fifty, appoint one of the sons of the king or of a satrap as leader of each company, and order them to follow their leader in a race, having marked off a distance of thirty or forty stadia. They require them also to give an account of each lesson, at the same time training them in loud speaking and in breathing, and in the use of their lungs, and also training them to endure heat and cold and rain, and to cross torrential streams in such a way as to keep both armour and clothing dry, and also to tend flocks and live outdoors all night and eat wild fruits, such as pistachio nuts, acorns, and wild pears. [They are called Kardakes, since they live on thievery, for "karda" means the manly and warlike spirit.] Their daily food after the gymnastic exercises consists of bread, barley-cake, cardamum, grains of salt, and roasted or boiled meat; but their drink is water. They hunt by throwing spears from horse-back, and with bows and slings; and late in the afternoon they are trained in the planting of trees and in the cutting and gathering of roots and in making weapons and in the art of making linen cloths and hunters' nets. The boys do not touch the meat of wild animals, though it is the custom to bring them home. Prizes are offered by the king for victory in running and in the four other contests of the pentathla. The boys are adorned with gold, since the people hold in honour the fiery appearance of this metal. (trans. H. L. Jones)

Despite some minor differences, the information given by Xenophon in the first book of the *Cyropaedia* generally confirms the picture of this Persian institution drawn by Herodotus and Strabo. The training is above all physical (gymnastic exercises and endurance tests) and military (hunting on horseback is an integral part of it) but leaves space for more intellectual lessons given by "wise men," that is, evidently, the magi. Their lessons essentially consist of the oral transmission of the mythic history of the Persian people and of the history of great men, that is, the Persian legends of the ancestral founders of the dynasty: the young men are trained to become competent soldiers and men devoted to the king and the dynasty.[18] It is certainly the latter aspect, expressed through "to speak the truth," by which the Greeks render the Persian term *arta*, a veritable nexus of political-religious conceptions, which is usually translated by "truth, justice," as opposed to *drauga*, "perjury, disloyalty, rebellion." *Arta* means above all conformity with the established order in heaven and on earth. In other words, by learning to "speak the truth," the young Persians are introduced to their duty to respect the intangible world order, including naturally the dynasty's rule.[19] It is, accordingly, the king himself who rewards the most deserving young men. Henceforth they are the king's men, his loyal followers, *pistoi* in Greek terminology, which probably corresponds quite closely to the (untranslatable) Persian term *banda-ka;* on the inscription of Behistun, Darius uses this term both for subjected peoples and for loyal and devoted satraps. Coming out of this kind of training, the young men see it as their supreme duty to obey the Great King unconditionally and, above all, to serve in the army; hence the drastic measures taken against fathers who tried to have their sons exempted from military service (Herodotus 4.84; 7.38–39).

Resemblances with the Spartan system of education (*agōgē*) were noticed already by ancient authors, especially Arrian (*Anabasis* 5.4.5), faithful reader and admirer of Xenophon. This comparison should not be viewed hypercritically: there is nothing extraordinary in finding remarkable similarities in the training of young men among various tribal societies.[20] It is precisely such resemblances that prompted Henri Jeanmaire's innovative research into the initiation of young men and then led Pierre Vidal-Naquet to develop the model of the "black hunter."[21] The two systems are perhaps even closer to each other than one might think. Strabo, in fact, differentiates neatly between two types of food: the normal, daily regimen (bread, barley, salt, meat) and a more exceptional regimen based on wild fruits. The latter probably marks a specific moment—of which Strabo is not fully conscious—that is, a phase in the training when the young are left alone during the night in the open country, forced to rely for survival on their physical qualities and their knowledge of nature. This quite probably is the Persian equivalent of the Spartan *krypteia.*[22] On the basis of this rite of passage the young men are admitted to the warrior class; hence no doubt the term *kardakes* used for them (see below, "The *Kardakes* of Darius III").

Education, Army, and Society

Xenophon insists that, although in principle the *agōgē* is open to all Persians, in fact only the sons of the great families have access to it (*Cyropaedia* 1.2.15), that is, those "who live of the work of others" (ibid. 8.1.16), also called "the Persian nobility" (*Anabasis* 1.9.3). Those whom Xenophon calls the "common people" are excluded because "they need to work for their living" (*Cyr.* 2.1.11). A case in point is Pheraulas, son of a poor Persian farmer who only manages to survive by borrowing seeds between two harvests (ibid. 8.3.36–38); although from childhood desiring to be a soldier, Pheraulas has not been able to enter the *agōgē.* It is difficult to decide whether or not this person represents, despite this handicap, an exceptional case of social mobility admired by Xenophon,[23] but generally it is clear that the highest positions in army and imperial administration were reserved for the sons of the great families. In describing the parade of Xerxes' army, for example, Herodotus opposes the indiscriminate mass of the ethnic contingents, who are not supposed to come close to the king, to the Persians, separated from them by an interval (7.40.1). Within the latter category, he distinguishes again between horsemen and spearmen "selected among all Persians" (7.40.2) and the thousand spearmen qualified as "the best and most noble of the Persians" (7.41.1). These certainly are the thousand "apple-bearers" of whom Heraclides Ponticus says: "They are chosen for their high birth (*aristindēn*) among the Ten Thousand Persians called the Immortals" (Athenaeus 12.514c).

This educational system was reduplicated in the courts of the provincial satraps, which were generally organized after the model of the central court. The noble Persians who held estates in these provinces visited the court of the satrap, and the sons of these families were entitled to receive the same education as their peers living in Persia (*Cyropaedia* 8.6.10). Because of increasingly close relations between Persian families in the imperial diaspora and local elites, perhaps eventually sons of mixed marriages were admitted to the *agōgē*—as is suggested by the case of Datames, known through Cornelius Nepos's novelistic biography.[24] Datames was of Carian origin (Nepos 1.1), which means either that he was Carian himself or that his father was a Persian living in Caria. The name of his father (Camisares) and his own name Datames indicate Persian origin. Datames' mother, Scythissa, belonged to an aristocratic family of Paphlagonia (1.3). Hence Datames issued from a mixed union between a Persian in Asia Minor and a woman of the local aristocracy. One of the first stages in Datames' rapid rise to prominence was "to belong to the corps of soldiers of Artaxerxes who served as guards of the palace" (1.1). Hence Datames probably was admitted to the Persian system of education, either in Asia Minor or at the central court, which served as the starting point for his remarkable career.

Persian Army and Imperial Army

The Catalogue of Xerxes' Army

As Herodotus does in two famous passages (1.183; 3.97), the royal inscriptions place emphasis on the status and role of the Persian people and country (*dahyu*) at the center of the empire. "These are the countries I conquered with the Persians," proclaims Darius (*DPe*), pointing to the power of Persia "with the good horses and good warriors" (*DPd*). Yet without doubt, gradually, as conquests and the organization of the Empire progressed, the Great Kings enrolled contingents levied among the subjected peoples. This clearly is the impression the ancient authors give in their descriptions of the armies of Darius III and, earlier, Xerxes. Often compared with Herodotus's list of the tributary districts organized by Darius I after his accession (3.89–98), the catalogue of Xerxes' army composed by the same author (7.60–99) continues to pose enormous problems of interpretation.

According to Herodotus, once arrived in Thrace near Doriskos, Xerxes decided to marshal and count his army (7.56, 100). There follows the list of ethnic contingents, serving in the infantry (61–83), cavalry (84–88), and navy (89–99), with the names of the commanders for each of these categories (81–83, 88, and 96–99, respectively). Of each contingent, he reports the ethnic origin (Persians, Medes, Hyrkanians, etc.), the type of clothing they wear, and the weapons they bear. The diversity of equipment and the modes of combat it suggests is astounding, so much so that the question is inevitable whether such an army was really functional and operational. The impression of disorder is increased further by the incredible numbers adduced by Herodotus: "The total of the land army amounted to 170 myriads" (60), that is, 1,700,000 men, to which must be added the totals of cavalry and navy (rowers and marines), of noncombatants, and of the contingents levied in Greece. All in all, Herodotus concludes (184–87), there were 1,700,000 infantry, 517,610 men on the different squadrons of the fleet, 80,000 cavalry, and 20,000 camel riders and charioteers from Arabia and Libya, totaling 2,317,610 men, "not mentioning army servants and the men in the food transports" (184), categories that in his opinion (186) matched the number of combatants. Adding the troops levied in Europe, Herodotus arrives at the astronomical number of 5,283,220 men (187), without "the eunuchs, female cooks, and concubines" (ibid.). Understandably, Herodotus was not surprised that some rivers ran out of water!

Specialists in military history and logistics have forever questioned Herodotus's figures, agreeing that they are unacceptable and proposing countless counterestimates. But, whatever the number retained at the end, the historical problem remains the same: even if reduced by 25, 50 or 60 percent, would such an army have been capable of executing effective military maneuvers, or would it have been condemned to irremediable ineffectiveness because of its diverse origin and lack of unity? To be sure, Herodotus observes, when the ethnic contingents were assembled, their indigenous leaders were replaced by Persian commanders (7.96), which suggests an attempt at unifying the army. But the measure was bound to remain insufficient if, as scholars generally assume, the different contingents continued to use in battle their heterogeneous armament and native fighting tactics. Traditionally, this is seen as the main reason for the defeat of Xerxes by the Greek city-states and that of Darius III by Alexander—an interpretation that, doubts about figures notwithstanding, remains firmly based on the logic of Herodotus's description. Another interpretation, however, is possible.[25]

Parade Army and War Army

According to Herodotus (7.184), all the ethnic contingents counted at Doriskos were present at Thermopylae. But did they all participate in the fighting? No source forces us to conclude that they did. On the contrary, none of the ethnic contingents described at Doriskos is specifically mentioned later on. At Thermopylae, the attack is led by Medes, Kissians, and the Persian "Immortals" (Herodotus 7.210–11, 215; Diodorus 11.6–8). The composition of the elite army Xerxes handed over to Mardonios after the defeat of Salamis is especially revealing:

> [Besides the Immortals Mardonios chose] the Persian spearmen and the picked cavalry squadron, a thousand strong; then the Medes, Sacae, Bactrians, and Indians, both horse and foot. These contingents he took over complete; from the other nationalities he picked a few men here and there, being guided in his choice either by their physical appearance or by his knowledge that they had distinguished themselves, until he had a total number, including the cavalry, of 300,000 men. The Persians with their necklaces and armlets provided the largest contingent; next were the Medes—although the Medes were not actually inferior in number, only in valour (Herodotus 8.113).

Apart from the numbers, the text is clear: Mardonios's elite army was composed primarily of Persian, Iranian, and Indo-Iranian contingents, and among these the Persians were considered an elite among the elite. Similarly, among the *epibatai* (marine infantry), we find essentially Persians, Medes, and Sacae (9.96, 184). At Plataea, Persians, Medes, Bactrians, Indians, and Sacae provided the first lines (9.31). At Mycale, the Persians received the frontal assault (9.31). Members of other ethnic contingents were added by Mardonios but only selectively. In other words, if, which remains to be proved, all the contingents Herodotus mentions at Doriskos followed the army on its invasion of Greece, they do not seem to have participated in battle. Why, then, did Xerxes order their enrollment, and why did the Great King burden himself with insurmountable logistical problems only for the sake of having supplementary troops?

The solution of the puzzle lies in the fact that Herodotus's catalogue should not be read as a fully realistic text. The great diversity of names, clothing, and armament suggests that the enumeration serves, above all, to illustrate the immense power of the Great King. A first spectacle of this type was organized at Abydos, where Xerxes "wanted to see his entire army" (Herod. 8.44), just as

Darius I had organized a parade of his army in Thrace thirty years earlier (4.85). The army review at Doriskos has the same purpose: Xerxes "drove in his chariot past the contingents of all the various nations, asking questions, the answers to which were taken down by his secretaries" (7.100). In this way, the king learns less about his army than about the infinite diversity of his empire, illustrated by this spectacle. Its primary function thus is that of a mirror in which the king can perceive and admire his own power. If this interpretation is correct, much of the discussion about numbers in Herodotus is irrelevant: what the historian provides is not intended as factual information about a real army. Another passage makes this quite clear: it refers to "two marble columns erected [by Darius], on one of which was an inscription in Assyrian characters showing the various nations which were serving on the campaign; the other had a similar inscription in Greek. These nations were, in fact, all over which he had dominion" (4.87). Even if such stelae were in fact put up on the shore of the Bosporus—which again is debatable—they certainly did not contain a catalogue of archival nature. In conclusion, I suggest that if Xerxes brought to Europe ethnic contingents from his empire, these were troops reduced in numbers and used primarily during reviews and parades in which the picturesque diversity of clothing and armament served mainly to demonstrate the immensity and diversity of the Great King's rule—comparable to the long lines of gift-bearing peoples who are represented on the stairs of the *apadana* (hall of audiences) in Persepolis, paying homage to the Great King. This parade army clearly must be distinguished completely from the fighting army.

The fighting army itself was composed of soldiers from diverse ethnic origins, but it was not lacking unity. Many soldiers came from Iranian countries that stretched to the Indus; but such Iranian homogeneity remained partial because other contingents participated as well; for example, Egyptians were among the marines used by Mardonios (9.32). Hence, if this army really was an effective fighting force, perhaps the diversity emphasized by Herodotus itself was partly fictitious. In fact, the Egyptians, Medes, and Sacae were not necessarily levied in Egypt, Media, or central Asia. Numerous garrisons and permanent military colonies existed throughout the Empire, and in these ethnic diversity was the rule. In the case of the military colonies established in Babylonia,[26] cuneiform documents suggest that at least some of the Sacae so often listed in the royal armies could perfectly well have been Sacae permanently installed in Babylonia.[27] In addition, Greek and Babylonian evidence indicates that the soldiers settled on military land allotments were regularly called up for royal reviews and that they had to bring the required equipment: "a horse with harness and reins, a *suhattu* coat with neckpiece and hood, an iron armor with hood, a quiver, 120 arrows, some with heads, some without, a sword (?) with its scabbard, 2 iron spears."[28]

The original ethnic diversity of the contingents was thus balanced to some extent by several unifying traits and measures, such as the deeply rooted unity of the Persian elite contingents welded together by a common education, the role of elite troops played by the Iranian contingents, the fact that commanding positions in most cases were held by members of the Persian aristocracy and royal family, the adoption and use of (at least partially) common armament in military colonies, and the frequency of military reviews and exercises.[29] All in all, the armies of the Great King thus certainly were not disorganized masses of soldiers completely lacking unity and homogeneity.

The Kardakes *of Darius III*

My examination of an army corps the Greek authors call *kardakes*[30] suggests that the imperial administration may have enacted even farther-reaching measures to strengthen the unity and effectiveness of the troops stationed permanently in a territory. These *kardakes* first appear in the ancient literature in the army commanded by Autophradates, who in the 360s was ordered by the king to fight against the satrap Datames. According to Nepos (*Datames* 8.2), Autophradates' army consisted of three elements: (1) contingents levied in the Anatolian satrapies (for example, troops from Cappadocia, Armenia, Lydia, and Pisidia); (2) 3000 Greek mercenaries; (3) "of barbarians he had 20,000 cavalry and 100,000 infantry, whom they [the barbarians] call *kardakes* (*Cardacae*), and 3000 slingers of the same people/category (*eiusdem generis*)." This passage offers first-class information on the composition of a satrapal army in the fourth century; in particular, it shows that, in contrast to a well-established view, the Greek mercenaries were a minority.[31] The Persians obviously provided a crucial part of the force, in both infantry and cavalry (50 percent according to the numbers reported by Nepos).[32] Nor, in contrast to another traditional view, did the Persians limit themselves to the cavalry, despite the high valuation of the horse, well attested for the Persian aristocracy and evidenced by Darius's expression "Persia of the good horses," mentioned earlier. In fact, we know from Strabo (15.3.19) that from age twenty to fifty, upon completing their long *agōgē*, the Persians "served in the army and held commands there, both as infantry and cavalry." As mentioned earlier as well, Darius himself boasts to be a good archer and spearman, "on foot and on horse."

There remains the term *kardakes*, obviously considered by Nepos or his source a technical term of Persian origin; the context seems to indicate, in addition, that these troops were themselves composed of Persians (*eiusdem generis*), but the term *barbarus* is used too widely and loosely to allow certainty. The term *kardakes* reappears in Arrian, speaking of the army of Darius III at Issos. During that battle, "60,000 of those called *kardakes*" were arranged next to the Greek mercenaries, facing the Macedonian phalanx, and Arrian explains, "the *kardakes* were also hoplites"; they are part of what Arrian calls "the barbarian phalanx," clearly distinguished from the ethnic contingents and the Greek mercenary corps (2.8.8). At Gaugamela, Arrian refers to the Persian infantry without using the term *kardakes* (3.11.3).

These texts, although informative, do not offer a precise definition of the *kardakes,* except that they are infantry-hoplites[33] and "barbarians": does this mean that they are all Persians? A definition of the term occurs first in the passage of Strabo (cited earlier), where a terminological explication (probably an interpolation)[34] is added to the description of the education of the young Persians: "They are called Kardakes, since they live on thievery, for 'karda' means the manly and warlike spirit." Whatever the value of the etymology proposed here, it contains a noteworthy detail, namely, that those called *kardakes* supported themselves by theft. This suggests that the term does not designate indiscriminately all young men in training but especially those who are in the stage of *kryptos,* that is, in the final period of initiation. During this phase, and only then, the young men, abandoned in the country, must survive by collecting and stealing what they can—just as in Sparta the young "kryptos" during his rite of passage had to "nourish himself by theft and the like."[35] Hence, if at some point the term was extended to a formation of infantry-hoplites, it must have lost its narrow sense emphasized by the interpolator in Strabo. Definitions found in late lexicographers confirm this hypothesis.[36] According to Photius, the *kardakes* were "the soldiers in Asia; the guards (or garrisons) are called *kardakes* as well"; as Hesychius puts it, they were "the barbarians campaigning under the command of Persians." All this suggests that the *kardakes* were an elite infantry corps furnished by subjects of the Great King.[37] Elsewhere, Hesychius adds: "And in Asia one calls thus the soldiers, after neither their ethnic origin nor place of origin." This definition, then, distinguishes the *kardakes* sharply from the contingents levied "by people" (*kata ethnē;* see Arrian 2.8.6, 8).[38] They certainly are troops not levied hastily but armed uniformly and trained carefully, so as to provide a true "phalanx of hoplites." We thus conclude that in the course of Achaemenid history, even if the education of the young Persians remained separate, its principles were extended to young men from other parts of the empire in order to create what one might call an *imperial infantry,*[39] the members of which received the name *kardakes,* whatever their ethnic or regional origins; they were "barbarians," that is, recruited among subjected peoples, but they served under the command of Persians.

If this hypothesis proves correct, the second part of Hesychius's definition (mentioned earlier) offers an extraordinary testimony on the effort of *territorialization* pursued in the course of Achaemenid history. Certainly, to the end, division "by peoples (*kata ethnē*)" remained in force (on both the tributary and the military level) but, at the same time, this seems not to have been the only method used to organize the peoples and territories controlled by the Great King's authority.[40] My hypothesis on the *kardakes* also throws new light on the relations the Persians cultivated with the various populations in the Empire—relations that seem to have been closer than thought so far. Finally, this hypothesis confirms that the stereotypical image of immovable stability or stagnation is particularly inappropriate for the analysis of the evolutionary dynamics working in the Achaemenid Empire.

From Darius III to Alexander the Great

The term *kardakes* survived in the period of the Seleucid and Attalid kingdoms, but the documentation available is rare, late, and allusive, and does not permit a reconstruction of the organization of these troops.[41] Worse, we do not have a scrap of reliable evidence illuminating the development between the Achaemenid and Hellenistic periods. What happened to the *kardakes* when Alexander designed and realized the great military reforms intended to enable Macedonian and Iranian troops to fight side by side? No text allows a confident response, but a few suggest a hypothesis. When campaigning in eastern Iran, Alexander made an important decision, reported by several ancient authors. According to Plutarch (*Alexander* 47.6), "he chose thirty thousand boys (*paidas*), ordering that they be taught Greek and given a military education, and delegating many educators to this task." Placing this order in the context of Alexander's Indian campaign, Quintus Curtius writes, "Lest there should be any disturbance in his rear which could interfere with his plan, Alexander ordered 30,000 of the younger men to be selected from all the provinces and brought to him under arms, intending to have them at once as hostages and as soldiers" (8.5.1; cf. 10.3.10–11; trans. John C. Rolfe). Arrian reports that these young men were led to Susa in 324: "He was also joined by the satraps from the new cities he had founded, and the other land he had conquered, bringing about thirty thousand boys now growing up, all of the same age, whom Alexander called Epigoni (Successors), dressed in Macedonian dress and trained to warfare in the Macedonian style" (7.6.1; trans. P. A. Brunt). The arrival in Susa of these thirty thousand young men is also noted by Diodorus, who gives them the ethnic label "Persians" and explains that they had been chosen "for their bodily grace and strength. They had been enrolled in compliance with the king's orders and had been under supervisors and teachers of the arts of war for as long as necessary. They were splendidly equipped with full Macedonian armament" (17.108.1–2).

One of the questions raised by this documentation is where Alexander received the inspiration for this project: what role did Achaemenid and Macedonian elements play in this new institution?[42] Interpreting all these texts in the framework of Macedonian institutions, N. G. L. Hammond recently proposed to see in Alexander's order an extension, to all the conquered countries, of the educational system of the Macedonian royal pages.[43] He bases his suggestion primarily on the entry *basileioi paides* (royal page boys) in the *Suda*-lexicon: "Numbering 6000, they were trained, on Alexander's order, intensely in Egypt in the military arts." Hammond thinks that Alexander had made his decision during his stay in Egypt in 332/1 and that the arrival of Lydian, Lycian, and Syrian contingents shows that Alexander had given orders, from the beginning of the conquest of Asia Minor, that young men selected from among the conquered peoples should be educated in the Macedonian style.[44] This is an interesting suggestion, but it runs into a number of problems that Hammond does not seem to have considered sufficiently.

First, the text of the *Suda* is important, but nothing indicates that it reports an order given by Alexander in 332. The arrival of Lydian, Lycian, and Syrian contingents may have nothing to do with such a policy, which, to repeat, is attested in the historical documentation only after Alexander's arrival in eastern Iran.[45]

Second, the thesis that a Macedonian institution was immediately and almost mechanically exported to all the countries of the Achaemenid Empire poses considerable and, in my view, almost insoluble difficulties.[46] It seems quite unlikely that Alexander would have been able to develop such a program so quickly out of nothing. The suggestion was made earlier that the institution of the Macedonian pages was copied from an Achaemenid model, but I have demonstrated elsewhere that this hypothesis is based on a wrong understanding of a passage in Arrian.[47] In spite of some analogies, the Persian and Macedonian educational systems differed profoundly from each other because the social and cultural practices were profoundly different.[48] In fact, certain aspects underlying the system of Macedonian pages were completely alien to Achaemenid customs and conceptions.[49] The methodological principle to be observed here is that the transfer of an institution to a different society is possible only if this society is ready to accept the transfer, that is, if there already exists a certain amount of social and cultural compatibility between donor and receiver. I am not ready to believe that these conditions applied, and that such compatibility already existed in the immense area between Aegean and Indus.

Third, we should take note that the *Suda* is the only source to use the expression *basileioi paides*. The authors who mention Alexander's initiative make it clear that this new corps of soldiers was to be called the *epigonoi*.[50] It is especially remarkable that this is true also of Arrian (4.13–14.1), who elsewhere gives a precise definition of the institution of Macedonian pages about which he had precise information, and of Quintus Curtius (8.6.2–6, with an internal reference to 5.1.42), who does not use a special term for the young Iranians. Hence, if the entry in the *Suda*, as is quite possible, refers to the eventual extension to Egypt of a system introduced as an experiment in eastern Iran, the source underlying this entry probably applied erroneously the term "royal pages" to a corps which its founder had explicitly called the *epigonoi*.

Fourth, we should keep in mind as well that the term "royal pages" was continually used after Alexander *in its original application.*[51] In conclusion, I find it difficult to believe that the same terminology could have been used to designate two entities that were so different from each other.

At the end, we should return to the texts and the context. Alexander was confronted with a problem of truly imperial dimensions: how to have regular access to a source of elite infantry soldiers who were well trained on a model imposed by the central government. It seems much more reasonable to assume that he adapted for this purpose a preexisting Achaemenid institution. Is it not likely that this would be the institution of *kardakes,* as I have reconstructed it here? In this view, the Achaemenid institution was modified and adapted to transform completely the armament and training of the young recruits in order to turn them into "Macedonian" hoplites (the *epigonoi*), whatever their ethnic and regional backgrounds.

Abbreviations

FGrH   see Jacoby 1923ff.
ML   see Meiggs and Lewis 1988.
For the abbreviations used for Persian royal inscriptions, see Kent 1953.

Notes

1. All dates are B.C.E. For abbreviations and bibliography, see the end of this chapter. The works of the Greek authors cited here are available in translation in the Penguin series and/or the Loeb Classical Library. I express my warmest thanks to Kurt Raaflaub for translating my text into English.
2. See, conveniently, Head 1992; Sekunda 1992, both popularizing works for nonspecialists but well informed and useful.
3. For my own answers, see Briant 1996.552–57, 886–91.
4. Briant 1996.314–35.
5. Briant 1990.
6. Briant 1987.21–22.
7. According to Ctesias, *Persika* 49 (*FGrH* 688 F15), of the thirteen children born to Darius by Parysatis, only four survived; "all the others died prematurely." When Artaxerxes I and his wife died, only one legitimate son was alive (Xerxes II), but Artaxerxes had seventeen bastard sons (Ctesias 44).
8. I do not enter here the long-standing debate on the question of whether the first inscription attributed to Arsames is authentic.
9. Translations of the royal Achaemenid inscriptions are taken from Kent 1953 (except

for *DSab*, published and translated into French by F. Vallat in *Cahiers de la Délégation Française en Iran* 4 [1974] 161–70). Kent translates *martiyā* with "man." In Old Persian, however, the meaning of *martiyā*-soldier is mixed with that of *martiyā*-man—just as in Greek one of the meanings of anēr-man tends toward "bravery" (*andreia*-energy, virility, courage).

10. Briant 1989.
11. See Briant 1996.840–43, 1069.
12. This is the translation (in my view very free and erroneous) of *megalopsychia* proposed by Goukowsky 1976, ad loc.
13. The term *megalopsychia* is absent from the account of Arrian (1.12.8), who explains Arsites' response differently: mirroring the king's responsibility, the satrap is the protector of the peasants' land; cf. Briant 1982.363–67.
14. On this inscription, see esp. Herrenschmidt 1985 (who, however, tries too systematically to demonstrate the closeness of this text to the Greek poem in honor of Arbinas of Xanthos); and see now Bousquet 1992.159–81.
15. Cf. the words Plutarch lends to Darius, who in composing his own eulogy affirms "that his mind became more active (*phronimōteros*) in battles and in the presence of danger" (*Moralia* 172c).
16. Briant 1991; 1996.242–44.
17. On all this, see the detailed analysis in Briant 1996.789–800, 1059–60.
18. The surprising obligation, as part of the training, to plant trees fits in well with what we know of the virtues of the "royal gardener" (Briant 1982.447–48; 1996.244–55); cf. also Gadatas's praise by Darius (ML 12.13).
19. On *arta*, see recently the decisive analysis by Kellens 1995.
20. Strabo (15.2.14) equally reports some sort of a rite of passage among the Carmanians: "Nobody may marry before having cut off the head of an enemy and brought it to the king."
21. See Vidal-Naquet 1986, 1989. On the Spartan *agōgē*, see Kennell 1995.
22. See Knauth-Nadjamabadi 1975.81–92 and, independently, Briant 1982.449.
23. For discussion, see Briant 1996.344–46.
24. The ethnic and social origin of Datames remains puzzling (Sekunda 1988; Briant 1987.19 with n. 47; 1996, index s.v.), especially if (although this is uncertain) he is the person known from coins under a Luwian name rendered in Aramaean as Tarkumuwa.
25. A preliminary version of the following discussion is in Briant 1990.81 n. 20, fully developed (with bibliography) in 1996.207–11.
26. I use the term *military colony* only for convenience. We are dealing in fact with the system of *hatru*, in which a community receives land for its use, sometimes in exchange for military service; accordingly, certain lots are described in military terms as "bow-land, chariot-land," etc.; see Cardascia 1951; Stolper 1985.
27. See Dandamaev 1979, 1982.
28. Translation P. A. Beaulieu, cited in Joannès 1995.1481; see also the French translation in Cardascia 1951.180–81 and the historical commentary in Briant 1996. 615–16, 1005–6. The text dates to the reign of Darius II, 422.
29. E.g., Diodorus 11.75.3; 17.53.4, 55.1.

30. I develop here an idea presented in Briant 1996.1063–64.
31. On this point, see Briant 1996.803–20.
32. Although this, of course, does not mean that we must accept Nepos's figures at face value, the proportions they reflect, particularly between mercenaries and Persian-Achaemenid regular troops, show that the traditional picture of a growing Greek mercenary component in Achaemenid armies cannot be accepted.
33. The sentence structure in Nepos's list of Autophradates' army does not allow the conclusion that the additional comment at the end ("the light-armed troops were innumerable") refers especially to the *kardakes*. On technical aspects, see Head 1992.42–43; I do not understand the suggestion of Sekunda (1992.27, 53) that the 120,000 soldiers sent against the Carduchians (Xenophon, *Anabasis* 3.5.16) could have been *kardakes* (his graphic reconstruction [pl. 12 and p. 53] is novelistic); nor do I see (despite Sekunda 1988.42; 1992.27) why Datames should be considered the promoter of this new army corps.
34. Knauth-Nadjamabadi 1975.83–84.
35. Thus a scholiast (ancient commentator) on Plato, *Laws* I.633B, cited in Jeanmaire 1913.140 n. 3, an article that is still fundamental.
36. Listed conveniently in Segre 1938.194 n. 2.
37. So too, briefly, Bosworth 1980.208, who curiously does not cite the second part of Hesychius's definition.
38. This interpretation is somewhat confirmed by a gloss of Aelius Dius (cited by Segre, loc. cit.): "the barbarians serving for pay (*misthos*)." This corresponds fairly closely to what I tried elsewhere (Briant 1996.812–15, without using this source) to describe as "royal mercenaries" (as opposed to the *Greek* mercenaries and the imperial levies by ethnic contingents), that is, soldiers enlisted among various peoples of the empire for paid service in the army.
39. Cf. Arrian 2.8.8, mentioning a "barbarian phalanx."
40. On this issue, see also generally, Briant 1996.402–4, 422–24.
41. See esp. Polybius 5.79.11 (the army of Antiochus III at Raphia): "1000 *kardakes* of the Galatian Lysimachos"; cf. Bar-Kochva 1976.50, 216–17, 229–30 (but the identification of *kardakes* with Carduchians [50] certainly is wrong). The "village of *kardakes*" in a letter of Eumenes II of Pergamum seems to refer to a military colony (cf. Segre 1938.193–97 and now Cohen 1995.330–31).
42. The problem is raised in Briant 1994.283–86. On Achaemenid-Hellenistic continuities, see also Briant 1982.291–330; 1996.956–57.
43. Hammond 1990.275–80.
44. Hammond 1990.275–76.
45. In basing his thesis particularly on the notice of the *Suda*, Hammond (1990.287 n. 71) refutes Bosworth (1988.272–73), who seems to think that Alexander's order was valid only for the Iranian countries. But, conversely, I do not see (pace Hammond, 275, 279) why the selection of Lydian, Lycian, or Syrian contingents should necessarily be seen as proof that Alexander issued such orders from his arrival in Asia Minor; these examples rather seem to confirm the principle of ethnic distribution (*kata ethnē*). For criticism of Hammond's interpretations, see also Thompson 1992.50 with nn. 15–16.

46. Hammond 1990.278 simply notes that the young men recruited in the Empire needed to be trained to become hoplites, like the Macedonian pages, and not horsemen.

47. Briant 1994.298–302; 1996.950.

48. On the Macedonian rites of passage, see Briant 1994.305–7; Hatzopoulos 1994.87–111.

49. Briant 1991.225–30; 1994.302–7.

50. Only Justin 12.4.11, certainly wrongly, uses this name for the children of unions between soldiers of Alexander and local women.

51. See esp. Diodorus 19.52.4 and other texts cited in Briant 1994.299–300; cf. Hammond 1990.269–72, who, however, frequently identifies pages (in the Macedonian sense of the term) with young men recruited among native peoples by the diadochs (cf. 280–84). On the policies of the diadochs on this issue and their relations to Alexander's policies, see Briant 1982.32–50.

Bibliography

Bar-Kochva, B. 1976. *The Seleucid Army: Organization and Tactics in the Great Campaigns.* Cambridge: Cambridge University Press.

Bosworth, A. B. 1980. *A Historical Commentary on Arrian's History of Alexander,* Vol. 1. Oxford: Oxford University Press.

———. 1988. *Conquest and Empire: The Reign of Alexander the Great.* Oxford: Oxford University Press.

Bousquet, J. 1992. "Les inscriptions du Létoôn en l'honneur d'Arbinas et l'épigramme grecque." In *Fouilles de Xanthos,* Vol 9. Paris: C. Klincksieck.

Briant, P. 1982. *Rois, tributs et paysans.* Paris: Les Belles Lettres.

———. 1987. "Pouvoir central et polycentrisme culturel dans l'Empire achéménide (Quelques reflexions et suggestions)." *Achaemenid History* 1, 1–31.

———. 1989. "Histoire et idéologie: Les Grecs et la 'décadence perse.'" In *Mélanges Pierre Lévêque,* edited by Marie-Madeleine Mactoux and Evelyne Geny, Vol. 2, 35–44. Paris: Les Belles Lettres.

———. 1990. "Hérodote et la société perse." In *Hérodote et les peuples non-grecs.* Entretiens sur l'Antiquité classique 35, 69–104. Geneva: Fondation Hardt.

———. 1991. "Chasses royales macédoniennes et chasses royales perses: le thème de la chasse au lion sur la *Chasse de Vergina.*" *Dialogues d'histoire ancienne* 17.1, 211–55.

———. 1994. "Sources grêco-hellénistiques, institutions perses et institutions macédoniennes: continuités, changements et bricolages." *Achaemenid History* 8, 283–310.

———. 1996. *Histoire de l'Empire perse. De Cyrus à Alexandre.* Paris: Fayard.

Cardascia, G. 1951. *Les archives des Murashu. Une famille d'hommes d'affaires babyloniens à l'époque perse (455–403 av. J.-C.).* Paris: Imprimerie Nationale.

Cohen, G. M. 1995. *The Hellenistic Settlements in Europe, the Islands and Asia Minor.* Hellenistic Culture and Society, 17. Berkeley and Los Angeles: University of California Press.

Dandamaev, M. 1979. "Data of the Babylonian Documents from the 6th to the 5th

Centuries B.C. on the Sakas." In *Prolegomena to the Sources on the History of Pre-Islamic Central Asia*, edited by J. Harmatta, 95–109. Budapest: Akadémiai Kiadó.

———. 1982. "Saka Soldiers on Ships." *Iranica Antiqua* 17, 101–3.

Goukowsky, P., ed. 1976. *Diodore de Sicile. Livre XVII*. Collection des Universités de France. Paris: Les Belles Lettres.

Hammond, N. G. L. 1990. "Royal Pages, Personal Pages, and Boys Trained in the Macedonian Manner during the Period of the Temenid Monarchy." *Historia* 39, 261–90.

Hatzopoulos, M. 1994. *Cultes et rites de passage en Macédoine*. Meletemata 19. Athens: Kentron Hellenikes kai Romaikes Archaiotetos Ethnikon Hydryma Ereunon; and Paris: De Boccard.

Head, D. 1992. *The Achaemenid Persian Army*. Stockport: Montvert Publications.

Herrenschmidt, C. 1985. "Une lecture iranisante du poème de Symmachos dédié à Arbinas, dynaste de Xanthos." *Revue des études anciennes* 87, 125–34.

Jacoby, F., ed. 1923ff. *Die Fragmente der griechischen Historiker*. Many vols. Berlin, then Leiden: E. J. Brill.

Jeanmaire, H. 1913. "La cryptie lacédémonienne." *Revue des études grecques* 26, 121–50.

Joannès, F. 1995. "Private Commerce and Banking in Achaemenid Babylonia." In *Civilizations of the Ancient Near East*, edited by J. M. Sasson et al., Vol. 3, 1475–85. New York: Scribner's.

Kellens, J. 1995. "L'âme entre le cadavre et le paradis." *Journal Asiatique* 283, 19–56.

Kennell, N. M. 1995. *The Gymnasium of Virtue: Education and Culture in Ancient Sparta*. Chapel Hill, N.C.: University of North Carolina Press.

Kent, R. G. 1953. *Old Persian Grammar, Texts, Lexikon*. 2d ed. New Haven, Conn.: American Oriental Society.

Knauth, W. and S. Nadjamabadi. 1975. *Das altiranische Fürstenideal von Xenophon bis Ferdousi*. Wiesbaden: F. Steiner Verlag.

Segre, M. 1938. "Iscrizioni di Licia." *Clara Rhodos* 9, 181-208.

Sekunda, N. 1988. "Some Notes on the Life of Datames." *Iran* 26, 35–53.

———. 1992. *The Persian Army, 560–330 B.C.* London: Osprey.

Stolper, M. 1985. *Entrepreneurs and Empire. The Murašû Archive, the Murašû Firm and Persian Rule in Babylonia*. Leiden: Institut Neérlandais du Proche-Orient.

Thompson, D. 1992. "Language and Literacy in Early Hellenistic Egypt." In *Ethnicity in Hellenistic Egypt*, edited by P. Bilde et al., 39–52. Studies in Hellenistic Civilization, Vol. 3. Aarhus: Aarhus University Press.

Vidal-Naquet, P. 1986. *The Black Hunter: Forms of Thought and Forms of Society in the Greek World*. Translated by A. Szegedy-Maszak. Baltimore, Md.: Johns Hopkins University Press.

———. 1989. "Retour au Chasseur noir." In *Mélanges Pierre Lévêque*, edited by Marie-Madeleine Mactoux and Evelyne Geny, Vol. 2, 387–411. Paris: Les Belles Lettres.

◳◳◳◳

Archaic and Classical Greece

KURT RAAFLAUB

Introduction and Background

This volume is concerned with the relationship between war and military organization on the one hand and, on the other, the economic, social, and political structures of the states or communities involved. This relationship can best be grasped in times of incisive changes on one side or the other. Scholars speak of three "military revolutions" in Greek history. Two of these are discussed in this chapter: the evolution of hoplite warfare and its connection with the rise of the polis in the eighth to sixth centuries and the emergence of naval warfare and its connection with imperialism and democracy especially in Athens in the fifth century. The third, the transformation of warfare in the late fifth and especially fourth century, will be analyzed in the subsequent chapter on the Hellenistic period.[1]

First, a brief sketch of the historical background. The Bronze Age "Mycenaean" civilization, centered in large palaces with hierarchical structures and centralized economies, perished by 1200. The extant evidence reflects a militaristic society and central organization of warfare but is too fragmentary to permit a clear reconstruction of military details.[2] The subsequent period, traditionally called the Dark Ages, was characterized in many areas by cultural decline, shrinking population, and increasing isolation. Small groups of families, led by their ablest member, a sort of chieftain, lived in scattered villages.[3] Warfare must have consisted of raids against neighboring lands and coasts, conducted by warrior bands under the command of local or regional leaders. Such raids are amply illustrated in the Homeric epics.[4]

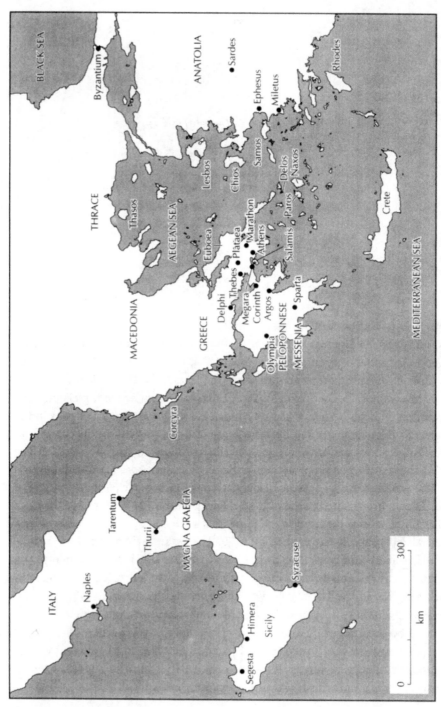

The Greek World, 7th to 5th cent. B.C.E.

From the tenth to the eighth century, the population increased and contacts with other peoples broadened; the eighth century in particular was a
period of rapid change. In the course of this process the "polis" evolved; in
many parts of the Aegean and abroad, where Greek emigrants settled ("colonized") from the eighth to the sixth century, it became the typical form of
community, different from the more loosely organized *ethnos* ("tribal state")
that prevailed in other areas. Politically and culturally, the polis dominated the
Greek world to the conquest of Greece by Philip II of Macedon in the late
fourth century.[5]

In the archaic period (750–480) many poleis evolved through a phase of
economic and social crisis toward a more balanced constitution. While private
or semipublic raids for cattle or booty continued, wars in this period became
increasingly communal. They were mostly local affairs, fought, on a fairly small
scale and in long intervals, between neighboring poleis over the control of fertile border lands, and usually decided in a pitched battle between citizen armies.
Such intercity rivalries, for example between Argos and Sparta, continued for
centuries. Sparta was the first polis to form a system of regional power. Following the conquest of Lakonia and Messenia (eighth century), some communities
became dependent poleis (*perioikoi*), while large parts of the subjected populations were enslaved (helots), cultivating the farms of the Spartan citizens
(Spartiates) but also posing a constant threat. As a consequence, the Spartiates
gradually developed a strictly regulated system of communal life. From about
550, Sparta dominated much of the Peloponnese through its hegemony, based
on military supremacy, in a system of alliances (the Peloponnesian League).
Despite its size, Athens played no major role before the late sixth century.[6] Until
the middle of that century, the Greeks remained outside the power sphere of
the Near Eastern empires, but then the Lydians under Croesus, followed by the
Persians under Cyrus, expanded their empires to the shores of the Aegean, subjecting the Greek poleis of Asia Minor to their rule.

The nature of politics and warfare changed dramatically in the fifth century, as a consequence of developments triggered by the war between Greeks and
Persians. This confrontation, highlighted by Greek victories in 490 and 480/79,
continued for thirty years. When Sparta and her allies withdrew from the war
in 478/77, a new alliance was established under Athenian leadership (the Delian
League). Its activities resulted in several victories over Persian forces and a vast
expansion of the Athenian sphere of influence. Within two decades the Delian
League was transformed into a tightly controlled and centralized naval empire
ruled by Athens, and, in Athens itself, democracy was fully realized.

Both the empire and democracy made conflicts with Sparta and her allies
inevitable. These conflicts, with several short intermissions, dominated the second half of the fifth century, from the 450s to the Peloponnesian War of 431–404.

The outcome of these conflicts was heavily influenced by the disastrous outcome of two large-scale Athenian naval expeditions: one in the 450s in support of an Egyptian revolt against Persia, the other in 415–13 in Sicily. In 404 Athens capitulated and lost its fleet and empire.[7]

The "military revolution" of the fifth century consisted of the emergence of large-scale naval warfare, which completely transformed the character of war and made it permanent, professional, and total. Certainly, traditional wars for the control of land continued to be fought between citizen armies of neighboring poleis, but politics and wars now increasingly involved large alliance systems and empires.

Apart from "tyrannies" (short-lived rules by individuals seizing power), monarchies were virtually absent in the Greek world during most of this period. This offers us an exceptional opportunity to study the questions that are central to this volume in the social context of nonhierarchical citizen communities—a context that was crucial for the specific achievement of ancient Greek civilization.[8]

Hoplites and Polis in Archaic Greece

Phalanx and "Hoplite Revolution"

Some of the questions raised in this volume were anticipated by Greek political theory. In the *Politics*, Aristotle sketches the evolution of Greek society, connecting military systems and constitutions: small numbers, the lack of a middle class, and monopolization of military expertise by the elite initially favored an aristocratic system based on cavalry forces. "When, however, states began to increase in size, and infantry forces acquired a greater degree of strength, more persons were admitted to the enjoyment of political rights" (*Politics* 1297b16–28). Aristotle's theories of constitutional change raise many problems.[9] Although horse breeding had long been a status symbol of the wealthy elites who dominated the early polis, and even in the classical period cavalries were largely an upper-class specialty, with few exceptions, such as Thessaly and Macedonia, Greece never witnessed a stage of true cavalry supremacy.[10] Aristotle's linking of aristocracy and cavalry warfare thus cannot be generalized, and the evolutionary connection in his scheme between growth of states, increasing importance of infantry forces, and extension of political rights to nonaristocrats is likely to be theoretical rather than empirical as well, perhaps derived from the observation of a similar connection between naval power and democracy.[11] Yet here lies the origin of the modern theory of the "hoplite revolution."

Phalanx fighting was a remarkable form of warfare, different from any other. Two armies met each other on level ground; they were arranged in dense formations, several ranks deep (the "phalanx"), the soldiers equipped uniformly with the panoply consisting of helmet, corslet and greaves, spear and short sword, and the big round shield (*hoplon,* hence hoplites). Mounted or light-armed troops, if involved at all, played a minor role. After the two armies clashed, heavy fighting with spear and sword went on for a while before the soldiers in the front ranks locked shields and tried to dislodge each other by pushing and shoving (*ōthismos*), those in the front being pressed forward by those in the back. All thus depended on maintaining the formation; as soon as one side gave in, the ranks were broken and the battle usually was over.[12] Since the goal was to defeat, not to annihilate, the enemy, the fleeing losers usually were not pursued and casualties, though potentially serious, often were limited.[13]

Herodotus indicates that the Greeks themselves around 430 were fully aware of the peculiar nature of hoplite fighting.[14] How, when, and why did this system come about? A common view long held that in early Greece a "heroic" mode of fighting prevailed—as it *seems* to be depicted in the *Iliad:*[15] the battle was decided by the elite leaders whose status depended on demonstrations of fighting skills and courage, while the masses of the common people mostly stayed in the background.[16] From about 750, the elements of the hoplite panoply, of various origin, were gradually combined and adapted. By about 650, the equipment, formation, and fighting tactics of the phalanx were fully developed. This phalanx required the involvement of larger masses of equally equipped and trained soldiers. Thus the free farmers who could afford the panoply were integrated into the polis army and eventually achieved political integration as well. This process, often called the "hoplite revolution," ended the phase of elite domination of the polis and ushered in an age of more egalitarian constitutions in which the free farmers played a decisive role.

Essentially, this model assumes that military change prompted political change. It has a venerable tradition, from Aristotle (above) to Eduard Meyer and Max Weber. In the 1960s it was strengthened by Anthony Snodgrass's seminal work on the evolution of early Greek military equipment and its political consequences; with slight modifications, it has been restated several times even recently.[17] Yet battles in the *Iliad* are decided by the entire army, and the poet's descriptions contain many references to mass fighting and egalitarian structures.[18] The hoplite equipment, appearing in tombs from approximately 725, shows unique characteristics that must have been developed for frontal fighting in dense mass formations. In particular, a double arm grip made it possible to carry the large round shield in a way that protected the left neighbor's right side as well, and the shield's extreme concavity allowed the fighter to let it rest on his left shoulder during the shoving match. The "Corinthian helmet" limited vision and hearing in exchange for maximum protection.[19] Mass fighting thus was common long before 725. In fact, to the poet of the *Iliad* it was so normal that he naturally incorporated it into his battle descriptions. It was then made more effective by the development of specific fighting tactics and of equipment that supported these tactics.[20] Hence the priority of military change is uncertain and the question is how this development relates to contemporaneous forms of warfare and social, economic, and political structures.

Elsewhere I have proposed that the extant evidence can be explained better by a model of polis evolution that assumes the interdependence of military and sociopolitical change: the polis, the phalanx, and the sphere of "the political" in the polis evolved in an interactive process over a long time; the concepts of landownership and "territoriality" were inseparable components of this inter-related process; and polis aristocracies emerged as part of the same process. Furthermore, if mass fighting was essentially egalitarian, the polis must have evolved on a foundation of considerable equality.[21] This model raises questions that need to be addressed.

Phalanx, Warfare, and Society

Apart from private and semiprivate raiding expeditions, the Homeric epics pay much attention to communal wars between neighboring poleis—conflicts that coexisted with private raids and sometimes appear to have been caused by them.[22] The setting of the Trojan War itself—but of course not its heroic story—resembles such a war: Troy and the temporary Achaean city on the shore[23] lie on two sides of a fertile plain, a constellation conducive to war throughout Greek history. In fact, the earliest historical wars attested in Greece took place between neighboring poleis in the late eighth century—the time of "Homer." Such wars, continuing for centuries, were usually fought over control of contested land.[24] This thematic and chronological correspondence between history and epics enables us to connect the evolution of polis and communal warfare.

Under the conditions of the Dark Ages (above at n. 4), there probably was neither need nor opportunity for wars between massed armies. As the population increased and economic conditions improved, settlements multiplied, previously unoccupied lands were cultivated, and the polis emerged. The polis territories were filled up, land became precious, the notions of "territoriality" and fixed boundaries assumed increasing importance, and neighboring poleis began to fight about land. Massed fighting in communal armies thus was the consequence of increased population densities, increasing and widespread wealth sufficient to afford the necessary equipment, the new organizational structures of the early polis,[25] and, most important, the citizens' need to defend their fields collectively and fight for the territory, if not the survival, of their polis. Ways were then sought to improve the effectiveness of the citizen army: technological and tactical changes interacted with economic and social changes to produce, at the end of a long process, the hoplite phalanx. This process was largely completed by 650. What was its impact on the poleis involved?

A long-standing scholarly consensus holds that at the height of phalanx warfare hoplite fighting was strictly regulated: all soldiers wore the same equipment, which they had to provide at their own expense, and "membership" in the "hoplite class" was often tied to a census requirement, measured by agrarian property and income. In some way or other, in such "timocratic systems" political participation was linked to military and economic capacity. In Athens (as in Rome) citizens were divided into "horsemen" (*hippeis, equites* [those who could afford horses and used them in war as well]);[26] hoplites (*zeugitai* [those owning a yoke of oxen or fighting in a tight, "yoked" formation], *classis*); and those who were neither and counted for little socially, militarily, and politically (*thetes, infra classem,* including small and tenant farmers, craftsmen, and traders, some of whom sometimes supported the phalanx as light-armed skirmishers).[27]

At some point in the development, therefore, the distinction between the citizens who mattered and those who did not was fixed; the criteria determining such distinctions included "membership" in the "hoplite class." Solon's property classes of 594 (although perhaps refining an earlier system) offer a terminus ante. Sparta's earliest "constitution," based on the hoplite class, was enacted around 650. Several new phenomena that emphasize the importance of hoplites, including the dedication of hoplite figurines and equipment in sanctuaries and vase paintings illustrating hoplite fighting, are clustered around the same time. Snodgrass plausibly concludes that all this must reflect an important shift in public conscience connected precisely with the phalanx.[28] I have proposed that, since mass fighting and citizen armies were an integral part of war long before the phalanx was fully developed and in fact provided the impetus for its development, this shift was probably prompted by the perfection and formalization rather than the introduction of phalanx warfare. Even after a long evolution, such formalization must have brought about incisive changes in the polis, including the introduction of organizational structures and the definition of who qualified.[29]

"Timocratic systems," then, resulted from a long evolution, not a "hoplite revolution"; they formalized, but did not introduce, the linking of the triad of functions typical of Greek polis citizens: the landowners (above a minimal subsistence level) fought in the polis army and sat in the assembly to share in the polis's decision making.

Phalanx and Exclusiveness

The distinction between evolution and formalization seems helpful in other respects as well. Many scholars have emphasized the great importance of the principle of self-equipment, and rightly so. To own the—not inexpensive—panoply and be a hoplite determined status and "belonging" in the community. As Paul Cartledge puts it, the principle of self-equipment meant that not only economic capacity but also the will to enroll was required—which turned the hoplites into a "civic corporation" and explains the apportionment of political prerogatives in accordance with military function.[30] But this principle, too, may have changed over time, handled differently by each polis. The equipment of the early citizen-soldiers must have been uneven and cheaper: shield, spear, and sword were essential, but the shield was simpler than the later hoplite shield, and many perhaps wore leather caps and corslets rather than metal ones.[31] Even after the panoply became the standard, it was perhaps often acquired through spoils or passed on through families and generations—fitting being cheaper than buying.[32] Moreover, since status and prestige were involved, citizens might have been willing to make sacrifices in order to qualify. All this suggests larger rather than smaller numbers. At least initially, economic capacity might have been a relative, not absolute, criterion; that is, all those naturally fought in the polis army who owned the (or some of the) equipment.

This raises several connected questions. (1) What was the ratio in the citizen body between those who qualified and those who did not? (2) Why did the polis not make better military use of its subhoplite citizens? (3) What was the purpose of defining the hoplite class in rigid economic terms, and were such definitions applied universally? Concerning the first question, scholars usually assume that throughout its history the polis was structured similarly, comprising a small minority of wealthy elite families, a much larger class (but overall still a minority) of farmers who qualified as hoplites, and a majority of subhoplites.[33] This is certainly true for poleis with a highly diversified economy and a developed secondary sector. But such conditions applied only from the late sixth and especially fifth century and only in exceptional cases, among which Athens was quite unique (below at n. 69). In the archaic period, when polis populations were almost completely agrarian and few other opportunities existed to earn a decent living, when the poor and dissatisfied often emigrated and thetes who depended on others for their livelihood were treated with utmost contempt, the proportion of small farmers and especially nonfarmers must have been much smaller.[34] If so, through most of the archaic period the hoplite-farmers would have represented the majority of polis citizens.

Historically, this would make sense. When poleis and polis territories were emerging and interpolis feuds began to be fought by citizen armies, it must soon have been obvious that numbers were decisive. Given the small size of the average polis, the general tendency must have been to field as large a proportion of the citizens as possible.[35] The view seems implausible, therefore, that the "will to enroll" was a major factor.[36] This view presupposes that hoplites might have been unwilling to serve in the phalanx; it is diametrically opposed to another, that hoplite fighting became so standardized because this proved a successful means to keep the despised lower classes out of the army and hence out of politics.[37] Both assumptions ignore the nature and purpose of hoplite warfare. If the enemy attacked their fields, any farmer would want to help defend them: put simply, the hoplites fought on their land for their land.[38] This aspect determined the social and ideological implications of the phalanx. If the defense of the polis could be made more effective by involving more citizens, this would certainly have been—and probably often was—done.[39] If the archaic polis relied on hoplites and not on light-armed troops, this was not the result of political conspiracy and manipulation but of compelling economic and practical factors.

The second question involves two aspects. First, given that in most of Greece plains are rare and mountain ranges separate the poleis, and that hoplite warfare often aimed at forcing the opponents to fight or submit by threatening their crops,[40] why did the communities not defend the mountain passes and use the terrain to their advantage rather than allowing the enemy to penetrate their territory, risking their fields to be ravaged, and relying on pitched battles? The best answer is that a system of border defense would have required fortifications and, considering the relatively short distances, the maintenance of a standing corps of border guards. The resulting financial burden would have exceeded the capacity of almost all early poleis.[41] Before the fifth century, only Sparta could afford a professional army; it was supported by the enslaved Messenians—a system unsuitable for general imitation. The hoplites were a citizen militia; phalanx fighting was adapted to the possibilities of the early polis and the needs of warfare between these poleis. As possibilities and needs changed, the methods of warfare and the personnel involved in war changed too.

In addition, even if the bulk of the polis armies consisted of hoplites, it might still have been useful to support the phalanx with cavalry and light-armed troops. To some extent this was done but rarely in an organized and systematic way.[42] Although in later periods both types of troops proved their effectiveness, Athens, for example, created a substantial cavalry corps only in the mid–fifth century and never took full advantage of it, and by 424 still had no organized light-armed corps.[43] Why such reluctance? Here all indications indeed point to tradition, values, and social prejudice. Throughout the archaic and classical periods, *once the principle was established,* the hoplite's achievement was valued more highly than other forms of fighting: true valor (*aretē*) was seen in facing the enemy in man-to-man combat and holding one's position in the battle formation. Warrior ethics were closely linked with those of tilling the land: the true citizen was farmer and soldier.[44] The reason for the predominance and persistence of such values most likely lies precisely in the nature of the polis as a citizen community of farmer-soldiers who shared strong interests and learned solidarity and discipline when fighting in defense of their community. These virtues were cemented by the phalanx. Those who did not share in them indeed did not matter. Hence there developed a tendency to stick to pure hoplite fighting, which—and this is crucial—was facilitated because the underlying values were generally accepted in the world of poleis and because hoplite fighting gradually changed its purpose.

This leads to the third question: Why, to what purpose, and how universally were definitions limiting the hoplite class to farmers above a certain property level used, and how restrictive were they really? One obvious explanation for such limitations, that the number of hoplites exceeded the level deemed necessary, would apply only to the largest poleis, if at all. Another may lie in the process of "ritualization" of hoplite warfare itself.

Before the fifth century, war among Greek poleis was endemic but not permanent (below at n. 61). Although such wars, fought in fairly regular intervals, were serious enough, their impact and function seem to have changed, once the polis system was in place and somewhat balanced (roughly by the late seventh century). Phalanx fighting was increasingly "ritualized," in the sense of both playing an important ritual role within the community and following widely agreed-upon principles.[45] In fact, this type of warfare was only possible because the values and behavior codes involved were shared widely and reinforced regularly at interstate festivals and by the ethics promoted by the Panhellenic sanctuaries. As a result, the brutality immanent in war was somewhat reduced, and in the particular world of Greek poleis between the late seventh and early fifth century the function of war—normally—was to determine the prestige rather than the survival of the polis. This helps explain why later tradition remembered so few destructions and enslavements of cities in the archaic period.[46]

The custom of limiting the hoplite class to property owners above a certain level thus may have been a Panhellenic phenomenon, reflecting shared ideals.[47] The question of where the limit was set, and how exclusive it was, then becomes all the more important. The Athenian example, as so often, may be atypical— or simply wrong. The tradition about its property classes certainly poses serious problems.[48] In fact, close examination shows that the census figure of two hundred *medimnoi* for hoplites, only one hundred *medimnoi* less than the *hippeis*, although accepted by most scholars, is far too high. Accordingly, I consider it probable that at least well into the fifth century the Athenian hoplite class was far less comfortably propertied, less exclusive, and perhaps less rigidly defined than the tradition suggests.[49] This is certainly true for most other poleis, which were small in size and population and able to field a decent hoplite force only if almost every independent farmer was enrolled.[50] This, in turn, confirms the suggestion made earlier that during most of the archaic period the hoplite farmers represented the bulk of the citizen body and all the citizens who mattered.

Phalanx, Polis, and Equality

If the polis citizens were militarily empowered from early on, the traditional view that these same citizens were essentially powerless poses difficulties. On the political side, this view is based on the assumption that early Greek assemblies were insignificant; this assumption, in turn, rests on a one-sided interpretation of several scenes in the Homeric epics that seem to describe the assembly as passive, depending on elite leaders, and easily manipulated. Recent studies, however, have refuted this assumption and made a strong case that even in the epics the assembly plays a crucial role and is communally indispensable.[51] On the social side, essential parts of archaic poetry (especially Hesiod and Solon) reflect elite predominance and various forms of dependence among the demos. Yet, why should this be incompatible in principle with the demos' fighting in the polis army—or with their participation, in elementary but important ways, in communal decision making? Elite ideology, visible already in the *Iliad* (2.200–202), aimed at enhancing aristocratic domination and increasing the distance between elite and masses.[52] Continuing economic and social differentiation would have reinforced such trends, resulting in a sense of superiority and abuses of power on the part of the elite, and, among the commoners, in both real and perceived dependence and powerlessness. The commoners' military involvement might not in itself suffice to stem this trend, especially if it predated the sketched developments by a long time. In other words, according to the interactive model proposed earlier in this chapter, Greek polis aristocracies emerged and rose to power as the polis evolved; their rivalries and abuses, amply attested in the poetry of the time, thus influenced and changed relations and structures that were in part long established, in part also still evolving. Such abuses, however, met with resistance precisely when they disturbed the egalitarian base on which the polis was built. Hence, not surprisingly, massive protest and resistance eventually forced the elite to compromise.[53] Dependence of parts of the demos thus was not identical with powerlessness of the demos as a whole.

Sparta provides an illuminating exception: here around the mid–seventh century an early constitution established regular meetings of the assembly and defined its place in the communal decision-making process, next to the kings and council of elders; eventually, the Spartiate citizen-hoplites were recognized as peers (*homoioi*).[54] In my view, this was less the result of the long and recurring war with Messenia itself than that of the continuous threat posed to the Spartiate community by the enslavement of the defeated (above at n. 6). The hoplites thus assumed permanent military responsibility for the security of their polis. The difference in warfare between "permanent and essential" versus "occasional and ritual" was decisive. Fifth-century Athens offers another example where the rise of citizen-soldiers to *permanent* and *essential* military significance had far-reaching political consequences.[55] In such cases the military factor indeed seems to have been the primary agent of sociopolitical change. In poleis that were less permanently threatened and where the army played a less crucial role, the military factor probably had less of an impact.

Nevertheless, toward the end of the archaic period egalitarian structures were institutionally fixed in many poleis, thereby enhancing and formalizing more extensively the political participation of at least the hoplite farmers.[56] Such formalization of equality potentially went far beyond earlier timocratic systems; in Athens, the difference is expressed by Cleisthenes' "order of equality" (*isonomia*) of 508/7 versus Solon's traditional "good order" (*eunomia*) reaffirmed almost a century earlier.[57] If this development was in most cases not directly related to the hoplite phalanx, what brought it about? Since it resulted in incisive innovations, strong pressures must have been at work, from the outside or from within the polis. In most cases, the latter may have been decisive: infighting among elite families, their abuse of social and economic power, and severe social conflicts threatened the polis as well. The formalization of institutions, the enactment of written law, and the appointment of mediators and legislators with extraordinary power served as means, supported by the entire polis, to overcome such crises.[58] So, too, the increased and formalized political empowerment of the farmers served the purpose of stabilizing the polis that was in danger of complete destabilization. The fact that these farmers were hoplites was less the cause than the condition of their integration: fighting in the phalanx was one of three interconnected factors that were crucial in determining who belonged among the essential part of the citizen body.

Conclusion

The evidence of Homeric and early Greek warfare leaves no space for a "hoplite revolution." The phalanx evolved with the polis and the emergence of communal warfare and represented the Greeks' response to the specific challenges of mostly localized and increasingly ritualized warfare in a fairly balanced system of poleis. From the very beginning, the landowning farmers formed an integral element, both militarily and politically, in the evolving polis. Their roles of landowners, soldiers, and assemblymen were interconnected and naturally made them the essential part of the citizen body. Although the early Greek polis was thus founded on essential elements of equality, economic and social differentiation continued and resulted in elite domination and abuse of power, which in turn provoked resistance and revolt. Eventually, the farmer-hoplites were formally integrated in egalitarian polis constitutions. Usually this happened not primarily as a result of their contribution to the phalanx but as a result of serious social crisis and in an effort, supported by the entire polis, to stabilize the community and set it on a broader base of citizen involvement and communal responsibility. In exceptional cases, especially that of Sparta, permanent outside pressure on the community resulted in a professionalization of the citizens' military function and, in close connection with this development, in their enhanced and formalized political participation in a system that emphasized their status as "peers" (*homoioi*).

Naval Warfare, Imperialism, and Democracy in the Fifth Century

The hoplites' significant role in fifth-century warfare should not be underestimated. Moreover, although political theorists included them among the supporters of oligarchy, the Athenian hoplites, with few exceptions, identified with and supported democracy hardly less than the lower-class "naval crowds."[59] Nevertheless, what revolutionized warfare in the fifth century was Athens's reliance on large-scale naval warfare. Many scholars have postulated a direct connection between naval warfare and democracy, assuming, again, that military change prompted political change. Again, however, things might be more complicated. The main questions we need to discuss are, What exactly is the connection between naval power and empire, and between both and democracy? And how did all this affect Athenian society?

The Nature of Naval Warfare

Naval warfare was radically different from traditional Greek land warfare. In the fifth century, it was based on the trireme, a formidable man-of-war, long and narrow, manned by 200 men (of whom 170 were rowers, tightly packed in three tiers), propelled by oars and two sails, very fast and highly maneuverable. Although invented earlier, it was used relatively rarely before the Persian Wars. In the archaic period, naval encounters were mostly fought with smaller ships that served both military and trade or transportation purposes. Even early naval powers (such as Corinth and Corcyra) had relatively small fleets. The Phoenicians, providing the bulk of the Persian fleet, were the dominant naval power in the eastern Mediterranean: in 494 they defeated the combined navies of the Ionian and island poleis that had revolted from Persia. This was one of the first great sea battles in Aegean waters fought with triremes. The Athenians' decision in the late 480s to entrust the survival of their community against the Persians to a fleet of triremes thus was not novel but daring.[60]

Naval warfare contributed decisively to making war more permanent, comprehensive, and brutal. Unlike hoplite campaigns that usually were short and took place only in fairly long intervals, naval expeditions lasted weeks if not months or years. Naval warfare was highly technical and required constant training; hence a small squadron was almost constantly on sea for patrol and training missions. In the fifth and fourth centuries, the Athenians were involved in serious military actions in no less than two out of every three years. Relying on their navy to transport soldiers and resources, they soon became the foremost Greek experts in siegecraft. Henceforth, warfare was more intense and "total": economic blockades and ravaging of the enemy's territory became frequent means of putting pressure on the opponent. Moreover, the Athenians reintroduced into Greek warfare the "Homeric" custom of destroying a captured city, killing the men, and selling women and children into slavery. Reliance on the navy changed their defensive strategy as well: they fortified the Piraeus and constructed the Long Walls, thereby turning their city and harbor into one big fortress; this enabled them to avoid pitched battles with the superior Spartan hoplite army and to yield the Attic countryside largely to the enemy while supplying the city by sea.[61]

Naval warfare was very expensive: one trireme cost roughly one talent, and one month's pay for the crew of 200 men between one-half and one talent. A three-month campaign with 150 ships thus would have devoured between 225 and 450 talents. For comparison, according to Thucydides (1.96), the first year's contributions of the Delian League amounted to 460 talents; 1,400 talents were spent on the nine-month siege of rebellious Samos—more than the 1,200 to 1,300 for the Parthenon, including Athena's statue of gold and ivory.[62] The crews consisted of citizens (especially volunteers of the lower classes), metics (resident foreigners), mercenaries, and slaves. Hence, although the proportion of citizens apparently declined over time, many thousands of them were frequently and over extended periods engaged in paid service for the community.[63] The accumulation of public funds and cash reserves, as well as financial planning, therefore assumed unprecedented importance. The required finances were normally provided, in varying combinations, by the allies' tribute and other imperial and domestic revenues, in exceptional cases by loans from the treasuries of Athena and other sanctuaries, or by a special tax (*eisphora*). In addition, wealthy citizens contributed through the institution of the "trierarchy," that is, the obligation to fit out, man, and command a trireme.[64]

Finally, the casualties caused by naval warfare could be astronomical. The records that survive from one year, 460/59, show that one of the ten *phylai* (civic subdivisions) alone lost 177 men (roughly 3.5 to 4.5 percent of its adult citizens) in various actions ranging from Aegina and Megara to Cyprus and Egypt. Comprehensive estimates are difficult, but probably about eight thousand citizens (one out of five or six adult men!) perished in the failed Egyptian expedition of the 450s, at least ten thousand in Sicily (415–413), and twenty-eight thousand overall in the Peloponnesian War.[65] Many of these died in land, not naval, battles; the essential point is that the vastly increased size and scope of operations, made possible by naval warfare, entailed much higher risks and losses.

Naval Warfare and Empire

The trireme was developed to make naval warfare more effective. Why was it not used more regularly in earlier decades? The answer must be that naval warfare, based on a fleet of triremes that could not be used for anything else, required tremendous resources and a highly developed infrastructure. Such resources included reliable and enforceable access to shipbuilding materials, most of which (timber, leather, metals) needed to be imported; safe harbors and large shipyards where hundreds of ships could be built, repaired, and kept dry in winter; and enormous numbers of crews, shipwrights, and other personnel. Up to twenty thousand men were needed to operate one hundred triremes, perhaps fifteen thousand to maintain and regularly replace the three hundred hulls of Athens's fifth-century fleet. Even if many rowers were part of that workforce when not on campaign, the manpower demands were staggering, especially since the number of adult male citizens reached five to ten thousand only in a few exceptionally large poleis and even in Athens probably never exceeded fifty thousand. Facilities and resources were needed to house, feed, and entertain such a workforce, an effective administration to organize the labor and materials, and a steady income of unprecedented size to finance it all.[66] Moreover, given the trireme's limited capacity to carry supplies, extended operations depended on constant access to coastal supply bases:[67] naval power and control of coastal areas depended on each other.

In all these respects, the potential of all but very few archaic poleis was severely limited. Just as permanent forces of light-armed border guards would have exceeded their resources (above at n. 41), so, too, even large poleis could not afford a permanent specialized war fleet. For occasional naval actions it was sufficient to use transport vessels borrowed from their owners. In fifth-century Athens, however, several unusual circumstances combined to make it possible to build and maintain a large war fleet. Various factors—including knowledge of the causes of the Ionians' failure against Persia, the threat of a massive Persian invasion by land and sea, and the discovery of a new silver mine at Laurium—created a favorable disposition toward naval warfare and provided both the initial stimulus and the funds necessary to build a fleet. After the war of 480/79, the Delian League provided both the necessary resources to maintain this fleet and a wide-flung coastal support network. By the time the Persian danger had vanished and some allies questioned the necessity of this expensive organization, the Athenians had built up their own navy, adjusted their economy and administration, and were determined to hold on to their power, no matter what. Such power depended on continuing access to the League's resources: naval and imperial power were thus interconnected.[68]

Naval Warfare and Society

After the Persian Wars, Athens's imperial role brought about a rapid and comprehensive transformation of economy and society. Although the result of these changes is better visible in the last third of the century, when literary and documentary sources are plentiful, we can make some inferences about causes and beginnings.[69]

A veritable industry must have emerged, encompassing many trades, that focused on building and maintaining warships. The frequent involvement of Athenian hoplites in the city's wars made sure that the manufacturers of arms and armor prospered as well. Major public construction took place especially in Athens and the Piraeus, capped by the building programs on Acropolis and Agora, and the private sector must have experienced a "building boom." Booty and indemnities from wars against Persians and recalcitrant Greek cities, as well as other imperial revenues, brought unprecedented material profits into Attica. Trade and other business activities increased rapidly along with the consolidation of the Athenian sphere of domination: the Piraeus quickly became the central port of the Aegean and far beyond. The labor force probably was mixed; the number of slaves and foreign residents (metics) increased greatly, but by far the largest component must have come from the farming population of rural Attica. As a result, Athens and the Piraeus, connected by the Long Walls, developed into large, densely populated cities with an exceptionally large number of people employed in all kinds of manufacture, industry, and trade, and in the "hotel and entertainment industry."[70]

The "balance sheet of empire" reveals that, despite hardships and setbacks, all Athenians profited greatly from their empire.[71] Economically, socially, politically, and mentally, they adjusted to their city's imperial rule and to the need to be constantly prepared for and frequently involved in war: as Thucydides puts it (1.70), they became activists, restless interventionists and aggressive expansionists. Athenian imperial ideology, too, presented the ideal citizen as incessantly striving to maintain and increase the freedom, power, and rule of his city and emulating the great martial deeds of the ancestors. Even the city's protectress, Athena, now presented herself as a mighty warrior goddess.[72] All this helps explain the extraordinary politicization and militarization of the entire citizen body and their commitment to public service that lasted well over two generations.

Naval Warfare and Democracy

The Athenian system of government changed considerably as a result of conditions that emerged after the Persian Wars.[73] Clearly, though, the great naval victory of Salamis by itself would have been insufficient to engender lasting change. Several allies contributed major fleets to the common war effort; none of them became a democracy. And, as the examples of Corinth, Aegina, and other large island poleis indicate, naval power per se did not necessitate democracy.[74]

The decisive difference, in the case of Athens, was the function assigned to the fleet and the composition of the crews rowing it. As pointed out earlier, naval warfare greatly increased the scope, duration, and frequency of wars. The continuation of the Persian Wars by the Delian League and its transformation into a naval empire turned the fleet into a crucial instrument for Athens's security and domination, made the thetes who mostly rowed this fleet responsible for their community's security and power, and—this is decisive—caused this new role of fleet and thetes to be *not an exception but the rule.* Accordingly, an entire class of citizens, who normally did not count for much, became *permanently indispensable* to their community and thereby acquired social prestige and self-confidence—which made it possible, even necessary, to integrate them politically. Their military ascendance disturbed the traditional interdependence between landownership, social status, military capacity, and political participation. Since this balance could not easily be restored in the social and economic spheres, its restoration on the political level became all the more urgent. Even opponents of democracy eventually recognized this connection, although it continued to be contested on ideological grounds.[75]

Not least the fact that other Greek poleis with strong navies did not develop democracy has prompted some scholars to question the link between democracy and naval power.[76] We know little about how other navies were operated. Even if they were rowed by citizens, however, they were fighting Athens's or the Delian League's wars and thus never assumed the role of permanent importance to their own communities that was typical of the Athenian fleet. In Athens, moreover, special circumstances made it possible to break through traditional class and mental barriers that otherwise might have prevented the involvement of lower-class citizens. In cases of "national emergency," class and status boundaries were often ignored; even slaves, liberated before or after the action, were recruited to supplement the numbers of citizens.[77] The Athenians, too, exposed to existential danger, could not afford to nurture old social prejudices. Once they decided to base their defense against the Persians on the fleet, they had no choice but to call upon all able-bodied citizens, whether noble, farmer-hoplite, or thete, and even to include the metics. During the war of 480/79 and its immediate aftermath, nobody worried about potential consequences of this policy, and then the Delian League offered Athens unique opportunities, too good to decline. After that, there was no way to turn back: the system had proved tremendously successful, and the thetes were to continue to play a crucial military role.

Several additional factors, however, interacted with military change and were necessary to translate it into political change. First, the allies' financial contributions brought much more money into the treasury than was spent on wars. Combined with other imperial revenues, they greatly relieved Athens's military budget, which must have facilitated the—truly revolutionary—decision to introduce pay for certain communal functions.[78]

Second, the imperial city's foreign relations expanded vastly and rapidly, and the agenda of the institutions concerned with this sphere (council, assembly, law courts) multiplied.[79] Their importance and prestige were enhanced, service in them became more demanding, and they needed to be adjusted structurally to their new range of responsibilities. All this was unparalleled elsewhere, inevitably challenged the traditional distribution of power in the community, and raised the question of what role the people should play in shaping and controlling policies that directly affected their lives and future.

Third, navy and empire transformed Athenian society (above at n. 69). Thousands of citizens changed their work habits, way of life, and outlook, from village to city, from local affairs to the polis and its policies. By the 460s the impact of a broad range of changes, massive, accelerating, and interacting with each other, must have been felt everywhere. Vast numbers of Athenians who had been marginalized before now assumed communally important functions. Others whose families had belonged among the hoplites all along but who had lived too far away to participate regularly, now moved close to the political center; they might now be counted as thetes, but their political aspirations remained the same. Overall, this enormous demographic shift in the citizen body cannot have left the political sphere unaffected; new ways had to be found for these citizens to articulate their voice in changed circumstances.[80]

Thus in several essential ways—by militarily empowering the thetes, providing unprecedented financial strength, enhancing importance and prestige of the institutions, and creating a large urban concentration of citizens whose work was important to the community—the empire created conditions that contributed decisively to making democracy possible.

Fourth, the Athenian elite was highly competitive, constantly fighting for influence and power. Such rivalries could result in institutional change, if one faction advocated it in order to gain followers and votes. Cleisthenes' reforms originated in such a constellation, and similar considerations perhaps played a role as well in the political integration of the thetes.[81]

At any rate, reforms introduced in 462 and supplemented by further measures during the next twelve years brought about dramatic changes in the city's government. The power of those institutions that represented the entire demos (assembly, the Council of 500, and the jury courts) was enhanced at the expense of the traditional aristocratic Areopagus Council; the operation of some of these institutions was modified, reflecting increased duties; pay was introduced for certain civic functions, census qualifications reduced for others, and citizenship defined more strictly. The purpose of these measures clearly was to enable all citizens to participate in their city's government and to determine exactly who was to enjoy these privileges.[82] The demos was thereby put fully in charge. Although institutional development continued thereafter,[83] for all practical purposes the middle of the fifth century marks the beginning of full democracy in Athens.[84] The realization of this type of democracy was inextricably linked with naval power and the empire, and therefore was possible only in Athens.[85]

Conclusion

The fifth-century "military revolution," brought about by naval warfare, originated in an extraordinary emergency in the Persian Wars. It resulted in deep and rapid economic, social, mental, and eventually political changes in Athenian society. Such changes, however, were caused not directly by the victories in the Persian Wars, but because through the Delian League and empire the Athenians were able to create an organizational framework that made it possible to maintain large-scale naval power. Adapting to the demands of their city's imperial rule, the Athenian citizens became professionals, in both their military and, after the democratic reforms of 462–450, their political capacity. Military change interacted with social and economic change to bring about political change. As in the case of archaic Sparta, here, too, the military factor assumed primary importance only because the citizens' military role became *permanently and decisively significant* to the community.

Due to the severely limited potential of the Greek polis to enfranchise new citizens and the Athenians' propensity to overextend themselves, their empire collapsed at the end of the fifth century. But the changes it imposed, in interaction with democracy, on Greek warfare were irreversible. The traditional brief, limited, and intermittent wars between individual poleis continued, but henceforth they were of secondary importance: the more significant wars were fought between alliance systems over predominance in Greece and, eventually, for the survival of the independence of Greece. The citizen militias continued to play an important military role, but besides them, and often overshadowing them, professional and specialized troops, mostly mercenaries, acquired rapidly increasing importance. Warfare became ever more endemic, "total," and expensive, vastly exceeding the resources of all but the largest poleis—and even these. Hence those who disposed of great financial resources—tyrants (such as Dionysius I of Syracuse) and foreign potentates (especially the Persian kings and Philip II of Macedon)—assumed an ever more decisive role in military affairs, in the advancement of military technology, and in deciding the fate of the Greek world.[86]

Epilogue: A Different Perspective

I have analyzed the interaction of two major innovations in Greek warfare with economic, social, and political changes. From a long-term perspective, one might distinguish two different developments. One, beginning in the Dark Ages and reaching its climax in fifth-century Athens, concerns the polis as a citizen state and the citizens' role as soldiers. Emerging with the formation of the polis, the concept of citizen-soldier was initially realized on the level of the independent farmers fighting as hoplites; under exceptional circumstances prevailing in

Athens, it was extended to the lower-class citizens rowing the fleet. This development is best explained by a model of interaction between military and economic, social, and political factors that took place largely (although not entirely) within the polis and seems responsible for the cohesion, strength, and political predominance, as well as military superiority, of polis-based Greek societies even in conflicts with seemingly far superior non-Greek states.

The second development had a forerunner in archaic Sparta, reached a first climax in fifth-century Athens, and dominated Greek warfare in the late fifth and fourth centuries. It transcended the structures of the polis, largely depended on outside resources in money and manpower, and eventually overtaxed the capacities of polis-based societies, resulting in the political demise and absorption of Greek poleis into larger territorial empires. This development is best characterized by the notions of the professionalization and specialization of warfare and the militarization of politics. These two developments overlapped, but, essentially, the former belongs in the context of intermittent warfare between poleis, the latter in that of permanent warfare between larger entities: leagues, federations, and empires. From this perspective, fifth-century Athens is a "hybrid," and a crucial transition in Greek history coincides, in the period from the mid–sixth to the mid–fifth century, with the intrusion of foreign imperialism into the Greek world and the subsequent emergence of Greek forms of imperialism.

Notes

1. All dates are B.C. I thank Paul Cartledge for sharing his excellent essay (1996b) with me before publication and for generous comments, and Nathan Rosenstein for valuable suggestions. Because of space limitations, I cite mostly recent publications where the reader will find fuller bibliographies. General works on archaic and classical Greek warfare: Kromayer and Veith 1928; Anderson 1970, 1988; Garlan 1975; Delbrück 1975; Ducrey 1985; Ferrill 1985; see also Pritchett 1971–91; Rich and Shipley 1993; Lloyd 1996.
2. Surveys: Chadwick 1976; Dickinson 1994. War: Snodgrass 1967, chap. 1; Lejeune 1968; Drews 1993.
3. Snodgrass 1971; 1987, chap. 6; 1996; Donlan 1989; Morris 1996a, 1997.
4. E.g., *Iliad* 6.414–27; *Odyssey* 9.39–61; 14.211–75; Nowag 1983; Welwei 1992b; Jackson 1993.
5. Eighth century: Snodgrass 1980; Morris 1998. Polis: Ehrenberg 1969.88–102; Starr 1986; its emergence: Snodgrass 1993b; Raaflaub 1993. Rather than a "city-state," the polis was a community of citizens, a "citizen-state": Runciman 1990.348; Hansen 1993.7–29. Colonization: Boardman and Hammond 1982, chaps. 37–39. *Ethnos:* Snodgrass 1980.42–44; Morgan 1991.
6. Welwei 1992a. Sparta: Cartledge 1979; Finley 1982, chap. 2; Murray 1993, chap. 10.

Neighborhood wars: below n. 23. League: Kagan 1969.9–30. Formation of power: Raaflaub 1990.

7. Surveys: Hornblower 1988; Powell 1988; Lewis et al. 1992.
8. Vernant 1982; Meier 1990a.51–90. Tyranny: Murray 1993, chap. 9.
9. Mulgan 1977.118–38; Polansky 1991.
10. Cartledge 1977.18 n. 60; Snodgrass 1980.98, 100; contra: Garlan 1975.119. Horses: Gschnitzer 1981.38–41. Cavalry: Greenhalgh 1973; Bugh 1988; Spence 1993.
11. E.g., *Politics* 1304a 22–24; Plutarch, *Aristides* 22.1. Pseudo-Xenophon, *Constitution of the Athenians* 1.2; Plato, *Laws* 706c–707a, observe this connection on the factual but not on the evolutionary level: Ceccarelli 1993; van Wees 1995.154–56.
12. Examples: Thucydides 5.66–74, 6.66–71. See Anderson 1970; Pritchett 1985; Hanson 1989, 1991. Cawkwell 1989 presents a different model of hoplite battle; see also Holladay 1982.94–97; Krentz 1985b; Lazenby 1991. His claim that extended fighting preceded the *ōthismos* should be taken seriously; contra: Anderson 1984; Hanson 1989. Krentz (1985b.55–57) explains *ōthismos* differently; cf. Luginbill 1994; Krentz 1994. Light-armed troops: below n. 42.
13. Average: 10 to 20 percent for the losers, 3 to 10 percent for the winners: Krentz 1985a; Strauss 1986.179; Spence 1993.172.
14. 7.9.2; cf. Polybius 13.3.4 with Walbank 1967.416.
15. Dated to the late eighth or early seventh century: discussion and bibliography in Raaflaub 1998a.
16. Garlan 1975.83.
17. Meyer 1937.512–17; Weber 1968.1352, 1359–60; cf. Nilsson 1929. Snodgrass 1964, 1965, 1967, chap. 3; Bryant 1990; Murray 1993, chap. 10; Cartledge 1996b.
18. Snodgrass 1993a; van Wees 1994, 1996.
19. Hanson 1991.63–84; Mitchell 1996.89–90.
20. Hanson 1991.63–67.
21. Hanson 1995, chap. 5; Morris 1996b; Raaflaub 1996a: 150–53, 1997a.
22. E.g., *Iliad* 18.509–40; 11.670–761; Baltrusch 1994.92–99; Raaflaub 1997b. 2–4.
23. Raaflaub 1993.47–48. Army as polis: Garlan 1975.91–92.
24. Raaflaub 1991.223–24; Parker 1997; de Ste. Croix 1972.218–20.
25. Destructiveness of early wars: van Wees 1992.183–99. Territories: de Polignac 1995; Snodgrass 1980.35–40; 1993b.37–39.
26. If only to ride to the battlefield: Greenhalgh 1973; see above n. 10.
27. *Zeugitai:* Whitehead 1981; Rhodes 1981.138. Skirmishers: below n. 42; thetes: below nn. 34, 56. Rome: Thomsen 1980, chap. 5.
28. Snodgrass 1980.99–100, 105–6; cf. Cartledge 1977.26–27; Salmon 1977.85–92. Solon: Andrewes 1982.384–86. Sparta: below n. 54.
29. Raaflaub 1997a.54; cf. Snodgrass 1967.61; 1993a.60–61; 1993b.34–35.
30. Cartledge 1996b.705. Cost: Connor 1988.10 n. 30 (75–100 drachmas); Jackson 1991.229 lists epigraphically attested figures (30 drachmas in late sixth-century Athens, 300 drachmas in fourth-century Thasos). The equivalents given by Plutarch, *Solon* 23.3 (1 sheep = 1 drachma = 1 *medimnos* [a grain measure; cf. Rhodes 1981. 141–42]) are problematic (Welwei 1992a.181–82); W. T. Loomis suggests for

Connor's figure "7–10 goats or 25–33 piglets; less certain would be 2–4 cattle or 5–10 sheep" (personal communication; cf. Loomis forthcoming).

31. As was usual again much later (but for different reasons: to increase mobility): Snodgrass 1967, chap. 4. Unevenness of early equipment: Snodgrass 1965.112–13; cf. now Storch 1998. Of course, reality may often have differed from the ideal, and the back of the phalanx been less heavily armed than the front.

32. Distribution of spoils: Pritchett 1971–91, Vol. 5. 375–401. It seems unlikely that all equipment retrieved by the victors from the battlefield went to the state and was dedicated to the gods (thus Connor 1988.16; cf. Jackson 1991).

33. Snodgrass 1965.114; 1980.107; Cartledge 1977.23; Starr 1982.423; Hanson 1995.411.

34. Similarly, Donlan 1997; cf. Hanson 1995.209. Thetes: *Odyssey* 11.489–91; 18.356–75; cf. *Iliad* 21.441–52; Finley 1977.57–58.

35. Ruschenbusch 1985; cf. below n. 50.

36. Cartledge 1996b.705.

37. Snodgrass 1965.114–16, 120–22; Cartledge 1977.23–24.

38. Snodgrass 1987.173–74; Ober 1991; Mitchell 1996.95–101.

39. See below at n. 77 for an obvious example.

40. De Romilly 1968; Foxhall 1993; Snodgrass 1967.62: a "game of agricultural poker."

41. Recent discussion: de Ste. Croix 1972.190–96; Holladay 1982.97–99, 103; Ober 1985a.33–35, 191–92; 1991; Anderson 1988.685–86.

42. Van Wees 1995.162–65.

43. Bugh 1988; Spence 1993; Best 1969; Anderson 1970.

44. Tyrtaeus 12 West; see Spence 1993.165–79 and the bibliography cited in Raaflaub 1994.138–42.

45. Connor 1988.18–29; cf. Burkert 1983.47; Meier 1990b.563–78; Cartledge 1996b.697–702.

46. Ducrey 1968.112; cf. above n. 13; Kiechle 1958. Destructiveness of early wars: above n. 25. Prestige, of course, did not exclude material interests; cf. Herodotus 1.82.

47. Hanson 1995, esp. chap. 5.

48. Rhodes 1981.137–46; Welwei 1992a.180–83.

49. So too de Ste. Croix, as cited in Rhodes 1981.143, 145; Jameson 1992.145; Welwei 1992a.182–83; Foxhall 1997.129–31. Connor 1987.47–49 offers a different solution. Although most scholars now think that *zeugitēs* refers to military function (above n.31), the zeugite property limit is set impossibly high for a broad-based hoplite class. My doubts, briefly, are based on the following considerations. In order to produce at least 200 *medimnoi* (probably not, as Aristotle [*Const. of the Athenians* 7.4] suggests, in a combination of barley and wine but rather in wheat; for sources and discussion, see Rhodes 1981.145; Welwei 1992a.180 n.113, and esp. Foxhall 1997.130–31), a zeugite's property needed to comprise at least ten hectars (ca. 25 acres; Ruschenbusch 1995.440-43 [with one quarter left fallow]; cf. Foxhall 1997.130 [8–13 hectars]; Starr 1977.154–56 [12 hectars]; Hignett 1952.100 n.10 [following De Sanctis and Beloch: 17.4 hectars = 43 acres]; French 1964.20–21 [even more]). Compared with the generally assumed size of the average Greek

family or hoplite farm (9–13 acres: cf. Ruschenbusch 1995.442; Hanson 1995.181–201; Welwei 1992a.183 n.120), even this minimal estimate puts the Athenian zeugites on the level of well-to-do farmers (so too Foxhall 1997.131). Given, however, that cultivable land in Attica is calculated at between 65,000 and 96,000 hectars (Ruschenbusch 1995.441 [64,800]; Starr 1977.155 [69,000], Garnsey 1988, ch. 6 [84–96,000]), that the members of the higher census classes owned considerably more land, and that the Athenian hoplite army counted 9,000 men at Marathon and 8,000 at Plataea (Beloch 1886.60), this census figure cannot be right (even if we allow for mitigating factors, such as a fair number of father-son pairs or settlement of some Athenian hoplites outside of Attica already at the time of the Persian Wars). Hence, if *zeugitēs* designates hoplite, the zeugite census of 200 *medimnoi* is far too high and must represent an inference from much later and perhaps not directly pertinent data; or else, if the census figure is correct, the zeugites are not identical with the hoplite class whose property qualification then probably was much lower, if one existed at all; in terms of the timocratic system, however, this would relegate most hoplites to the thetic class, which, given the values and ideologies mentioned above, is plainly impossible. The conclusion presented in the text (**at n.49**) therefore seems inevitable. This problem needs to be investigated more thoroughly.

50. Ruschenbusch 1995.436–39: more than half of all poleis were too small to field meaningful hoplite armies or, because of their location, did not need one. The census for hoplites in Boeotian Orchomenos was approximately 45 *medimnoi*; in many places such requirements may have fluctuated (cf. Hanson 1995.210–11).

51. Havelock 1978, chap. 7; Gschnitzer 1991; Raaflaub 1997b with bibliography.

52. Van Wees 1992 (index under "idealization"); 1995.165–70. Incompatible: Bryant 1990.492.

53. Aristocracy: e.g., Starr 1977, chaps. 6, 8; Donlan 1980; Stein-Hölkeskamp 1989. Solonian Athens offers a good example of conflict and compromise: Andrewes 1982.375–91; Murray 1993, chap. 11; Raaflaub 1996b. Frost 1984 argues that the Athenian hoplites' role was very limited before the late sixth century.

54. See n. 6 and Raaflaub 1993.64–68 with bibliography; Cartledge 1996a.

55. Below at n. 75.

56. Morris 1996b; Robinson 1997. I consider it doubtful that the thetes shared full political rights in Cleisthenes' system of the late, let alone in Solon's in the early, sixth century: Raaflaub 1997c; cf. Rhodes 1981.141; Bleicken 1994.23–24.

57. Solon, fr. 4 West (*eunomia*); *isonomia:* Raaflaub 1995.49–51; 1996a.143–45. *Isos* versus *homoios:* Cartledge 1996a.

58. Stein-Hölkeskamp 1989.94–103; Meier 1990a, chaps. 3–4; Gehrke 1993, and the bibliography in Raaflaub 1993.68–75. See also van Wees 1995.169–70. Crisis (best known from Athens): Welwei 1992a.150–61, and above n. 53.

59. Ridley 1979; Hanson 1995, chap. 8; 1996. Oligarchy: Raaflaub 1994.139–40 with bibliography.

60. Naval warfare: Rodgers 1937; Morrison and Williams 1968. Trireme: Morrison and Coates 1986; Wallinga 1993. Battle: Herodotus 6.7–17.

61. Hanson forthcoming. Frequency: Garlan 1975.15. Brutality: Ducrey 1968; Karavites 1982; Rosivach forthcoming. Strategy: Ober 1985b; Starr 1989, chap. 3; Spence 1990.

62. Gabrielsen 1994, chaps. 5–6. Samos: Meiggs 1972.192. Parthenon: Stanier 1953. Daily wages: one-half to one drachma (1 talent = 6000 drachmas).

63. Amit 1965; Jordan 1975; Rosivach 1985; van Wees 1995.160–61. Metics: Whitehead 1977.84–86. Slaves: Welwei 1974.65–104.

64. Thomsen 1964; Kallet-Marx 1993, 1994. Trierarchy: Gabrielsen 1994.

65. Meiggs and Lewis 1988, no. 33. Ruschenbusch 1979.153–56; Strauss 1986.179–82; Hansen 1988.14–28.

66. Materials: Morrison and Coates 1986, chap. 10; Meiggs 1982, chap. 5; Finley 1982.53–57. Maintenance: Blackman 1968; Garland 1987.95–100; Gabrielsen 1994, chap. 6. Administration: Jordan 1975, pt. 1. Funding: above n. 64. Number of citizens: Ruschenbusch 1985 and esp. 1983a, 1983b. Athens: Hansen 1988.7–10; French 1993.

67. Gabrielsen 1994.6.

68. Ionian Revolt and Persian Wars: Boardman et al. 1988, chaps. 8–11. Laurium: Herodotus 7.144. Delian League: Meiggs 1972; Rhodes 1992b.

69. Surveys: Davies 1992a, 1992b; Raaflaub 1998b.

70. Demography: Frost 1976.70–71; Garland 1987.59–61; Hansen 1988.7–13. Industry and trade: French 1964; Garland 1987. 83–95; Gabrielsen 1994, chaps. 6–7. Building and city planning: Boersma 1970, chap. 5; Hoepfner and Schwandner 1994.22–50. Population of Athens: 36,000 to 45,000 (Drögemüller 1969.97); up to 50,000: Kolb 1984.83 (75 percent occupied in the secondary sector); Piraeus: above 30,000 (Garland 1987.58).

71. Meiggs 1972, chap. 14; Finley 1982, chap. 3; Schmitz 1988.

72. Herington 1963; Raaflaub 1994, forthcoming.

73. Fornara and Samons 1991, chap. 2; Rhodes 1992a; Morris and Raaflaub 1997.

74. Raaflaub 1995.35; 1997c.44–50, 95–97; cf. Bleicken 1994.52; contra: Bleicken 1995.

75. Above n. 11; cf. Strauss 1996; Raaflaub 1994.138–44; van Wees 1995.158–60. Thetes as crews: above n. 63.

76. Beloch 1922.134–35; Amit 1965.57–71; Ceccarelli 1993. Van Wees 1995.157–62 uses other arguments.

77. Welwei 1974.

78. Aristotle, Constitution of the Athenians 27.3–4; Finley 1982.48–51; Schmitz 1988.57–70. Income: Kallet 1998.

79. Schuller 1984.88–90; cf. Ruschenbusch 1979.15–17.

80. See above at nn. 70 (demography), 49 (hoplites); Frost 1976.72; Davies 1992b.291–302.

81. Thus Eder 1997, but see Raaflaub 1995.44–46. Cleisthenes: Herodotus 5.66.2.

82. Fornara and Samons 1991.58–75; Rhodes 1992a.67–77; Bleicken 1994.43–46; Raaflaub 1997c. 48–50, 97–101.

83. Eder 1995, 1997.

84. On the political exclusion of women and reliance on slaves, common to ancient societies and far beyond, see Strauss 1997.

85. Bleicken 1994.47, 64.
86. Militias versus mercenaries: Burckhardt 1996. "Total" warfare: Ober 1985a, chap. 2. Specialized troops: Best 1969; cavalry: above n. 9. See generally, Anderson 1970; Garlan 1994; Austin 1994; Hamilton 1995. See further Hamilton, this volume.

Bibliography

Amit, Moshe. 1965. *Athens and the Sea: A Study in Athenian Sea Power.* Brussels: Latomus.

Anderson, John K. 1970. *Military Theory and Practice in the Age of Xenophon.* Berkeley and Los Angeles: University of California Press.

———. 1984. "Hoplites and Heresies: A Note." *Journal of Hellenic Studies* 104, 152.

———. 1988. "Wars and Military Science: Greece." In Grant and Kitzinger 1988, Vol. 1.679–701.

Andrewes, Antony. 1982. "The Growth of the Athenian State." In Boardman and Hammond 1982.360–91.

Austin, Michael M. 1994. "Society and Economy [in the Fourth Century]." In Lewis et al. 1994.527–64.

Baltrusch, Ernst. 1994. *Symmachie und Spondai: Untersuchungen zum griechischen Völkerrecht der archaischen und klassischen Zeit, 8.-5. Jh.v.Chr.* Berlin: De Gruyter.

Beloch, Karl Julius. 1886. *Die Bevölkerung der griechisch-römischen Welt.* Leipzig: Duncker und Humblot. Reprint Rome: L'Erma, 1968.

———. 1922. *Griechische Geschichte,* Vol. 2, pt. 2. 2d ed. Berlin: De Gruyter. Reprint, 1931.

Best, J. G. P. 1969. *Thracian Peltasts and Their Influence on Greek Warfare.* Groningen: Wolters-Noordhoff.

Blackman, David J. 1968. "The Ship-sheds." In Morrison and Williams 1968.181–92.

Bleicken, Jochen. 1994. *Die athenische Demokratie.* 2d ed. Paderborn: Schöningh.

———. 1995. "Wann begann die athenische Demokratie?" *Historische Zeitschrift* 260, 337–64.

Boardman, John, and N. G. L. Hammond, eds. 1982. *The Cambridge Ancient History.* Vol. 3. pt. 3, *The Expansion of the Greek World, Eighth to Sixth Centuries B.C.* 2d ed. Cambridge: Cambridge University Press.

Boardman, John, N. G. L. Hammond, D. M. Lewis, and Martin Ostwald, eds. 1988. *The Cambridge Ancient History.* Vol. 4, *Persia, Greece and the Western Mediterranean c. 525 to 479 B.C.* 2d ed. Cambridge: Cambridge University Press.

Boedeker, Deborah, and Kurt Raaflaub, eds. 1998. *Democracy, Empire, and the Arts in Fifth-Century Athens.* Center for Hellenic Studies Coll. 2. Cambridge, Mass.: Harvard University Press.

Boersma, J. S. 1970. *Athenian Building Policy from 561/0–405/4 B.C.* Groningen: Wolters-Noordhoff.

Bryant, J. M. 1990. "Military Technology and Socio-Cultural Change in the Ancient Greek City." *Sociological Review* 38, 484–516.

Bugh, Glenn R. 1988. *The Horsemen of Athens.* Princeton, N.J.: Princeton University Press.

Burckhardt, Leonhard. 1996. *Bürger und Soldaten. Aspekte der politischen und militärischen Rolle athenischer Bürger im Kriegswesen des 4. Jahrhunderts v. Chr. Historia* Einzelschriften 101. Stuttgart: Steiner.

Burkert, Walter. 1983. *Homo necans: The Anthropology of Ancient Greek Sacrificial Ritual and Myth.* Translated by Peter Bing. Berkeley and Los Angeles: University of California Press.

Cartledge, Paul. 1977. "Hoplites and Heroes: Sparta's Contribution to the Technique of Ancient Warfare." *Journal of Hellenic Studies* 97, 11–27.

——. 1979. *Sparta and Lakonia: A Regional History 1300–362 B.C.* London: Routledge and Kegan Paul.

——. 1996a. "Comparatively Equal." In Ober and Hedrick 1996.175–85.

——. 1996b. "La nascita degli opliti e l'organizzazione militare." In Settis 1996.681–714.

Cawkwell, George L. 1989. "Orthodoxy and Hoplites." *Classical Quarterly,* n.s. 39, 375–89.

Ceccarelli, Paola. 1993. "Sans thalassocratie, pas de démocratie? Le rapport entre thalassocratie et démocratie à Athènes dans la discussion du Ve et IVe siècle av. J.-C." *Historia* 42, 444–70.

Chadwick, John. 1976. *The Mycenaean World.* Cambridge: Cambridge University Press.

Connor, W. R. 1987. "Tribes, Festivals and Processions: Civic Ceremonial and Political Manipulation in Archaic Greece." *Journal of Hellenic Studies* 107, 40–50.

——. 1988. "Early Greek Land Warfare as Symbolic Expression." *Past & Present* 119, 3–29.

Davies, John K. 1992a. "Greece after the Persian Wars." In Lewis et al. 1992.15–33.

——. 1992b. "Society and Economy." In Lewis et al. 1992.287–305.

Delbrück, Hans. 1975. *Warfare in Antiquity.* Translated by Walter J. Renfroe Jr. Lincoln: University of Nebraska Press.

Dickinson, Oliver. 1994. *The Aegean Bronze Age.* Cambridge: Cambridge University Press.

Donlan, Walter. 1980. *The Aristocratic Ideal in Ancient Greece.* Lawrence, Kans.: Coronado Press.

——. 1989. "The Pre-State Community in Greece." *Symbolae Osloenses* 64, 5–29.

——. 1997. "The Relations of Power in the Pre-State and Early State Polities." In Mitchell and Rhodes 1997.39–48.

Drews, Robert. 1993. *The End of the Bronze Age: Changes in Warfare and the Catastrophe ca. 1200 BC.* Princeton, N.J.: Princeton University Press.

Drögemüller, Hans-Peter. 1969. *Syrakus: Zur Topographie und Geschichte einer griechischen Stadt. Gymnasium* Beiheft 6. Heidelberg.

Ducrey, Pierre. 1968. *Le traitement des prisonniers de guerre en Grèce ancienne.* Paris: de Boccard.

——. 1985. *Warfare in Ancient Greece.* Translated by Janet Lloyd. New York: Schocken Books.

Eder, Walter. 1995. "Die athenische Demokratie im 4. Jh. v. Chr.: Krise oder Vollendung?" In *Die athenische Demokratie im 4. Jahrhundert v. Chr. Vollendung oder Verfall einer Verfassungsform?* Edited by Walter Eder, 11–28. Stuttgart: Steiner.

——. 1997. "Aristocrats and the Coming of Athenian Democracy." In Morris and Raaflaub 1997.105–40.

Ehrenberg, Victor. 1969. *The Greek State.* 2d ed. London: Methuen.

Ferrill, Arther. 1985. *The Origins of War from the Stone Age to Alexander the Great.* London: Thames and Hudson.

Finley, Moses I. 1977. *The World of Odysseus.* 2d ed. London: Chatto and Windus.

——. 1982. *Economy and Society in Ancient Greece.* New York: Viking.

Fisher, Nick, and Hans van Wees, eds. 1998. *Archaic Greece: New Approaches and New Evidence.* Swansea and London: Classical Press of Wales and Duckworth.

Fornara, Charles W., and Loren J. Samons II. 1991. *Athens from Cleisthenes to Pericles.* Berkeley and Los Angeles: University of California Press.

Foxhall, Lin. 1993. "Farming and Fighting in Ancient Greece." In Rich and Shipley 1993.134–45.

——. 1997. "A View from the Top: Evaluating the Solonian Property Classes." In Mitchell and Rhodes 1997.113–36.

French, Alfred. 1964. *The Growth of the Athenian Economy.* London: Routledge and Paul.

——. 1993. "The Population of Fifth-Century Athens." *Ancient History: Resources for Teachers* 23, 74–94.

Frost, Frank J. 1976. "Tribal Politics and the Civic State." *American Journal of Ancient History* 1, 66–75.

——. 1984. "The Athenian Military before Cleisthenes." *Historia* 33, 283–94.

Gabrielsen, Vincent. 1994. *Financing the Athenian Fleet: Public Taxation and Social Relations.* Baltimore, Md.: Johns Hopkins University Press.

Garlan, Yvon. 1975. *War in the Ancient World: A Social History.* Translated by Janet Lloyd. London: Chatto and Windus.

——. 1994. "Warfare [in the Fourth Century B.C.]." In Lewis et al. 1994.678–92.

Garland, Robert. 1987. *The Piraeus from the Fifth to the First Century B.C.* Ithaca, N.Y.: Cornell University Press.

Garnsey, Peter. 1988. *Famine and Food Supply in the Graeco-Roman World: Responses to Risk and Crisis.* Cambridge: Cambridge University Press.

Gehrke, Hans-Joachim. 1993. "Konflikt und Gesetz: Überlegungen zur frühen Polis." In *Colloquium aus Anlass des 80. Geburtstages von Alfred Heuss,* edited by Jochen Bleicken, 49–67. Frankfurter Althistorische Studien 13. Kallmünz: M. Lassleben.

Grant, Michael, and Rachel Kitzinger, eds. 1988. *Civilization of the Ancient Mediterranean: Greece and Rome.* 3 vols. New York: Scribner's.

Greenhalgh, P. A. L. 1973. *Early Greek Warfare: Horsemen and Chariots in the Homeric and Archaic Ages.* Cambridge: Cambridge University Press.

Gschnitzer, Fritz. 1981. *Griechische Sozialgeschichte von der mykenischen bis zum Ausgang der klassischen Zeit.* Stuttgart: Steiner.

——. 1991. "Zur homerischen Staats- und Gesellschaftsordnung: Grundcharakter und geschichtliche Stellung." In Latacz 1991.182–204.

Hamilton, Charles. 1995. "From Archidamus to Alexander: The Revolution in Greek Warfare." *Naval War College Review* 48.1, 84–95.

Hansen, Mogens H. 1988. *Three Studies in Athenian Demography.* The Royal Danish Academy of Sciences and Letters, Meddelelser 56. Copenhagen: Munksgaard.

——, ed. 1993. *The Ancient Greek City-State.* The Royal Danish Academy of Sciences and Letters, Meddelelser 67. Copenhagen: Munksgaard.

Hanson, Victor D. 1989. *The Western Way of War: Infantry Battle in Classical Greece.* New York: Oxford University Press.

——. 1995. *The Other Greeks: The Family Farm and the Agrarian Roots of Western Civilization.* New York: Free Press.

——. 1996. "Hoplites into Democrats: The Changing Ideology of Athenian Infantry." In Ober and Hedrick 1996.289–312.

——. Forthcoming. "Democratic Warfare." In McCann and Strauss forthcoming.

——, ed. 1991. *Hoplites: The Classical Greek Battle Experience.* London: Routledge.

Havelock, Eric A. 1978. *The Greek Concept of Justice from Its Shadow in Homer to Its Substance in Plato.* Cambridge, Mass.: Harvard University Press.

Herington, C. John. 1963. "Athena in Athenian Literature and Cult." In *Parthenos and Parthenon,* edited by G. T. W. Hooker. *Greece and Rome* 10, suppl., 61–73.

Hignett, Charles. 1952. *A History of the Athenian Constitution to the End of the Fifth Century* B.C. Oxford: Clarendon Press.

Hoepfner, Wolfram, and Ernst-Ludwig Schwandner. 1994. *Haus und Stadt im klassischen Griechenland.* 2d ed. Munich: Deutscher Kunstverlag.

Holladay, A. J. 1982. "Hoplites and Heresies." *Journal of Hellenic Studies* 102, 94–103.

Hornblower, Simon. 1988. "Greece: The History of the Classical Period." In *The Oxford History of the Classical World,* Vol. 1: *Greece and the Hellenistic World,* edited by John Boardman, Jasper Griffin, and Oswyn Murray, 118–49. Oxford: Oxford University Press.

Jackson, Alastar. 1991. "Hoplites and the Gods: The Dedication of Captured Arms and Armour." In Hanson 1991.228–49.

——. 1993. "War and Raids for Booty in the World of Odysseus." In Rich and Shipley 1993.64–76.

Jameson, Michael H. 1992. "Agricultural Labor in Ancient Greece." In *Agriculture in Ancient Greece,* edited by Berit Wells, 135–46. Stockholm: Paul Åströms Förlag.

Jordan, Borimir. 1975. *The Athenian Navy in the Classical Period.* Berkeley and Los Angeles: University of California Press.

Kagan, Donald. 1969. *The Outbreak of the Peloponnesian War.* Ithaca, N.Y.: Cornell University Press.

Kallet (-Marx), Lisa. 1993. *Money, Expense, and Naval Power in Thucydides'* History *1–5.24.* Berkeley and Los Angeles: University of California Press.

——. 1994. "Money Talks: Rhetor, Demos, and the Resources of the Athenian Empire." In Osborne and Hornblower 1994.227–51.

——. 1998. "Accounting for Culture in Fifth-Century Athens." In Boedeker and Raaflaub 1998.43–58.

Karavites, Panayotis. 1982. *Capitulations and Greek Interstate Relations.* Hypomnemata 71. Göttingen: Vandenhoeck and Ruprecht.

Kiechle, Franz. 1958. "Zur Humanität in der Kriegführung der griechischen Staaten." *Historia* 7, 129–56.

Kinzl, Konrad H., ed. 1995. *Demokratia: Der Weg zur Demokratie bei den Griechen.* Wege der Forschung 657. Darmstadt: Wissenschaftliche Buchgesellschaft.

Kolb, Frank. 1984. *Die Stadt im Altertum.* Munich: Beck.

Krentz, Peter. 1985a. "Casualties in Hoplite Battles." *Greek, Roman and Byzantine Studies* 26, 13–20.

———. 1985b. "The Nature of Hoplite Battle." *Classical Antiquity* 4, 50–61.

———. 1994. "Continuing the *Othismos* on *Othismos*." *Ancient History Bulletin* 8, 45–49.

Kromayer, Johannes, and Georg Veith. 1928. *Heerwesen und Kriegführung der Griechen und Römer*. Handbuch der Altertumswissenschaft, Vol. 4.3.2. Munich: Beck.

Latacz, Joachim, ed. 1991. *Zweihundert Jahre Homer-Forschung: Rückblick und Ausblick*. Coll. Rauricum 2. Stuttgart: Teubner.

Lazenby, John F. 1991. "The Killing Zone." In Hanson 1991.87–109.

Lejeune, Michel. 1968. "La civilisation mycénienne et la guerre." In Vernant 1968.31–51.

Lewis, David M., John Boardman, John K. Davies, and Martin Ostwald, eds. 1992. *The Cambridge Ancient History*. Vol. 5, *The Fifth Century B.C.* 2d ed. Cambridge: Cambridge University Press.

Lewis, David M., John Boardman, Simon Hornblower, and Martin Ostwald, eds. 1994. *The Cambridge Ancient History*. Vol. 6, *The Fourth Century B.C.* 2d ed. Cambridge: Cambridge University Press.

Lloyd, Alan B., ed. 1996. *Battle in Antiquity*. Swansea and London: Classical Press of Wales and Duckworth.

Loomis, William T. Forthcoming. *Talents to Chalkoi: A Catalogue of Athenian Monetary Figures*. Ann Arbor, Mich.: University of Michigan Press.

Luginbill, R. D. 1994. "*Othismos:* The Importance of the Mass-Shove in Hoplite Warfare." *Phoenix* 48, 51–61.

McCann, David, and Barry S. Strauss, eds. Forthcoming. *Democracy at War: The Peloponnesian War and the Korean War*. Washington, D.C.: Wilson Center Press.

Meier, Christian. 1990a. *The Greek Discovery of Politics*. Translated by David McLintock. Cambridge, Mass.: Harvard University Press.

———. 1990b. "Die Rolle des Krieges im klassischen Athen." *Historische Zeitschrift* 251, 555–605.

Meiggs, Russell. 1972. *The Athenian Empire*. Oxford: Clarendon Press.

———. 1982. *Trees and Timber in the Ancient Mediterranean World*. Oxford: Clarendon Press.

Meiggs, Russell, and David Lewis. 1988. *A Selection of Greek Historical Inscriptions to the End of the Fifth Century B.C.* Rev. ed. Oxford: Clarendon Press.

Meyer, Eduard. 1937. *Geschichte des Altertums*. Vol. 3. 2d ed. Stuttgart: Cotta.

Mitchell, Lynette, and Peter J. Rhodes, eds. 1997. *The Development of the Polis in Archaic Greece*. London: Routledge.

Mitchell, Stephen. 1996. "Hoplite Warfare in Ancient Greece." In Lloyd 1996.87–105.

Morgan, Catherine. 1991. "Ethnicity and Early Greek States: Historical and Material Perspectives." *Proceedings of the Cambridge Philological Society* 37, 131–63.

Morris, Ian. 1996a. "Periodization and the Heroes: Inventing a Dark Age." In *Inventing Classical Culture?* Edited by Mark Golden and Peter Toohey, 96–131. London: Routledge.

———. 1996b. "The Strong Principle of Equality and the Archaic Origin of Greek Democracy." In Ober and Hedrick 1996.19–48.

——. 1997. "Homer and the Iron Age." In Morris and Powell 1997.535–59.

——. 1998. "Archaeology and Archaic Greek History." In Fisher and van Wees 1998.1–91.

Morris, Ian, and Barry Powell, eds. 1997. *A New Companion to Homer*. Leiden: Brill.

Morris, Ian, and Kurt Raaflaub, eds. 1997. *Democracy 2500? Questions and Challenges.* Archaeological Institute of America, Colloquia and Conference Papers 2. Dubuque, Iowa: Kendall/Hunt.

Morrison, John S., and J. F. Coates. 1986. *The Athenian Trireme: The History and Reconstruction of an Ancient Greek Warship.* Cambridge: Cambridge University Press.

Morrison, John S., and R. T. Williams. 1968. *Greek Oared Ships, 900–322 B.C.* Cambridge: Cambridge University Press.

Mulgan, R. G. 1977. *Aristotle's Political Theory.* Oxford: Clarendon Press.

Murray, Oswyn. 1993. *Early Greece.* 2d ed. Cambridge, Mass.: Harvard University Press.

Murray, Oswyn, and Simon Price, eds. 1990. *The Greek City: From Homer to Alexander.* Oxford: Clarendon Press.

Nilsson, Martin. 1929. "Die Hoplitentaktik und das Staatswesen." *Klio* 22, 240–49. Reprinted in Martin Nilsson, *Opuscula selecta*, Vol. 2, 897–907. Lund: Gleerup.

Nowag, Werner. 1983. *Raub und Beute in der archaischen Zeit der Griechen.* Frankfurt am Main: Haag and Herchen.

Ober, Josiah. 1985a. *Fortress Attica: Defense of the Athenian Land Frontier, 404–322 B.C. Mnemosyne* supplement 84. Leiden: Brill.

——. 1985b. "Thucydides, Pericles, and the Strategy of Defense." In *The Craft of the Ancient Historian: Essays in Honor of Chester G. Starr,* edited by John W. Eadie and Josiah Ober, 171–88. Lanham, Md.: University Press of America.

——. 1991. "Hoplites and Obstacles." In Hanson 1991.173–96.

Ober, Josiah, and Charles Hedrick, eds. 1996. *Demokratia: A Conversation on Democracies, Ancient and Modern.* Princeton, N.J.: Princeton University Press.

Osborne, Robin, and Simon Hornblower, eds. 1994. *Ritual, Finance, Politics. Athenian Democratic Accounts Presented to David Lewis.* Oxford: Clarendon Press.

Parker, Victor. 1997. *Untersuchungen zum Lelantischen Krieg und verwandten Problemen der frühgriechischen Geschichte. Historia* Einzelschr.109. Stuttgart: Steiner.

Polansky, Ronald. 1991. "Aristotle on Political Change." In *A Companion to Aristotle's Politics,* edited by David Keyt and Fred D. Miller, 323–45. Oxford: Blackwell.

Polignac, François de. 1995. *Cults, Territory, and the Origins of the Greek City-State.* Translated by Janet Lloyd. Chicago: University of Chicago Press.

Powell, Anton. 1988. *Athens and Sparta: Constructing Greek Political and Social History from 478 B.C.* London: Routledge.

Pritchett, William K. 1971–91. *The Greek State at War.* 5 vols. Berkeley and Los Angeles: University of California Press.

——. 1985. "The Pitched Battle." In Pritchett 1971–91, Vol. 4, 1–93.

Raaflaub, Kurt A. 1990. "Expansion und Machtbildung in frühen Polis-Systemen." In *Staat und Staatlichkeit in der frühen römischen Republik,* edited by Walter Eder, 511–45. Stuttgart: Steiner.

——. 1991. "Homer und die Geschichte des 8. Jh.s v. Chr." In Latacz 1991.205–56.

——. 1993. "Homer to Solon: The Rise of the Polis (the Written Evidence)." In Hansen 1993.41–105.

——. 1994. "Democracy, Power, and Imperialism in Fifth-Century Athens." In *Athenian Political Thought and the Reconstruction of American Democracy,* edited by J. Peter Euben, John R. Wallach, and Josiah Ober, 103–46. Ithaca, N.Y.: Cornell University Press.

——. 1995. "Einleitung und Bilanz: Kleisthenes, Ephialtes und die Begründung der Demokratie." In Kinzl 1995.1–54.

——. 1996a. "Equalities and Inequalities in Athenian Democracy." In Ober and Hedrick 1996.139–74.

——. 1996b. "Solone, la nuova Atene e l'emergere della politica." In Settis 1996.1035–81.

——. 1997a. "Citizens, Soldiers, and the Evolution of the Early Greek Polis." In Mitchell and Rhodes 1997.49–59.

——. 1997b. "Politics and Interstate Relations in the World of Early Greek *Poleis:* Homer and Beyond." *Antichthon* 31, 1–27.

——. 1997c. "Power in the Hands of the People: Foundations of Athenian Democracy," "The Thetes and Democracy." In Morris and Raaflaub 1997.31–66, 87–103.

——. 1998a. "A Historian's Headache: How to Read 'Homeric Society'?" In Fisher and van Wees 1998.169–93.

——. 1998b. "The Transformation of Athens in the Fifth Century." In Boedeker and Raaflaub 1998.15–41.

——. Forthcoming. "Father of All, Destroyer of All: War in Late Fifth-Century Athenian Discourse." In McCann and Strauss forthcoming.

Rhodes, Peter J. 1981. *A Commentary on the Aristotelian* Athenaion Politeia. Oxford: Clarendon Press.

——. 1992a. "The Athenian Revolution." In Lewis et al. 1992.62–95.

——. 1992b. "The Delian League to 449 B.C." In Lewis et al. 1992.34–61.

Rich, John, and Graham Shipley, eds. 1993. *War and Society in the Greek World.* London: Routledge.

Ridley, Ronald T. 1979. "The Hoplite as Citizen: Athenian Military Institutions in their Social Context." *L'Antiquité classique* 48, 508–48.

Robinson, Eric. 1997. *The First Democracies: Early Popular Government Outside Athens. Historia* Einzelschr.107. Stuttgart: Steiner.

Rodgers, William L. 1937. *Greek and Roman Naval Warfare.* Annapolis, Md.: U.S. Naval Institute. Repr. 1964.

Romilly, Jacqueline de. 1968. "Guerre et paix entre cités." In Vernant 1968.207–20.

Rosivach, Vincent. 1985. "Manning the Athenian Fleet." *American Journal of Ancient History* 10 (published 1993), 41–66.

——. Forthcoming. "Enslaving *Barbaroi* and the Athenian Ideology of Slavery." Forthcoming in *Historia.*

Runciman, W. G. 1990. "Doomed to Extinction: The *Polis* as an Evolutionary Dead-End." In Murray and Price 1990.347–67.

Ruschenbusch, Eberhard. 1979. *Athenische Innenpolitik im 5. Jh. v. Chr. Ideologie oder Pragmatismus?* Bamberg: aku-Verlag.

——. 1983a. "Das Machtpotential der Bündner im ersten athenischen Seebund (Überlegungen zu Thukydides 1,99,2)." *Zeitschrift für Papyrologie und Epigraphik* 53, 144–48.

——. 1983b. "Tribut und Bürgerzahl im ersten athenischen Seebund." *Zeitschrift für Papyrologie und Epigraphik* 53, 125–43.

——. 1985. "Die Zahl der griechischen Staaten und Arealgrösse und Bürgerzahl der 'Normalpolis.'" *Zeitschrift für Papyrologie und Epigraphik* 59, 253–63.

——. 1995. "Zur Verfassungsgeschichte Griechenlands." In Kinzl 1995.432–45.

Ste. Croix, G. E. M. de. 1972. *The Origins of the Peloponnesian War.* Ithaca, N.Y.: Cornell University Press.

Salmon, J. 1977. "Political Hoplites?" *Journal of Hellenic Studies* 97, 84–101.

Schmitz, Winfried. 1988. *Wirtschaftliche Prosperität, soziale Integration und die Seebundpolitik Athens.* Munich: tuduv Verlag.

Schuller, Wolfgang. 1984. "Wirkungen des Ersten Attischen Seebunds auf die Herausbildung der athenischen Demokratie." In J. M. Balcer et al., *Studien zum Attischen Seebund*, 87–101. Xenia 8. Konstanz: Universitätsverlag.

Settis, Salvatore, ed. 1996. *I Greci*, Vol. 2. pt. 1. Turin: Einaudi.

Snodgrass, Anthony M. 1964. *Early Greek Armour and Weapons from the End of the Bronze Age to 600 B.C.* Edinburgh: University Press.

——. 1965. "The Hoplite Reform and History." *Journal of Hellenic Studies* 85, 110–22.

——. 1967. *Arms and Armour of the Greeks.* London: Thames and Hudson.

——. 1971. *The Dark Age of Greece. An Archaeological Survey of the Eleventh to the Eighth Centuries BC.* Edinburgh: University Press.

——. 1980. *Archaic Greece: The Age of Experiment.* Berkeley and Los Angeles: University of California Press.

——. 1987. *An Archaeology of Greece: The Present State and Future Scope of a Discipline.* Sather Classical Lectures 53. Berkeley and Los Angeles: University of California Press.

——. 1993a. "The 'Hoplite Reform' Revisited." *Dialogues d'histoire ancienne* 19, 47–61.

——. 1993b. "The Rise of the *Polis:* The Archaeological Evidence." In Hansen 1993.30–40.

——. 1996. "I caratteri dell'età oscura nell'area egea." In Settis 1996.191–226.

Spence, Iain G. 1990. "Perikles and the Defence of Attika during the Peloponnesian War." *Journal of Hellenic Studies* 110, 91–109.

——. 1993. *The Cavalry of Classical Greece: A Social and Military History with Particular Reference to Athens.* Oxford: Clarendon Press.

Stanier, R. S. 1953. "The Cost of the Parthenon." *Journal of Hellenic Studies* 73, 68–76.

Starr, Chester G. 1977. *The Economic and Social Growth of Early Greece, 800–500 B.C.* New York: Oxford University Press.

——. 1982. "Economic and Social Conditions in the Greek World [in the Archaic Age]." In Boardman and Hammond 1982.417–41.

——. 1986. *Individual and Community: The Rise of the Polis, 800–500 B.C.* New York: Oxford University Press.

——. 1989. *The Influence of Sea Power on Ancient History.* New York: Oxford University Press.

Stein-Hölkeskamp, Elke. 1989. *Adelskultur und Polisgesellschaft: Studien zum griechischen Adel in archaischer und klassischer Zeit.* Stuttgart: Steiner.

Storch, Rudolph H. 1998. "The Archaic Greek Phalanx, 750–650 B.C." *The Ancient History Bulletin* 12, 1–7.

Strauss, Barry S. 1986. *Athens after the Peloponnesian War: Class, Faction and Policy, 403–386 B.C.* Ithaca, N.Y.: Cornell University Press.

———. 1996. "The Athenian Trireme, School of Democracy." In Ober and Hedrick 1996.313–25.

———. 1997. "Genealogy, Ideology, and Society in Democratic Athens." In Morris and Raaflaub 1997.141–54.

Thomsen, Rudi. 1964. *Eisphora: A Study of Direct Taxation in Ancient Athens.* Copenhagen: Gyldendal.

———. 1980. *King Servius Tullius: A Historical Synthesis.* Copenhagen: Gyldendal.

Vernant, Jean-Pierre. 1982. *The Origins of Greek Thought.* Ithaca, N.Y.: Cornell University Press.

———, ed. 1968. *Problèmes de la guerre en Grèce ancienne.* Paris: Mouton.

Walbank, Frank W. 1967. *A Historical Commentary on Polybius.* Vol. 2. Oxford: Clarendon Press.

Wallinga, H. T. 1993. *Ships & Sea-Power before the Great Persian War: The Ancestry of the Ancient Trireme.* Mnemosyne supplement 121. Leiden: E. J. Brill.

Weber, Max. 1968. *Economy and Society: An Outline of Interpretive Sociology,* Vol. 3. Edited by Günther Roth and Claus Wittich. London: Bedminster Press.

Wees, Hans van. 1992. *Status Warriors: War, Violence and Society in Homer and History.* Amsterdam: Gieben.

———. 1994. "The Homeric Way of War: The *Iliad* and the Hoplite Phalanx." *Greece & Rome* 41, 1–18, 131–55.

———. 1995. "Politics and the Battle Field: Ideology in Greek Warfare." In *The Greek World,* edited by Anton Powell, 153–78. London: Routledge.

———. 1996. "Heroes, Knights and Nutters: Warrior Mentality in Homer." In Lloyd 1996.1–86.

Welwei, Karl-Wilhelm. 1974. *Unfreie im antiken Kriegsdienst.* Vol. 1, *Athen und Sparta.* Forschungen zur antiken Sklaverei 5. Wiesbaden: Steiner.

———. 1992a. *Athen: vom neolithischen Siedlungsplatz zur archaischen Grosspolis.* Darmstadt: Wissenschaftliche Buchgesellschaft.

———. 1992b. "Polisbildung, Hetairos-Gruppen und Hetairien." *Gymnasium* 99, 481–500.

Whitehead, David. 1977. *The Ideology of the Athenian Metic. Proceedings of the Cambridge Philological Society* supplement 4. Cambridge.

———. 1981. "The Archaic Athenian *zeugitai.*" *Classical Quarterly* 31, 282–86.

The Hellenistic World

CHARLES D. HAMILTON

Introduction

Macedon's conquest of the Greek world under Philip II altered the course of Greek history.[1] His son and successor, Alexander the Great, conquered the Persian Empire and changed the direction of world history. The historian may well ask, therefore, how these two monarchs accomplished these feats, and the answer surely must be that a military system superior to those that existed in the fourth century, either in the Greek world or in the Persian Empire, is in large measure responsible for this development.[2] To be sure, political, diplomatic, and economic considerations played their part, but it is undeniable that the Macedonians possessed an extraordinary military system that was the creation of Philip. These achievements, however, have to be viewed within the context of the Greek world of the fourth century.[3]

Sparta's victory over Athens in the Peloponnesian War was a turning point in Greek history. Although dominant for several decades, Sparta saw its hegemony challenged by other Greek states, most notably Athens, Thebes, Corinth, and Argos. The opposition of these powers to Spartan high-handedness led to a coalition that opposed Sparta in the Corinthian War (395–386), in which the Persian Empire served as paymaster to the allies. Persia's interest was to force the withdrawal from Asia Minor of a Spartan-led army, which, under King Agesilaus, had succeeded in capturing the satrapal capital of Sardis (395) and was threatening to secure control of much of Asia Minor. The war ended in the King's Peace (386) when Sparta, unable to prosecute a two-front war against

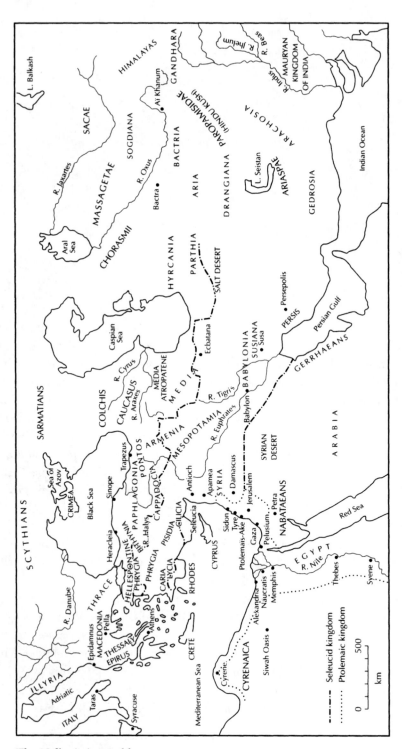

The Hellenistic World

overwhelming odds, agreed to surrender the Greek cities of Asia to Persian control, while the remainder of the Greek world was to enjoy autonomy, guaranteed by the Persian king. Sparta thus assured its dominant position within Greece, and especially the Peloponnesus, for another fifteen years.[4]

But Thebes and Athens continued to resent Spartan arrogance and control, and another conflict broke out in 378, the Boeotian War, which led ultimately to a signal Spartan defeat at Leuctra in 371.[5] That battle and subsequent conflicts demonstrated that the Spartan military system was experiencing grave difficulties. For reasons that are not entirely clear, the numbers of full citizens in Sparta, the primary component of its professional army, had been declining, and the state was unable to regain its position in Greek affairs. The defection of numerous states from Sparta's centuries-old Peloponnesian League, which was the result of the failure of Spartan diplomacy and foreign policy, contributed to this decline. For the next decade Thebes tended to dominate affairs in Greece, but not without opposition from Athens at the head of a revived Second Athenian League.[6] By the time of the battle of Mantinea in 362, in which no clear victor emerged from the general war that involved most of Greece, the states were exhausted and unable to resolve their perennial conflicts, through either diplomacy or war.

In the four decades since Athens's defeat, important changes had also occurred in Greek warfare and society. Citizen hoplite forces, which were still the core of Greek armies, had begun to give way to semiprofessional, light-armed infantry specialists, called *peltasts.* These troops were first seen in the Peloponnesian War, and a corps was used to great effect by the Athenian general Iphicrates against a Spartan detachment in the Corinthian War. Furthermore, cavalry had begun to play a more significant role in warfare as well, thus giving somewhat greater prominence to the wealthier classes who alone could afford horses. Finally, the use of mercenaries was becoming more frequent than previously.[7] Even the Spartans, in a reform of their system of levying troops from their Peloponnesian allies, substituted monetary contributions for individual service so that their armies became composed of mercenaries to a far greater extent after 382.[8] Since mercenaries served for pay, the states had now to consider other means of financing their wars than merely calling upon citizen levies. All of these developments formed the background to Philip's conquest of Greece, and Alexander's of Persia.

Following the breakup of Alexander's empire after his death, a new historical period began. This Hellenistic era, as modern historians call it, was characterized politically by the existence of three great kingdoms, Macedon, Syria, and Egypt, and a host of lesser states.[9] The conquests of Alexander had exported the Macedonian military system and Macedonian institutions, which were grafted onto native ones in Egypt and Asia to form the Hellenistic monarchies. These entities maintained a tentative balance of power for approximately a century, from the battle of Ipsus (ca. 301) until approximately 200. In that year the Romans invaded Macedon in the Second Macedonian War, and Philip V suffered defeat in the battle of Cynoscephalae (197).[10] In the aftermath of the war, the Romans returned time and again to the east until they, in their turn, conquered and incorporated into their empire first Macedon (146), then Syria (63), and finally Egypt (30).[11] Although the chronological scope of this period runs from the time of Philip II and Alexander the Great through the Roman conquest of the Greek east, constraints of space preclude even coverage.

This chapter will focus on and discuss such questions as how and why Macedon was able to succeed in defeating first the Greek poleis and then the mighty Persian Empire; how the great Hellenistic monarchies mobilized their resources and especially their military power to pursue their aims in politics and diplomacy; and, finally, why the Hellenistic monarchies failed to withstand the Roman military system, based on the manipular legion, which defeated the hitherto largely invincible Macedonian-style phalanx (although this latter topic falls more properly within the essay in this volume by Rosenstein). Among the central questions to be explored will be the nature of the Macedonian kingdom and its military system, that is, the interaction between war and society in Macedon; the extent to which the two other major successor states, Syria and Egypt, differed from Macedon in political, social, and especially military structures; and the increasing reliance on mercenary troops in the Hellenistic world.

The Macedon of Philip II and Alexander the Great

In 359 King Perdiccas and four thousand of his army perished on the field of battle, slaughtered by the invading Illyrians who had long been pressing on the western borders of the kingdom. Macedon was beset by pressures in the east from the Thracians as well, and the succession to the throne was disputed. In this situation of dire peril, with the very survival of the kingdom in question, the Macedonian army assembly elected Amyntas, the young son of Perdiccas, as their king and put power into the hands of Philip, Perdiccas's younger brother, as regent.[12] It was Philip's great achievement that the kingdom survived the numerous threats it was facing, and he accomplished this by a combination of military and political innovations that transformed Macedonian society. In order to appreciate his contributions, it will be necessary to examine the nature of the Macedonian state and society before Philip's accession to power.

Macedon in the fourth century was a tribal state whose institutions were generally regarded by contemporary Greeks as backward, or at least primitive. The kingdom consisted geographically of a number of districts north of Thessaly, which extended in an arc from the foothills of Mount Olympus in the southwest along the shore of the Thermaic Gulf toward Thrace and the Chalcidic peninsula in the northeast. Most of its territory lay in the valleys of the rivers Haliacmon and Axius and was farmed by the tribesmen who had moved down from the mountains to the west in the sixth century and settled in the coastal plains. To the west and northwest lay the districts of Upper Macedonia, which possessed separate kingships before the time of Philip II.[13] The baronies of Upper Macedonia in particular exhibited a strong aristocratic social structure and resisted the tendency of the monarchs of Macedon's Argead dynasty to limit the powers of the nobles. In Macedon proper this tension had led to the establishment of a link between the king and his nobles, who were called his Companions and who fought with him, on horseback, when called upon to do so. The Companions claimed numerous social privileges, including the right of free association with their king, and they hunted, dined, and drank with him.[14] The predilection for hunting, fighting, and especially heavy drinking was criticized by some Greeks, like Demosthenes and Theopompus. In their view the Macedonians had not advanced to that stage of civilization which the Greeks experienced in the polis.[15]

The bulk of the population of Macedon around 400 consisted of farmers, who were engaged in animal husbandry and agriculture. They lived for the most part in rural villages and conducted little trade, commerce, and manufacture; such activities were carried out by their Greek neighbors. The farmers had an obligation to fight for their lands and families when called upon to do so, and pressures from hostile neighbors made fulfillment of this obligation easy for their king to accomplish. Hammond insists that the state consisted of the king and his people in arms, and that a Macedonian did not possess citizenship until he had taken up arms and sworn an oath to his sovereign.[16] While the human resources of Macedonian society were extensive, they had to be marshaled and focused for war if the state were to survive. That would be the principal challenge for the monarchy.

The monarchy was central to the Macedonian state and was its single most important institution. The king was the military leader, both titular and actual commander in chief.[17] As such he was responsible for raising, training, and leading his troops into battle. He was expected to be in the forefront of the melee and, if necessary, to die with his men, as Perdiccas had done. Thus the personal qualities of the king, including daring and bravery in battle, were an integral element of Macedonian monarchy. Philip demonstrated his personal bravery on numerous occasions, and he proudly bore many scars, including the loss of an eye, to attest to his hardiness in battle.[18] Alexander the Great was equally brave in battle, some might even say reckless: he was almost killed at the battle of the Granicus in the first year of his invasion of the Persian Empire, and he too suffered wounds, including an arrow in his lung in the assault on an Indian city during his campaign in the Indus River valley.[19] It is important to recognize this aspect of Macedonian kingship because the rank and file expected their king above all to provide effective military leadership, both to protect them from their enemies and to advance the fortunes of their kingdom. If a king failed to fulfill this obligation, he might forfeit his throne, as seems to have happened when Philip usurped power from his nephew in 356, largely on the basis of his substantial military successes by that date.[20]

The Macedonian king was also expected to render justice to his subjects. Custom demanded that the king make himself available on a regular basis to review petitions for redress of grievances, and he was expected to display fair-mindedness, if not wisdom, in his judicial decisions.[21] The king was furthermore the formal representative of the state in relation to the gods. This responsibility meant that he had to perform various sacrifices and prayers on behalf of the people to ensure divine blessings for them.[22] The effectiveness of a Macedonian king, therefore, was directly related to his ability to fulfill these obligations.

In the forty years between the death of King Archelaus the Philhellene (399) and that of Perdiccas (359), Macedon had experienced by and large a series of reigns of weak kings who had failed particularly to fulfill their obligations to protect the state from invasion and military threat. Contemporary observers in 359 might have been tempted to predict the disappearance of the kingdom entirely in the face of military weakness and inept kings.

The Macedonian military system before Philip seems to have relied on an infantry levy of the ordinary folk, most of whom were simple farmers or shepherds, and a cavalry contingent furnished by the aristocrats. Thucydides reports that the Macedonian infantry at the beginning of the Peloponnesian War was virtually useless, melting away as it did at the first sign of the enemy.[23] The cavalry was more reliable, but cavalry alone could not stand effectively against a Greek hoplite phalanx, bristling with extended spear points and defensive armor. Archelaus, at the end of the fifth century, did much to improve the infrastructure of his kingdom, effecting some military reforms, which included the construction of straight roads and other such enhancements to rapid deployment of troops, communication, and transportation. But his reforms do not seem to have endured under his successors, and the army that was cut to pieces under Perdiccas seems to have been a relatively ineffective peasant militia, stiffened by some cavalry. Philip immediately undertook a radical reform of the Macedonian military system, although it took years for the social effects of these reforms to become effective.

He began by recruiting a new army of infantry, which he equipped at royal expense with standard weapons and armor, thus transforming, as Arrian says, rude shepherds dressed in skins into mighty warriors.[24] The great innovation was the introduction of the *sarissa*, a thrusting spear much longer than the typical hoplite spear, reaching to some five meters or more (sixteen to eighteen feet) in length. This fearsome weapon was composed of a shaft of the light but tough cornel-wood, tipped with a double-edged iron blade about twelve inches long, and balanced with an iron butt with a sharpened tip, which could be rammed into the ground when its owner was at rest. The length and weight of the *sarissa* necessitated that its wielder use both hands to manipulate it, so the heavy shield that Greek hoplites carried on their left arm was replaced by a lighter, round shield slung from a strap worn around the soldier's neck and shoulder. The defensive armor of the Macedonian soldier was completed by a helmet, a *kottybos*, which was either a stomach band (like a cummerbund) or a cuirass or breastplate of stiffened linen and/or leather instead of the typical hoplite's bronze corselet, and either metal greaves or high leather boots to protect the shins and lower leg.[25] The warrior also had a short sword, which could be used in close combat if the phalanx was breached and the *sarissa*'s use became impractical. This description of the soldier's armament depends on literary sources for the reigns of Philip and Alexander, and inscriptions of royal rescripts from the second century (the military regulations of Philip V).[26] Scholars continue to argue over points of detail, such as the construction of the *sarissa* and the material of the corselet, but there is no disputing the two principal changes introduced: the *sarissa*, a much more effective offensive weapon than the standard hoplite spear, and lighter defensive armor, which made it easier for the soldier to move about. Collectively, these changes emphasized a new aggressive and offensive attitude, on the part of the king, the soldiers, and their society.

The *sarissa* was designed to be employed in the infantry formation known as the *phalanx*, in which the soldiers stood shoulder to shoulder in long ranks across the field of battle, with additional soldiers in files behind them, the whole forming a dense mass (see Raaflaub, this volume). The files were called *dekades*, but in fact they had from eight to twelve men in them. The points of the pikes protruded in front of the formation, four or five of them in serried ranks, so that the enemy would encounter a bristling array of *sarissa* points before they could come into contact with the troops themselves. The extra length of the *sarissa* meant that the Macedonian phalanx of pikemen would strike a phalanx of hoplites armed with the traditional spear before the hoplites could reach them, thus giving the Macedonians the advantage and stressing their offensive posture. And, of course, such a formidable array of pikemen would be especially effective against the barbarian tribesmen of Illyria or Thrace, who were not organized in hoplite phalanx and with whom the Macedonians had first to deal. Those in the ranks farther back than the first four or five held their *sarissas* vertically and were able to use them to deflect any projectiles, javelins, or arrows the enemy might launch. The men in each file normally stood about two meters from one another, but the phalanx could be made more compact by moving men from the rear of the files forward and filling in the spaces; this technique was known as *synaspismos,* or dense shield formation. It was also possible to bunch the front ranks into a wedge-shaped protrusion that would cut through enemy infantry ranks.

Of course, extensive training was essential to the successful use of this formation. In the early years of Alexander's reign we hear that he gave a demonstration to the Thracian Triballi that displayed the precision with which the Macedonian phalanx could wheel about, change from regular to dense formation, and face front either to right or to left.[27] The ability to execute such precise movements, especially while carrying the awkward *sarissa,* betokens a great deal of skill, training, and discipline on the part of the Macedonian infantry. Among contemporaries, only the Spartans and the reformed Theban armies of Pelopidas and Epaminondas could begin to compete with the Macedonians in such maneuvers. One drawback to the effective use of the phalanx, of course, was the necessity to select one's ground for engagement carefully. Terrain that was flat, unbroken, and relatively unencumbered by streams or other obstacles was the ideal battleground, and the Greeks had preferred to fight on such terrain for centuries. If a commander could select his site, however, the phalanx could prevail over other formations; if he could not, as at Cynoscephalae, an enemy force could exploit the disorder and disarray of a phalanx attempting to fight on rough ground.

While the pikemen phalanx formed the core of Philip's army, he continued to employ cavalry. The bulk of these were Macedonians wealthy enough to own a horse and military equipment, either aristocrats or gentry, those who possessed landed wealth but could not claim a pedigree by birth. Philip armed his cavalry also with the *sarissa,* and they became a formidable force, especially in deflecting attacks on the flanks of the phalanx and in pursuit of defeated and fleeing enemies. On several occasions the cavalry pursued enemies in flight for up to twenty miles in a day, and more than once the slaughter of enemy infantry, broken by the Macedonian pikemen and in headlong flight, was extensive.[28] This combination of well-trained, well-equipped cavalry together with the pikemen phalanx proved to be the key to the military achievements of Philip and Alexander, and of their successors.

A new and special bond was forged between the king and his soldiers, who were called *pezhetairoi,* or Foot Companions.[29] It is probable that Alexander II (369–368) effected this reform during his brief reign, and that his successors, most notably Philip II, perfected it. In any event, what was involved was the extension of the notion of companionship of the king from the narrow circle of the aristocrats to that of the commoners, those whom the sources call the *Macedones.* Bravery in battle could bring distinctions, promotion, and other rewards to the *pezhetairoi.* These new Foot Companions of the king may also have been rewarded with plots of land as the kingdom expanded to the east against hostile Paeonians and Thracians. Their loyalty would thus have been solidified by personal gain. A social transformation seems, therefore, to have taken place within Macedon, whereby ordinary foot soldiers reaped benefits, psychological as well as social and economic, from service under aggressive kings such as Philip and Alexander.[30]

The wealth of which Philip disposed as king, especially from the royal monopolies on the export of timber from the Balkan hinterland and on the mining of precious metals, gave him the ability to equip, train, and pay a reformed, highly effective army, thus focusing the loyalty of his subjects. Payment for extended service meant that the soldiers did not have to worry unduly about their farms during their absence; they could purchase slaves or hire laborers to attend to agricultural work. Philip did not keep troops under arms constantly, however; they were called up for varying periods of time, from several months to several years, as requirements necessitated. Philip took his new army into the field in 358 against the Illyrians and crushed his enemy in battle.

He then made another fateful decision, that of incorporating the baronies of Upper Macedonia directly into his kingdom, so that in future any threatened invasion from Illyria would fall upon these territories first, thus shielding Lower Macedonia from direct attack. This step increased the manpower resources, although by how much is difficult to estimate. In Alexander's army at the Hellespont three of the six *taxeis* (brigades) were from Upper Macedonia. Nonetheless, he was probably the first king to bring the commoners of Upper Macedonia, the regions called Lyncestus, Orestis, and Elimiotis, into the royal armies, and he probably used the new designation of *pezhetairoi* to win them over. In any case, the expanded and reformed army was highly successful in the next several years.

The secrets of the success of these Macedonian troops were loyalty and commitment to their king, excellent training, and superb and uniform equipment, provided by the state from royal revenues, especially from the mines at Mount Pangaeus. All subjects of the king were liable to serve, but they were also raised to embrace military service willingly from the time of Philip II onward. The young Macedonian recruit was integrated into the army through a number of means: an oath of loyalty to the sovereign, which made him a fully fledged citizen-soldier; common uniform, arms, and extensive training; and the status of *pezhetairos*, which involved pay at least, and possibly a grant of land as well.[31] Thus the entire adult male population of Macedon was available as a reserve to be recruited into the military as needed. This army was supplemented by contingents from other ethnic groups such as the Thracians.

Through skillful diplomacy, bribery, and the application of force when he judged it expedient, Philip managed to separate and isolate his enemies in such a way that he was able to defeat them piecemeal: Illyrians, Thracians, Paeonians, the Chalcidians of Olynthus, and finally the mercenary armies of Phocis by 346. His diplomacy secured him the military leadership of the Thessalian cities and a seat on the council that supervised the affairs of the Delphic shrine of Apollo. Over the next several years he expanded his power further, despite opposition in Athens, led by Demosthenes.[32] At Chaeronea in 338 he finally faced a significant coalition of Greek forces in which the Theban and Athenian contingents matched his own army. In that conflict the superiority of the Macedonian phalanx and the dashing charge of the cavalry, led by the eighteen-year-old Alexander, decided the day.[33]

After his victory, Philip treated his defeated enemies generously and established a new organization of Greek states. The so-called League of Corinth was in theory a voluntary alliance of Macedon and the majority of Greek states; Sparta decided to stand aloof. The League's representatives met in Corinth to determine common objectives of foreign policy—in the first place an expedition against Persia to liberate the Greek poleis on the western coast of Asia Minor. Philip, elected leader of the expedition, was assassinated in 336 before he could complete plans for the invasion.[34]

Alexander's Conquests

Alexander succeeded to the throne, the position of hegemon of the Corinthian League, and the legacy of the expedition against the Persian Empire.[35] It is beyond the scope of this chapter to examine Alexander's victories and conquests in detail. Suffice it to say that he launched the planned invasion across the Hellespont in 334 and within three years overcame the organized resistance of the Persian king Darius III. Alexander initially commanded probably only some forty thousand troops, of which less than half were Macedonian regulars. The remainder represented contingents from the various Greek states of the League of Corinth, and some mercenary forces, including barbarian elements, Thracians, and others. With this motley array he met and defeated the Persians in three decisive battles: at the River Granicus, near the Hellespont in 334, at Issus on the Syrian coast in 333, and at Gaugamela, in northern Mesopotamia, in 331. The Granicus was a brief though major and decisive battle over the western Persian field army that secured Alexander's progress across Asia Minor.[36] Issus and Gaugamela were full-scale battles in which the Persian king pitted his full forces against the invader. Among decisive elements in Alexander's victories are his personal courage and reckless bravado in battle, which certainly inspired his troops although it almost cost him his life at the Granicus; the steadfast discipline and reliability of the Macedonian phalanx; and the use of cavalry both to turn the tide of battle and to effect the pursuit of fleeing enemies.[37] After

Gaugamela in October 331, organized resistance to Alexander ceased, and Darius was soon killed by one of his own officers. Some troops, grumbling about the length of service away from Macedon, were sent home, while others were summoned as replacements. The original purpose of the expedition, to liberate the Greek cities of Asia Minor, had been accomplished, but Alexander pushed on for the next eight years, slogging across the deserts of Iran and the mountains of Bactria (Afghanistan) down into the Indus River valley of northwest India (modern Pakistan) until his mutinous troops, homesick and tired of his adventuring, finally forced him to turn back. He had conquered the vast Persian Empire, and more; the question was, what would he do with his conquests?

Certain policies had already begun to emerge: the settlement of military veterans, the old and injured or infirm, in colonies, new poleis, across Asia; the employment of officials and bureaucrats from the old Achaemenid Empire in Alexander's newly conquered realm; the training of Persians and other non-Greeks in the Macedonian manner of warfare and Greek speech and customs; and the encouragement of intermarriage of Greeks and Macedonians with local women. Alexander himself married Roxane, who was pregnant when he fell ill in Babylon and died suddenly of fever in June 323. His plans for the future remain matter for debate, as does the question of how he might have coped with the staggering difficulties of governing and administering a huge and complex empire that stretched from the Balkan Peninsula and the Aegean to the borders of India, and included ancient Persia, Mesopotamia, Syria-Palestine, Egypt, and the diverse populations of Asia Minor within its frontiers, not to mention Macedon proper and Greece. It fell to his marshals to deal with this situation, and for almost a quarter of a century, from 323 until 301, they fought among themselves over whether, first, the empire could be kept together, and then, who would govern it, a member of the old Argead dynasty, or another. Alexander's widow, his posthumous son Alexander IV, his mother Olympias, and his half-brother Philip Arrhidaeus had all been murdered by 310; the Argead dynasty was no more. Then the dynasts struggled among themselves for control. The battle of Ipsus in 301 decided the issue: the empire would be divided. The only remaining question was who would govern what elements of Alexander's short-lived empire.[38]

The Hellenistic Kingdoms

The Hellenistic kingdoms emerged out of the fragmentation of Alexander's realm. The two principal components were the old Achaemenid Persian Empire and the Macedonian Kingdom. Of these kingdoms, Macedon alone was and remained a relatively homogeneous, integrated state, in which the institutions displayed great continuity from the age of Philip and Alexander until the

Roman conquest. We need not, therefore, spend much time in analyzing Macedon. The other two major kingdoms, Ptolemaic Egypt and especially Seleucid Syria, will require greater examination. All of these kingdoms, and the smaller Kingdom of Pergamum in Asia Minor, faced common problems in raising and financing armies of adequate size to meet their needs.

One of the most vexing problems concerning the Macedonian military is to determine the extent of manpower resources. Unfortunately, our sources do not give us precise numbers for the armies of Philip or Alexander in relation to the total population. We do not even know whether the Macedonians, like the Athenians and the Romans, carried out a census of the population to determine the numbers available for military service, although I think this likely. Errington puts it well: "An indication is given by the number of Macedonians who, under certain circumstances—in battle, say—could be mustered, but in no single instance do the sources put it in relation to the potential army size."[39] We do, however, know how many men were available at certain points in this period. The army that Alexander inherited from Philip and took with him to conquer the Persian Empire is enumerated by Arrian, whose ultimate sources are trustworthy. Alexander had about 12,500 Macedonian hoplites, and several thousand cavalry, out of some 35,000 to 40,000 total troops that he mustered at the Hellespont; he left behind an equal number of Macedonians with Antipater, and he collected another several thousand Macedonians who had crossed over to Asia earlier. That would suggest roughly 30,000 as the total number of Macedonian troops available in 334, which compares favorably with the 30,000 infantry and 2,000 cavalry Philip disposed of at Chaeronea in 338.[40]

From the time of Alexander onward, however, when the king took more than half the resources of his kingdom with him on his expedition into Asia, the manpower resources of Macedon were subject to attrition as a result of emigration.[41] This was an intermittently recurring theme in Macedonian history, and it is impossible to gauge exactly how many Macedonians left the homeland in the century and a half between Alexander's time and the Roman conquest. The process began under Alexander and continued during the wars of the successors, in which Macedonian troops played a major role in the armies of all the contenders. Loyalty to the king had broken down, or become clouded, when it was not clear who the legitimate king was. The Macedonian generals who went on to carve out kingdoms for themselves desired trained and effective troops, and they stimulated emigration by offering new and better economic opportunities than existed at home to soldiers willing to migrate to military colonies abroad.[42] Our sources report regularly on the existence of "Macedonian hoplites" in the armies of the monarchs of the Hellenistic successor states. Some scholars understand this term to mean merely "soldiers trained and equipped as Macedonian hoplites," regardless of their ethnic origins,[43] while others see them as the products of periodic emigration from the homeland during the late fourth and third centuries.[44] In any case, Bosworth's view that Alexander bled Macedon white and did irreparable damage to the manpower resources of the kingdom seems much exaggerated.

At later dates in Macedon's history, numbers roughly comparable to those of Alexander's time are recorded. At Krannon in 322 Antipater commanded 40,000 infantry and 5,000 cavalry, of whom two-thirds were probably Macedonians. At Ipsus in 301 Cassander had 29,000 infantry and 2,000 cavalry, the majority of whom were probably Macedonians. Antigonus Doson had 13,000 foot and 300 horse at Sellasia in 222, but he commanded 20,000 and 1,300, respectively, two years earlier. At Cynoscephalae in 197 Philip V had 18,000 infantry and 2,000 cavalry, with another 2,000 infantry on garrison duty; soon after the battle he raised another 6,500 infantry. At Pydna in 168 the casualty figures for the Macedonians were 20,000 killed and 11,000 taken prisoner; and Livy records 43,000 men in 171, half of whom were Macedonian phalangites. Errington's conclusion that "for a period of more than 150 years after the Macedonian state had taken firm shape under Philip II, the kings and their deputies were regularly in a position to muster between twenty thousand and thirty thousand Macedonian troops" seems sound.[45]

The chief objective of the Antigonid dynasty, which succeeded the Argead in approximately 275, was to maintain Macedonian dominance in the Aegean area. This involved continuing hegemony over the Greek states to the south, many of which had rebelled, first while Alexander was in Asia and then, upon news of his death, in the Lamian War. In addition to their concerns to maintain dominance in Greece proper, the Antigonids had to protect their kingdom from their traditional enemies to the north, Thracians and Illyrians in particular, and to guard against the aggressions and depredations of the other two great Hellenistic monarchies, Egypt and Syria.[46] Thus, for the better part of a century, from the accession of Antigonus II until the end of the reign of Philip V, Macedonian kings struggled against a host of potential enemies, sometimes giving in to the temptation to intervene militarily in affairs to the south, and at other times operating in Thrace, across the Aegean in Asia Minor, or within the Aegean itself.

These challenges meant that the dynasty had to maintain an aggressive military stance, or, in contemporary terms, to learn "power projection." Thus the acquisition of a navy, and its support and maintenance, became a factor of importance for the Antigonids.[47] Egypt, for example, maintained a presence within the Aegean on behalf of many of the lesser Greek states, and Ptolemaic naval operations in the area required Macedonian countermeasures. Furthermore, the Antigonids followed a policy of attempting to control Greece by garrisoning cities at the three choke points within Greece: Demetrias on the Gulf of Pagasae near the borders of Thessaly and Phocis; Chalcis on Euboea, near the narrow channel known as the Euripus; and Corinth at the Isthmus, which controlled access by land from central Greece to the Peloponnesus. This policy necessitated access to an adequate supply of mercenary troops, because long-term garrison duty was unsuitable for citizen-soldiers.

The nature of Macedonian military service for citizen-subjects of the Antigonids had not changed much from that under the Argeads. The core of the army was formed by levies of Macedonian phalangites and cavalry, who might serve for extended campaigns but could not be kept in the field, or on garrison duty, for indefinite periods of time, since they needed to tend to the farms and estates that supported them. Thus, for example, Macedon retained close ties to the island of Crete, which had become famous for its supplies of excellent archers. Many were recruited either as specialty troops for major campaigns or for garrison duty. These needs created an added expense for the Macedonian crown, but revenues from traditional sources such as control of timber supplies and the mines to a large degree enabled Macedon to pursue its foreign policy objectives.[48]

Egypt, by contrast to Macedon, was a composite, more heterogeneous entity, at least in terms of population.[49] The bulk of the population seems always to have remained composed of native peasants who spent most of their time in cultivating the land and working on flood control measures, dikes, and irrigation canals, much as their ancestors had done for thousands of years under the pharaohs. They were compliant subjects who accepted the Macedonian dynasty which Ptolemy founded as legitimate rulers and viewed them as Egyptians had viewed their rulers from the inception of the Egyptian state: as divine in the person of the god Horus incarnate. The Ptolemies were also able to exploit an extensive and effective bureaucratic system, which was a legacy from the ancient past. This meant, in practice, that the Ptolemies were constrained in their rule only by such practical realities as money or other resources. As Rostovtzeff has shown, however, the Ptolemies were adept at controlling state monopolies of all sorts of industries, and, in general, they did not lack for funds, since Egypt was wealthy in the basic foodstuff of antiquity, edible grains.[50] Egypt was, in fact, one of the three principal granaries of the ancient Mediterranean world. Possession of its enormous wealth could confer enormous power, as the Roman emperor Augustus discovered later. As for the rest of the population, it was divided among immigrants, such as groups of Jews who had fled there from persecution in Judaea, and, of course, the Greco-Macedonian immigrants who flocked to Egypt to exploit opportunities in the Ptolemaic bureaucracy, in the military system, and in trade and commerce. Alexandria became perhaps the busiest and most important city in the eastern Mediterranean not long after its founding, and it offered manifold economic and other opportunities to its inhabitants.

Geographically speaking, the heart of Egypt remained the Nile valley and the delta, where the river branched out to empty into the Mediterranean through several mouths, or channels.[51] The valley was protected by mountains stretching away to the Red Sea in the east and by the western, or Libyan, desert on the left bank of the Nile. These geographic features continued to serve as natural barriers to invasion, as they had done in pharaonic times. To the south numerous cataracts made invasion from that direction difficult as well. Egypt's principal area of vulnerability was in the north, where an enemy possessing a fleet could attack the delta or could invade overland from the northeast, through the Sinai. Not surprisingly, therefore, the Ptolemies maintained a vigorous naval policy, and they extended their control over Cyrene to the west and over the island of Cyprus. But their chief weakness lay in their common borders with the Seleucids, and for much of the third century Egypt and Syria struggled for control of what was known at that time as Coele Syria, the region of Lebanon, Palestine, and the Gaza Strip. This corridor had long been a funnel for armies marching in one direction or another between Egypt, Asia Minor, and Syria and Mesopotamia.[52] Rivalry between the two led to several battles in our period, perhaps most notably the battle of Raphia in 217 and that of Panion in 200.

The Ptolemies established a military system that was based on employment of Macedonian phalangites. These men were furnished primarily by military colonists established in the Arsinoite nome near the delta, who could easily be activated in times of need or trouble.[53] Their weapons and tactics were those that had worked so well for Philip and Alexander and had also been adopted by their rivals, the Seleucids in Syria, as well as, of course, by the Macedonian Antigonid dynasty. The Ptolemaic government, however, employed Jewish mercenaries and also relied on native Egyptian troops to a significant extent, for example at the battle of Raphia. These Egyptian levies, however, revolted soon thereafter. By contrast, the Seleucid military colonies were much more successful in furnishing trained and reliable troops when a crisis struck.[54]

The case of Syria provides a striking contrast to both Macedon and Egypt. First, the very extent of the kingdom, stretching as it did from the Mediterranean eastward to the borders of India, made it much less manageable, although its manpower resources were potentially vast.[55] The bane of the Seleucid realm was its size and diversity, and especially the centrifugal tendency of peripheral provinces, particularly in the east. The core of the kingdom was the area formed of ancient Mesopotamia, Syria and Palestine, and the central portions of Asia Minor. As we have observed, Coele Syria was an object of contention between Syria and Egypt for much of this period, and many of the provinces east of the Zagros range, the heartland of modern Iran and Afghanistan, were often either in open rebellion from the government at Antioch or following policies of de facto autonomy.[56] Following his unsuccessful attempt to wrest Coele Syria from

Egypt at Raphia in 217, Antiochus III the Great (223–187) undertook a great eastern campaign from 212 to 205 during which he subdued many of the eastern lands that had been invaded and conquered by Alexander but had more recently broken away from Seleucid control. Flushed with success, Antiochus plunged again into western politics and warred upon his neighbors, Egypt and the Kingdom of Pergamum in the west of Asia Minor. This time he exploited temporary Egyptian weakness following the death of Ptolemy IV and the accession of a minor in 203, which led to court intrigue during a regency and Egyptian inability to pursue a vigorous foreign policy. Antiochus managed to defeat Egypt in battle at Panion in 200 and seized control of Coele Syria. The policies of his successors, particularly Antiochus IV Epiphanes, would lead to Jewish discontent, immigration to Egypt, and ultimately the revolt of the Maccabees. The successes of Antiochus III reflected the relative strengths and weaknesses of his kingdom.

Syria was not only far larger than either Egypt or Macedon but also far more heterogeneous than either. Whereas Macedon was fundamentally populated by ethnic Macedonians, with elements of neighboring peoples, such as Thracians, Illyrians, and Greeks intermixed among them, and Egypt was composed of a majority of native peasants ruled by a minority of Greco-Macedonians, with some other elements such as Jews mixed in, Syria had no single and predominant distinct ethnic composition. The old Persian Empire had consisted of Iranians (Medes and Persians), Babylonians, Assyrians, Aramaeans, Jews, Phoenicians, Lydians, Carians, Paphlagonians, Cappadocians, Greeks and others in the central and western regions, and various other semicivilized peoples on the northern and eastern fringes; Egypt had once belonged to it, as had Macedon itself for a brief period in the late sixth and early fifth centuries. Babylonians, Assyrians, Medes, and Persians had each in their turn ruled over empires that included more or less of Seleucid Syria. This congeries of distinct and disparate ethnic groups, most of them with languages and cultural and religious traditions of their own, made the process of governing and integrating them into a single empire enormously difficult.[57] The Achaemenid dynasty had made great strides under its early kings, especially Darius I. The satrapal system of regional administration, widespread acceptance of the Persian gold *daric,* and a network of royal roads helped bind the empire together. Alexander had adopted much of the Achaemenid infrastructure and reappointed many officials who had served Darius III, but he died before it was clear what shape he would give to his vast empire. The Seleucids therefore faced distinct difficulties in organizing and coordinating their resources, but they had the examples of the Persians and of Alexander before them in attempting to cope with these difficulties.

The dynasty of Seleucus, which ruled sometimes from Antioch in Syria, the city Antiochus had founded and named for himself, but more often from

Babylon, laid claim to an ancient tradition of monarchy that reached far back in time, to the first Mesopotamian empire, that of Sargon of Agade, in the later third millennium. The various native peoples within the empire therefore had long been accustomed to a kingship in which the ruler was viewed as divinely appointed, and whose duties included direction of traditional religious observances.[58] Alexander, toward the end of his life, seems to have sought and received divine honors.[59] It was not difficult, then, for the Seleucids to develop a theory of divine kingship in which their various subjects could all relate to them on a single plane. This development produced an ideological basis for loyalty to the dynasty on the part of the many native peoples of Asia, not unlike that in Ptolemaic Egypt. The Seleucids combined other aspects of the heritage of the Persians and of Alexander in forming their system of government. Many of the practical aspects of Persian rule were retained, including Aramaean as the lingua franca of business, trade, and government; but alongside it the Koine Greek imported by Alexander became an important working language of the empire.

The military system of Seleucid Syria has been examined in a detailed monograph, and the policy of military colonies has also been studied in detail.[60] We know rather more, therefore, about how the Seleucids responded to military problems that were more acute for them than for the Antigonids in Macedon or the Ptolemies in Egypt. Alexander's policy of settling many of his Greek and Macedonian veterans in poleis throughout Asia was retained and developed by the Seleucids. These military settlements served both as focal points from which to radiate Greek cultural ideas to neighboring non-Greek peoples and as sources of recruitment for the Seleucid military. The Seleucid armies seem to have employed a core of Greco-Macedonian phalangites, recruited from the military colonies, and supplemented as necessary either with native levies or with mercenaries. In short, their practice was not unlike that of the other two Hellenistic states, except that they probably placed greater reliance on various native contingents.

It is likely that the Seleucid military colonists, many of whom enjoyed special privileges of citizenship through the institutions of the polis in their colonies, served for a time on active service before becoming reservists liable to military service for a lengthy period. This appears to be true of cavalry units as well as of hoplite phalangites.[61] The colonies seem to have been concentrated in two general areas, one along the western borders of the empire in Asia Minor, where the Seleucids shared a frontier with the Attalid dynasty of Pergamum; and another in northern and eastern Mesopotamia, where danger often threatened from tribesmen living in the mountainous fringes of the valley of the Two Rivers.[62] In addition, the Seleucids often called upon native levies whose status is difficult to ascertain: sometimes they appear to be mercenary corps, at other times allied contingents obliged to fight for the dynasty by treaties of one sort or another, and sometimes native conscripts. Such contingents may have constituted about one-half of the effective military forces of the Seleucids, but they were not always as reliable as the core units composed of the descendants of the Greco-Macedonian settlers. Thus all three of the great Hellenistic kingdoms shared this feature: they all relied primarily on a core of phalangites, trained and equipped in the Macedonian manner, and composed often, although not necessarily exclusively, of Macedonians or descendants of Greco-Macedonian settlers; but they all also employed, to a greater or lesser degree, native contingents and especially mercenary troops.

The Role of Mercenaries in Hellenistic Warfare

"Another consistent characteristic of the Macedonian military," as Errington puts it, "was the incorporation of contingents from the Balkans, Illyrians, Thracians, and Paeonians, and the employment of mercenaries."[63] The phenomenon of mercenary service came to be increasingly important in the fourth century and throughout the ensuing Hellenistic period, although it was not new to the fourth century. We know of Greek and Carian mercenaries from the western seaboard of Asia Minor who took service with various oriental monarchs, Assyrian and Egyptian, in the seventh century; indeed there are Greek graffiti from the Saite period in Egypt far up the Nile at Abu Simbel that attest to this development. In Greece proper, many tyrants in the sixth century employed Greek mercenaries in support of their regimes, finding them perhaps more loyal than citizen troops from their own cities. But the practice was not particularly widespread in the classical period, when citizen troops, particularly as hoplites, formed the core of the armies of the poleis. Mercenaries, where they did exist, tended either to supplement regular armies or to serve in special forces, as the Athenian navy, or in small standing units, as bodyguards for rulers or as garrison troops to occupy key locations like the acropolis of a city. It was in the aftermath of the great Peloponnesian War that mercenaries came into their own in the Greek world.[64]

Isocrates paints a lurid picture of the plague of mercenaries that scourged the Aegean in his day.[65] Bands of unemployed professional soldiers wandered about, preying on the weak and undefended, and ready to serve whoever could pay their wages. Many, but hardly all, of them were Greeks. The economic dislocations of the protracted struggle between the Spartans and Athenians (431–404), and the conflict that broke out soon thereafter between the Spartans and the Persian Empire, fueled this phenomenon. Almost thirty years of constant warfare had produced a class of soldiers who were skilled at their craft but unable to find a livelihood through traditional means—farming, trade, or manufacture at home—and who turned to the profession of arms as an alternative. The earliest and best-known example of such mercenary activity is afforded by the story of the army the Persian prince Cyrus raised in his bid to overthrow his brother, King Artaxerxes. Some thirteen thousand Greek soldiers of fortune, recruited from various parts of the Greek world, gathered on the coast of Asia Minor in 401. Xenophon tells us that Cyrus had one of his recruiting agents raise an army in Arcadia, the desolate and impoverished interior of the Peloponnesus, and many Arcadians served in the Ten Thousand, as the survivors of the battle of Cunaxa were known.[66] When Cyrus perished in the battle and their generals were treacherously murdered afterward by the Persians, the Ten Thousand elected new leaders and fought their way out of the heart of the Persian Empire, from Assyria across the mountains of Armenia to the shores of the Black Sea. This celebrated event, immortalized in the pages of Xenophon's *Anabasis,* became the prototype for later Greek service in the armies of Persian kings or Egyptian rebels. The veterans of this corps were absorbed into the army which the Spartan king Agesilaus formed to operate in western Asia Minor in 396.[67] Thereafter, contingents of Greek mercenaries were to be found in Persian or Egyptian employ down to the time of Alexander the Great.

They were much sought after, and the Persian King brought an end to the Corinthian War in part because he wanted to recruit Greek troops for his own forces. The series of diplomatic agreements, known as the Common Peace, which followed the original King's Peace of 386 all had as their purpose, at least in part, the cessation of hostilities within the Greek world so that the recruiting agents of the Persians could secure adequate numbers of troops.[68] For sixty years, from the 390s to the 330s, various Greek commanders, including the Athenians Iphicrates, Timotheus, and Chares, and even two Spartan kings, Agesilaus and his son Archidamus, served abroad in the service of Thracian kings, Persian satraps, Egyptians in rebellion against Persian power, or the Greek cities of south Italy. There were plenty of opportunities for mercenaries to enrich themselves during the virtually incessant warfare of the period, but in the intervals groups of mercenaries drifted around the Aegean basin, seeking employment and often causing disturbances in Greece.

Isocrates bemoaned this situation, which he blamed on the impoverishment of Greece proper and the lack of adequate lands to support the population. He advocated the plan of a crusade against the Persian Empire, which would have the beneficial effect of focusing the efforts and energies of Greek mercenaries on the hereditary enemy and, in the event of successful campaigning to liberate portions of western Asia Minor, provide new lands where these mercenaries could settle down, never to trouble the peace of Greece again. Although Isocrates was never able to convince the Greeks to put aside their differences and to adopt his scheme, his ideas may in fact have stimulated Philip's and later Alexander's ambitions to attack the Persian Empire.[69] In any event, both the army of Alexander and that of his opponent, Darius III, contained contingents of Greek mercenaries. The Macedonian army also contained elements of various barbarian nations, Illyrians, Thracians, and Paeonians, who may have been serving as auxiliary troops, allied to Macedon, or as mercenaries. The frequent use of mercenaries gave rise to a military manual by Aeneas Tacticus dealing with treason, siegecraft, and other aspects of warfare. By the time of Alexander's invasion of Asia in 334, the presence of mercenary corps in the armed forces of the day was commonly accepted and had become a fact of life. It would be intensified in the Hellenistic period.

We know something about the social origins of these mercenaries.[70] Many were Greek exiles or refugees who had fled their native states for political reasons, while others were adventurers who had gone abroad in search of economic advantage. They came from various parts of the Greek world, from the Peloponnesus, Ionia, and particularly from Crete, with which Macedon established and maintained close relations throughout the Hellenistic period. The principal reason for taking mercenary service must have been economic necessity. Aristotle in the *Politics* speaks of a growing gap between rich and poor, and his picture of economic conditions leading to *stasis* (class conflict) agrees with that of Isocrates.[71] Perhaps the most notable example of the impact of mercenaries on society in this period is afforded by the history of the conflict known as the Third Sacred War (356–346). The people of Phocis seized the treasuries of Delphi, and they were able to employ a mercenary army of some ten thousand. Despite the best efforts of the Thebans, the Thessalians, and even of Philip, the mercenaries could not be dislodged for almost a decade.[72]

Mercenaries, by definition, serve for pay and not out of loyalty or ideology. Griffith has collected the evidence bearing on this question, and he shows conclusively that most mercenaries expected to have their daily needs met in the first instance, in the form of either grain rations (*sitos*) or money to purchase rations. Next they expected pay or wages (*misthos*), and their normal pay, together with subsistence allowance, approximated that of skilled workmen. Finally, there was always the hope that they would realize substantial bonuses, in the form of plunder while on campaign or even in grants of land for service rendered. Large cities like Athens and Corinth were places where mercenaries gathered while unemployed and could be recruited by those in need of them. Cape Taenarum at the tip of the Peloponnesus also became a noted mercenary depot, and several times recruiting agents in the late fourth century visited there in search of recruits.[73] In addition to Greek mercenaries, the principal ethnic groups that were favored by Hellenistic employers were Illyrians, Thracians, and, after the invasion of 278, Gauls. Many of the latter were settled in the interior of Asia Minor, in Galatia, and they served many Seleucid monarchs of Syria over two centuries as effective troops.

Mercenaries tended to play a double role in warfare. When a general simply needed to stiffen his forces in combat, they could be recruited for a given campaign and could be either integrated into the regular army, whatever its composition, or kept as distinct, native elements. In times of peace, mercenaries were most often employed as garrison troops to hold key areas, against either internal or external threat. This practice had certainly begun in the latter years of the Peloponnesian War, when King Agis garrisoned the fortified post of Decelea in Attica.[74] In the Hellenistic period many monarchs also required mercenary garrisons to hold key spots for them. The Macedonian Antigonids sought over two centuries to control Greece by garrisoning the fetters of Greece: Demetrias, Chalcis, and Corinth. In Asia Minor the Attalids of Pergamum had numerous garrisons in place along their precarious borders with the Seleucid realm, and the Ptolemies of Egypt maintained military strongholds in the Aegean and along the southern coast of Asia Minor to protect the Greek cities there against Antigonid or Seleucid aggression. All these garrisons needed a constant supply of skilled and trained mercenary troops.

How were the mercenaries equipped? Did they possess their own weapons and armor, or were these supplied to them by their employers? It is possible, at least in the early fourth century, that some of them were once ranked as hoplites and had become impoverished in the course of the Peloponnesian War, as we know to have occurred in Corinth, resulting in the revolution of 392.[75] Alternatively, many of them who took service as peltasts would have found it easier and cheaper to obtain the weapons and equipment required for these more lightly armed soldiers. The increasing role and success of light-armed troops against hoplites seems to have begun in certain phases of the Peloponnesian War, under the influence of Thracians.[76] The peltasts had much lighter body armor than the hoplites and carried a smaller shield called the *pelta.* But their secret to success lay in their mobility and their offensive weapon, the javelin. A body of peltasts could be moved much more rapidly against the slower, more cumbersome hoplite phalanx, and once the peltasts had discharged a volley of javelins with often harrowing effect, they could be withdrawn before the phalanx could advance to engage them. The Athenian mercenary commander Iphicrates first used peltast tactics to good effect in 392 against a Spartan contingent in the vicinity of Corinth.[77] Thereafter the employment of peltasts, whose equipment was much less costly than that of hoplites, became almost routine in Greek warfare. The peltasts, however, were vulnerable because they could not stand against cavalry, so that an army strong in that element, such as the Macedonian, could threaten to sweep them from the field before they could inflict much damage on their opponents. Overall, it seems, the majority of mercenaries were hoplites, at least in the service of the Persian Empire and in the Hellenistic armies that arose after Alexander.

Conclusions: The Coming of Rome

In the year 200 the Romans dispatched envoys to Greece and Macedon to order Philip V to desist from military operations directed against the Kingdom of Pergamum, the Republic of Rhodes, and Athens, among other Greek states. Philip refused and, on the Senate's orders, the consul Galba took a legionary army across the Adriatic Sea to the Balkan Peninsula.[78] The opening of this war, the Second Macedonian War, was the beginning of the end for the Hellenistic military system. In their wars against the hardy Samnite tribesmen of the mountains of southern Italy in the late fourth century, the Romans had learned to modify their tactics and formations from the rather rigidly organized phalanx to more mobile, smaller units that could be detached from the mass of the army to operate independently, especially in rough terrain (see Rosenstein, this volume). These maniples could be dispatched over rocky areas where a Greco-Macedonian phalanx could not operate successfully. Thus the Romans gained the advantage of being able to take the phalanx in flank or in the rear, if they could choose their battlefields.

In the Hellenistic period phalanx warfare had become somewhat ritualized, rather as scholars write of the agonal ritual of hoplite warfare in classical Greece.[79] In particular, commanders demanded that the terrain on which they conducted battles between phalanxes be level and contain adequate space for the proper deployment of their troops. The decisive battle of the Second Macedonian War was not waged on such terrain. After several years of tracking one another's armies across the Balkans, the Roman army of Flamininus finally made contact with that of Philip in southern Thessaly, in the vicinity of a range of hills called Cynoscephalae. The respective armies were positioned on opposite sides of the ridge, and the Macedonians were in the process of attempting to cross over to engage the Romans on level ground when Flamininus struck. The armies were evenly matched in size, but the greater flexibility of the Roman maniples allowed them to scramble up the slopes of the hill and to attack the phalanx before it could form its defensive ranks. The result was chaotic for the Macedonians, who suffered such losses that Philip sued for terms after the battle.[80] In the first instance, therefore, Cynoscephalae appears to be a tactical victory, and that it was. The phalanx simply could not operate successfully on rough, broken terrain, and its vulnerability to the more flexible Roman formation became apparent. The question arises why the Macedonians did not recognize the limitations of the phalanx and undertake reforms to make it more effective against the legion. The answer probably is that they did not yet recognize the inherent limitations of the phalanx because they had not yet met the legion on terrain best suited to the phalanx, as they would do at Pydna. By then, it was too late to attempt tactical reform or modifications.

A shift occurred in the relationship between warfare and society in this period. The Macedonians of Philip II were pledged by oath to fight for their king and their country; they were well trained and well equipped, and they fought well. Alexander took them to the end of the earth, and they helped him to create the largest empire the West had ever known. In the aftermath of his death, his generals fought among themselves for the spoils of his empire, but they relied primarily on trained Macedonian phalangites or cavalrymen for the core of their armed forces. Since in two of the three major Hellenistic kingdoms the bulk of the population was not of Greek or Macedonian descent, the Ptolemies and Seleucids had to depend on a minority to supply the essential elements of their armies. This they did by forming a class of settlers who had hereditary obligations to fight. They also made few modifications in the tactics of phalanx warfare, which had worked so well for the founders of the system, Philip and Alexander. Unfortunately for them, their commanders became inflexible in their tactics and strategy and proved incapable of adapting to new circumstances, especially those associated with the arrival of the Roman legionary army.[81] It was not this alone that hastened the decline of the Hellenistic monarchies: external pressures, internal weaknesses, and diplomatic reversals all played their role in the process. But a military system that placed overreliance on what had worked in the past did not improve the situation. Perhaps the Ptolemies, the Seleucids, and the Antigonids held their predecessors, Philip and Alexander, in too high esteem.

Notes

1. The principal literary sources for the fourth century include Xenophon's *Hellenica;* Diodorus of Sicily's *Universal History,* which is based on the lost fourth-century works of Ephorus and Theopompus; the speeches of the Attic orators, especially Demosthenes, Isocrates, and Aeschines; numerous lives by Plutarch; passages in Polyaenus's *Stratagems;* several lives by Cornelius Nepos; and epigraphical sources. For the history of Alexander the Great, Arrian is particularly valuable in addition to Diodorus and Plutarch, Justin, and Curtius. For the period of the Diadochs (the successors to Alexander) and the third and second centuries Plutarch is valuable, as are the histories of Polybius and Livy, as well as epigraphy and papyrology, especially for Egypt. Biblical sources shed some light on Seleucid history, especially relations with the Jews. Many other contemporary historians wrote, but their works survive only in fragments.
2. For general studies of Philip's career, see Ellis 1976; Cawkwell 1978; Borza 1990; on Alexander's, see Lane-Fox 1973; Green 1974 (1991); Bosworth 1988.
3. See Tritle 1997 for recent discussion of the Greek world in the fourth century.
4. See Hamilton 1979 for discussion of the Corinthian War.
5. See Hamilton 1991 for this period.
6. See Buckler 1980 and Cargill 1981 for detailed treatment.

7. See Anderson 1970 for traditional hoplite warfare; Best 1969 on peltasts; Bugh 1988, Spence 1993, and Worley 1994, on cavalry; and Hamilton 1995.84–95 for a brief overview of these developments.

8. See Hamilton 1991.138–39.

9. See Walbank 1993 for a general introduction to the period, and Green 1993 for recent studies on special aspects of the topic.

10. See Gruen 1984, Vol. 2.382–98 for discussion of the Second Macedonian War.

11. See Gruen 1984, Vol. 2.481–528 for Rome and Syria, and 2.611–719 for Rome and Egypt.

12. Hammond 1989.75, 137.

13. See Borza 1990.30–50 for a discussion of the geography of Macedonia.

14. Hammond 1989.53–58; Borza 1990.241–44.

15. Cawkwell 1978.79–80; Sealey 1993.125–26, 174–85; Flower 1994.104–30.

16. Hammond 1989.58–59, 62–66.

17. Hammond 1989.64–70; Borza 1990.237–41.

18. Cawkwell 1978.37.

19. Arrian, *Anabasis of Alexander* 1.13–16; 6.8–11.

20. For a discussion of the source controversy over Philip's accession, see Hammond 1989.137–38; Errington 1990.37; Cawkwell 1978.27–28. I accept Hammond's argument that Philip first served as regent for the young Amyntas, despite the objections of Cawkwell.

21. Hammond 1989.65; Errington 1990.219–20, 222.

22. Hammond 1979.155–56.

23. Thuc. 2.100.5; 4.124.1; 4.125.1; 4.126.3.

24. See Arrian, *Anabasis of Alexander* 7.9.2.

25. Hammond 1989.100–103; Errington 1990.40–41.

26. Errington 1990.241.

27. Hammond 1989.103–4; Arrian, *Anabasis of Alexander* 1.6.1–3.

28. Hammond 1989.104–7; Errington 1990.243–44.

29. Bosworth 1988.259–60; Hammond 1989.104, 148–51; Errington 1990.244.

30. Borza 1990.203.

31. See Lloyd 1996 for discussion of the importance of such elements in turning raw recruits into an effective army, especially in Macedon in this period.

32. Ellis 1976.168–80.

33. See Griffith 1979.596–603 for discussion of many of the problems of this battle.

34. Ellis 1981.99–137; Borza 1990.227.

35. Bosworth 1988.25–28.

36. See the discussion of Harl 1997.303–26.

37. For evaluations of Alexander's generalship, see Hammond 1980; Fuller 1960; on logistics, see Engels 1978.

38. See Adams 1997.

39. Errington 1990.239.

40. Errington 1990.239.

41. Bosworth 1986.1–12 decries the negative effects of such policies.

42. Briant 1978 analyzes this process especially for the Seleucid realm.
43. Launey 1987 makes this point quite forcefully.
44. See Bosworth 1986; Adams 1996; contra Billows 1995.
45. Errington 1990.241; he has collected the sources for Macedonian military strength.
46. Errington 1990.162–204.
47. See Tarn 1930.122–52 for naval policy and related developments.
48. For a discussion of royal finance for military purposes, see Austin 1986.
49. Rostovtzeff 1941 and Bevan 1927, although older, are still fundamental studies on this topic.
50. Rostovtzeff 1941, Vol. 1.351–406.
51. On Egyptian geography, see Gardiner 1961.27–45.
52. Redford 1992 discusses relations among Egypt, Canaan, and Palestine in the pre-Persian period, emphasizing the importance of this area to major states, especially as a corridor.
53. See Lévêque 1968.265–66.
54. See Bar-Kochva 1976.47–48 and 45–46 for these points.
55. Sherwin-White and Kuhrt 1993 provide good recent insight into this topic.
56. Holt revises and updates Tarn 1984, the essential study on this topic.
57. See Olmstead 1948; Cook 1983; Sherwin-White and Kuhrt 1993.
58. Hammurabi's code, which the god Shamash delivers to the ruler, indicates his divine mandate; see Roux 1966.183–88.
59. On Alexander's divinity, see Balsdon 1950; Badian 1981.
60. Bar-Kochva 1976, Cohen 1978, and Billows 1995 present this material.
61. Bar-Kochva 1976.54–62.
62. Bar-Kochva 1976.47; Cohen 1978.14–19.
63. Errington 1990.241.
64. The fundamental study of this subject is still Griffith 1935, which follows upon Parke 1933 (limited to developments prior to the battle of Ipsus in 301). More recently, see Marinovic 1988 on mercenaries in fourth-century Greece.
65. Isoc. 4.167.
66. See Perlman 1976–77.241–84.
67. Hamilton 1991.60.
68. Ryder 1965 is the fundamental study of this topic.
69. Isoc. 5.122.
70. See Griffith 1935.236–54.
71. Arist. *Politics* 1295b.
72. See Buckler 1989 for modern discussion of this conflict, its chronology, and its significance.
73. Griffith 1935.259–60.
74. On Agis at Decelea, see Parke 1932.42–46.
75. Hamilton 1979.264–72.
76. See Best 1969 for discussion of Thracian peltasts and their influence on Greek warfare.
77. Hamilton 1995.89–90.

78. See Hamilton 1993.559–67 for the argument that the Roman senate deliberately decided on this war.
79. See Raaflaub, this volume, and Hanson 1989 for discussion of the nature of hoplite warfare in Classical Greece. But see now Krentz 1997.55–61, who disputes this model of agonal warfare.
80. See Walbank 1940 for this aspect of Philip V's career.
81. See especially Bar-Kochva 1976.1 and his study of Magnesia.

Bibliography

Adams, W. Lindsay. 1996. "In the Wake of Alexander the Great. The Impact of Conquest on the Aegean World." *Ancient World* 27, 29–37.

——. 1997. "The Successors of Alexander." In *The Greek World in the Fourth Century*, edited by Lawrence A. Tritle, 228–48. London: Routledge.

Anderson, John K. 1970. *Military Theory and Practice in the Age of Xenophon*. Berkeley and Los Angeles: University of California Press.

Austin, M. M. 1986. "Hellenistic Kings, War, and the Economy." *Classical Quarterly* 36, 450–66.

Badian, Ernst. 1981. "The Deification of Alexander the Great." In *Ancient Macedonian Studies in Honor of Charles F. Edson*, edited by Harry J. Dell, 27–71. Thessaloniki: Institute for Balkan Studies.

Balsdon, J. P. V. D. 1950. "The 'Divinity' of Alexander." *Historia* 1, 363–88.

Bar-Kochva, Bezalel. 1976. *The Seleucid Army: Organization and Tactics in the Great Campaigns*. Cambridge: Cambridge University Press.

Best, Jan G. P. 1969. *Thracian Peltasts and Their Influence on Greek Warfare*. Groningen: Wolters-Noordhoff.

Bevan, Edwyn R. 1902. *The House of Seleucus*. Reprint, Chicago: Ares Press, 1985.

——. 1927. *The House of Ptolemy*. Reprint, Chicago: Ares Press, 1985.

Billows, Richard A. 1995. *Kings and Colonists: Aspects of Macedonian Imperialism*. Leiden: E. J. Brill.

Borza, Eugene N. 1990. *In the Shadow of Olympus: The Emergence of Macedon*. Princeton, N.J.: Princeton University Press.

Bosworth, Alan B. 1971. "Philip II and Upper Macedonia." *Classical Quarterly* 21, 93–105.

——. 1986. "Alexander the Great and the Decline of Macedon." *Journal of Hellenic Studies* 106, 1–12.

——. 1988. *Conquest and Empire: The Reign of Alexander the Great*. Cambridge: Cambridge University Press.

Briant, Pierre. 1978. "Colonisation hellénistique et populations indigènes." *Klio* 60, 57–92.

Buckler, John. 1980. *The Theban Hegemony*. Cambridge, Mass.: Harvard University Press.

——. 1989. *Philip II and the Third Sacred War*. Mnemosyne supplement 109. Leiden: E. J. Brill.

Bugh, Glenn. 1988. *The Horsemen of Athens.* Princeton, N.J.: Princeton University Press.

Cargill, Jack. 1981. *The Second Athenian League: Empire or Free Alliance?* Berkeley and Los Angeles: University of California Press.

Cawkwell, George W. 1978. *Philip of Macedon.* London: Faber.

Cohen, Getzel M. 1978. *The Seleucid Colonies: Studies in Founding, Administration and Organization. Historia* Einzelschriften 30. Wiesbaden: Steiner.

Cook, John M. 1983. *The Persian Empire.* New York: Schocken.

Ellis, John R. 1976. *Philip II and Macedonian Imperialism.* London: Methuen.

———. 1981. "The Assassination of Philip II." In *Ancient Macedonian Studies in Honor of Charles F. Edson,* edited by Harry J. Dell, 99–137. Thessaloniki: Institute for Balkan Studies.

Engels, Donald. 1978. *Alexander the Great and the Logistics of the Macedonian Army.* Berkeley and Los Angeles: University of California Press.

Errington, Robert M. 1973. "The Nature of the Macedonian State under the Monarchy." *Chiron* 8, 77–78.

———. 1981. "Review-Discussion: Four Interpretations of Philip II." *American Journal of Ancient History* 6, 69–88.

———. 1990. *A History of Macedonia.* Berkeley and Los Angeles: University of California Press.

Flower, Michael A. 1994. *Theopompus of Chios: History and Rhetoric in the Fourth Century BC.* Oxford: Oxford University Press.

Fuller, John F. C. 1960. *The Generalship of Alexander the Great.* New York: Da Capo.

Gardiner, Alan. 1961. *Egypt of the Pharaohs.* Oxford: Oxford University Press.

Green, Peter. 1974 (1991). *Alexander the Great: A Historical Biography.* Berkeley and Los Angeles: University of California Press.

———, ed. 1993. *Hellenistic History and Culture.* Berkeley and Los Angeles: University of California Press.

Griffith, Guy T. 1935. *Mercenaries of the Hellenistic World.* Cambridge: Cambridge University Press.

———. 1979. *A History of Macedonia 550–336 B.C.* Vol. 2. Oxford: Clarendon Press.

Gruen, Erich S. 1984. *The Hellenistic World and the Coming of Rome.* 2 vols. Berkeley and Los Angeles: University of California Press.

Hamilton, Charles D. 1979. *Sparta's Bitter Victories: Politics and Diplomacy in the Corinthian War.* Ithaca, N.Y.: Cornell University Press.

———. 1986. "Amyntas III and Agesilaus: Macedon and Sparta in the Fourth Century." *Ancient Macedonia* 4, 239–45.

———. 1991. *Agesilaus and the Failure of Spartan Hegemony.* Ithaca, N.Y.: Cornell University Press.

———. 1993. "The Origins of the Second Macedonian War." *Ancient Macedonia* 5, 559–67.

———. 1995. "From Archidamus to Alexander: The Revolution in Greek Warfare." *Naval War College Review* 48, 84–95.

Hammond, Nicholas G. L. 1979. *A History of Macedonia 550–336 B.C.* Vol. 2. Oxford: Clarendon Press.

———. 1980. *Alexander the Great: King, Commander and Statesman.* Park Ridge, N.J.: Noyes.

——. 1981. "The Western Frontier of Macedonia in the Reign of Philip II." In *Ancient Macedonian Studies in Honor of Charles F. Edson,* edited by Harry J. Dell, 199–217. Thessaloniki: Institute for Balkan Studies.

——. 1983. "Casualties and Reinforcements of Citizen Soldiers in Greece and Macedonia." *Journal of Hellenic Studies* 109, 56–68.

——. 1989. *The Macedonian State: The Origins, Institutions and History.* Oxford: Oxford University Press.

Hanson, Victor D. 1989. *The Western Way of War.* New York: Oxford University Press.

Harl, Kenneth. 1997. "Alexander's Cavalry Battle at the Granicus." In *Polis and Polemos,* edited by Charles D. Hamilton and Peter Krentz, 303–26. Claremont, Calif.: Regina Books.

Krentz, Peter. 1997. "The Strategic Culture of Periclean Athens." In *Polis and Polemos,* edited by Charles D. Hamilton and Peter Krentz, 55–72. Claremont, Calif.: Regina Books.

Lane-Fox, Robin. 1973. *Alexander the Great.* London: Allen Lane.

Launey, Marcel. 1987. *Recherches sur les armées hellénistiques.* Edited by Y. Garlan, P. Gauthier, and C. Orrieux. 2d rev. ed. 2 vols. Paris: De Boccard.

Lévêque, Pierre. 1968. "La guerre à l'époque hellénistique." In *Problèmes de la guerre en Grèce ancienne,* edited by J.-P. Vernant, 261–87. Paris: Mouton.

Lloyd, Alan B. 1996. "Philip II and Alexander the Great: The Moulding of Macedon's Army." In *Battle in Antiquity,* edited by Alan B. Lloyd, 169–98. London: Duckworth.

Marinovic, Ludmila. 1988. *Le mercénariat grec au IVe s. av. n. è. et la crise de la polis.* Paris: Belles-Lettres.

Olmstead, A. T. 1948. *History of the Persian Empire.* Chicago: University of Chicago Press.

Parke, Herbert W. 1932. "The Tithe of Apollo and the Harmost at Deceleia, 412–404 B.C." *Journal of Hellenic Studies* 52, 42–46.

——. 1933. *Greek Mercenary Soldiers from the Earliest Times to the Battle of Ipsus.* Oxford: Oxford University Press.

Perlman, Shalom. 1957. "Isocrates' Philippus: A Reinterpretation." *Historia* 6, 306–17.

——. 1976–77. "The Ten Thousand: A Chapter in the Military, Social, and Economic History of the Fourth Century." *Rivista Storica dell'Antichità* 6–7, 241–84.

Redford, Donald B. 1992. *Egypt, Canaan and Israel in Ancient Times.* Princeton, N.J.: Princeton University Press.

Rostovtzeff, Michael I. 1941. *Social and Economic History of the Hellenistic World.* 3 vols. Oxford: Clarendon Press.

Roux, Georges. 1966. *Ancient Iraq.* Harmondsworth: Penguin.

Ryder, Timothy T. B. 1965. *Koine Eirene.* Oxford: Oxford University Press.

Sealey, Raphael. 1993. *Demosthenes and His Time: A Study in Defeat.* Oxford: Oxford University Press.

Sherwin-White, Susan, and Amélie Kuhrt. 1993. *From Samarkhand to Sardis: A New Approach to the Seleucid Empire.* London: Duckworth.

Spence, I. G. 1993. *The Cavalry of Ancient Greece.* New York: Oxford University Press.

Tarn, William W. 1930. *Hellenistic Military and Naval Developments.* Berkeley and Los Angeles: University of California Press.

———. 1948. *Alexander the Great.* 2 vols. Cambridge: Cambridge University Press.

———. 1984. *The Greeks in Bactria and India.* 3d ed. revised by Frank Holt. Chicago: Ares Press.

Tritle, Lawrence, ed. 1997. *Greece in the Fourth Century.* London: Routledge.

Walbank, Frank W. 1940. *Philip V of Macedon.* Cambridge: Cambridge University Press.

———. 1993. *The Hellenistic World.* Rev. ed. Cambridge, Mass.: Harvard University Press.

Worley, Leslie J. 1994. *Hippeis: The Cavalry of Ancient Greece.* Boulder, Colo.: Westview Press.

Republican Rome

NATHAN ROSENSTEIN

Introduction

Wars and conquest were the hallmarks of Republican Rome.[1] Nearly every year
for almost five hundred years, the city's armies marched off to war; their efforts
won Rome first hegemony in central Italy, then dominance within the peninsula, and finally rule over the length and breadth of the ancient Mediterranean.
Long, relentless warfare profoundly affected the Roman people, yet what most
impelled and sustained this massive undertaking was nothing less than the very
character of Republican Rome itself. No case therefore more strikingly illumi-
nates the continuous interplay of war and society as they acted and reacted
upon one another. This chapter centers on two fundamental and related questions: first, what features of the Republic's economy, society, politics, and ideology enabled Rome's armies to win this vast imperium and, second, what impact
its acquisition in turn had on Rome.

To begin with some background, the Republic's expansion falls into three
broad phases. Rome became prosperous and powerful under the monarchs
who ruled it in the late seventh and sixth centuries as well as at the outset of
the Republic established in 509 when a group of dissident aristocrats overthrew
Rome's last king. Its territory at the close of the sixth century was perhaps 820
square kilometers, and scholars usually put the total population between twenty-five and forty thousand. Temple construction and the archaeological record
reveal affluence as well as cultural sophistication, while a treaty struck with
Carthage in the first year of the Republic demonstrates Rome's status as the

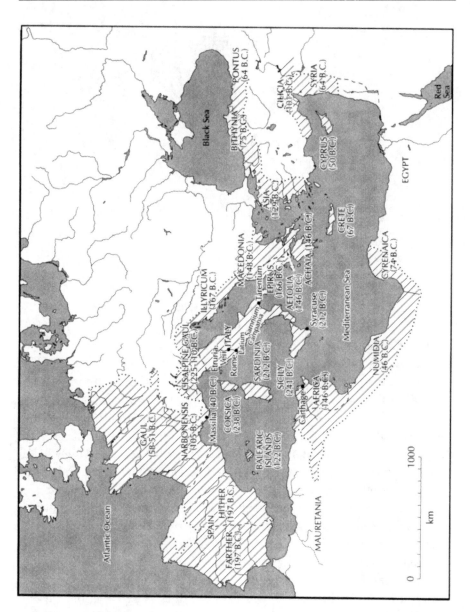

The Roman Empire, ca. 44 B.C.E.
(Dates of provinces are given in parentheses)

region's dominant power. The city was on a par with the largest of its Etruscan neighbors and all but the grandest poleis in the contemporary Hellenic world.[2] Yet the ensuing decades would sorely test the city's strength. Large-scale migrations out of the Apennine highlands, probably in response to population growth and famine, created widespread dislocation throughout Italy and drove tribes living in the mountains east and south of Latium and Rome down into the plain in search of food and land at the expense of earlier settlers. During the mid–fifth century the city found itself locked in a complex, desperate struggle with these migrants as well as its various Latin and Etruscan neighbors. Rome's territory shrank, and the archaeological record indicates precipitous economic decline as well. Rome's military situation seems to have improved toward the end of the century, although reliable details are scarce. One solid fact, however, emerges at the close of the fifth century: the city's conquest of Veii, its powerful Etruscan neighbor to the north and chief rival for dominance in the region. Unfortunately, Rome's humiliating loss at the Allia River (traditionally 390) to a large war band of Gauls soon followed, and although the Gauls departed after pillaging the city, the defeat seems to have badly shaken Rome's standing in central Italy. Thereafter local warfare continued down to the latter part of the fourth century.

A new phase opens at this point, marked by swift, dramatic growth over the next two centuries. In 338 Rome gained decisive control over Latium after crushing a revolt of its former allies and incorporating many of them among its citizens. Rome's territory now leapt to 5,525 square kilometers, with a total free population of perhaps 347,300.[3] At about the same time, the focus of Roman warfare began to shift to more distant theaters, particularly Campania, a rich agricultural region to the south. Involvement here set in motion a long series of wars with the Samnites who occupied the mountains east of Campania. Increasing Roman success eventually brought most of the rest of Italy's peoples into the struggle on one side or the other, either fearing the growth of Roman power or in an attempt to employ it in local conflicts. Rome's great victory at Sentinum in 295 over a combined army of Samnites, Etruscans, and Gauls turned the tide decisively in Rome's favor. Fighting continued intermittently down through 272, particularly when Tarentum, the last major city free of Roman dominion, enlisted the Epirote king Pyrrhus against Rome in 281. However, by 264, on the eve of the city's first war with Carthage, its control over Italy south of the Appenines was unchallenged. Rome's territory was now perhaps 26,805 square kilometers, and the total free population around 900,000.[4] In addition, the city had forced nearly every other state in the peninsula into alliance with itself, whether by intimidation, conquest, or by offering protection against a powerful neighbor. Allies surrendered control of their foreign relations to Rome and allowed it to draw on their manpower for its armies. Together with the city's colonies (see later discussion), this network of alliances nearly tripled Rome's military manpower.[5] Two great struggles with Carthage followed: the first (264–249) gave Rome control of Sicily; the second, the war with Hannibal (218–201), brought mastery of the western Mediterranean. Wars in the east ensued, against Macedon twice (200–196 and 171–167), and with Syria and the Aetolian League (191–189). At the same time, Rome completed the conquest of Gallic northern Italy, begun before the Hannibalic War, and undertook the pacification of Spain. By the last third of the second century, after renewed conflicts in Spain, Greece, and Macedon, and against Carthage, Rome controlled the entire Mediterranean basin.

Conquests well beyond the Mediterranean characterize the final phase of Republican expansion, most notably Gaul, initiated in the last decades of the second century but principally the work of Caesar in the 50s, and Anatolia and Syria by Pompey during the 60s. Fighting also occurred in Africa and the Balkans, and Rome withstood a grave threat at the close of the second century from migrating Germanic tribes, the Cimbri and Teutones, defeated in southern Gaul and northern Italy under Marius's leadership. A backdrop of social and political conflict at Rome distinguishes this phase of Rome's expansion, most dramatically revealed in the revolt of Rome's Italian allies in 91–89 and two civil wars: between Marius, his successors, and Sulla, 89–81, and then in 49–45 between Caesar and Pompey and then Caesar and Pompey's heirs. The latter, along with the renewed civil wars following Caesar's assassination, effectively ended the Republic and laid the basis for the establishment of the monarchy.

War and Society in the Early and Middle Republic

Rome could sustain this arduous burden of conquest over so many generations because war greatly helped the city mitigate socioeconomic and political conflicts. The origins of this pattern lie far back in the Republic's earliest years. Scholars dispute nearly everything about this era owing to the lack of contemporary sources and the distortions introduced, wittingly or not, by ancient authors writing centuries after the fact. What follows claims only to be a fair reconstruction based on current scholarship but one, it is hoped, that avoids building too much on hotly disputed premises. Most Romans in the fifth century were farmers, as they would remain throughout the city's history, producing crops destined almost exclusively for their own consumption, principally *far* (emmer wheat). Since the average size of their holdings appears to have been quite small—in the range of 1.5 to 2.5 hectares—they also probably exploited some portion of Rome's public land, the *ager publicus,* in order to survive and, in many cases, flourish, for a considerable number of these farmers grew wealthy enough to serve as hoplites. As in contemporary Greece, a phalanx of citizens able to equip themselves with a full panoply defended early Rome. This group, the *classis,* formed the core of the city's armed might, numbering at the beginning of the Republic probably between three and six thousand hoplites in all.[6] Below them, *infra classem,* poorer citizens fought as light-armed skirmishers, while those with the greatest wealth, principally a small aristocracy known as the *patricians,* served as cavalry and supplied the army's officers and generals. The patricians also derived their income from agriculture via control over large tracts of land and the dependent labor necessary to work them. All citizens served without pay and supplied not only their own weapons and armor but also food while on campaign in keeping with the rudimentary state of Rome's financial structures and public fisc.[7]

The military crisis confronting Rome during the fifth century brought tensions latent in this arrangement to the surface. Enemy raids and loss of territory probably hurt the city's small farmers the most, since they had few resources to fall back on in the event they lost all or even part of a year's crop, while losing their land meant complete ruin.[8] Those so affected had little choice but to seek a livelihood and protection by placing themselves in the debt of wealthy aristocrats, who could probably mobilize private military resources among kinsmen and dependents to defend themselves and their lands. Under the institution of debt bondage (*nexum*), a free man offered his labor to another on the security of his person in return for support. He thereby ceased to be completely free, for the penalty for failing to perform his part of the bargain was sale into slavery. For the aristocratic creditor, on the other hand, the fifth-century troubles were both bad and good: his lands, too, were threatened, but he was more able to sustain losses and to protect his crops, while the availability of debtors increased. And because such men possessed few other options, a creditor was in a position to dictate terms and impose burdens beyond what was customary. More debtors from whom more labor could be extracted enabled aristocrats to cultivate more land and so grow richer. The land they exploited, however, was usually *ager publicus,* and their appropriation of it further undermined the economic viability of the small farms that sustained most of the populace, the plebs. The latter therefore agitated throughout this period both for limits to the abuses debtors could suffer under *nexum* and especially for land to enable farmers to avoid or escape debt. But war was shrinking Roman territory, and the rich, who controlled the public lands that might have gone to satisfy plebeian demands, were naturally reluctant to give it up or to see the supply or powerlessness of dependent laborers for their estates limited. Yet as the ranks of prosperous smallholders dwindled, the number of men able to serve in the city's phalanx diminished with it. Some debtors may have continued to serve as hoplites, but if so their oppression scarcely made them eager defenders of a polity that allowed their merciless exploitation against its foes. Fears that a similar fate might someday await them probably affected even those plebeians who had not yet fallen into debt and made them, too, reluctant warriors. Hence as Rome's military crisis increased the bitter antagonism between the plebs and the patricians over debt and landlessness, the city's ability to defend its remaining territory declined, leading to further shrinkage, increasing internal conflict over land and debt, and consequently greater military weakness in a steadily downward spiral.

But war also offered a way out of the impasse. The military pressure on the Republic furnished the plebs with a weapon capable of forcing concessions from the patricians: the *secessio,* a general strike that included refusal of military service. This made the two sides somewhat more equal in their struggle and impelled compromise, initially the creation of plebeian magistrates, the tribunes of the plebs, to protect debtors from abuse. Subsequently in the late fifth and fourth centuries, as Rome slowly built up a network of alliances that could mobilize enough manpower to turn the tide in Latium, conquered territory became available for distribution to landless plebeians, creating an alternative to debt-bondage and so limiting the labor force aristocrats could use to monopolize public lands needed by plebeian smallholders to sustain themselves. Yet patrician aristocrats benefited not only because the pressure on the public land they already held thereby eased but also through the overall increase in the amount of public land available for exploitation, for not all conquered land was parceled out to colonists or among individual settlers. The problem of supplying labor for their domains remained, but to meet this need the former occupants of conquered lands, many of whom defeat had reduced to slavery, were now available. Consequently, aristocrats could afford to yield to demands to let their debt bondsmen go and, ultimately, acquiesce in the abolition of *nexum* itself. Moreover, the economic independence and prosperity of Rome's small farmers expanded the pool of manpower available for the legions and thereby facilitated further conquests.

Successful war thus allowed the Republic to avoid any permanent solution to the competition for access to public land between rich and poor; instead, the creation of ever more *ager publicus* simply palliated that conflict. This link between conquest and profit—both land and the movable booty that victory also brought—became a fundamental incentive leading the Romans to war year after year.[9] Moreover, this expansion also contained a self-perpetuating dynamic in the continuous supply of poor peasants that it concurrently produced. Not all of those the city defeated faced slavery. Much depended on circumstances, and these not infrequently led Rome to allow many of the conquered to keep their freedom, but at the cost of surrendering a significant portion of their lands and becoming Roman allies. Others struck treaties to forestall attack or strengthen themselves against enemies closer to home. Alliance imposed a significant military burden: an ally's principal obligation was to supply troops to fight alongside the legions. However, allies also shared in the spoils of victory, including colonies. These provided a place for impoverished allied citizens— particularly those whose land had gone to Rome as the price of peace—but also required further conquests to acquire new territory for colonies, conquests that the allies' contribution to Roman military power would in turn help facilitate. New conquests, however, brought new allies and newly impoverished peasants and began the cycle again.

In the fourth century and particularly following the suppression of the Latin revolt, Rome also began to use the extension of its own citizenship as an instrument of imperial expansion, forcing cities whose loyalty it particularly wished to secure to merge into the Republic.[10] This openness to new citizens set Rome apart from many other city-states, particularly the Greek poleis, which prided themselves on their homogeneity and exclusiveness.[11] On the contrary, the Romans' foundation myth emphasized the highly disparate character of the first settlers Romulus and Remus brought together when they established their city, and this sense of themselves as a composite people certainly helped minimize friction as the Romans absorbed ethnically distinct peoples into their citizen body.[12] This practice probably accounts for much of the growth of Rome's population, since preindustrial agrarian populations do not increase naturally very quickly, and we know of no reason to impute extraordinary fertility to the Romans of the early and middle Republic. It also certainly helped expand the number of men available for the legions. But at the same time this increase continuously renewed the numbers of small farmers and landless among the citizens who looked to Rome's conquests to better their lots, thereby placing further pressure on the city to expand.

As long as the supply of enemies whose land they could conquer and distribute lasted, therefore, the Romans could find social peace at home and at the same time satisfy their allies' needs in order to keep together the alliance system that underpinned their military power. War fostered political peace, too, within the Republic's ruling class, and transformed its character. The aristocracy of the early Republic, the patricians, had by the mid–fifth century formed themselves into a closed caste in response both to pressures on them for concessions from the plebs and the military exigencies of the era.[13] They controlled Rome's government through the senate, technically only an advisory body to the Republic's magistrates but in fact possessing great authority by virtue of its members' prestige, their collective experience and expertise, and the fact that magistrates were drawn exclusively from its ranks and returned to it following their year in office. Patricians also occupied all priesthoods; in addition, they alone knew Rome's unwritten laws and, even after these were codified and published around 450 B.C., the complex procedural formulas essential to conduct suits before the courts. Yet toward the end of the fifth century and increasingly throughout the fourth, some plebeians challenged these pillars of patrician domination, seeking particularly access to the city's chief magistracy, the consulate. These men, to be distinguished from the mass of small and middling plebeian farmers, acquired the estates necessary to aspire to aristocratic status in the course of the extraordinary increase in Rome's territory that accompanied its conquests. The same warfare also enabled them to gain the prestige essential to lead their fellow plebeians and so claim a place among the city's ruling elite. The army drew its cavalry and officers from the wealthiest citizens, including rich plebeians, and constant warfare afforded the latter many opportunities to win the military laurels that allowed them, back in Rome, to become tribunes of the plebs and spokesmen for plebeian demands. Because plebeians constituted the bulk of Rome's population, their tribunes soon sought a role in the leadership of the whole community and access to the consulate itself. And since their followers were essential to victory in the wars that patrician consuls led, leading plebeians could link agitation for a share of political power to the economic demands of small farmers and gradually force the patricians to open first the consulate (367), later the priesthoods (300), and finally almost all positions of authority to plebeians.[14]

Not surprisingly, as these wealthy plebeians claimed their share of political power at Rome, opportunities arose for them to forge marriage alliances with families from the old patrician aristocracy. The result was the creation of a new elite, the *nobilitas,* for whom war continued to play a vital role. Its members defined themselves through both high birth and an ideology that stressed possession of *virtus* (manly excellence) displayed in the pursuit and acquisition of *gloria* and *fama* (glory and renown) won through service to the *res publica* (Rome's public affairs). War constituted by far the city's most important public business, and hence war offered the greatest scope for accumulating *gloria* and *fama.* These and the *virtus* they bespoke most of all demonstrated a man's fitness for leadership and paved the way to high public office, particularly election to the consulate. Tenure of this magistracy, in turn, stamped a man and his descendants as noble or confirmed the elite status of a scion from a family already distinguished in this way. Consequently, competition for the office was always intense, and possession of the greater military prestige frequently determined its outcome. The victories that consuls won thereafter helped underwrite the *auctoritas* (influence) that their voices carried in senatorial and public debate. Hence the city's constant warfare served as a theater for competitive aristocratic performance, and its opportunities for personal distinction were vital to the ambitions of the *nobilitas.* This dependence of Republican political culture on war contributed greatly to encouraging a fundamental belligerence among the city's elite.[15]

Thus war at Rome became the nexus linking the interests of rich and poor, Roman and ally, patrician and wealthy plebeian, junior senator and distinguished ex-consul. This fact goes a long way toward explaining the harmony of Republican and Italian society during the third and much of the second centuries, the era of the city's greatest conquests. One should not, however, go on to claim that structural factors fully account for Rome's wars during this period. Proximate causes played a critical role throughout. The actions of Rome's enemies and allies more than once drew the city into conflicts.[16] The tactical and strategic imperatives that shaped individual commanders' short-term decisions also significantly affected the course of Republican foreign policy.[17] At times even simple fear, most notably of the Gauls in northern Italy, may have incited Rome to war.[18] Also, because the allies' obligations to Rome were purely military, continuous warfare may have been essential simply so that by availing itself of the allies' military cooperation Rome thereby maintained and strengthened its hegemony over them.[19]

The final ingredient that made this system work so successfully was a military instrument capable of winning the victories that would satisfy all the constituencies at Rome that war served. However, its development first required significant changes in the economic basis of the Republic's war-making. Early Rome's yeomen-hoplites could campaign only for a fairly brief period both because of their agricultural work in the spring and fall, but especially because they paid their own expenses while on campaign.[20] Among subsistence farmers operating in a poorly developed market economy that offered few opportunities to raise cash crops, ready money was in chronically short supply, and that, in turn, limited their ability to wage war. Because wheat is bulky and laborious to transport, soldiers on campaign usually took along only enough for a few days.[21] Once these supplies were gone, they relied on local markets or pillaging to feed themselves. But wheat in Italy is ripe enough to harvest only for a comparatively short time during June and July.[22] Before that it is inedible, and afterward in antiquity it had usually been gathered and secreted behind city walls out of reach. Consequently, markets supplied food much more dependably, although in hostile territory even these might be scarce. However, buying food meant spending money, and because subsistence farmers, even comparatively prosperous ones, were reluctant to part with what little cash they had, their campaigns tended to be brief and consequently close to home.[23]

This limitation mattered little as long as the Republic warred principally against its neighbors, who fought under similar economic constraints. In the latter decades of the fourth century, however, Rome began to challenge more distant and difficult enemies; campaigns in Samnium especially required armies to remain longer in the field. Accordingly, the way wars were funded had to change as well.[24] The solution, payment for military service (*stipendium*), not only solved the immediate problem but also set in motion a series of changes that fundamentally altered the nature of Roman warfare. Soldiers could now buy the food necessary to remain in the field for months or even years at a time, allowing the Republic's armies to undertake wars not only throughout Italy but also across the entire Mediterranean basin.[25] As campaigns required troops to fight throughout the fall and winter, warfare in turn began to impinge on the requirements of the agricultural cycle and impelled changes in the composition of the legions. Men who bore primary responsibility for their farms simply could not stay away from them until late autumn or winter and still expect to plow and plant enough to support themselves and their families. Only younger men who had not yet taken up primary responsibility for a farm were able to absent themselves on campaign for six or seven months at a time. Roman men seem to have married fairly late—in their middle to late twenties—and before that age many in addition will still have had living fathers, meaning they had some time to wait before they inherited the family farms.[26] So between coming of age at eighteen and being able to start families of their own, they were available for extended military service that conflicted with the agricultural requirements of a subsistence farm.[27]

The economic strength that permitted the Republic to offer such payments therefore represents the cornerstone in Rome's military expansion. War, of course, to some extent funded itself: Rome frequently required defeated foes to provide indemnities that compensated the city for the cost of a war, and booty as well represented an important source of income to offset the sums disbursed for pay. But whatever return a war brought came only at the victorious conclusion, while commencing and sustaining it until then required cash up front. The tax that funded military pay, the *tributum*, seems to have accompanied *stipendium* from its inception; only with the massive booty from the conquest of Macedon in 167 in the treasury did the senate cease its collection. But the senate's ability to collect the tax stemmed not from any qualitative change in the Roman economy, which remained primarily agrarian throughout the Republic, but from an increase in the number of prosperous farmers who could afford to pay it.[28] In part, their numbers and wealth resulted directly from Rome's success in resisting the incursions of its neighbors in the fifth century, in the warfare that enlarged its own territory in the fourth and the third, and from the practice of using this conquered land to succor poor and landless citizens. However, it seems more than coincidence that the introduction of payment for military service occurred only following Rome's defeat of the Latin League in 338 and the incorporation of most of its members among its own citizenry, vastly increasing the size of that body and, accordingly, the number of taxpayers.

Pay and longer service in turn allowed Rome in the last decades of the fourth century to develop the sophisticated manipular army of the middle Republic. This involved changes in both weapons and tactics.[29] Heavy infantrymen now adopted an oblong shield, a short stabbing sword, and throwing spears in place of the hoplite's round shield and thrusting-spear. The bronze breastplate and greaves disappeared: those who could afford it wore mail armor, otherwise a metal pectoral, while a more open helmet permitting greater lateral vision replaced the closed hoplite-type helmet.[30] These changes were closely connected with innovations in Rome's order of battle. The Romans broke up the unitary mass of their phalanx into small squads, the maniples, in which legionaries arrayed themselves more loosely than hoplites in a phalanx, since soldiers wielding swords or throwing spears require more room around them than densely packed phalangites. A more open formation for the thirty maniples constituting a legion also evolved, the so-called *quincunx,* an arrangement of three lines of ten maniples each, each maniple separated from the maniple to its left and right by a distance equal to its own front, and each maniple of the second and third lines placed behind the gap between two maniples in the line in front of it. The arrangement resembled the five spots on a die or the diamonds, clubs, and so forth, on a five in a deck of cards. The maniples themselves fell into one of three age-groups, which in turn correspond to the position each held in the Roman line of battle. Younger men, the *hastati,* in maniples of 120, occupied the front rank; those next in age, the *principes,* also grouped in maniples of 120 men each, constituted the second line; while at the rear the oldest formed the reserve, the *triarii,* whose maniples contained only 60. All of these were armed as described previously except for *triarii,* who still carried heavy thrusting spears. Thus 3,000 heavy infantry normally constituted a legion, in addition to 1,200 of the youngest and poorest recruits who served as light-armed *velites* and 300 cavalry, as before drawn from the upper class. A Roman army normally comprised two legions accompanied by an equal or greater number of allies. What the legions lost in solidity in consequence of these changes they more than made up for in increased tactical flexibility and maneuverability.

Precisely how this formation operated in battle remains controversial, but the key seems to have been the ability of the maniples to fall back or move forward to reinforce one another through the gaps in each line, as well as the looser arrangement within a maniple that permitted its soldiers successively to move up to and retire from a battle's front lines. The result was by far the most effective infantry the ancient world ever knew, as the longevity of the manipular army and especially its successor, the cohort army operating on the same tactical principles, demonstrates. This is not to say that Rome won every battle its legions ever fought nor to deny that its massive reserves of manpower were critical in allowing the Romans to absorb punishing losses and still continue to fight. The Romans, in fact, only gradually realized the full potential of the tactical system they had created. But in the end the legions won every decisive battle and every war, and their ability to do so gained Rome its empire. For our purposes, the important point is that pay was essential to this system's success, for it allowed

Roman armies to become much more proficient at arms than levies of farmers who only assembled in response to trouble. The heavy infantry of a manipular legion along with its *velites* and cavalry, together for several months on campaign, had considerable time to drill and otherwise cultivate the skills and discipline they would need in battle. The result was by no means professional armies, but armies unquestionably far better versed in the art of war than many of their opponents.[31] In achieving this extraordinary level of proficiency, the manipular system itself also played a critical role. The power of a Greek polis's phalanx lay in the strength of the bonds among its citizen-hoplites, men who had long lived with one another and knew each other well. Rome was by this time no longer a simple city-state: its territory extended over much of central Italy, and public life for many citizens was mediated through the *municipia* (communities of Roman citizens who also managed their local affairs) rather than Rome itself. The men annually levied for a Roman phalanx might have little familiarity with one another and hence did not bring to war the intense mutual loyalty necessary to cohere under the pressure of combat. Breaking the phalanx into smaller blocks allowed the men of each maniple to develop a far greater degree of cohesiveness among themselves than they would have had as individuals within the mass of a phalanx.[32] Thus by constructing their legions out of many small, tough, easily replicated maniples and keeping them in the field for long periods, the Romans found a way to overcome the limitation on military effectiveness inherent in annual levies of citizen-soldiers from among a large and diverse population, and to create a powerful instrument of war.

Yet the ramifications of the manipular army extend far beyond simply winning battles, as important as this was. The legions' remarkably consistent success was vital to aristocratic cohesion and the stability of the Republic's highly competitive political system. The concentration of honor and authority among a small number of its members was always a threat to an aristocracy like Rome's, breeding jealousy and resentment among those excluded and raising the specter of divisions developing that would ultimately lead to civil strife. Avoiding this problem meant ensuring that a few men did not monopolize the magistracies, particularly the consulate, that conferred prestige and power on those who held them. Instead, tenure of such offices needed to circulate widely within the elite. Yet these posts usually entailed military command, and access to them came through victory in hotly contested elections in which many of the voters would follow the winner off to war. Nothing would have been more natural than for citizen-soldiers to prefer tried and tested former consuls who had already demonstrated their ability to win battles. Yet the trend at Rome was precisely the reverse as repetition of the consulate became less and less frequent during the middle and late Republic, allowing more and more aristocrats to reach this supreme honor. No coincidence, then, that this trend began in the early decades of the third century, following the creation of the manipular system. Its effectiveness allowed the Romans to develop an ideology of victory that placed little weight on the tactical or strategic skills of the commander but instead saw victory as principally won by the soldiers themselves along with the city's gods. The general served mainly to inspire his men by setting an example of courage and determination in the fighting, a role that most aristocrats, trained throughout their lives to exhibit *virtus*, were capable of performing. Hence elections were won or lost on the basis of the respective *fama* and *gloria* of the candidates and their ancestors, not skill at managing armies in combat, something only experienced and successful former generals could plausibly claim to possess. The Romans anticipated their armies would win no matter who was in command provided only that he possess the requisite moral character.[33]

The army also played a vital role in fostering and strengthening a common civic identity among the Romans. The mechanisms that promoted unity in a polis, such as participation in religious festivals or at political events, tended to operate with diminished efficacy in a widely dispersed citizen body such as Rome's in the middle Republic, for usually citizens had to come to Rome to take part and many lacked the resources to make the long journey with any frequency. Military service was different. It brought together men from all over Roman territory in their late teens and twenties for many months each year over several years. It emphasized to them the special status they shared as Romans, in contrast not only to the enemies they conquered but also to the cohorts of allies who shared their campaigns but whose conditions of service were patently worse. It crosscut local identities and allegiances, since men were enrolled in the legions without regard for where they came from, and ties to hometown patrons counted for little or nothing. Military service entailed a direct interaction between the citizen and his state, one of the few an ordinary man might ever experience in a society pervaded by the mediating links of patronage and where, as in most preindustrial states, the government's overall intrusion into his daily life was minimal at best. At the same time, since the political and social elite of Rome continued to supply the armies' officers and generals, the legions' command structure reflected and at the same time reinforced the social and political hierarchies of the society at large.[34]

The Late Republic

Changes in tactical organization and social composition mark the advent of the late Republican army. In the final decade of the second century, after two hundred years of success, the manipular system finally met its match against the Cimbri and Teutones, whose numbers simply overwhelmed the maniples. In response, the Romans made the cohort, a larger formation that had been used from time to time during the preceding century when the tactical situation warranted, their basic tactical unit, allotting ten to a legion.[35] The characteristic *quincunx* formation they retained, but the cohorts of each line ceased to be composed of soldiers from specific age-groups. Instead, whatever dynamic this arrangement by ages had contributed to the legions' effectiveness henceforth became internalized within the cohorts themselves: one maniple each from the *principes, hastati,* and *triarii* now comprised a 480-man cohort, making it, in effect, a microcosm of the old manipular legion.[36] In addition, the number of heavy infantry within each legion was increased through the elimination of its light-armed component; those who had formally served as *velites* now became heavy infantrymen. The system proved highly durable, forming the bedrock of Roman military power not only during the Republic's last half-century but also throughout the early and middle empire.[37]

Second, these late Republican legions drew their recruits mainly from the large number of poor and landless men among Rome's rural population. Scholars usually trace the origins of this group to social and economic changes attendant on Rome's conquests in the first half of the second century.[38] Wars waged, often simultaneously, in Greece, the Hellenistic Near East, Spain, and northern Italy required levying great numbers of men into the legions: from 200 to 168, a yearly average of about 47,850 Romans from a total adult male citizen population of around 300,000. Rome's effort during the worst of the Hannibalic War, only a few years earlier, had certainly been greater, but those troops had served mostly in Italy. Following the war, many legions served abroad for several years, since transportation back to Italy, dismissal for the winter, and then reassembly the following spring was highly impractical. The middle years of the century saw some easing of the military burden, but never below an annual average of 30,000 citizens after 167, mostly serving overseas.[39]

These two factors, it is thought, combined to undermine the viability of Italy's small farmers. Because yeomen-soldiers transported to distant wars could not return to their farms when active campaigning ceased, particularly for plowing and planting in the fall, their farms failed for lack of their labor. And because so many smallholders were under arms during these years, farms failed in vast numbers. Soldiers finally mustered out returned to ruined fields or farms encumbered with debt and had no choice but to sell them, becoming part of a growing, impoverished rural proletariat. At the same time, however, Rome's victories brought unprecedented wealth to those in the city's and Italy's upper classes who had officered the armies or profited from the disposal of booty. Because the Roman economy was still largely agrarian, few outlets existed for this cash other than land. Consequently, as ruined farmers were selling out, the upper classes were in the market for properties on which to establish large estates manned by the slaves that Rome's conquests had also created in record numbers in order to produce cash crops—principally cattle, wine, and olives—for new urban markets like Rome itself.[40] The result was not simply a social crisis owing to widespread displacement of Rome's small farmers from the land by slaves but a military problem as well, since possession of a minimum amount of property was a prerequisite for service in the legions, and landless men could not meet it. Rome's pool of potential recruits consequently began to shrink, even though the number of citizens did not decline. The problem became apparent toward the middle of the second century, and various reformers, beginning with Tiberius Gracchus in 133, came forward attempting to solve the problem only to encounter fierce resistance in the senate. Its members feared the political consequences of the popularity that would accrue to any successful reformer and opposed limiting the amount of public land anyone could control because this would hurt their economic interests and those of their friends.

Increasingly, however, doubters have questioned this reconstruction.[41] Little evidence points unequivocally to a shortage of recruits. While complaints about the levy did arise from time to time and draftees occasionally resisted conscription, the difficulty and unprofitability of the wars in prospect and a general distaste for military service seem best to explain such episodes rather than the undue burden that Rome's demands for manpower placed on property owners still liable to the draft. When victory and booty seemed in the offing, plenty of volunteers came forward to serve.[42] Moreover, archaeology has conspicuously failed to confirm an overall picture of declining numbers of small farms in the second and first centuries B.C. While smallholdings are scarce in some areas, they abound in others, suggesting that independent small farmers survived there as well. A complex situation in Italy resists blanket characterization and cautions against monocausal explanations for declines where these occurred, particularly since high manpower demands and overseas wars do not necessarily undercut the needs of subsistence agriculture. The absence of a man from his farm is a problem only when his labor is essential, but, as suggested earlier, most Roman men did not marry before their late twenties; thus, few men drafted at eighteen will have had wives and children dependent on their husbandry to feed them. Perhaps as many as half had fathers yet living who would continue to work the farm while they were gone. Nor would the loss of their labor have represented a serious hardship, for subsistence agriculture is not necessarily labor-intensive. On the contrary, underemployment is typical on small farms, and if a son left for several years, this would mean less food had to be grown and so less labor would be needed. Yet even if the fields did go out of cultivation for a time, that did not necessarily mean they could not be brought back to productivity. In fact, in a world of little fertilizer and imperfect knowledge of crop rotation, long fallowing could be beneficial.[43] Finally, the contrast between the character of Rome's wars in the second century and the city's conquests in the third or even the fourth should not be exaggerated. Lengthy campaigns, some even requiring troops to winter in camp, were common. If farms were going to fail because continuous warfare kept soldiers from their fields, they would have been failing much earlier than the second century. Yet everything we know suggests that recruits were, if not eager, at least willing to serve throughout the third century and most of the second.[44] Had they perceived going to war as a threat to their livelihoods, one would expect evidence of widespread resistance, particularly since the Republic lacked the means to coerce large numbers of recalcitrant recruits. None, however, is apparent.[45]

Poverty and landlessness certainly troubled late Republican society, but warfare's role in their creation may have been only indirect. Great wealth undeniably flowed from Rome's victories in the early second century into the hands of the upper classes, and these men certainly did have few ways to invest it other than in land, but the land they sought to transform into capitalist estates probably comprised not mosaics of tiny smallholdings but extensive tracts of the city's *ager publicus.*[46] Competition over access to this land had roiled social relations in the early Republic, and only the Republic's success in increasing its overall supply through conquest had alleviated that conflict. But this strategy offered no permanent solution to the problem of apportioning a finite public resource among citizens with widely divergent ends in view and highly unequal means to achieve them. Once the Romans ran out of enemies in Italy and hence a supply of new *ager publicus,* as they did in the early decades of the second century, the problem of access was bound to recur, and the upper class, with its growing wealth, political connections, and social prestige, was in a far stronger position to enforce its claims than small farmers. Since access to some public land was essential to the latter, once the rich blocked this, smallholders either found their farms unable to support them or experienced a dramatic decline in their standard of living. At the same time, because conquest and colonization within Italy had ceased, the traditional mechanism for meeting the needs of Rome's poor no longer functioned.

Whatever their origins, however, landlessness and poverty are central to any understanding of the late Republican army and that army's impact on Roman society. In 107, C. Marius chose to ignore the property qualification for legionary service in raising troops, and in the crises that followed—the war with the Cimbri and Teutones, and particularly the great revolt of Rome's Italian allies—urgent manpower needs led recruiting officers to draft impoverished citizens wholesale. The practice of filling the legions exclusively with property owners thereafter went by the board, and Roman armies ceased to reflect the social and economic makeup of the society as a whole, although Marius's innovation probably did not represent a sharp break with previous practice so much as its culmination: the property requirement had apparently been quite small for some time, so that eliminating it produced no sudden alteration in the social origins of the legionaries.[47] Certainly, their circumstances did not tempt destitute farmers to look upon military service as an alternate career. While the legions may have offered some a temporary livelihood, no professional army developed at this stage. The bulk of the soldiers wanted above all to return to civilian life as prosperous landowners.[48] Nor did poverty produce a spate of client-armies loyal only to their generals to whom they looked for wealth and land.[49] Most legionaries served Rome faithfully and then returned to civilian life. Only Sulla, Pompey, and perhaps Marius were able to bestow lavish grants of land on their soldiers, and only Pompey was in a position to employ his veterans in subsequent political struggles. Yet he ultimately found the loyalty evoked by the benefits he conferred evanescent.[50] Finally, their economic circumstances never led the soldiers to develop a revolutionary or class-consciousness. Even Sulla's legionaries, the first ever to march on Rome, were following a duly elected consul attempting to suppress rioting and lawlessness in the city. If they also saw their own material interests at stake because those responsible for the violence had passed legislation depriving Sulla and themselves of the lucrative campaign in Asia then in prospect, that does not make them in their own minds any the less defenders of public order and traditional government. In the civil war that followed, each side claimed legitimacy as the champion of the Republic against its enemies. No soldier fought to overthrow the state. Yet men from identical class backgrounds constituted these armies, and when Sulla's legions won the contest, they felt no compunction about seeing their leader confiscate other small farmers' land to provide them their rewards and create a new class of landless poor in the process. They were eager to join the status quo, not overthrow it.

Poverty did, however, strongly reinforce the ancient belief among the soldiers that those who won wars ought to obtain land from their success, providing a powerful economic push to complement the ideological pull of tradition. This connection constitutes a leitmotif running through late Republican politics, from legislation to settle Marius's veterans in Africa after their victory there to the arrangements Caesar made to secure land for the veterans of his Gallic wars.[51] In the same era, two critical events conjoined war and politics in a different way. In the late 90s Rome's Italian allies agitated for Roman citizenship and full equality with the people whose partners in conquest they had long been. Their motives were various; one widespread complaint may have been the harsher treatment and inferior conditions under which allied soldiers served.[52] When Roman intransigence frustrated attempts to win the concession politically, they took up arms, and, although they lost the Social War, they won their point: desperation impelled the senate to offer the allies citizenship to secure the allegiance of those still loyal to Rome and induce rebels to lay down their arms. The second event was Sulla's march on Rome, already noted, when the consul turned to his soldiers after his enemies had carried the day in the assembly, and its corollary, his return from Asia at the head of his troops after his enemies had seized the reins of government and declared him an outlaw. These precedents taught that war could be a continuation of internal political competition by other means (as Clausewitz might have put it had he treated civil war), while the soldiers' indigence made it possible to win their support for such a step through promises of wealth and especially land in the event of victory. Moreover, because the senate largely failed to take meaningful steps toward alleviating landlessness among the rural poor in the years following the Sullan civil war, the perception of aristocratic indifference to their plight may also have eroded the loyalty that armies recruited from among the dispossessed felt toward Rome's ruling class.[53]

No socioeconomic crisis, however, precipitated the Republic's fall. Paradoxically, the legitimacy and strength of the traditional order stood unquestioned in the minds of nearly all who lived under it.[54] Most modern scholars see the prevalence of rural poverty and the incorporation of landless men into the army as only a necessary, not a sufficient, cause for the conflagration of the civil wars.[55] Some even argue that in its own slow, erratic, but quite customary way the Republican establishment was in fact moving toward solutions to some of Rome's social ills.[56] But, if so, reform did not come fast enough to prevent the sparks of political conflict from igniting the blaze. A central component of the traditional order was vigorous, intense competition among the city's elite and a political culture that stressed equilibrium within their ranks by limiting the stature and influence that any single figure could gain. Caesar had won unprecedented *gloria* and *fama* along with stupendous wealth in Gaul. The immensity of his achievement and the enormous prestige it conferred brought together many aristocrats in an effort to prevent him from dominating political life by cutting him down to size. This was no more than the way politics had always worked. However, the Italians and Sulla had demonstrated that no political defeat need be final, and when Caesar's opponents in Rome gained the upper hand in the senate, he did not hesitate to follow Sulla's precedent. He claimed before his soldiers to be defending his dignity and the ancestral constitution against his enemies who had violated its central tenets, but he also promised his legions, already loyal by virtue of the Gallic riches he had lavished upon them, even greater bounties for their help against his enemies. Which was uppermost in their minds we cannot say, but their willingness to follow him ended the Republic in the long years of civil war that ensued.

Epilogue

Hard, bitter combats convulsed Italy and the Mediterranean for almost a generation: between Caesar and Pompey, Caesar and Pompey's followers after the latter's death, Caesar's assassins and his supporters in the wake of Caesar's murder,
and finally between Octavian—the future Emperor Augustus—and Marc Antony
for supreme power at Rome. In the end, both war and society were transformed.
A monarchy replaced the Republic, and free political competition ceased forever.
Augustus, once firmly in power, found a solution to the social turmoil that had
roiled the Republic's final decades in a massive demobilization of legions and the
establishment of their veterans in colonies in Italy and overseas. That move effectively ended the problem of landlessness in Italy and thereby eliminated both its
role in politics and its impact on the army. Rome enjoyed social and political
peace for the first time in decades, and that peace underwrote public support for
Augustus's rule. Change came to the city's military establishment as well.
Although citizen-soldiers had fought one another for nearly twenty years, the
armies of the civil wars were the last to be so constituted. Caesar had survived the
attempts to destroy him only because of the loyalty and proficiency of his
legionaries, and his heir Augustus learned that lesson well. Long-serving, well-
paid professionals, loyal to the emperor, their commander in chief, and permanently stationed for the most part on the empire's distant frontiers, would
henceforth fight Rome's wars, breaking once and for all the connection between
citizenship and military service that had been the bedrock of the Republic's military power. Command could no longer be left to the outcome of political competition among the aristocracy; the legions were too essential to Augustus's hold
on power. The emperor handpicked his army's officers, still drawing them from
the upper classes as under the Republic but now carefully screened for loyalty.
The most critical posts went to members of his own family.[57] Wars did not cease:
under Augustus Rome's legions were on the march again. But now their victories,
as in the good old days of the Republic, came against foreign foes. By the end of
his reign, Augustus's conquests had eclipsed even Caesar's. Interestingly, and significantly, however, the fundamental link between military service and land
endured: upon their discharge, the emperor bestowed colonial allotments on his
veterans or the cash with which to purchase substantial farms, a last reward for
meritorious service and the final guarantee of their loyalty. From this point on,
however, soldier and civilian became separate and distinct in the Roman world,
acting and reacting upon one another in quite new and complex ways.[58]

Notes

1. All dates B.C.E. Notes are deliberately minimal, intended principally to direct readers to recent scholarship in English where they can find references to earlier literature, full citations of the ancient evidence, and/or further argument and discussion of the points made in the text. Readers should note the detailed surveys of many of the points and issues touched on here in volumes 7.2, 8, 9, and 10 of the *Cambridge Ancient History*, 2d edition. I thank my coeditor, Kurt Raaflaub, for the many helpful comments and criticisms he has offered on this chapter.
2. Raaflaub 1986a.40–45; Cornell 1995.204–14.
3. Cornell 1995.351.
4. Cornell 1995.380.
5. Cf. Brunt 1971.44–60, esp. 54, and Baronowski 1993, for 225.
6. Evans 1981; de Neeve 1984b.30; Spurr 1986.82–86; Drummond 1989.118–24.
7. Raaflaub 1986a.44; Cornell 1995.179–86.
8. Cf. Garnsey 1988.8–86, 167–73, and Gallant 1991 on the tenuousness of subsistence agriculture under normal circumstances.
9. Harris 1979.
10. Sherwin-White 1973.
11. Sallares 1991.109.
12. Cornell 1995.60.
13. Raaflaub 1993.
14. Raaflaub 1986b.
15. Harris 1979. Whether ordinary citizens perceived military service as an opportunity for upward mobility through displays of valor, as was the case, for example, among the Aztecs (Hassig, this volume) or the Chinese (Yates, this volume), is unclear.
16. Gruen 1984.
17. Eckstein 1987.
18. Rich 1993.
19. Momigliano 1975.44–46; Oakley 1993.16–18.
20. Cf. Greek hoplites: Raaflaub, this volume; and levies in the medieval West: Bachrach, this volume.
21. Cf. Greek practices: Anderson 1970.43–59; Pritchett 1971.30–52; Engles 1978. 11–25, 123–30, and the Aztecs: Hassig, this volume.
22. Spurr 1986.66–67.
23. Cf. Thuc. 1.141.3–5.
24. Scholars debate when and why payment for military service began. Some follow the ancient sources and date the practice to the last years of the fifth century, in connection with Rome's siege of Veii, but others believe this is far too early and suggest a point a century later, during Rome's wars with the Samnites: late fifth century: e.g., Crawford 1985.22–24; late fourth century: e.g., Raaflaub 1996.290. A diplomatic solution might be to suggest that the siege of Veii did require the year-round presence of troops and so some type of subvention, but that pay did not become a regu-

lar feature of Roman warfare until lengthier campaigns in more distant Samnium and elsewhere necessitated keeping armies in the field for several months each year.

25. Poly. 6.39.12–15. Cf. Erdkamp 1995. Cf. the importance of pay to the development of the Athenian naval power.
26. Saller 1994.
27. See further, Rosenstein forthcoming.
28. Nicolet 1976; 1980.149–69.
29. Meyer 1924.195–224; Keppie 1984.19–21.
30. Bishop and Coulston 1993.48–64.
31. Cf. again the importance of pay to the development of Athenian naval power.
32. Lee 1996.207–10.
33. Rosenstein 1990; cf. Goldsworthy 1996.116–70.
34. Nicolet 1980.89–148.
35. Bell 1965.
36. On the importance of age-solidarity, cf. the Spartans' organization of their army by age classes.
37. Goldsworthy 1996.12–38, 171–247; Keppie 1984.63–67.
38. Brunt 1962.
39. Brunt 1971; Hopkins 1978.33–36.
40. Hopkins 1978.1–98.
41. Dyson 1992.23–55; Evans 1980.19–47; Rich 1983.287–331.
42. Rich 1983.316–21.
43. Spurr 1986.120–22.
44. Harris 1979.46–50.
45. On this whole problem, see Rosenstein forthcoming.
46. De Neeve 1984a.150–51.
47. Rich 1983.297–99; Rathbone 1993.144–46.
48. Brunt 1962.
49. Brunt 1988.257–65.
50. Gruen 1974.374–79; Brunt 1988.278–80 for Marius.
51. Brunt 1988.265–73.
52. In general: Brunt 1988.93–143.
53. Brunt 1962; Brunt 1988.68–81.
54. Meier 1995.26–28, 349–63.
55. E.g., Brunt 1988.1–92.
56. Gruen 1974.358–404.
57. Raaflaub 1987.
58. See Campbell, this volume.

Bibliography

Anderson, John K. 1970. *Military Theory and Practice in the Age of Xenophon.* Berkeley and Los Angeles: University of California Press.

Baronowski, D. 1993. "Roman Military Forces in 225 B.C. (Polybius 2.23–4)." *Historia* 42, 181–202.

Bell, M. J. V. 1965. "Tactical Reform in the Roman Republican Army." *Historia* 14, 404–22.

Bilancio critico. 1993. *Bilancio critico su Roma arcaica fra monarchia e repubblica.* Atti dei Convegni Lincei 100. Roma: Accademia Nazionale dei Lincei.

Binder, G., ed. 1987. *Saeculum Augustum* I: *Herrschaft und Gesellschaft.* Wege der Forschung, Volume 512. Darmstadt: Wissenschaftliche Buchgesellschaft.

Bishop, M. C., and J. C. N. Coulston. 1993. *Roman Military Equipment from the Punic Wars to the Fall of Rome.* London: B. T. Batsford.

Brunt, Peter A. 1962. "The Army and the Land in the Roman Revolution." *Journal of Roman Studies* 52, 69–86. Republished with revisions in Brunt 1988.240–80.

———. 1971. *Italian Manpower.* Oxford: Clarendon Press.

———. 1988. *The Fall of the Roman Republic and Related Essays.* Oxford: Clarendon Press.

Cornell, Timothy. 1995. *The Beginnings of Rome: Italy and Rome from the Bronze Age to the Punic Wars (c. 1000–264 B.C.).* London: Routledge.

Crawford, Michael. 1985. *Coinage and Money under the Roman Republic: Italy and the Mediterranean Economy.* London: Methuen.

De Neeve, Pieter W. 1984a. *Colonus: Private Farm-Tenancy in Roman Italy during the Republic and the Early Principate.* Amsterdam: J. C. Gieben.

———. 1984b. *Peasants in Peril: Location and Economy in Italy in the Second Century B.C.* Amsterdam: J. C. Gieben.

Drummond, A. 1989. "Rome in the Fifth Century I: The Social and Economic Framework." In Walbank 1989.113–71.

Dyson, Stephen L. 1992. *Community and Society in Roman Italy.* Baltimore, Md.: Johns Hopkins University Press.

Eckstein, Arthur M. 1987. *Senate and General: Individual Decision-making and Roman Foreign Relations, 261–194 B.C.* Berkeley and Los Angeles: University of California Press.

Engles, Donald. 1978. *Alexander the Great and the Logistics of the Macedonian Army.* Berkeley and Los Angeles: University of California Press.

Erdkamp, Paul. 1995. "The Corn Supply of the Roman Armies during the Third and Second Centuries B.C." *Historia* 44, 168–91.

Evans, John K. 1980. "*Plebs Rustica:* The Peasantry of Classical Italy I." *American Journal of Ancient History* 5, 19–47.

———. 1981. "Wheat Production and Its Social Consequences in the Roman World." *Classical Quarterly* 31, 428–42.

Gallant, Thomas W. 1991. *Risk and Survival in Ancient Greece.* Stanford, Calif.: Stanford University Press.

Garnsey, Peter. 1988. *Famine and Food Supply in the Graeco-Roman World.* Cambridge: Cambridge University Press.

Goldsworthy, Adrian. 1996. *The Roman Army at War: 100 B.C.–A.D. 200.* Oxford: Clarendon Press.

Gruen, Erich. 1974. *The Last Generation of the Roman Republic.* Berkeley and Los Angeles: University of California Press.

———. 1984. *The Hellenistic World and the Coming of Rome.* Berkeley and Los Angeles: University of California Press.

Harris, William V. 1979. *War and Imperialism in Republican Rome, 327–70 B.C.* Oxford: Clarendon Press.

Hopkins, Keith. 1978. *Conquerors and Slaves: Sociological Studies in Roman History.* Vol. 1. Cambridge: Cambridge University Press.

Keppie, Lawrence. 1984. *The Making of the Roman Army from Republic to Em₁'ire.* London: B. T. Batsford.

Lee, A. D. 1996. "Morale and the Roman Experience of Battle." In Lloyd 1996.199–217.

Lloyd, Alan B., ed. 1996. *Battle in Antiquity.* London: Duckworth.

Meier, Christian. 1995. *Caesar: A Biography.* Translated by David McLintock. New York: Basic Books.

Meyer, Eduard. 1924. *Kleine Schriften.* Vol. 2. Halle: Niemeyer.

Momigliano, Arnaldo. 1975. *Alien Wisdom.* Cambridge: Cambridge University Press

Nicolet, Claude. 1976. *Tributum: Recherches sur la fiscalité directe sous la république romaine.* Bonn: Habelt.

———. 1980. *The World of the Citizen in Republican Rome.* Translated by P. S. Falla. Berkeley and Los Angeles: University of California Press.

Oakley, Stephen. 1993. "The Roman Conquest of Italy." In Rich and Shipley 1993.9–37.

Pritchett, W. Kendrick. 1971. *The Greek State at War.* Part I. Berkeley and Los Angeles: University of California Press.

Raaflaub, Kurt. 1986a. "The Conflict of the Orders in Archaic Rome: A Comprehensive and Comparative Approach." In Raaflaub 1986c.1–51.

———. 1986b. "From Protection and Defense to Offense and Participation: Stages in the Conflict of the Orders." In Raaflaub 1986c.198–243.

———, ed. 1986c. *Social Struggles in Archaic Rome: New Perspectives on the Conflict of the Orders.* Berkeley and Los Angeles: University of California Press.

———. 1987. "Die Militärreformen des Augustus und die politische Problematik des frühen Prinzipats." In Binder 1987.246–307.

———. 1993. "Politics and Society in Fifth-Century Rome." In *Bilancio critico* 1993.129–57.

———. 1996. "Born to Be Wolves? Origins of Roman Imperialism." In *Transitions to Empire: Essays in Greco-Roman History, 360–146 B.C., in Honor of E. Badian,* edited by Robert W. Wallace and Edward M. Harris, 273–314. Norman: University of Oklahoma Press.

Rathbone, Dominic. 1993. "The *Census* Qualifications of the *Assidui* and the *Prima Classis.*" In Sancisi-Weerdenburg, et al. 1993.121–52.

Rich, John. 1983. "The Supposed Manpower Shortage of the Later Second Century B.C." *Historia* 32, 287–331.

———. 1993. "Fear, Greed and Glory: The Causes of Roman War-making in the Middle Republic." In Rich and Shipley 1993.38–68.

Rich, John, and Graham Shipley, eds. 1993. *War and Society in the Roman World.* London: Routledge.

Rosenstein, Nathan. 1990. *Imperatores Victi: Military Defeat and Aristocratic Competition in the Middle and Late Republic.* Berkeley and Los Angeles: University of California Press.

————. Forthcoming. *War, Agriculture, and the Family in Mid-Republican Rome ca. 320–100 B.C.*

Sallares, Robert. 1991. *The Ecology of the Ancient Greek World.* London: Duckworth.

Saller, Richard P. 1994. *Patriarchy, Property and Death in the Roman Family.* Cambridge: Cambridge University Press.

Sancisi-Weerdenburg, Heleen, et al., eds. 1993. *De Agricultura: In Memoriam Pieter Willem de Neeve (1945–1990).* Amsterdam: J. C. Gieben.

Sherwin-White, Adrian N. 1973. *The Roman Citizenship.* 2d ed. Oxford: Oxford University Press.

Spurr, M. S. 1986. *Arable Cultivation in Roman Italy c. 200 B.C.–c. A.D. 100. Journal of Roman Studies* Monographs No. 3. London: Society for the Promotion of Roman Studies.

Walbank, Frank W., et al., eds. *The Cambridge Ancient History.* Vol. 7, Part 2. 2d ed. Cambridge: Cambridge University Press.

The Roman Empire

BRIAN CAMPBELL

The Historical Background

After the years of civil war that followed the murder of Caesar in 44 B.C., Augustus finally emerged as the most successful of the military leaders who had fought for supremacy using armies of Roman citizens in their personal pay. By 31 B.C. he controlled the resources of the Roman world and had under his command the largest army of skilled and experienced Italian soldiers ever assembled. This army, bound in loyalty to his person, was from the start linked to imperial politics and the personal survival of the emperor. So, the system of government that emerged in the imperial period functioned in many crucial aspects as a military autocracy, in which the main players were the leader and the army.[1]

The Leader

The Roman emperor was an autocrat subject to few restraints except his own discretion and the desirability of finding a satisfactory relationship with the upper classes, who provided most of the army commanders and senior administrators. He was effectively commander in chief of the army, controlling appointments to military commands, and the disposition and emoluments of the troops. The emperor also directed foreign policy and the use of the army, and was therefore responsible for all victories, which were credited to him, not to his commanders. However, the close association of the emperor with the army and military decisions meant that he was increasingly drawn into conducting major campaigns in person. This enhanced his military image and

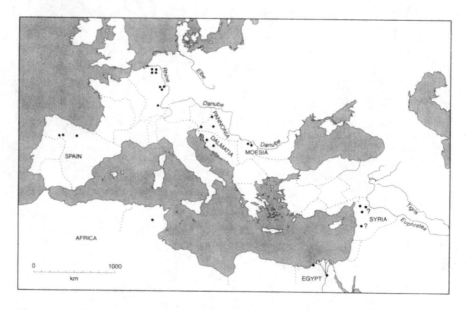

The Roman Legions in A.D. *14*

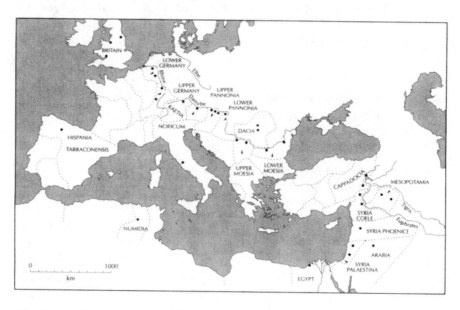

The Roman Legions in A.D. *200*

brought more opportunities for contact with the troops but undoubtedly made it more difficult for the emperor to distance himself from military failure.

The Army

Augustus reorganized the Roman army while preserving its traditional structure and practices. The system he established remained largely intact into the third century A.D. and shows, therefore, how society in the Roman world was organized for war during a crucial period for the development and consolidation of Rome's Mediterranean empire. The imperial army was to be a standing, professional force whose soldiers normally served for twenty-five years. First, it contained legions, each comprising about fifty-two hundred heavy infantry; legionaries were Roman citizens, but increasingly of non-Italian extraction, that is, they were recruited from citizens in the provinces of the empire. Second, there were *auxilia* units, either infantry or cavalry (there were some mixed units, and some specialist fighters, e.g., archers and camel riders); they were noncitizens, recruited from the less-Romanized provinces or the periphery of the empire. The *auxilia* infantry may have had somewhat lower pay and a lower status than legionaries,[2] which perhaps reflects the old idea that service in the Roman army was a *privilege* as well as a duty (in the army of the Republic, citizen-soldiers were originally required to have some property). Third, the army included the praetorian cohorts (the emperor's personal bodyguard, largely recruited from Italian citizens), and additional forces in Rome consisted of the urban cohorts (a kind of paramilitary police force also recruited from Italians) and the Vigiles (the fire brigade recruited originally from freedmen). The praetorians were an elite force with higher pay and better service conditions; and they symbolized the emperor's close personal association with the army and his political dependence on it.[3]

Many of the soldiers' duties were routine, since in part they made up an army of occupation that had to keep order in Rome's territories, perform guard and semipolice duties, and maintain and administer itself. However, the army was primarily a professional fighting force, which as well as repelling incursions into the empire also conducted campaigns of aggrandizement and expansion.

The Empire

After Augustus's reign, which saw more territory added to the empire than ever before, the long rule of the Julio-Claudian dynasty settled into a pattern of substantially untroubled military loyalty and little intervention by emperors in military campaigns, although Claudius visited Britain in person for the climax of the war of annexation. The civil wars of 68–69 were a great break with what had gone before, and out of the political disorder emerged the Flavian dynasty, which had a background of considerable military experience because of the role of Vespasian and Titus in the suppression of the Jewish Revolt of 66. Domitian,

Vespasian's younger son, as emperor conducted extensive campaigns on the Rhine and Danube, and the emperor's personal involvement in military activity became more common in the second century. After Domitian's murder, Nerva's brief rule was notable in that, by either design or compulsion, he chose a successor (Trajan) from outside his family. Thereafter, for a time emperors chose the man they wanted as their successor, until Marcus Aurelius was succeeded by his son Commodus, whose murder in 192 precipitated a further period of civil war (193–97) and the emergence of the Severan dynasty. There was no policy that an emperor should choose his successor for any presumed military qualities, although Trajan and Hadrian had experience as governors and army commanders. Nevertheless, in this century external warfare became more prevalent. Trajan annexed Dacia (105) and unsuccessfully attempted to overthrow the Parthian empire. Further campaigns in the east by Lucius Verus were followed by the great northern wars of Marcus Aurelius, which began as a response to threats to the stability of Roman influence beyond the Rhine and Danube rivers but which, by the time of Marcus's death, may have moved to a plan to annex more territory. Commodus abandoned the campaign. At the end of the second century there was more territorial expansion as Septimius Severus annexed Mesopotamia in 195–97, after another war with Parthia. From the late first century onward, the crucial areas of military interest were to remain the zones around the rivers Rhine, Danube, and Euphrates.

Despite the importance of the army, and the role of military prowess in Roman ideology, which went back to the Republic, the system of government established by Augustus, with its balance between the emperor and army, the institutions of the Republic, and the traditional prerogatives of the ruling class, proved to be relatively stable. In a period of over two hundred years there were only two civil wars in which the army was successfully used by a provincial governor to overthrow the ruling emperor.[4] The military resources of the empire were therefore conserved for use against external enemies, and not against other Romans, although the destructive impact of the campaigns in Italy in 68–69 should not be underestimated, nor should the damage done by the costly battles in 193–97. Cassius Dio comments on the loss to Roman power and the battlefield strewn with dead at Lugdunum.[5] In the third century, by contrast, much more effort was expended in civil conflict.

Army and Society

Numbers, Disposition, and Role

After the battle of Actium in 31 B.C., Augustus found himself with sixty legions comprising about a quarter of a million men under arms. Such numbers could not be supported in the long term, and he pensioned off many of them, creating an army of twenty-eight legions, which was intended to be a standing army from which all the military needs of the empire could be met without the requirement to recruit additional men in emergencies. The loss of Quinctilius Varus and his three legions in a military disaster in Germany in A.D. 9 reduced the army to twenty-five legions. Thereafter, the legionary force was only slowly augmented, numbering thirty-three legions by A.D. 193. This seems to bear out Augustus's initial judgment. By the end of his reign the *auxilia*, according to Tacitus (*Annals* IV. 5), equaled the legionaries in numbers. Auxilia units developed in a much more haphazard way than the legions, but they maintained their share of the army's complement (about four hundred thousand men by the third century A.D.).

The disposition of this army is of great importance for subsequent developments (see maps on page 218). From the start, legions and auxilia were permanently stationed in certain provinces (about nineteen by the end of the second century A.D.), with small detachments in many other provinces. Some provinces contained two or even three legions with auxiliaries, commanded by a senator of consular rank; others contained one legion and auxiliaries, commanded by a senator of praetorian rank. Initially, there was a considerable degree of movement and transfer of troops, but eventually things settled down and greater continuity was established. In the early imperial period, the troops were mainly located in winter camps, from which they emerged when the campaigning season resumed. Gradually, however, they were placed in permanent camps. The army therefore came to be like an army of occupation or a garrison army, with the potential for long-standing contacts with local communities. In the eastern provinces, the troops seem to have been temporarily billeted in cities, which would have brought them even closer to the local population, but this situation was considered injurious to discipline. Nevertheless, in the second century A.D. many legionary detachments in the east were stationed away from legionary headquarters, near urban settlements.

The Roman army had an effective monopoly of military power. Even if Rome did not formally disarm her subjects, the cities and the rural areas in Rome's dominions had no military forces at their disposal, except perhaps occasionally a small militia for police duties. In most parts of the empire, the army was likely to encounter little organized armed resistance or nationalist rebellions (with the notable exception of Judaea). The cities had lost their ability to protect themselves, so they relied on the army for protection against banditry, internal unrest, or attacks from peoples outside the empire. It is not surprising that rich Greeks like Dio Chrysostomos and Aelius Aristides saw the Roman emperor and his army as shepherdlike guardians of the grateful peoples of the empire. In fact, the army had a crucial role in preserving the city-based culture and the social, political, and economic structure of the Mediterranean world and its ruling elite.

There was a price to pay. This professional, standing army involved a huge annual cost in the payment of salaries, perhaps more than 40 percent of the empire's income in the first century A.D., financed to a large extent from taxation, which was borne mainly by the subject peoples of the provinces, but also by Roman citizens, who faced direct taxes on inheritances and auctions to finance the military treasury set up by Augustus.[6] In addition, soldiers received irregular income from imperial handouts (donatives) to celebrate certain occasions (e.g., the emperor's birthday), and when on the move, either individually or in groups or in armies, had to be supported by the local population with food, shelter, and the means for their journey. A large quantity of evidence shows how burdensome and oppressive this arrangement was for ordinary people, especially those living near the great military roads.[7] It is of great importance that Roman soldiers at all times were present among the population of the empire and cannot be separated from social, political, and economic developments.

Recruiting, Assimilation, and Integration

Service in the army attracted volunteers, but at least in the first two centuries conscription was common. It is likely that this was most often applied to the provinces and not to Italy itself,[8] which can help to explain the gradual decline in the number of Italians serving in the Roman legions.[9] Italians presumably preferred not to serve far from home and chose to enter the praetorian cohorts. That recruitment policy could affect society directly, at least in popular perception, we can see from the comments of Cassius Dio, who thought that the emperor Septimius Severus's decision to recruit the praetorians from legionaries incidentally ruined the youth of Italy, since they turned to banditry from want of any employment (LXXV.2.5). By the mid–second century A.D. (in the reign of the emperor Hadrian), there were hardly any Italians serving in the legions, which were now manned by provincial Roman citizens, or legionaries' sons who had been granted citizenship on joining up (legionaries tended to live with non-Roman women and so produced noncitizen children). In the early period, recruiting centered on the more Romanized provinces, such as Narbonese Gaul, Spain, and Asia Minor. Later, more men were recruited from the frontier zones, and also from Syria and Egypt.[10] Although some citizens were admitted to auxiliary units as the distinctions became blurred, the majority of auxiliaries were recruited from non-Roman peoples. It is beyond doubt that the vast majority of Roman soldiers came from a lower-class background. Upper-class contempt for the soldiery and their capacity for destruction is inherent in the account of the civil wars of A.D. 68–69 written by Tacitus, who was himself a senator. Cassius Dio, writing in the third century A.D., dismisses rank-and-file soldiers as "mere carriers of bundles of wood."[11] It was apparently a plausible, although exaggerated, taunt against Vitellius's army of the Rhine during its march on Rome in the civil war against Otho in A.D. 69 that it consisted of foreigners and aliens.[12]

What were the advantages of military service, and how were soldiers from varied, non-Italian backgrounds assimilated into Roman ideology and persuaded to fight for Rome in a professional army whose rates of pay were never high? Naturally, military discipline and the habit of obedience would be important factors in soldiers' behavior. Furthermore, men from a poor background will have appreciated the regularity of military pay (in three installments, although in the first century less per day than that received by a skilled worker),[13] the discharge payment on retirement (about thirteen times a year's salary for a legionary),[14] the comforting regimentation of military life with the uniform application of Roman training methods and techniques, and the use of clothing, equipment, regalia, and military standards, all of which expressed Roman ideology. This was backed up by the adoption of a military calendar in the camps, which, by concentrating attention on Roman deities and the emperor himself and his family, instilled respect for Roman customs. For a man from the lower classes, life in the army enabled him to rise above the usual lifestyle associated with his status. In some respects he had a privileged position (e.g., in certain legal matters) and a source of assistance in his officers, or even in the emperor himself. Moreover, in the long term there was a degree of social mobility in the army, with opportunities for promotion to the rank of centurion, and a way forward for men of low degree, who could with some luck progress by this route to equestrian rank, the second most senior social group.[15]

Most significant was the assimilation of soldiers into the Roman way of life by the granting of Roman citizenship to *auxilia* on discharge, or after twenty-five years' service. This recalls the practice of the Republic when foreign soldiers who had given sterling service to Rome were rewarded with grants of citizenship. However, by the end of the first century A.D., there was a regular process of rewarding not only auxiliary soldiers in this way but also their children and descendants. Furthermore, the children of praetorians, and probably also of legionaries, born after military service to noncitizen mothers, received citizenship. Although soldiers were forbidden to marry during service, in practice the government turned a blind eye to liaisons formed by soldiers with local women.[16] It may have hoped to find potential recruits among the children of serving soldiers, who perhaps had no better prospects elsewhere. Anyway, there was created among serving soldiers some opportunity for family life even if there were many difficulties, both legal and practical. Now, if soldiers were based in military camps, what happened to their "wives" and children? It is time to turn to the integration of soldiers into local society and the consequences of this process.

The establishment of permanent military camps in which the same units were stationed on a long-term basis must have created a great stir among the local population and also attracted people from outside. Naturally, the presence of large numbers of soldiers in an area had a significant economic effect in offering a market for produce and the provision of other services. The soldiers needed grain, foodstuffs, meat, wine, iron, timber, building materials, replacement draft animals and horses, leather, and clothing. The army was not self-sufficient, and it has been calculated that three hundred thousand soldiers would require about 100,000 tonnes of wheat annually, rising to 150,000 tonnes by the end of the second century with the increase in army numbers.[17] Some supplies had to be brought over long distances; for example, in Britain at the camp at Caerleon, remains of wheat have been discovered containing Mediterranean weeds.[18] However, many supplies would be brought to military camps from the immediate locality, or over relatively short distances (encouraged by various tax concessions to suppliers), and the presence of so many grain consumers should have had an impact on the rather static agricultural setup of local communities, and may have encouraged the production of more grain. Since not all this grain was in the form of taxes or rents in kind, there will have been scope for profit. Moreover, military bases, although sometimes set up in sparsely inhabited and underexploited areas, were often located at a communications center, and could be well placed for trade. There is evidence for commerce and mutual contact with peoples beyond Roman territory. For example, north of Hadrian's wall in east Lothian, there are indications that both the growing of grain and the rearing of cattle increased significantly after the arrival of the Romans.[19] Everywhere the soldiers brought protection, building activity, technical assistance, and new facilities which, although in the first instance designated for their own enjoyment, demonstrated a fresh dimension of organized life in a settled environment.[20]

Above all, soldiers attracted people. Merchants, traders, artisans, innkeepers, and women came in the wake of the camps. In many places temporary settlements (*canabae*) grew up right at the edge of legionary camps, providing an area with a military ambiance where civilians and soldiers could mix. The *canabae* obviously attracted large numbers of Roman citizens, and since soldiers often formed liaisons with local women during service, they would also contain military families, that is, the "wives" and children of soldiers and their relatives. Moreover, after discharge, veteran soldiers often preferred to settle in the *canabae* with their families, close to the comrades with whom they had served, rather than be part of a military colony in some other region.

These *canabae*, which were under the jurisdiction of the local legionary commander, gradually acquired a more permanent structure and better amenities, and began to have the air of fully fledged communities. In time, some were extended and developed into independent communities with their own magistrates. For example, at Carnuntum on the Danube, in the province of Pannonia, a military camp was built in the reign of Tiberius. On the division of Pannonia into two provinces under Trajan, Carnuntum became the seat of the governor of Upper Pannonia. From the end of Trajan's reign, legion XIV Gemina was stationed here, where it remained to the end of Roman control in the area. The *canabae* grew up in an unsystematic fashion on three sides of the military camp, close to which an amphitheater and a forum were built. Then a separate civilian settlement developed to the west of the camp, with several large buildings, including a new amphitheater with a capacity of about thirteen thousand (see Figure 9.1). In A.D. 124, during his visit to Pannonia, Hadrian granted municipal status to Carnuntum, and in A.D. 194 Septimius Severus, who as governor of Upper Pannonia had launched his successful bid for power from here, made it a colony with the title *Septimia Carnuntum*. This illustrates how the social, economic, and political development of communities could be bound up with the army and the ambitions of powerful governors.[21]

Settlements similar to *canabae* emerged on a smaller scale around camps and forts housing auxiliary soldiers, who often occupied outposts where larger

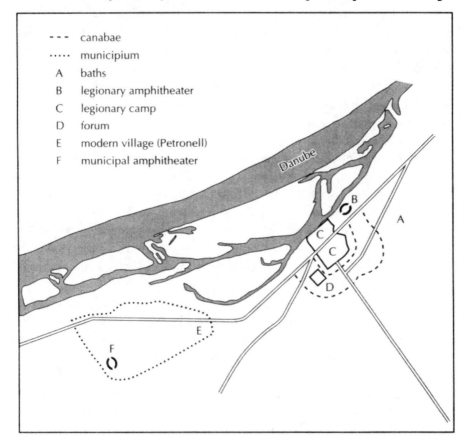

Figure 9.1. Carnuntum

concentrations of troops were either unnecessary or impracticable. These civilian settlements were called *vici*, were smaller than *canabae*, and had fewer Roman citizens in them. We can see such a development near Rapidum (Sour Djouab) in Mauretania, where the second cohort of Sardians was based.[22]

Some of the most striking examples of social upheaval and change in the pattern of landholding in the Roman world were brought about by the settlement of veteran soldiers in military colonies (i.e., an urban center with surrounding agricultural land) from the late Republic up to the reign of Hadrian. On one level this process left great physical remains, in the division of the land into large squares (*centuriae*, 706 meters by 706 meters, containing about 124.6 acres = 50.4 ha) by means of *limites* (roadways or balks), in preparation for distribution.[23] Traces of these field systems remain in the topography of Europe and North Africa to this day. More important, the work of the land surveyors influenced the siting of towns in Italy and the provinces, the establishment of rural communities, the place of soldiers in those communities, and the development of the relationship between town, country, and central government. Between A.D. 14 and 117, about fifty colonies were founded, although it has been calculated that around three hundred would have been needed for the presumed number of veterans.[24] Presumably, then, more soldiers received a monetary discharge payment and found their own place to settle than were planted in colonies. Nevertheless, expensive and sophisticated new towns continued to be founded, offering more facilities and attracting more people, who saw the arrival of Roman citizens with money in their pockets as a good opportunity for profit. For example, at Timgad, founded by Trajan in A.D. 100 for veterans of the legion III Augusta, which was stationed nearby at Lambaesis, the planners created a sophisticated urban environment in a desert setting. The town is laid out like a military camp, a square with rounded corners, one gate in each side, straight roads intersecting at right angles, and regimented barracklike squares for the houses, which would make the soldiers feel at home. Within the walls were all the amenities of civilized urban life, including baths, a theater, and even a library.[25]

All these developments—permanent military camps, the growth of *canabae* and *vici*, the settlement of veteran soldiers in colonies or in local communities—contributed to a greater integration of soldiers into local society. We may reasonably conclude that settled family life will have bound the troops more closely to the area where they served. In addition, by the second century A.D. recruiting was conducted largely on a local basis. So, perhaps soldiers would be more willing to perform their military service for Rome and fight in a region where they had a vested interest and where they subsequently hoped to settle. However, this pattern was by no means uniform, and it is important not to exaggerate the positive role of the army in social and economic developments. In some areas the presence of the army, its exploitation of rural areas, and the emergence of military settlements will have impeded the development of the local civilian urban economy, as apparently in Brigantia (in northern England), where the urban-villa economy prevalent in the south of Britain did not emerge.[26] Moreover, in Britain and in parts of the German provinces, where local recruiting was initially limited, the army existed in comparative isolation from the rest of the population, and *canabae* or *vici* retained a largely military, self-contained character, with a degree of urban civilization distinct from other local communities.[27] There is another, related question that is very difficult to answer, namely, how far Romanization and the influence of the military and those associated with it percolated into local life in the frontier zones. It may be the case that elite groups in the Roman or Romanized settlements had more in common with elite groups on the other side of the frontier zone outside Roman control than with rural dwellers in the countryside within Roman control.[28]

The development of permanent garrisons in a settled environment may have raised questions about the long-term mobility of the army. At times, soldiers who had a long-standing association with the area around their camp had to be transferred to another province. From the second century A.D. the government resorted to using *vexillationes,* that is, detachments of legions rather than whole legions, that could be moved to another location, initially for a limited time. This practice worked as long as the empire did not suffer a series of simultaneous military threats from different quarters. In the third century, however, the changing strategic and political picture led to the appearance of a field army, which originally was not strictly tied to a territorial area.[29]

It should be emphasized that the period from Augustus to Septimius Severus was one of substantial change: from an Italian to a non-Italian army, from a citizen army to one in which citizens made up barely half the numbers, from an army of occupation to a force that had many of its roots in the areas where it served. It is indeed plausible to argue that in this period the traditional separation of soldier and civilian was of much less significance than sometimes supposed, or than that which occurred at other times.[30] Soldiers had families, mostly from a rural background, often lived in the vicinity of other families in local society, and returned to these same areas after service, sometimes to a plot of land. Serving soldiers and veterans had a role to play in local communities. Veterans, for example, appear as patrons and benefactors; they could blend into local society and culture, some becoming traders, like the soldier who became a pottery trader at Lugdunum,[31] others entering business and providing employment; we find a legionary veteran settled in Egypt in A.D. 99 owning an olive farm and making a contract to hire a local woman to carry olives to his olive press.[32] They held office in their communities, like Annaeus Balbus of the fifth legion, who was a member of the Board of Two at Thuburnica in Africa,[33] and

Lucius Absens, who was priest of the emperor at Madaura, also in Africa.[34] A striking example of cross-cultural influences that we can only dimly understand is found in the recently published bilingual inscription set up on the banks of the Tigris in Greek and Aramaic by a veteran soldier with a Roman name (Antonios Domittianos), in honor of Zeus.[35]

For the local civilian population, the presence of the Roman army quartered in close proximity was not always a boon. Since in general the government had difficulty in controlling its agents, it is not surprising that there is much evidence throughout the imperial period of the widespread oppression of the local population by soldiers who exploited their superior power and status. This abuse ranged from casual theft to extortion and violence, and was prolonged, repeated, and extensive, despite attempts by emperors to prevent it.[36]

The Emperor and His Commanders

Almost all senior provincial governorships involving the command of troops were held by men of the upper classes (at the end of the second century only Egypt and Mesopotamia were governed by *equites,* the next most senior social group), who had held a series of offices, both civil and military, in various parts of the administration. They had also held the senior magistracy (the consulship) and were generally at least in their forties. What is striking is that Roman army commanders underwent no formal training and often had little experience of active service when they took up their posts. Furthermore, they generally held a top command (involving perhaps up to three legions and *auxilia* units) for no more than three years, and it was unusual for a man to hold more than two such commands in his career. Some guidance was apparently offered by military handbooks, which explained how past commanders had succeeded or failed and provided a series of stratagems for dealing with particular situations. Frontinus (senator and army commander ca. A.D. 100) comments on his collection of *Strategemata:* "For in this way commanders will be furnished with specimens of wisdom and foresight, which will serve to foster their own power of conceiving and executing similar exploits. There will be the added benefit that a general will not fear the result of his own stratagem, if he compares it with experiments already successfully made."[37]

Therefore, society and custom had much to do with the way in which the Romans organized their senior army commands. Consequently, it was difficult for younger but able men, or talented men from outside the senatorial class, to be promoted quickly to military commands. Emperors were constrained by social and political factors in their appointment of commanders, but in some ways that suited them because the nonspecialist approach meant that in the Roman Empire there was no military hierarchy of senior commanders that could threaten the emperor. For a senator, to command an army was still an important ambition because military ideology continued to have a significant role in Roman life, but the paradox was that the real political influence was wielded in Rome and a man returned there only after surrendering his command. Nevertheless, the emperor needed to choose carefully the men who were to hold army commands (they should be competent but not overly ambitious), and he also needed to keep the support of the upper classes (which would reduce the chance of a successful rebellion), while retaining the affection and loyalty of the troops (which could dissuade any potential usurper from trying his luck).

In military life, increasing significance was attached to the person of the emperor himself, who, when he took command, fitted the profile of upper-class commanders, since most had little or no military experience. Yet by the second century A.D., the emperor acted as a genuine commander in chief, taking charge of major campaigns and directing operations in person. In some cases this was the personal preference of an emperor. But we may also note that the behavior of emperors approximated more and more to the many military trappings of their position. Furthermore, an emperor might well be hesitant about allowing a senatorial commander to conduct a major campaign on his own initiative, as he could win military glory and the affection and respect of the troops. Because of his increasing personal involvement, the emperor's status as a commander became of greater significance in any judgment of his capacity to rule.

In terms of military strategy, emperors seem to have been essentially conservative in their use of the armed forces, and military aggrandizement involving the annexation of substantial territory and the creation of a new province was comparatively rare. Yet they could exploit the army in order to boost their prestige through military victories. There is little doubt that Claudius (A.D. 41–54) ordered the conquest of Britain in order to prop up his weak political position. He appeared in person in Britain for a mere two weeks of the campaign and then celebrated the victory spectacularly, with a triumph, a triumphal arch, and a special issue of coins. Trajan seems to have added Dacia to the empire mainly as an expression of his personal desire for military renown. His attack on Parthia, which ended in disastrous failure, had no discernible explanation other than the emperor's military vanity and his desire for a soldier's life. It seems likely that Septimius Severus launched his attack on Parthia in 195, and subsequently annexed Mesopotamia, largely to distract attention from the prolonged civil wars that brought him to power. In these examples of Roman aggression there is little sign of long-term strategical planning or concerted objectives. From the point of view of the Roman emperor, the potential glory of victory would have to be balanced against the risk of military defeat or loss of territory, which could be politically very damaging and perhaps encourage revolt among army commanders. Major campaigns involved huge expenditure of resources (which might or might not be recouped), the logistical problems of moving large numbers of troops, possibly over long distances, since the legions were widely dispersed, and the need to give some military responsibility to the emperor's senior commanders.

Indeed, in certain cases the Romans carefully avoided war. For example, what is striking about Roman relations with Parthia (an area well suited for the realization of militaristic fantasies because of its association with the exploits of Alexander the Great, the role model for military commanders) is the use of sophisticated diplomacy to avoid war, up until the time of Trajan.[38] We see this even in the case of Augustus, who rightly has the reputation of being a great conqueror in his early years. But in his dealings with Parthia he assiduously avoided war, instead using diplomatic pressure to achieve the return of Roman military standards previously lost, which he presented to the public as a great military success. He surely did not lack the resources or will to fight a war against Parthia. But he shrewdly reckoned that military glory could be better obtained elsewhere, for example, in Germany, where the campaigns of Caesar had shown possibilities, rather than in the east, where Roman armies had recently had a pretty disastrous record.

The absence of a formal military hierarchy, or government machinery for dealing with foreign affairs, probably made it difficult to formulate a consistent policy for dealing with peoples on the periphery of Rome's territory. Each emperor would have to rely on his immediate advisers and whatever recollection there was of previous decisions. It is worth noting that the lack of professional and highly experienced commanders may also have hampered the development of new techniques of fighting or the adoption of new weapons. In fact, tactical innovations and changes to weaponry were very slow in this period.[39] The only clear development was forced on the Romans by the success of armored cavalry and mounted archers used by the Parthians and other peoples. The defensive technique adopted involved the use of a new longer spear and a formation of legionaries resembling the old Greek phalanx, to resist the shock of an armored cavalry charge.[40] Perhaps significantly, this "innovation" looked backward, and in general the emperor and his advisers seem not to have initiated long-term strategies. Instead, they reacted to events and stimuli from below and dealt in an ad hoc fashion with problems that arose. While we should not underestimate the element of irrationality in decision making (an emperor could always exercise his inexplicable whim), it is probably correct to think that in the main emperors were guided by a shrewd desire to maintain Roman power and prestige, and to avoid large-scale offensive commitments that might threaten their established status, wealth, and power. We should not ignore the possibility that the Romans believed the peace and prosperity of the empire's peoples to be an important objective. So, the distinguished military commander of the first century A.D., Plautius Silvanus, records in his memorial inscription how he preserved the "peace of the province" by his military actions.[41]

The Later Empire

When Septimius Severus, the governor of Upper Pannonia, marched on Rome in 193 and captured it, this was the first time for almost 125 years that a military commander had seized power in this way. He precipitated a period of civil war that ended only in 197 with the defeat of his last rival, Clodius Albinus, governor of Britain. Although Severus won the army's favor by increasing military pay and allowing soldiers to marry, in the main he himself succeeded in keeping discipline in his armies. Nevertheless, the manner in which he seized power enhanced the role of the army by openly demonstrating its importance in the maintenance of political power. The balance between emperor, army, and upper classes, so carefully arranged by Augustus, was significantly altered. The last words of Severus to his sons were prophetic: "Stick together, enrich the soldiers, and despise everyone else."[42] The turbulent period of the Severan dynasty ended with the murder of Severus Alexander in 235 by an army officer, Maximinus, who came from Thrace and was allegedly of low birth. Alexander was seemingly overthrown by purely military discontent, because the soldiers were infuriated at his feebleness as a commander and his miserliness. Significantly, during Alexander's campaign against the Persians, some of the troops who had been transferred from Illyricum almost mutinied, since their wives and children had been put at risk by an invasion of German tribes where they had been stationed.[43]

The growing political instability between 235 and 284 was increased by an unprecedented number of raids and serious incursions into Roman territory, the death of one emperor and the capture of another in battle against foreign enemies, and substantial economic and social disruption, although this has sometimes been exaggerated.[44] Indeed, the empire held together remarkably well. Significant territorial loss was confined to a small area between the Rhine and the Danube, Dacia, and Mesopotamia. The empire survived as a political unit partly because its army was still capable of winning substantial victories and because the military structure did not disintegrate, despite its misuse in frequent civil wars. The military reorganization carried out by Diocletian (284–305) and Constantine (307–37) provided a sound basis for securing the empire in the changed strategical situation of the fourth century.[45] In brief, there are three crucial areas of change and development in this period, all of which are linked to themes explored earlier in this chapter: the role of the emperor, the command structure, and army organization.

Maximinus (235–38) was the first Roman emperor who fought in battle personally, and by now the close identification between emperors and their military duties encouraged the belief that to be an effective emperor a man needed to be an effective leader in war. Maximinus came from the Danube area, and emperors were increasingly associated with the militarily tough Danubian provinces. Diocletian himself came from Dalmatia, and the family of Constantine was of Illyrian pedigree. Moreover, it may be that the rapid turnover of emperors in the mid–third century A.D. reflects the idea that the military crises and incursions in various parts of the empire could be dealt with only by a man of imperial rank. It is possible to argue that the eventual political reorganization of the empire by Diocletian was influenced by these concerns. He established the so-called Tetrarchy, in which he had a fellow emperor with equal powers and prerogatives, and each of them had a *Caesar,* a kind of junior emperor and obvious successor. In practice each of the four rulers could take responsibility for part of the empire's territory. Therefore, there would in theory always be someone of imperial rank relatively close to the scene of the action and ready to deal with military expeditions or rebellions. Given the situation in the empire, it stands to reason that all emperors would depend very much on their military officers.

In the third century the disloyalty of many army commanders and the feeble ineffectiveness of many ephemeral emperors, drawn in the main from the senatorial class, must have raised doubts about the competence and suitability of senators in top military posts. The emperor Gallienus (253–68) made increasing use of men of equestrian rank (*equites*) in command of detachments of troops. He also used them in posts normally held by senators, for example, commanding a legion. It is unlikely that this was a comprehensive policy, but in the end Gallienus apparently decided unofficially not to consider senators for legionary commands. In time this could be observed by other emperors as a kind of rule. *Equites* tended to have more military experience than senators, and so the consequence was a move toward a more specialized army command. Since the military experience of senators was now still further restricted, it made less sense than before to appoint a senator as governor of a province where he was commander in chief of several legions and *auxilia.* Indeed, it seems that by the end of Gallienus's reign the process had begun of phasing senators out of provincial governorships involving the command of legionary troops and replacing them with *equites.* This obviously happened gradually. Nevertheless, the last clear example of a senator in command of a campaign is Decianus, governor of Numidia probably in 260 (*ILS* 1194). Moreover, from the mid–third century *equites* were being appointed to more senior posts, with the title *dux.* The *dux* had charge of a substantial body of soldiers and some initiative in their deployment—a role that would normally have been filled by a senator. The *dux* was subsequently to acquire responsibility for large territorial areas embracing the land of several provinces, thereby ending the established practice that military command went with responsibility for a single province. The relative success of Gallienus's armies demonstrated the competence of governors of equestrian rank. This was the pattern for the future, and the *equites* used tended to be schooled in military affairs and often promoted from highly experienced centurions and senior centurions. Therefore, in this period something like a military hierarchy of experienced officers does begin to emerge, which could of course constitute a threat to an emperor, and itself become the most likely source of a new emperor.

In my view, one reason for the resilience of empire and army in the third century was the close bond that had been created in the first two centuries between many soldiers and the area in which they served, by local recruitment, by permanent camps and related settlements, and by family life that linked soldiers closely to the local social and economic environment. These bonds could perhaps make soldiers reluctant to leave the area where they were stationed, and certainly caused them to have a local loyalty and willingness to fight to protect the area and the society with which they identified. It can be argued that at the end of the Severan dynasty soldier and civilian had important links, in that they frequently lived and worked side by side, even though the soldiers were formally separate as a professional army. It is in this context that we need to consider certain changes in army organization in the third century.

Two significant developments occurred gradually and are very difficult to date precisely, but should most likely be associated with the reign of Gallienus. First, there was an increased use of detachments of legions (*vexillationes*) on temporary assignment. Sometimes *vexillationes* from several legions were concentrated at vital points, for example, at Aquileia, a key stronghold for the defense of northern Italy, which received detachments from the Pannonian legions. Second, additional cavalry regiments were developed and seemed to serve as a special force under their own commander. These moves should be seen as an ad hoc reaction to immediate strategic problems, and not as part of an overall plan to change the military structure. However, they were pointers to the way forward to deal with a potential problem present since Augustus's military dispositions. The army was not large, given that it was permanently stationed in fixed locations in a huge empire that extended from Scotland to Egypt and from Spain to the Euphrates. Launching a campaign or dealing with a military crisis involved the expensive and disruptive movement of large numbers of soldiers, which became more problematic as soldiers became emotionally attached to particular locations.[46] In the third century the problem was that the empire faced long-term strategic threats in two areas simultaneously—the Rhine/Danube and the Euphrates, where the Persians had replaced the Parthians as a potent enemy east of the river. One possible answer was the creation of an army group consisting of infantry and cavalry, which could act independently of any territorial connection and be available to strike anywhere in the empire. This force, known as the field army (*Comitatus* or *Comitatenses*), existed in the time of Diocletian, although possibly its structure had not been formalized. Constantine increased the size and importance of the field army, conferring privileges on its soldiers and appointing two new senior officers, to command the infantry and the cavalry of the *Comitatenses*. The field army was combined with the traditional method of stationing troops permanently in certain key provincial areas. These troops (often called *limitanei*) were probably the more important element of Diocletian's arrangement, although it is likely that Constantine reversed this emphasis. Diocletian's strong territorial forces were backed up by increased building of forts, more easily defensible structures with fewer gates, thicker walls, more towers, and fighting platforms where large numbers of men and artillery could be stationed. They protected communications by road and river, facilitated internal control and patrolling, but still formed part of a system that could be used to initiate attacks. Even in the late third and early fourth centuries, the Roman Empire should not be seen as a defensive structure.[47] The Romans did not recognize any frontiers or formal limits to their power, and the army retained a significant capacity for offensive operations.

Diocletian also continued a process begun in the third century and increased the number of provinces by subdividing them. His purpose was primarily to enhance the control of the central government, and the military infrastructure of the empire remained intact, with armed and unarmed provinces. However, there is no doubt that Diocletian considerably increased the number of legions. For example, there were 28 legions, 70 cavalry units, 54 auxiliary *alae*, and 54 cohorts in the eastern provinces. In all, the 33 legions of the Severan era had been increased to at least 67. So, if the legions were of the traditional size, there will have been a huge increase in the number of soldiers. This is disputed, but there is no doubt that the pressure to find recruits was greater than ever. Lactantius (a Christian apologist of the late third to early fourth century), criticizing what he thought was a great increase in the army, highlights the intolerable burden of providing men for the levy (*De Mortibus Persecutorum* VII.5). It seems that government policy was to enforce conscription and insist that veterans' sons join up. A decision by Constantine in 313 probably confirms the practice under Diocletian: "Of veterans' sons who are fit for military service, some indolently refuse to perform compulsory military duties and others are so cowardly that they wish to evade the necessity of military service by mutilation of their own bodies" (*Codex Theodosianus* VII.22.1). City governments or individual landholders were responsible for providing a quota of recruits. This may be connected with the developing third-century practice of compelling civilians to remain in certain occupations and even to make the occupation hereditary. On the other hand, such measures may have been temporary, a response to the military crisis at the end of the third century and the subsequent civil wars; the government had always encouraged by various devices the sons of serving soldiers to join up. The real problem was not finding recruits but maintaining them. The social and economic dislocation of the third century brought an increasing debasement of the coinage and inflation. The center had less secure contact with the periphery of the empire, communities found it harder to administer their territories, and the tax base declined (Diocletian's reorganized provincial system was partly aimed at more efficient tax collecting). Indeed, the government moved toward a system of paying soldiers in kind. However, the territorial troops (*limitanei*), although inferior in status in the fourth century to the *comitatenses,* were not merely a kind of territorial militia of peasant farmers who tilled the soil where they were stationed. Although recruited locally and perhaps owning land in a private capacity, they were professional soldiers, separate from the local civilian population, until well into the sixth century.

Throughout this period the government supplemented the usual recruiting methods by the employment of large numbers of fighting peoples from the periphery of the empire. They were paid with money accepted from provincials in lieu of providing recruits, and settled on specially provided land. On the eastern frontier *alae* and cohorts are found bearing the names of tribes who had fought against Rome: Alamanni, Franks, Vandals. They remained together in their own units and fought in their traditional way. The consequence of this in the long term was that the Roman army assumed more of the character of a non-Roman mercenary force, in which the bond between locally recruited soldiers and the local population was broken and the whole concept of loyalty to Rome altered.

Epilogue

In the three-hundred-year period between Augustus and Constantine, the essential features of what Augustus called "the foundations that I have laid for the state" remained in place. But by the early fourth century, although the senatorial class retained its privileged position, it was no longer dominant in administration and military commands. The emperor nearly always had to prove himself in war and sometimes came from a military background, outside the traditional aristocracy. His military officers were tough and experienced soldiers from an equestrian background or lower (many coming from the Danubian area), and as emperors came to rely on them, their influence in government increased. For the soldiers, Roman citizenship no longer mattered; the army was increasingly non-Roman, even "barbarian," and in some cases was commanded by non-Roman officers, which may represent a decline in Roman authority and an attempt to bargain for military loyalty. It remained in the main a professional force, but its link with Roman ideology had been undermined, and it became more and more divorced from the Roman people and provincial society. It was just at this time that the tax base was declining and the support of the army was more burdensome for the communities in the empire; economic management consisted in transferring the produce of peasant farmers to the military hierarchy, and government no longer seemed to be primarily in the interests of the city-based elite. As the demand for good soldiers increased, warlords appeared in command of private armies, who chose to serve or oppose Rome's interests as suited their personal inclinations. In the east, where systems were devised to maintain and develop the tax base and hence to support the army, Constantinople emerged as the center of a revitalized empire. In the west, however, imperial power eventually collapsed through an inability to find and maintain reliable soldiers.[48]

Notes

1. The best account of the fall of the Roman Republic is still that of Syme 1939. For the transformation of the legions of the civil wars into the army of Augustus, see Rosenstein, this volume.
2. Alston 1994 has challenged the traditional view (see, e.g., M. A. Speidel 1992) that auxiliary soldiers were paid less than those serving in the legions.
3. Military organization: Cheesman 1914; Durry 1938; Passerini 1939; Parker 1958; Watson 1969; Holder 1980; Saddington 1982; Keppie 1984b; Webster 1985; Le Bohec 1989; Dixon and Southern 1992; Bishop and Coulston 1993; M. P. Speidel 1994.
4. For a survey of the development of the empire, and the position of the emperor in this period, see Millar 1977; Garnsey and Saller 1987; Wells 1992.
5. LXXV.7. Dio was a senator from Nicaea in Bithynia.
6. Cost of army: Hopkins 1980.124–25; Campbell 1984.161–76; military treasury: Dio LV.24–25; Augustus, *Res Gestae* 17.2; this treasury was for the payment of discharge benefits (see below).
7. Mitchell 1976.
8. Brunt 1974.
9. Forni 1953, 1974.
10. See n. 9 and Mann 1983.12–68.
11. For Tacitus, see Campbell 1984.365–67; Dio, LII.25.6.
12. Tacitus, *Hist.* II.21; cf. II.56.
13. For recent discussion of the evidence for military pay, see n. 2.
14. See above n. 6 and also below.
15. Legal privileges: Campbell 1984.207–314; military careers: Campbell 1994.28–56.
16. Campbell 1978.
17. Garnsey and Saller 1987.88–92.
18. Jones 1984.43–45.
19. Whittaker 1994.114.
20. Campbell 1994.141.
21. For Carnuntum, see Mócsy 1974.126–29, 162–65, 218.
22. A civilian settlement was set up adjoining the camp at Rapidum (built in A.D. 122), and in 167 a wall was constructed around this settlement by "the veterans and civilians dwelling in Rapidum . . . ": *Inscriptiones Latinae Selectae*, edited by H. Dessau

(Berlin, 1892–1916 [hereafter *ILS*]) number 6885. It became a *municipium* in the third century but was at the mercy of troop movements, and when around A.D. 270 the camp was abandoned, the settlement was destroyed and only partially reoccupied subsequently; see Laporte 1989.

23. Methods of Roman land survey: Dilke 1971; Campbell 1996.
24. See Mann 1983; Keppie 1983, 1984a; Campbell 1994.210–21.
25. Mann 1983.14; Sear 1989.205–6.
26. Higham 1986.175, 199–201.
27. However, note the *canabae* at Chester, which abutted on the military camp, and where some of the inhabitants had tapped into the camp's water supply; see Mason 1987.
28. Cf. Whittaker 1994.121–31.
29. See below.
30. The theme of the integration of the army into local provincial society has recently been explored in the case of Egypt by Alston 1995.
31. *ILS* 7531.
32. *Select Papyri*, Vol. 1, No. 17, edited by A. S. Hunt and C. C. Edgar (Cambridge, Mass.: Harvard University Press, 1932).
33. *ILS* 2249.
34. *Inscriptions Latines de l'Algérie*, edited by S. Gsell et al. (Paris, 1922–76) number 2201.
35. Healey and Lightfoot 1991.
36. See above, n. 7; Campbell 1984.246–54.
37. *Strat.* I *prooem;* for a survey of senatorial career patterns, see Campbell 1975; 1984.317–47; and from a different viewpoint, Birley 1981.4–35.
38. Campbell 1993.213–240.
39. Roman weapons and armor: Bishop and Coulston 1993; development of tactics in the Republic: Keppie 1984b.14–131; Rosenstein, this volume. For speculation on the relevance of the training and experience of commanders in the introduction of new weapons and tactics, see Campbell 1987.25.
40. Campbell 1987.24–27; for other references to battle tactics in the imperial period, see Campbell 1987.28–29.
41. *ILS* 986.
42. Dio, LXXVI.15.2. For the reign of Septimius Severus, see Birley 1988.
43. Herodian VI.7.3.
44. Whittaker 1976; see also below.
45. For the later empire in general, see Jones 1964; Williams 1985; Cameron 1993; for the late Roman army, see Southern and Dixon 1996.
46. For the problem of transferring soldiers in the reign of Severus Alexander, see above at n. 43.
47. See Mann 1979, Isaac 1992, modifying the contentions of Luttwak 1976.
48. For the resilience of the eastern part of the empire, see Haldon, this volume.

Bibliography

Alston, R. 1994. "Roman Military Pay from Caesar to Diocletian." *Journal of Roman Studies* 84, 113–23.

———. 1995. *Soldier and Society in Roman Egypt: A Social History*. London: Routledge.

Austin, N. J. E., and N. B. Rankov. 1995. *Exploratio: Military and Political Intelligence in the Roman World from the Second Punic War to the Battle of Adrianople*. London: Routledge.

Birley, A. R. 1981. *The Fasti of Roman Britain*. Oxford: Oxford University Press.

———. 1988. *The African Emperor: Septimius Severus*. London: Batsford.

Bishop, M. C., and J. C. N. Coulston. 1993. *Roman Military Equipment from the Punic Wars to the Fall of Rome*. London: Batsford.

Brunt, P. A. 1974. "Conscription and Volunteering in the Roman Imperial Army." *Scripta Classica Israelica* 1, 90–115.

Cameron, A. 1993. *The Later Roman Empire AD 284–430*. London: Fontana.

Campbell, J. B. 1975. "Who Were the 'Viri Militares'?" *Journal of Roman Studies* 65, 11–31.

———. 1978. "The Marriage of Soldiers under the Empire." *Journal of Roman Studies* 68, 153–66.

———. 1984. *The Emperor and the Roman Army 31 B.C.–A.D. 235*. Oxford: Oxford University Press.

———. 1987. "Teach Yourself How to Be a General." *Journal of Roman Studies* 77, 13–29.

———. 1993. "War and Diplomacy: Rome and Parthia, 31 B.C.–A.D. 235." In *War and Society in the Roman World*, edited by J. Rich and G. Shipley, 213–40. London: Routledge.

———. 1994. *The Roman Army, 31 B.C.–A.D. 337: A Sourcebook*. London: Routledge.

———. 1996. "Shaping the Rural Environment: Surveyors in Ancient Rome." *Journal of Roman Studies* 86, 74–99.

Cheesman, G. L. 1914. *The Auxilia of the Roman Imperial Army*. Oxford: Oxford University Press. Reprint, Hildesheim: Olms, 1971.

Connolly, P. 1988. *Greece and Rome at War*. Reprint, London: Macdonald.

Dilke, O. A. W. 1971. *The Roman Land Surveyors: An Introduction to the Agrimensores*. Newton Abbot: David and Charles.

Dixon, K. R., and P. Southern. 1992. *The Roman Cavalry from the First to the Third Century A.D.* London: Batsford.

Durry, M. 1938. *Les cohortes prétoriennes*. Paris: de Boccard.

Forni, G. 1953. *Il reclutamento delle legioni da Augusto a Diocleziano*. Milan: Bocca.

———. 1974. "Estrazione etnica e sociale dei soldati delle legioni nei primi tre secoli dell'impero." In *Aufstieg und Niedergang der römischen Welt*, edited by H. Temporini, Vol. II.1, 339–91 Berlin: De Gruyter.

Garnsey, P., and R. Saller. 1987. *The Roman Empire: Economy, Society and Culture*. Berkeley and Los Angeles: University of California Press.

Healey, J. F., and C. S. Lightfoot. 1991. "A Roman Veteran on the Tigris." *Epigraphica Anatolica* 17, 1–7.

Higham, N. 1986. *The Northern Counties to* A.D. *1000.* In *A Regional History of England,* edited by B. Cunliff and H. David, Vol 1. London: Longman.

Holder, P. A. 1980. *Studies in the Auxilia of the Roman Army from Augustus to Trajan.* BAR International Series 70. Oxford: Oxbow.

Hopkins, K. 1980. "Taxes and Trade in the Roman Empire (200 B.C.–A.D. 400)." *Journal of Roman Studies* 70, 101–25.

Hyland, A. 1993. *Training the Roman Cavalry: From Arrian's* Ars Tactica. Stroud.: Alan Sutton.

ILS: see n. 22.

Isaac, B. 1992. *The Limits of Empire: The Roman Army in the East.* Rev. ed. Oxford: Oxford University Press.

Jones, A. H. M. 1964. *The Later Roman Empire 284–602.* Oxford: Blackwell.

Jones, M. L. 1984. *Society and Settlement in Wales and the Marches 500* B.C. *to* A.D. *1100.* BAR British Series 121. Oxford: Oxbow.

Keppie, L. 1983. *Colonisation and Veteran Settlement in Italy 47–14* B.C. Rome: British School at Rome.

———. 1984a. "Colonisation and Veteran Settlement in Italy in the First Century A.D." *Papers of the British School at Rome* 52, 77–114.

———. 1984b. *The Making of the Roman Army: From Republic to Empire.* London: Batsford.

Laporte, J.-P. 1989. *Rapidum: Le camp de la cohorte des Sardes en Maurétanie césarienne.* Sassari: Università degli studi di Sassari.

Le Bohec, Y. 1989. *L'armeé romaine sous le haut-empire.* Paris: Picard.

Luttwak, E. N. 1976. *The Grand Strategy of the Roman Empire from the First Century* A.D. *to the Third.* Baltimore, Md.: Johns Hopkins University Press.

Mann, J. C. 1979. "Power, Force and the Frontiers of the Empire." *Journal of Roman Studies* 69, 175–83.

———. 1983. *Legionary Recruitment and Veteran Settlement during the Principate.* Institute of Archaeology Occasional Publication No. 7. London: University of London.

Mason, D. J. P. 1987. "Chester: The *Canabae Legionis.*" *Britannia* 18, 143–68.

Millar, F. 1977. *The Emperor in the Roman World.* London: Duckworth.

Mitchell, S. 1976. "Requisitioned Transport in the Roman Empire: A New Inscription from Pisidia." *Journal of Roman Studies* 66, 106–31.

Mócsy, A. 1974. *Pannonia and Upper Moesia: A History of the Middle Danube Provinces of the Roman Empire.* London: Routledge and Kegan Paul.

Parker, H. M. D. 1958. *The Roman Legions.* Rev. ed. Cambridge: Heffer.

Passerini, A. 1939. *Le coorti pretorie.* Rome: Signorelli.

Saddington, D. B. 1982. *The Development of the Roman Auxiliary Forces from Caesar to Vespasian (49* B.C.–A.D. *79).* Harare: University of Zimbabwe.

Sear, F. 1989. *Roman Architecture.* Rev. ed. London: Batsford.

Southern, P., and K. R. Dixon. 1996. *The Late Roman Army.* New Haven, Conn., and London: Yale University Press and Batsford.

Speidel, M. A. 1992. "Roman Army Pay Scales." *Journal of Roman Studies* 82, 87–106.

Speidel, M. P. 1994. *Riding for Caesar: The Roman Emperor's Horse Guards.* London: Batsford.

Syme, R. 1939. *The Roman Revolution.* Oxford: Oxford University Press.

Watson, G. R. 1969. *The Roman Soldier.* London: Thames and Hudson.

Webster, G. 1985. *The Roman Imperial Army.* 3d ed. London: A. C. Black.

Wells, C. M. 1992. *The Roman Empire.* 2d ed. London: Fontana.

Whittaker, C. R. 1976. "*Agri deserti.*" In *Studies in Roman Property,* edited by M. I. Finley, 137–65. Cambridge: Cambridge University Press.

———. 1994. *Frontiers of the Roman Empire: A Social and Economic Study.* Baltimore, Md.: Johns Hopkins University Press.

Williams, S. 1985. *Diocletian and the Roman Recovery.* London: Batsford.

The Byzantine World

JOHN HALDON

The term "Byzantine Empire" refers to the eastern Roman Empire from the fourth (or sixth, as some prefer) century to the fifteenth century, that is to say, from the time when a distinctively East Roman political formation began to evolve with the recognition of the cultural divisions between "Greek East" and "Latin West" in the empire's political structure, to the fall of Constantinople on May 29, 1453, at the hands of the Ottoman Sultan Mehmet II "Fatih," "the Conqueror." And although within this long period there were many substantial transformations, the elements of structural continuity are marked enough to permit such a broad chronological definition. In this chapter I will deal with the period from the sixth to the twelfth century, a period marked out in the seventh century by a dramatic contraction as a result of the expansion of Islam, followed by a recovery of some former territories in the Middle East and Balkans between the later ninth and early eleventh centuries, and a further and more permanent contraction in the later eleventh and twelfth centuries.[1]

Late Roman and Early Byzantine
State and Society: Structures

The Christian Roman state was structured as a hierarchy of administrative levels: at the top was the emperor, understood to be God's representative, surrounded by a palatine and household apparatus, the center of imperial government and administration. Civil and fiscal government was delegated from the emperor to the praetorian prefects, whose prefectures were the largest territorial circumscriptions in the state; each prefecture was further divided into

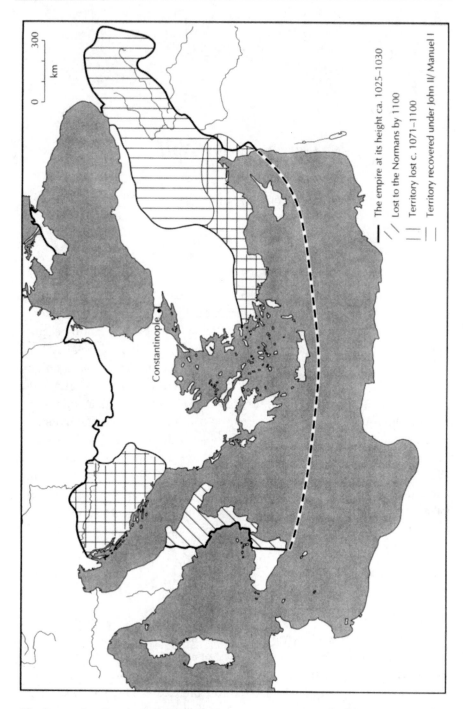

The Byzantine Empire ca. 1025–1180

dioecesae, or dioceses, which had a predominantly fiscal aspect; and each diocese was divide into *provinciae,* or provinces, territorial units of fiscal and judicial administration. These were further divided into self-governing *poleis* or *civitates,* the cities, each with its *territorium* or hinterland (which might be more or less extensive, according to geographic, demographic, and other factors). Cities were the basic tax-collecting units, and the leading landowners of the cities were responsible for collecting taxes of varying sorts, assessed on a yearly basis according to estimates of state budgetary requirements for the year ahead. This pattern was slowly transformed after the third century, so that by the middle of the sixth century, the state intervened directly to ensure that taxes were properly assessed and collected.[2]

Rural production dominated the economy, of course; but the cities were the homes of a literate elite of landowners (although in the less heavily urbanized regions ranchlike country estates with fortified villas could be found), many of whom were members of what has been called the "senatorial aristocracy." Social status was largely determined by one's relationship to the system of imperial titles and precedence, whether one had held an active post in the imperial bureaucracy, and at what level, and so forth, although regional variations were marked.

The Church and the theological system it represented (from the late fourth century the official religion of the Roman state and, probably by the mid–sixth century, the majority religion within the empire) played a central role in the economy of the Roman world—it was a major landowner—as well as in imperial politics, in influencing the moral and ethical system of the Roman world, and in directing imperial religious policy. Emperors were inextricably involved in the conflicts generated by theological disagreements, given the prevailing view that the emperor was chosen by God, that he had to be Orthodox, and that his role was to defend the interests of Orthodoxy and the Roman (i.e. Christian) *oikoumenē* (the inhabited, civilized—Roman—world). The political implications were such that heresy was construed as treason, and opposition to the (Orthodox) emperor could effectively be treated as heresy. The late Roman state was thus a complex bureaucracy, rooted in and imposed upon a series of overlapping social formations structured by local variations on essentially the same social relations of production across the whole central and east Mediterranean and Balkan world. Social and political tensions were exacerbated by religious divisions, local economic conditions, imperial politics, and the burden placed upon the taxpaying population as a result of the state's needs in respect of its administrative apparatus and, in particular, its armies.

This situation was radically transformed between the later sixth and the early ninth century, as the result of a number of factors. In spite of the problems faced by the eastern half of the empire in the middle and later fifth century, its greater structural cohesiveness and flexibility enabled it to survive both external attacks and the disruption of economic and trading patterns;[3] indeed, in the late fifth and early sixth century a major reform of the bronze coinage was undertaken that was to provide the basic framework for the monetary system of the empire until the twelfth century.[4] The strength of the empire enabled it during the sixth century to take the offensive and to recover large regions that had been lost to invaders or settlers. Although the cost of this expansionism was very great, the East Roman state in the early 630s still embraced North Africa, Egypt, modern Syria, western Iraq, and western Jordan, along with Lebanon and Palestine, Anatolia, much of the Balkans, Sicily, Sardinia, and considerable areas of Italy, although reduced by the Lombards. Most of the Balkans was out of effective central control, dominated by Slav or other invaders. But in the 630s the Arabs emerged from the Arabian peninsula under the banner of Islam and the holy war, and imperial resistance was little more than token. By 642 all of Egypt and the Middle Eastern provinces had been lost, Arab forces had penetrated deep into Asia Minor and Libya, and imperial forces had been withdrawn into Asia Minor, to be settled across the provinces of the region as the only available means of supporting them. Within a period of some twelve years, therefore, the empire lost something over half its area and three-quarters of its resources—a drastic loss for an imperial state that still had to maintain and equip a considerable army and an effective administrative bureaucracy if it was to survive at all.[5] While many of the developments that led to this transformation were in train long before the seventh-century crisis, it was this conjuncture that served to bring things to a head and promote the structural responses that followed.

From Defense to Offense: The Forging of the Middle Byzantine Army

The defeats and territorial contraction that resulted from the expansion of Islam from the 640s in the East, on the one hand, and the arrival of the Bulgars and establishment of a permanent Bulgar Khanate in the Balkans from the 680s,[6] on the other, radically altered the political conditions of existence of the East Roman state. The resulting transformation of state administrative structures produced an army that was based almost entirely on defensive principles, for which offensive warfare became a rarity until the middle of the eighth century, and which was encouraged by the imperial government to avoid pitched battles and open confrontation with enemy forces wherever possible. The field armies of the late Roman state were transformed in effect into provincial militias, although a central core of full-time "professional" soldiers seems always to have been maintained by each regional military commander. A strategy of guerrilla warfare evolved, in which enemy forces were allowed to penetrate the borderlands before being cut off from their bases and harried and worried until they broke up or until they were forced to return to their own lands. Byzantine officers conducted a "scorched-earth" policy in many regions, and local populations in endangered regions were encouraged to keep lookouts posted, so that they could gather their livestock and other movable possessions and take refuge in mountain fortresses, thereby depriving enemy units of forage and booty.[7] Although individual emperors did launch offensive expeditions in the period from approximately 660 to 730, these were generally designed to forestall a major enemy attack into Roman territory in Asia Minor, or had a punitive nature, designed more as ideologically motivated revenge attacks on important enemy targets, and with no lasting strategic value (although they did have implications for military morale). Although a few notable successes were recorded, many of these expeditions failed and resulted in substantial defeats and loss of men and materials. The differentiation between arms at the tactical level—between light and heavy cavalry or infantry, archers, lancers, or spearmen—appears to have lessened, surviving only in a few contexts, associated with imperially maintained elite units. Byzantine armies and Arab armies looked very much the same.[8]

Only from the 730s on, during the reign of Leo III, an emperor from a military background who seized the throne in 717, and more particularly that of his son and successor Constantine V (741–75), a campaigning emperor who introduced a number of administrative reforms in the army and established an elite field army at Constantinople in the 760s, did this situation begin to change. Political stability internally, the beginnings of economic recovery in the later eighth century, and dissension among their enemies enabled the Byzantines to reestablish a certain equilibrium by the year 800. In spite of occasional major defeats (for example, the annihilation of a Byzantine force following a Bulgar surprise attack in 811, and the death in battle of the emperor Nicephorus I), and an often unfavorable international political situation, the Byzantines were able to begin a more offensive policy with regard to the Islamic power to the east and the Bulgars in the north—in the latter case, combining diplomacy and missionary activity with military threats. By the early tenth century, and as the caliphate was weakened by internal strife, the Byzantines were beginning to establish a certain advantage; and in spite of the fierce and sometimes successful opposition of local Muslim warlords (such as the emirs of Aleppo in the 940s and 950s), there followed a series of brilliant reconquests of huge swathes of territory in North Syria and Iraq, the annihilation of the second Bulgarian empire, and the beginnings of the reconquest of Sicily and southern Italy. By the death of the soldier-emperor Basil II "the Bulgar-slayer" (1025), the empire was once again the paramount political and military power in the eastern Mediterranean basin, rivaled only by the Fatimid Caliphate in Egypt and Syria.[9]

But the offensive warfare that developed from the middle of the ninth century reacted, in its turn, upon the administration and organization of the imperial armies. The provincial militias became less and less suited to the requirements of such campaigning, tied as they had become to their localities, to what was in effect a type of guerrilla strategy, and to the seasonal campaigning dictated by Arab or Bulgar raiders. Instead, regular field armies with a more complex tactical structure, specialized fighting skills and weapons, and more offensive élan began to develop, partly under the auspices of a new social elite of military commanders who were also great landowners, partly encouraged and financed by the state. Mercenary troops played an increasingly important role as the state began to commute military service in the provincial armies for cash with which to hire professionals: by the middle of the eleventh century, a large portion of the imperial armies was made up of indigenously recruited mercenary units together with Norman, Russian, Turkic, and Frankish mercenaries, mostly cavalry, but including infantry troops (such as the famous Varangian guard).[10] The successes achieved between approximately 900 and 1030 were thus based not only on effective organization and better resources than in the preceding period. Morale and ideology also played a key role; and in particular the increase in the tactical complexity of Byzantine field armies played a significant part, with the various types of arms familiar from the late Roman period, which had all but vanished in the period of crisis of the seventh and eighth centuries, reappearing once more. Arab commentators remark on the effectiveness of the Byzantine heavy cavalry "wedge," employed with, literally, crushing effect in the Byzantine wars with both Muslims and northern foes such as the Bulgars and the Rus' of Kiev.[11]

The expansionism of the period of approximately 940 to 1030 had its negative results, however. Increasing state demands clashed with greater aristocratic resistance to paying taxes; political factionalism at court, reflecting in turn the development of new social tensions within society as a whole, and in the context of weak and opportunistic imperial government, led to policy failures, the overestimation of imperial military strength, and neglect of defensive structures. When Seljuk Turkish raiding parties were able to defeat piecemeal a major imperial force in 1071 and capture the emperor Romanos IV (bringing about further factional strife at Constantinople), the empire could offer no organized counterattack, with the result that central Asia Minor was slowly occupied by pastoral nomads and their herds and lost permanently to the empire. Major military and fiscal reforms under the emperors of the Komnenos dynasty (a military aristocratic clan) from 1081 reestablished stability and, to a degree, the international position of the empire. While foreign mercenary units continued to play a prominent role, the recruitment of indigenous Byzantine units specializing in a variety of arms restored the ability of the imperial armies to fight external enemies on their own terms. This was partly based on a reformed fiscal administration and the raising and maintenance of troops on the basis of grants of revenue to certain individuals in return for the provision of trained soldiers, both infantry and cavalry. Increasing western influence, in the form of the introduction of weapons such as the crossbow and the adoption of western heavy cavalry tactics, differentiate this period from the preceding century. But the successes of the new dynasty were relatively short-lived: overexpansion, the loss of Bulgaria and much of the Balkans to what might be dubbed "nationalist" rebellions, and the collapse of the empire into renewed factional strife in the 1180s and 1190s laid it open to external threat, and this materialized in the form of the Fourth Crusade.[12] The capture and sack of Constantinople in 1204 and the subsequent partition of the empire among the Venetian and western victors ended the empire's role as a major political and military power, although it survived after the recovery of Constantinople in 1261 and reestablishment of an imperial regime, on an ever smaller territorial scale, until only Constantinople and a few Aegean islands remained. And in 1453 the Ottoman sultan Mehmet II extinguished even this remnant.

The period with which we are concerned here, therefore, covers in effect three phases of military development: contraction, localization, and a primarily defensive character in the seventh through eighth centuries; expansion, reconquest, and a more offensive approach in the ninth through early eleventh centuries; and the breakdown and reform of the structures inherited from the late ancient period during the eleventh and twelfth centuries.

Middle Byzantine State and Society: Structures

The changes that accompanied the developments of the seventh century affected all areas of social, cultural, and economic life. There occurred a "ruralization" of society, promoted by the fact that cities were already losing their role in the state fiscal system by the later sixth century. Coupled with the devastation, abandonment, shrinkage, or displacement of many cities in Asia Minor as a result of invasions and raids, especially from the 640s but also during the period of the Persian wars (602–26), the state transferred its fiscal attention to the village community, which became the main unit of assessment by the later seventh century.[13] The defensive properties of "urban" sites, their direct relevance to military, administrative, or ecclesiastical needs, and so on, now played the key role in whether a city survived. At the same time, the evidence shows the preeminent position taken by Constantinople. The establishment of a new imperial capital in the year 330, on the site of the ancient city of Byzantion, with the imperial court, a senate, and all the social, economic, and administrative consequences, had far-reaching implications for the pattern of exchange and movement of goods in the Aegean and east Mediterranean basin.[14]

The social elite was transformed. The so-called senatorial aristocracy of the later Roman period was replaced by an elite of "new men" selected by the emperors on a more obviously meritocratic basis, a group that undoubtedly included some members of the older elite, although the sources tell us very little on this point. The newcomers into the administrative and military hierarchy of the state were initially heavily dependent on the emperor and on imperially sponsored positions.[15] But as a result of its increasing grip on state positions and the lands it accrued through the rewards attached to such service, this elite soon turned into an aristocracy, during the eighth and ninth centuries still very dependent on the state, during the tenth and especially the eleventh increasingly independent. The court had to compete directly with a social class whose enormous landed wealth and entrenched position in the apparatuses of the state meant that it posed a real threat to central control of fiscal resources.[16]

The events of the seventh century also produced a reassertion of central state power over late Roman tendencies toward decentralization.[17] The state was both limited by, and in its turn partly defined, the nature of key economic relationships. This is exemplified in the issue and circulation of coin, the basic mechanism through which the state converted agricultural produce into transferable fiscal resources.[18] Coin was issued chiefly to oil the wheels of the state machinery, and wealth was appropriated and consumed through a redistributive fiscal mechanism: the state issued gold in the form of salaries and largesse to its bureaucracy and armies, who exchanged a substantial portion thereof for goods and services in maintaining themselves. The state could thus collect much of the coin it put into circulation through tax, the more so since fiscal policy generally demanded tax in gold and offered change in bronze. There were periods when this system was constrained by circumstances, resulting in the ad hoc arrangements for supplying soldiers and raising tax in kind, for example (as in the seventh century), and it also varied by region.[19] But in a society in which social status and advancement (including the self-identity of the aristocracy) were connected with the state, these arrangements considerably hindered economic activity not directly connected with the state's activities. For the continued power and attraction of the imperial establishment at Constantinople, with its court and hierarchical system of precedence, as well as the highly centralized fiscal administrative structure, consumed the whole attention of the Byzantine elite, hindering the evolution of a more highly localized aristocracy that might otherwise have invested in the economy and society of its own localities and towns, rather than in the imperial system.[20]

The Army and Resources

The army and its needs represented central concerns of the state.[21] A series of ancillary structures, in particular the public post, served both military and bureaucratic needs. As an anonymous sixth-century treatise on strategy notes, "The financial system was set up to take care of matters of public importance that arise on occasion, such as the building of ships and of walls. But it is principally concerned with paying the soldiers. Each year most of the public revenues are spent for this purpose."[22]

The methods evolved to deal with these requirements were, of course, determined to a degree by factors of a geopolitical and ecological character: conditions determining transport, terrain, climate, all affecting the maintenance of either livestock or human populations to service the institutions of the state, the availability of materials for construction (roads, bridges, posting stations), of fodder for beasts of burden or post-horses, and of food for both imperial servants and those who maintained the system, and so on.[23] In addition, the methods of payment for such services played a role: where (and when) a developed system of market exchange operated, goods and services will have been exchanged quite easily. In contrast, when money transactions were limited by the unreliability or unavailability of coin, especially in low denominations, exchange relationships will have been cumbersome, labor-intensive, and relatively inefficient.[24] These conditions directly affected the forms which those institutions connected with resources took, and the ways in which they operated.

Throughout the period in question two basic methods of supplying soldiers existed, although their institutional/bureaucratic forms varied. Apart from occasional and regular cash donatives, garrison units were issued with rations, although from the later fifth century in the East these were actually commuted at locally fixed tariffs into gold, so that the regimental commissaries bought the necessary requirements at local markets or directly from the producers before issuing them to the soldiers. In the case of mobile units, actuaries and special officers were allowed to draw supplies from the regular revenues of the provinces affected in return for receipts. The whole system was operated by the praetorian prefecture at its various administrative levels, so that the supplies demanded for the army could be taken into account when making the regular land-tax assessment. For expeditionary or moving forces, the numbers of soldiers and animals that needed provisions had to be submitted to the central and local administrations in advance, so that the necessary supplies could be deposited in storehouses or otherwise made available along the route of march.[25]

Equipment—clothing, mounts, weapons—was provided by a combination of taxation or levy in kind and through state manufactories. A number of arms factories were situated at towns throughout the provinces. Weapons and clothing were, by the later sixth century, bought by the soldier, either directly or through the regimental actuary, with a cash allowance issued for the purpose. Mounts were provided partly by levy, partly through purchase at fixed prices, some provided by imperial stud farms. At the end of the sixth century, generals were advised to establish winter quarters in areas where such supplies were available for purchase, or to make it possible for traders and others to reach the army to provide the required provisions and equipment. Iron ore, charcoal, and wood were also provided by levy, sometimes remitted from the tax burden of the area or community in question, sometimes raised through extraordinary impositions on certain categories of taxpayer.[26]

Transporting military supplies was expensive. Water transport (sea or river) was cheapest, but this was rarely relevant to inland campaigns, either on the eastern front or in the Balkans (although the *quaestura exercitus* provides an example of a solution to a problem specific to the Danube frontier).[27]

The seventh-century economic and political crisis brought changes to these arrangements. Much of the burden of supporting the armies was transferred directly onto local populations. Cash salaries were reduced to a nominal and occasional sum, while a system of supporting troops in kind, similar to that which had operated in the fourth century, reappeared. Troops were distributed over wide areas to facilitate this system, resulting in an increasing dependency on soldiers' households for provisions and even weapons. By the later eighth century many provincial soldiers were called up for only part of the year. Weapons were produced through levies on provincial craftsmen, to supplement the remaining armaments factories;[28] military clothing and mounts and pack animals were raised in the same way.[29]

Yet the system operated in the ninth and tenth centuries for provisioning and supplying moving forces was still remarkably similar to that which pertained in the later Roman period.[30] In spite of what was in effect a localization and "farming-out" of the production of arms and other military equipment, and the reversion to a system of levies of provisions in kind, imperial authority remained, effected through the supervision of centrally appointed officials to the staffs of thematic commanders. Assessments of military needs were measured against the ability of the population to support such demands; demands for provisions for moving forces were carefully recorded, so that they could be balanced against the total fiscal demand for taxes for the areas in question. By the ninth century it was thus a shrunken and somewhat bastardized late Roman system that was still operating, on the same fundamental principle of centralized state authority, in which resources were appropriated by the state through tax and other impositions or services, but directly redistributed to those elements of the state's apparatus where they were needed.

From the later tenth century there evolved a system of resource management that was in some ways quite different. Reflecting the offensive warfare and expansionism of the period, the number of full-time, "professional," and mercenary soldiers, both foreign and indigenous, increased, inducing further shifts in the ways in which the armies were maintained, in particular during noncampaigning times. Until the middle of the tenth century, a large proportion of the burden of maintaining the traditional thematic[31] forces had come to rest upon the households of the soldiers themselves or their neighbors within the community to which the soldiers belonged. The cost of maintaining the armies was thus distributed across each province, even if a body of standing troops, which might on occasion have been substantial, had also to be maintained at central government expense. The administration of this system involved not only fairly close supervision of productive capacity but also the direct allocation of resources to individual soldiers. And even though the costs of large-scale expeditions were met by extraordinary levies in supplies, manpower, and livestock, until the middle of the tenth century such undertakings were not frequent. The change in emphasis that took place over the tenth century and into the eleventh century—in effect, from a provincially supported and provincially raised indigenous "militia-like" army to an increasingly professionalized mercenary army supported through direct taxation—had important consequences for relations between the state and the dominant elite, to which we will return later.

The Armies: Basic Organization and Structures

The late Roman armies in the sixth century can be divided into two categories, mobile field forces (*comitatenses*) and stationary frontier units (*limitanei*). The former were composed for the most part of units created during the later third and fourth centuries; the latter were composed predominantly from the older legions and associated auxiliary units that had been posted along the frontiers. Units based near the imperial capital or serving in the presence of the emperor were referred to as *palatini*; but, in fact, there was so much cross-posting, and so many field units became entrenched in their garrison towns on a more or less permanent basis, that these divisions are in practice very artificial. These notionally more mobile forces were then grouped into divisions under regional commanders, or *magistri militum*, each covering a major defensive hinterland, and under each of whom the commanders of the stationary units were based. In the later sixth century there were nine such major divisions, including two based around Constantinople. Naval units for both seaborne and riverine activities were based at key Balkan and Syrian ports, maintained on the same basis as the field armies.[32]

Soldiers were recruited partly on a voluntary basis, partly on the basis of a relationship between tax assessments, land, and manpower, although the latter was increasingly replaced by the former as the sixth century drew on. Soldiers in the *limitanei* had the privilege of putting down their sons' names for recruitment to a more or less guaranteed place if they wished, a reflection of the relative security a soldier's career was seen to represent, at least in such garrison units.[33]

The mobile field armies were complemented by more localized forces, including the *limitanei*, along and behind the frontiers, commands that also included provinces in which local trouble—brigandage, for example—might be expected, also subject to the regional field-army commander. In the 560s there were some twenty-five such commands covering the frontiers and their hinterlands.[34]

This two-tier "system," which had evolved directly out of changes that took place in the third century, was premised upon a particular mode of tax collection and assessment, upon particular institutional arrangements for surplus redistribution, and upon the particular contours of late Roman relations of political power.[35] It functioned relatively well up until the great war with the Sassanid Persian kingdom from 602 to 626 but broke down under the pressures placed on it by the early Islamic conquests and the ensuing massive loss of tax revenue and resources from the eastern provinces between 634 and 642.

During the seventh century these late Roman forces evolved into more provincialized militia-like armies, each with a central core of full-time professionals supported by both Constantinopolitan and local funds. The empire's territory came to be divided into a number of military regions, or *themata*, each commanded, from the military perspective (there is some debate about their wider authority), by a general, or *stratēgos*.[36] The "theme" or "thematic" system, as it has become known, initially came into being as armies were billeted across Asia Minor in the period of approximately 637 to 640, through a process by which the groups of provinces occupied by each field army came collectively to be known by the name of that army. Later *themata* received purely geographic names. The civil administration, modified in various ways, especially in respect of fiscal administration, which was the state's overriding interest,[37] subsisted in an increasingly altered form until, probably in the early ninth century, the state introduced a series of measures to update the thematic administration and recognize the nature and form of the changes that had taken place.

Although the armies continued to function as regular field divisions, they evolved increasingly in the direction of a militia. It is clear that the state faced enormous difficulties in maintaining its armies after the loss of the eastern provinces, and especially Egypt, to the Arabs, and the withdrawal of the field armies into Anatolia. The government was already very hard-pressed for cash in the 630s and 640s;[38] and the way in which the soldiers were garrisoned across the provinces of Asia Minor thereafter suggests that the state reverted on an increasing scale to raising tax in kind in order to maintain the troops, rather than paying them in cash, as had hitherto been the case for those units not on campaign or in transit. Partial corroboration of this practice lies in the distribution of the late Roman field armies across Anatolia, for there is a close correlation between the size of the forces occupying a given region and the known resources of the regions concerned.[39]

One of the results of this change was the localization of the soldiers in respect of residence and patterns of recruitment, so that over the following decades a sizable element became little more than a local militia, demonstrating highly localized loyalties and competitiveness with the troops from other regions for rewards and imperial favor. At the same time, the means employed by the state to support and maintain its armies became more diverse. Hereditary conscription was at some point, probably during the seventh century, reintroduced. Connected with a revision of fiscal registers during the later seventh and eighth centuries, soldiers with landed property were encouraged to provide a proportion of their arms, equipment, and mounts, and were granted certain tax benefits in return. By the later eighth or ninth century, several categories of soldier existed, including regular and irregular professional and militia-like units, as well as full-time "professional" regiments such as the imperial guards units at Constantinople.[40] Similar considerations in respect of regionalization, provincialization, and recruitment applied to the imperial naval forces, also radically restructured during the later seventh and eighth centuries.[41]

The Role of the Army in Society

There is a significant shift in the political role of the army and of soldiers in the period from the sixth to the ninth century. The relationship between soldiers and the state in the period up to approximately 630 can be characterized as fairly direct: the intermediaries between these two elements were relatively few, and were on the whole themselves part and parcel of the state's apparatus, whether civil or military. The state retained a fairly strict control over the production and issue of weapons, which were a state monopoly.[42] Further, the state directly supervised the provisioning of the field armies; and it paid and rewarded its soldiers directly, through cash salaries, quinquennial and accessional donatives, and field or campaign awards.[43] Soldiers had a specific legal status, inscribed in Roman-Byzantine law and inherited from the late Republic, including a protected and privileged status in terms of inheritance law.[44] They were in many ways independent of other social loyalties, serving the state in a more or less unmediated way. In the late Roman period, soldiers' rebellions against authority were connected mostly with conditions of service rather than with any sort of "political/ideological" consciousness or desire to intervene in politics. "Politics" remained a predominantly metropolitan or urban phenomenon, in which soldiers were only marginally implicated as an independent element. Officers were similarly uninvolved in political activity other than in respect of immediate grievances regarding service conditions, pay and emoluments, and so forth. Officers as a body seem on the whole to have been thoroughly integrated into the sociocultural and political status quo.[45]

This general situation changed by the later seventh century. Soldiers and their leaders were actively involved in challenging and overthrowing emperors on what can only be called an almost regular basis, for a while at least. Whether involving officers or not, soldiers became engaged in imperial politics, and in voicing their own particular points of view.[46] The key issues seem to have been fundamental questions about the nature of the state they lived in and the political-ideological issues of the times.[47] Partly, this reflected the loosening of the fairly direct relationship between the state and its armies. The regular field armies of the empire—now withdrawn into the regions that supported them after the Arab victories of the late 630s—became increasingly ideologically and psychologically distanced from the center. Central authority over recruitment or conscription of soldiers was relaxed as recruitment became more highly localized. Soldiers became a more integral part of provincial society. Soldiers recruited from particular localities served in the same units, so they tended to hold both similar loyalties and similar views.[48]

In addition, a consequence of the decline in the social function of provincial towns was that only the army remained as a metaphorical site on which large numbers of people regularly came together, and where views, fears, and anxieties could be expressed or formed in a public context. In effect, soldiers replaced the urban populace of the empire as the voice of opposition or discontent.[49] The army thus became "political" in a way that it really had not been before, directly responding to changes in imperial rule or to defeats at the hands of external foes.

This politicization of the military can be demonstrated in several ways.[50] The creation of the *tagmata* (imperial guards units) in the middle of the eighth century and the evolution of a "guards" army at Constantinople is illustrative of attempts by emperors to counteract the political power of provincial armies and an evolving opposition between center and province.[51] There was an explicit politicization of the army from above during the second half of the eighth century, evidenced in the creation of a two-tier army: *tagmata* as contrasted with *themata*.[52]

These changes cannot be divorced from what was happening in Byzantine society in general, of course, especially the evolution of a rather different political and social elite, promoted by the state from the middle of the seventh century.[53] They reflect also economic recovery and political stabilization, as well as the emergence of new political and economic relationships, including those between the provincial soldiery and their modes of recruitment, on the one hand, and on the other the elite of magnates and imperial office- and title-holders.[54]

Thus from the "professional" and non-politicized armies of the sixth century, there occurred a progressive politicization of armies and soldiers: during the seventh and eighth centuries, as soldiers recruited locally identified with, and acted on behalf of, local loyalties, local ideological perspectives, and political or economic concerns; and during the later eighth and ninth centuries, as the opposition between the central tagmatic forces and the provincial thematic forces evolved. This contrast was heightened by sociopolitical tensions within the power elite, especially between those elements that invested in the central administrative establishment and those that concentrated on establishing a provincial power base. From the middle of the tenth century, this polarization intensified as the central establishment tried to prevent provincial magnates from alienating provincial military resources through its construction of networks of patronage and clienteles, a process that also involved the swallowing up of thematic soldiers' smallholdings.[55] The conflict was exacerbated by the offensive warfare of the tenth century and the opportunities this offered to the military elements of the elite. An increased, but willing, dependency of the central establishment on both indigenous and foreign mercenary units, in order to counterbalance the strength of this elite, was a logical concomitant, a dependency that had the effect of centralizing military power and reinforcing, for a while, the authority and policies of the rulers.

The result was, in its turn, a twofold polarization within the military establishment of the empire: between the traditional provincial or thematic armies under their local officers and leaders, the latter drawn from different and often competing families of the magnate class, and the tagmatic or centrally controlled forces. There was also a contradiction between the interests of the dominant elite as a social group, whatever its internal divisions may have been, and the interests of the state, which is to say, of the faction dominating the center and imperial politics at any given moment. In all these respects, the army and the network of political, economic, and social interests of which it formed the center played a crucial role in Byzantine social and political history.

Soldiers in Society

The status of soldiers varied across time in respect of the attitudes of people from different areas or sections of society. From the sixth to the later ninth and early tenth century, soldiers had a relatively privileged position in comparison with the ordinary inhabitants of towns or countryside, and they constituted a more or less clearly identifiable group in juridical-institutional respects. And in spite of the obvious differences in economic status and situation between and among soldiers, the mostly indigenous Byzantine armies were relatively homogeneous, rooted in local society, recruited regionally from peasant communities, and officered largely by local men.[56] Until the later tenth century, foreign mercenary soldiers were led by Roman officers, while non-Byzantine soldiers recruited from foreign refugee settlers were assimilated and subjected to the same conditions of fiscal and civil administration as native Byzantine populations.[57]

This homogeneity was reinforced by the fact that the property of soldiers acquired through their military service was protected by a special legal status and protected by state law. Troops received donatives and a share of booty; in ideological terms they occupied a special position, along with the Church and the peasantry.[58] The emperors saw themselves symbolically as fathers of their soldiers, the soldiers' wives as their daughters-in-law; some emperors referred to the soldiers as their own *systratiōtai,* or comrades-in-arms.[59]

There were also practical advantages to being a soldier, especially in the area of fiscal privileges, for soldiers and their immediate families were always exempted from extraordinary fiscal burdens and state obligations. They paid only the basic taxes, the land tax (*synonē*) and the hearth tax (*kapnikon*). The differences between military and nonmilitary reflected the standard and entirely normal Roman distinction between those groups who enjoyed immunities in respect of certain state demands and those who did not.[60]

As well as this special fiscal and juridical position, soldiers and their immediate dependents had the right to have cases tried by their own commanders for offenses relating to their duties, again reflecting standard Roman juridical practice, whereby members of any juridically defined corporate body could possess similar rights.[61] On the other hand, there is some evidence that soldiers suffered through victimization at the hands of imperial officials and powerful landlords or other such persons, just as other members of rural society.[62] Yet, just as in the late Roman period and earlier, for which the evidence is somewhat better, soldiers were also able to bully civilians, either in their own communities when on or off duty, or in the regions through which they passed when on campaign. And the presence of soldiers in either towns or countryside was usually felt to be oppressive by local populations.[63]

Of course, in reality there were many more subdivisions within the broad category of "soldiers" than historians have often seen. Consequently, it is to a degree rather artificial, and even misleading, to try to speak about the status of "soldiers" en bloc without further defining the term.

As already noted the word can represent a whole range of economic and functional strata. Social status obviously attaches to wealth, for example. Yet, while it seems that the better-off among the thematic armies occupied a position of some import in their communities, membership of the *axiōmatikoi*— those who possessed an imperial title—was just as significant in securing social recognition, and it is clear from the surviving documents that most *stratiōtai* did not belong to this group.[64] On the other hand, functional military issues also played a role. Heavily armed cavalrymen, whether supported by the state or partly through their own means, may have been able to improve their social position in their own communities, where they had such, through their military service. Border garrisons and watchtowers were manned by local forces of relatively humble status,[65] who were socially far inferior to the wealthy heavy cavalrymen of the themes and also the mercenaries paid by the state. Nevertheless, they will all, in theory, have shared the same juridical status and privileges.

The sources are ambiguous regarding the social standing and economic status of soldiers, a fact that probably reflects these sorts of differences. In some texts, soldiers are regarded as belonging to the wealthy and/or the oppressors of the rural smallholders.[66] In much of the imperial legislation, on the other hand, provincial soldiers are bracketed with other less well-off peasants, whose livelihood was threatened by the *dynatoi* and by natural calamities. It is possible that this reflects a particular situation, evident in other aspects of imperial legislation, pertaining to the middle years of the tenth century only.[67] Yet according to other legislation of the same period, soldiers hold a relatively high position in the hierarchy of the rural community; and it is clear from some of the evidence that many of those registered in the military rolls were relatively well-off compared with much of the rural population.[68]

There is, in addition, the fact that there was within each thematic force a differentiation between light and heavy cavalry and infantry as well as other arms—slingers, archers, and so on. What happened to the different specialist arms after the distribution and localization of the armies had begun during the 640s and after is unknown; but this is a factor that must have had implications for the social status, relative wealth, and economic position of soldiers.[69]

These issues are still in need of much more discussion; and while the regular provincial soldiery, the *stratiōtai,* cannot be said to have formed a distinct social group as such, many of them probably belonged to a stratum of petty landlords and some to the lower reaches of the "powerful." On the other hand, the extent to which a particular juridical status gave poorer soldiers a slightly higher social position in anything other than legal fiction is very difficult to determine. The position of the wealthiest theme soldiers may have been enhanced by the legislation of the emperor Nicephorus II (963–69), which placed great emphasis on such troops.[70] It appears to have dramatically hastened the fiscalization of military service—the conversion of actual service into a cash payment or tax—in general (since the state used the cash thus obtained to hire smaller numbers of full-time professional or "mercenary" units), with the result that the regular theme forces, whose real military value was in defensive warfare, were more and more neglected. One of the results of this was that the more professional, full-time soldiers, whether indigenous or not, had few local loyalties and no embryonic associations with provincial Byzantine society.

The general position of thematic soldiers as a special category in the late Roman sense thus begins to deteriorate from the tenth century. There was an increasing tendency, except in certain border *themata* or provinces, to fiscalize the burden of military service, generalized by the time of the reign of Constantine Monomachos (1042–55),[71] so that military service on the basis of a hereditary registered obligation came to represent merely one fiscal obligation among several.[72] In addition, as full-time mercenary units predominated, so the peasants who had previously supplied the core of the theme armies were no longer differentiated from the mass of the rural population. But soldiers as such continued to enjoy a particular legal status, whether they were non-Byzantine or indigenous: it was the name and title of soldier that continued to be crucial, not the methods by which a soldier was originally recruited.[73]

As I have suggested, one of the reasons for the important position of soldiers in practical terms in the period from the seventh to the tenth century was the absence of any other focus save the armies for nonmetropolitan or provincial opinion, and the central position of the *stratēgoi*, the thematic commanders, in imperial politics. From the tenth century these conditions were altered: greatly increased economic stability accompanied the military expansion and reconquests of the period; there was a recovery of commerce and provincial urban fortunes and a "civilianization" of thematic administration, particularly in the less militarized regions behind the frontier zones. At the same time, a provincial magnate class, with the disposable wealth and the influence of all who held imperial titles, became increasingly dominant in the state apparatuses, bringing with it the factionalism and vested interests that served to introduce instability and conflict to the central government.

As a result, the structural position of soldiers in society as a whole changed. The developments of the middle and later seventh century had meant an increasing integration of soldiers into rural provincial society. One of the effects of such integration may also have been the lessening of traditional forms of civil-military tension, as provincial soldiers increasingly stayed in or near the communities from which they were raised, living for much of the year within the context of normal rural social relations rather than those of the military camp or garrison town where large numbers of soldiers and the military aspect dominated. The "military lands," soldiers' landed property protected by specific legal regulations that had come into being by the tenth century, were a by-product of this integration; and as the state's demands for soldiers in the offensive and expansionist campaigns of the tenth century and the political considerations of the eleventh century stimulated radical changes in both the mode of supporting the armies, on the one hand (fiscalization of the *strateia*), and the sources of soldiers, on the other, so these legally protected forms of landed property and the provincial armies or militias they had supported passed away, although there remain several unresolved questions in this connection. During the course of the tenth century, there set in a process of separation of the regular troops of the empire from the mass of the ordinary, rural population, a process that was completed by the last quarter of the eleventh century.

While these changes affected the soldiers' position in society, however, they did not necessarily affect their position in the ideological scheme of things. They brought a greater distance between provincial society and the armies, although this does not mean that full-time units recruited from the provinces were never based in their own districts, nor that traditional thematic forces could not still be raised.[74]

The shift from a system of partly self-supporting soldier-militias, raised and maintained on a local basis, to that of an essentially mercenary army that had to be supported by cash and by corvées imposed upon the ordinary population, is well illustrated by the regular occurrence in the surviving archival documents of exemptions from billeting and supplying units of mercenary and other soldiers.[75]

Such soldiers were as important as ever to the defense and security of the state, Orthodoxy, and the dominant social groups, of course, and in the official ideology still held their significance. But the transformation of the structures of state administration, and of the relationship between the state, the ruling elite of magnate clans, holders of imperial dignities, the wealthy and middling urban and landowning families, on the one hand, and the depressed rural population, on the other, lent to the armies and to those who made them up a very different character and position in the structure of late Byzantine society and politics. In spite of the dramatic changes that affected Roman administration and institutions during and after the seventh century, there survived until the tenth century a highly evolved version of the late Roman state, together with the institutional norms and structures that were inherited from that time. Thereafter, from the tenth to the twelfth century, these institutions are further radically transformed, with the result that the military comes to occupy a very different position in society, and to represent a very different set of institutions and social relationships from those that had gone before.

Conclusions

I would emphasize the following main points in respect of the evolution of Byzantine military institutions in their social and political context.

First, soldiers and military institutions, the fiscal arrangements necessary to support the imperial armies, and the demands of the armies on campaign and for regular supplies and pay, were all crucial factors influencing the ways in which the late Roman and Byzantine state functioned. These factors also affected imperial politics and the relations between different elements within the power elite of the Byzantine world, as well as the economic and social position of the peasantry from which the bulk of soldiers were drawn. Indeed, it would be reasonable to suggest that, given the overriding demands of defense and the requirements for survival that dominated the early period of Byzantine history in the seventh and eighth centuries, the institutional arrangements associated with the army in all its aspects were the dominant features that determined the ways in which the state and its structures could develop, as well as the forms in which Byzantine society at large and, in particular, a social-economic elite could evolve.

Second, there always existed a number of parallel modes of recruiting and maintaining soldiers, varying across time in the emphasis placed on different modes according to state requirements and the economic and fiscal exigencies that constrained imperial policy. Both the *themata* as administrative regions and the connection between military service and the private or family income of soldiers (land) had their origins in the crisis period of the second half of the seventh century, although there is no evidence for any deliberately planned, institutional connection between them. The withdrawal of armies into Asia Minor and the development of territorial *themata* resulted in a localization of recruitment that led in turn to the evolution of a connection between the possession of land and the obligation to support military service for certain soldiers and their heirs. When cash resources and manpower were in short supply, these two complementary developments were the best the rump of the late Roman state could offer in respect of managing its military and fiscal needs. Side by side with the provincial soldiers supported wholly or partly by their own resources and registered in the state muster lists, there existed both mercenary soldiers recruited from outside the empire or from among warlike groups within the empire as well as mercenary (i.e., full-time) regular soldiers in each theme. This process of localization and provincialization had other sociopolitical results too: in particular, it led to the evolution of links of patronage and clientship, as well as economic and social dependency, between the provincial officers and their soldiers, or at least a proportion of these two groups. This, in its turn, had consequences for the political relations between regions and their armies and between the provinces and the center.

This network of modes of recruiting and maintaining soldiers worked comparatively well in the situation that engendered it; but once conditions changed, the nature of the demands made upon it changed also. A first stage in the process of transformation was marked by the reforms undertaken by Constantine V (mid–eighth century), especially the establishment of an imperial "guards" division, the *tagmata*, at Constantinople; then by the policies relating to the ways in which soldiers were to be supported by communal subscription introduced during the ninth century. A watershed was reached with the legislation of the tenth-century emperors, whose promulgations represented not just the rulers' concern with the welfare of the peasantry and the soldiers drawn from them, nor with the increasing threat posed by powerful persons—landowners or officeholders with resources to invest—to the resources at the state's disposal. It also reflects the last, failed efforts of the central administration to shore up a mode of recruiting and maintaining soldiers that was already obsolete, because circumstances vastly different from those in which it was first made possible had evolved, and because of the demands imposed on it by the expansive warfare and campaigning necessitated by imperial policy with regard to both the caliphate and the empire's western neighbors in the tenth century.

The move away from reliance on armies made up of locally recruited conscripts supported by local resources, and the transformation of those resources into fiscalized revenues, had as its result the fact that resources for the maintenance of armies were once more routed through and concentrated at the center of imperial power. This is apparent from the changes that took place between the sixth and ninth centuries in particular. But it is also apparent in the history of the empire thereafter. For when the "theme" armies disappeared, to be replaced by units of full-time soldiers recruited from all the provinces of the empire as well as from outside, paid and maintained through central government agents and the imposition on the provincial populations of a wide range of extraordinary demands and corvées, these changes had a direct effect on the political power struggles within the dominant social elite of the empire and, in consequence, on the later political and social structure of the imperial state. At the root of the shifts in administrative practices that took place in the tenth and eleventh centuries was the process of transformation of the Byzantine Empire from a strong state that determined both the social and the ideological orientation of its personnel into a centralized but very much weaker state, in which the once-subordinate and dependent state elite came to constitute, in part at least, an economically semi-independent social class able to challenge the state for the control of resources. The army and its demands played a crucial role in determining the pace and character of that transformation.

Notes

1. For historical surveys see Ostrogorsky 1969; Jones 1964; Brown 1971; *CMH* Vol. 4, pt. 1; Angold 1984. For the Arab conquests and the various arguments attempting to explain their success, see Donner 1981 and Kaegi 1992.
2. The literature on all these aspects of later Roman history is vast. An accessible brief introduction can be found in Brown 1971. For more detailed analyses, see the essays in Jones 1974, 1964; Haldon 1990a.
3. On the political events, Jones 1964.217–37; Stein 1959.351–64; 1949.7–76, 177–92.

4. For these developments, see Hendy 1985.475–92; Jones 1964.207–8, 235–36.

5. For a brief political-military history of the period, see Ostrogorsky 1969.83–95, 100–117; and in more detail Stratos 1968, 1972, 1975. For the proportion of the revenue lost, see Hendy 1985.620.

6. The Balkans up to the Danube was claimed by the empire, and when imperial armies appeared, the local, predominantly Slav, chieftains and leaders acknowledged Roman authority. But this lasted only as long as the army was present. The Bulgars were a new element whose nomadic military organization and technology enabled them quickly to establish a political hegemony over the region south of the Danube delta, from which their khans rapidly expanded their power, so that by the end of the seventh century they were a substantial threat to imperial claims in the region. See Obolensky 1971.63–68.

7. The strategy is described in considerable detail by a mid-tenth-century writer just as it was becoming redundant and the empire was firmly on the offensive again: the text (De velitatione bellica) is edited and translated in both Dagron and Mihaescu 1986 and Dennis 1985. Dagron and Mihaescu offer a detailed historical commentary and discussion. For further discussion, see Haldon and Kennedy 1980.

8. See Dagron and Mihaescu 1986; Haldon 1975; McGeer 1995.

9. A useful brief survey of the history of this period is presented in Whittow 1996.

10. See Whittow 1996.310–61, on the reconquests; and Oikonomidès 1976.125–52 for administrative and military organizational developments.

11. See the relevant discussion of these developments in McGeer 1995.

12. See Cheynet 1990; Vryonis 1971 for internal politics and factionalism; and for the general history of the period, see the relevant chapters in Angold 1984, 1995, and Magdalino 1993.

13. See the list and discussion in Brandes 1989.120–24.

14. See Brandes 1989; Spieser 1989.97–106; Kaplan 1986.198–232; 1982; Köpstein 1978.56–60. For surveys of Byzantine fiscal administration for the period from the seventh to eleventh centuries: Dölger 1927; Lemerle 1979. See also Haldon 1990a.137–38, 142–53. For a good summary of the fiscal-institutional function of cities in the Roman state, see Jones 1967.89; 1964.716–19. On the long-term consequences of the rise of Constantinople, see Brandes 1989.152–60; Mango 1986.118–36; Hunger 1965; and Spieser 1989.106. For the localization of exchange and the centrality of Constantinople, see Hayes 1980.375–87; Abadie-Reynal 1989.156–58; for Syria/Palestine the valuable survey of Kennedy 1985.141–83; Hayes 1992.203–16 with the modified views, 1968.7.

15. I have discussed these questions at length in Haldon 1990a.153–72 and 395–99, where the sources and relevant literature are to be found.

16. On the political structure of the Byzantine elite in the period from the tenth to twelfth centuries, see Cheynet 1990.

17. Hendy 1985.602–13, 662–67; 1989b. Note also Haldon 1985, esp. 80–83; and although one can modify the point according to the historical context (e.g., pointing out that the role and significance of commercial exchange and cash crops increased very considerably during the period after the tenth century), it remains valid for the whole Byzantine period up to the thirteenth century.

18. I stress transferable because a substantial proportion of the surplus wealth extracted by the state was always in the form of raw materials, state services of one sort or another, labor, and so forth.

19. See Haldon 1994.116–53; 1995.

20. All these elements are discussed in greater detail in Angold 1985 and Harvey 1989. For a survey of the different functions of gold and bronze coinages and their position in the state's fiscal considerations, see Haldon 1985.80–84; Hendy 1989a.

21. See the discussion in Haldon 1995.

22. Dennis 1985.12, 18–21 (trans. 13). The sources for the late Roman and Byzantine army are many and varied. They include also technical manuals compiled by both scholars and military men, the information from which can be very important but must also be carefully assessed in respect of genre, context, and function. See Hunger 1978, Vol. 2.323–40.

23. These points are made quite clear in Hendy 1985.21–138

24. See my comments in Haldon 1985.80–83.

25. See Jones 1964.623–30, 672–74; Teall 1959.87–39, see 93–94.

26. For horses and stud farms (both late Roman and Byzantine), see Haldon 1984.117–18 and notes 137–40 for sources; Haldon 1990b.184–87. See Jones 1964.834–39 for the arms factories and the supply of raw materials. On the question of the decline of wheeled transport in the Middle East from the fifth and sixth centuries, see Bulliet 1975; and on prices of animals and transportation, Cheynet, Malamut, and Morrisson 1991. For rates of movement, see Jones 1964.830–32; Nesbitt 1963; and in general on Mediterranean transport and movement in preindustrial times, Braudel 1975.276–80, 355–60.

27. For the transport of arms and weapons, see Haldon 1984.114 and notes. A special arrangement, the *Quaestura exercitus,* to supply troops on the Danube by sea from the Aegean area was established by Justinian: see Haldon 1990a.12.

28. Haldon 1984.318–22; 1990a.238–44 for a detailed discussion of the evidence for these changes.

29. For provincial arms production, see Haldon 1984.318–322, where the evidence is discussed in detail. There is no room to discuss the question of late Roman and Byzantine military technology, except to note that, while it retained a certain independence, it was also open to outside influence (introduction of the stirrup in the late sixth century, of the single-edged saber in the eighth or ninth, and of the crossbow in the twelfth), until overwhelmed by western military ideas and practice in the later twelfth and thirteenth centuries. Apart from "Greek Fire" (called "liquid fire" by the Byzantines, introduced during the later seventh century and representing a type of medieval flamethrower: see Haldon and Byrne 1977), it was not particularly innovative. Traditional Roman engineering skills seem to have declined from the seventh century on, although a clear notion of, and some practical attempt to maintain, a "science" of warfare, including technical knowledge of artillery engineering, was retained into the eleventh and twelfth centuries. See Haldon 1975; Kolias 1988.

30. See Haldon 1990b: text (C) 349–58, and commentary 236–37.

31. That is to say, the armies of the militarized provinces, or *themata:* see below.

32. See Jones 1964.280, 655–57, 671, 679, 834–37; and the contribution of Campbell, this volume.

33. See Whitby 1995.61–124, for a detailed analysis of these aspects.

34. Haldon 1990a.209–11.

35. There is an enormous literature on the various aspects of these structures. Major works include MacMullen 1963; Jones 1964.607–80, which provides one of the best modern surveys up to the year 602. To these one might add the collection *Armées et fiscalité dans le monde antique* (1977); Carrié 1986.449–88, 760–71; 1976.159–76; Ravegnani 1988. Relevant and useful older works are listed in Haldon 1993.

36. For the origin and meanings of the word *thema*, see Koder 1990.

37. See Hendy 1985.157–59, 406–29; Haldon 1990a.173–75 and 218–27 for the process of withdrawal.

38. Hendy 1985.640–54, 625–26; Morrisson, Barrandon, and Poirier 1985.113–87, see 125–26. For the implications of these developments in their wider context: Haldon 1990a.

39. Haldon 1990a.227–28, 251–52.

40. For detailed analysis and further literature, see Haldon 1979, 1984.

41. See the brief entry with further literature in *Oxford Dictionary of Byzantium* (1991), 1444.

42. See Jones 1964.670–71; Haldon 1984.114.

43. For the administrative structures that supported the army in the sixth and the early seventh century, see in general Jones 1964.671–74 (with 623–25 as background); Haldon 1984.113–15; 1990a.221–22; Kaegi 1982.103–5.

44. Privileges attached to military service: Jones 1964.617, 675; Patlagean 1977. For the Roman period proper, in which these privileges are rooted, see Campbell 1984.210–29 (on testamentary privileges), 229–36 (on *peculium castrense*); Garnsey 1970.245–47; MacMullen 1963.107–9; and Sander 1958.152–234.

45. These conclusions are clearly supported by Kaegi's analysis of military unrest in the fifth and sixth centuries (1981.14–40); see also Jones 1964.677–78, 1035–37; and Haldon 1986.141–42. For the "constitutionally" inscribed position of soldiers in the formal structures of the expression of imperial power—their "traditional" role in respect of imperial accessions, along with the senate and people, was generally recognized—see the discussion with literature in Haldon 1986. The centrality of the military in this respect was reduced over the fifth and sixth centuries: see Beck 1970.28–30. Some groups, such as semiprivate bodyguards, were an exception, although only marginally so: see Gascou 1976.143–56; 1985.

46. See Haldon 1986, esp. 178–90; and 1990a.355–75, for detailed analyses.

47. See Haldon 1986.161–70, 180–88; also Cameron 1979.3–35; 1978.79–108.

48. See Haldon 1993.45 and n.111; 1990b.256–58.

49. For the role of soldiers and the armies in this context, see Haldon 1986.172, 187–90 and the discussion of related evidence in Haldon 1993.46.

50. See Kaegi 1966; 1981.209–43 (esp. 232–43), 270–92.

51. See Haldon 1984, esp. 245–56.

52. This is clearest where the *tagmata* and similar units are concerned, but it applies to the provincial armies too: Kaegi 1981.244–69.
53. Haldon 1990a.153–72, 395–402.
54. Treadgold 1988 and the critical responses of Lilie 1987.
55. Such smallholdings seem to have evolved slowly and at different rates in different parts of the empire from the later seventh century, as the state first permitted, and then came to expect, some soldiers to support themselves from their own resources. See the discussion above (text at n.28), and literature cited in the accompanying notes.
56. See, for example, Haldon 1984.331 and n. 1021.
57. See Haldon 1993.54–55.
58. Haldon 1993.54–55.
59. For example, Haldon 1990b: text (C) 453–54, and commentary, 242–44.
60. On fiscal privileges, see the texts cited at Haldon 1979.54 n. 94, 60 n. 104; Dagron and Mihaescu 1986.264–66; Patlagean 1977, for the late Roman origins of these special categories.
61. For detailed discussion of soldiers' privileges, and particularly the question of *praescriptio fori*, see Haldon 1984.304–7, with nn. 915–26; Dagron and Mihaescu 1986.269–72.
62. See Haldon 1993.55.
63. Haldon 1984.232–33 for some examples. For conflicts over billeting and supplying soldiers in the late Roman period, see in general MacMullen 1963.86–88, as well as Jones 1964.631–32.
64. It is significant that all those bearing imperial titles, whether civil or military, were expressly prohibited from purchasing land subject to a *strateia*: e.g., *JGR* i, coll. iii, nov. v, 209; nov. viii, 223.
65. See Dagron and Mihaescu 1986.254–57 with literature; also Lemerle 1979.135 and n. 1; Ahrweiler 1960.14.
66. Examples in Haldon 1993.57.
67. Lemerle 1979.85–87, 224, 225.
68. Lemerle 1979.115–56; Ahrweiler 1960, esp. 9–10.
69. Haldon 1993.59.
70. Dagron and Mihaescu 1986.186, 267–72.
71. Haldon 1979.59–63; and esp. Ahrweiler 1960.19–21.
72. See Ahrweiler 1960.21–23.
73. See Dagron and Mihaescu 1986.259–74, and esp. 284–86; Kolia-Dermitzakē 1989.39–55, on the notion of a Christian "holy war" in the tenth century. The sources appear to treat all soldiers as more or less equal, although reference to their privileges and legal status is never direct.
74. See Haldon 1993.63.
75. See Oikonomidès 1976.144; Hohlweg 1965.46–48.

Bibliography

Abadie-Reynal, C. 1989. "Céramique et commerce dans le bassin Égéen du IVe au VIIe siècle." In *Hommes et richesses dans l'Empire byzantin, IVe–VIIe siècles,* 143–62. Paris: Centre Nationale de la Recherche Scientifique.

Ahrweiler, H. 1960. "Recherches sur l'administration de l'empire byzantin aux IXe-XIe siècles." *Bulletin de Correspondance Hellénique* 84, 1–109.

Angold, M. 1984. *Byzantium 1025–1204: A Political History.* London: Longman.

———. 1985. "The Shaping of the Medieval Byzantine 'City.'" *Byzantinische Forschungen* 10, 1–37.

———. 1995. *Church and Society in Byzantium under the Comneni, 1081–1261.* Cambridge: Cambridge University Press.

Armées et fiscalité dans le monde antique, 1977. Colloques nationaux du CNRS no. 936. Paris: Centre Nationale de la Recherche Scientifique.

Beck, H.-G. 1966. "Senat und Volk von Konstantinopel. Probleme der byzantinischen Verfassungsgeschichte." *Sitzungsber. d. Bayer. Akad. d. Wiss.,* phil.-hist. Kl., Heft 6, 1–75. Reprinted in H.-G. Beck. 1972. *Ideen und Realitäten in Byzanz.* London: Variorum, XII.

———. 1970. "Res publica Romana. Vom Staatsdenken der Byzantiner." *Sitzungsber. d. Bayer. Akad. d. Wiss.,* phil.-hist. Kl., Heft 2. Reprinted in H. Hunger, ed. 1975. *Das byzantinische Herrscherbild,* 379–414. Darmstadt: Wissenschaftliche Buchgesellschaft.

Brandes, W. 1989. *Die Städte Kleinasiens im 7. und 8. Jahrhundert.* Berliner Byzantinistische Arbeiten 56. Berlin: Akademie Verlag.

Braudel, F. 1975. *The Mediterranean and the Mediterranean World in the Age of Philip II.* Vol. 1. English translation by S. Reynolds. London: Fontana/Collins.

Brown, P. 1971. *The World of Late Antiquity.* London: Thames and Hudson.

CMH = *Cambridge Medieval History.* Vol. 4, *The Byzantine Empire.* 2 parts. Rev. ed. J. M. Hussey, 1966. Cambridge: Cambridge University Press.

Bulliet, R.W. 1975. *The Camel and the Wheel.* Cambridge, Mass.: Harvard University Press.

Cameron, Averil. 1978. "The Theotokos in Sixth-Century Constantinople: A City Finds Its Symbol." *Journal of Theological Studies* 29, 79–108. Reprinted in Cameron 1981, chap. XVI.

———. 1979. "Images of Authority: Elites and Icons in Late Sixth-Century Byzantium." *Past and Present* 84, 3–35. Reprinted in Cameron 1981, chap. XVIII.

———. 1981. *Continuity and Change in Sixth-Century Byzantium.* London: Variorum.

Campbell, J. B. 1984. *The Emperor and the Roman Army.* Oxford: Blackwell.

Carrié, J.-M. 1976. "Patronage et propriété militaire au IVe siècle. Objet rhétorique et objet réel du Discours 'Sur les Patronages' de Libanius." *Bulletin de Correspondance Hellénique* 100, 159–76.

———. 1986. "L'esercito: Trasformazioni funzionali ed economie locali." In *Società romana e impero tardoantico: Istituzioni, ceti, economie,* edited by A. Giardina, 449–88, 760–71. Rome: Laterza.

Cheynet, J.-Cl. 1990. *Pouvoir et contestations à Byzance (963–1210)*. Byzantina Sorbonensia 9. Paris: Sorbonne.

Cheynet, J.-Cl., E. Malamut, and C. Morrisson. 1991. "Prix et salaires à Byzance (X^e–XIe siècles)." In *Hommes et richesses dans l'empire byzantin (VIIIe-XVe siècle)*, 339–74. Paris: Centre Nationale de la Recherche Scientifique.

Dagron, G. 1969. "Aux origines de la civilisation byzantine: Langue de culture et langue d'état." *Revue Historique* 241, 23–56. Reprinted in Dagron 1984, chap. I.

———. 1984. *La romanité chrétienne en Orient*. London: Variorum.

Dagron, G., and H. Mihaescu, eds. 1986. *Le traité sur la Guérilla (De velitatione) de l'empereur Nicéphore Phocas (963–969)*. Paris: Centre Nationale de la Recherche Scientifique.

Dennis, G. T., ed. 1985. *Three Byzantine Military Treatises*. Washington, D.C.: Dumbarton Oaks.

Dölger, F. 1927. *Beiträge zur Geschichte der byzantinischen Finanzverwaltung besonders des 10. und 11. Jahrhunderts*. Byzantinisches Archiv 9. Leipzig: Teubner, 2nd ed. 1960. Hildesheim: Olms.

Donner, Fred M. 1981. *The Early Arabic Conquests*. Princeton, N.J.: Princeton University Press.

Enßlin, W. 1942. "Zur Torqueskrönung und Schilderhebung bei der Kaiserwahl." *Klio* 35, 268–98.

Gabba, E. 1968. "Ordinamenti militari del Tardo Impero." In *Ordinamenti militari in Occidente nell'alto medioevo*. Settimane di Studio del Centro Italiano di Studi sull'alto Medioevo. Vol. 15, 1, 79ff. Spoleto: Centro Italiano di Studi sull'alto Medioevo.

Garnsey, P. 1970. *Social Status and Legal Privilege in the Roman Empire*. Oxford: Blackwell.

Gascou, J. 1976. "L'Institution des Bucellaires." *Bulletin de l'Institut français d'archéologie orientale* 76, 143–56.

———. 1985. "Les grands domaines, la cité et l'état en Égypte byzantine (Recherches d'histoire agraire, fiscale et administrative)." *Travaux et Mémoires* 9, 1–89.

Haldon, J. F. 1975. "Some Aspects of Byzantine Military Technology from the Sixth to the Tenth Centuries." *Byzantine and Modern Greek Studies* 1, 11–47.

———. 1979. *Recruitment and Conscription in the Byzantine Army c. 550–950: A Study on the Origins of the stratiotika ktemata*. Sitzungsber. d. Österr. Akad. d. Wissenschaften 357. Vienna: Austrian Academy.

———. 1984. *Byzantine Praetorians: An Administrative, Institutional and Social Survey of the Opsikion and Tagmata, c. 580–900*. Poikila Byzantina 3. Bonn: Habelt.

———. 1985. "Some Considerations on Byzantine Society and Economy in the Seventh Century." *Byzantinische Forschungen* 10, 75–112.

———. 1986. "Ideology and Social Change in the Seventh Century: Military Discontent as a Barometer." *Klio* 68, 139–90.

———. 1990a. *Byzantium in the Seventh Century: The Transformation of a Culture*. Cambridge: Cambridge University Press.

———. 1993. "Military Service, Military Lands and the Status of Soldiers: Current Problems and Interpretations." *Dumbarton Oaks Papers* 47, 1–67.

————. 1994. "*Synōnē*: Reconsidering a Problematic Term of Middle Byzantine Fiscal Administration." *Byzantine and Modern Greek Studies* 18, 116–53.

————. 1995. "Pre-Industrial States and the Distribution of Resources: The Nature of the Problem." In *The Byzantine and Early Islamic Near East.* Vol. 3, *States, Resources and Armies,* edited by Averil Cameron, 1–25. Princeton, N.J.: Darwin Press.

————, ed. 1990b. *Constantine Porphyrogenitus, Three Treatises on Imperial Military Expeditions. Introduction, edition, translation, and commentary.* Corpus fontium historiae Byzantinae 28. Vienna: Austrian Academy.

Haldon, J. F., and M. Byrne. 1977. "A Possible Solution to the Problem of Greek Fire." *Byzantinische Zeitschrift* 70, 91–99.

Haldon, J. F., and H. Kennedy. 1980. "The Arab-Byzantine Frontier in the Eighth and Ninth Centuries: Military Organisation and Society in the Borderlands." *Zbornik Radova Vizantoloskog Instituta* 19, 79–116.

Harvey, A. 1989. *Economic Expansion in the Byzantine Empire 900–1200.* Cambridge: Cambridge University Press.

Hayes, J. W. 1968. "A Seventh-Century Pottery Group." In R. M. Harrison and N. Firatli, "Excavations at Saraçhane in Istanbul: Fifth Preliminary Report." *Dumbarton Oaks Papers* 22, 203–16.

————. 1980. "Problèmes de la céramique des VIIᵉ-IXᵉ siècles à Salamine et à Chypre." In *Salamine de Chypre, histoire et archéologie: État des recherches.* Colloques internationaux du CNRS no. 578, 375–87. Paris: Centre Nationale de la Recherche Scientifique.

————. 1992. *Excavations at Saraçhane in Istanbul.* Vol. 2, *The Pottery.* Princeton, N.J.: Princeton University Press.

Hendy, M. F. 1985. *Studies in the Byzantine Monetary Economy ca. 300–1450.* Cambridge: Cambridge University Press.

————. 1989a. "Byzantium, 1081–1204: The Economy Revisited." In Hendy 1989c, chap. III.

————. 1989b. "Economy and State in Late Rome and Early Byzantium: An Introduction." In Hendy 1989c, chap. I.

————. 1989c. *The Economy, Fiscal Administration and Coinage of Byzantium.* London: Variorum.

Hohlweg, A. 1965. *Beiträge zur Verwaltungsgeschichte des oströmischen Reiches unter den Komnenen.* Miscellanea Byzantina Monacensia 1. Munich: University of Munich.

Hommes et richesses dans l'Empire byzantin, IVᵉ–VIIᵉ siècles. 1989. Paris: Sorbonne.

Hunger, H. 1965. *Reich der neuen Mitte. Der christliche Geist der byzantinischen Kultur.* Vienna: Austrian Academy.

————. 1978. *Die hochsprachliche profane Literatur der Byzantiner.* 2 vols. Handbuch der Altertumswissenschaft. Vols. 12. 5.1 and 2 = Byzantinisches Handbuch. Vols. 5. 1 and 2. Munich: Beck.

Jones, A. H. M. 1954. "The Cities of the Roman Empire: Political, Administrative and Judicial Functions." *Recueils de la Société Jean Bodin* 6, 135–73. Reprinted in Jones 1974.1–34.

————. 1963. "The Social Background of the Struggle between Paganism and Christianity." In *The Conflict between Paganism and Christianity in the Fourth Century,* edited by A. Momigliano, 13–37. Oxford: Blackwell.

————. 1964. *The Later Roman Empire 284–602: A Social, Economic and Administrative Survey.* Oxford: Blackwell.

————. 1967. *The Greek City from Alexander to Justinian.* Oxford: Blackwell.

————. 1974. *The Roman Economy: Studies in Ancient Economic and Administrative History,* edited by P. A. Brunt. Oxford: Blackwell.

JGR = *Jus Graecoromanum.* Edited by I. Zepos and P. Zepos. 8 vols. Athens 1931. Reprint Aalen 1962.

Kaegi, W. E. 1966. "The Byzantine Armies and Iconoclasm." *Byzantinoslavica* 22, 48–70.

————. 1981. *Byzantine Military Unrest 471–843: An Interpretation.* Amsterdam: Hakkert.

————. 1982. "Two Studies in the Continuity of Late Roman and Byzantine Military Institutions." *Byzantinische Forschungen* 8, 87–113.

————. 1992. *Byzantium and the Early Islamic Conquests.* Cambridge: Cambridge University Press.

Kaplan, M. 1982. "Les villageois aux premiers siècles byzantins (VIe–Xe siècles): Une société homogène?" *Byzantinoslavica* 43, 202–17.

————. 1986. "L'économie paysanne dans l'empire byzantin du Ve au Xe siècle." *Klio* 68, 198–232.

————. 1992. *Les hommes et la terre à Byzance du VIe au XIe siècle.* Paris: Sorbonne.

Kennedy, H. 1985. "The Last Century of Byzantine Syria: A Reinterpretation." *Byzantinische Forschungen* 10, 141–83.

Koder, J. 1990. "Zur Bedeutungsentwicklung des byzantinischen Terminus *Thema.*" *Jahrbuch der Österreichischen Byzantinistik* 40, 55–165.

Kolia-Dermitzakē, A. 1989. "Hē idea tou 'Hierou polemou' sto Byzantio kata ton 10o aiōna. Hē martyria tōn taktikōn kai tōn dēmēgoriōn." In *Kōnstantinos 7 ho Porphyrogennētos kai hē epochē tou,* 39–55. Athens: Athens Academy.

Kolias, T. 1988. *Byzantinische Waffen.* Vienna: Austrian Academy.

Köpstein, H. 1978. "Zu den Agrarverhältnissen." In H. Köpstein, F. Winkelmann, H. Ditten, I. Rochow, *Byzanz im 7. Jahrhundert: Untersuchungen zur Herausbildung des Feudalismus,* 1–72. Berliner Byzantinistische Arbeiten 48. Berlin: Akademie Verlag.

Lemerle, P. 1979. *The Agrarian History of Byzantium from the Origins to the Twelfth Century: The Sources and the Problems.* Galway: Galway University Press.

Lilie, R.-J. 1987. Review of Treadgold 1988, in *Byzantinoslavica* 48, 49–55.

MacMullen, R. 1963. *Soldier and Civilian in the Later Roman Empire.* Cambridge, Mass.: Harvard University Press.

Magdalino, P. 1993. *The Empire of Manuel I Komnenos, 1143–1180.* Cambridge: Cambridge University Press.

Mango, C. 1986. "The Development of Constantinople as an Urban Centre." In *Seventeenth International Byzantine Congress: Major Papers,* 118–36. New York: Caratzas.

McGeer, E. 1995. *Sowing the Dragon's Teeth: Byzantine Warfare in the Tenth Century.* Dumbarton Oaks Studies 33. Washington, D.C.: Dumbarton Oaks.

Mommsen, Th. 1889. "Das römische Militärwesen seit Diocletian." *Hermes* 24, 195–279.

Morrisson, Cécile, Jean-Noël Barrandon, and Jacques Poirier. 1985. "La monnaie d'or byzantine à Constantinople: Purification et modes d'altérations (491–1354)." In

Cécile Morrisson, Cl. Brenot, J.-P. Callu, J.-N. Barrandon, J. Poirier, and R. Halleux, *L'or monnayé*, Vol. I, 113–87. Paris: Centre Nationale de la Recherche Scientifique.

Müller, A. 1912. "Das Heer Iustinians nach Prokop und Agathias." *Philologus* 71, 101–38.

Nesbitt, J. 1963. "The Rate of March of Crusading Armies in Europe: A Study and Computation." *Traditio* 19, 167–81.

Obolensky, D. 1971. *The Byzantine Commonwealth: Eastern Europe, 500–1453*. London: Weidenfeld and Nicholson.

Oikonomidès, N. 1976. "L'évolution de l'organisation administrative de l'Empire byzantin au XIe siècle (1025–1118)." *Travaux et Mémoires* 6, 125–52.

Ostrogorsky, G. 1969. *History of the Byzantine State*. New Brunswick, N.J.: Rutgers University Press.

Patlagean, E. 1977. "L'impôt payé par les soldats." In *Armées et fiscalité dans le monde antique*, 303–9. Paris: Centre Nationale de la Recherche Scientifique.

Ravegnani, G. 1988. *Soldati di Bisanzio in età Giustinianea*. Materiali e Ricerche, nuova Serie 6. Rome: Jouvence.

Rémondon, R. 1965. "Militaires et civils dans une campagne égyptienne au temps de Constance II." *Journal des Savants* 132–43.

Russell, J. 1986. "Transformations in Early Byzantine Urban Life: The Contribution and Limitations of Archaeological Evidence." In *Seventeenth International Byzantine Congress: Major Papers*, 137–54. New York: Caratzas.

Sander, E. 1958. "Das Recht des römischen Soldaten." *Rheinisches Museum* 101, 152–234.

Spieser, J.-M. 1989. "L'évolution de la ville byzantine de l'époque paléochrétienne à l'iconoclasme." In *Hommes et richesses dans l'Empire byzantin, IVe–VIIe siècles*, 97–106. Paris: Sorbonne.

Stein, E. 1949. *Histoire du Bas-Empire*, Vol. 2: *De la disparition de l'empire d'Occident à la mort de Justinien (476–565)*. Paris: Desclee de Brouwer.

———. 1959. *Histoire du Bas-Empire*, Vol. 1: *De l'état romain à l'état byzantin (284–476)*. French ed. by J.-R. Palanque. Paris: Desclee de Brouwer.

Stratos, A. N. 1968, 1972, 1975. *Byzantium in the Seventh Century*. Vols. 1–3. Amsterdam: Hakkert.

Teall, J. L. 1959. "The Grain Supply of the Byzantine Empire." *Dumbarton Oaks Papers* 13, 87–139.

———. 1965. "The Barbarians in Justinian's Armies." *Speculum* 40, 294–322.

Treadgold, W. 1988. *The Byzantine Revival, 780–842*. Stanford, Calif.: Stanford University Press.

Vryonis, Sp. 1971. *The Decline of Medieval Hellenism in Asia Minor and the Process of Islamization from the Eleventh through the Fifteenth Century*. Berkeley and Los Angeles: University of California Press.

Whitby, M. 1995. "Recruitment in Roman Armies from Justinian to Heraclius (ca. 565–615)." In *The Byzantine and Early Islamic Near East*. Vol. 3, *States, Resources and Armies*, edited by Averil Cameron, 61–124. Princeton, N.J.: Darwin Press.

Whittow, M. 1996. *The Making of Orthodox Byzantium*. London: Macmillan.

Early Medieval Europe

Bernard S. Bachrach

Introduction

The European Middle Ages encompasses the period from the dissolution of Roman imperial power in the West during the fifth century to the Protestant Reformation during the sixteenth century. This chapter deals only with the first five or so centuries of this era (ca. 400–ca. 900), which fall into two subperiods. The first may be considered the age of the empire's Romano-German successor states. These polities flourished more or less until the Islamic conquests, which during the eighth century destroyed the Visigothic kingdom in Spain, undermined the long-distance trade segment of the Merovingian economy in Gaul, placed Italy under extreme pressure, and severely undermined the efforts of the eastern rump of the Roman Empire to play a sustained or even a significant role in the West.

The second subperiod is the Carolingian world that itself contains two stages. In the first, Charlemagne (768–814), building upon the great military successes of his father, Peppin (d. 768), and his grandfather, Charles Martel (d. 741), brought under his control much of what had been the Roman Empire in the West. Charlemagne conquered the Lombard kingdom in northern Italy, much of northern Spain, the Balearic Islands, great parts of the Balkans, and northwestern Germany, which Augustus had lost following the famous defeat in the Teutoburg Forest suffered by Varus in A.D. 9. Indeed, following Peppin's initiative, Charlemagne interfered in the East Roman government's sphere of influence by pursuing diplomatic relations with the caliph in Baghdad, Haroun al

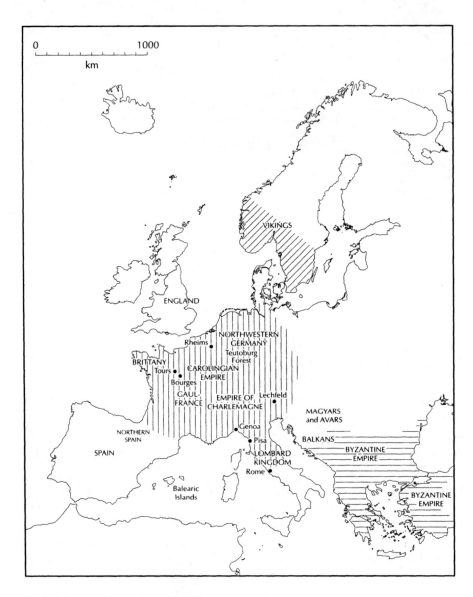

Early Medieval Europe and Its Environs

Rashid, securing trading rights for Jewish merchants in the caliphate, and winning privileges for Western pilgrims in Jerusalem. Charlemagne's acceptance of the imperial title for the Western half of the empire, which was formalized in Rome on Christmas Day 800, was recognized, despite initial reservations, by the East Roman government in 812.

The later stage embraces the dissolution of the Carolingian empire through the final two-thirds of the ninth century and into the early tenth century. The later part of the ninth century saw the unity of the Western empire dissolve once again as had happened during the fifth century. Just as before, the would-be political heirs of the emperor and their descendants fought to obtain a greater share of the empire than had been allotted to them. The damage caused by these dynastic wars among Charlemagne's grandsons and their successors was exacerbated by external military pressure of Viking and Muslim invasions.[1]

The Romano-German Kingdoms:
The Imperial Roots of State and Society

The kings who ruled the new Romano-German *regna* that emerged in the West were men closely connected to the old imperial order, and they worked diligently to preserve both the substance and the image of what they had inherited. Thus, for example, Clovis (d. 511) was the son of a Salian Frankish king and imperial general named Childeric who had been the Roman ruler of Tournai. Clovis was granted an (honorary?) consulship in 508 by the emperor Anastasius, which ostensibly confirmed his rule in Gaul. Following Clovis's victory over the Visigoths, the emperor also granted him permission to celebrate at Tours a triumph of the type accorded to a successful Roman general.[2] The Lombard kings in Italy and the Visigothic rulers in Spain took the *cognomen* Flavius to demonstrate their imperial connections and like most other Romano-German rulers continued the issuance of coinage in the imperial style. Indeed, the Visigothic king, Athaulf, who had been given the very high rank of *magister militum* (the Roman equivalent of field marshal), vowed to dedicate his career to the use of his Visigothic soldiers in the support of Roman civilization.[3]

The Romano-German kings, like Roman emperors and imperial generals, required all their male armsworthy subjects to take oaths of faithfulness to them. In addition, these kings, following later Roman precedent, issued law codes for the various peoples who lived in their kingdoms. Personality of the law was maintained following imperial traditions, for example, Roman Jewry law. The so-called Germanic or barbarian law codes on the mainland were very heavily influenced by Roman law and were published exclusively in Latin. The hand of Roman lawyers has been well documented in the redaction of these new "Germanic" law codes. In this context it is noteworthy that the king's court was the highest court in the *regnum*. Finally, the Merovingian and Carolingian Franks, in obvious imitation of later Roman imperial tradition exemplified by the well-known actions of Constantine the Great, the first Christian emperor, divided their *regna* among their male heirs. The Visigoths, Lombards, and Anglo-Saxons would seem to have followed what may appear to have been a more Germanic tradition of having a single successor. However, it is possible that they too were simply influenced by a Roman tradition that was different from the Constantinian model.[4]

In Rome's successor states *imitatio imperii* (imitation of the empire) carried well beyond the secular realm. The Roman emperors in the West—following the policy of Constantine the Great (d. 337)—had been regarded as the Christian God's representatives on earth, and in the East the emperor continued to be viewed in this light. In the West, the Visigoths were the first to formulate a very close relation to God through the Christian Church by adopting the ceremony of anointing a new king at the royal coronation found in the Hebrew Bible. Among the Franks, when Bishop Remigius of Rheims baptized Clovis in 496, he likened him to Constantine. Where the latter was regarded in the early Middle Ages as having made Christianity the religion of the empire, Clovis was seen to do the same for the Franks, whom both the Franks themselves and the pope regarded as God's new "Chosen People." Thus, Gregory of Tours, at the end of the sixth century, likened Remigius to Pope Sylvester I, the bishop who baptized Constantine, and exclaimed that like David, Clovis walked in the way of the Lord and the Lord was pleased.[5]

The Carolingians also adopted the ceremony of anointing at their royal and then subsequently at their imperial coronations. Einhard, Charlemagne's contemporary, wrote a biography of his lord, king, and emperor, which was modeled on the *Lives of the Caesars* by Suetonius. He not only makes the great Carolingian ruler out to be God's representative on earth and at least the equal of the emperor in the East but also portrays him as the bearer of triumphal Christianity. In addition, Einhard treated Charlemagne in a much more positive light than Suetonius had treated the twelve pagan Caesars about whom he wrote.[6] In this context of reestablishing the Western empire, the forged "Donation of Constantine" (ca. 751) provided the pseudolegal basis for Charlemagne's later elevation to the imperial title, which was depicted in this seminal document as being in the gift of the pope.[7]

The basis for political, religious, economic, and social organization in the West remained the Roman *civitas*. This is the western counterpart of the Greek *polis* and generally was composed of a massively fortified urban center, the *urbs*, and its *territorium*, or hinterland. The *urbes* contained the greatest agglomerations of population. They served, as well, as centers of local civil and military administration under a count who usually made his headquarters in the erst-while *praetorium* or *arx,* that is, citadel, located within the walls of the city. In some regions a viscount was appointed to help the count. These Roman-based circumscriptions continued to dominate the administrative structures of western Europe until modern times; in England the count is referred to as earl and the viscount as sheriff. When Charlemagne conquered much of Germany, he effectively established this imperial system beyond the frontiers of what had been the Roman Empire.[8]

Local administration was based on the *civitas.* The count headed a bureau-cracy that collected taxes of various types on land, persons, and trade. He also administered justice through a system of regional courts that worked all the way down to the village level. Many hundreds of thousands of lambs were slaugh-tered to produce the tons of parchment required to sustain the workings of sec-ular government. The count himself presided over the highest of the local courts. In addition, the count was responsible for mustering the army for the local defense; this force is the analogue of the great *fyrd,* or "nation in arms," in Anglo-Saxon England. The count also commanded that part of the army that was locally raised for offensive operations, or *expeditio.* This was the select levy, an analogue of the Anglo-Saxon select *fyrd,* which was based on a minimum wealth qualification. In addition, the count supported a personal military house-hold, or *obsequium,* that was composed of professional soldiers.[9]

Christianity in the West as in the East was the official religion, and strong kings such as Clovis and Charlemagne clearly headed the church just as the emperor did in Byzantium. Much effort was made both to convert pagans to Christianity and to maintain standards of Christian behavior. The Church was regarded as the arbiter of moral behavior, and, among other matters, continued the development of a Christian just-war doctrine. The Church government was based on the diocese or see, which generally was conterminous with the *civitas.* The hierarchy, headed by the bishop, was based in the *urbs,* where the cathedral seat was usually established within the walls that had been built during the lat-er empire. Monasteries were established both in the *urbes* and lesser fortress centers, for example, *castra,* as well as in the "wilderness."[10]

While the largest agglomerations of population dwelled in the *urbes* and other fortified centers in the West, the vast majority of the population in west-ern Europe, as until very recent times, lived in a rural setting and was engaged in agriculture. Most people were dependent on one or another magnate, whether secular or clerical, that is, bishop, abbot, or abbess. The Church likely controlled more than half of the land in Gaul and at least a similar amount in Anglo-Saxon England.[11] Indeed, the early tendency to exempt Church land in England from providing soldiers, doing work on fortifications, and maintaining bridges, that is, the *trinoda necessitas,* was reversed because the kings could not defend the land without this necessary church support. Thus, the *trinoda necessitas,* or "common burden," was established as a universal royal tax on all land.[12]

In the course of the early Middle Ages, most of Spain, much of southern Italy, and the islands of the western Mediterranean were more or less lost to the Muslims for lengthy periods. Indeed, it is arguable that the loss of tax revenues from long-distance Mediterranean-based trade played a marginal but not unimportant role in the decline of Merovingian royal power.[13] However, the great events that radically transformed the East between the later sixth and early ninth centuries, of which the success of the Islamic invasions was the most important, by comparison affected the West far less. Indeed, the general theme stressed in this chapter is one of continuity from the later Roman Empire through the early Middle Ages.

This emphasis on continuity should not be understood to mean sclerotic stasis but rather gradual change over a long period within the framework that had been established in the West during the later Roman Empire. Economically, the great estate, with its slaves, dependent cultivators, and satellite freeholders, continued to dominate the economy.[14] Public land, that is, government estates (*res publica*) and the emperor's private wealth (*res privata*) were administered separately under the empire. However, these became merged under their royal successors into the royal fisc, which was as important as the estates held by the secular magnates.[15] Throughout this period, the economic strength of the Church grew dramatically as ecclesiastical institutions, in addition to their spiritual responsibilities, played the primary role in providing services in the areas of health, education, and welfare.[16] However, Church wealth was often siphoned off to help sustain government projects, especially war.[17]

The continued economic dominance of the large estate played an important role in maintaining an aristocratic social structure in western Europe. However, the entry of many newcomers into the empire, Germans and others, in rather large numbers altered somewhat the ethnic composition of the aristocracy.[18] Culturally, the aristocracy of the erstwhile Roman parts of the Carolingian empire in the ninth century, although fundamentally Christian, surely was different from that of the fifth century. However, the lines along which the Carolingian aristocracy developed clearly lead back through the Merovingian era to the later Roman Empire.[19] This surely is what should be expected in light of the impact of continuity on developments in other vital sectors of society such as religion, economic organization, and war.

From Defense to Offense to Defense Again

From the early third century A.D., at the latest, the western half of the Roman Empire was on the defensive. The later Roman emperors put in place a grand strategy to protect the empire that today quite correctly we call "defense in depth."[20] The primary requirement of the new grand strategy was the radical transformation of the cities and other major population centers of the later Roman Empire into urban fortresses. In the defense-in-depth system these new "hardened" centers had four interrelated military functions. They served as supply depots, control points at key land and water routes, loci for coordination of rear area security and intelligence, and self-contained strongholds with mobile field forces.[21]

This decision had an obvious and profound effect on military topography throughout the West. In Gaul, for example, some 80 percent of the 115 *urbes* that are listed in the *Notitia Galliarum* were drastically reduced in size and became the beneficiaries of massive walls that averaged ten meters in height and four meters in thickness at the base, with stone foundations four or five meters below ground level. These fortifications were generally strengthened with equally massive projecting semi-circular towers that on average were placed at twenty-five-meter intervals along the walls and elaborate fortifications to protect the gates, which all provided carefully calculated "overlapping fields of fire" for archers, crossbowmen, and light artillery. This entire complex was usually further reinforced with an internal citadel (the *arx* or *praetorium*). Finally, in order to enhance the defenses, not uncommonly ditches were dug around the walls and then filled with water by diverting nearby streams or rivers.[22]

This system of defense in depth was generally successful in the West. When the so-called barbarians met the armies of the empire on the field of battle during the later fourth and fifth centuries, the latter were usually successful. A lengthy series of victories in the field won by the armies of Roman generals such as Stilicho, Constantius, and Aetius highlight the military history of the first half of the fifth century in the West. Indeed, the culmination of the success of this defensive policy was demonstrated in 451 on the field at Châlons, where Aetius defeated Attila the Hun and his allies.[23]

Continuing on the Defensive

The imperial government had seen the building of these great fortified cities as a way to thwart the "barbarians," who were perceived to lack both the technology and the organization to undertake siege warfare. However, these putative "primitives" learned very rapidly. Thus, in less than a hundred years, the Visigoths, who were warned late in the fourth century by their general Fritigern "to be at peace with the walls," are seen during the second half of the fifth century by the younger Merobaudes, a Romano-Frankish general, to have learned "the mature skills of the art of warfare"; these, he makes clear, included learning how to defend and to build great stone fortifications.[24]

The leaders of the empire's Romano-German successor states, once having been delegated authority in various parts of the West, remained essentially on the defensive throughout what we have come to consider the first phase of the early Middle Ages. The men responsible for making military policy or grand strategy worked diligently to maintain and improve the physical infrastructure of fortress cities, lesser strongholds, ports, and roads that had dominated imperial military topography.[25] The walls that had been built following the crash of the third century not only survived but continued more often than not and in more places than in fewer to be maintained in defensible condition.[26]

Indeed, even in Anglo-Saxon England, so far from the erstwhile center of the empire, Roman fortress cities remained a vital part of military strategy. During the later eighth century, Alcuin wrote with great pride of York, "with its high walls and lofty towers" that were "first built by Roman hands" and that continued to serve as a "bastion against enemy attacks" as well as being "a haven for ocean-going ships."[27] For Alfred the Great (d. 899) the massive Roman fortress city of Winchester served as a key element in his strategy to defend Wessex. Alfred created a system of defense in depth with thirty-three "hardpoints," some originally of Roman construction, that on the regional level was as sophisticated as the strategy that Diocletian and his successors had developed for the empire as a whole.[28]

The argument being made here is not that the armies of the Visigothic, Lombard, and Frankish kingdoms never went on the offensive, but, like the armies of the later Roman Empire in the West, they did not sustain long-term offensive actions over the course of many years in campaigns of significant territorial conquest. If we use the Merovingians as representative, it is clear that offensive war aims were, in general, very limited, both in terms of the relatively few major offensive operations they undertook and in the strategic targets of these campaigns. Clovis, who commanded a multiethnic army, was able only to conquer northwestern Gaul (that is, the future Neustria) and Aquitaine in a series of intermittent campaigns between approximately 486 and 508. In this effort there was only one noteworthy battle in the field, his victory over the Visigoths at Vouillé in 507. The conquests of his sons were the result of fewer than a dozen sustained campaigns aimed at bringing large stretches of territory held by their adversaries under Merovingian control.[29] The Merovingians also largely ignored Spain after the failed campaign against Saragossa in 541 led by King Childebert I and King Chlothar I.[30] By contrast, Charlemagne's armies, often led by his son Louis the Pious, operated there with great success for some two decades on an annual basis through the later eighth and early ninth centuries.[31] In a similar vein, one may contrast the Merovingians' failed campaigns in Italy with the great success enjoyed by Charlemagne, who conquered the Lombard kingdom and subsequently bullied both the pope and the Byzantines throughout his reign.[32]

Why the Merovingians as well as the Ostrogoths, Lombards, and Visigoths adhered to what was the imperial defensive policy in the West is explained by the continued diplomatic dominance and, when required, military might of the empire in the East. The Romano-German kingdoms, while exercising a certain amount of autonomy, were not fully independent. Thus, for example, Clovis's war against the Visigoths, mentioned earlier, was fought in support of imperial policy. His conquest of Aquitaine was legitimized by the emperor Anastasius through the award of a Roman triumph and consular honor.[33] Examples of Romano-German military operations being orchestrated by the emperor, for example, the Merovingian invasions of Italy, already discussed, could be multiplied many times over.[34]

A balance of power existed in the West that originally had been structured by the empire in recognizing the rulers of the new Romano-German *regna* in Italy, Gaul, and Spain as imperial officials. The final arbiter of these diplomatic and by extension military equilibria throughout the West, in general, and within the Frankish kingdoms of Gaul, in particular, was, of course, the Eastern empire. By holding the potential to provide military and/or financial support to one or another state in the West, the emperor in Constantinople controlled the balance of power. The credibility of imperial intervention was demonstrated consistently throughout the fifth century and dramatically illustrated, if such an illustration were needed, by Justinian's reconquest of North Africa, Italy, and a part of Spain, which quite obviously went well beyond the mere manipulation of the diplomatic situation.

However, the great losses suffered by the empire during the Islamic invasions undermined its ability to intervene in the West or even credibly to threaten military intervention there on a consistent basis. This does not mean that the Byzantines stopped trying, only that by and large they failed. During the early eighth century the situation in Gaul dramatically changed as well. The tradition adopted by the Franks of dividing the royal power and the kingdom into several *regna* came to a temporary end, not because the Carolingians abandoned the imperial tradition that was so forcefully symbolized for them by the Constantinian model, but because for more than a century the Carolingians produced only a single heir. Thus, the great material and human resources of Gaul effectively remained under the control of a single ruler.

Within the kingdoms of the Merovingians, warfare was by and large limited on the offensive side to forays by the expeditionary forces of one *civitas* against another *civitas*. Sometimes these operations resulted from the policy of a particular count, influenced locally by his secular and/or ecclesiastical supporters, since the *civitas* was in many ways a city-state, which had its own diplomatic goals in relation to other *civitates*. The weakness of the Merovingian kings, especially during the seventh and early eighth centuries, encouraged independent local action, and these local initiatives often had the reciprocal effect of further weakening the central government.[35] A similar pattern can be discerned during the tenth and early eleventh centuries, especially in the French kingdom (*Francia occidentalis*), following the dissolution of Carolingian central power and the weakened position of the newly elected Capetian monarchs.[36]

At other times in Merovingian Gaul, the forces of a *dux*, who led the expeditionary forces of several *civitates*, attacked one or another local target.[37] Here again the alliances of combinations of city-states in tenth- and eleventh-century France or even later medieval Italy are useful in a very general manner for comparative purposes. In such cases, of course, the military ineffectiveness of the central government is usually, at base, the reason that local warfare on a relatively large scale was possible. This helps us to understand, as well, why one finds relatively few concerted efforts by one or another king to put armies on a consistent basis into the field for offensive purposes aimed at substantial territorial conquest.

However, sometimes the Merovingian kings did manage to orchestrate a major military operation that was executed by large troop concentrations. In addition to the operations beyond the Frankish frontiers by the Merovingians, mentioned previously, the expeditionary forces of several *civitates* along with some professional forces were joined from time to time to lay siege to one or another of the great fortress cities that had been built during the later Roman Empire.[38] For example, Gundovald's "Little War" included the siege of Bourges in 583 and later the siege of Saint Bertrand de Comminges, which ended the war.[39]

The pattern of small wars and inconsistently engineered offensive operations lasted in Gaul until the death of the Merovingian ruler Dagobert I in 638. For a half century or so following his death, during the era of the so-called *rois fainéants*, or "do-nothing kings," raiding and counterraiding by relatively small groups both within the various Merovingian kingdoms and between kingdoms dominated the military scene. The very limited and localized nature of military affairs was punctuated from time to time by raids that were undertaken by enemies living beyond the frontiers of the highly fragmented *regnum Francorum*. Thus Saxons, Thuringians, Muslims, and Frisians all at one time or another penetrated Frankish territory with relative impunity to attack the countryside. Generally, however, these forces saw little success against the fortress cities, with the noteworthy exception of the Muslims in southern Gaul, who by and large survived comparatively unscathed.[40]

The Offensive

In contrast to the Merovingians, the Carolingian mayors of the palace gradually began to mobilize forces in order to go on the offensive. The move from the defensive to the offensive during the later seventh century probably began with the conquest of Neustria by Peppin II. The battle of Tertry in 687 seems to mark a beginning, at least from hindsight.[41] That Peppin and his advisers, in fact, had in mind a grand strategic design for the conquest of the entire *regnum Francorum* is surely not impossible, but such an overall plan cannot be proven to have existed. Thereupon, Peppin and his successors gradually asserted their control over the entire *regnum Francorum*. Charles Martel led armies on a series of offensive campaigns on a regular annual schedule for a quarter century until his death in 741, and Charles's son, King Peppin I, completed the Carolingian "reconquest" of the *regnum Francorum* in 768. Following the deaths of his father, Peppin I, in 768 and his brother, Carloman, in 771, Charlemagne subsequently more than doubled the size of the territory that he had inherited.[42]

The Carolingians' success in sustaining major offensive action over more than a century was due to the fact that they were united, for the most part, under a single ruler. The crippling effects of political division can be graphically illustrated, on the other hand, in the very brief period during which Charlemagne and his brother, Carloman, succeeded to a divided kingdom upon the death of their father. The two brothers not only found it impossible to develop unified military operations but also were thought by contemporaries to be on the verge of civil war.[43] The premature death of Carloman of natural causes in 771 saw the reunification of the Carolingian kingdoms under Charlemagne, and the rest is a history of consistent and sustained military conquest leading to the reestablishment of the western half of the Roman Empire and the acquisition of the imperial title, that is, Western Roman emperor, in 800.

In part, the success of unified Carolingian rule was undergirded by resuscitating a basic kingdom-wide administrative system that depended heavily on the use of extensive inventories of both private and public resources compiled both by the government and by private landholders (often called *polyptychs* by scholars), which were not dissimilar to those used during the later empire and in her Romano-German successor states. With a rather detailed knowledge of available resources, comparable in gross to William the Conqueror's Domesday Book, the Carolingian kings were able to keep track of the manpower resources of their kingdom in order to raise very large armies and of the material resources in order to levy substantial taxes for the support of their wars.[44]

The Defensive Again

Charlemagne's successors by and large found it impossible to maintain the pattern of sustained offensive warfare at which the early Carolingians had been so successful. Dynastic disputes beginning during the reign of Louis the Pious (814–40), Charlemagne's only surviving son and thus his sole successor, intermittently distracted the Carolingians from undertaking a great many major offensives.[45] In 843, three years after Louis's death, the empire was decisively divided between his three surviving sons by the Treaty of Verdun, with Lothair, the eldest, being recognized as the senior partner.[46] This imitation of the later Roman tradition of having senior and junior rulers worked no better in the ninth century than it had in the fourth.

The Carolingians, of course, did not immediately appreciate the weaknesses inherent in such a division because Charlemagne also had allotted kingdoms to his various sons—Louis the Pious inherited a unified empire in 814 because all of his brothers had predeceased him. The division of the empire in 843 had also not precluded further sustained offensive operations; each of the heirs was provided with an opportunity for continued expansion of his territory against ostensibly non-Christian enemies.[47] The division of the empire in 843 did, however, have negative effects on military mobilization. We have numerous examples of armies recruited by Charlemagne in places far distant from the theater of operation in which they ultimately were deployed. However, the division of the empire among essentially noncooperative rulers substantially diminished the Carolingians' ability to use their traditional tactic of deploying overwhelming force against their enemies.[48] Alliances were occasionally made between the brothers, but a lingering sense of hostility that had been fostered by previous frequent struggles among them and their supporters undermined the possibilities for sustained or even frequent military cooperation.[49]

The impact of the division of the empire and the dynastic wars that followed was exacerbated by an increase in hostile actions by the Muslims in the western Mediterranean and especially by the Vikings in the north. Although some expansion did go forward, these attacks forced the West fundamentally to return to the defensive. The Viking raids played a key role in increasing the power of royal officials on the local level. Regional defenses over time were to prove more effective than those of the royal government in France at combating the rapidly hitting seaborne raids of the Vikings. However, the Vikings in France never really threatened to conquer large segments of the kingdom. The establishment of the Norman Duchy in 910 by Charles the Simple was more in the nature of the co-option and the settlement of "barbarians" for military purposes to be used against other "barbarians" and in the ongoing local wars.[50] This strategy is strongly reminiscent of imperial efforts carried on during the later fourth and fifth centuries.

By contrast with the military situation in France, the Vikings were far more successful in England. There they managed to establish a colony in the northeast with the great fortified city of York as its capital.[51] Alfred the Great and his immediate successors, by unifying most of the rest of England, stemmed the tide of Viking success. In this context, Alfred reorganized the army, developed an effective navy—perhaps incorporating new ship designs—and, as noted earlier, established a system of defense in depth that was of exceptional sophistication.[52]

In Germany the defensive is to be emphasized as well. Indeed, the great victories in the field by Henry I at Riade in 933 and by Otto the Great at the Lechfeld in 955 were, in fact, won against invading Magyar armies on German soil. Despite Otto I's "renovatio" of the empire in 962, German expansion into Italy during the later tenth century did not go very well. The decisive defeat inflicted by Muslims on the army of Otto II at Cap Colonna in 982 was a disaster not only because of the massive casualties suffered by the emperor's elite heavily armed mounted forces at the hands of enemy light cavalry using the feigned retreat tactic but also because it severely stunted German enthusiasm for further operations in Italy. Comparatively minor offensive advances, however, were accomplished by various German magnates at the head of expeditionary levies in the northeast against the Slavs.[53]

Only in the eleventh century with sustained multinational military operations in Spain, attributed in legend to El Cid (d. 1099), did the West move forward in dramatic fashion. The conquest of the western Mediterranean islands by Genoa, Pisa, and the Normans, who also seized southern Italy and Sicily, and finally with the great success enjoyed by the massive multinational armies of the First Crusade did the West once again place its armed forces consistently on the offensive. Operations in the Mediterranean were mirrored, although on a considerably smaller scale, in the east of Europe by the German *Drang nach Osten,* that is, the drive to the East, against the Slavs.[54]

The Army

In consonance with the vast alteration of the military topography of the later Roman Empire through the creation of fortress cities, an effort was made to militarize the civilian population.[55] This process of creating urban militias was driven, in part, by the need to have large numbers of troops available to man the walls of the newly fortified centers of population. Thus, for example, the legislation establishing urban militia forces was already very well in train by 440 when the Emperor Valentinian III clarified, in the following manner, the existing but now lost regulations regarding the situation at Rome itself:

> We decree . . . that all are to know . . . that no Roman citizen [living in Rome] or member of a guild [in the same city] is to be compelled to do [expeditionary] military service. Indeed, he is required to do armed service only on the walls and at the gates [for the defense of the city] whenever the necessity arises. The regulations made by the Illustrious Prefect of the City are to be obeyed by all. (*Nov. Val.* V.2)

Proper defense of fortifications required one man for approximately every four feet of wall.[56] The fortress city of Bourges in northern Aquitaine, for example, had a 2,900-meter circuit wall,[57] which required a defense force of something in excess of 2,350 local militia men. Conversely, an attacking force, in order to pose a credible threat to storm the walls, had to have at least a four-to-one numerical advantage over the defenders.[58] Thus, if Bourges were defended simply by its local militia, as estimated above, an attacking force on the order of 10,000 effectives was required. These calculations remained valid throughout the early Middle Ages because the military technology that was available to those who defended the walls and to those on the offensive largely remained constant.[59]

However, the process of the militarization of the civilian population moved on apace in the countryside as well.[60] In 440, for example, Emperor Valentinian III, upon receiving intelligence regarding a projected Vandal invasion of Italy by sea, took steps for his regular soldiers and his federate allies to guard the cities and shore and for a mobile force to be put in the field. He then observed:

> [B]ecause the opportunities that are available for navigation during the summer make it uncertain where the enemy ships are going to land, we issue a warning that each and every landholder is to defend his property with his own men against the enemy should the circumstances require it. (*Nov. Val.* 9.1)

After noting that these rural militia forces served under the command of the great landowners upon whose lands they lived, Valentinian makes clear that they already were armed adequately: "They are to use those weapons that they have available," and with these weapons the militia forces are "to guard our province and their own fortunes." The emperor's concluding statement regards the disposition of the spoils of war: "Whatever a victor takes away from an enemy shall belong to him without any doubt." This legislation at once emphasizes the emperor's expectation that the militia forces will acquit themselves very well against the invaders and at the same time encourages them by granting to them the right to keep all of the booty that they capture (*Nov. Val.* 9.1).

The militarization of the rural population flourished in consonance with the need to defend the countryside against local bandits, in the first instance, and then, following the development of the defense-in-depth strategy, more heavily against organized units of barbarian invaders from beyond the frontier.[61] An important element of this local defense was the fortified villa. These were planned and financed by the great magnates, who owned vast estates, and were constructed by the free and unfree workers who cultivated these lands. These same workers were trained to defend the walls and towers of the fortified villas where they congregated with their families when the enemy attacked. The rural militias were supported by small groups of professional soldiers composed of erstwhile imperial soldiers and even barbarian mercenaries who served in the military household of the magnate.[62]

The militarization of the civilian population put weapons into the hands of a vastly increased number of Romans. In addition, these men received a modicum of training in their use, especially urban dwellers for the purpose of defending the massive fortifications in which they lived, since these centers of wealth were high-priority targets for invaders bent on obtaining loot. At the end of the sixth century, the emperor Maurice reiterated what, in light of the texts cited previously, apparently was a long-standing imperial regulation regarding the training of citizens; that is, all Roman men were to train in the use of archery until they reached the age of forty.[63]

While the civilian population was in the process of being militarized, the army was taking on civilian characteristics. Indeed, a gradual process of creating soldier-farmers and soldier-townsmen was taking place.[64] This pattern of "domesticating" the military was well in train when a late fourth-century writer observed that "lands were taken from the enemy and these were handed over to the commanders and to the soldiers who served as auxiliary troops." These tenures were governed by "the provision that they should continue to belong to the soldiers only if their heirs entered military service." Further, the imperial edict stipulated that these lands "should never belong to civilians." Finally, legal provision was made so that in addition to the lands, "animals and slaves were provided so that the *milites* would be able to cultivate what they had been given (*Scriptores Historiae Augustae, Severus Alexander*, 58.4–5).[65] By the early fifth century it was widely recognized that the slaves who belonged to regular soldiers, as well as those who belonged to *foederati* and *dediticii*, were already thoroughly engaged in "making war alongside their owners." Therefore the emperor Honorius made an effort to "encourage especially" these men to join the "imperial armed service." Indeed, Honorius went so far as to decree that, in general, "slaves shall offer themselves for war" (*CTh*, VII, 13.16).[66]

By the fifth century, it was the usual practice of imperial officials to provide large groups of immigrants such as Visigoths, Burgundians, Ostrogoths, and Lombards with one-third of the tax revenues and homesteads (*sortes*), usually in places that had been deserted by the owners.[67] Thus, for example, Pacatius emphasized in praise of Theodosius I's 383 treaty that settled the Goths in Thrace: "You received into your service Goths to provide soldiers for your army and cultivators for the land" (*Pan.* II, 22.3). More than two generations later, Vortigern and the *consilium* of Roman Britain came to be widely condemned for the mercenary contract (*foedus*) that they had made with Hengst and Horsa. It was agreed that these Saxons would be provided with a food supply (*annonae*) on a monthly basis (*epimenia*) and be established in homesteads (*domus*) of their own. Those Romano-Britons responsible for providing this support, like their counterparts throughout the West, were styled *hospites.*[68]

The late imperial practice of providing land to soldiers for their support continued into the early medieval era, as did in many cases the very units in which these soldiers had served. For example, the expeditionary forces that Clovis led in the wars he conducted to unify the greater part of *Gallia* were essentially of imperial origin. They were organized in many different ways and included not only military settlers (*laeti*), erstwhile prisoners of war (*dediticii*), and mercenary-allies (*foederati*) but regular Roman troops as well.[69] Procopius, writing toward the mid–sixth century, describes in considerable detail the fate of one group, perhaps frontier troops (*limitanei*), that had been serving in Armorica and subsequently was amalgamated into Clovis's armies. Procopius writes: "They handed themselves over along with their military standards and the lands that they had been guarding for the Romans for a long time to the *Arborychoi* [Armoricans] and to the Germans [Merovingian Franks]." These Roman soldiers, Procopius continues, "handed down to their offspring all of their fathers' customs . . . and this people held them in reverence . . . even up to my time" (*Bellum Gothicum*, 2.64ff.).[70]

Indeed, the Salian Franks, the group of which Clovis is accounted *rex* and from which he is thought to have obtained the core of his military forces, would seem to have had their ethnogenesis as Roman allies in the late third century.[71] Thus, for example, the often discussed Title LIX.5 of *Lex Salica*, where the inheritance of land "shall pertain to the male sex" and "shall not go to a woman," is very likely the result of the legislation of Constantius Chlorus, the father of Constantine the Great, for German *laeti*, including Franks, whom he settled in the northeastern part of Gaul.[72] These lands were held by men who performed military service, and their inheritance was entailed to ensure that the military obligations owed by the possessors were maintained.[73] The obvious similarity of this requirement to that noted earlier concerning *limitanei* is indicative of normal imperial policy with regard to the tenure of "military land."

The process of militarizing the civilian population in medieval Europe, as had been the case during the later Roman Empire, was grounded on the assumption that all able-bodied men were responsible for defending their homes. Indeed, contemporaries even discussed whether the Christian clergy owed armed service. Constantine's inauguration of a Christian chaplain service may well have muted some criticism.[74] However, efforts to get priests to fight remained controversial during the later Roman Empire and throughout the early Middle Ages.[75] In addition, each man was to provide greater or lesser service on the basis of his wealth. Thus, all able-bodied men were required to serve in a general levy, a locally based militia (*Landwehr*) for the defense of the region in which they lived.[76] Men who lived in a fortified city, or town, or other lesser stronghold played the primary role in numerical terms for the defense of the walls.[77] This aspect of a general military obligation was ubiquitous in Rome's successor states. The Anglo-Saxon version of the general levy, for example, often rather romantically labeled "the nation in arms," was the great *fyrd*.[78]

Civilians of sufficient means, regardless of their ethnic backgrounds, had military obligations that went well beyond participation in the general levy for local defense. They formed a great part of the select levy that was called upon for expeditionary service (*expeditio*).[79] The basic unit of wealth measurement, the manse (a landed estate capable of supporting a family), was the initial basis for such service. However, during the century-long period of offensive war carried out by the Carolingians in lengthy campaigns far from home, many of the rank and file of the expeditionary militia could not afford such service[80] and gradually were brought to the brink of poverty. Thus, Charlemagne raised the basic unit of wealth required for *expeditio* first to three and then to four manses.[81]

To augment the select levies, the Romano-German kingdoms and later the Carolingians used men who had been given military land by the Roman government to support them so they could go to war on a regular basis. For example, those men who were ethnically *Franci*, or Franks, and who held *terra Salica* were required to provide from their own resources for their arms, armor, and transport. In addition, they also were required to sustain their personal food costs for three months of campaigning each year and their clothing costs for six months of campaigning each year.[82]

In order to augment the recruits for the army raised from *terra Salica*, the Carolingians developed a new type of military land, the *beneficium*. More often than not the men who held these *beneficia* were called *vassali*, or vassals. It is important to note that most of these vassals were landless men and often unfree men (*servi*) who were granted military land to support them in arms.[83] As noted earlier, men who had land in sufficient quantity to provide for their own weapons and supplies already owed military service. Thus, the grant of military lands, *terra Salica*, by the empire to able-bodied but landless Franks and later the grant of *beneficia* to men from the lower strata of society by the Carolingians saw the raising up over the course of the early medieval centuries of many tens of thousands of impoverished or at the least land-poor men to the status of small landholders.

From a numerical perspective, the general levy composed of all able-bodied men of the militarized civilian population provided the overwhelming majority of the armed forces for local defense. The select levy provided the rank and file of the armies that carried out major offensive operations that were aimed at permanent conquest. However, these citizen-soldiers were significantly strengthened both for the purposes of local defense and while on *expeditio* by the addition of units of professional troops that were organized in a wide variety of ways.

First and foremost among the professional soldiers were the armed followers who served in the king's household. These groups may be considered the analogue of the *praesentales*, the units of the late imperial army that served in the presence of the emperor. Other members of the royal army were established with their families in military colonies or as garrisons in local strongholds, and sometimes even on lands of their own.[84] These groups frequently were structured in imitation of and sometimes were in direct continuity with institutions that had flourished during the later empire.[85] Analogues to these structures can be identified in Byzantium, the empire's successor state in the East.[86]

Other important men in society, lay and clerical alike, commonly supported a military household in accord with what was the late imperial tradition. The importance of such armed followings was well understood by the imperial government and flourished in Rome's successor states. For example, the great Byzantine general Belisarius, a contemporary of Clovis's sons, is reported by a contemporary on his staff to have had seven thousand effectives in his military household. Most of the members of such a military *familia*, like the *presentales* of the emperor, served in the household of the man who supported them.[87]

Constitutionally, the role of such powerful men as servants of the state is most clearly seen with regard to the princes of the Church. During the period of transition from direct imperial rule to the derivative constitutions of Rome's successor states in the West, the episcopate gradually became one of the dominant elements in local government.[88] Thus, important ecclesiastics, as great landholders, played a key role in the military organization of medieval Europe. It was the norm, for example, for each bishop to support a military component in his *familia* or household.[89] The bishops, the abbots, and even the abbesses also had the responsibility for seeing to it that their dependents, both free and unfree, performed service in the general levy and in an *expeditio* when either of these was required by royal or comital command.[90]

Toward the latter part of the ninth century, Archbishop Hincmar of Rheims, who arguably was the most ferocious defender of Church rights against government encroachment during the entire Carolingian era, attempted to codify the long-standing military obligations that were owed to the state by the Church. Thus, he made it clear that according to custom a full two-fifths of episcopal income as well as an equal percentage of the income that was collected by other religious institutions was to be made available to the government for the defense of the state.[91] Hincmar's efforts apparently were intended to scale back existing practices. Indeed, on average more than half of the income from major ecclesiastical institutions such as the monastery of St. Germain-des-Prés in Paris were collected for the purpose of supporting the army.[92]

It is very important to emphasize that the armed forces controlled by the magnates were legitimized solely in terms of the service they performed, either directly or indirectly, for the state. This rationale held whether the forces were led by generals, lay government officials, high-ranking ecclesiastics, or merely rich landowners, such as those who were addressed by Valentinian's rescript of 440, discussed earlier. In addition, the role of the magnate, who commanded and supported a group of such fighting men, whether civilian-soldiers or professionals, was legitimized in terms of the service he performed for the government. In this context, it is important to emphasize that rulers such as Charlemagne required all able-bodied men, that is, those who served in the retinue of a magnate, those who served as select levies, and those who only served in the general levy, to take an oath of loyalty to the king.[93] In short, those who were obligated to bear arms in defense of the state, both in the Roman Empire and in her successor states, had to swear loyalty to the leader of the state.[94]

The Nature of War

In the Romano-German kingdoms the focus of war was upon gaining control of and holding the *civitates* with their fortified *urbes* and lesser fortified centers of population.[95] The overpowering presence of the Roman fortress cities assured that sieges would dominate warfare both at the strategic and at the tactical level, and the centrality of siege warfare throughout the Middle Ages in those parts of the West that had been part of the Roman Empire is massively documented.[96] In Rome's successor states, for example, Clovis's success during the later fifth and early sixth centuries in imposing his rule on what is now the greater part of France was based on the ability of his armies to capture great fortress cities such as Verdun, Paris, Avignon, Albi, Rodez, Clermont, Bordeaux, Toulouse, and Angoulême.[97]

Campaign strategy, and to a lesser extent battle tactics, recognized the primary importance of keeping the destruction of both people and resources to a minimum and of avoiding unnecessary damage when possible. Massacred farmers and artisans, burned buildings, devastated vineyards, broken canals, and ruined bridges merely undermined the value of victory as taxes would fall in arrears and productivity would slump.[98] The destruction and disaster wrought by military operations is traditionally exaggerated by ecclesiastical authors throughout the Middle Ages. These "monkish" histories and chronicles often were written to lament the sinfulness of worldly society in contrast to the model behavior of holy people.[99] The failure of modern scholars to account properly for this bias has led to a serious overemphasis on disorder, violence, and destruction.[100]

For the early Carolingians, the strategic and tactical importance of the great fortress cities remained constant in those areas that had been a part of the Roman Empire in the West. During the eighth century, effective control of the government in Gaul passed from the Merovingian *roi fainéants* to the Carolingian mayors of the palace and other great regional magnate families. So, for example, the independent dukes of Aquitaine, Eudo, and Waiofar, based their entire strategy for the defense of their state on control of the twenty great fortress cities of the region. Waiofar's ultimate failure to defend these cities against King Peppin I, who developed an impressive siege train with massive support services, sounded the death knell of Aquitanian independence.[101]

Laying siege to massive late antique fortress cities that were well defended by large numbers of urban militia and trained regulars, such as Pavia, captured by Charlemagne in 774, and Barcelona, captured by Louis the Pious in 802—both after lengthy investments—required a logistic infrastructure capable of sustaining large armies.[102] Through a matrix of taxes levied on agricultural production and resources throughout the kingdom, as well as through the use of the products and resources from the very extensive lands of the royal fisc, the Carolingians, using cheaper and faster water transportation when possible, systematically mobilized what was needed to sustain forty to fifty thousand men for lengthy siege operations.[103] The administrative reforms, mentioned previously, provided the "paperwork" that undergirded these efforts. Indeed, the Carolingian policy of not ravaging friendly lands for forage succeeded, in large part, because religious establishments already paid on a regular basis more than 50 percent of their surplus income to sustain the state at war.

Siege warfare was also facilitated by the availability of proper technology. Machines for investing great fortresses had been developed in the West during antiquity, and Rome's successor states inherited knowledge of this technology from the later empire. Stone-throwing devices such as the onager, battering rams, and crossbows were not exceptionally difficult to construct and maintain, but they were effective.[104] These were used by the Byzantines and the Muslims as well as in the Romano-Germanic kingdoms. Indeed, even peoples from beyond the frontiers such as the Avars and the Saxons acquired the technology for building stone-throwing machines.[105] Technical manuals, such as the *Mappae Clavicula*, contained recipes for constructing incendiary devices among a host of other useful "scientific" aids for carrying on siege warfare.[106] The training of men to build and operate machines required the same type of specialization and professionalization in the early medieval West that it had required in the later Roman Empire.[107] Early Carolingian conquests under Charlemagne saw the sieges of Verona and Pavia along with the capture of the remaining cities of northern Italy as the basis for securing control of the Lombard kingdom.[108] The great success of the Carolingians in northeastern Spain rested, as well, on the capture of the great fortress cites of the region and especially of Barcelona, which was invested for almost two years.[109] By contrast, however, offensive warfare in Saxony and against the Avars was in territory that lacked the massively developed military topography of the empire with its highly prized road system and fortress cities.[110] Thus, Charlemagne systematically built *urbes* such as Paderborn as early as 776 and other fortifications in his newly conquered territories. He systematically strengthened his logistic capabilities by building roads, bridges, and canals while maintaining infrastructure components of imperial origin such as the communications system (*tractoria*).[111] In such newly conquered lands, Charlemagne and his advisers built upon the model of what was already available to them in the West as Rome's legacy and also upon what they learned from the Roman histories that they frequently had copied and even read aloud at court.[112]

Warfare of the later Carolingian era in France and Italy saw a reversion to the fundamentally defensive tactics and strategy of the sixth and early seventh centuries. Germany, however, where the physical infrastructure of fortified cities, roads, and bridges was considerably less developed than in the West, saw fewer sieges and more battles in the field.[113] However, the great administrative developments that had accompanied early Carolingian military success provided the later Carolingians with very effective means of keeping track of those who owed military service. Thus, for example, the armies of Charles the Bald (840–77) were usually well organized and effective. In addition, he worked vigorously to build fortifications to support local and regional defense, and to improve bridges and roads to strengthen his logistics.[114]

Numbers and Costs

The requirement that the walls of the great fortress cities and of the lesser centers of habitation be defended by large numbers of troops meant that the militarization of the civilian population continued and even accelerated in the early Middle Ages. At the same time, since even larger military forces were required to invest a fortress city, it was necessary to mobilize very large relief forces if sieges were to be raised or otherwise thwarted by engaging the invaders in the field.[115] This need for military manpower therefore required throughout the Middle Ages a consistent policy of maintaining all able-bodied civilian males in a state of military readiness. However, as noted previously, the greater part of the regular military in Rome's successor states, both East and West, at the same time gradually adopted a more civilian way of life. The total number of soldiers who might be considered professionals was greatly reduced from what had been the case during the later Roman Empire. Such men became a relatively small part of those who performed one or another type of military service.[116]

These two developments, when evaluated over time, resulted for the central governments of Rome's successor states in the West in massive decreases in the direct cost of maintaining their armed forces. For example, rulers such as Clovis, Charlemagne, Alfred the Great, and Otto the Great relied on the universal military obligation of their subjects, weighted by wealth, some elite troops supported by "military lands," the personal followings of their great magnates, and the forces of the royal military households to provide the field armies for their operations. By contrast, the government of the Byzantine emperor Justinian I (527–65) paid out on an annual basis some eighty thousand pounds of gold to sustain the field forces of his army and supporting services. This figure fell during the reign of his successor Heraclius (610–41) to about forty thousand pounds of gold and hovered between ten and twenty thousand pounds from Constans II in approximately 668 to Constantine VII in approximately 959.[117]

However, it is somewhat perplexing that the percentage of professional mounted troops, who were considerably more expensive to support than foot soldiers, increased substantially as a result of later Roman grand strategy over what it had been during the early empire.[118] The decision to increase the number of mounted troops is a paradox not only in economic terms but militarily as well, because these men played a small role, at best, in the normal conduct of a siege.[119] Nevertheless, during the Middle Ages, when the able-bodied male civilian population was fully militarized and siege warfare was the norm, policy decisions continued to be made consistently to maintain this expensive weapon system of obviously limited value.[120]

Writers who comment on military strategy and tactics from the later fourth century on, however, consistently justify, at least in part, what might appear to have been an unreasonable allocation of resources. These observers make it clear that the mounted troops under consideration were not subject to some doctrine or social convention that required them to refuse to fight on foot. It was well recognized by military thinkers such as Vegetius, not long after the decision had been taken to increase both the proportion and the actual number of mounted troops in the armies of the later Roman Empire, that these men were to be trained to dismount and fight on foot when the tactical situation required it (*De re militari* 1.18). Likewise, during the Middle Ages, most battles in the field saw most of the men who came to the battlefield on horseback dismount and fight on foot. Indeed, according to Rhabanus Maurus, writing in 856, Carolingian horsemen were trained to do this through the late Roman training methods described by Vegetius. Rhabanus, in fact, while commenting on Vegetius's text, makes clear "[t]hat, indeed, the exercise of jumping [on and off one's horse] has flourished greatly among the Franks."[121] Even Norman horsemen of the post-Conquest era, who are considered to have been among the most accomplished mounted fighting men in western Europe, far more often than not dismounted in battle in order to fight on foot. For example, in *all* of the major battles of the Anglo-Norman era—Tinchbrai in 1106, Brémule in 1119, Bourg Théroulde in 1124, Northallerton in 1138, and Lincoln in 1141—most of the mounted forces dismounted to enter combat.[122] Such a pattern would seem to reflect something approaching doctrine.

During sieges, horsemen certainly had the potential to play important auxiliary roles. Mounted troops were useful as scouts and spies, for guarding foraging operations, carrying messages, providing escorts, and a myriad of other minor though not unimportant tasks that helped to make a siege fully effective.[123] Perhaps most important, however, mounted troops could be used to deter invading forces from carrying out foraging operations. Thus, units of mounted troops were deployed to "shadow" an enemy army and undermine its means of supply. This tactic arose out of the great efforts that competent medieval commanders made to avoid combat whenever possible and to defeat the enemy by depriving them of logistic support instead.[124]

These tactical assignments, however, would hardly seem to require that all or even very many mounted troops be heavily armed and equipped with expensive and well-trained war horses.[125] Yet, from the very early Middle Ages onward, it is clear that in most of Rome's successor states it was important to maintain stocks of war horses.[126] Charlemagne, whose administration was very sophisticated, made a concerted effort to control the breeding of war horses for the armies of the Carolingian empire. Indeed, throughout the Middle Ages, kings, dukes, counts, and even lesser magnates worked diligently to breed and maintain costly war horses.[127]

Anglo-Saxon England affords an instructive contrast. There, policies were in place to ensure the availability of good horses for military purposes. These were not, however, war horses trained for battle, a difficult, time-consuming, and very expensive process at all times.[128] Indeed, the English vigorously sustained a doctrine that severely limited the flexibility of their forces; they excluded mounted combat from their tactical repertoire.[129] A careful examination of the military capabilities of the adversaries whom the English traditionally faced (Picts, Scots, and especially Vikings) indicates that these enemies were foot soldiers. In addition, it is clear that mounted troops, for a variety of reasons, usually were of marginal value in combat against these adversaries.[130] Indeed, the Vikings arguably were the best soldiers in western Europe for the greater part of two centuries, and their infantry formations could not be broken up easily by the charge of western Europe's best mounted forces.[131] In short, the English, who themselves were among the best foot soldiers in Europe, had no pressing need to raise and maintain expensive war horses or to develop mounted combat techniques.[132]

On the European mainland, however, two considerations would seem to have converged to require or, at least, to stimulate the maintenance of these very expensive but highly specialized heavily armed mounted units. Unlike the English, whose adversaries presented a very limited repertoire of combat techniques, the mainland states faced a variety of enemies who possessed a wide assortment of armaments and a broad spectrum of tactics. Beginning in the later empire and extending well into the tenth century, central Asian mounted archers (Huns, Avars, and Magyars) provided a continuing problem for the armies of the West. These problems were compounded from the eighth through the eleventh century by Muslim armies, which provided tactical problems in the field to western commanders not unlike those presented by the central Asian light cavalry.[133] Thus the military policy makers in Rome's successor states simply continued the imperial strategy of maintaining substantial mounted forces in order to deal with these enemies. However, once they had been defeated, none of the plethora of post-Carolingian states that supported such forces could give them up as long as their potential domestic adversaries did not. Without a broad and enforceable general agreement regarding the elimination of this weapons system, any government that might undertake partial disarmament unilaterally would face the risk of placing itself in a disadvantaged position.[134]

Second, Western leaders, shortly after freeing their states from central Asian and Muslim enemies at home, undertook a broad policy of military expansion. The Crusades, the *Drang nach Osten,* and the *Reconquista* were but the three most important of these efforts which continued throughout the Middle Ages. Western European armies therefore continued to maintain hostile contact with peoples who presented tactical problems to commanders that could be dealt with successfully, although only in part, by the use of appropriately deployed heavily armed mounted combat forces.[135] It must be admitted, however, that these troops, whether deployed on horseback to take advantage of their heavy armament or on foot as was far more common, were always a very small part of any large army.[136]

Conclusions

The construction of massive fortress cities and lesser fortifications during the later Roman Empire thoroughly altered the military topography of the West. Sieges came to dominate warfare in the medieval West, and the civilian population was militarized for local defense. Large forces were needed to carry out siege operations, and thus most armies were numerically dominated by citizen-soldiers who owed expeditionary service. In order to mount sieges and sustain them, a wide variety of technology was required and specialists were needed. In addition, an elaborate system of logistics was employed and maintained to feed and supply these large armies over lengthy periods of time on a consistent basis.

The massive reliance on citizen-soldiers in the West lowered the demands on the central government for expenditures to support the military. In this context, the need for a massive central bureaucracy similar to that which flourished in Byzantium was considerably diminished. Decentralization provided the impetus for the development of local and regional institutional structures with concomitant financial savings due to the avoidance of much of the great expense of overland transportation and the difficulties of long-distance communications. Indeed, the flexibility of the West in building on developments that took place during the later Roman Empire resulted in immense military strengths, which, for example, proved their worth in the success for two centuries of the crusader states against overwhelming odds.

The great majority of effectives in any siege, both among those on the defense and among those on the offense, fought on foot. This was the case in battles in the field as well, which in any case were rare. Indeed, many of the major battles in the field were fought in the context of a siege. Nevertheless, the decision had been taken at the highest level of government during the later Roman Empire to increase the proportion of horsemen in the regular armed forces, despite the great expense involved. During the Middle Ages a plethora of policy makers reaffirmed this decision throughout the greater part of western Europe. These decisions were sustained, regardless of the very specialized and limited tactical role allotted to heavily armed mounted troops in combat and the great expense they incurred, as efforts at arms control had a sad history of failure. Overall, like much else in Europe during the Middle Ages and beyond, the art of warfare reflects the massive influence of the later Roman Empire, recycled in a continuing pattern of creative conservatism leading to gradual changes that mark military matters in the history of the West.

Notes

1. Bachrach 1997b; cf. Leyser 1993.87–108, who sees a military world inhabited by primitive Germanic warriors and chiefs.
2. The best treatment of Clovis is now Rouche 1996. The seriously flawed textbook by Wood 1994 cannot be recommended, especially to students. Concerning Clovis's consulship, see McCormick 1989.155–80.
3. Wallace-Hadrill 1967 is an excellent introduction to the general practice of *imitatio imperii*.
4. Cf. Wallace-Hadrill 1967.
5. *Hist.* bk. II, chap. 31. For a list of abbreviations and editions of sources, see the first part of the bibliography at the end of this chapter.
6. Einhard, *V. Karoli* passim.
7. A useful review of this very controversial text is provided by Noble 1984.134–37.
8. Hubert 1959.529–58; Février 1973.41–138. Readers must be wary of some recent archaeologists who, working with seriously flawed methods both in regard to the material finds and especially in the treatment of the written sources, argue that major walled cities in this period became "urban shells," e.g., Halsall 1995.228 concerning Metz ca. 400 to ca. 550.
9. Cam 1912; Hollister 1962.
10. For the church in general, see Wallace-Hadrill 1983; McKitterick 1977; and Russell 1975 in regard to the "Just War."
11. Church possessions: Lesne 1910.224 regarding Gaul.
12. Abels 1988.53–54, 61–62, 91–93, 116–31, 146–59.
13. Cf. Pirenne 1939, who tends to exaggerate the overall economic impact of the tax losses suffered by the royal treasury as a result of the diminution of Mediterranean trade.

14. Verhulst 1995.481–509.
15. Durliat 1990; Goffart 1982b.
16. Lesne 1910.
17. Bachrach 1970a; cf. Reynolds 1994.1–114 on the use of church lands. Additional views: Magnou-Nortier 1997.253–348.
18. Goffart 1980; Werner 1984a, 1984b.
19. Werner 1984b.
20. Luttwak 1976.126–90. This major contribution to our understanding of Roman military strategy has had its critics whom Wheeler 1993.7–41, 215–40, however, has effectively answered.
21. Luttwak 1976.132–34. Luttwak's "defense in depth" contains five major elements. However, the fifth, "conservation of the strength of *mobile* forces," can reasonably be subsumed under point four.
22. Regarding the monumental physical infrastructure, see, e.g., the general survey by Johnson 1983. For special focus on Britain, Gaul, and the Rhineland, see Petrikovits 1971.178–218. Special attention to Gaul in Butler 1959.25–50. Also valuable: Grenier 1934; Brühl 1975, 1990; and Blanchet 1907.
23. Bachrach 1992.205; 1994b.
24. Bachrach 1995a.
25. Bachrach 1993d, 1995b; Ganshof 1928.
26. Johnson 1983; Brühl 1975, 1990; Février 1973; Hubert 1959. Bachrach 1994a for a regional case study.
27. Alcuin, *Versus*, lines 19–27. Note how Alcuin effectively merges both the military and the commercial importance of York.
28. Abels 1988.68–72.
29. Bachrach 1972, 1993c, 1997a.
30. On Saragossa: Bachrach 1972.26, where the date needs correction.
31. Bachrach 1974.
32. Bachrach 1998 concerning Charlemagne.
33. Bachrach 1997a.
34. Bachrach 1994a.
35. Bachrach 1972.
36. Bachrach 1985b; 1993b.
37. Bachrach 1972.
38. Bachrach 1972.
39. Bachrach 1994a chaps. 4 and 5.
40. Bachrach 1972 chap. 5.
41. Cf. Fouracre 1984.1–31.
42. In general: McKitterick 1983.41–76, and Riché 1993.92–116. But see also Bachrach 1972 chap. 5.
43. Lintzel 1929.1–22; Delaruelle 1932.213–24.
44. Goffart 1972, 1982a; and, on the great importance of written documents in Carolingian administration: McKitterick 1989. Cf. Davis 1987.15–39, who provides a partial list of polyptychs.

45. Cf. Reuter 1985, 1990, who sets the period of defensive orientation a bit too early and sometimes exaggerates the inability of the later Carolingians to mount offensive operations.
46. Ganshof 1956.313–30; McKitterick 1983.172–73; and Riché 1993.165–71.
47. Bowlus 1995 provides an excellent discussion of German expansion into the Balkans.
48. Bachrach 1999a.
49. McKitterick 1983.144–205.
50. Nelson 1992, cf. Bates 1982.
51. Sawyer 1971.
52. Abels 1988.63–66, 74–75, 99–100.
53. Reuter 1991.
54. Bartlett 1993 is thought-provoking on this topic.
55. Bachrach 1993c; cf. Elton 1996.102–3.
56. Bachrach and Aris 1990.
57. Claude 1960.40–47 remains the basic work, but cf. Brühl 1975.163–64.
58. Bachrach and Aris 1990.
59. Bradbury 1992; Rogers 1992; Bachrach 1994a.
60. Bachrach 1993c; cf. Elton 1996.102–3.
61. Luttwak 1976.132–33.
62. Bachrach 1993c; MacMullen 1967.99–118.
63. *Strat.* bk. I, chap. 2.
64. See the fine study by Brown 1984.
65. Further discussion in Brown 1984; Bachrach 1995b, 1999b.
66. Further discussion: Bachrach 1995b.
67. Goffart 1980; Durliat 1988.
68. Bachrach 1988b, 1991.
69. Bachrach 1972.1–17.
70. Bachrach 1970b.28–29; Anderson 1995.129–44; Bachrach 1997a.26.
71. Anderson 1995.129–44; cf., however, Poly 1993.287–320.
72. Anderson 1995.143 rightly argues this on the basis of *Pan. lat.* VIII, 21.1. See in addition the notes in Nixon's and Rodgers's edition of this text: 142–43, of which Anderson apparently was unaware.
73. Bachrach 1999b.
74. Jones 1953.
75. Prinz 1971, 1979.
76. Cam 1912; Ganshof 1968; Bachrach 1999b. But cf. Reuter 1985, 1990.
77. Bachrach 1972, 1993c.
78. Hollister 1962.
79. Bachrach 1972, 1993c.58–59.
80. In England the relevant unit was termed a "hide."
81. Müller-Mertens 1963 provides a reasonable economic explanation, but cf. Reuter 1985, 1990, who argues for a strategic cause. Reuter's strategic argument, however, has unresolved chronological problems.

82. Bachrach 1999b.

83. Bachrach 1999b; Odegaard 1945; Reynolds 1994.

84. Bachrach 1999b.

85. Bachrach 1995b.

86. Bachrach 1999b.

87. Bachrach 1995b; cf. Le Jan-Hennebicque 1990.

88. Heinzelmann 1976, 1988.

89. Bachrach 1993b.

90. Prinz 1971, 1979.

91. Nelson 1986.123–25.

92. Durliat 1983.

93. Ganshof 1971a.

94. Magnou-Nortier 1997.320.

95. Bachrach 1994a for a case study.

96. Bradbury 1992; Bachrach 1994c.

97. Bachrach 1972.1–17; Harrison 1993.

98. Bachrach 1995b.

99. Goffart 1998.219–20; Bachrach1994c.xviii–xix; Strickland 1996.7–16. Regarding the general mistreatment of the Vikings by clerical writers, see Sawyer 1971.

100. Bisson 1994.6–42 and Magnou-Nortier 1992.58–79 for a valuable corrective.

101. Bachrach 1974.

102. Very large armies: Werner 1968 and, on the general acceptance of Werner's arguments, Contamine 1994.102–3. Sieges: Bachrach 1974 and Harrison 1993.

103. Bachrach 1993d.

104. The basic works by Köhler 1893 and Huuri 1941 are in serious need of correction. See, e.g., Bachrach 1994a regarding the Merovingian background. Schneider 1910.1–26 overreacts to Köhler and is well wide of the mark.

105. Gillmore 1981; Bradbury 1992.

106. *Mappae Clavicula*, chaps. 162, 266–76.

107. Bachrach 1993d.

108. Harrison 1993 for siege warfare as the norm in Lombard Italy. On military organization in early medieval Italy: Rasi 1937; Patlagean 1974; Tabacco 1966.

109. Bachrach 1974.

110. Avars: Pohl 1988. Saxons: Lintzel 1934.30–70 and Halphen 1921.

111. Hofmann 1965.437–53; Ganshof 1928.69–91; and Haywood 1991.82, 88 are a useful representative sample concerning these matters.

112. Reading aloud: Einhard, *V. Karoli* chap. 24; for libraries and *scriptoria*, see McKitterick 1989.165–210.

113. Reuter 1991.

114. Nelson 1992.

115. See above for discussion of the numbers required.

116. Bachrach 1993c.

117. Treadgold 1995, Table 12. The relative stability of the price of gold in the Eastern Roman Empire during this period makes the figures comparable.

118. Elton 1996.108–16.
119. Bachrach 1994c.
120. Bachrach 1983.181–87; 1995b.
121. Rhabanus, chap. XII and the "dedication," where he notes that he has included from Vegetius's text only those items of interest in modern times ("tempore moderno"). Discussion on the use of Vegetius in Bachrach 1983. On the controversial matter of Carolingian cavalry: Bachrach 1983. Ganshof 1952.531–37 and Verbruggen 1965.420–34.
122. Hollister 1962.130–32; further examples in Bachrach 1988a.184.
123. Bachrach 1985a.727–29.
124. Gillingham 1990.145–55 develops these ideas very well.
125. Werner 1968.814–22 on heavily and lightly armed mounted troops.
126. Bachrach 1985a.711–13.
127. Davis 1989, although he neglects the earlier Middle Ages, is on the right track. Although Ayton 1994 has discovered an immense amount of information about horses, he propagates old myths concerning their tactical and strategic importance.
128. Gillmore 1992.7–29.
129. Brown 1967.123–26.
130. Hollister 1962.127–52.
131. Bachrach 1988a.185.
132. Hollister 1962.127–52. Indeed, it bears emphasis that until the Normans learned from the Byzantines how to build horse transports that permitted landing their mounts *in battle-ready condition,* the English did not have to deal with large numbers of mounted fighting men: Bachrach 1985b.
133. The impact of the threat these central Asian enemies posed on military policy in the West from the fourth through tenth centuries has yet to be properly assessed. For specialized studies see, e.g., Bachrach 1986.5–27; Bowlus 1995.
134. Medieval leaders had had very little success in trying to "legislate" regarding war. Neither the "Peace of God" nor the "Truce of God" may be considered to have been a success: Bachrach 1987. Note that the specific "arms control" efforts of the Second Lateran Council to ban the use of the crossbow by Christians against Christians totally failed: Contamine 1984.71–72.
135. France 1994.
136. Bachrach 1988a, 1989.

Bibliography

Sources

Alcuin, *Versus de patribus regibus et sanctis euboricensis ecclesiae.* Edited and translated by Peter Godman. In *The Bishops, Kings, and Saints of York.* Oxford: Oxford University Press, 1982.

Einhard, *V. Karoli* = Éginhard, *Vie de Charlemagne.* Edited and translated by Louis Halphen. Paris: H. Champion, 1947.

Gregory of Tours, *Hist.* = *Historiarum libri X.* Edited by Bruno Krusch and Wilhelm Levison. *Monumenta Germaniae Historica, Scriptores Rerum Merovingicarum,* vol. I.1. Hannover: Impensis Bibliopolii Hahniani, 1951.

Lex Salica = *Pactus legis Salicae.* Edited by Karl August Eckhardt. *Monumenta Germaniae Historica, Leges,* Vol. I, 4.1. Hannover: Impensis Bibliopolii Hahniani, 1962.

Mappae Clavicula: A Little Key to the World of Medieval Techniques. Edited and translated by Cyril Smith and John Hawthorne. Philadelphia: American Philosophical Society, 1974.

Maurice, *Strategicon* = *Das Strategikon des Maurikios.* Edited by G. Dennis, translated by Ernst Gamillscheg. Vienna: Österreichische Akademie der Wissenschaften, 1981; and *Maurice's Strategikon: Handbook of Byzantine Military Strategy.* Translated by G. Dennis. Philadelphia: University of Pennsylvania Press, 1984.

Pan. = *In Praise of Later Roman Emperors: The Panegyrici Latini. Introduction, Translation, and Historical Commentary with the Latin Text of R. A. B. Mynors.* Edited by C. E. V. Nixon and Barbara Saylor Rodgers. Berkeley and Los Angeles: University of California Press, 1994.

Rhabanus Maurus, *De procinctu Romanae militiae.* Edited by Ernst Dümmler. In *Zeitschrift für deutsches Alterthum* 15 (1872), 413–51.

Severus Alexander. In *Scriptores Historiae Augustae,* edited by E. Hohl. Leipzig: Teubner, 1927.

Vegetius, *De re militari* = *Epitoma rei militaris.* Edited by Carl Lang. Leipzig: Teubner, 1885.

Scholarly Works

Abels, Richard. 1988. *Lordship and Military Organization in Anglo-Saxon England.* Berkeley: University of California Press.

Anderson, Thomas, Jr. 1995. "Roman Military Colonies in Gaul, Salian Ethnogenesis and the Forgotten Meaning of *Pactus Legis Salicae* 59.5." *Early Medieval Europe* 4, 129–44.

Ayton, Andrew. 1994. *Knights and Warhorses: Military Service and the English Aristocracy under Edward III.* Rochester: Boydell Press.

Bachrach, Bernard S. 1970a. "Charles Martel, Mounted Shock Combat, the Stirrup and Feudalism." *Studies in Medieval and Renaissance History* 7, 49–75. Reprinted in Bachrach 1993a. XII, 49–75.

———. 1970b. "Procopius and the Chronology of Clovis's Reign." *Viator* 1, 21–31. Reprinted in Bachrach 1993a. VII, 21–31.

———. 1972. *Merovingian Military Organization 481–751.* Minneapolis: University of Minnesota Press.

———. 1974. "Military Organization in Aquitaine under the Early Carolingians." *Speculum* 49, 1–33. Reprinted in Bachrach 1993a. XIII, 1–33.

———. 1983. "Charlemagne's Cavalry: Myth and Reality." *Military Affairs* 47, 181–87. Reprinted in Bachrach 1993a. XIV, 1–20.

———. 1985a. "Animals and Warfare in Early Medieval Europe." In *Settimane di studio del Centro Italiano di Studi sull'alto Medioevo* 31, 1, 707–51. Spoleto. Reprinted in Bachrach 1993a. XVII, 707–51.

———. 1985b. "Geoffrey Greymantle, Count of the Angevins, 960–987: A Study in French Politics." *Studies in Medieval and Renaissance History* 17, 1–67. Reprinted in Bernard S. Bachrach, *State Building in Medieval France: Studies in Early Angevin History*, 505–31. London: Variorum, 1995.

———. 1985c. "The Practical Use of Vegetius' *De Re Militari* during the Early Middle Ages." *The Historian* 47, 239–55.

———. 1986. "A Picture of Avar-Frankish Warfare from a Carolingian Psalter of the Early Ninth Century in Light of the *Strategicum*." *Archivum Eurasiae Medii Aevi* 4,5–27. Reprinted in Bachrach 1993a. XVI, 5–27.

———. 1987. "The Northern Origins of the Peace Movement at Le Puy in 975." *Historical Reflections/Reflexions Historiques* 14, 405–21.

———. 1988a. "*Caballus et Caballarius* in Medieval Warfare." In *The Study of Chivalry: Resources and Approaches*. Edited by Howell Chickering and Thomas H. Seiler, 173–211. Kalamazoo, Mich.: Medieval Institute Publications, Western Michigan University.

———. 1988b. "Gildas, Vortigern and Constitutionality in Sub-Roman Britain." *Nottingham Medieval Studies* 32, 126–40. Reprinted in Bachrach 1993a. I, 126–40.

———. 1989. "Angevin Campaign Forces in the Reign of Fulk Nerra, Count of the Angevins (987–1040)." *Francia* 16.1, 67–84.

———. 1991. "The Questions of King Arthur's Existence and of Romano-British Naval Operations." *The Haskins Society Journal* 2, 13–28. Reprinted in Bachrach 1993a. II, 13–28.

———. 1992. "Some Observations on the 'Goths' at War." *Francia* 19.1, 205–14.

———. 1993a. *Armies and Politics in the Early Medieval West*. Aldershot: Variorum.

———. 1993b. *Fulk Nerra, the Neo-Roman Consul: A Political Biography of the Angevin Count (987–1040)*. Berkeley-Los Angeles: University of California Press.

———. 1993c. "Grand Strategy in the Germanic Kingdoms: Recruitment of the Rank and File." In *L'Armée romaine et les barbares du IIIe au VIIe siècle*, edited by Françoise Vallet and Michel Kazanski, 55–63. Rouen: Association française d'archéologie merovingienne; Musée des Antiquités Nationales.

———. 1993d. "Logistics in Pre-Crusade Europe." In *Feeding Mars: Logistics in Western Warfare from the Middle Ages to the Present*, edited by John A. Lynn, 57–78. Boulder, Colo.: Westview Press.

———. 1994a. *The Anatomy of a Little War: A Diplomatic and Military History of the Gundovald Affair (568–586)*. Boulder, Colo.: Westview Press.

———. 1994b. "The Hun Army at the Battle of Chalons (451): An Essay in Military Demography." In *Ethnogenese und Überlieferung: Angewandte Methoden der Früh-mittelalterforschung*, edited by Karl Brunner and Brigitte Merta, 59–67. Vienna-Munich: Oldenbourg.

———. 1994c. "Medieval Siege Warfare: A Reconnaissance." *Journal of Military History* 58, 119–33.

———. 1995a. "The Education of the 'Officer Corps' in the Fifth and Sixth Centuries." In *La noblesse romaine et les chefs barbares du IIIe au VIIe siècle*, edited by Françoise Vallet and Michel Kazanski, 7–13. Rouen: Association française d'archéologie merovingienne; Musée des Antiquités Nationales.

————. 1995b. "On Roman Ramparts, 300–1300." In *The Cambridge Illustrated History of Warfare: The Triumph of the West*, edited by Geoffrey Parker, 64–91. Cambridge: Cambridge University Press.

————. 1997a. "The Imperial Roots of Merovingian Military Organization." In *Military Aspects of Scandinavian Society in a European Perspective, A.D. 1–1300*, edited by Anne Norgard Jorgensen and Birthe L. Clausen, 25–31. Copenhagen: National Museum Society.

————. 1997b. "Medieval Military Historiography." In *Companion to Historiography*, edited by Michael Bentley, 203–220. London-New York: Routledge.

————. 1998. "Pirenne and Charlemagne." In *After Rome's Fall. Narrators and Sources of Early Medieval History. Essays presented to Walter Goffart*, edited by Alexander Callendar Murray, 214–31. Toronto: University of Toronto Press.

————. 1999a. "Early Medieval Military Demography: Some Observations on the Methods of Hans Delbrück." Forthcoming in *The Realm of Fact and Theory in Medieval Military History*, edited by Donald Kagay. Woodbridge, Suffolk: Boydell and Brewer.

————. 1999b. "Military Lands in Historical Perspective." Forthcoming in *The Haskins Society Journal*.

———— and Rutherford Aris. 1990. "Military Technology and Garrison Organization: Some Observations on Anglo-Saxon Military Thinking in Light of the Burghal Hidage." *Technology and Culture* 31, 1–17.

Bartlett, Robert. 1993. *The Making of Europe: Conquest, Colonization, and Cultural Change, 950–1350*. London: Allen Lane.

Bates, David. 1982. *Normandy before 1066*. London-New York: Longman.

Bisson, Thomas. 1994. "The 'Feudal Revolution.'" *Past and Present* 142, 6–42.

Blanchet, Adrien. 1907. *Les enceintes romaines de la Gaule*. Paris: E. Leroux.

Bowlus, Charles R. 1995. *Franks, Moravians, and Magyars: The Struggle for the Middle Danube, 788–907*. Philadelphia: University of Pennsylvania Press.

Bradbury, Jim. 1992. *The Medieval Siege*. Woodbridge, Suffolk-Rochester: Boydell Press.

Brown, R. Allen. 1967. "The Norman Conquest." *Transactions of the Royal Historical Society* 5th ser. 17, 109–30.

Brown, T. S. 1984. *Gentlemen and Officers: Imperial Administration and Aristocratic Power in Byzantine Italy A.D. 554–800*. London: British School at Rome.

Brühl, Carl-Richard. 1975. *Palatium und Civitas: Studien zur Profantopographie spätantiker Civitates vom 3. bis zum 13. Jahrhundert*. Vol. 1, *Gallien*. Cologne-Vienna: Böhlau.

————. 1990. *Palatium und Civitas: Studien zur Profantopographie spätantiker Civitates vom 3. bis zum 13. Jahrhundert*. Vol. 2, *Belgica I, Beide Germanien und Raetia II*. Cologne-Vienna: Böhlau.

Butler, R. M. 1959. "Late Roman Town Walls in Gaul." *Archaeological Journal* 116, 25–50.

Cam, Helen Maud. 1912. *Local Government in "Francia" and England: A Comparison of the Local Administration and Jurisdiction of the Carolingian Empire with that of the West Saxon Kingdom*. London: University of London Press.

Claude, Dietrich. 1960. *Topographie und Verfassung der Städte Bourges und Poitiers bis in das 11. Jahrhundert*. Historische Studien, Vol. 380. Lübeck-Hamburg: Matthiesen.

Contamine, Philippe. 1984. *War in the Middle Ages,* translated by Michael Jones. Oxford: Blackwell.

———. 1994. *La guerre au Moyen Age.* 4th revised edition. Paris: Presses Universitaires de France.

Davis, R. H. C. 1987. "Domesday Book: Continental Parallels." In *Domesday Studies: Papers Read at the Novocentenary Conference of the Royal Historical Society and the Institute of British Geographers: Winchester, 1986,* edited by J. C. Holt, 15–39. Woodbridge, Suffolk: Boydell Press.

———. 1989. *The Medieval Warhorse: Origin, Development, and Redevelopment.* London-New York: Thames and Hudson.

Delaruelle, E. 1932. "Charlemagne, Caroloman, Didier et la politique du mariage Franco-lombard 770–771." *Revue Historique* 170, 213–24.

Durliat, Jean. 1983. "Le polyptyque d'Irminon pour l'armée." *Bibliothèque de l'École des Chartes* 141, 183–208.

———. 1988. "Le salaire de la paix sociale dans les royaumes barbares (V^e–VIe siècle)." In *Anerkennung und Integration: zu den wirtschaftlichen Grundlagen der Völkerwanderungszeit 400–600: Berichte des Symposions der Kommission für Frühmittelalterforschung, 7.bis 9. Mai 1986, Stiftzwettl, Niederösterreich,* edited by Herwig Wolfram and Andreas Schwarcz, 21–72. Vienna: Verlag der Österreichischen Akademie der Wissenschaften.

———. 1990. *Les finances publiques de Dioclétien aux Carolingiens (284–889).* Sigmaringen: Jan Thorbecke.

Elton, Hugh, 1996. *Warfare in Roman Europe, A.D. 350–425.* Oxford: Clarendon Press.

Févier, Paul-Albert. 1973. "Permanence et héritages de l'antiquité dans la topographie des villes de l'occident durant le haut moyen âge." *Settimane di studio del Centro Italiano di Studi sull'alto Medioevo* 20, 41–138.

Fouracre, Paul J. 1984. "Observations on the Outgrowth of Peppinid Influence in the 'Regnum Francorum' after the Battle of Tertry (687–715)." *Medieval Prosopography* 5.2, 1–31.

France, John. 1994. *Victory in the East: A Military History of the First Crusade.* Cambridge: Cambridge University Press.

Ganshof, F. L. 1928. "*La Tractoria:* Contribution à l'étude des origines du droit de gîte." *Tijdschrift voor rechtsgeschiedenis* 8, 69–91.

———. 1952. "A propos de la cavalerie dans les armées de Charlemagne." *Académie des Inscriptions et Belles-Lettres: Comtes rendus des séances* 21, 531–37.

———. 1956. "Zur Entstehungsgeschichte und Bedeutung des Vertrages von Verdun (843)." *Deutsches Archiv für Erforschung des Mittelalters* 13, 313–30. Translated as "The Genesis and Significance of the Treaty of Verdun (843)." In Ganshof 1971b. 289–302.

———. 1968. "Charlemagne's Army." In Ganshof, *Frankish Institutions under Charlemagne.* Translated by Bryce Lyon and Mary Lyon, 151–61. Providence: Brown University Press.

———. 1971a. "Charlemagne's Use of the Oath." In Ganshof 1971b. 111–24.

———. 1971b. *The Carolingians and the Frankish Monarchy: Studies in Carolingian History.* Ithaca-London: Cornell University Press.

Gillingham, John. 1990. "War and Chivalry in the *History of William the Marshall.*" In *Thirteenth Century England,* edited by P. R. Cross and S. D. Lloyd, 1–13. Woodbridge, Suffolk: Boydell Press.

Gillmore, Carroll. 1981. "The Introduction of the Traction Trebuchet into the West." *Viator* 12, 1–8.

———. 1992. "Practical Chivalry: The Training of Horses for Tournaments and Warfare." *Studies in Medieval and Renaissance History,* n.s. 13, 7–29.

Goffart, Walter. 1972. "From Roman Taxation to Medieval Seigneurie: Three Notes: 1. The *Iugum* in Ostrogothic Italy; 2. The Ambulatory Hide; 3. Flodoard and the Frankish Polyptych." *Speculum* 47, 165–87, 373–94. Reprinted in Goffart 1989. 167–211.

———. 1980. *Barbarians and Romans A.D. 418–584: The Techniques of Accommodation.* Princeton: Princeton University Press.

———. 1982a. "Merovingian Polyptychs: Reflections on Two Recent Publications." *Francia* 9, 55–77. Reprinted in Goffart 1989. 233–53.

———. 1982b. "Old and New in Merovingian Taxation." *Past and Present* 96, 3–32. Reprinted in Goffart 1989. 213–31.

———. 1988. *The Narrators of Barbarian History (A.D. 550–800): Jordanes, Gregory of Tours, Bede, and Paul the Deacon.* Princeton: Princeton University Press.

———. 1989. *Rome's Fall and After.* London: Hambledon Press.

Grenier, Albert. 1934. *Manuel d'archéologie gallo-romaine,* Vol. 6.1. Paris: A. Picard.

Halphen, Louis. 1921. *Études critiques sur l'histoire de Charlemagne.* Paris: F. Alcan.

Halsall, Guy. 1995. *Settlement and Social Organization: The Merovingian Region of Metz.* Cambridge-New York: Cambridge University Press.

Harrison, Dick. 1993. *The Early State and the Towns: Forms of Integration in Lombard Italy, A.D. 568–774.* Lund: Lund University Press.

Haywood, John. 1991. *Dark Age Naval Power: A Re-assessment of Frankish and Anglo-Saxon Seafaring Activity.* London-New York: Routledge.

Heinzelmann, Martin. 1976. *Bischofsherrschaft in Gallien. Zur Kontinuität römischer Führungsschichten vom 4. bis zum 7. Jahrhundert: soziale, prosopographische und bildungsgeschichtliche Aspekte.* Munich: Artemis Verlag.

———. 1988. "Bischof und Herrschaft vom spätantiken Gallien bis zu den karolingischen Hausmeiern. Die institutionellen Grundlagen." In *Herrschaft und Kirche. Beiträge zur Entstehung und Wirkungsweise episkopaler und monastischer Organisationsformen,* edited by Friedrich Prinz, 23–82. Stuttgart: A. Hiersemann.

Hofmann, Hans Herbert. 1965. "*Fossa Carolina.* Versuch einer Zusammenschau." In *Karl der Grosse: Lebenswerk und Nachleben,* edited by Wolfgang Braunfels and Helmut Beumann, 1:437–53. Düsseldorf: L. Schwann.

Hollister, C. Warren. 1962. *Anglo-Saxon Military Institutions on the Eve of the Norman Conquest.* Oxford: Clarendon Press.

Hubert, Jean. 1959. "Evolution de la topographie de l'aspect des villes de Gaule du Ve au Xe siècle." *Settimane di studio del Centro Italiano di Studi sull'alto Medioevo* 6, 529–58.

Huuri, K. K. 1941. *Zur Geschichte des mittelalterlichen Geschützwesens aus orientalischen Quellen.* Studia orientalia 9. Helsinki: Societas Orientalis Fennica.

Johnson, Stephen. 1983. *Late Roman Fortifications*. Totowa: Barnes and Noble Books.

Jones, A. H. M. 1953. "Military Chaplains in the Roman Army." *Harvard Theological Review* 46, 239–40.

Köhler, G. 1893. *Die Entwickelung des Kriegswesens und der Kriegführung in der Ritterzeit von Mitte des 11. Jahrhunderts bis zu den Hussitenkriegen.* 3 vols. Breslau: W. Koebner.

Le Jan-Hennebicque, Régine. 1990. "Satellites et bandes armées dans le monde franc (VIIe–Xe siècles)," In *Le combattant au moyen âge*, 97–109. Histoire ancienne et médiévale 36. 2d ed. Paris: Publications of the Sorbonne.

Lesne, Emile. 1943. *Histoire de la propriété ecclésiastique en France.* 6 vols. Lille: R. Girard; Paris: H. Champion.

Leyser, Karl. 1993. "Early Medieval Warfare." In *The Battle of Maldon*, edited by Janet Cooper, 87–108. Reprinted in Leyser, *Communications and Power in Medieval Europe: The Carolingian and Ottonian Centuries*, edited by Timothy Reuter, 29–50. London and Rio Grande: Hambledon Press, 1994.

Lintzel, Martin. 1929. "Karl der Grosse und Karlmann." *Historische Zeitschrift* 140, 1–22. Reprinted in Lintzel 1961. 2:10–26.

———. 1934. "Die Unterwerfung Sachsens durch Karl den Grossen und der sächsische Adel." *Sachsen und Anhalt* 10, 30–70. Reprinted in Lintzel 1961. 1:96–127.

———. 1961. *Ausgewählte Schriften.* 2 vols. Berlin: Akademie-Verlag.

Luttwak, Edward N. 1976. *The Grand Strategy of the Roman Empire from the First Century A.D. to the Third.* Baltimore: Johns Hopkins University Press.

MacMullen, Ramsey. 1963. *Soldier and Civilian in the Later Roman Empire.* Cambridge, Mass.: Harvard University Press.

Magnou-Nortier, Elisabeth. 1992. "The Enemies of the Peace: Reflections on a Vocabulary, 500–1100." In *The Peace of God: Social Violence and Religious Response in France around the Year 1000*, edited by Thomas Head and Richard Landes, 58–79. Ithaca: Cornell University Press.

———. 1997. "La féodalité en crise. Propos sur "Fiefs and Vassals" de Susan Reynolds." *Revue Historique* 216, 253–348.

McCormick, Michael. 1989. "Clovis at Tours, Byzantine Public Ritual and the Origins of Medieval Ruler Symbolism." In *Das Reich und die Barbaren*, edited by E. K. Chrysos and A. Schwarcz, 155–80. Vienna-Cologne: Böhlau.

McKitterick, Rosamond. 1977. *The Frankish Church and the Carolingian Reforms, 789–895.* London: Royal Historical Society.

———. 1983. *The Frankish Kingdoms under the Carolingians: 751–987.* London: Longman.

———. 1989. *The Carolingians and the Written Word.* Cambridge: Cambridge University Press.

Müller-Mertens, Eckhard. 1963. *Karl der Grosse und Ludwig der Fromme und die Freien.* Berlin: Akademie-Verlag.

Nelson, Janet. 1986. "The Church's Military Service in the Ninth Century: A Contemporary View." In Nelson, *Politics and Ritual in Early Medieval Europe*, 117–32. London: Hambledon Press.

————. 1992. *Charles the Bald.* London: Longman.

Noble, Thomas F. X. 1984. *The Republic of St. Peter: The Birth of the Papal State, 680–825.* Philadelphia: University of Pennsylvania Press.

Odegaard, C. E. 1945. *Vassi and Fideles in the Carolingian Empire.* Cambridge, Mass.: Harvard University Press.

Patlagean, Evelyne. 1974. "Les armes et la cité à Rome du VIIe au IXe siècle, et le modèle européen des trois fonctions." *Mélanges d'archéologie et d'histoire* 86, 25–62.

Petrikovits, H. von. 1971. "Fortifications in the North-Western Roman Empire from the Third to the Fifth Centuries A.D." *Journal of Roman Studies* 61, 178–218.

Pirenne, Henri. 1939. *Mohammed and Charlemagne.* Translated by Bernard Mial. New York: W. W. Norton.

Pohl, Walter. 1988. *Die Awarenkriege Karls des Grossen 788–803.* Vienna: Bundesverlag.

Poly, Jean-Pierre. 1993. "La corde au cou: Les Franks, la France, et la Loi Salique." In *Genèse de l'état moderne en Méditerranée: Approches historique et anthropologique des pratiques et des représentations,* 287–320. Collection de l'Ecole française Rome 168. Rome: École française de Rome.

Prinz, Friedrich E. 1971. *Klerus und Krieg im früheren Mittelalter.* Stuttgart: Hiersemann.

————. 1979. "King, Clergy and War at the Time of the Carolingians." In *Saints, Scholars and Heroes: Studies in Medieval Culture in Honour of Charles W. Jones,* edited by Margot H. King and Wesley M. Stevens, 2:301–329. Collegeville: Hill Monastic Manuscript Library, St. John's Abbey and University.

Rasi, Piero. 1937. *"Exercitus Italicus" e milizie cittadine nell'alto Medioevo.* Padua: Casa Editrice Dott Antonio Milani.

Reuter, Timothy. 1985. "Plunder and Tribute in the Carolingian Empire." *Transactions of the Royal Historical Society,* 5th ser. 35, 75–94.

————. 1990. "The End of the Carolingian Military Expansion." In *Charlemagne's Heir: New Perspectives on the Reign of Louis the Pious (814–840),* edited by Peter Godman and Roger Collins, 391–405. Oxford: Clarendon Press; New York: Oxford University Press.

————. 1991. *Germany in the Early Middle Ages, c. 800–1056.* London-New York: Longman.

Reynolds, Susan. 1994. *Fiefs and Vassals: The Medieval Evidence Reinterpreted.* Oxford-New York: Oxford University Press.

Riché, Pierre. 1993. *The Carolingians: A Family Who Forged Europe.* Translated by M. I. Allen. Philadelphia: University of Pennsylvania Press.

Rogers, R. 1992. *Latin Siege Warfare in the Twelfth Century.* Oxford: Clarendon Press; New York: Oxford University Press.

Rouche, Michel. 1996. *Clovis.* Paris: Fayard.

Russell, Frederick H. 1975. *The Just War in the Middle Ages.* Cambridge-New York: Cambridge University Press.

Sawyer, Peter H. 1971. *The Age of the Vikings.* 2d ed. London: Edward Arnold.

Schneider, R. 1910. *Die Artillerie des Mittelalters.* Berlin: Weidmannsche Buchhandlung.

Strickland, Matthew. 1996. *War and Chivalry: The Conduct and Perception of War in England and Normandy, 1066–1217.* Cambridge-New York: Cambridge University Press.

Tabacco, Giovanni. 1966. *I Liberi del Re nell'Italia carolingia e post-carolingia.* Spoleto: Presso la Sede del Centro.

Treadgold, Warren. 1995. *Byzantium and Its Army, 284–1081.* Stanford: Stanford University Press.

Verbruggen, J. F. 1965. "L'armée et la stratégie de Charlemagne." In *Karl der Grosse: Lebenswerk und Nachleben,* edited by Wolfgang Braunfels, 1:420–34. Düsseldorf: L. Schwann.

Verhulst, Adriaan. 1995. "Economic Organisation." In *The New Cambridge Medieval History: c. 700–c. 900,* edited by Rosamond McKitterick, 2:481–509. Cambridge-New York: Cambridge University Press.

Wallace-Hadrill, J. M. 1967. *The Barbarian West, 400–1000.* 3d rev. ed. New York: Hutchinson.

———. 1983. *The Frankish Church.* Oxford: Clarendon Press.

Werner, Karl Ferdinand. 1968. "Heeresorganisation und Kriegführung im deutschen Königreich des 10. und 11. Jahrhunderts." *Settimane di studio del Centro Italiano di Studi sull'alto Medioevo* 15, 791–843.

———. 1984a. "Conquête franque de la Gaule ou changement de régime?" In Werner, *Vom Frankenreich zur Entfaltung Deutschlands und Frankreichs,* 1–11. Sigmaringen: J. Thorbecke.

———. 1984b. *Les Origines avant l'an mil. Histoire de France.* Vol. 1. Paris: Fayard.

Wheeler, Everett L. 1993. "Methodological Limits and the Mirage of Roman Strategy." *Journal of Military History* 57, 7–41, 215–40.

Wood, Ian. 1994. *The Merovingian Kingdoms, 450–751.* London-New York: Longman.

The Early Islamic World

PATRICIA CRONE

This chapter is concerned with the Muslim army in the first two centuries after the Arab conquests, and especially with changing sources of recruitment. The Arabs, as the nonspecialist reader may wish to be reminded, were a tribal people who had inhabited the Syrian Desert and Arabian peninsula since at least the ninth century B.C. and who acquired political and religious unity at the hands of Muḥammad in the early seventh century A.D. Between approximately 630 and 656 they invaded the Sasanid empire and the eastern parts of the Byzantine empire, and although they proceeded to fight no less than three civil wars in the next hundred years, the Byzantines and Sasanids never recovered their possessions. The first civil war resulted in the transfer of power to the Umayyad family (661–750), who ruled from Syria rather than Arabia; the Umayyads survived the second civil war (684–92), but the third (744–50) transferred power to another family, the ʿAbbāsids (750–1250), who ruled from Iraq and under whom it soon became clear that the Middle East had changed too much to be recoverable by its former rulers in a recognizable form.[1]

The military developments of the first two centuries are known primarily from chronicles compiled from the late ninth century onward on the basis of earlier accounts, which in their turn were compiled between approximately 750 and 850 and which codified the oral tradition of the invaders. The early Muslims are not known to have engaged in theoretical reflections on the nature of war, but they devoted much attention to the legal rules and religious merit of holy war (jihād), that is, war aimed at the subjection of infidels to Muslim sovereignty. They also wrote military manuals, although none survives from

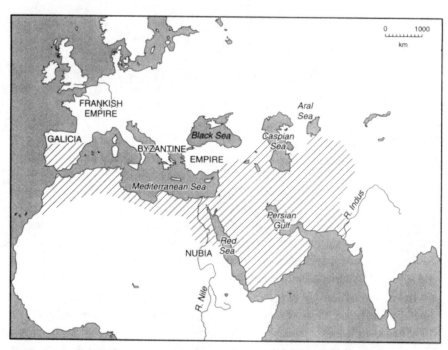

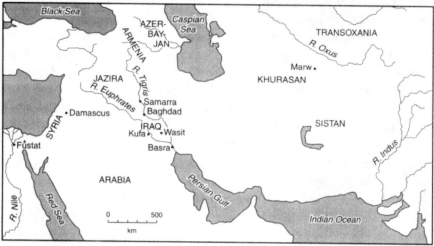

The Early Islamic World

the early centuries.[2] Some of the manuals appear to have been translations or loose adaptations of Persian and Indian works, and at some point Aelian's *Tactica* was also translated.[3] The Muslims had no compunctions about borrowing either ideas or equipment from their enemies as far as warfare was concerned. Some religious scholars did denounce stirrups as a non-Arab device likely to render the Arabs effete, because they would no longer have to jump onto their horses,[4] but military men ignored them.

The Conquest Society (ca. 630–750)

Garrison Cities

Unlike the barbarian invasions of the western Roman Empire, the Arab invasions of the eastern Roman and Sasanid empires were coordinated (within the limits imposed by the means of communication) from a single center, initially Medina. The caliphs' motives in launching the wars of conquest are disputed, as are the reasons for their success,[5] but the existence of a unitary leadership matters greatly for the manner in which the conquerors organized themselves. Contrary to what one might expect, they did not disperse as landlords and peasants over the conquered lands but stayed together as soldiers in garrison cities (*amṣār*) and military districts (*ajnād*). The decision to found such military centers is credited to the second caliph 'Umar (634–44), who allegedly persuaded the invaders not to divide up the conquered lands among themselves by invoking the interests of future generations,[6] and who certainly made the garrison cities attractive to the invaders by offering payments in cash and kind to those who settled in them.[7] Set apart from the conquered people by their Arab ethnicity, tribal organization, separate religion, and astonishing military success, the conquerors do not appear to have been greatly tempted to disperse among their subjects; insofar as we can tell, they accepted 'Umar's offer of a subsidized existence as warriors in the military centers with alacrity.

The Arabs located their first garrison cities on the edge of the desert for easy retreat in case of trouble (much as the British were later to locate theirs on the coast): thus Kufa and Basra in Iraq, Fusṭāṭ in Egypt, and Qayrawān in North Africa, which were new foundations. Some garrison cities were old cities adapted for new use, notably Marw in Khurasan; and in Syria no one garrison city was established at all: here the Arabs settled in several existing cities, and even on the land, dispersed in the four (later five) military districts into which this province was divided. But all garrison cities and military districts were in the nature of camps. Each accommodated a regional army from which garrisons were dispatched and expeditions sent out, be it for the suppression of revolts or further expansion.

At first the camps in the conquered lands were the outposts of Muslim society. But the conquered lands were vastly richer than Arabia and soon had a larger Arab population too, so the center was bound to shift. In the first civil war (656–61) all the contenders were based outside Arabia. Since the victor of this war was Muʿāwiya, the governor of Syria who became the founder of the Umayyad dynasty, it was to Syria that the capital was transferred. A century later the ʿAbbāsids moved it to Iraq, but it never returned to Arabia. From the end of the first civil war onward, in other words, Muslim society means the community established by the Arabs in the conquered Middle East rather than that of the Arabs who stayed behind in Arabia and the Syrian Desert and who merely formed an appendage to it. Some first-century Muslims did not even see them as appendages. True Muslims were *muhājirūn*, that is, emigrants who had left their homes to serve their new religion as soldiers; those who stayed put were mere "bedouin" (a term applied to stay-behinds regardless of whether they were pastoralists, agriculturalists, or urbanites), and the extent to which "bedouin" counted as members of Muslim society was controversial. In principle, all Muslims were soldiers. In principle, there was no Muslim army distinct from Muslim society. The Muslims *were* an army.[8]

The conquered peoples were left to administer themselves under their own leaders, typically members of the preconquest nobility or religious dignitaries. A fair number of punitive expeditions had to be dispatched against them in the early days, especially in Iran, and there were pockets of unsubdued tribes and local rulers here and there. But the Iranian resistance was uncoordinated; the Syrians, Egyptians, and Iraqis had been under foreign rule for too long to remember anything else, and although all the conquered peoples complained of exorbitant taxation,[9] they proved relatively easy to rule. It was far more difficult for the Muslims to keep their own ranks in order. Even so, they were free to devote most of their military energy in the first hundred years to expansion.

The Military Roll

All emigrants in the garrison cities were registered in the *dīwān*, a Persian word for "register," also used for the office in which the register was kept. A registered soldier was entitled to monthly rations in kind (*rizq*) for himself and his family, as well as to an annual cash payment (*ʿaṭāʾ*, normally translated "stipend") ranging from three hundred to two thousand dirhams. His wife could also claim a small stipend, typically one hundred dirhams a year, and until approximately 700 the same sum was paid for every child of either sex.[10] Soldiers paid no taxes, only alms (*zakāh*, which developed into a tax).

In return, the soldier had to be available for military service from spring to winter, although he was not necessarily called up every year; and once called up, he had to supply his own equipment.[11] For a trooper, this consisted of a horse, lance, sword, shield, bow, quiver, helmet, and armor (usually envisaged as mail).[12] As a rule, the soldier also had to maintain himself while on campaign.[13] Unless he had been settled on land with express permission to cultivate, he was forbidden to engage in agriculture.[14]

Once registered, a soldier seems to have remained on the military roll until he died. No special provisions (or even special word) for veterans are recorded. Soldiers too old for active service might transfer to administrative work or send substitutes.[15] If they were disabled, they would be registered as cripples and continue to draw their pay, or perhaps some fraction of it, without further obligations.[16]

The *dīwān* is explicitly said to have been modeled on the military roll of the Byzantines and/or Persians, and the similarities between Arab military organization and that of the defeated empires are obvious.[17] But the Arab understanding of the military roll was quite new. As they saw it, it was not so much an institution for the maintenance of armies as one for the maintenance of Muslims. Stipends were not simply military pay in their view, but rather a right that every emigrant and his descendants could claim by way of reward for his participation in the conquests; the revenue from the conquered lands was their booty (*fay'*): they could have taken it by dividing up the conquered lands among themselves; the government was merely administering it on their behalf.[18] Eventually, they endowed every Muslim with a right in the "booty" and presented ʿUmar as the creator of a perfect welfare state in which every believer of whatever ethnicity, age, or sex was provided for out of the wealth with which God had rewarded Muḥammad's followers for embracing his cause. This is obviously an idealization, but there is no disputing its starting point: initially, the emigrants were indeed subsidized by the government.

The political counterpart to universal subsidies was a consensual style of government, which was also to be greatly idealized. Since the provincial revenues were mostly spent on the soldiers and their families, there was not much to send on to the caliph;[19] and since the latter had no army separate from Muslim society, he could rule only by agreement with the tribal chiefs on whom his control of the mass of Arab tribesmen depended. The early caliphate was thus a federation of semi-autonomous armies over which the caliph presided as a "first councilor" (*prōtosymboulos*, as a Byzantine chronicler famously calls Muʿāwiya).[20] Muʿāwiya's governors were mostly chosen from among his kinsmen and friends, and his governors in their turn relied on the tribal chiefs to keep control of Muslim population. The chiefs were the intermediaries in an indirect system of government.[21] Of direct control there was very little. When Muʿāwiya executed a Kufan dissident in 672, the Kufans were outraged even though their own chiefs had signed the charges against him.[22] The caliph's task was to keep them united by formulating and maintaining a consensus, not to coerce them. To take the life of a free Arab Muslim who had not disgraced himself as a common criminal was to act as a tyrant.

The Reception of the Natives

Both the welfare state and the consensual style of government were predicated on the fact that the conquest elite was small, tribal, homogeneous, and warlike. But it did not retain these characteristics for long.

The total number of Arabs who left their homes can hardly have exceeded, or even totaled, five hundred thousand. The conquered peoples numbered perhaps twenty to thirty million.[23] To stay in power the Arabs thus needed native help, and they readily employed non-Arabs (including non-Muslims) as bureaucrats and tax collectors. They were less happy about using them in the army. In the early wars of conquest, it is true, they had welcomed deserters, and a number of Iranian troops became Muslims after negotiating favorable terms for themselves. Where difficult terrain and local resistance slowed down their further expansion, as in eastern Iran, they also made treaties with non-Muslim rulers, which obliged the latter to provide auxiliaries.[24] But they did not conscript their non-Muslim subjects, except in the case of the Copts for service in the navy;[25] nor did they set out to convert and recruit the able-bodied men of the conquered peoples by way of consolidating their hold on their provinces, except in the case of Berber North Africa, which they could not otherwise pacify.[26] They did, however, acquire a huge number of captives in the course of their campaigns, and although they viewed them with contempt, captives soon permeated their army and society.

Some captives were enrolled collectively in regiments of their own with special skills, such as the Iranian Bukhāriyya or the Indian Qīqāniyya, who were archers.[27] There was a long tradition in the Middle East, and indeed elsewhere, for using resettled captives as soldiers.[28] The Arabs rarely resettled them on the land, but rather took them with them to a Muslim center, where those enrolled in special regiments would serve their manumitter, normally the ruler or a general. They thus have the appearance of private guards, but the above-mentioned regiments were public forces and primarily used in urban policing, like the Scythian archers in classical Athens.[29]

Most captives ended up as domestic and semidomestic slaves, converted, and were eventually manumitted, so that Muslims of non-Arab origin must have outnumbered their erstwhile captors within a generation or two of the conquests. Like Roman freedmen, they became clients (mawālī) of their former masters. They generally took up civilian occupations after their manumission, thus creating a civilian Muslim society where previously there had been none; but they also appear in the army, initially in the service of their patrons, then in their own right.

Slaves and freedmen served their masters as grooms, weapon-bearers, and the like on campaign, and as bodyguards and other armed retainers. All persons of importance would surround themselves with retinues of kinsmen and/or slaves, freedmen, and other protégés. They were not always armed, but no caliphal objections are recorded to those that were, and their inclusion of slaves rarely gives rise to comment. The Muslims were decidedly less cautious about arming their slaves than the Greeks and Romans,[30] presumably because they had less to fear: captives almost always became Muslims and fought as such when they were armed, not as slaves against their masters. In civil wars and other crises, rebels and rulers alike would regularly arm their own slaves and attract other people's with promises of freedom (although the subversion of other people's slaves was regarded as wrong); and no great difference seems to have been perceived between arming one's slaves and one's freedmen. The retinues of slaves, freedmen, and other dependents (which were soon maintained by Arab and non-Arab soldiers alike) were usually of modest size, but that of the late Umayyad prince Sulaymān b. Hishām numbered some three thousand men.[31]

Freedmen could also register as soldiers in their own right, at least from the mid-Umayyad period onward. It is more commonly their sons that we meet in the client units, and free converts occasionally figure too (they also became clients, i.e., of the person "at whose hands" they had converted); but most free converts were runaway peasants, who were rarely accepted. All clients were paid less than Arabs, but they do not seem to have suffered other formal disabilities, and they soon rose to military governorships and commands, in their patron's service or otherwise.[32]

The Dilution of the Arabs

The children of the Arab conquerors had no direct experience of the warlike society in which their fathers had grown up, nor had they felt the exhilaration of converting. They were born under caliphs, took their religion for granted, and were required to be soldiers rather than warriors. Unlike Roman soldiers, however, they did not live in barracks; as soldiers for life, they could not be forbidden to marry;[33] in Egypt and Iraq, which had no major frontiers to defend, they might not be called up for years, and it is not clear how far they engaged in training. In short, there was not much to give them a sense of being members of an army, as opposed to simply of a society. Hence many of them soon became reluctant and incompetent soldiers. They did not voluntarily come off the military roll, which ensured them their right to stipends, but in Iraq, the province about which we are best informed, they would react to mobilization orders by sending substitutes or deserting, and they performed poorly against their own sectarian (Khārijite) rebels in 685–95, although they did not sympathize with the rebels.[34] In 699 the governor of Iraq sent a splendidly equipped

Iraqi army to Sīstān to deal with a troublesome local ruler in what is now Afghanistan. The task was arduous and unpopular, and when the troops were told to stay on in Sīstān, they rebelled and returned to Iraq, driven by longing for their families, to be defeated by Syrian troops in 701 or 702.[35] Thereafter Syrian troops were permanently stationed in Iraq, where the city of Wāsiṭ was built for them. The old regional army of Iraq was reduced to a local gendarmerie that was irregularly paid, infrequently called up, and recruited largely or wholly on a hereditary basis. New troops continued to be recruited in Kufa and Basra for service in Khurasan, but Iraq had effectively been demilitarized. The Arabs of Iraq became traders, shopkeepers, scholars, and (usually absentee) landowners on a par with their non-Arab converts.

Assimilation thus caused the old citizen armies to give way to professional troops, in the sense of full-time soldiers distinct from society at large. Of such professional troops there were two kinds. The Syrians provided the field army used for garrison service and emergencies all over the empire; the armies of the Jazira (Upper Mesopotamia, originally part of Syria) and Khurasan (eastern Iran), which had major frontiers to defend, continued to be largely or wholly confined to local use. Both types of army were recruited from Arabs and non-Arabs alike, although Arabs continued to predominate in both until the fall of the Umayyads; both were in constant action, the winter months apart; and both appear to have been regularly paid. Elsewhere the old regional armies survived in varying states of obsolescence.[36]

Assimilation also undermined the tribal cohesion of the Arabs. When members of the same tribal group in a given military center took up different occupations, they acquired different interests and lost their ability to act as a unit. They did not forget their tribal affiliation—far from it. But tribal ties lost their former political value in the sense that tribal chiefs could no longer use them to control the groups in question. Indirect rule via tribal chiefs thus had to be replaced by direct military control.[37] Further, as the Arabs struck roots in their diverse provinces and mixed with the locals, they ceased to be a single homogeneous people. Their increasing social and geographic differentiation made the formulation and maintenance of consensus difficult to achieve and endangered the survival of their makeshift empire, for there was, of course, nothing to hold it together apart from the Arabs themselves. The second civil war of 684–92 was a considerably longer and more complex affair than the first, and the Umayyad victory was much more of a military conquest than it had been the first time around. The sequel was also different, for this time the Umayyads responded by using the Syrians as a new conquest elite, subjecting Muslims and non-Muslims alike to the same military regime.

The Syrian army was dominated by "bedouin," that is, recruits from the Arab tribes of the Syrian Desert who had stayed put instead of emigrating.

(Many were undoubtedly bedouin in the literal sense of the word as well.) The Umayyads had close relations, often cemented by marriage alliance, with tribal chiefs of the Syrian Desert who must be presumed to have provided them with a regular supply of recruits in return for fiscal and political privileges for themselves and their tribes. Such recruits also formed the bulk of the Jaziran frontier army, which was run by members of the Umayyad house, and Syrians and Jazirans took most of the commands and governorships of the later Umayyad period. As the Arab conquest elite began to disappear in a general mass of Muslim subjects, the Umayyads would thus seem to have tried to rescue it with an infusion of fresh desert Arabs noted equally for their tribal solidarity and their devotion to the caliphal house. Emigration from Arabia had petered out by the 680s, and no attempts to raise new armies in Arabia are recorded.

With the emergence of the Syrian field army, the caliphate ceased to be a federation of autonomous regional armies, while at the same time the caliph ceased to be a *prōtosymboulos*. Muʿāwiya (661–80) had made himself deeply unpopular toward the end of his reign by designating his son Yazīd as his successor, although the alternative to hereditary succession was civil war whenever a caliph had to be elected. (Civil war came anyway because Yazīd died prematurely in 683.) Hereditary succession was quite correctly seen as a move away from consultative government. But there was worse to come. Having won two civil wars, the Umayyads could hardly go on pretending that they were ruling without coercion; and having acquired an army distinct from Muslim society, they were able to adopt a more authoritarian style of government. More provincial revenues must have been sent on to Syria, for although we do not have any figures, we have numerous protests at the removal of provincial surpluses and government monopolization of the "booty." Consultation with tribal chiefs, apart from those of Syro-Jazira, had become pointless inasmuch as the chiefs neither represented nor controlled the Muslim masses any longer. Goverment also became more brutal as Muslim society ceased to be a network of friends and allies. The days when a single execution could cause outrage were long gone.

Deprived of their stipends and pushed around by military governors, the Muslims reacted by looking back to the period before the first civil war and building it up in a primitivist vein as an era of lost perfection. Once upon a time, a mere two or three generations ago, the Muslims had been free, autonomous, and egalitarian tribesmen ruled without jails, police, executioners, taxes, and privileged elites, by caliphs who still resided in the Prophet's Medina and would have none of dynastic succession; in those days the caliphate had been elective, government had been consultative, and policies had been based on what was true and right, making disagreement impossible; all Muslims had worked of their own accord in the path of God, and God had richly rewarded them by granting them victory over the infidels and settling them in the conquered lands.[38] What, then, had gone wrong?

Some blamed the progeny of captives (*abnā' al-sabāyā*).[39] Most blamed the Umayyads, who were accused of having transformed the leadership of the Prophet's polity into *mulk*, "kingship," that is, coercive government for the benefit of rulers rather than consensual government for the benefit of all, *mulk* being the type of government that the Byzantines and Sasanids had been saddled with and that Islam had come to destroy.[40] Since there were fewer Syrians than there had once been Arabs, and since the ranks of the Muslims continued to expand, the Umayyads were fighting a losing battle. Having won the first two civil wars, they were defeated and fell in the third.

The Early 'Abbāsids (750–861)

The 'Abbāsids were enthroned by rebel armies raised in Khurasan.[41] Of mixed Arab and Iranian origin, and originally Persian-speaking, these troops settled in Iraq, where the second 'Abbāsid caliph al-Manṣūr (754–75) housed them in his new capital, Baghdad, and where they replaced the Syrians in the role of imperial troops. It was now Khurasanis who garrisoned the empire, provided troops wherever there were emergencies, and took the highest governorships and commands (insofar as they were not taken by members of the 'Abbāsid family itself). The Syrians were demoted to regional troops and the Jazīrans continued in that capacity, while the Egyptians kept their local gendarmerie. The age of large-scale conquest having come to an end in the late Umayyad period, the main task of the army was now to maintain the political unity and internal order of the caliphate.

The 'Abbāsids did not prove able to maintain the caliphate intact, however, and their Khurasani army lasted for only fifty years. Spain seceded in 757 under an Umayyad prince; the areas roughly corresponding to modern Morocco and Algeria seceded in 777 and 789 under sectarian leaders; and in 800 Hārūn al-Rashīd invested a Khurasani general as autonomous ruler of the rest of North Africa. Hārūn al-Rashīd's death was followed by the fourth civil war (811–13), which pitted his son and successor al-Amīn against al-Ma'mūn, another son of his who was governor of Khurasan. Al-Ma'mūn recruited new Khurasanis and allied himself with Transoxanian princes and other Iranian (possibly also Turkish) grandees, who brought their own troops in a resumption of the relationship between the Sasanid emperor and his royal vassals; and these troops defeated al-Amīn's Baghdadi Khurasanis, who were thus reduced to a secondary role. Two years later, al-Ma'mūn granted Khurasan autonomy under a hereditary dynasty, the Ṭāhirids, who held so many posts outside Khurasan as well that the caliphate turned into a veritable 'Abbāsid-Ṭāhirid condominium.

But the caliphal army was modified yet again when al-Ma'mūn died. His brother and successor al-Mu'taṣim (833–42) had accumulated a retinue of some three or four thousand Turks, whom he had bought as slaves and freed for military service already before his accession, and he continued to collect Turkish slaves thereafter, thus introducing what is known in Islamicist parlance as the Mamluk institution, that is, the systematic reliance on soldiers of servile and non-Muslim origin. When friction between the old Khurasanis and the Turks in Baghdad caused al-Mu'taṣim to build a new capital at Samarra, his army consisted of (1) Turks, kept in strict isolation from home-born troops; (2) a mysterious regiment of Maghāriba, "Westerners," said by one source to have consisted of Arab tribesmen from Egypt, but shown by an incidental reference to have included slaves;[42] (3) Transoxanian regiments inherited from al-Ma'mūn's reign and now known as Farāghina, Ushrūsaniyya, and so forth, after their place of origin; and (4) other Khurasanis (new and old) plus miscellaneous recruits, all registered together under the label *al-jund wa'l-shākiriyya*, "the army and the retinue."[43] Most of the old Khurasanis stayed in Baghdad, where they furnished the police force insofar as they remained in military service at all. To these units, Daylamī and bedouin mercenaries were soon to be added, but the Transoxanians did not remain prominent for long. In 838 a number of them plotted to replace al-Mu'taṣim with al-Ma'mūn's son (who had been expected to succeed him). The plot was foiled, its participants executed, and in 841 the leading Transoxanian general, who was prince of Ushrūsana, was tried for apostasy and killed.[44] Thereafter the Farāghina and Ushrūsaniyya dwindled into insignificance. Meanwhile, the Syrian and Jazīran frontier troops had been disbanded and the native Egyptian gendarmerie dropped.[45] All areas under direct caliphal control were now policed by soldiers of Turkish and other foreign origin, and all major commands and governorships were increasingly assigned to Turks.

Al-Mu'taṣim's experiment cannot be described as successful. In 861, a mere nineteen years after his death, the Turks assassinated his son and second successor in Samarra and turned the caliphs into puppets, whereupon the fragmentation of the caliphate accelerated. But the Mamluk institution nonetheless spread to become a standard feature of the Muslim Middle East down to modern times. The Ottoman variety of the Mamluk institution was suppressed in 1826; the last slave soldiers fought in South Arabia in the 1940s.[46]

Why Slave Soldiers?

The Explicandum   The Mamluk institution clearly has its origins in the armed retinues of slaves, freedmen, and other clients with which people in positions of command were in the habit of surrounding themselves thanks to the wide availability of captives.[47] Al-Mu'taṣim's Turks began as just such a retinue, for he collected them unaware that he would eventually succeed to the throne.[48] His

retinue was of much the same size as Sulaymān b. Hishām's, from which it differed mainly in its exclusively Turkish composition.

Given that Iranian captives, appreciated for their skills as archers, had been
enrolled in private retinues and public regiments alike in the Umayyad period,
it is not surprising that Turkish captives, also famed as archers, should have
appeared in the same roles when they became widely available in their turn: the
army may have included Turkish archers already by the 770s.[49] Nor is there anything unusual about the presence of slaves, freedmen, and other foreigners in
an imperial guard. Roman emperors regularly included German captives and
other slaves and freedmen, as well as gladiators, in their horseguard; of
Caracalla we are told that he "kept Goths and Germans about him, not only free
men but also slaves whom he had taken away from men and women and armed.
These he trusted more than the soldiers."[50] In Tang China (618–906) the ruling
Li family likewise put slaves of their own in the horse guard.[51] What is problematic in the Muslim case, then, is not that the caliph's horseguard included
men of this kind but that it expanded in size and function to become the cornerstone of the public army.

Negative Points   The explanation is not that the Turks were cheap to run.
Islamicists call them slave soldiers because they owed their military career to the
fact that they were or had been slaves, but they did not supply forced labor, nor
were they menial servants. Converted to Islam and usually (at first) manumitted before taking up service, they received stipends for themselves, their wives,
and their children alike, and the army swallowed up colossal sums after their
arrival.[52] Besides, al-Muʿtaṣim went out of his way to shower honors on his
favorites. He even adopted the son of one of his Turks, apparently a free ruler,
and had him brought up together with the future al-Mutawakkil (847–61);[53] he
passed the sister of the slave girl who bore him al-Mutawakkil to another Turk,
a former slave, whose son was thus al-Mutawakkil's cousin;[54] and both al-
Mutawakkil and al-Mustaʿīn (862–66) had sons of their own brought up in
Turkish households.[55] The relationship was far more honorary than is customary with slaves and freedmen (and far more intimate than is customary with
mercenaries), but it can hardly be argued that servility was incidental to it: the
Turks were ultimate slaves, as Patterson puts it.[56]

Ayalon, the veteran of Mamluk studies, sees the adoption of Turkish slave
soldiers as a response to manpower shortage arising from the Islamic commitment to holy war: the entire world had to be conquered, but Arabs were few in
number and the Iranians with whom they were supplemented prepared the
ground for the recruitment of Turks.[57] But al-Muʿtaṣim recruited his Turks at a
time when concerted attempts at expansion had come to an end; the Turks sup-
planted existing forces instead of augmenting them; and it is not obvious why

the Iranians inside the caliphate should have proved a mere stepping-stone to the Turks outside it.

Ayalon also stresses that the Turks were appreciated for their military skills, and this is certainly correct. Warfare in the Muslim Middle East, as in that of the Sasanids and Byzantines, was dominated by heavy cavalry. It is true that the Arabs had conquered the Middle East with light cavalry and infantry (horses were prestige items in Arabia, and camels were used only for transport),[58] but they adopted their enemies' equipment as fast as they could, and by the Umayyad period heavy cavalry predominated. Iron stirrups were introduced in the 680s to replace wooden ones (mostly, the conquerors seem to have used none at all),[59] and the typical soldier was now a "composite cavalryman" trained to be equally skilled with the lance and the bow and to dismount for close combat with the sword when the initial charge was over.[60] The Arabs were not particularly skilled as horse archers, however (although the Romans had recruited them as such),[61] and the Khurasanis were also composite cavalrymen rather than mounted archery specialists. Neither could stand comparison with the Turks.

But this is merely to say that the caliphs had good reason to enroll Turkish captives and allies in their guard and army, as the Romans had enrolled Gauls and Germans from the first century onward, not that a Turkish takeover was to be expected. No Turkish invasions were in progress, forcing the Muslims to use barbarians against barbarians; and for purposes of maintaining internal order it is not obvious that the Turks were better soldiers than the Transoxanians, who had won the fourth civil war for al-Ma'mūn and who suppressed a number of major revolts for al-Ma'mūn and al-Mu'taṣim alike. But al-Mu'taṣim clearly distrusted the Transoxanians, whose princes enjoyed power and prestige independently of him and whom he suspected of nursing separate aims as well, accusing their leading figure of plotting to restore the political and religious organization of preconquest Iran. Distrust must have played a greater role than military skills in the emergence of the Mamluk institution, for when Turks were in short supply, they were replaced by, or supplemented with, slaves of other origins such as Indians, Slavs, and Blacks.

The Problem of Legitimation   For this reason the emergence of the Mamluk institution has been linked with problems of legitimation.[62] The Umayyads had damned themselves by presiding over the dissolution of the conquest society, but the 'Abbāsids could not turn the clock back, for all that they presented the revolution as a rerun of the rise of Islam. On the contrary, they had to complete the developments of the Umayyad period by reorganizing their possessions along the imperial lines that had prevailed before the conquests, persuading their subjects that their organization was Islamic rather than a reversion to pre-Islamic *mulk*. This could not be done. The religious scholars who had emerged as the bearers of Islam were the chief exponents of the primitivist ideal from which the Umayyads were seen as having departed. Although they generally liked the 'Abbāsids better than the Umayyads, their political ideals were diametrically opposed to those of the caliphs, and they had enshrined these ideals in the legal and other normative literature on which every educated Muslim was brought up. The 'Abbāsids could not be both imperial and Islamic; they could not have both might and right. The religion they represented had developed in a manner incompatible with their political task. Hence they handed over military and political power to outsiders with minimal commitment to Islamic norms.[63] The unpopular tyrant, as Plato observed, will recruit at home "by robbing the citizens of their slaves, freeing them, and enrolling them in his bodyguard" and by importing a "mixed swarm of drones from abroad."[64]

Differently put, the Arab conquests had resulted in a drastic shift in the locus of religious authority: in a polity predisposed by its size, economy, and preconquest tradition alike for agrarian-based and hierarchical rule, religious leadership had devolved unto urban and largely mercantile groups. The Arab conquerors had settled in garrison cities, where they formed a new elite of scholars and urban notables, and the non-Arab elites of the countryside had not been islamized. The conquests had generally been too swift and too effortless for the Arabs to have to co-opt them. Those who did become members of Muslim society entered mostly as captives stripped by slavery of their preconquest positions, while those who remained non-Muslims were left to look after their own communities, only to disappear as the local communities converted. The upshot was the formation, under the aegis of Islam, of an agrarian society without a landed aristocracy or gentry.

The religious scholars and urban notables were absentee landowners, if they had land at all; they preferred commerce and education to government service, and their outlook was in general bourgeois rather than aristocratic. The originally tribal vision of egalitarian and consultative Medina expressed their interests very well. The political values they upheld were in one sense too archaic and in another sense too modern for the task at the rulers' hands. (It would have been a different story if the Muslims had somehow passed straight from tribal conquest to industrial, or at least early capitalist, society; but for all the cultural predominance of the Muslim bourgeoisie, the capitalist sector remained minute, and the state continued to be financed by agrarian revenues.) Neither the values nor the social order represented by the urban elite lent themselves to imperial state building of the preindustrial kind.[65]

The Problem in Action   But how did the inability of the 'Abbāsids to secure Islamic legitimation for their imperial aims affect government on the ground? Some initial difficulties notwithstanding, they certainly did not fail to gain the loyalty of the Khurasanis in Baghdad. They did, however, have problems with the relationship between the central government and local elites.

Like other pre-modern rulers, the 'Abbāsids were unable to govern without local cooperation.[66] It was leading men of local communities, usually urban notables, who kept the peace, passed on government orders, saw to their execution (or nonexecution), collected the local taxes, dispensed local welfare, and generally kept their communities running on a day-to-day basis. One would have expected the 'Abbāsids to co-opt these notables, for example, by giving them formal office as district magistrates[67] or by appointing them to government office anywhere in the empire, from which they could either rise in rank or return to their local communities loaded with honor and glory. But the 'Abbāsid caliphate was remarkably lacking in such mechanisms, as had indeed been the case of the Umayyad caliphate too. No local office such as that of district magistrate existed, and both dynasties awarded the bulk of their governorships and military commands to members of their field army, which in its turn was recruited from a single province, Syro-Jazīra and Khurasan respectively. Secretarial positions were only marginally more open, normally being awarded to men originating within or around the capital. Natives of other provinces, however eminent, had to make do with local careers. They might well travel to the center and return loaded with honor and glory, but the honor and glory came from their acquisition of religious learning from private scholars, not from government service. Most provincials cherished the caliphate as a continuation of the Prophet's polity, and all appreciated order, but they had no concrete stake in the maintenance of the unitary state. Local order might be better served by rulers closer by, and so indeed might their careers.

Given the caliphal policy of recruiting government servants from a single province, the only way the 'Abbāsids could give the local elites a stake in the caliphate was by closely tying the religious institution to the state. But this was precisely what they could not do. The religious scholars regarded all rulers as doomed by their office to violate the law, deemed cooperation with them to be incompatible with religious integrity, refused the judgeships with which the 'Abbāsids hoped to turn them into salaried officials, and generally counseled a combination of active avoidance and passive obedience. Owing their livelihood and prestige to popular support rather than government patronage and lacking formal organization, they were too amorphous for the caliph to have any leverage on them. Since both the religious scholars and the local notables were urban residents who owed their position to local support, they were closely entwined and often identical. The religious institution thus reinforced the distance between local elites and the state instead of bridging it.[68]

The 'Abbāsids responded by appointing governors with extremely short tenures to prevent them from going local, but this of course meant that they could not get anything done. In North Africa and Khurasan, where prolonged ineffectual government would have led to loss of the provinces to local rebels, the caliphs eventually recognized their inability to represent local interests by tacitly granting autonomy (in 800 and 821) to hereditary governors. The latter were chosen from families with too many interests in Baghdad to be likely to turn against the center, and they did in fact continue to recognize 'Abbāsid over-lordship, although the extent to which they continued to send tribute is unclear.[69] But the empire to which al-Muʿtaṣim fell heir was already in a state of dissolution.

Why the Provincial Bias?   By relying on public servants from a single province, the caliphs would seem to have made things unnecessarily difficult for themselves. Why, then, did they do it? As far as the Umayyads are concerned, the answer is that there was no Muslim empire when they acceded, only a federation of regional armies, each one of which was recruited and employed within its own region, maintained from its own revenues, and administered by such local bureaucrats as it contained. It was by using the regional army of Syria outside Syria that the Umayyads turned the Syrians into imperial troops, and it is hard to see how else they could have centralized the increasingly heterogeneous conquest society.

But one would have expected the 'Abbāsids to recruit their public servants from all over the empire. They did, of course, have to favor the Khurasanis: having come to power in a revolution, they were not in a position to risk the loyalty of the soldiers who had raised them to the throne by throwing open the army to all and sundry. (Membership was a privilege.)[70] But there was no trend toward greater use of non-Khurasani troops as time passed, although the islamization of the countryside meant that the number of potential recruits was expanding, nor does there appear to have been any attempt to use the civil administration as a focus for provincial aspiration.

The explanation for this peculiar fact seems to lie in a combination of three factors. Firstly, the army was based on cavalry. Since horses are expensive and lifelong training is required for their effective use, cavalry armies are biased in favor of aristocrats and/or particular ethnic groups. The legions of the Roman republic brought together men of diverse social and geographic origin, being infantry, but the *alae* were socially biased from the start, being cavalry, and ethnic units made an early appearance, to predominate in tandem with the rise of cavalry in the later empire.[71] In principle the 'Abbāsids could have created institutions for the training of cavalry, as did the Byzantines, who never relied on ready-made horsemen in the form of barbarians alone; but the idea never seems to have suggested itself to them, in part no doubt because ready-made horsemen were amply available within their realm. The main reservoirs were the horse-rearing bedouin of Syro-Jazira, the Khurasani troops taken over from the Umayyads, and the local rulers and aristocrats who survived on the fringes of Iran. The early 'Abbāsids relied on the Khurasanis and retained the services of Arab tribesmen in the local armies in the west; al-Ma'mūn added Iranian aristocrats. But all three options excluded the bulk of mainstream Muslims.

Secondly, the 'Abbāsids assumed unit cohesion to arise from common kinship and/or geographic origin. In fact, this always seems to have been the assumption in the Middle East, and the tribal tradition of the Arabs reinforced it. Where the early Roman legions crosscut local identities and allegiances, 'Abbāsid units were based on them:[72] Khurasanis could not be mixed with, or commanded by, non-Khurasanis (interlopers were weeded out).[73] To create an opening for their subjects in general, the 'Abbāsids would have had to establish special units for them, led by their own commanders; but the excluded provincials had no special skills of interest to them, so they left them out.

Thirdly, it is clear that the caliphs found it difficult to establish relationships of trust outside a narrow circle of people with whom they were personally acquainted. The Umayyads had relied on personal links, reinforced by marriage alliances, with tribal chiefs. The 'Abbāsids relied on personal links, sometimes reinforced by fosterage, between themselves and Khurasani families in Baghdad; the latter in their turn relied on personal links of their own. Everyone, in fact, took it for granted that one could only trust people who formed part of one's network of friends and allies. This preference for personal networks over formal institutions was to become a standard feature of Muslim society, and it is hard not to credit it with a tribal origin; but in any case, it meant that eminent Muslims outside the metropolis could not be employed on a systematic basis.[74] The army was run by what would nowadays be known as a Khurasani mafia, the bureaucracy by an Iraqi one. The bureaucracy was in any case so strongly associated with pre-conquest culture that it would have been difficult to use it as a focus for provincial aspiration even if the networks had been absent.

Overall By approximately 800, then, Muslim society was dominated by urban scholars and notables who disapproved of imperial government and who had no real stake in it, while government was exercised by military and political leaders disproportionately drawn from a single province thanks to their skills as cavalrymen and alliance with the caliph. The latter were the nearest the 'Abbāsids got to an elite representative of Muslim society. But the alliance was broken in the fourth civil war, leaving the caliphs with the question of where they were going to find a replacement; the answer had to be from groups that combined military skills with relative immunity to religious leaders of the scholarly type, or, in other words, from groups marginal to mainstream society. Al-Ma'mūn found them in his new Khurasanis and Transoxanians, who were representative enough of their own world, being aristocrats at home, but whose aristocratic credentials were mostly too pre-Islamic in origin to validate their status to the Muslims at large. The ease with which a charge of apostasy could be trumped up against one of them illustrates the degree to which they were perceived as aliens.[75] Shortly before his death, al-Ma'mūn decided to challenge the authority of the scholars, presumably in the hope of endowing Islam with a religious leadership more sympathetic to caliphal designs,[76] but it was a hopeless venture, and although al-Mu'taṣim kept it up, he effectively acknowledged that the military and political elite could not be legitimated. It thus had to be bound to him by personal ties alone. For this purpose freedmen were more promising than princes with power of their own, and so his private guard turned into the core of the public army.

Differently put, the 'Abbāsids harvested the fruits of the conquests. The Muslims had arrived in the non-Arabian Middle East with a tribal solidarity and religious distrust of the conquered peoples that made them keep their distance from pre-conquest institutions and saved them from cultural absorption; but now that they could no longer rely on tribal solidarity to keep an empirewide elite together, they lacked the resources to create a new one of the traditional, pre-conquest type. The very attempt to reorganize the Muslim world along pre-conquest lines was viewed with suspicion, given that Islam was seen as having come to replace traditional empires with a simple polity of its own. In a sense the 'Abbāsids were in the same boat as the Carolingians. Both were confronted with the task of creating polities for which their tribal past offered no models, but which could not simply be revised versions of the empires their ancestors had overrun, in the west because the fiscal and administrative machinery had collapsed even though the desire to preserve (or revive) the empire was present, in the east because the desire was absent even though the machinery had survived. Both fell back on private ties, and in both cases the outcome was political fragmentation. But because the fiscal and administrative machinery survived in the east, the 'Abbāsids could simply buy the retainers they needed, and so they lost their power not to lords and vassals but to freedmen.

Epilogue

The rise of the freedmen completed the transformation of Muslim society from a polity with an unusually high military participation ratio to one with an unusually low one. This is not to say that the Muslims at large had been disarmed. Muslim rulers never claimed a monopoly on the exercise of violence,[77] and their subjects continued to wield arms in holy war, faction fighting, policing, and the like; but they did so under their own organization, in response to their own appreciation of right and wrong, not in response to the demands of the state. Their aims did, of course, converge with those of the state at times, above all in connection with holy war, but fundamentally state and society had separated. Of power standoffs between state and society there are many examples in history, but few have taken quite so distinctive a form.

Notes

1. For surveys, see Hawting 1986; Kennedy 1986.
2. For a possible exception, see al-Harthamī (still unstudied), said to be an epitome of a work addressed to the caliph al-Ma'mūn (d. 833). For later manuals, see *EI2*, s.v. "*ḥarb*"; Scanlon 1961.
3. Ibn al-Nadīm, *Fihrist*, 376f. There is no sign of Aelian until the fourteenth century (cf. Tantum 1979.194), but one would assume the translation, now lost, to have been made in the ninth or tenth.
4. Cf. their mouthpiece 'Umar in Jāḥiẓ, *Bayān*, iii, 23.
5. Cf. Donner 1981; Kaegi 1992.
6. E.g., BF, 384.
7. Cf. *EI2*, s.v. "*dīwān*."
8. For all this, see Crone 1994a.
9. Crone 1980, note 383.
10. BF, 451ff.
11. Jūda 1979.212ff.
12. BA, xi, 273; 'Abd al-Ḥamīd b. Yaḥyā, 509ff. = Schönig, 51ff.
13. E.g., Ibn A'tham, viii, 30.
14. IAH, 162 (Egypt); Kister 1991.282f; BF, 178 (Syria, Jazīra); Jāḥiẓ, *Bayān*, ii, 286 (Iraq).
15. IQ, 417; Tab. ii, 869; BA, xi, 275f.
16. BA, xi, 276; cf. Tab. ii, 873; *Aghānī*, ii, 417.
17. BF, 449.-8, 457.-5; Ibn Sa'd, iii, 295 (Byzantine); Jahshiyārī, 17 (Persian); BF, 453.-7; Ibn Sa'd, iii, 300 (non-Arab); cf. Haldon 1979; Zakeri 1995.52ff.
18. E.g., BF, 542.-5, 453.3; BA, iva, 97.13. Cf. also *EI2*, s.v. "*fay*."
19. Cf. *EI2*, s.v. "Mu'āwiya," col. 267a.
20. Theophanes 1883–85, anno mundi 6171.
21. Cf. Crone 1980, chap.3.
22. *EI2*, s.v. "Ḥudjr b. 'Adī."
23. For guesses, see Russell 1958.88ff.; McEvedy and Jones 1978, and the comments of Blankinship 1994.273f.
24. Gibb 1923.40f.
25. Contrast Hsiao 1978.18ff., on the Mongols.
26. Contrast Isaac 1992.59, on the Romans.
27. Zakeri 1995.193ff.
28. Cf. Gnirs, this volume (ancient Egypt); Dalley 1995.419, 421 (Assyria); Christensen 1944.369f. (Sasanid Iran); Elton 1996.129ff.(late Rome); Charanis 1961.143 (Byzantium); Loewe 1974.102f. (Han China); Farris 1992.95, 113 (ninth-century Japan).

29. Cf. Spence 1993.56f.
30. Cf. Welwei 1974, 1977, 1988 (but there are numerous parallels).
31. Crone 1980.53.
32. *EI2*, s.v. "*mawlā.*"
33. Cf. Campbell, this volume.
34. Hawting 1986.66f.; cf. Crone 1994b.37ff.
35. Hawting 1986.67ff.
36. Crone 1980.37f.
37. Crone 1980.39f.
38. There is no monograph on the Muslim (primarily Sunnī) image of the golden past, also known as the age of "the Rightly Guided Caliphs'" (Rāshidūn). But almost any account of this age in the primary, and to some extent even the secondary, literature could serve as an illustration. So, too, could accounts of the "innovations" introduced by the Umayyads (cf., e.g., YT, ii, 276, on Muʿāwiya). Muslim primitivism is both chronological ("the best age is the first") and cultural ("the best society is a simple one") but it differs from that of antiquity in hardly ever focusing on foreign societies (cf. Lovejoy and Boas 1955).
39. Sayf, 18, no. 21; Abū Zurʿa, no. 1339.
40. Hawting 1986.12f.
41. There is a large literature on this; cf. Humphreys 1991, chap. 4.
42. MM, vii, 118; Tab. iii, 1369f.
43. YB, 258ff.
44. Tab., iii, 1256ff., 1303ff.; *EI2*, s.v. "Afshīn."
45. Kindī, 193f.; cf. Tab. iii, 1164.
46. Cf. *EI2*, s.v. "*djaysh*," col. 513a; Ingrams 1949.52.
47. Beckwith 1984 believes it to originate in the Turkish equivalent of the Germanic *comitatus*. But the Muslims had their own equivalents; the Turkish use of free retainers is hardly reminiscent of the caliphal use of Turkish slaves, and the argument is marred by factual mistakes.
48. He collected them in Iraq, not in Khurasan, as Beckwith asserts (1989.32, 39) and Paul repeats (1994.25n). Both believe him to have stayed in Khurasan with his brother al-Maʾmūn, but he stayed in Iraq, where he supported the anticaliph raised up against al-Maʾmūn in 817 (*EI2*, s.v. "al-Maʾmūn," col. 335a).
49. Khalīfa, 701 (year 160/776f). But variant versions of this incident are set as early as 137/754f (BA, iii, 252, cf. Tab. iii, 120) and as late as 180/796f (Khalīfa, 724) without mention of the Turks.
50. Speidel 1994.14, 23, 25, 28, 52, 66 (citing Dio 79.6); cf. also 27 (Parthian prince), 78 (handsome servants in private elite army).
51. Pulleyblank 1955.64f.
52. Cf. Tab. iii, 1685.
53. *EI2*, s.v. "al-Fath b. Khākān."
54. Al-Mutawakkil's mother was a Khwārizmian slave girl called Shujāʾ (cf. *EI2*, s.v. "al-Mutawakkil"). Her sister was the mother of Mūsā b. Bughā (Tab. iii, 1459.6).
55. Tab. iii, 1513.1, 1659.7. Al-Muʿtasim had himself been brought up by a Turk

(Shābushtī, 225).

56. Patterson 1982, chap. 11. Differently Kennedy 1986.159f., who sees no significant difference between the slave soldiers of the Muslims and the Armenians and other marginal recruits of the Byzantines.
57. Ayalon 1964.1975.
58. Hill 1975; Jandora 1990. The Arabs only fought on camels in flight (cf. Macdonald 1995.1363).
59. White 1964.18f. (with fictitious leather stirrups thrown in).
60. Cf. Haldon 1975.12.
61. Jāḥiẓ, *Rasā'il*, i, 45; Speidel 1994.84.
62. Crone 1980, Pipes 1981; cf. also Paul 1994.28, 33, on the spread of the institution to Sāmānid Khurasan.
63. Crone 1980.63ff. (where "settled states" is a misnomer for "imperial organization"); cf. Pipes 1981.62ff.
64. *Republic*, 567.
65. Cf. Hodgson 1974.1:i, 354ff; Crone 1986.73ff.
66. Cf. Crone 1989.44ff.; Kennedy 1981.
67. Compare Farris, this volume.
68. Pipes 1981.69ff. (with some conflation of cause and effect).
69. Talbi 1966; *CHIr*, iv, 90ff.
70. As in Rome, but for different reasons (cf. Campbell, this volume).
71. Rosenstein, this volume; Speidel 1984; 1994.85.
72. Cf. Rosenstein and Ferguson, this volume.
73. Cf. Jāḥiẓ, *Rasā'il*, ii, 206f.
74. This was acknowledged by a ninth-century theologian who held that several rulers would be preferable to one, inter alia, because a single ruler could not know the meritorious men in distant provinces, who were thus unable to participate in government (Nāshi', 60f.).
75. Cf. above, note 42.
76. *EI2*, s.v. "*miḥna*"; Nawas 1994.
77. Stressed by Paul 1994.

Bibliography

'Abd al-Ḥamīd b. Yaḥyā. 1937. "Risāla 'an Marwān ilā ibnihi 'Abdallāh b. Marwān." In *Jamharat rasā'il al-'arab*, edited by A. Z. Ṣafwat, ii, 473–533. Cairo. = H. Schönig (trans.), *Das Sendschreiben des 'Abdalḥamīd b. Yaḥyā (gest. 132/750) an den Kronprinzen 'Abdallāh b. Marwān II*. Stuttgart: Steiner, 1985.
Abū Zur'a. 1980. *Ta'rīkh*. Edited by Sh. al-Qawjānī. Damascus.
Aghānī = Abū 'l-Faraj al-Iṣbahānī. 1927–74. *Kitāb al-aghānī*. Cairo.
Ayalon, D. 1964. "The Military Reforms of Caliph al-Mu'taṣim." Paper presented at the Congress of Orientalists, New Delhi 1964 (stenciled pamphlet); printed in D. Ayalon, *Islam and the Abode of War*, 1–39. Variorum Reprints. Aldershot: Variorum, 1994.

——. 1975. "Preliminary Remarks on the *Mamlūk* Military Institution in Islam." Parry and Yapp 1975.44–58. London: Oxford University Press.

BA= al-Balādhurī, *Ansāb al-ashrāf*, vol. iii, ed. 'A.-A. al-Dūrī, Beirut and Wiesbaden 1978; vol. iva, ed. M. J. Kister, Jerusalem 1971; vol. xi, (*Anonyme arabische Chronik*), ed. W. Ahlwardt, Greifswald 1883.

Beckwith, C. I. 1984. "Aspects of the Early History of the Central Asian Guard Corps in Islam." *Archivum Eurasiae Medii Aevi* 4, 29–43.

BF = al-Balādhurī. 1866. *Futūḥ al-buldān*. Edited by M. J. de Goeje. Leiden: Brill.

Blankinship, K. Y. 1994. *The End of the Jihad State*. Albany: State University of New York Press.

Charanis, P. 1961. "The Transfer of Population as a Policy in the Byzantine Empire." *Comparative Studies in Society and History* 3, 140–54.

CHIr = *The Cambridge History of Iran,* vol. 4, edited by R. N. Frye. Cambridge: Cambridge University Press, 1975.

Christensen, A. 1944. *L'Iran sous les Sassanides*. 2d ed. Copenhagen: E. Munksgaard.

Crone, P. 1980. *Slaves on Horses, the Evolution of the Islamic Polity*. Cambridge: Cambridge University Press.

——. 1986. "The Tribe and the State." In *States in History,* edited by J. A. Hall, 48–77. Oxford: Blackwell.

——. 1989. *Pre-industrial Societies*. Oxford: Blackwell.

——. 1994a. "The First-Century Concept of Hiğra." *Arabica* 41, 352–87.

——. 1994b. "Were the Qays and the Yemen of the Umayyad Period Political Parties?" *Der Islam* 71, 1–57.

Dalley, S. 1995. "Ancient Mesopotamian Military Organization." In *Civilizations of the Ancient Near East,* vol. 1, edited by J. M. Sasson, 413–22. New York: Scribner.

Dixon, 'A.-A. 'A. 1971. *The Umayyad Caliphate. 65–86/684–705*. London: Luzac.

Donner, F. M. 1981. *The Early Islamic Conquests*. Princeton, N.J.: Princeton University Press.

EI2 = *The Encyclopaedia of Islam*. 2d ed. Leiden: Brill, 1960–.

Elton, H. 1996. *Warfare in Roman Europe AD 350–425*. Oxford: Clarendon Press.

Farris, W. W. 1992. *Heavenly Warriors. The Evolution of Japan's Military, 500–1300*. Cambridge, Mass.: Council on East Asian Studies, Harvard University.

Gibb, H. A. R. 1923. *The Arab Conquests in Central Asia*. London: Royal Asiatic Society.

Haldon, J. F. 1975. "Some Aspects of Byzantine Military Technology from the Sixth to the Tenth Centuries." *Byzantine and Modern Greek Studies* 1, 11–47.

——. 1979. *Recruitment and Conscription in the Byzantine Army c. 550–950*. Vienna: Österreichische Akademie der Wissenschaften.

al-Harthamī. 1964. *Mukhtaṣar siyāsat al-ḥurūb*. Edited by 'A.-R. 'Awn and M. M. Ziyāda. Cairo.

Hawting, G. 1986. *The First Dynasty of Islam*. London: Croom Helm.

Hill, D. R. 1975. "The Role of the Camel and the Horse in the Early Arab Conquests." Parry and Yapp 1975.32–43.

Hodgson, M. G. S. 1974. *The Venture of Islam*. Chicago: University of Chicago Press.

Hsiao, C. 1978. *The Military Establishment of the Yuan Dynasty*. Cambridge, Mass.: Council on East Asian Studies, Harvard University.

Humphreys, R. S. 1991. *Islamic History: A Framework for Inquiry.* London: I. B. Tauris.

IAH = Ibn 'Abd al-Ḥakam. 1922. *Futūh Miṣr wa-akhbāruhā.* Edited by C. C. Torrey. New Haven, Conn.: Yale University Press.

Ibn A'tham. 1968–75. *Kitāb al-futūḥ.* Hyderabad.

Ibn al-Nadīm. 1971. *Kitāb al-fihrist.* Edited by R. Tajaddud. Tehran.

IQ = Ibn Qutayba. 1969. *al-Ma'ārif.* Edited by Th. 'Ukkāsha. Cairo.

Ibn Sa'd. 1957–60. *al-Ṭabaqāt al-kubrā.* Beirut: Dar Sadir.

Ingrams, D. 1949. *A Survey of Social and Economic Conditions in the Aden Protectorate.* Eritrea.

Isaac, B. 1992. *The Limits of Empire. The Roman Army in the East.* 2d ed. Oxford: Clarendon Press.

al-Jāḥiẓ. 1960–61. *al-Bayān wa'l-tabyīn.* Edited by 'A.-S. M. Hārūn. 2d printing. Cairo.

———. 1964–79. *Rasā'il.* Edited by 'A.-S. M. Hārūn. Cairo.

al-Jahshiyārī. 1938. *Kitāb al-wuzarā' wa'l-kuttāb.* Edited by M. al-Saqqā and others. Cairo.

Jandora, J. W. 1990. *The March from Medina: A Revisionist Study of the Arab Conquests.* Clifton N.J.: Kingston Press.

Jūda, J. 1979. *al-'Arab wa 'l-arḍ fī 'l-'Irāq.* Ammān.

Kaegi, W. E. 1992. *Byzantium and the Early Islamic Conquests.* Cambridge: Cambridge University Press.

Kennedy, H. 1981. "Central Government and Provincial Elites in the Early 'Abbāsid Caliphate." *Bulletin of the School of Oriental and African Studies* 44, 26–38.

———. 1986. *The Prophet and the Age of the Caliphates.* London: Longman.

Khalīfa b. Khayyāṭ. 1967–68. *Ta'rīkh.* Edited by S. Zakkār. Damascus.

al-Kindī. 1912. *The Governors and Judges of Egypt.* Edited by R. Guest. Leiden: Brill.

Kister, M. J. 1991. "Land Property and Jihād." *Journal of the Economic and Social History of the Orient* 34, 270–311.

Loewe, M. 1974. "The Campaigns of Han Wu-ti." In *Chinese Ways in Warfare,* edited by F. A. Kiernan and J. K. Fairbank, 67–122. Cambridge, Mass.: Harvard University Press.

Lovejoy, A. O., and G. Boas. 1955. *Primitivism and Related Ideas in Antiquity.* Baltimore: Johns Hopkins University Press.

Macdonald, M. C. A. 1995. "North Arabia in the First Millenium BCE." In *Civilizations of the Ancient Near East,* vol. 2, edited by J. M. Sasson, 1355–69. New York: Scribner.

McEvedy, C., and R. Jones. 1978. *Atlas of World Population History.* Harmondsworth: Penguin.

MM = al-Mas'ūdī. 1861–77. *Murūj al-dhahab.* Edited and translated by A. C. Barbier de Meynard and A. J.-B. Pavet de Courteille. Paris: Imprimerie Impériale.

Nāshi' = J. van Ess, ed. 1971. *Frühe mu'tazilitische Häresiographie. Zwei Werke des Nāsi' al-Akbar (gest. 293 H).* Beirut.

Nawas, J. A. 1994. "A Reexamination of Three Current Explanations for al-Ma'mūn's Introduction of the Miḥna." *International Journal of Middle East Studies* 26, 615–29.

Parry, V. J., and M. E. Yapp (eds.). 1975. *War, Technology and Society in the Middle East.* London: Oxford University Press.

Patterson, O. 1982. *Slavery and Social Death.* Cambridge, Mass.: Harvard University Press.

Paul, J. 1994. "The State and the Military: the Samanid Case." *Papers on Inner Asia* (Bloomington, Indiana) 26, 1–40.

Pipes, D. 1981. *Slave Soldiers and Islam.* New Haven, Conn.: Yale University Press.

Pulleyblank, E. G. 1955. *The Background of the Rebellion of An Lu-Shan.* London: Oxford University Press.

Russell, J. C. 1958. *Late Ancient and Medieval Populations.* Transactions of the American Philosophical Society, n.s., 48, no. 3.

Sayf b. ʿUmar al-Tamīmī. 1995. *Kitāb al-ridda wa'l-futūḥ.* Edited by Q. Al-Samarrai. Leiden: Smitskamp Oriental Antiquarium.

Scanlon, G. T. 1961. *A Muslim Manual of War.* Cairo: American University at Cairo Press.

al-Shābushtī. 1966. *al-Diyārāt.* Edited by K. ʿAwwād. Baghdad.

Speidel, M. 1984. "The Rise of Ethnic Units in the Roman Imperial Army." In M. Speidel, *Roman Army Studies,* vol. 1, 117–48. Amsterdam: Gieben.

———. 1994. *Riding for Caesar.* London: Batsford.

Spence, I. G. 1993. *The Cavalry of Classical Greece.* Oxford: Clarendon Press.

Tab. = al-Ṭabarī. 1879–1901. *Taʾrīkh al-rusul wa'l-mulūk.* Edited by M. J. de Goeje and others. Leiden: Brill.

Talbi, M. 1966. *L'Emirat aghlabide.* Paris: Librairie d'Amérique et d'Orient.

Tantum, G. 1979. "Muslim Warfare: A Study of a Medieval Muslim Treatise on the Art of War." In *Islamic Arms and Armour,* edited by R. Elgood, 187–201. London: Scolar Press.

Theophanes. 1883–85. *Chronographia.* Edited by C. de Boor. Leipzig: Teubner.

Wellhausen, J. 1927. *The Arab Kingdom and Its Fall.* Translated by M. Weir. Calcutta: University of Calcutta (German original Berlin: Reiner, 1902).

Welwei, K.-W. 1974, 1977, 1988. *Unfreie im antiken Kriegsdienst.* Vols. 1–3. Wiesbaden: Steiner.

White, L. 1964. *Medieval Technology and Social Change.* Oxford: Clarendon Press.

YB = al-Yaʿqūbī. 1892. *Kitāb al-buldān.* Edited by M. J. de Goeje. Leiden: Brill.

YT = al-Yaʿqūbī. 1883. *Taʾrīkh.* Edited by M. Th. Houtsma. Leiden: Brill.

Zakeri, M. 1995. *Sāsānid Soldiers in Early Muslim Society.* Wiesbaden: Harrassowitz.

THIRTEEN

Ancient Maya Warfare

DAVID WEBSTER

Introduction

The term Maya refers (1) to a set of thirty related languages and dialects established since very ancient times in southern Mexico, Guatemala, Belize, western Honduras, and El Salvador; and (2) to the general traditions of culture associated with Maya speakers. Classic Maya culture developed between A.D. 250 and 800 in the low-lying (i.e, under one thousand meters above sea level) tropical forest zones of Yucatán, northern Guatemala, Belize, and parts of Honduras. Its military traditions and history are the main subjects of this chapter.

The Classic Maya developed the most sophisticated calendars and writing systems in the New World and so in the strict sense are a "historical" civilization.[1] Nevertheless, our ability to extract historical information from Maya texts is constrained by several factors. First, texts are comparatively rare. Only four pre-Spanish books have survived. Other texts were carved or painted on stone, pottery, shell, and bone, but they do not remotely approximate in length or comprehensibility those available for most Old World civilizations. Finally, Maya literacy was effectively confined to elite and royal persons, and inscriptions focus almost entirely on their concerns. Because the ancient Maya are only incipiently historical from our perspective, inscriptions, archaeological data, studies of iconography, and ethnohistorical and ethnographic information all must be used to make sense out of the Maya past.

Cultural History

Maya cultural history can be broken down into the following general chronological framework.[2]

The Maya Region of Mesoamerica

Early hunter-gatherers	Before 2500 B.C.
Preclassic Period	2500 B.C.–A.D. 250
Classic Period	A.D. 250–800
Terminal Classic	A.D. 800–1000
Early Postclassic Period	A.D. 1000–1200
Late Postclassic Period	A.D. 1200–1500
Contact Period	A.D. 1500–1545

Ancient hunter-gatherer populations probably inhabited the Maya Lowlands as early as 9000 B.C. Palynological indicators of what may be forest clearance for agriculture appear about 2000 B.C. or a little before, but the first direct archaeological traces of farming communities date to a millennium later. Populations increased rapidly during the latter part of the Late Preclassic period, and by about 600–300 B.C. there was major architectural activity in emergent royal centers such as Mirador and Nakbe. Shortly thereafter, we detect traces of other quintessentially Maya cultural elements—art that expresses both political and cosmological themes, complex calendars, and hints at the inception of writing. The first inferential evidence for warfare, the apparent sacrificial burials of large numbers of mutilated men of military age, appears during the Late Preclassic period.

By A.D. 300, when the first large monument inscriptions appear (the earliest at Tikal in A.D. 292), Classic Maya civilization was in full career, although our best insights derive from archaeological remains of the Late Classic period (A.D. 250–800). Inscriptions, dates, and iconography became most abundant, widespread, and intelligible during this time; scores of elite centers dominated the landscape; and regional populations peaked at overall densities of at least one hundred people per square kilometer. Between about A.D. 750 and 900, Classic Maya centers in the central and southern Lowlands were largely abandoned, as the so-called Maya collapse proceeded.

The Maya of northern Yucatán were largely unaffected by the crisis in the south. The Puuc region experienced a major cultural florescence between about A.D. 750 and 1000, and later the successive capitals of Chichén Itzá and Mayapán dominated events until approximately 1450. Influences and perhaps actual military intrusions from elsewhere in Mesoamerica, especially from highland Mexico, are evident during the late Postclassic. When the Spanish arrived in the early sixteenth century they encountered sixteen Maya polities in northern Yucatán, with a total population estimated between six hundred thousand and one million. In some of them, kings, surrounded by a class of hereditary nobles, still ruled from impressive capitals with masonry temples and palaces. Architecture, art, calendrics, and writing still thrived, albeit in forms rather different from those of the Classic period.[3] Warfare was common among and within these late polities, which the Spanish described in detail.

Warfare and Maya Civilization

Until quite recently Maya civilization was envisioned by most scholars as peaceful and non-warlike, although there were some notable exceptions to this view.[4] To be sure, early Spanish expeditions were beset by large and effective Maya armies, and during the Contact period Maya fought incessantly among themselves.[5] Such bellicosity was usually seen, however, as the unfortunate legacy of Mexican intrusions of the Late Postclassic. Military imagery in Classic period art was ignored or explained away as portrayals of ritual conflict. Intellectual priest-bureaucrats rather than kings purportedly held sway over Classic Maya polities, exercising their theocratic benevolence from essentially vacant ceremonial centers. Huge temples, built by masses of devoted commoners, dominated a tranquil political landscape. Monuments portrayed gods, and associated dates and inscriptions conveyed religious and astronomical information.

Beginning in the 1950s, developments rapidly undermined this charming if unconvincing set of conceptions. First, some temples were shown to be burial monuments for important individuals.[6] Shortly thereafter, breakthroughs in decipherment of Maya texts demonstrated the existence of dynasties of kings who recorded their deeds, including military exploits, in public inscriptions. Third, the rapid maturation of Maya archaeology revealed much new data about the character and chronology of Maya centers, polities, and populations that were impossible to reconcile with the traditional theocratic view. For example, major fortifications appeared in the Maya Lowlands at least by the end of the Preclassic period.[7] Reevaluation has accelerated even more rapidly since 1980, and nothing has changed more radically than our perceptions of Maya warfare, which, along with its attendant rituals and sacrifices, is now recognized as perhaps the single largest theme of Late Classic texts and art. While the pendulum of opinion has perhaps swung too far toward an almost Aztec-like conception of the Maya as compulsively warlike, at least we can no longer envision them as a uniquely peaceful ancient civilization.

Epigraphic Evidence for War

Although Early Classic Maya art has plenty of war-related themes, associated inscriptions and dates lack the specificity and intelligibility of Late Classic texts; hence our understanding of most events for the early period is fragmentary and controversial.[8] Despite the prominence of war themes in Early Classic art, "war is present in the inscriptions only after the sixth century A.D."[9] Thereafter references to war occur with increasing frequency throughout the Late Classic, and especially the eighth century, although there are different regional styles of warfare expression, some so highly metaphoric that it is difficult to understand their historic import.

Because the Maya are only incipiently historical, the archaeological record must provide much of the evidence for the existence and nature of war, whether as a general process or as sets of particular historical events. Unfortunately, warfare is very difficult to document and analyze using only archaeological remains, and few field projects have ever been designed specifically to investigate it. Many of the debates about the nature and character of Classic Maya war are occasioned by poor or ambiguous data. The most basic issues are the following: (1) Who participated in wars, and in whose interests were they fought? (2) How was warfare organized and carried out? and (3) What were the purposes and functions of warfare? We will return to these issues after discussing the broader contexts of Maya war.

Environmental and Sociocultural Background of Classic Maya Warfare

Maya warfare developed and operated in environmental and sociocultural settings that were in some respects similar to those of the classical cultures of the Mediterranean world, but also profoundly different from them.

Environment

Lowland Maya civilization evolved over a region of 250,000 square kilometers (about twice the size of the modern nation-state of Greece) that lies entirely in the New World tropics.[10] Temperatures are high year-round (a range of 18–35°C). Annual precipitation varies from about 500 to 4000 millimeters, with heaviest rainfall in the south and west. In most areas there is a strong wet-season/dry-season pattern, with most rain falling in the months from May to December. Unless irrigated, the primary annual crops are grown during the rainy season, although dry-season crops are possible in some areas.

Most of the Lowlands are underlain by limestone formations, and topography is typically flat or rolling except in the Maya Mountains of Belize, in the old ranges of the southeast frontier, and the escarpment and ridge country of the southwest. Although various kinds of cherts and igneous rocks are locally available, there are few mineral resources. Because of the lack of sharp relief, there is comparatively little topographic partitioning of the physical landscape. Rivers are largely absent except in Belize and along the southwestern margins of the Lowlands because water seeps through the surface bedrock and forms subsurface drainage channels. Permanent or seasonal swamps (*bajos*) cover much of the landscape, and water is also available in *cenote* features where the surface limestone has collapsed to expose underground water.

Thin but fertile upland soils develop on the limestone bedrock, and in the absence of human interference support dense, semideciduous tropical forest, varying from scrub in the dry north to triple canopy forest as high as fifty meters in the south. As in most of the humid tropics, nutrients are heavily concentrated in the plant biomass rather than the soil, which can quickly lose its fertility and erode when cleared of natural vegetation and cultivated too frequently.

Economy and Technology

The Maya, like the classical Greeks, medieval Europeans, Chinese, and Japanese, were essentially agrarian people. Although dozens of domestic plant species were cultivated, the most important staple was maize, heavily supplemented by beans. Except for dogs, stingless bees, and turkeys, there were no domestic animals, so the economy lacked a pastoral element and no animal energy was available for traction or transport. Agricultural production seems to have been carried out by the small, rural, domestic unit. Although localized forms of intensive agriculture utilized drained fields and hillside terracing, opinion is currently divided on how important these were to the agrarian or political economy. Various orchard crops and vegetables were undoubtedly grown in house-lot gardens, but with the exception of cacao (chocolate) there were no specialized bulk commercial crops such as the olives and grapes of the Old World. Among the Contact period Maya, rights to land were held both collectively by communities or families, and in some cases by important individuals. We have no direct evidence for patterns of land tenure among the Classic Maya.

Technology, based on stone, wood, and fiber, was remarkably simple from the Old World perspective. There were no metal tools or weapons, nor were there wheeled vehicles, plows, sails, or mills powered by wind or water. In the absence of metal tools, animal energy sources, and laborsaving devices, most work was laboriously accomplished by human muscles.[11] All aspects of Maya society, including warfare, were strongly conditioned by such technological and energetic constraints.

Trade and commerce were much less developed than in Mediterranean, medieval, or oriental civilizations. Cheap, bulk commodities such as grain could not effectively be moved long distances, so staple economies were highly localized. Materials of high value and low weight, such as fine pottery, precious stones, salt, cotton, animal skins, jade, obsidian, feathers, cacao, and shell, all were exchanged over long distances, but were utilized mainly by elites. There was no all-purpose currency, and although there seem to have been specialized merchants, there was certainly no powerful, profit-seeking mercantile element in the Maya economy as there was in Greece, China, or Rome, nor any similar development of occupational specialization or specialized production.

Large seagoing trading canoes were observed by Europeans in the sixteenth century, but the most sophisticated vessels were dugouts with no sails that seem generally to have hugged the coast. There was consequently no maritime technology and commerce comparable to that of Mediterranean cultures, navies did not project force across large bodies of water, nor were cheap bulk commodities shipped over great distances.

Polities and Centers

For over a century some archaeologists have utilized an explicitly Greek-derived concept—the city-state—to characterize Classic Maya political organization.[12] I prefer not to use this term because I do not believe that the Maya had either cities or state-type institutions in the Old World sense, but the analogy is nevertheless in some ways a useful one. Certainly the Maya had impressive central places dominated by huge temple-pyramids (some fifty to sixty meters high), palaces, and ball courts, all typically arranged around spacious public plazas. Carved and inscribed royal monuments in the form of stone stelae and altars were set up in the plazas, and also adorned the facades and interiors of buildings. A few of these great centers covered several square kilometers, although most were much smaller. Large centers were as little as fifteen to thirty kilometers apart in the core Petén region of northeastern Guatemala.

Instead of vacant ceremonial places, we now recognize sites such as Tikal, Calakmul, Copán, and Palenque to be royal capitals—essentially the remains of grandiose royal households, with all of their associated ritual, political, and symbolic accoutrements.[13] Basically, the "city" in the Maya conception, as elsewhere in Mesoamerica, was the place where principal lords resided. Because of the ideological importance of kingship, which was related to royal ancestral cults and rituals that ensured cosmic order, the royal household was essential to the well-being of people in outlying dispersed communities. No doubt more mundane political and economic functions were also discharged by rulers, but we have no direct evidence for them except, as we shall see, for war. The monumental architectural cores of many of these regal-ritual places grew by accretion over hundreds of years and were heavily embellished by inscribed stelae, altars, and facade sculpture that conveyed complex political/religious messages to commoners and lords alike.

What centers lacked were the high population densities and range of functions that we associate with some Old World urban traditions. Maya centers more closely approximated in function Bronze Age Greek centers such as Mycenae rather than true cities such as Rome, although they were generally not fortified and probably had more religious significance—at any rate their ritual facilities are more massive and obtrusive. Another important difference is that the economic functions of Maya centers (e.g., trade or specialized production) seem to have been much less well developed. Although Maya elites probably did control some economic activities, and did so from centers that in some sense can be considered palaces, there was probably nothing comparable to the "palace economies" of the Mycenean world.

Politics and Society

The many polities of the Classic Maya Lowlands, like those of sixth- through fifth-century B.C. Greece, were never politically unified. All shared the same basic set of cultural traditions, albeit with some important regional variations. For example, although the Classic Maya generally recognized the same pantheon of deities, patron gods seem to have been identified with particular royal centers. Each polity was probably quite ethnically homogeneous. Inscriptions show that kings, their immediate relatives, and perhaps other persons of prestigious descent used the title *ahaw,* usually translated as "lord," but there were important distinctions among holders of the *ahaw* title. Most conspicuous are hereditary royal individuals who held the most exalted titles (such as *k'ul ahaw,* or "holy lord," and the poorly understood *kalomte*) and associated offices, or the highest social rank, as in *na ahaw,* or noble lady. Some kings seem to be responsible for the installation of others, or are said "to possess" them, indicating hierarchical relationships among rulers.

Kings (and Maya elites more generally) were probably polygynous. Descent, inheritance, and succession seem to have been linked to patrilineages, although texts do not clearly reveal kinship structure.[14] Royal wives were of very high status and played extremely important roles in succession at some centers, occasionally ruling in their own right. Some dynastic lines can be traced back through as many as fifteen to thirty-nine successive rulers over periods as long as six to seven hundred years. Royal lines proliferated in the Early Classic as cadet branches founded their own centers and polities, and this process continued into the eighth century. While Classical Mediterranean polities experienced considerable flux in forms and degree of political centralization and leadership, the Maya throughout their history seem to have emphasized the importance of hereditary kingship. In Postclassic times several royal confederates rather than an individual sovereign might have reigned at some centers.

Maya royal families and possibly lesser elites exchanged spouses across political boundaries, negotiated political alliances, visited and entertained one another, participated in collective rituals, and exchanged elaborate gifts and courtesies. All these activities created a suprapolity network of privileged people who shared a common elite Great Tradition and, by the end of the Classic period, complex sets of kinship relations and often conflicting claims to titles, offices, and resources. As in Greece, people probably made pilgrimages to important shrines, and there also seem to have been multipolity athletic events (ball games) with ritual and political overtones, although we know of no sites comparable to Olympia or Delphi. Religion was highly animistic, and deities were associated with powerful forces or elements of nature. Ancestors (especially royal ones) were venerated, and kings were semidivine and ritually responsible for maintaining the order of the cosmos and the prosperity of their people.[15]

Kings, their families, and their lesser elite retainers and associates dominated events and formed the highest social stratum that collectively constituted ten percent or less of the population. The bulk of the people were commoners, mostly farmers, although there were probably low-level occupational specialists among them as well, and no doubt some were materially better off than others. Commoners supported elites through contributions of labor and taxes in kind, and most lived in small farmsteads or agricultural hamlets dispersed over the countryside. There was no concept of the citizen comparable to that of the Greek or Roman worlds, and no known codified sets of laws. Slaves were present in the sixteenth century, although apparently in small numbers. Certainly slaves were much less socially or economically important than in the Mediterranean world, and we are not sure if they even existed in Classic times.

Two important unresolved issues relating to Classic Maya politics and society will later become important for our consideration of Maya warfare. The first concerns the size of Maya polities. Mayanists are currently divided into two camps on the issue of how big the largest Maya polities were. At the risk of some oversimplification, advocates of the little-polity perspective envision fairly small basic political territories (averaging, say, about twenty-five hundred square kilometers) with populations ranging from a few thousand to one hundred thousand people, each essentially subject to a single capital and ruling dynasty. Big-polity advocates believe there were very large and stable political units, created by alliances or by conquest warfare, that embraced tens of thousands of square kilometers of territory, populations in the hundreds of thousands, and hierarchies of dependent and subordinate rulers and capitals. Evidence for such large polities is seen in the recorded conquests some lords achieved, and also in the "overlord" expressions on some monuments, which clearly show that some kings ranked above others, and that they or their proxies manipulated events and lesser rulers far from their own capitals. The big-polity model resembles (although on a smaller scale) the political arrangements of the Aztec empire in the early sixteenth century described by Hassig elsewhere in this volume.

This is not a debate primarily about demographic or territorial scale. All Mayanists do agree that by the eighth century, and long before, centers such as Tikal, Calakmul, and Caracol were unusually powerful and had large dependent populations and probably territories (although even the largest territorial entity envisioned by advocates of the big-polity perspective would be only about the size of a respectable north Italian city-state of the fifteenth to sixteenth centuries). The fundamental issue, rather, is whether there were well-developed multicenter hierarchies of domination and dependency presided over by such giants, or whether sociopolitical ties between polities of all sizes were looser and more egalitarian. Secondary issues are whether centralized big polities, if they existed, were created by hegemonic warfare, and whether big polities contended militarily with one another for generations.[16]

The main reason for the big-polity/little-polity debate is that while we can see historical interactions between rulers in the epigraphic record, it is not clear what kinds of political relationships these imply, and especially if they were strongly hierarchical in terms of the exercise of real power or economic advantage. A middle position between these two extremes is that some dynamic kings were situationally able, through alliance and conquest, to carve out large polities, but that these were inherently unstable. An example is the Dos Pilas polity in the western Maya Lowlands that achieved short-lived regional dominance between A.D. 670 and 760.[17] Schele and Freidel offer a lively discussion of how complex the intrigues and wars of Maya kingdoms might have been.[18]

The second debate concerns relationships between elites and commoners. Essentially, this issue is one of social differentiation. One possibility is that a wide social gap separated Classic Maya hereditary elites from commoners—that is, there were very marked social strata, with no kin linkages between them (although such linkages were very important among the nobles). A second reconstruction emphasizes ranking rather than stratification. In this model, some kin groups were more highly ranked than others (with a royal lineage at the apex of the social pyramid), but kinship ties linked people of commoner and elite rank. Each of these models (see later discussion) has rather different implications for how and why Maya wars were fought.

Maya Warfare

For the purposes of this chapter I define warfare as *planned confrontations between organized groups of people who share (or believe they share) common interests, and who are prepared to pursue these interests using forms of intimidation and violence that may involve deliberate killing.* Combatants and their constituents form political communities, or factions, that seek to defend or augment their collective interests through war. At least one such political community initiates conflict with the intent of maintaining the status quo or bringing about a shift in power relations. Many or most antagonists have no personal animosities and may even be anonymous to one another. Warfare so defined can include conflicts between antagonists who fight in the interests of territorially and politically distinct polities, but also between factions internal to such polities, as in civil or dynastic wars. It also encompasses a range of conflicts from small-scale raids to large engagements between highly organized forces.

Military incursions by people with highland Mexican affinities affected the Postclassic Maya, but until the Spanish conquest there were no foreign military intrusions into the Maya Lowlands comparable to the Persian attacks on Greece, nor did the Maya launch sizable military campaigns against non-Maya people.

Most warfare thus had the character of *internal war*—that is, combatants shared a high degree of linguistic and cultural similarities.[19] There may have been a linguistic boundary between Tikal and Calakmul in Classic times, with Yucatecan languages spoken to the north and Cholan languages to the south, and other linguistic boundary zones on the southwest and northwest frontiers.

The Technology of Classic Maya War: Weapons

Maya armament was quite simple compared with that of ancient classica' or medieval cultures. Weapons were made of stone, wood, and fiber. For close combat the Maya used clubs, sword or poleaxe-like implements consisting of flint or obsidian blades set in wooden shafts, as well as knives and axes. Short thrusting spears were also used, and some spears might possibly have been thrown. Projectile weapons included slings and atlatls (throwing sticks for darts or small spears). Although the latter are shown in Classic Maya art, there is disagreement over whether they were actually used in battle. Bows and arrows were used by the Postclassic Maya but are not shown in Classic art. Small shields are depicted, but they might have been symbolic rather than practical defensive weapons. Cotton armor provided personal defense during the Postclassic, but we do not know how widely it was used before that time. At least elite warriors wore elaborate headdresses that probably provided some protection. Many of these weapons no doubt had their origins in Preclassic times, and except for bows and cotton armor there seems to have been only modest innovation in armament throughout Maya cultural history.

One interesting implication of this range of weaponry is that none of it was technologically specialized, expensive, or particularly difficult to learn to use. Old World elites could monopolize metal swords, helmets, armor, shields, chariots, and horses (considering the horse a weapon) and received special training in their use. Privileged access to highly effective weapons could defend or augment elite interests against those of less well-equipped commoners, and also served as symbols of status and wealth. No such disparity existed in Maya society. Although elites might have possessed weapons of particularly fine quality, Maya commoners could easily have made reasonably effective versions of any weapons, some of which were in any case probably routinely used in hunting. Moreover, ethnohistoric accounts strongly suggest that Maya warriors of all ranks kept weapons in their houses, and so had them easily accessible.[20]

War canoes are the one exception to the egalitarian character of Maya military technology. Postclassic art shows military engagements involving canoes, which probably were used both on rivers and along the coast. Large canoes were extremely expensive to make and might have been monopolized by elites.[21] War canoes are not shown in Classic Maya art, and in any case the rarity of large, easily navigable rivers would have restricted their usefulness.

The Technology of Classic Maya War: Fortifications

Throughout much of the Old World, cities were characteristically protected by walls, and it is tempting generally to equate the presence or absence of warfare with the presence of formal fortifications. Unfortunately, this reasoning does not work for ancient Mesoamerica. Although some fortified places certainly existed, most political centers did not have defenses even where warfare was intense (e.g., in the Postclassic Basin of Mexico). The Spanish did encounter several kinds of Contact period Maya fortifications. In some cases political centers were built in defensible positions such as on islands. Ditches were dug around some centers, often supplemented by wooden palisades and sometimes dense hedges of thorny plants. A few centers were surrounded by formal stone walls, probably topped by palisades. Quickly erected barriers were also positioned along paths in the forest to delay enemy forces and make them vulnerable to ambush.

Many of these same strategies were situationally used by the Maya throughout pre-Spanish times but were never universally present. A major difficulty is archaeological detection of fortifications. Wooden palisades, plant hedges, or even small ditches might leave few traces, and in any case the long occupation and continued growth of many Maya centers probably obliterated fortifications present during earlier phases. My own opinion is that fortifications were quite common components of the Maya landscape from Preclassic to Postclassic times, but other scholars would disagree.

Fortunately, we do have direct archaeological evidence for many pre–Contact period centers protected by earthworks, ditches, stone walls and/or palisades, defensible position, or some combination of these. One of the earliest known fortifications, the great earthwork at Becan, was probably built at the end of the Late Preclassic.[22] One of the latest is the stone wall around the city of Mayapán, abandoned only two generations before the Spanish arrived. Most known fortifications date to the Postclassic period, but this is probably as much an artifact of the archaeological record as any shift in military activity or strategy.

There were several defensive arrangements. In some cases, whole centers were fortified with artificial barriers as at Becan. Elsewhere, walls were built only around the innermost monumental cores of centers. Ridge-top or peninsula sites were defended by walls or ditches. At Tikal not only the site core but also the immediate hinterland of about 120 square kilometers was protected by ditches and natural swamps.[23] Some ramshackle fortifications, as at Dos Pilas and Aguateca, were erected around site cores using scavenged building material, and obviously represent last-ditch defensive measures.

In all cases fortifications are simple in design and inexpensive to build, and the Maya seem to have evolved no distinctive tradition of sophisticated military architecture. Defenses generally served to protect the ruling apparatus of a polity, and only rarely any sizable residential population. Very few centers seem to have been fortified from their beginnings. However amateurish they were by Old World standards, Maya fortifications were probably quite effective given the low technological and logistical capabilities of Maya armies.

Who Fought Maya Wars?

Fortifications aside, most of our direct evidence for how warfare was conducted comes from art and inscriptions, which are most abundant between A.D. 600 and 900. Protagonists of inscriptions were usually rulers, who listed their personal military exploits, their distinguished victims or captives (including other kings), victories over particular enemy polities, and participation in war-related rituals that often involved human sacrifice. Lesser elites obviously fought as well. Depictions accompanying texts typically show victorious rulers and elites in resplendent warrior costumes dominating debased victims, often shown naked, or the rituals that preceded or followed conflict. In some cases exalted royal women, especially as proxies for their young sons, are shown dominating defeated enemies.[24] As elsewhere in Mesoamerica, most able-bodied noble men were probably expected to be warriors (it is for this reason, and because of the widespread availability of weapons, that I use the term warrior rather than soldier throughout this chapter). Titled war leaders and distinguished warrior roles are known for the Contact period, but Classic texts have as yet produced little evidence for specialized military titles, offices, or roles, although the important Classic title of *sahal*, which refers to a subordinate ruler, is thought by some epigraphers to have strong military overtones.[25]

There are no clear references in texts to commoner participation, and whether commoners fought is hotly debated.[26] Some Mayanists believe that war was entirely an elite enterprise.[27] It is unclear whether common warriors are shown in the very few known large-scale representations of battle scenes or their sacrificial aftermaths, but there are three reasons to think that they frequently took part. First, the Spanish were obviously beset by such large forces that mobilization of much of the adult male population must have occurred.[28] This is probably a much older pattern of recruitment. Second, some fortifications are so formidable as to suggest very large attacking forces. If only elites fought, even large Maya polities could have mustered only a few thousand men, and many as few as some hundreds. Finally, some polities at least situationally subjugated and dominated others, and it is hard to imagine how this was possible unless large forces were involved.

How Were Maya Wars Organized and Conducted?

Mayanists agree that Classic warfare was initiated by Maya elites and that elites organized and commanded campaigns. Three kinds of political entities seem to have been potentially involved. First, independent polities of equal or unequal rank—what we might call city-states—engaged in war on behalf of their rulers and associated nobles. Second, rulers of independent polities made military alliances among themselves and jointly conducted defensive or offensive operations, possibly under the hegemony of a dominant king. Third, factions internal to polities fought for control of offices, titles, or privileges, or sought to break away and become independent. All these sorts of warfare are documented for the ethnohistoric Maya—that is, those observed and described by Europeans in the sixteenth and seventeenth centuries.[29] The first two patterns are most conspicuous in Classic texts and art, and the latter is largely inferential. In some cases military "alliance" might have involved lords of dominant and subordinate political status within the same multicenter polity rather than sovereign lords.

Some ancient Old World societies developed professional armies that were maintained and rewarded for their services by the ruler or state. Such armies consisted of permanently mobilized, strategically stationed units, each with its own command structure, composed of specially trained and equipped men of all ranks who identified themselves as full-time military specialists. Rulers could also hire such professionals as mercenaries. We have no evidence for any professional military organizations for the Maya. Rather, elite men served as a core of military participants and leaders, supplemented, I believe, by conscripted commoners who were situationally mobilized for war—essentially a militia pattern of organization and recruitment.

Wars apparently ranged from small-scale raids to large engagements, depending on the situation, and organization would have varied accordingly. While there was probably considerable advance planning and good discipline while on the march, battles once joined quickly broke down into small, comparatively unstructured engagements among individuals or small groups, with little overall coordination. Exploits of distinguished warriors, or unexpected loss of them, heavily affected the outcome. Some Mayanists think that various kinds of standardized weaponry imply highly organized, cohesive, and disciplined combat units with different tactical capabilities and roles, but the evidence for this view is very weak. No direct evidence in the form of skeletal samples tells us how lethal battles were, but certainly large numbers of captives or sacrificial victims are depicted in Classic Maya art.

Preparations for war, campaigns themselves, and follow-up ceremonies were all heavily ritualized. According to some reconstructions, initiation of conflict was conditioned by auspicious dates, astronomical events, and divination. A class of particularly important conflicts is symbolized in the inscriptions as "star-shell" (or "earth-star") events, purportedly associated with the Venus cycle. These events are rare in inscriptions before the seventh century, then multiply greatly.[30]

Ritual constraints on the conduct of war, to the extent that they existed, did not cause imbalances in military capability (at least until the Spanish arrived) because opponents strongly shared the same cultural understandings and proclivities. Formal combats might have had highly choreographed and stylized phases, and perhaps even been prearranged in some cases, but these things are difficult to detect in texts and art.

There are many well-dated references to specific campaigns or battles, particularly during the seventh and eighth centuries. These are probably the tip of the iceberg, with many lesser conflicts unlisted. Within a single four-month period in A.D. 799, the center of Naranjo seems to have engaged in at least eight successive war events.[31] Yaxchilan seems to have engaged in major conflicts at average intervals of about thirteen years, although this might be an extreme case.[32]

Where multiple events are recorded, it is clear that some centers or dynasties had traditional enemies with whom they fought repeatedly over extended periods. Some big-polity advocates believe they can discern protracted struggles for supremacy between major regional polities and their allies, perhaps comparable to those between the Athenian and Spartan confederations in fifth-century B.C. Greece.[33] Under these conditions, large forces would have been feasible.

Maya warfare must have been strongly seasonal, especially if any large number of commoners was involved.[34] Farmers could have been efficiently detached from their agricultural pursuits only during the dry season (roughly December through May in the southern heartland of the Lowlands), and terrain would have been most passable at this time. Another consideration was logistics. Unless they were in friendly territory or had water transport, Maya forces had to carry their food on their backs. Reents-Budet illustrates a Classic vessel apparently showing elite warriors being helped by women to load up with arms and provisions for a campaign.[35] Commoner porters may have carried supplies, but in any case they had to eat, too. This energetic constraint severely limited the duration and spatial extent of Maya campaigns. One partial solution was probably to forage food from dispersed farmsteads and fields in enemy territory, which could most efficiently have been done just before the crops were harvested or just after they had been stored. Foraging for wild resources would have been ineffective to support sizable bodies of warriors.

Distances between sixteen paired antagonist centers involved in specific conflicts average 57.5 linear kilometers, with a range of 19 to 109.5 kilometers.[36] Unfortunately, it is not clear exactly where battles took place, except where fortifications or other evidence suggests that one center was actually attacked. Hassig calculates that large groups of men carrying their own military equipment, and perhaps accompanied by food-bearing porters, could travel overland only about nineteen kilometers per day.[37] At this rate, even if battles took place in boundary zones roughly midway between two polities, the duration of campaigns probably was two weeks or less. Obviously, long sieges were not very feasible, which partially accounts for the seeming effectiveness of even light, unsophisticated fortifications.

In Whose Interests Were Maya Wars Fought?

There is little doubt that successful war most directly served elite, and particularly royal, interests. Insofar as coordination and leadership guaranteed the integrity of the polity and its dynasty, the population in general probably benefited as well. I observed earlier that there was no concept of the citizen in Maya society like that in Greece and Rome. Also, as already noted, we are unsure about how people of different social and political statuses related to one another. Commoners probably saw themselves as low-ranking people in divinely sanctioned hierarchical systems, with few or no rights over against the interests of hereditary elites, and they had little or no consciousness of themselves as a social class. This perspective would be strongest if the stratified model of sociopolitical relationships, discussed previously, obtained. The alternative model, which emphasizes ranking, implies that low-ranked people had legitimate claims on their higher-ranking kin, and perhaps more ability to influence decisions, negotiate their own participation in war, and possibly receive some direct benefits from it.

The two models also have different implications for recruitment, assuming that commoners were mobilized. If the commoner population was politically atomized into small producer-households with no larger effective corporate identities, they could be directly recruited by officials of the polity, and would have little ability either to resist demands for military service or to assert claims over the fruits of victory. In the kin-based model, recruitment presumably would have been via their senior kinsmen, who had obligations to king and polity but also to their kin-constituents, and who thus acted as intermediaries between them. Under these circumstances, commoners would have been more informed and influential participants.

In fifth-century B.C. Greece there existed what one could reasonably call a proletariat with its own identity and interests. According to some interpretations, the Persian Wars and the wealth created by the Athenian empire made proletarian service to the state not only more strategically necessary but also more affordable.[38] The resulting political leverage enabled people of low social status to promote their own interests and helped democratize the whole society. Nothing like this collective promotion seems to have occurred among the Classic Maya, nor anywhere else in Mesoamerica. Aztec commoners who were successful in war were rewarded with titles, status objects, and even estates, but such upward social mobility affected individuals, not groups, and never raised them to the ranks of the hereditary nobility. Whether the Maya had any similar system of institutionalized rewards and incentives for common warriors is uncertain, but it seems more likely as epigraphic evidence accumulates.[39]

What Were the Purposes and Functions of Maya War?

Contact period conflicts were carried out for land, slaves, control of trade routes, and for elite prestige, revenge, intrapolity political advantage, and tribute in objects such as cotton mantles. Whether the same range of purposes obtained earlier is uncertain, and here Classic texts do not help much. As Stuart remarks: "Unfortunately the inscriptions that we can read are not at all explicit about the motives for warfare, nor its character."[40] Although some post-Conquest books include descriptions of earlier Postclassic wars, the Classic Maya left us no surviving reflective, historical narratives remotely like accounts by Herodotus and Thucydides of the Persian and Peloponnesian Wars.

War and Ritual   Reconstructions of Maya war emphasize its superstructural dimensions. Warfare was heavily ritualized and ideologically charged, and had special symbolic implications for Classic Maya concepts of kingship. Mayanists widely accept that a fundamental duty of ancient kings was to guarantee order and balance in an animate cosmos prone to disorder. Order and balance, in turn, ensured the well-being of the king's realm, his subjects, his royal person, and his line. Success in war reflected the supernatural efficacy of the ruler, and no doubt failure detracted from it. Participation in war thus was an essential part of the royal role and also figured in life crisis ceremonies such as accession and heir designation. Capture, public humiliation, and eventual ritual sacrifice of distinguished enemies demonstrated the royal warrior's prowess, and the most suitable captive was another ruler.[41] Subordinate warriors sometimes seem to have "adorned" their prisoners and presented them as gifts to rulers, who in return rewarded them with status objects.[42]

Inscribed stone monuments recorded war events and the exploits of kings, and conspicuous themes are the numbers and identities of captives. For example, three generations of Yaxchilan kings list no fewer than thirty-four captured enemies.[43] Sometimes such monuments were erected by victors at the defeated center. Elite costume and regalia included the heads and other body parts of slain enemies.

While no one doubts this heavy ritual component, some scholars have emphasized it as almost the only, or at least the most fundamental, purpose of Classic Maya war. For example, Schele and Miller write of conflict that "the capture of sacrificial victims was its fundamental goal."[44] Stuart cautions, however, that "deciphered warfare events are not explicit in emphasizing ritual over more material motivations."[45] Many scholars, myself included, think that war had many more materialistic and infrastructural dimensions. To the extent that warfare was driven by ritual considerations and the sacred ideological postulates underlying them, it was about essentially nonnegotiable or nonresolvable issues.

War as Competition for Resources   I believe that warfare over resources, including agricultural land and labor, began as early as Late Preclassic times and was an important factor in the emergence of Maya political centralization and hierarchy.[46] Unfortunately, Maya elites throughout their history generally neglected to record (at least in durable form) information concerning the extents of their territories, numbers of taxpayers, resources extracted from them, or other information necessary for reconstructing basic economic motivations for war or their historical consequences.

Emerging conceptions of conflicting Late Classic Maya "superstates" emphasize large-scale patterns of hegemonic warfare presided over by regionally dominant centers and dynasties such as Calakmul, Tikal, Caracol, and Dos Pilas.[47] These polities, supported by their lesser allies, dependents, and proxies, purportedly contended with each other for several generations. Evidence for the prolonged wars of these titans comes almost entirely from textual evidence that is still widely debated among epigraphers. Unfortunately, the published material on these conflicts is almost entirely concerned with identifying the protagonist polities, alliances, and cultural history of conflicts rather than motivations, functions, and outcomes. Nor can we yet determine if the supra-city-state aggregations involved in such conflicts were strongly structured in hierarchical terms, or instead consisted of associations of convenience in which each player sought political advantage. In at least one case, however, the captured ruler of a defeated polity was not sacrificed, but rather returned to his own center, where presumably he ruled as a subordinate to his captor.[48]

What were the purposes of such hypertrophied conflicts if they indeed occurred? Among the few who have addressed this problem are Diane and Arlen Chase, who believe that the polity of Caracol benefited very materially in tribute and labor after defeating Tikal in A.D. 562.[49] Unfortunately, their detailed data have not yet been published. The general implication of such "superstate" warfare is, though, that it was fought for territory, for strategic advantage, and for control of centers that could provide support not just in elite tribute items but also in more basic and tangible forms. Transfers of cheap, bulk foods, as well as labor, could certainly have been made over short distances, although they are not mentioned in deciphered texts. There is no convincing evidence that war was fought to control specific centers of trade or trade routes.

We do not know how the farmers who constituted most of the population were affected by war. One possibility is that, situational seizure of their products and occasional demands for military service aside, they were largely unaffected by wars or their outcomes. It was, after all, in the interests of rulers and elites not to disrupt severely the agrarian producers who supported them, and over whose control they contended. From the perspective of the farmer it might have mattered comparatively little which elites one paid taxes to. In any case, effective escape from regional warfare was impractical by Late Classic times. Populations were dense and royal centers were many. Moreover, the landscape was highly variegated in terms of agricultural productivity, with few vacant zones which it would have been attractive for refugees to colonize. Most people could not simply move away from the theaters of war, even had they been motivated to do so. The same social circumscription, however, would have allowed them to vote with their feet, deserting weak lords for strong ones.

War as Status Rivalry   Stuart believes that the sudden appearance of explicit war-related inscriptions after A.D. 600 reflects the creation of many small polities for whose rulers war was an essential expression of royal identity and political sovereignty.[50] By the eighth century the political and dynastic landscape of the Classic Lowlands must have been extraordinarily complex. The maximum number of major centers and polities existed at this time, population densities were at their highest, and agricultural productivity was probably declining due to deleterious anthropogenic effects on the environment.

War, intermarriage, and political alliances over hundreds of years created cosmopolitan and interlinked sets of royal and elite persons. I believe this setting to have been a potent environment for mature dynastic warfare motivated by elite status rivalry.[51] By this I mean the active competition among elites or would-be elites for restricted titles, offices, honors, and privileges that were the symbolic correlates of rank, status, and authority. These symbols could be objects of competition in and of themselves, but they also guaranteed access to the more fundamental resources of land and labor, which in any agrarian society are the foundation of the political economy. Low-ranked commoner-producers supplied elites with food, built their houses, provided some kinds of prestige goods, and fueled such enterprises as monument construction and war. The most important economic considerations of any elite person or faction were acquiring and maintaining claims to rights of disposal over the labor and products of producers and being able to enforce these claims if challenged. A convenient late medieval analogy is the English Wars of the Roses.

Central to status rivalry war are ambiguities of power and authority. The proliferation of Maya dynastic lines and their cadet branches, polygyny, elite intermarriage, and the high status of women (which added dimensions of bilateral descent) all must have created ambiguities of power and privilege that served as pretexts for many kinds of inter- and intrapolity conflicts. As Oliver noted for Tahitian war: "The political interests of socially important individuals [and] ambitions to extend or efforts to curb political power accounted for most of the larger and more devastating armed conflicts."[52] As in Polynesia, hereditary rank and inheritance could be counterbalanced by achievement, and the mobilization of political supporters or factions was the most tangible expression of political potency and the key to success in status rivalry. Resort to conflict was especially efficacious in the absence of institutions such as professional state armies that centralized the apparatus of coercion. If Maya polities consisted of kin-based segments, then powerful elite personages had natural constituencies that could support their interests in status struggles. We know from historical accounts that conflicts of this sort occurred among the Contact period Maya.

Unfortunately (but understandably), no royal texts clearly celebrate the successful usurpation of rulership or the defeat of upstart claimants to the throne, although some Mayanists have suggested archaeological evidence for violent dynastic competition, including possible elimination of one royal faction.[53] Close scrutiny of intertwined dynastic wars, marriages, and alliances during the eighth century strongly hints at the complexities of status warfare.[54] Periodic cessation of monument erection and building projects at some centers such as Tikal and Caracol suggest dynastic weakness and possible conflict, as do several recorded incidents of long intervals between the death of one ruler and the accession of his successor. Defeated rulers sometimes appear to have been kept for years in the centers of their captors, and it is easy to imagine the dynastic problems in their original polities created by this practice.[55]

Even though the direct evidence is weak and the details will probably always elude us in the absence of a more complete historical record, I think status rivalry war was one of the most potent forces in structuring Late and Terminal Classic Maya civilization and contributed significantly to its downfall.

Warfare and the Classic Maya Collapse

Most people envision the famous Maya collapse as a dramatic and sudden catastrophe that uniformly caused the abandonment of the great Classic centers and the disappearance of their supporting populations. Events as reconstructed by archaeologists are much different—to the point that some prefer not to use the word "collapse" at all. It is true that a process of political disruption and demographic decline broadly afflicted the Lowland Maya, but it was far from uniform. Northern Yucatán was not much affected—we already saw that a variant of Lowland civilization still thrived there when the Spanish arrived. It is in the central and southern Lowlands, the heartland of Classic civilization, that the notion of a collapse applies best. At some polities, political and demographic collapse does seem to have been abrupt. Elsewhere royal dynasties, subroyal elites, and commoner populations disappeared gradually over hundreds of years. Some polities and populations survived the collapse, particularly in Belize. Nevertheless, the old Classic social, political, economic, and cultural patterns were certainly severely disrupted, and overpopulation and environmental degradation are heavily implicated in this process of decline.

War and violence were postulated as at least partial causes of the Classic collapse of the eighth and early ninth centuries long before we could effectively understand Maya inscriptions. J. E. S. Thompson, the most influential Maya scholar for thirty years, believed that elite demands so oppressed and overtaxed peasants that they overthrew the ancient dynasties of one polity after another.[56] Others later tried to show that chronological patterns support Thompson's view.[57] Although the internal revolt theory can account for some of what happened, such as the abandonment of building projects, the cessation of royal inscriptions, and monument defacement, it does not explain where all the people went, why there was no recovery under new emergent elites, why the pace and character of the collapse were so variable, or why some centers continued to thrive. There are no convincing indications of large-scale, exogenous environmental changes, such as drought and desiccation, that can account for the patterns of the collapse, although local, anthropogenically produced alterations of landscape certainly occurred, as did possibly local microclimatic changes.

Some Mayanists advanced ceramic and sculptural evidence for the invasions of non-Classic Maya military adventurers along the southwestern frontier during the Terminal Classic period.[58] David Stuart finds no iconographic or epigraphic support for this hypothesis in the purportedly "foreign" stelae of Seibal, the principal center in question.[59] While there still may well have been some foreign influences in this region, we cannot detect convincing evidence for large-scale invasions, which in any case would have been too localized to affect the Lowlands as a whole drastically.

The Late Classic was traditionally regarded as the most mature, prosperous, and sophisticated phase of Maya cultural history. As we have seen, it was also characterized by conflicts of unprecedented frequency and scale, especially after A.D. 700. The latter view suggests another perspective—namely, that the glittering façade of Classic culture masked fundamental and ultimately unresolvable and destructive weaknesses. As David Stuart has cogently noted, the whole of the Late Classic period might fruitfully be regarded as a protracted collapse.[60] Accelerating warfare, in this view, is one symptom of these weaknesses. The questions then become why the Maya faced more intractable problems late in their history, and exactly what these were?

I think the answers are generally quite obvious. There were more closely juxtaposed polities of disparate character than ever before. Dynastic and elite entanglements, rights claims, and counterclaims were very complex and often ambiguous. Population densities reached unprecedented levels on landscapes that were inherently fragile, and that had been utilized intensively for hundreds of years. Deleterious anthropogenic changes such as erosion, deforestation, and perhaps even alterations of microclimates resulted in lowered agricultural productivity and increased risk. Peasants were hard-pressed, and elites, more numerous than ever, pursued their self-serving and conflicting interests through territorial and status rivalry wars. Kings found it increasingly difficult to deliver the balance and productivity so ideologically essential to their roles as magical guarantors of cosmic order.

In this view, war of many kinds is only one factor in a complex series of destructive processes, and it operated variably in different regions at the end of the Classic period. The Petexbatun region on the southwestern margin of the Lowlands went down in a welter of protracted conflicts.[61] Far to the east, at Copán, a better case can be made for internal struggles that dethroned the royal dynasty, leaving some elites to hold on for generations in a general environment of agricultural and demographic decline.[62] Documenting such variation, and the reasons for it, is our next big challenge.

Conclusions

The Classic Maya were long perceived to have been a peaceful people who somehow lacked the warfare that plagued other great civilizations. Archaeological research, along with studies of Maya epigraphy and art, reveal that, to the contrary, warfare occurred frequently and was an essential process in the emergence and organization of Classic polities and society.

Maya warfare developed in contexts unlike those of the other societies reviewed in this volume. Not only did the Maya inhabit a distinctive tropical environment, but their technology, as well as their subsistence and economic systems, were very different from those of Old World civilizations, most importantly in their technological simplicity and reliance on human muscle. Also distinctive were their sociocultural systems, which emphasized divine kings, reverence for ancestors, animistic religions that included human sacrifice, and social arrangements probably characterized more by kinship ranking than by class stratification. Still, there were many similarities. Like all the other societies described in this volume, the Maya were an agrarian people. Hereditary kings ruled large territories. Some people were powerful and wealthy, and most were not. Some people worked hard to support others. Access to land and labor were keys to privilege and prominence. Agricultural productivity was fundamental but precarious. Individuals and factions vied for titles and offices that guaranteed rank, positions, and resources, and they often did so through warfare.

We have come a long way in our understanding of warfare in ancient Maya civilization despite the paucity of historical data and our own wishful thinking. Sometimes the greatest impediment to new, better knowledge is old, bad ideas, and by the early 1970s the "peaceful Maya" theory, always suspect from the perspective of any broad, comparative view of complex societies, had been largely laid to rest. We are now in a second and very exciting phase of research—the epigraphic and iconographic documentation of the cultural history of Maya war. Full appreciation of the role of warfare in the rise and decline of Maya civilization will result from the eventual understanding of the broader economic, social, and political processes underlying the internecine conflicts only now coming to light.

Notes

1. For the best recent summary of Classic Maya writing and its themes see Stuart 1995.
2. See Sharer 1994.46–47 for a more detailed version.
3. The environment of northern Yucatán contrasts markedly with that of the south in terms of hydrology, rainfall, vegetation, and topography. For this reason, and also because the northern Maya fall into a different linguistic family from those who lived farther to the south and wrote the Classic inscriptions, sixteenth-century Spanish accounts must be used very carefully to interpret and reconstruct Classic Maya society and culture.
4. Rands 1952.
5. Landa 1941; Roys 1943.
6. Ruz Lhuillier 1973.
7. Webster 1976.
8. For example, some epigraphers postulate a fourth-century conflict between Tikal and Uaxactun that was one of the first full-scale wars of conquest (Schele 1991). Others strongly reject this reconstruction (Stuart 1993.334; 1995.315–320) and cite an A.D. 652 conflict between Caracol and Tikal as the first explicit war that is glyphically well attested (Miller 1993.408).
9. Stuart 1995.329.
10. Rice 1993.11–63.
11. Most tasks carried by nonindustrial Old World peoples were also accomplished by the Maya, albeit less efficiently. For example, we know from both ethnographic observations from many parts of the world and experimental archaeology that trees can be felled using either stone or metal tools. Metal tools, however, do the job three to four times more efficiently.
12. Webster 1995.
13. Sanders and Webster 1988.521–46.
14. Hopkins 1988.87–121.
15. Freidel, Schele, and Parker 1993.
16. Martin and Grube 1995.41–46.

17. Mathews and Willey 1991.30–71; Houston 1993.
18. Schele and Freidel 1990.
19. Otterbein 1973.
20. Identifiable weaponry is seldom, if ever, recovered from Maya graves, but only the most durable parts (e.g., stone blades) would be recoverable in any case, and these would be difficult to distinguish from other classes of tools or ritual objects.
21. This is a widely known ethnographic pattern, particularly in Polynesia and Southeast Asia, where elites commissioned specialists to make such war craft, which were paddled by common warriors.
22. Webster 1976.
23. Puleston and Callender 1967.40–48.
24. See for example Schele and Freidel 1990.193.
25. Stuart 1993.330–31.
26. Who participated in Maya conflicts is potentially testable through the examination of large skeletal series for signs of war-related trauma. Unfortunately, however, the Maya did not bury people in cemeteries, but rather in and around residences, or in royal/elite tombs in ritual structures, so large numbers of burials cannot be recovered quickly. Skeletal remains are also often in poor condition because of the humid tropical climate. So far only a few large skeletal series have been examined, and none of the samples comes from centers that we know were heavily involved in war. There is considerable, although scattered, skeletal evidence from Preclassic times on for the human sacrifices that we know followed military victories.
27. Freidel 1986.93–108.
28. Cortés 1986.
29. Marcus 1993.111–84.
30. Miller 1993.414–63.
31. Stuart 1995.359–61.
32. Hassig 1992.219–21.
33. Martin and Grube 1995.
34. Roys 1943.67; Marcus 1992a.
35. Reents-Budet 1994.
36. Webster 1998.
37. Hassig 1992.44.
38. Jones 1960.233–34. See also Raaflaub, this volume.
39. Stuart 1995.297.
40. Stuart 1995.358–59.
41. A recently discovered depiction from Tonina suggests that elite women were sometimes made captive as well. New epigraphic insights also strongly suggest that the capture and destruction of images of the patron deities of an enemy polity were major goals of war.
42. Stuart 1995.296–97.
43. Miller 1993.407.
44. Schele and Miller 1986.220.
45. Stuart 1995.324.

46. Webster 1977.335–72.
47. For example Martin and Grube 1995.
48. Stuart 1995.324–26.
49. Chase and Chase 1989.5–18.
50. Stuart 1995.329.
51. Webster 1998; 1993.415–44; 1995.
52. Oliver 1974, 1.376.
53. Laporte and Fialko 1990.33–66.
54. Miller 1993.
55. Status-rivalry conflict is an emergent theme in Maya scholarship. Such conflict is consistent with the ever-increasing textual information we have for the Classic Maya. On another level it is a comparative inference postulated on the basis of our more general knowledge of Classic society, and of the nature of warfare in other historically documented societies with similar features—for example, Polynesia. Direct evidence is clearest where long-term regional projects have been undertaken. At Copán, where I have worked for many years, the royal dynasty suffered setbacks in the mid–eighth century, at which time the establishments of lesser nobles became greatly enlarged and embellished in ways normally reserved for royalty. About A.D. 800–850 the royal household was abandoned and parts of it deliberately burned. Some other elite establishments were also abandoned about this time, but others survived and even grew for another century or so. All this strongly suggests status rivalry conflict on an intrapolity level.
56. Thompson 1954.
57. Hamblin and Pitcher 1980.46–67.
58. Sabloff and Willey 1967.311–36; Sabloff 1973.107–32; Henderson and Sabloff 1993.
59. Stuart 1993.336–44.
60. Stuart 1993.
61. Houston 1993; Sharer 1994.220–32; Demarest 1993; Inomata 1995.
62. Webster, Sanders, and van Rossum 1992; Webster 1994.

Bibliography

Chase, Arlen, and Diane Z. Chase. 1989. "The Investigation of Classic Period Maya Warfare at Caracol, Belize." *Mayob* 5, 5–18.

Cortés, Hernan. 1986. *Letters from Mexico.* New Haven, Conn.: Yale University Press.

Demarest, Arthur. 1993. "Violent Saga of a Maya Kingdom." *National Geographic Magazine* 183:2, 95–111.

Freidel, David. 1986. "Maya Warfare: An Example of Peer-Polity Interaction." In *Peer-Polity Interaction and Sociopolitical Change,* edited by Colin Renfrew and John Cherry, 93–108. London: Cambridge University Press.

Freidel, David, Linda Schele, and Joy Parker. 1993. *Maya Cosmos.* New York: William Morrow.

Hamblin, R. L., and B. L. Pitcher. 1980. "The Classic Maya Collapse: Testing Class Conflict Theories." *American Antiquity* 45:2, 46–67.

Hassig, Ross. 1992. *War and Society in Ancient Mesoamerica.* Berkeley and Los Angeles: University of California Press.

Henderson, John S., and Jeremy A. Sabloff. 1993. "Reconceptualizing the Maya Cultural Tradition: Programmatic Comments." In Sabloff and Henderson 1993.445–76.

Hopkins, Nicholas. 1988. "Classic Mayan Kinship Systems: Epigraphic and Ethnographic Evidence for Patrilineality." *Estudios de Cultural Maya* 17, 87–121.

Houston, Stephen D. 1993. *Hieroglyphics and History at Dos Pilas: Dynastic Politics of the Classic Maya.* Austin: University of Texas Press.

Inomata, Takeshi. 1995. "Archaeological Investigations at the Fortified Center of Aguateca, El Petén, Guatemala: Implications for the Study of the Classic Maya Collapse." Ph.D. diss., Vanderbilt University.

Jones, Tom. 1960. *Ancient Civilization.* New York: Rand McNally.

Landa, Diego de. 1941. *Landa's Relacion de las Cosas de Yucatan.* Edited and annotated by Alfred M. Tozzer. Papers of the Peabody Museum 18. Cambridge, Mass.: The Peabody Museum.

Laporte, Juan Pedro, and Vilma Fialko C. 1990. "New Perspectives on Old Problems: Dynastic References for the Early Classic at Tikal." In *Vision and Revision in Maya Studies,* edited by Flora S. Clancy and Peter D. Harrison, 33–66. Albuquerque: University of New Mexico Press.

Marcus, Joyce. 1992a. *Mesoamerican Writing Systems.* Princeton, N.J.: Princeton University Press.

———. 1992b. "Political Fluctuations in Mesoamerica." *National Geographic Research and Exploration* 8:4, 392–411.

———. 1993. "Ancient Maya Political Organization." In Sabloff and Henderson 1993.111–84.

Martin, Simon, and Nikolai Grube. 1995. "Maya Superstates." *Archaeology* 48:6, 41–46.

Mathews, Peter, and Gordon R. Willey. 1991. "Prehistoric Polities of the Pasion Region: Hieroglyphic Texts and Their Archaeological Settings." In *Classic Maya Political History,* edited by T. Patrick Culbert, 30–71. New York: Cambridge University Press.

Miller, Mary Ellen. 1993. "On the Eve of the Collapse: Maya Art of the Eighth Century." In Sabloff and Henderson 1993.355–414.

Oliver, Douglas L. 1974. *Ancient Tahitian Society.* Vols. 1–3. Honolulu: University Press of Hawaii.

Otterbein, Keith. 1973. "The Anthropology of War." In *Handbook of Social and Cultural Anthropology,* edited by J. Honigmann. Chicago: Rand-McNally.

Puleston, Dennis, and D. W. Callender, Jr. 1967. "Defensive Earthworks at Tikal." *Expedition* 9:3, 40–48.

Rands, Robert. 1952. *Some Evidences of Warfare in Classic Maya Art.* Ph.D diss., Columbia University.

Reents-Budet, Dorie. 1994. *Painting the Maya Universe: Royal Ceramics of the Classic Period.* London: Duke University Press.

Rice, Don S. 1993. "Eighth-Century Physical Geography, Environment, and Natural Resources in the Maya Lowlands." In Sabloff and Henderson 1993.11–63.

Roys, Ralph. 1943. *The Indian Background of Colonial Yucatan.* Carnegie Institution of Washington Publication 548. Washington D.C.: Carnegie Institution.

Ruz Lhuillier, Alberto. 1973. *El Templo de las Inscripciones, Palenque.* Colleción Cientifica Arquelogia 7. Mexico City: Instituto Nacional de Antropologia e Historia.

Sabloff, Jeremy A. 1973. "Continuity and Disruption during Terminal Late Classic Times in Seibal: Ceramic and Other Evidence." In *The Classic Maya Collapse,* edited by T. Patrick Culbert, 107–32. Albuquerque: University of New Mexico Press.

Sabloff, Jeremy A., and John S. Henderson, eds. 1993. *Lowland Maya Civilization in the Eighth Century A.D.* Washington, D.C.: Dumbarton Oaks Research Library and Collection.

Sabloff, Jeremy A., and Gordon R. Willey. 1967. "The Collapse of Maya Civilization in the Southern Lowlands: A Consideration of History and Process." *Southwestern Journal of Anthropology* 23, 311–36.

Sanders, William T., and David Webster. 1988. "The Mesoamerican Urban Tradition." *American Anthropologist* 90, 521–46.

Schele, Linda. 1991. "The Owl, Shield, and Flint Blade." *Natural History,* November, 6–11.

Schele, Linda, and David Freidel. 1990. *A Forest of Kings.* New York: William Morrow.

Schele, Linda, and Mary Ellen Miller. 1986. *The Blood of Kings.* New York: G. Braziller in association with the Kimbell Art Museum, Fort Worth.

Sharer, Robert. 1994. *The Ancient Maya.* Palo Alto, Calif.: Stanford University Press.

Stuart, David. 1993. "Historical Inscriptions and the Maya Collapse." In Sabloff and Henderson 1993.321–54.

———. 1995. "A Study of Maya Inscriptions." Ph.D. diss., Vanderbilt University.

Thompson, J. Eric S. 1954. *The Rise and Fall of Maya Civilization.* Norman: University of Oklahoma Press.

Webster, David. 1976. *Defensive Earthworks at Becán, Campeche, Mexico: Implications for Maya Warfare.* Publication 41. New Orleans: Middle American Research Institute, Tulane University.

———. 1977. "Warfare and the Evolution of Maya Civilization." In *The Origins of Maya Civilization,* edited by R. E. W. Adams, 335–72. Albuquerque: University of New Mexico Press.

———. 1993. "The Study of Maya Warfare: What It Tells Us about the Maya and about Maya Archaeology." In Sabloff and Henderson 1993.415–44.

———. 1994. "Cultural Ecology and Culture History of Resource Management at Copán, Honduras." Manuscript prepared for the Advanced Seminar on the Archaeology of Copán. Santa Fe: School of American Research.

———. 1995. "Status Rivalry and Late Classic Maya Warfare." Paper presented at the 1995 Palenque Round Table on Maya Warfare, Palenque, Mexico.

———. 1997. "City-States of the Maya." In *The Archaeology of City-States: Cross-Cultural Approaches,* edited by Deborah Nichols and Thomas Charleton, 135–54. Washington D. C.: Smithsonian Institution Press.

————. 1998. "Status Rivalry Warfare: Some Maya-Polynesian Comparisons." In *Archaic States,* edited by Gary Feinman and Joyce Marcus, 311–52. Santa Fe: School of American Research.

Webster, David, William T. Sanders, and Peter van Rossum. 1992. "A Simulation of Copán Population History and Its Implications." *Ancient Mesoamerica* 3:1, 185–98.

FOURTEEN

The Aztec World

Ross Hassig

The Aztec empire is, by far, the best known in Mesoamerica—the area of high indigenous civilizations in Mexico, Belize, Guatemala, El Salvador, and Honduras. It owes its fame not merely to its exceptional character but also to the historical accident of Spanish contact that produced many descriptions and chronicles of its history and accomplishments. The Aztecs were, in fact, the fourth major expansion—three of them imperial—that linked much of Mesoamerica, and the last in a series of such expansions stretching back some twenty-five hundred years.

The Aztec empire developed from earlier societies, both technologically and organizationally. But our knowledge of these empires is limited because it is based primarily on physical remains. Nevertheless, this evidence yields a sweeping cultural history of Mesoamerica within which Aztec developments must be placed and against which they can be assessed.

Complex warfare began with the rise of the Olmecs around 1150 B.C. on the Gulf Coast of Mexico and accompanied their cultural expansion, which was the first of three pre-Aztec expansions that gave Mesoamerica its cultural unity. The Olmecs expanded throughout much of Mesoamerica, apparently for trade purposes, although they were aided by the introduction of specialized military arms, including clubs, maces, and spears.[1] By 550 B.C., however, the Olmecs withdrew into their homeland and Mesoamerica lapsed into a period of conflict between independent city-states.

In the first century A.D., Teotihuacan emerged as the first true empire in Mesoamerica, penetrating far north into the desert and south into Guatemala, linking much of Middle America. Driven by trade, Teotihuacan's expansion

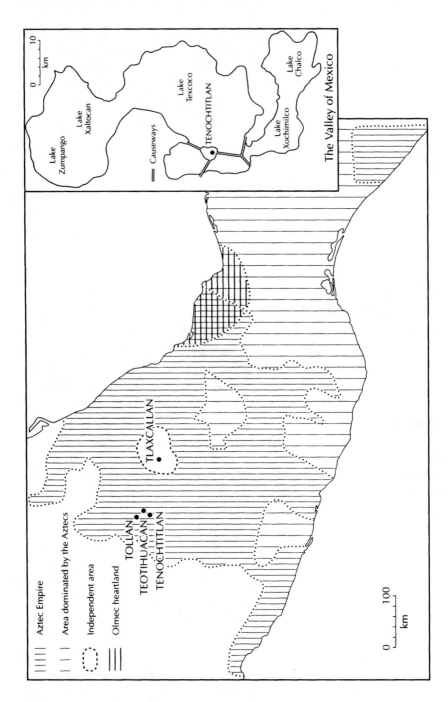

The Aztec Empire

was backed by the most formidable army in Mesoamerica at that time, which was also associated with new weapons, including thrusting spears, atlatls (spear-throwers), and darts and later, quilted cotton armor. But more important than its technological edge in arms and armor, Teotihuacan drew on commoners and nobles alike for its army, allowing it to field the largest in Mesoamerica. Equipped by the state, its soldiers were trained to fight in complementary arms units.[2] But, by A.D. 500, Teotihuacan began withdrawing from its colonies, and the city collapsed around A.D. 750.[3]

For the next two centuries, city-states again vied for local dominance, until the rise of the Toltec empire centered at Tollan after A.D. 900.[4] Like Teotihuacan, Tollan also drew broadly from all social classes to field a large army,[5] aided by yet another new weapon, the short sword. Coupled with the atlatl and wielded by the same soldiers, the short sword effectively doubled the impact of Toltec troops. But the Toltec empire fell when progressive desiccation undermined its agricultural base and drove nomadic barbarians armed with bows and arrows south into the area, disrupting the trade on which it depended.[6] Thereafter, small empires and confederacies rose and fell, but no major empire emerged until the Aztecs.

The Aztecs migrated into the Valley of Mexico at the end of the twelfth century A.D., established their capital of Tenochtitlan (now Mexico City) in the first half of the fourteenth century, and became political dependents and tributaries of the small Tepanec empire that dominated the west side of the valley. Taking advantage of the political fragmentation that followed the death of its founder, the Aztecs and their allies overthrew the now politically isolated Tepanec capital and emerged as the new power in the Valley of Mexico. Although there were other confederacies (e.g., Tlaxcallan) and regional empires (e.g., Tarascan) that presented obstacles, the Aztecs nevertheless expanded and became the dominant tributary empire in the following ninety years. After conquering the fragmented remains of the Tepanec empire, the Aztecs consolidated their hold on the Valley of Mexico, then expanded against the city-states to the south before challenging the Tlaxcallan confederacy to the east and the Tarascan empire to the west, a confrontation that was ongoing when Cortés arrived.

All four of the major Mesoamerican expansions had similar histories. But two factors ensured that their expansion-contraction cycles were not merely repetitions of the same pattern. First, population throughout Mesoamerica increased dramatically over time. Each successive empire controlled more people, which gave them access to larger armies, greater tribute, and increasingly efficient logistical support, all of which propelled further expansion.[7]

Second, the technology of war also improved. There was a growing reliance on projectiles used not just by specialists but also by hand-to-hand combatants in the early phases of battle. As armor improved, cutting arms displaced crushers, and their bladed edges expanded, producing progressively lighter yet more effective weapons.[8] Moreover, the growing sophistication of arms in Meso-america increased the size and deadliness of the kill zone—the area between armies in which the opposing weapons were effective.

Even though the materials to construct these arms were widely available and the skills needed to do so were relatively simple, the advantages of new arms were felt primarily by empires rather than by city-states, since the former's population increases were absolutely and proportionally much greater. What polity adopted which weapons was largely a function of size. However, it was not the technological innovations themselves that were important, but how they affected organization.

Specialized weaponry required formal training, but empires also empha-sized arms and tactics favoring organized units rather than individual combat, an effective chain of command, and standardized weapons. Moreover, these armies were large and relied heavily on commoners, which generated a major social dynamic of Mesoamerican empires, since military success provided a rare avenue for social mobility: commoner participation was rewarded, which en-couraged rapid population growth through immigration that fueled further expansion. City-states, by contrast, neither needed nor possessed large armies, relying instead on elite soldiers and offering neither social mobility nor mater-ial rewards to the commoners. Reflective of this, nonstandardized arms were employed, which further indicates individual rather than state ownership, the importance of individual combat skills, less emphasis on unit operations, and markedly less centralized political control.[9]

Although a larger army and broad conscription gave them the upper hand, empires nevertheless lacked the long-term stability of city-states. Although city-states too could collapse, they were not so precariously dependent on external trade, and they generally persisted longer than the more complex social systems of empires.[10] Larger systems have shorter developmental cycles because, as they expand beyond the normal economic and political hinterlands of city-states, the friction of distance raises the costs of trade, warfare, political administra-tion, and even tribute. And nowhere is this more evident than in Mesoamerica, where there were neither wheeled vehicles nor draft animals.

Even in the absence of significant opposition, imperial expansion is not merely a mechanical process of adding comparable units; rather, each expan-sion causes internal changes in the empire, and especially in the capital, as the number of people involved in such activities as manufacturing, trade, and ad-ministration increases proportionally. These internal changes allow greater control over, and benefit from, the empire, but they are also hostage to its main-tenance. Imperial expansion does not mean just subordination; contact stimu-lates local developments, especially social stratification, which creates local competition, and, since even small competitors cut into imperial revenue, the empire is forced to divert resources to control them. Even if the empire succeeds in maintaining control, its position nevertheless erodes because the same income is maintained at a greater cost, effectively reducing the actual return. As costs increase and returns decline, empires begin to contract. And once the empire contracts, the internal developments that occurred during expansion cannot be sustained, and social disruption follows.

The general fragility of empires was even more pronounced in the Meso-american case because of the historical circumstances of their expansions. They faced relative political vacuums, which encouraged them to expand much farther and produced greater initial internal development than could be sustained once these peripheral areas developed and became competitors. City-states, by contrast, usually expand only far enough to control a symbiotic city/hinterland area. Thus they sustain internal social and economic systems appropriate to their size and experience few pressures from competing elites that would force contraction.

Lasting many centuries, both the Olmecs and Teotihuacan experienced the entire expansion-contraction cycle. The Toltec and Aztec empires, by contrast, were cut short, the former by the ecological and social catastrophe that struck their capital, and the latter by the Spanish conquest.

Aztec War and Society

Perhaps since Olmec times, and certainly during the Aztec era, warfare was endemic in central Mexico. Virtually every city-state had traditional enemies against which it waged war, and although this may have led to minor shifts in tributary alliances, these conflicts persisted for decades and even centuries without fundamentally altering the prevailing political situations or relationships. Rather, these wars were fought to legitimate the succession and rule of kings and to reassert boundaries. If warfare was endemic, yet did not fundamentally alter the political landscape, why then did some city-states expand, conquer foreign areas, and become empires?

Theories purporting to explain why empires emerge and expand have been grouped into three fundamental types. The first type sees imperialism as internal: certain social structures possess an inherent need to expand, as, for instance, capitalism has been viewed as necessarily expanding in search of new markets. The second type sees imperialism as the result of external conditions: expansion is caused by the weakness of the periphery; chaos and lawlessness in foreign areas force stronger polities to impose order so stable relations can be maintained. Here, too, social structures may be causal, but of the periphery rather than the center. The third type sees imperialism not in a particular social structure but simply as a natural consequence of power differences between polities, with the more powerful one inevitably expanding at the expense of the weaker.[11]

Because there is so little information on internal political and social dynamics of earlier empires, there are too few data to apply either internal or external theories convincingly; so I have attempted to explain pre-Aztec Mesoamerica in terms of the power differential approach.[12] But when social behavior is better documented, these starkly drawn theoretical distinctions are less exclusive. And since this is the case with the Aztec empire, each theory can be assessed more directly in relation to the data.

The merit of the external theory of imperialism rests on the fact that no complex society is entirely independent of others. Mesoamerica is extremely diverse ecologically, ranging from arid deserts to tropical jungles, and rising from sea level to well over five thousand meters (18,000+ feet) in remarkably short distances.[13] As a result, the many products needed in complex societies were widely scattered but could be acquired through trade. Relying on others, however, renders a polity vulnerable, especially if it must depend on them for strategic resources—actual, such as obsidian for weapons, or perceived, such as quetzal feathers that served as status markers.[14] Expansion to control the sources of supply allows empires to control and to guarantee their influx in a predictable manner without depending on the goodwill of independent polities.[15]

Increasing the quantity and reliability of trade was, indeed, one of the goals of Aztec imperial expansion, since that allowed their merchants to travel and to trade safely. Each time the empire expanded, so too did the types and amounts of goods merchants could import, and craftsmen from other cities flooded into the capital, creating a manufacturing center unequaled in central Mexico.[16] But while controlling trade is a compelling reason for expansion in many cases, the relative inefficiency of Mesoamerican transportation reduced trade to a secondary imperial purpose.

While small groups of porters could travel somewhat faster than armies at some twenty-six to twenty-nine kilometers (sixteen to eighteen miles) per day, basic commodities, such as maize, could nevertheless be brought to market only from short distances—little more than one day's walk. Thus, Tenochtitlan's economic hinterland for staple foodstuffs was quite restricted, and even trade in elite goods was constrained. Imperial expansion could make trade safer and more reliable, but it could not, of itself, increase its efficiency. Instead, the primary economic benefit of Aztec expansion was from tribute, which did not feel the friction of distance so directly because the cost of both production and shipment was borne not by the consumers but by the producers.

The potential benefits of trade and tribute were available to all city-states, but few expanded to take advantage of them, so the mere plausibility of financial gain does not explain why some city-states became empires and others did not. For that, other theories of imperialism must be addressed.

The second approach to imperial expansion, the power differential theory, finds support in an assessment of Mexican armies and military technology. Aztec armies relied on a combination of tactics and arms that were not used by city-states. Specifically, atlatls and darts had been displaced by bows and arrows in smaller armies. The Aztec retention of these weapons, however, gave their frontline troops an impact far greater than that of their enemies; so a power differential did exist. But whether this alone caused, or permitted, their expansion demands a deeper assessment of the Mesoamerican arms industry.

Mesoamerican arms and armor used little metal but were nevertheless finely crafted of such materials as stone, bone, wood, leather, cotton, and vegetable fibers. Some of these materials were found locally, but others, such as cotton, had to be imported from more tropical regions. As a result, many of the arms and materials for their construction and repair were available through the flourishing market trade: stimulated by the demand in centers such as Tenochtitlan, distant, noncombatant towns produced such arms as quilted cotton armor for export.[17] And warfare was sufficiently pervasive that it gave rise to a pan-Mesoamerican military-preindustrial complex responsive not to polities but to the market. And when trade was inadequate to meet demand, additional arms were exacted as tribute from subordinate polities and others were manufactured in state armories.[18]

Differences in military technology may explain imperial expansion, when one side has a monopoly on a decisive weapon.[19] But, given the level of Mesoamerican technology, any material innovation in warfare diffused rapidly and came within the grasp of every group. The barriers to the spread of arms in Mesoamerica were social and organizational, not technological. A craftsman anywhere in Mesoamerica could construct a broadsword. But only states could afford to support specialists who would spend the time necessary to learn how to wield the weapon in hand-to-hand combat. And while the Aztecs' success is clear evidence of their military superiority and of a power difference, emphasizing arms ignores the reasons for it, which were internal to Aztec society.

The internal theory of imperialism best fits the Aztec case, since what drove their expansion was internal to Aztec society. One widely touted motivation was religion, and there is some evidence of this. In the famous creation myth, after the last of three or four worlds had been destroyed, the gods gathered together and decided that one of them would have to leap into a bonfire to become the new sun. When none of the greater gods did so, a lesser god, Nanahuatzin, jumped in and rose from the flames as Tonatiuh, the sun god. But he would not begin his travels across the skies; so the remaining gods all pierced themselves for blood, which they offered to Tonatiuh, who then began the journey from east to west that he has followed ever since.[20] This myth is widely regarded as the fundamental supernatural charter between the gods and the Aztecs—that people are dependent on the gods, but the gods are also dependent on people to provide blood sacrifices. This myth serves as a supernatural charter to explain the necessity of war: it is needed to secure captives for human sacrifice to the gods so the world will continue. But despite this myth, the question remains, did religious purposes lie at the basis of Aztec wars?

Two well-documented Aztec patterns suggest that religion did not drive war in any direct way. First, the Aztecs did not withdraw in the face of defeat but attacked cities that were unconquered the first time again and again, which suggests that they did not view the outcome of battle as signaling divine favor or disfavor. And second, one would expect tributary rebellions to be infrequent occurrences if conquest was believed to signal the superiority of the conquerors' gods, but, in fact, they were common. Thus, the Aztecs treated both war and tributary control as political, not religious, matters.

Although religion may have provided an ideological justification for warfare, it cannot simply be taken as a supernatural charter for long-term behaviors that crosscut all social and occupational groups in Aztec society. Doubtless, many Aztecs believed in a supernatural justification for war, and this belief may have aided the state in motivating soldiers.[21] But Aztec religion was not messianic. The Aztecs neither spread their gods to conquered peoples nor imposed their beliefs on others. So the relation between religion and warfare was, at most, an internal one, motivating the individual participants rather than driving the endeavor. The elites, whatever their beliefs, used religion for political purposes, relying on religious justifications for fundamentally political actions, which suggests a conscious manipulation of the Aztec masses.

The intermixture of the political and religious in Aztec society makes identifying the motivating cause of many acts difficult. Nevertheless, four examples show the underlying political purposes of what appear to be religiously motivated actions. In the first example, the Aztecs sometimes requested building materials for temples from independent cities. This was ostensibly a religious request made to honor the gods, but to comply and bring the goods sought was a tacit acknowledgment of subservience and acquiescence to future tribute demands. Only weak cities complied, and, when strong ones rejected the demand, the Aztecs used this to justify launching a war of conquest.[22]

The second example is the Aztec practice of burning the temple of defeated cities,[23] which suggests a religious motivation, at least to the extent that it signals the defeat of the local gods. But beyond this symbolism, burning the temples was a devastating practical blow, since they were usually the most heavily fortified sites within the city. And if it happened during a battle, it showed that the Aztecs had reached the center of their opponents' city, which meant that the enemy soldiers were now deprived of a safe haven, their political leadership was likely captured, and the armories associated with the temples were now destroyed or in Aztec hands. In short, burning the temples deprived the city's army of refuge, political direction, and additional arms, and can thus be more profitably seen as a military strategy than a religious one.

The third example of ostensibly religious behavior in war was the Aztec practice of seizing the gods of captured cities and taking them to their capital of Tenochtitlan to be housed in a special temple.[24] But was taking vanquished gods a way of controlling dominated populations? Perhaps; but there is scant evidence that the Aztecs worshiped these captured gods, and they did not take them from all conquered cities. In fact, they apparently did so when it would have been least necessary; that is, the recorded examples are from cities that were relatively close to Tenochtitlan, where control should have been easier than in more distant regions.

Given these anomalies, I suggest that, since all temples and their associated priests were supported both by offerings of supplicants and by lands dedicated to that cult, taking these gods to Tenochtitlan also meant moving the associated priests and redirecting the flow of wealth from temples in the vanquished cities to the temple in Tenochtitlan. In short, whether or not there were supernatural benefits in capturing foreign gods, the economic gains were direct and significant.

The fourth example is King Ahuitzotl's massive human sacrifices at the rededication of the Great Temple in Tenochtitlan in 1487. Ahuitzotl returned from a military campaign with a reported 80,400 prisoners who were all sacrificed during a four-day rededication celebration for the Great Temple. Although the ceremony was ostensibly religious, it was primarily motivated by political concerns. Ahuitzotl succeeded a weak king who failed to project Aztec power during his five-year reign, with the result that many tributaries had stopped paying tribute, and most failed to attend Ahuitzotl's coronation to repledge fealty as was customary. Faced with this disintegrating control, Ahuitzotl had two options: he could reconquer each tributary at enormous cost in time and manpower, or he could do what he did—invite his tributaries into the capital and demonstrate his power by sacrificing captives on an unprecedented scale, using a religious occasion as a pretext. This exercise in state terrorism was immediately effective, Aztec power was again demonstrated, and virtually all of the tributaries repledged their fealty.[25]

The extent to which individuals believed that religion motivated warfare doubtlessly varied by groups and individuals. Individual commoners may have believed and, reassured by that belief, been more willing to go to war. But whether or not they believed it, the political leadership manipulated religion for state purposes. And because war offered other advantages to so many groups and people, it is difficult to disentangle their motivations.

A careful assessment of the historical data does not support the idea that supernatural ideological motivations paved the way for imperial expansion, at least not strongly. But there are nevertheless other significant, though less exalted, motivations for both individual and group behavior. And in the case of most Aztecs, these are to be found in the structure of their society.

The most salient social consequence of war was its effect on the social classes in Tenochtitlan at all levels. Aztec society was divided into nobles (upper [teuctin] and lower [pipiltin]) and commoners (macehualtin), with the latter organized by ward (calpolli). Perhaps originally clans, calpollis had become residential units that held land in common and were overseen by their own leaders, or ward heads (calpoleque). The influx of tribute that began as soon as the Aztecs became an empire shifted their class structure solidly in favor of the nobility. Both nobles and commoners shared the booty of war,[26] but the nobles, and especially the king, received the vast bulk, providing them with wealth independent of that received from their own commoners.[27] Now less dependent on the tribute of their own people, the king was freer to decide matters of war and peace without as much regard for the commoners' wishes, which shifted the role of ward heads from relatively powerful and autonomous representatives of commoner interests to functionaries through whom royal dictates were transmitted.

War also affected the position of the upper nobility. They gained enormously in wealth, power, and a lessened dependence on the commoners. But the most significant war-driven changes were in the internal Aztec political structure that altered the prospects of the various segments of society.

Of the nine pre-Hispanic Aztec kings (see chart 1), three ruled before the Aztecs were an empire. Acamapichtli, a noble from the nearby city of Colhuacan, was selected as the first king, but he had little power. The Tepanecs, to whom the Aztecs were tributary, dictated external relations, while internal matters were largely in the hands of the ward heads. From this inauspicious beginning, Aztec political history was a multigenerational power struggle between competing interest groups. Acamapichtli first shifted the power balance by marrying the daughters of the calpolli leaders,[28] thereby uniting his noble status with the de facto authority of the ward heads and paving the way for the eventual consolidation of both internal and external decision making in the hands of the king.

Little else changed through three reigns: royal succession was patrilineal, with sons succeeding fathers. Acamapichtli was succeeded by his son, Huitzilihuitl, who was in turn succeeded by his son, Chimalpopoca. But when Chimalpopoca was assassinated as a young man without a suitable heir, Itzcoatl became the fourth king in a major shift in the principles of succession.

Whereas the early kings succeeded by direct male inheritance, beginning with Itzcoatl, kings were now chosen by the upper nobility from among themselves, based on military experience and ability. This shift was less a cause of

Chart 1   Aztec Kings and Their Reigns

1372–91   Acamapichtli ("Reed-fist")
1391–1417 Huitzilihuitl ("Hummingbird-feather")
1417–27   Chimalpopoca ("He-smokes-like-a-shield")
1427–40   Itzcoatl ("Obsidian-serpent")
1440–68   Moteuczoma Ilhuicamina ("He-frowned-like-a-lord
           He-pierces-the-sky-with-an-arrow")
1468–81   Axayacatl ("Water-mask")
1481–86   Tizoc ("Chalk-pulque")
1486–1502 Ahuitzotl ("Otter")
1502–20   Moteuczoma Xocoyotl ("He-frowned-like-a-lord
           The-younger")
1520   Cuitlahua ("Excrement-owner")
1520–25   Cuauhtemoc ("He-descends-like-an-eagle")

major changes in the internal Aztec political system than a reflection of them. The growth in numbers and power of the upper nobles enabled them to seize and retain control over succession, and Aztec kingship never reverted to patrilineal succession. Although he remained the most powerful Aztec, the king was forced to treat the upper nobles more deferentially, since succession was no longer monopolized by his family line, and his successor would be chosen by and from among the upper nobles. At the same time, expanding the ranks of who was eligible produced a large number of pretenders who could easily become disaffected once someone else was crowned. So while the office of king was strengthened by its greater emphasis on competence, broadening the pool of potential successors also weakened it by shifting more power into the hands of the upper nobles generally and by greatly enlarging the number of potential competitors.[29] Thus, this change produced better kings, but it simultaneously gave them an Achilles' heel: any royal action or inaction that struck at the interests of the nobility helped potential challengers and fostered the emergence of dissident factions. The most serious kind of threat to the nobility's interests was economic, and, because the Aztecs' empire was hegemonic, sustaining or increasing the influx of tribute depended on maintaining a successful show of strength and continuing to expand the empire.

The first major expansion beyond the Valley of Mexico occurred during the reign of Moteuczoma Ilhuicamina, following the devastating famine of 1454. He also embarked on a significant reorganization of the economy of the entire Valley of Mexico. Because Tenochtitlan's growing population could not be fed by current local production or by trade and tribute, the Aztecs converted the southern lakes to *chinampa* agriculture, an intensive form of farming on artificial islands constructed in the shallow lake bed that permitted year-round cultivation and thus greatly increased production. The Aztecs also flooded their markets with tribute goods, which they could do at or below the cost of production, and effectively undermined crafts production elsewhere in the valley, since these goods could now be purchased more cheaply than they could be manufactured. This, in turn, forced a shift away from craft production and toward agriculture,[30] effectively employing tributary wealth to convert the Valley of Mexico from a series of craft-producing city-states with their own peripheral agricultural areas into an integrated valley-wide economic sphere with Tenochtitlan as its manufacturing and trade center and the rest of the valley as its agricultural periphery.[31]

War brought a major influx of wealth that underwrote Aztec society as well as further imperial expansion. And while acquiring wealth was one factor that drove war, it was not the most direct concern. Everyone benefited from the booty of war: nobles gained wealth, but for the commoners, it was the potential social mobility that gained their support.

Moteuczoma Ilhuicamina's reign witnessed the first major expansion of the empire, which also increased the need for more and better soldiers. Accordingly, the king instituted schools for commoners (*telpochcalli*), where they could be trained in warfare.[32] This innovation greatly increased the number of formally trained troops available to the Aztecs, both absolutely and per capita, giving their armies a significant advantage over those of their competitors. But this act had unanticipated consequences for the Aztec social system, as became apparent during the reign of Tizoc.

These formally trained commoner soldiers increased Aztec military success, which made another shift in the power balance among the classes likely. To forestall this, the king awarded especially successful commoners the status of meritocratic nobles (*cuauhpipiltin*), similar to knights in Europe.[33] This status conferred the right to own land, be supported by the king, and hold high political and military office. Moreover, this new status was inheritable, opening up a new avenue for social mobility that had both good and bad consequences for the traditional nobles. These new meritocratic nobles were supported by the king, which meant dividing the wealth generated by the empire, although creating more nobles may well have paid for itself, since it led to great support for imperial wars by commoners. At the same time, new meritocratic nobles were removed from ward command and placed directly under the king. Systematically shifting the best soldiers from the wards to the king reduced the power of ward heads and enhanced that of the throne. And the king further used these meritocratic nobles, who owed their good fortunes to him, against the increasingly powerful upper nobles.

Because most of the upper nobles were potential competitors to the king, they could not be entirely trusted. Using them as royal surrogates, such as tribute collectors, would have given them access to potentially independent economic bases and political alliances, which they might have used to challenge the king. Instead, the king placed the meritocratic nobles in these roles because they had the noble status to deal with tributary kings but lacked the hereditary support needed to challenge the king for the throne. Despite the usefulness of meritocratic nobles and the way the Aztecs had channeled their potential to challenge the sociopolitical status quo into support for the monarchy, the *telpochcalli*-trained soldiers were so successful that, within a generation, King Tizoc was forced to increase the requirements to become a noble to avoid being swamped by upwardly mobile commoners.

This system of upward mobility appears to be an imperial creation and differs markedly from opportunities in city-states. Since the latter relied largely on nobles for elite warriors, leaving commoners to more pedestrian support roles, there was no need for the institution of meritocratic nobles. By contrast, Aztec imperial society readied the entire society for war by inducements that ultimately ensured an upward penetration of society by commoners and their interests.

The benefits of war were available to all the citizens of Tenochtitlan, which was the largest city in Mesoamerica by several orders of magnitude. Not old enough to have grown that large by normal rates of birth, much of Tenochtitlan's size was the result of immigration. This immigration could only have been in the crafts and laborer ranks, since all land was already owned by wards and could not be alienated. So what would account for a citizen of another city relinquishing his ward property rights there and migrating to a place where he could hope for none? The single most apparent factor is the real opportunity for social mobility that was absent from other cities. Migrants could aspire to meritocratic noble status in Tenochtitlan; so, quite apart from the wealth expansion generated, imperial wars created a rare opportunity for social mobility that fueled the influx of population.

The most important event of Tizoc's reign, however, was his own death. Tizoc ruled for less than five years, during which he engaged in few wars, and given the hegemonic nature of the Aztec empire, the prolonged failure of a king to demonstrate his power encouraged rebellions and the cessation of tribute payments. This, in turn, reduced the income on which the king, nobles, and cults depended, and directly undermined noble interests and support. A king could survive a few setbacks, but sustained failure eroded his internal support and could lead to his untimely death and replacement. As a result of Tizoc's inaction, many tributaries rebelled, tribute decreased, and he was poisoned. Tizoc was succeeded by Ahuitzotl, perhaps the most fearsome of the Aztec kings, but after five years of relative neglect, few tributaries even bothered to attend his coronation, a situation he deftly reversed through the massive sacrifices at the Great Temple rededication discussed earlier.

The lesson of Tizoc's demise was not lost on Ahuitzotl, nor on his successor, Moteuczoma Xocoyotl, whose reign was marked by two other notable features. First, he attempted to remove all commoners from royal service, presumably to stem their growing power relative to the hereditary nobles. And second, he initiated a policy of bringing the sons of tributary kings to Tenochtitlan and educating them as Aztecs. This has been interpreted as an effort to hold them hostage to their fathers' obedience, and doubtless they could have been used in this fashion. But more important, Moteuczoma was attempting to extend the base of his support to nobles throughout the empire, and to lessen the hold of his own nobility, who had been the cause of Tizoc's downfall.

Mesoamerican Political Organization

The Aztec empire was thus built less for strategic purposes than for domestic ones. As a result, the Aztecs made little attempt to integrate the groups they conquered, extracting tribute and minimal loyalty without otherwise meddling in their social, political, economic, or religious affairs. Instead, the way they organized their empire likewise arose to a great extent out of the particular constraints of Mesoamerican society.

The Aztecs did not conquer new areas and consolidate their hold by replacing local leaders and their armies with imperial governors and garrisons, even though such a system allows the extraction of large quantities of goods in tribute, because of the high political and administrative costs involved, particularly in maintaining troops in the conquered cities. Moreover, even though such a territorial empire offers direct control of subordinate groups, it has limited ability to expand because the available manpower is quickly consumed in garrison duty. Instead, the Aztecs left the conquered governments intact and imposed neither imperial rulers nor troops. Without direct control, the amount that could be extracted as tribute was limited, but so too were the political and administrative costs. Furthermore, a hegemonic empire does not consume its forces in garrison duty and so frees the army for further expansion.[34]

The more a hegemonic empire relies on power (the perception that desired goals can be achieved) rather than force (direct physical action), the more efficiently it functions because the subordinates police themselves.[35] But the tributaries must not perceive the costs of compliance as outweighing the benefits or the imperial power must rely more heavily on force, which reduces the system's efficiency. In short, the basic Mesoamerican imperial pattern was one of domination exercised not through structural changes in the subordinated societies but through the ability of empires to defeat decisively anyone acting contrary to imperial wishes. Nevertheless, the differences between hegemonic and territorial systems can be overstated. Both should be seen as modes of control rather than as conceptually discrete entities, since part of the difference between the two systems is a matter of scale.

Both empires and city-states exercise direct, or territorial, control over their immediate hinterlands, but beyond each city's immediate hinterland control becomes more difficult and is generally beyond the ability of city-states to maintain. Empires, however, do exercise more distant control hegemonically, because their disproportionate size enables them to muster far larger armies and to encourage compliance by local rulers. But because Mesoamerican empires depended on the perception of power, their expanded areas of hegemonic control fluctuated more than those of territorial systems.

Since there are no institutional changes in the form of puppet rulers or locally stationed imperial troops to maintain control directly, hegemonic empires are vulnerable to collapse at any point that weakness is exposed or perceived. Thus, a king's military prowess is not simply a matter of ideology or honor but is an essential element in sustaining the empire. Similarly, royal deaths were often followed by tributary rebellions because the successor king's military ability and ruthlessness were uncertain.[36]

Aztec Warfare

As a hegemonic system, the Aztec empire necessarily depended on a strong military, and the practice of war was tightly woven into the fabric of Aztec society. Rather than relying on foreign mercenaries or on a socially isolated professional elite, the Aztecs drew the bulk of their army from their own citizenry, based on their traditional organization, which in turn structured the army.[37]

Aztec society was divided into nobles (upper [*teuctin*] and lower [*pipiltin*]) and commoners (*macehualtin*), with the latter organized by ward (*calpolli*). Perhaps originally clans, calpollis had become residential units that held land in common and were overseen by their own leaders, or ward heads (*calpoleque*).

To muster an army, the king (*tlatoani*) solicited a specific number of men who were then summoned by the ward heads, based on a rotating service roster so that this obligation was borne equitably by all the eligible men.[38] Each ward's soldiers thus formed a tight-knit unit with residential and kin ties that marched and fought under its own leaders and banner within the overall Aztec army.[39]

The call-up was announced in the marketplace, and each ward mustered its troops, supplied them with weapons from the armories, and began retraining for battle. Although the army was assembled, supplies were gathered, and the troops were prepared to march within five days, the campaign preparations nevertheless required considerable advance planning. And in this the king exercised overall authority, determining the army's route, the number of days it would march, and the battle plan once the target was reached.[40]

The standard Aztec army unit was eight thousand men (a *xiquipilli*), with the total army being composed of multiples or divisions of these. On the march, the army was proceeded by priests carrying the gods on their backs,[41] and each *xiquipilli* departed on a separate day, a practice dictated by practical considerations, not religious ones.

Since there were no wheeled vehicles or draft animals in Mesoamerica, simply moving large numbers of men posed enormous problems. Like preindustrial armies elsewhere, the Aztec army moved slowly, probably averaging no more than 2.4 kilometers (1.5 miles) per hour, or 19 kilometers (12 miles) per day.[42] And since the Aztecs did not systematically construct roads except in their cities,[43] they relied on roads meant for local trade, and these were wide enough to accommodate no more than double files. Each xiquipilli thus stretched out over a minimum distance of 12,000 meters (7.5 miles), which meant the last men would not begin marching until five hours after the first had started. Thus, while a second xiquipilli could theoretically begin its march on the same day as the first, it could not reach that night's camp until well after nightfall, with the additional slowness and problems associated with travel in darkness. Although dispatching each xiquipilli on a successive day greatly increased the time needed to assemble the entire command on site for the attack, to do otherwise was impractical.

This problem could be minimized, although not completely eliminated, by dispatching armies along several alternative routes simultaneously, which the Aztecs commonly did. Moreover, stalling an attacking force for even a few days could thwart it because of the logistical constraints that made speed crucial to Aztec success.[44] Individual soldiers might bring some of their own supplies, but most food was transported by accompanying porters (*tlamemes*) who carried two *arrobas* (twenty-three kilograms or fifty pounds) each.[45] At the most favorable recorded ratio of one porter for every two warriors and a daily per capita consumption rate of .95 kilograms of maize,[46] the army could carry food for no more than eight days, giving it an effective combat radius of about thirty-six miles—three days going, one day fighting, one day recuperating, and three days returning. So approaching a target along several lines of march prevented the enemy from bottling up the army in a pass where they could not bring all of their forces to bear, until their supplies were exhausted.

To reduce this logistical constraint, the Aztecs demanded supplies from subordinate towns en route. Two days before the march, messengers were sent along the designated route to alert all tributary towns, which then gathered foodstuffs from the surrounding area for the passing Aztecs.[47] Thus, while the armies of city-states were limited to the normal thirty-six-mile combat radius, imperial armies could travel unimpeded throughout their empires and then thirty-six miles beyond.

Nevertheless, the slow rate of march, the time needed to assemble the entire army in camp, the clouds of dust kicked up by tens of thousands of feet on dirt roads, as well as the presence of spies, foreign merchants, and the advance word the Aztecs sent to their tributaries, meant that strategic surprise was virtually impossible to achieve. But even with advance warning, there was little a city-state could do to take advantage of it, and, the rare instances of wholesale flight aside, city-states typically awaited the Aztecs' arrival. Some cities were notified of an impending attack by Aztec emissaries, and surrender at that point meant a relatively modest tribute payment. But even without a formal request, cities could surrender at any time from the point they learned they had been targeted, although the tribute demanded increased the longer they delayed. If there was no surrender, battle was joined.[48]

Aztec battlefield assaults against other armies typically began at dawn, signaled by the commander's drum or trumpet, and involved an orderly sequence of weapon use and tactics. Fighting began with a projectile barrage once the armies closed to around sixty meters (two hundred feet), with arrows and stones hurled by unarmored archers and slingers who remained behind the frontline troops and did not advance.[49]

When the barrage began, soldiers advanced carrying broadswords (*macuahuitl*) and thrusting spears (*tepoztopilli*). Made of oak and obsidian, these weapons had keen stone blades tightly glued into grooves along the edges, producing weapons that the Spanish conquistadors noted could cut the head off a horse with a single blow. The most experienced and accomplished warriors were also well protected by shields, helmets, and various types of armor.[50]

The military shields (*yaochimalli*) were typically round, over seventy centimeters (twenty-eight inches) in diameter, made of hide, wood, or woven cane with heavy double cotton backing, and covered with feathers. Armor (*ichca-huipilli*) was constructed of unspun cotton quilted between two layers of cloth and made into a sleeveless jacket that hugged the body. One and a half to two fingers thick, the armor could not be penetrated by arrows;[51] it was worn alone or, if status merited it, under a war suit (*tlahuiztli* suit) that encased the arms and legs as well as the torso. Helmets made of quilted cotton or wood were sometimes used as well.

The opposing armies closed quickly, casting darts with their atlatls as they advanced. These lacked the distance of arrows or slingstones, but, with greater striking force at close range, they could penetrate the cotton armor of the front-rank soldiers and potentially disrupt the opposing formations. Only a few atlatl darts were carried, since they were used only until the armies met, at which point the combatants switched to broadswords and thrusting spears and were so intermingled that the slingers and archers ceased massed fire.[52]

Battle was heaviest between the soldiers at the front of the armies because only the first few ranks could engage the enemy, and the Aztecs extended their front to take advantage of their numerical superiority to envelop the opposing troops and cut them off from reinforcements and resupply. In battle, units were rotated in and out of combat roughly every fifteen minutes, with fresh troops also bringing more arms. Wounded enemy soldiers were seized and passed back through the ranks until they reached the rear, where they were bound. Wounded Aztec soldiers were tended by medical specialists who set broken bones, applied medicines, and sutured wounds.[53]

Very large cities in Mesoamerica consistently lacked comprehensive fortifications, since they were protected by their size. But smaller city-states occasionally erected defensive works to multiply the effectiveness of their limited forces. When there were fortifications, defenders sometimes stayed behind them rather than fight the Aztecs in the open. Unless the Aztecs gained entry through deceit or treason, or simply withdrew, fortifications presented the Aztec with the standard three options: breach them, scale them, or besiege the city. Breaching the fortifications was difficult and time-consuming; scaling walls with ladders was a quicker alternative but was dangerous and required many men. The remaining option was to lay siege to the town. This was feasible within the Valley of Mexico, where the besiegers could be resupplied by canoe, but elsewhere sieges were rare because logistical constraints made supplying a stationary army extremely difficult.[54]

Fortifications were seldom used, however, because, even if they were effective, the city could not be divorced from its wider social networks.[55] The fields and stores beyond its walls were still vulnerable, as were the smaller towns on which the city depended. Only an active defense in which the enemy was met and vanquished would guarantee the city's continuation as the hub of a social network. Cities were occasionally laid waste and a scorched-earth policy employed, but this was not common Aztec practice, since it was in the interests of both sides to maintain the city as a viable social and economic enterprise. Except in the face of extraordinary provocation, the goal was not to devastate the enemy but to incorporate them into the empire and to benefit from their tribute.

Word of victory or defeat was sent to the king in Tenochtitlan by runner. After the battle, the dead were identified so their families could be notified, the ward rolls adjusted, and payments made to the affected households. If the army was far from home, the bodies of the Aztec dead could not be returned and were cremated there. Enemy captives were bound, and the entire party began its march home.[56]

The significance of a battle's outcome differed greatly between empires and city-states. If a city-state won the battle, it merely gained a reprieve because the Aztecs would return another year; defeat, however, meant subjugation of the city-state and all its dependencies. But this was not the case for confederacies and empires. Because they controlled large hinterlands, advance warning allowed these polities to marshal their armies and march to their borders to meet the enemy, which profoundly altered the consequences of the battle. Victory against an empire did not mean its defeat, but rather the conquest of only the battle site. Even if beaten in battle, confederated and imperial armies could withdraw into their interiors, where the Aztecs could not safely pursue because there were no tributaries on whom they could rely for logistical support. Because of these logistical limitations, sizable hinterlands offered large polities a protection their armies could not. So while losing a battle meant subjugation for a city-state, it meant only the loss of a limited peripheral area for a confederacy or an empire. Thus, conquering the latter was a long-term project achieved only by gradually chipping away at the edges of the polity. A single, decisive blow to the heart of an empire was usually beyond the Aztecs' ability.

Some opponents were so strong that even victory would leave the Aztecs too weakened to maintain the perception of power needed to control their tributaries elsewhere. The costs of such a "victory" were too high for an empire that had to balance many strategic interests. So the Aztecs' strategic emphasis was on easy conquests and targets of opportunity, which reflected broad political considerations rather than specific military weakness. This did not mean the Aztecs ignored powerful opponents, since doing so would leave them intact as significant threats. But rather than risking outright wars of conquest, the Aztecs engaged these large, formidable opponents in flower wars (*xochiyaoyotl*).

Early accounts claim that, unlike traditional wars of conquest, flower wars were fought for military training, to take captives for sacrifice to the gods, and to display individual military skill.[57] This was all true, but flower wars were also part of a larger military strategy for dealing with major powers.

Flower wars began as shows of strength in which relatively few combatants fought to demonstrate individual military prowess. An impressive display showed the Aztecs' capabilities and the ultimate futility of resistance, and could lead to the enemy's capitulation without further conflict. But if the opponent remained unintimidated, additional flower wars would be fought—often over many years—gradually escalating in ferocity. In the first flower wars, injuries and deaths were not deliberate and no prisoners were sacrificed. But as the wars escalated, captives were sacrificed rather than returned, the number of combatants was increased, and bows and arrows introduced indiscriminate death rather than individual demonstrations of hand-to-hand skill and bravery until, eventually, flower wars resembled wars of conquest. Thus, flower wars began as low-cost exercises in military intimidation, but both costs and consequences escalated until they became wars of attrition. And with that, the numerically superior Aztecs could not lose, since even equal losses took a greater toll on the military elite of the smaller side and gradually undermined its ability to resist.

It could take considerably longer to defeat an enemy this way than through wars of conquest, but flower wars had significant advantages. By engaging the enemy in limited but enervating warfare, the Aztecs could pin down strong opponents and reduce their offensive threat. They then conquered the surrounding cities, gradually encircled their opponents, cut them off from allies, and reduced their areas of logistical and manpower support. As they escalated the flower wars, the Aztecs slowly chipped away at the enemy territory, reducing their allies and manpower, until they could attack their cities directly, and they fell. Thus, the Aztecs' weak-opponent-first strategy generated tribute revenue and increased their logistical capability at low cost, while the flower wars isolated and slowly reduced opponents too strong to be attacked directly.

Despite widespread warfare, Mexican cities were not in a constant state of alert. The Mesoamerican campaign season was limited by the May-to-September rainy season.[58] Major wars could not be waged during the summer or early fall when the commoners who made up most of the army and its support personnel were occupied in their fields. Moreover, adequate food supplies were not available until after harvest, at the beginning of the dry season. Only then did the dirt roads dry out and allow large groups to march without being mired in muddy quagmires, and to cross now-shrunken streams that were swollen during the summer rains. As a consequence, Aztec warfare was concentrated in a campaign season running from early December to late April.

The Aztec empire, like nearly every other empire, was not a fully integrated and logical structure from its inception but was, rather, the result of a historical development. It grew out of a social system that was altered and adapted to the task of empire. Aztec military capabilities were thus based on their original social system, but modifications effected in an effort to increase their military capability—selecting kings by ability, training commoners better, and elevating meretricious ones to noble status—all took on lives of their own and forced changes in Aztec society that further affected its military ability. Moreover, these social considerations began to drive military policy.

The Conquest

But how was such a large and well-organized empire brought down by a few hundred Spaniards in just two years? The answer lies not in Spanish actions but in how groups opposed to the Aztecs, as well as factions acting in their own self-interests, used the Spaniards' presence for their own purposes. The Spaniards were too few and too weak to bring about the conquest on their own, even with superior arms and technology. What was perhaps the pivotal event of the conquest was the Tlaxcaltec decision to ally with Cortés. And the reasons were internal: the Tlaxcaltecs could have defeated the Spaniards and were on the verge of doing so when they pulled back and initiated an alliance for reasons that had almost nothing to do with the Spaniards' political situation, but with their own. The Tlaxcaltecs were entirely encircled by the Aztecs, and their allies were gradually being defeated or switching sides in the conflict. Their own defeat by the Aztecs was imminent, and what the Tlaxcaltecs saw in the Spaniards was a potential solution to their own precarious situation.

A key goal in Mesoamerican warfare was breaking through the opposing lines, turning their flanks, and routing the enemy, which is difficult to accomplish when both sides use comparable arms and tactics. Spanish arms, such as harquebuses, cannons, crossbows, and mounted lancers, by contrast, could consistently penetrate the opposing army, although the Spaniards could not exploit this advantage, owing to their small numbers. The Tlaxcaltecs could, however, and it was their recognition of this potentially pivotal role the Spaniards could play—not on their own but as the tip of a large Tlaxcaltec force—that motivated their search for an alliance. Thus allied, a small Spanish force could punch through the Aztec lines, which the much larger Tlaxcaltec forces could then exploit. This altered the tactical balance in central Mexico, but the strategic shift was primarily political and was the result of the Aztecs' hegemonic imperial organization.

Once Tenochtitlan itself was attacked, most of the Aztec empire was now behind enemy lines. But since these cities were merely tributaries—and often reluctant ones at that—rather than well-integrated parts of a coherently structured empire, they acted in their own interests rather than those of the Aztecs, and, beyond the Valley of Mexico, no tributaries came to the Aztecs' aid. The hegemonic system functioned as expected: when Tenochtitlan was unchallenged, the tributaries were obedient, but when another power emerged, it effectively neutralized Aztec control. Tenochtitlan was left alone to fight this new threat, with future tributary allegiances going to the victor. The conquest of Mexico was a battle fought with a European edge, but it was a war of indigenous interests, indigenous motivations, and indigenous goals. Indians won the battle of Tenochtitlan, but it was the Spaniards who won the war. The various Indian goals were immediate, seeking local advantage, whereas those of Cortés were strategic. He sought to control Mexico completely, by playing off his many competing Indian allies against each other, and he was able to consolidate his gains politically.

Notes

1. Anderson 1978.158; Bernal 1969.188; Coe 1965.764–65; 1968.47, 86; Coe and Diehl 1980, 1.387, 392; 2.149; Grove 1981.61–64; Lowe 1989.50; Stirling 1943.19.
2. Cf. the arms with those of the armies of Macedonia in Hamilton, this volume; ancient Greece in Raaflaub, this volume; and Rome in Rosenstein, this volume.

3. Bernal 1965, 1966; Diehl 1989. 9, 11; Diehl and Berlo 1989.2–3; Linné 1942.134, 136; Miller 1973.fig. 363; Pasztory 1988.168–76.
4. Davies 1977.25–75; Healan 1989.5–6; Paddock 1983.210.
5. This assessment is based on the similarities of these two archaeologically known empires with the copiously chronicled Aztec empire.
6. Armillas 1969.697–701; Diehl 1974.194–95.
7. Sanders 1972.
8. Hassig 1992.172–73, and below. Cf. the development of arms and armor in ancient Japan in Farris, this volume.
9. Andreski 1968.88; Creveld 1989.12.
10. Galtung, Heistad, and Rudeng 1980.115–17.
11. Doyle 1986.20–30.
12. Hassig 1992.3.
13. Contrast this ecological diversity with that of the Maya area in Webster, this volume.
14. This analysis derives largely from Cohen 1973.
15. Cohen 1973.242; Mann 1987.131–32.
16. Calnek 1978.316; Sahagún 1950–82, 9.80–83.
17. Acuña 1982–87, 5.190.
18. Aguilar 1977.79; Díaz del Castillo 1977, 1.274; López de Gómara 1965–66, 2.143–44; Tapia 1950.58–59.
19. Cipolla 1965.144; Creveld 1989.19; Dupuy 1984.6; Raudzens 1990.
20. Ruiz de Alarcón 1984.70–72; Sahagún 1950–82, 7.4–7; Velázquez 1975.119–28.
21. Cf. the ideology underlying warfare with that of ancient Japan in Farris, this volume.
22. Torquemada 1975–83, 1.207.
23. *Crónica mexicana* 1975.404, 518–27, 608; Dibble 1980, 1.91; Durán 1967, 2.128, 429; Torquemada 1975–83, 1.198, 208–9.
24. Durán 1967, 2.273, 439.
25. Durán 1967, 2.340.
26. Durán 1967, 2.170.
27. Cf. the distribution of wealth in Rome in Rosenstein, this volume.
28. Carrasco 1984.57–59.
29. See Burling 1974 for a consideration of the consequences of various systems of succession.
30. Brumfiel 1976.200–207.
31. Hassig 1985.127–44.
32. Durán 1967, 2.211–14.
33. Carrasco 1971.351–56.
34. Hassig 1985.92–94; 1988.17–19.
35. Luttwak 1976.
36. Hassig 1988.157, 245–46.
37. Cf. recruitment in the armies of Macedonia in Hamilton, this volume, and ancient Greece in Raaflaub, this volume.
38. Durán 1967, 2.80. On the ward system, see above.

39. *Crónica mexicana* 1975.307; Díaz del Castillo 1977, 1.401; Durán 1967, 2.167. Cf. the theoretical claim for the importance of kinship in states in Ferguson, this volume.
40. Sahagún 1950–82, 8.51.
41. Clark 1938, 1.94; Sahagún 1950–82, 2.75; 1977, 1.162.
42. Clausewitz 1943.276–77.
43. The lack of formal road construction in central Mexico cannot be explained by the lack of draft animals or wheeled vehicles because the Maya constructed stone roads and the Inca built extensive roadways under essentially the same technological constraints.
44. *Crónica mexicana* 1975.307, 605; Durán 1967, 2.319; Torquemada 1975–83, 1.259.
45. Díaz del Castillo 1977, 1.177.
46. *Boletín* 1940, 11.16; Borah and Cook 1963.90; Cuevas 1975.52–53; *Archivo General de la Nación, Reales Cédulas Duplicadas* 3.17.9.
47. *Crónica mexicana* 1975.582. Cf. the supply system of the late Roman army in Haldon, this volume.
48. Hassig 1988.112.
49. Hassig 1988.98.
50. Anawalt 1981.11, 55–56; Broda 1978.121–23, 126; Cortés 1971.133; Díaz del Castillo 1977, 1.227, 274; Durán 1967, 1.115; González Rul 1971; Hassig 1988.81–85; Nickel n.d.; Pasztory 1983.278.
51. Anawalt 1981.39–46; "The Chronicle of the Anonymous Conquistador," in de Fuentes 1963.169; Clark 1938, 1.20; Clavigero 1787, 1.365–66; Díaz del Castillo 1977, 1.113; Durán 1967, 2.208; Nuttall 1891.34–35, 47; Seler 1960, 2.546–47, 575–77.
52. Hassig 1988.99.
53. Mendieta 1971.131.
54. Hassig 1988.107–9.
55. Cf. the role of cities in relation to warfare in the Middle Ages in Bachrach, this volume, and in ancient China in Yates, this volume.
56. *Crónica mexicana* 1975.544, 606, 613; Durán 1967, 2.168; Sahagún 1950–82, 8.53, 73, 12.57; Torquemada 1975–83, 1.259.
57. Tapia 1950.55–56.
58. Broda 1976.61; Castillo Farreras 1969. Cf. the seasonality of warfare among the Maya in Webster, this volume.

Bibliography

Acuña, René. 1982–87. *Relaciones Geográficas del Siglo XVI.* 9 vols. Mexico City: Universidad Nacional Autónoma de México.

Aguilar, Francisco de. 1977. *Relación breve de la conquista de la Nueva España.* Mexico City: Universidad Nacional Autónoma de México.

Anawalt, Patricia Rieff. 1981. *Indian Clothing before Cortes: Mesoamerican Costumes from the Codices.* Norman: University of Oklahoma Press.

Anderson, Dana. 1978. "Monuments." In *The Prehistory of Chalchuapa, El Salvador,* edited by Robert J. Sharer. Vol. 1, 155–80. Philadelphia: University of Pennsylvania Press.

Andreski, Stanislav. 1968. *Military Organization and Society.* Berkeley and Los Angeles: University of California Press.

Armillas, Pedro. 1969. "The Arid Frontier of Mexican Civilization." *Transactions of the New York Academy of Sciences,* 2d ser. 31, 697–704.

Bernal, Ignacio. 1965. "Notas preliminares sobre el posible imperio Teotihuacano." *Estudios de Cultura Náhuatl* 5, 31–38.

———. 1966. "Teotihuacán ¿Capital de imperio?" *Revista Mexicana de Estudios Antropológicos* 20, 95–110.

———. 1969. *The Olmec World.* Berkeley and Los Angeles: University of California Press.

Boletín. 1940. *Archivo General de la Nación, Boletín.* Mexico City: Archivo General De la Nación.

Borah, Woodrow, and Sherburne F. Cook. 1963. *The Aboriginal Population of Central Mexico on the Eve of the Spanish Conquest.* Ibero-Americana 45. Berkeley and Los Angeles: University of California Press.

Broda, Johanna. 1976. "Los estamentos en el ceremonial Mexica." In *Estratificación social en la Mesoamérica prehispánica,* edited by Pedro Carrasco and Johanna Broda, 37–66. Mexico City: Secretaria de Educacion Publica/Instituto Nacional de Antropologia e Historia.

———. 1978. "El tributo en trajes guerreros y la estructura del sistema tributario Mexica." In *Economía política e ideología en el México prehispánico,* edited by Pedro Carrasco and Johanna Broda, 113–72. Mexico City: Editorial Nueva Imagen.

Brumfiel, Elizabeth. 1976. "Specialization and Exchange at the Late Postclassic (Aztec) Community of Huexotla, Mexico." Ph.D. diss., University of Michigan.

Burling, Robbins. 1974. *The Passage of Power: Studies in Political Succession.* New York: Academic Press.

Calnek, Edward E. 1978. "El sistema de mercados de Tenochtitlan." In *Economía política e ideología en el México prehispánico,* edited by Pedro Carrasco and Johanna Broda, 95–112. Mexico City: Editorial Nueva Imagen.

Carrasco, Pedro. 1971. "The Peoples of Central Mexico and Their Historical Traditions." In *Handbook of Middle American Indians.* Vol. 11, *Archaeology of Northern Mesoamerica,* part 2, edited by Gordon F. Ekholm and Ignacio Bernal, 459–73. Austin: University of Texas Press.

———. 1984. "The Extent of the Tepanec Empire." In *The Native Sources and the History of the Valley of Mexico,* edited by J. de Durand-Forest. British Archaeological Reports, International Series 204. Oxford: British Archaeological Reports.

Castillo Farreras, Victor M. 1969. "Caminos del mundo náhuatl." *Estudios de Cultura Náhuatl* 8, 175–87.

Cipolla, Carlo M. 1965. *Guns, Sails and Empires: Technological Innovation and the Early Phases of European Expansion 1400–1700.* New York: Minerva Press.

Clark, James Cooper, ed. 1938. *Codex Mendoza: The Mexican Manuscript Known as the Collection of Mendoza and Preserved in the Bodleian Library Oxford.* 3 vols. London: Waterlow and Sons.

Clausewitz, Karl von. 1943. *On War.* New York: Random House.

Clavigero, Francisco. 1787. *The History of Mexico.* 2 vols. Translated by Charles Cullen. London: G. G. J. and Robinson.

Coe, Michael D. 1965. "The Olmec Style and Its Distribution." In *Handbook of Middle American Indians.* Vol. 3, *Archaeology of Southern Mesoamerica,* part 2, edited by Gordon R. Willey and Michael D. Coe, 739–75. Austin: University of Texas Press.

———. 1968. *America's First Civilization: Discovering the Olmec.* New York: American Heritage Publishing.

Coe, Michael D., and Richard A. Diehl. 1980. *In the Land of the Olmecs.* 2 vols. Austin: University of Texas Press.

Cohen, Benjamin J. 1973. *The Question of Imperialism: The Political Economy of Dominance and Dependence.* New York: Basic Books.

Cortés, Hernán. 1971. *Hernan Cortes: Letters from Mexico.* Translated by A. R. Pagden. New York: Grossman.

Creveld, Martin van. 1989. *Technology and War: From 2000 B.C. to the Present.* New York: Free Press.

Crónica mexicana. 1975. In Hernando Alvarado Tezozomoc, *Crónica mexicana y Códice Ramírez.* Mexico City: Editorial Porrúa.

Cuevas, P. Mariano, ed. 1975. *Documentos inéditos del siglo XVI para la historia de México.* Mexico City: Editorial Porrúa.

Davies, Nigel. 1977. *The Toltecs: Until the Fall of Tula.* Norman: University of Oklahoma Press.

DeFuentes, Patricia. 1963. *The Conquistadors: First-Person Accounts of the Conquest of Mexico.* New York: Orion Press.

Díaz del Castillo, Bernal. 1977. *Historia verdadera de la conquista de la Nueva España.* 2 vols. Mexico City: Editorial Porrúa.

Dibble, Charles E., ed. 1980. *Códice Xolotl.* 2 vols. 2d ed. Mexico City: Universidad Nacional Autónoma de México.

Diehl, Richard A. 1974. "Summary and Conclusions." In *Studies of Ancient Tollan: A Report of the University of Missouri Tula Archaeological Project,* edited by Richard A. Diehl, 190–95. University of Missouri Monographs in Anthropology, no. 1. Columbia, Mo.: Department of Anthropology, University of Missouri, Columbia.

———. 1989. "A Shadow of Its Former Self: Teotihuacan during the Coyotlatelco Period." In *Mesoamerica after the Decline of Teotihuacan A.D. 700–900,* edited by Richard A. Diehl and Janet Catherine Berlo. Washington, D.C.: Dumbarton Oaks.

Doyle, Michael W. 1986. *Empires.* Ithaca, N.Y.: Cornell University Press.

Dupuy, Trevor N. 1984. *The Evolution of Weapons and Warfare.* Fairfax, Va.: Hero Books.

Durán, Diego. 1967. *Historia de las Indias de Nueva España e islas de la tierra firme.* 2 vols. Mexico City: Editorial Porrúa.

Galtung, Johan, Tore Heistad, and Erik Rudeng. 1980. "On the Decline and Fall of Empires: The Roman Empire and Western Imperialism Compared." *Review (of the Fernand Braudel Center at SUNY-Binghamton)* 4, 91–153.

González Rul, Francisco. 1971. "El macuahuitl y el tlatzintepuzotilli: dos armas indígenas." *Anales del Instituto de Antropología e Historia*, época 7, 2, 147–52.

Grove, David C. 1981. "Olmec Monuments: Mutilation as a Clue to Meaning." In *The Olmec and Their Neighbors: Essays in Memory of Matthew W. Stirling*, edited by Elizabeth P. Benson, 49–68. Washington, D.C.: Dumbarton Oaks.

Hassig, Ross. 1985. *Trade, Tribute, and Transportation: The Sixteenth-Century Political Economy of the Valley of Mexico.* Norman: University of Oklahoma Press.

———. 1988. *Aztec Warfare: Imperial Expansion and Political Control.* Norman: University of Oklahoma Press.

———. 1992. *War and Society in Ancient Mesoamerica.* Berkeley and Los Angeles: University of California Press.

Healan, Dan M. 1989. "Tula, Tollan, and the Toltecs in Mesoamerican Prehistory." In *Tula of the Toltecs: Excavations and Survey*, edited by Dan M. Healan, 3–6. Iowa City: University of Iowa Press.

Linné, Sigvald. 1942. *Mexican Highland Cultures: Archaeological Researches at Teotihuacan, Calpulalpan and Chalchicomula in 1934/35.* Publication No. 7. Stockholm: The Ethnographical Museum of Sweden.

López de Gómara, Francisco. 1965–66. *Historia general de las Indias.* 2 vols. Barcelona: Obras Maestras.

Lowe, Gareth W. 1989. "The Heartland Olmec: Evolution of Material Culture." In *Regional Perspectives on the Olmec*, edited by Robert J. Sharer and David C. Grove, 33–67. Cambridge: Cambridge University Press.

Luttwak, Edward. 1976. *The Grand Strategy of the Roman Empire.* Baltimore, Md.: Johns Hopkins University Press.

Mann, Michael. 1987. *The Sources of Social Power.* Vol. 1, *A History of Power from the Beginning to A.D. 1760.* Cambridge: Cambridge University Press.

Mendieta, Gerónimo de. 1971. *Historia eclesiástica indiana.* Mexico City: Editorial Porrúa.

Miller, Arthur G. 1973. *The Mural Painting of Teotihuacán.* Washington, D.C.: Dumbarton Oaks.

Nickel, Helmut. N.d. "A Note on the *Macquauitl*." Manuscript, Metropolitan Museum of Art, New York.

Nuttall, Zelia. 1891. "On Ancient Mexican Shields." *Internationales Archiv für Ethnographie* 5, 34–53.

Paddock, John. 1983. "The Rise of the Ñuiñe Centers in the Mixteca Baja." In *The Cloud People: Divergent Evolution of the Zapotec and Mixtec Civilization*, edited by Kent V. Flannery and Joyce Marcus, 208–11. New York: Academic Press.

Pasztory, Esther. 1983. *Aztec Art.* New York: Harry N. Abrams.

———. 1988. "Small Birds with Shields and Spears and Other Fragments." In *Feathered Serpents and Flowering Trees: Reconstructing the Murals of Teotihuacan*, edited by Kathleen Berrin, 169–83. San Francisco: Fine Arts Museums of San Francisco.

Raudzens, George. 1990. "War-Winning Weapons: The Measurement of Technological Determinism in Military History." *Journal of Military History* 54, 403–33.

Ruiz de Alarcón, Hernando. 1984. *Treatise on the Heathen Superstitions That Today Live among the Indians Native to This New Spain, 1629.* Translated by J. Richard Andrews and Ross Hassig. Norman: University of Oklahoma Press.

Sahagún, Bernardino de. 1950–82. *General History of the Things of New Spain: Florentine Codex.* Translated by Arthur J. O. Anderson and Charles E. Dibble. 13 vols. Salt Lake City: University of Utah Press.

———. 1977. *Historia general de las cosas de Nueva España.* Translated by Angel María Garibay. 4 vols. Mexico City: Editorial Porrúa.

Sanders, William T. 1972. "Population, Agricultural History, and Societal Evolution in Mesoamerica." In *Population Growth: Anthropological Implications,* edited by Brian Spooner, 101–53. Cambridge, Mass.: MIT Press.

Seler, Eduard. 1960. *Gesammelte Abhandlungen zur amerikanischen Sprach- und Altertumskunde.* 5 vols. Graz, Austria: Akademische Druck- und Verlagsanstalt.

Stirling, Matthew W. 1943. *Stone Monuments of Southern Mexico.* Bureau of American Ethnology, Bulletin 138. Washington, D.C.: United States Government Printing Office.

Tapia, Andrés de. 1950. "Relación de Andrés de Tapia." In *Cronicas de la conquista de México,* edited by Agustín Yáñez, 41–96. Mexico City: Ediciones de la Universidad Nacional Autónoma.

Torquemada, Juan de. 1975–83. *Monarquía indiana.* 7 vols. Mexico City: Universidad Nacional Autónoma de México.

Velázquez, Primo Feliciano, trans. 1975. *Códice Chimalpopoca: Anales de Cuauhtitlán y leyenda de los soles.* 2d ed. Mexico City: Universidad Nacional Autónoma de México.

A Paradigm for the Study
of War and Society

R. BRIAN FERGUSON

Introduction

If most studies of war focus too exclusively on campaign and combat, anthropology tilts in the other direction. Anthropology focuses on the cultural connections of war more than its actual practice, which makes the discipline particularly relevant for this volume. Anthropology's distinctive contribution for understanding war derives from the twin disciplinary pillars of holism and cross-cultural comparison. All aspects of life fit together into sociocultural systems. Contours of pattern integration are relatively clear in the smaller, less complex societies anthropologists typically study, especially if seen in comparison to each other. Because of the scale of the societies considered in this volume and the enormous literature about each, holistic synthesis and comparison are difficult to imagine or attempt. This chapter is an application to the cases presented in this volume of a holistic model of the sociocultural ramifications of war developed through the cross-cultural study of stateless peoples. Not a theory but a framework for theory, it might best be called a paradigm.

This general model or paradigm has been developed in other publications.[1] It categorizes sociocultural phenomena into infrastructure, structure, and superstructure, which are conceptualized together as a complex hierarchy of progressively more limiting constraints. Somewhat simplified, infrastructure is a broad conjuncture of variables involving interaction with the physical environment, population characteristics and trends, technology, and the labor techniques of applying technology, which affect a people's physical existence and relation to nature. Structure consists of organized social life, patterns of interpersonal connections and divisions sorted into social organization, economics, and politics. Superstructure includes the mental constructs of culture, its belief systems, and patterned emotional dispositions. Each level is hugely complex, and each is equally important for human existence. But they relate to different aspects of the culture of war and can provide answers to different sorts of questions.

As an analytical tool, the paradigm shows how to combine different approaches dealing with different topical questions, with both causes and effects of war, with different time frames and levels of analysis, and with both system and process. It may seem like a catalogue of war-society connections, but one with coherence and a theoretical structure that is capable of generating contrasting hypotheses. It provides a common framework usable for cross-cultural comparison, or for wide-ranging investigation of war-society connections in one case. Prior to this essay, however, generalizations had been derived almost entirely from research into non-state societies, with simple states as the end point in the range. This chapter is a test of the paradigm's applicability to war and society in the ancient and medieval world. Regarding the case material presented here, does it apply, and does it help make sense of the bewildering rush of histories that have preceded?

The paradigm as presented here departs from earlier presentations. Previous discussions were couched in terms of relationships between war and society, although "intersocietal" interactions were also discussed (Ferguson 1984a.54). I would now argue that, in developing a holistic perspective on war, it is useful to distinguish explicit relations between war and sociocultural systems—or "society"—that occur *within* polities (war-making units) from those that occur *among* polities. This distinction opens up new areas for investigation and makes the paradigm potentially applicable to "international relations" approaches, while drawing attention to the internal-external dialectics that so frequently dominate war politics.

The plan of this presentation is to discuss the interconnections of war and society first within polities, going from infrastructure through structure to superstructure, then to do the same as those interconnections apply to inter- or transpolity relations. Ethnographic citations are of single exemplary cases. As each point is made, I will present applicable information from this volume (parenthetical references by name without year thus concern chapters in this volume). The fit is variable. In some cases, anthropological theory is more extensive and suggests areas where historical research might be pursued. In the other direction, several issues in this volume suggest extension of the paradigm beyond where tribal peoples could take it. The conclusion is a unified summary of points from both parts as they apply to the cases in this volume.

Sociocultural Ramifications of War within Polities

Intrapolity Infrastructure

The broad characteristics of physical existence, the practicalities of survival and reproduction in a real world—ever changing but at any moment inescapable—say much about major differences in war from one society to another. That point is illustrated again and again in this volume. Subsistence practice, the way food is extracted from nature, is intertwined with broad features of violent conflict. Hunters can and do use their weapons and skills to hunt men. Although small bands of hunter-gatherers may be least likely to make war (Knauft 1991. 402–3), as illustrated dramatically in the contrast of foraging and agricultural Japan (Farris 49–50), hunting techniques could be called a preadaptation to war (Shang kings sent their soldiers to hunt [Yates 14]). Nomadic pastoralists can strike at distances and are hard to attack, and livestock gives them a built-in incentive for raiding. Empire builders from Shang China (Yates 28, 33) to Imperial Rome (Campbell 219) and Byzantium (Haldon 260) have recognized the value of such life experience, employing archers and riders from their peripheral regions in specialized units. Where peasant farmers make up armies, even farm implements can become weapons (Yates 10).

In the New Guinea highlands, where "pigs are our hearts," pig husbandry permeates the processes of war—thefts and garden damage generate conflicts and grudges, exchanges and debts of pigs knit together allies, the size of herds affects timing of war and return to peace, and so forth (Rappaport 1968. 153–223). When gardening must be nutritionally supplemented by game, as in interriverine Amazonia, extensive uninhabited hunting ranges between villages encourage sneak attacks and ambushes (Ferguson 1995b.46–49), in contrast to the open field fighting that dominates in the more densely settled Grand Valley of New Guinea (Heider 1979.109–12). The productivity of agriculture and its frequent assignment as women's work may free men for extended military operations, sentry duties, and role specialization as warriors, as in the American Southwest (Kroeber and Fontana 1986.169–74). Where men tend the fields, there may be alternating seasonality of cultivation and wars (Trelease 1997.74–76), although neighbors can fight between farming (Meggitt 1977.207).

Seasonality of combat seems more general and pronounced with state armies of cultivators, as with the Aztecs (Hassig 380), in tenth-century Japan (Farris 59), Macedonia (Hamilton 171), and Rome (Rosenstein 201–202). In Sparta, the freeing of hoplites to be full-time warriors after the enslavement of the Messenians was a critical shift, as was the institution of pay for military service in Macedonia and Rome (see also Saggs 1963.146–47). Such moves gave rise to specialized soldier armies, the necessary basis of many technological and organizational developments discussed in this volume. By Hellenistic times, large numbers of men were detached from any means of support except their arms (Hamilton 180–182). Arab soldiers of the conquest period were actually forbidden to engage in agriculture (Crone 313). The intensified and extended production systems of expanding empires are able to generate food surpluses capable of supporting huge armies, reaching 150,000 tons of wheat annually in the second-century Roman Empire (Campbell 224). (The cost of supplying grain was a critical factor affecting the limits of Roman expansion in England [Goldberg and Findlow 1984.374].) As the days of empire waned in medieval western Europe, soldiers went back to being farmers as well, and military aims became much more local (Bachrach 271–280, 285, 291). Thus the organization and capabilities of a military force are closely linked to the societal system of provisioning, in states no less than tribes, but in states an important watershed is passed when soldiers are removed from food production during their time of active duty.

State armies are connected to farming in another way. In Old and Middle Kingdom Egypt, armies were regularly applied to productive labor, including agriculture (Gnirs 78, 81). In China from Shang to late Han, men were called into the army via the same system that drafted men and women for corvée labor (Yates 13, 25). Similar overlap of military and labor drafts are reported for African states, notably the Zulu—where regimented warriors and their female age-mates tended the fields and herds of their king (Guy 1981.40–44)—and elsewhere in the ancient Middle East such as the Assyrian empire (Postgate 1974.226–27). This overlap certainly merits further study, which might ask the question, is it only soldier–food producers who are regularly drafted for mass labor, or do professional soldiers get put to such work too?

In terms of the objectives, tribal wars may be generated by some critical scarcity of subsistence resources, although not as commonly as might be imagined. Scarcity of game animals was argued to be the cause of wars in Amazonia (Harris 1974.100–105), but while specific postulates of that theory have been confirmed, it does not seem capable of explaining war (Ferguson 1989c). Land scarcity was postulated as a major impulse to war among slash-and-burn agriculturalists (Vayda 1961), but this has been seriously challenged (King 1976). Yes, some wars are fought to gain garden land (Brookfield and Brown 1963), especially in situations of extremely restricted availability (Kirch 1997. 33), but in overt form they are unusual (Billman 1997; Sillitoe 1977). Land becomes a more inviting target as production systems develop and invest more labor in it (Wolf 1987.136), especially when political structures are evolved enough to incorporate the bounty of land and its tillers into tribute or tax (Reyna 1994a.49–50). In tightly circumscribed areas such as islands, however, even simple chiefdoms may be separated by clear-cut boundaries, which are defended by force (Bonnemaison 1994.30, 35–36).

When physical space is at issue in war by noncentralized polities, it often involves more concentrated and critical resources than cropland. Competition for limited water sources in arid environments may be the root of collective violence among some simple hunter-gatherers in ancient southern California and northern Australia (Lambert 1997.100–102; Tacon and Chippindale 1994.225–27). Sharp local concentrations of particularly valuable resources, such as mouths of salmon streams with rich marine zones and ample stored food on the Pacific Northwest coast, can invite raids generation after generation (Ferguson 1984b.312). But access to materials such as gems and metal ores is typically dealt with through trade rather than war, even in advanced chiefdoms (Gunawardana 1992.62–63).

In the societies discussed here, acquisition of resource territory is important in various ways. Capture of sources of raw material is noted as a persistent goal only in Egypt's efforts toward gold mines and quarries (Gnirs 77, 84), but Athenians were constantly embroiled in war to control mines and timber in Thrace (Raaflaub, 142–143 and personal communication), and no doubt similar things happened elsewhere. Scarce, precious farmland was contested in ancient Greece, where hoplites "fought on their land for their land" (Raaflaub 134, 137). Shang armies were sent to capture and prepare farm fields (Yates 14). In Romano-German times, the goal of war was to seize control of producing agricultural systems (Bachrach 289). Rewards of farmland were used as an incentive to motivate soldiers in New Kingdom Egypt (Gnirs 87), Republican Rome (Rosenstein 198), Carolingian western Europe (Bachrach 287), and for Japanese samurai (if they could keep hold of it, Farris 62–63)—although if this was itself the reason behind the war, it is only after land availability was filtered through stratification systems.

Having title to land sometimes was linked to an inherited duty of military service (Bachrach 285–286; Haldon 260; Raaflaub 137; Rosenstein 207). The creation of farming military colonies, for strategic defense and to produce a base of recruits, is reported for Egypt from the late second millennium B.C. (Gnirs 90), Seleucid Syria (Hamilton 179), and Rome from the late Republic onward (Campbell 226). A new dimension regarding land is added by the territorial character of states. Among early Greek poleis, constant jostling over land led to development of distinct borders, which of course became subject to military adjudication (Raaflaub 134), as also occurred among Mesoamerican city-states (Hassig 365). With territorial states, such as Egypt, border defense is a primary task of the army (Gnirs 78, 81). All this considered, the war of ancient and medieval states seems much more territorial than that of non-state peoples.

In some situations it is not land or other resources that are scarce, but people (Price 1984.222–23). In Native North America, people were captured to be laborers or marriage partners, or to replace losses (Starna and Watkins 1991).

The history of colonial Ibero-America is a history of forcibly appropriated indigenous labor, and the Atlantic slave trade comes unpleasantly to mind. Outside the European tradition, the nineteenth-century Sulu Sultanate of the Philippines was built on slave labor (Warren 1982). In cases presented here, the capture of large numbers of slaves was common around the eastern Mediterranean. Sparta rose to prominence on the backs of slaves (Raaflaub 137), and the reign of the Abbasids depended on a constant supply of enslaved tribesmen-warriors from their periphery (Crone 319–320). Japan stands out for the extent of violence used to make peasants work the land, probably because epidemics and other disasters led to a series of population crashes from the eighth to the eleventh century (Farris 53, 56–57, 60–63). Old Kingdom Egypt (Gnirs 77–78) and others relocated defeated populations where they would be more useful (Dalley 1995.419). Also worth noting is the fact that Hittites counted as booty the skilled craftsmen of defeated cities (Goetze 1963.129). Thus in both land and people, ancient and medieval states used war to obtain vital resources.

Population numbers determine the maximum size of armed forces. In non-state situations, full mobilization of autonomous groups and their allies may still produce forces that number only dozens (Ferguson 1995b.48), although armies of a thousand or more can be fielded by large confederacies (Otterbein 1979.146). Small numbers limit the tactics that may be employed (Keeley 1996.42). Cross-cultural statistics show that increasing scale of polities correlates with more sophisticated military practices (Otterbein 1985.75). Here, scale is more grand, with armies starting at several thousand and reaching hundreds of thousands. Advantages of scale are still apparent in the contrast of major imperial centers and local polities. Mesoamerican imperialists and especially the Aztecs created professional armies including a variety of fighters well beyond what any individual city-state could muster (Hassig 367), and it was only the combination of poleis under Athens in the Delian League that provided the resources and manpower to support its famed navy (Raaflaub 142–145). Carolingian imperial expansion was based on its ability to martial overwhelming numbers (Bachrach 282), and the expanded field armies of ninth-century Byzantium revived specialized weapons and tactics dormant since the Arab conquests (Haldon 246).

A long-standing issue in anthropology is the impact of war on population. Theory from the 1960s and 1970s posited that war was an adaptive mechanism, slowing population growth and redistributing people for a sustainable balance with nature. Further consideration called these relationships into question and noted maladaptive effects of war, including forced nucleations, large danger zones that cannot be exploited, and occasionally the breakdown of social structures which contributed to collective provisioning (Ferguson 1989b). Similarly, Adams asserts that the entire history of Mesopotamia demonstrates that military danger leads to nucleation and military security to dispersion of people to farmland (Adams 1981.88). In terms of direct casualties, tribal warfare, where all adult males are mobilized, can produce a very high death rate, exceeding 25 percent of adult males in a number of recently investigated cases. Usually, these add up over time from few individuals lost in any engagement, although slaughter is not rare (Keeley 1996.83–97).

On the impact of war on population, only a few points appear in this book, and as in non-state situations, these suggest mixed effects. No information is provided on casualties as percentage of population, but the report that Chinese Warring States general Bai Qi executed four hundred thousand prisoners (Yates n.97) suggests they could be a major demographic factor. War led to the devastation and abandonment of many cities in Asia Minor after A.D. 640 (Haldon 247) and played a major role in the demographic collapse of some Maya regions after A.D. 700 (Webster 353–354). More indirectly, war may have a negative demographic impact by reducing agricultural production. Under Masakado, Japanese armies practiced a scorched-earth policy against their noble enemies' peasant foot soldiers, which may have contributed to population decline (Farris 59), and a weakened Byzantine Empire fell back on scorched earth as a self-destructive form of defense (Haldon 245). Roman imperial expansion sent up to a fifth of the adult population away for years, although the impact of this back home is debated (Rosenstein 206–208). On the other hand, the Great King of Persia strongly encouraged a high birth rate to produce more soldiers (Briant 109–110). The presence of Imperial Roman armies stimulated agriculture in a region (Campbell 224), and in medieval western Europe the army was used to expand cultivation, and destruction of crops was diligently avoided (Bachrach 287, 289).

Turning to the material technology of war, fortification is in a class by itself. Fortifications are common among non-state peoples (Keeley 1996.55–58), and siege, although unusual, is not unknown (Vayda 1960.76–80). There are interesting variations on fortifications described here. In Mesoamerica, fortifications may be more common than once thought (Hassig 378; Webster 344), but they are surprisingly limited by Old World standards. Middle Kingdom Egypt, in contrast, had "a dense network of forts" across its southern frontier (Gnirs 81; cf. Lawrence 1965). In China, walls appear around villages in the Neolithic, develop as fortifications through the early Bronze Age, and seem proof against rudimentary siege techniques through the Eastern Zhou (Yates 10, 19, 26). The later Roman Empire saw an intensification of fort building as part of a defense-in-depth strategy (Campbell 234). Romano-German polities continued this trend, building more and better forts, using engineering that they were unlikely to have developed de novo. The presence of these massive structures was the central reality of all the combat that swirled around them, and the walls necessitated development of the massive logistical systems of siege warfare (Bachrach

276–278, 283, 289–291). Perhaps the relative absence of fortifications in Meso-america is related to the fact that even Imperial armies did not have the logistical resources to stick around more than a few days. Or perhaps the spread of walls in the Old World was a reaction to the development of pastoralist raiding (O'Connell 1989).

Weapons technology is both a major determinant of military practice and an expression of overall level of technological development (O'Connell 1989), as is well illustrated by the engineering of siege warfare (Bachrach 290). Although tribal peoples, as noted earlier, may use everyday tools to kill, development of specialized weapons and armor occurs even with relatively simple technologies (Keeley 1996.49–53). Development of technology goes in tandem with changes in combat practices, as visible in the shortening of the Zulu spear to make it work for close fighting infantry (Morris 1965.47). In anthropology, the main illustration of the interaction of weapons and the labor of combat concerns the introduction of guns, which from the early years of European colonialism have transformed the practice of war by indigenous peoples (Ferguson and Whitehead 1992a.20). The varying trajectories of military development on Africa's west coast during the slave trade makes the important point that one weapon can be integrated into very different military structures, to very different effect (Law 1992.104–5).

Changing weapons systems, and the interaction of technology, combat practice, and military organization are prominent themes in these chapters. Japan from the late third through fifth centuries illustrates the evolution of weapons and armor beyond what non-state peoples could attain (Farris 49–50), as illustrated by comparison with the peoples of the Pacific Northwest (Gunther 1972). The long history of Chinese warfare illustrates technological innovation, borrowings and continuities, differentiation of elite and mass arms, the significance of overall technological level as with metallurgy, and the greater importance of troop preparation over sheer technology by itself (Yates 10, 13–14, 18–19, 28–29). The panoply of the Greek hoplite exemplifies the interaction of technological changes with changes in formation and tactics (Raaflaub 132–134). Philip of Macedon equipped the hoplite phalanx with the extraordinarily long sarissa, which, with intensive training and drill, allowed his armies to best more conventionally armed foes (Hamilton 168–170). But the dominance of this system ended when they encountered Roman soldiers armed with short swords, organized into flexible manipular units that could take advantage of broken terrain (Hamilton 184; Rosenstein 202–203). The technological development most extensively discussed here is the Greek trireme, a marvel that required a large and intensively trained crew. The enormous expense of maintaining a fleet of triremes led to intensified efforts to extract revenue within and outside the Delian League, to structural changes and a continuous hegemonic thrust (Raaflaub 142–144).

One obvious but important point is that, with rare exceptions, combat is men's work (Adams 1983). On the gender division of labor in tribal societies, some anthropologists argue that it is tasks that require greater strength and stamina that go to men, others that it is tasks that are incompatible with pregnancy and child rearing. Either way, men get war (Kelekna 1994). Beyond that role foundation, war-making must be made to fit with the other activities of males, and it involves specialized training from an early age (Briant 108, 113–114; Meggitt 1977.61–64), as well as inculcation of appropriate emotional dispositions (Koch 1974b.166). Thus readiness for war may become a central component of male identity and gender relations (Divale and Harris 1976). There are only male warriors in this book, with very few exceptions (Yates 13). Although not discussed here (Cartledge 1981), the interaction of military roles and gender relations is surely an important aspect of society in all cases. A hint of the possible ramifications is the suggestion that late Roman law prohibited inheritance of land by women as a measure to ensure a supply of landed soldiers (Bachrach 286).

Intrapolity Structure

Institutionalized patterns of personal interaction guide the processes that lead up to and through war, and account for much of military variations during normal historical times. Structure can be divided into social organization, economics, and politics, and each will be considered in turn.

Internal Social Organization   Social organization—also called social structure—is broadly equated with kinship in tribal societies; it includes socially defined categories of people and patterned relationships between them. It determines what kind of groupings can become friends or enemies, and how men can be marshaled and sent to fight. Marriage is often discussed in relation to war, although relationships are complicated. Within groups, marriage is a basis for solidarity and cooperation among men—except when marriage is a source of conflict (Brown 1978.167). Postmarital residence has major implications. Virilocality, where men remain at home with fathers, brothers, and uncles, thus creating "fraternal interest groups," is strongly associated with local violence (Otterbein 1977). Uxorilocality, where men move into their wives' homes and work with other in-married men there, can create crosscutting ties that reduce local violence, but encourage a broader solidarity good for war over longer distances (Murphy 1957).

Unilineal descent groups provide another form of unification, again in complex variations. Patrilineality is sometimes associated with segmentary systems, where higher levels of organization can come together against collective enemies, to later revert back into autonomous local polities (Sahlins 1961). Matrilineality seems able to join together more permanent tribal unions, such as the Iroquois (Abler 1992.152). Other structural features, such as non-kin sodalities, age grades, and men's houses, also affect what collectivities of males can be brought together in war parties (Fukui and Turton 1979.5; Maybury-Lewis 1974.306). But it should not be imagined that recruitment follows mechanically along structural lines. Typically, war leaders use all their skills to enlarge their personal following (Langness 1973.308–14). War can have a major effect on social organization, and in one view, fraternal interest groups are the product of local conflict (Ember and Ember 1971). Protracted, intensive war can destroy the complex social structures linking extended networks of peoples (Whitehead 1992.133–39).

In classical theory, states leave kinship behind as class emerges as the main frame of social organization. All the developed social systems described here are stratified, although some only recently. The local elites of the Classic Maya (Webster 340), Shang China (Yates 11), and Fourth Dynasty Egypt (Gnirs 76) were distinctly set apart from the commoners below. By the mid–fifth century B.C. Roman patricians had become a virtual caste (Rosenstein 199). The emergence of stratification has a clear spatial dimension. For the Maya (Webster 335) and Shang (Yates 11), the first population centers that appear, some centuries after the advent of agriculture, were the grandiose homes of the local noble and his retainers, surrounded by his cultivators. This urban social dominance is still apparent after Western Rome fell apart (Bachrach 274–275).

Stratification, however, does not mean that kinship loses all military significance. Among elites, intermarriage is a frequent basis of solidarity and alliance (Webster 340; Yates 16, 31). Descent also continues to play a major role. The early Egyptian state was run by the king's clan (Gnirs 76). Among Shang (Yates 11) and Maya, rule was passed by patrilineal inheritance. In the latter case, cadet lineages branched off to start new centers, and succession disputes, which conferred control over people and resources, may have been a primary reason for war (Webster 340–341, 351–352). An important factor in the development of the Carolingian empire was that there was for a century only one legitimate claimant to rule (Bachrach 279, 281). In developed empires such as the patrilineal Aztecs (Hassig 370–371) and Persians (Briant 113), inherited claims to rule were still crucial but were ratified or overturned by martial prowess. (The ambilineal inheritance of leadership among Japanese [Farris 49] would provide great flexibility, and may be connected to the sometimes difficult demographic situation noted earlier.)

Local social organization continues to play a role in state military mobilizations. Lineage organization is the military order in incipient states (Mair 1977.129–30), and is still apparent here in Maya (Webster 348) and Shang armies. By China's Springs and Autumns periods some thousand years later, the lineage middleman had been eliminated, and the draft was bureaucratized down to five-family units, with local men kept together as soldiers (Yates 13,

23–24). Doubtless they brought along a lot of back-home social relations—kinship and everything else. The same is certainly true of Greek hoplites, and probably so of geographically based Aztec units (Hassig 375). The Roman Republican army, in contrast, stands out as operating more along the lines of armies today, bringing together soldiers from all over but giving them a new and enduring social structure in army squadrons (Rosenstein 202–205). When Rome's western successor states were unable to sustain that form, their mobilization of local forces reflected (and probably reinforced) the complex social-institutional landscape of medieval society, with urban militias, church forces, slaves, landed estates, and so forth (Bachrach 275, 283–289).

Recognition of the continuing role of "civilian" social organization on military formations does not diminish the overwhelming importance of stratification. Stratification is associated with two tiers (at least) of soldiers, elite and mass. The splendid Maya warrior depicted in art may have done most of the fighting, but he was, we can infer, supported by his peasants (Webster 345). Shang kings had a few hundred elite, specially equipped *zhong* troops, and maybe three thousand *ren* from the general population (Yates 13). Japan (Farris 50–59) and Macedonia before Philip (Hamilton 168) both had elite mounted troops and a mass army that would flee at first trouble. Archaic Greeks, too, had a mounted elite and infantry, but *this* infantry would fight. The shifting balance between archaic "knights" and emergent hoplites is a crucial and controversial issue in the development of Greek democracy (Raaflaub 132–135). Both Macedonians and the Roman Republican army combined a mounted elite and farmer hoplites, with poorer citizens or landless mercenaries as light skirmishers (Hamilton 170; Rosenstein 197). As the empire declined in western Europe, a distinction of elite and mass troops was once again fundamental (Bachrach 275, 286–287). In ascendant Byzantium, the same distinction is evident, although within a more complex diversity of soldiers (Haldon 256–257). Striking for its absence in this volume is any mention of a revolt of the militarized masses against the elite (except perhaps in late Egyptian riots [Gnirs 90–91] and in the murky Maya collapse [Webster 353–354]). It may be that the integration of both strata in armies, with the clear superiority of elite forces, is one thing that kept the masses in line.

Military service worked against revolution in another sense. A striking commonality across these diverse cases is that war offered an avenue of social mobility for men (not women) from lower classes. In a variety of ways, the successful, surviving military man could affect a permanent, often inheritable, elevation of social and material position (Bachrach 287; Briant 109; Campbell 223; Crone 320, 322; Gnirs 79, 87; Haldon 255–258; Hamilton 170–171; Raaflaub, personal communication; Rosenstein 200; Yates 27). A major advantage of the Aztecs against simple city-states is that the latter had a severely limited ability to expand elevated positions, so their serious fighters were restricted to the existing elite (Hassig 372–373). Thus a stratification system itself can provide great motivation for fighters from lower strata, and, conversely, this upward mobility of able men would increase the stability of a stratification system. Beyond the elevation of soldiers, expanding military forces and campaigns underwrote and made necessary the development of a broad literate bureaucracy in New Kingdom Egypt (Gnirs 85), Han China (Yates 35), Carolingian western Europe (Bachrach 281, 290), and no doubt elsewhere. The war machine, then, is part and parcel of the class structure.

Armies are themselves formal institutions, which stand in defined relations to institutions of civil administration and organized religion. The variable interrelationships of these three institutional systems have been crucial determinants of social formations from the first civilizations (Scarre and Fagan 1997), with roots back to the differentiation of headman, shaman, and war leader. Cases here demonstrate both the variability and the social importance of this triadic balance. In Chinese history, the demands of armies fostered growth of governmental institutions that later became "civil-ized," with the military given a subordinate social position (Yates 9, 35). Japan saw the differentiation of a military and civil nobility, with the former kept from the highest decision-making posts (Farris 58). The Abbasids were military rulers of the state, but they left much of civil society to somewhat antimilitary clerics (Crone 322–323). In Sparta and Athens, the military and civilian rule were closely linked because soldier-citizens dominated government (Raaflaub 140–141, 144–148). In post-Roman western Europe, religious and civil institutions were distinct but coordinate, and both doubled as military administrations (Bachrach 274–275, 288–289). Byzantine and Egyptian cases, where sovereigns are closely identified with state religions, demonstrate complexities in changing relations between military and political institutions that are beyond the scope of capsule summary (Gnirs 76–82; Haldon 243, 255–261). Future studies of war and society may identify regularities in this triadic relationship, which is clearly a most important aspect of the social organization of states.

Internal Economics   To turn now from social organization to the economics of war within polities, anthropology has had little to say on the relationship of war to the circulation and distribution of goods and services. Still, the patterning of who provides and who receives what will necessarily shape the way that any scarcity is experienced by different categories of people in a society. Closely intertwined with social organization, economics creates specific interests associated with different social positions. In Amazonia, game scarcity is translated through social organization to emerge as hostility between men and women, and sometimes fighting between men over women (Siskind 1973)—although this rarely reaches the level of war (Ferguson 1989c). Economic structure can generate scarcities and demands beyond subsistence needs that lead to war. This becomes more significant with developing complexity (Ferguson 1990b.48–49), but has been argued for relatively egalitarian people, such as the demands of cattle bride price payments among the cattle-raiding Nuer (Kelly 1985.112–18). War can also affect economies. On the Pacific Northwest coast, lineage chiefs had to spur production, and commoners accept a rather centralized economy, because of the need to amass food and wealth to potlatch military allies (Ferguson 1983). Less dramatic feasting is often a prelude to war, which is one reason that Amazonian headmen often maintain larger gardens (Chagnon 1983.67).

Similarities are suggested here, although in similarly limited exposition. If land is an incentive for landless soldiers, as noted previously, it is because of unequal distribution of land rather than any absolute scarcity. In stratified societies, scarcities may not be experienced by elite decision makers directly, but in the form of political unrest, as Rosenstein (197–199) argues for the Roman expansion. Isocrates described a growing gap between rich and poor that generated a surfeit of landless mercenaries, and Alexander's thrust through Persia was stimulated by the need to focus these men elsewhere (Hamilton 181–182).

As for impact on the economy, the connection between chronic warmaking and the development of taxation has been identified as crucial in the rise of national states in western Europe (Tilly 1975) and is noted in a few cases here.[2] The cost of its trireme navy led to the development of Athens's system of public finance (Raaflaub 143), and tax changes associated with military developments are noted for Republican, Imperial, and Holy Rome (Rosenstein 202; Campbell 235; Bachrach 290). Tax collection and fighting wars over nonpayment are major responsibilities of the Japanese military in the eighth through eleventh centuries (Farris 57, 65). The enormous expenditures on the military under the Byzantines drove endless efforts to increase state revenue, generating resistance by local elites (Haldon 246–253). Support of the Mamluk institution and other soldiers for the Abbasids (Crone 320) certainly must have stimulated efforts to raise taxes. Beyond even taxation, imperial centers transformed the entire system of production and commerce around them to provide both material support for armies and a continuing supply of troops (Bachrach 277, 284–285, 290–291; Campbell 224–228; Haldon 248, 258–259; Hassig 371–372; Yates 26, 34). Such basic economic restructuring well illustrates the power of war.

Internal Politics   In contrast to economics, internal political dimensions of war are well studied in anthropology.[3] In relatively egalitarian societies, most men make up their own mind about participating in an attack, and leaders can only manipulate deliberations (Sillitoe 1978.253–54). (Women play varying but lesser roles in decision making, both public and "backstage" at all levels of complexity.

War is, after all, men's work.) More prominent leaders in non-state societies, such as big men and chiefs, often meeting in counsels, have considerable influence among their followers but are usually bound by consensus (Hulme and Whitehead 1992.124). All leadership will be tied to those aspects of social organization and economic circumstances that create groups to be led. Koch (1974a) emphasizes that it is the absence of authoritative third parties that enables dyadic conflicts to escalate into war—which is another way of saying that development of more expansive and cohesive polities cuts down on localized fighting (Cooney 1997).

The role of leadership increases in times of war. Even in relatively egalitarian societies, once war is on, leaders are given more latitude to "call the shots" (Chagnon 1974.162). Often considerable authority is handed over to more aggressive men (Kracke 1978.76–79) or recognized war chiefs (Moore 1990.323–24). In situations of endemic conflict, war leaders may act arbitrarily, even despotically (Feil 1987.103–11). Leaders during war must carefully evaluate and navigate a course balancing internal factional alignments and oppositions with external alliances and conflicts (Ferguson 1995b.295–305). Critical matters of internal and external support are bound up with specific individuals, and may die with them. For all these reasons, a common tactic is to target the enemy leader because his death will disrupt and immobilize his forces (Chagnon 1983.179). But if leaders take special risks in war, they also get special benefits. New Guinea big men, although tightly bound by demands of public consensus, consider the ramifications of war for themselves and use all their influence to promote self-beneficial courses of action (Sillitoe 1978, 253–54). Success in war can often be an avenue to wealth, status, and influence (Brown 1978.197), and so we see the emergence of military entrepreneurs. Although simple war leaders' influence typically recedes with the restoration of peace, self-aggrandizing men may stir up trouble to generate continuing support and use periods of war to modify political structures to their own lasting benefit (Kracke 1978.77–80).

Thus war can act as an evolutionary ratchet, a factor that, in combination with all others, promotes incremental elaboration of centralization and hierarchy (Ferguson 1994.102). With the development of chiefly hierarchies comes the possibility of violent conflict over succession to high-status offices (Ferdon 1981.255). With incipient states, internal political determination of military policy reaches new heights (Cohen 1984.344–51). Rulers may even send an ambitious rising star off to a battle likely to prove fatal, as Saul did with David against the Philistines (*Old Testament, Samuel* 18: 20–29). With development of tribute, prominent even in some tribes and chiefdoms (Pershits 1979), leaders may require successful wars just to remain in power (Wolf 1987.141–44).

Cases collected here show great variation in centralization of decision making. Early Maya may have retained elements of the vertical integration of pre-state days, but this appears to be a vestigial check, if that, on the rule of elites (Webster 348). Homeric groups may have been chiefdoms, where the mixture of hierarchy and consensus in decision making is normal (Raaflaub 129, 139). What is remarkable, of course, is the development of democracy in classical times, through which decisions on war were made by those who would go to fight—although that may not have seemed so wonderful to the slaves. The conquering Muslim armies began as relatively egalitarian tribal forces, but within half a century rule by a consensus of chiefs gave way to centralized coercive rule over a demilitarized population (Crone 313–314, 316–317). Before Philip II, the command of Macedonian kings was tempered by close noble "companions." Alexander's rolling conquests—over lands previously assembled into an empire by Cyrus (Briant 105)—demonstrate the degree to which decision-making power could concentrate in one charismatic leader, although even Alexander's officers would not follow him into India (Hamilton 167, 173). Major imperial expansions typically are associated with powerful individual rulers (Sinopoli 1994.163), yet the "routine" autocrats of Imperial Rome generally eschewed grand adventures for more conservative military policies (Campbell 218, 229–230).

External military affairs have a major impact on the internal political position of military leaders. War enabled Egyptian military men to advance in position and esteem, as individuals and as a class (Gnirs 79, 85–86, 90–91). Ambitious men of Achaemenid Persia and Rome went to war to elevate their political status (Briant 115–116; Rosenstein 200, 205, 210). A major cause of Maya war was the rivalry of different contenders to the high positions that gave control over land and labor (Webster 350–352). The Roman emperor Claudius invaded Britain to prop himself up at home, and Severus attacked Parthia to restore unity after the civil war that brought him to power (Campbell 229–230). Conversely, an external defeat could fuel internal political divisions, as in the political scheming of the Aztec court (Hassig 372–374) or the factional fighting of Byzantium (Haldon 246). The threat of far-flung enemies enabled Athens's leaders to convert the Delian League from a voluntary confederacy to a centrally controlled empire (Raaflaub 131–132, 144–145). Lord Shang used a permanent state of war to destroy his rivals and establish an empire (Yates 26–27). Political stability within Ramesside Egypt depended on continuing military victories over its neighbors (Gnirs 88–90), and Aztec kings would not last long without constant infusions of tribute (Hassig 373). On the other hand, it was the critical military participation of archaic Greek citizens that made possible the institutionalization of egalitarian structures (Raaflaub 140).

Interpolity or external dimensions of war will be discussed later in this chapter. But as the previous paragraphs suggest, there is a complex dialectic between internal and external politics in war. Moreover, internal and external become relative terms within nested arenas of political organization, from local community to political universe, each with its own relationships and rules. Political interests in any situation reflect this vertical integration, as well as more obvious horizontal, interpolity relations. Conflict can lead to either fusion or fission of polities along a variety of social organizational lines, making internal into external or vice versa. Sovereignty—a major element in political ideologies, especially of states—may be qualified, contingent, and contested, within networks of political relationships.

Other aspects of war-society connections have not been well explored in anthropology because they are more particular to state-level polities. Three aspects of state-level military force can be noted. A hallmark of a state is the ability to compel men to fight, even on pain of death. States are also distinctive in the ability to suppress independent military initiatives by local forces—although the state's monopoly on legitimate force may be more complete in ideology than in practice. Finally, state armies often act as highly coercive internal police.

The state's ability to compel men to fight is taken for granted here. Governments in Warring States China combined detailed population records and harsh punishments in a system that called on all men from age sixteen to sixty (Yates 25). Japanese district magistrates used wide powers to compel peasants to serve in armies from the eighth century into the more centralized Masakado period (Farris 54–56, 59). Although Egypt relied heavily on Nubian troops, mass recruitment was also practiced, and frequent desertion was countered with devastation of deserters' families (Gnirs 87). Despite Persia's heavy valorization of the warrior life, it still used drastic measures against parents who tried to keep their sons out of the army (Briant 115). The Roman Empire and its Romano-German successors grappled with problems of mass mobilization (Campbell 235; Bachrach 281). Conference discussions touched on the Roman army's (rare) practice of decimation—killing one in ten of a cohort that did not fight effectively (Watson 1969.119). Whatever incentives were offered to soldiers, their very lives depended on military obedience, and this is one of the most significant differences between state and non-state societies.

On a polity's ability to suppress independent war-making by local strong men, again there is great variation. Homeric groups, in typical non-state fashion, could not suppress raids by ambitious individuals, and the fighting such men started could spread to involve entire groups, as in the Trojan War. Later poleis suppressed private wars only with great difficulty (Raaflaub 131, 134, personal communication). Muslim rulers did not claim a monopoly on violence, and their subjects often resorted to arms in their own interests (Crone 326–327). Egyptian pharaohs claimed sole prerogative to use violence, but control collapsed in intermediate periods, and was hard won back (Gnirs 78, 83, 85). The Western Zhou king claimed the exclusive right to raise an army, but many local elites did so anyway.

Later Han imperialists eliminated local military powers, only to lose control again later (Yates 23, 31, 34). In Japan after 791, the Chinese-style state attempted to centralize military control, but it could not sustain the costs and reverted to more localized forces (Farris 53–54). The government of the early Roman Empire had a true monopoly on force, with independent local powers eliminated (Campbell 221). Byzantine and Romano-German successors of the western Roman Empire both saw localization of forces followed by recentralization (Haldon 244, 250–254; Bachrach 274–275, 279–280, 283–285, 291–292). One of the central historical dynamics throughout the chapters of this book is the changing balance between central and local control of war-making, a tension that may be related to declining marginal returns for investment with increasing complexity (Tainter 1988).

It is often assumed, without much discussion, that ancient armies also served as internal police. Again, structural variations appear here. The Spartan hoplite assembly developed in response to the existential threat posed by so many slaves (Raaflaub 139). Japanese military were used to keep the peasants working in fear and prevent their flight (Farris 55–59). Ramesside army units were posted at important civil institutions to maintain order and suppress riots (Gnirs 90). Arab regional armies became local gendarmes, and the central army shifted attention from conquest to maintenance of internal order (Crone 318). The Imperial Roman Army had urban police units, and its garrisons rested heavily on occupied lands (Campbell 219, 228; Nippel 1995). In the early Middle Ages, elite-led rural forces defended not only against barbarian invaders but also against local brigands (Bachrach 284; Haldon 251–252). (Perhaps an internal policing role is part of the answer to the question why post-Roman states maintained seemingly inefficient mounted soldiers [Bachrach 292–294].) Warring States China may have had the most elaborate system of militarized policing, with the administrative structure used to draft soldiers and corvée laborers, also operating as a structure for compulsory self-policing (Yates 28). Much work needs to be done on internal policing by armies.[4]

Intrapolity Superstructure

If infrastructure encompasses physical existence, and structure the social order, superstructure deals with the mental world, with cultural psychology. Probably more anthropological attention has gone to this area than to any other in the study of war, from early works that regularly explained war as an expression of cultural values (Turney-High 1971.141–68), to very current hermeneutic studies that detail the local logics of war (Viveiros de Castro 1992)—which is why the two other anthropologists in this volume take pains to dispute ritual-religious explanations of war (Hassig 367–370; Webster 349–350).[5] Compared with anthropology, superstructural variables receive little attention in the papers collected here. The references that do occur, however, suggest strong

parallels to findings from non-state peoples, in terms of the inculcation of martial values, the development of justifying political ideologies, and the harness-
ing of spiritual beliefs to the idol of war.

Ethnographically, it is frequently although far from universally reported
that chronic warfare is accompanied by belligerent, aggressive male personali-
ties (Koch 1974b.166), although the hottest heads are oftentimes excluded from
actual decisions to fight (Fadiman 1976.23–24). Child-rearing patterns of close
association of boys with their mother, followed by a harsh switch to expectations of manliness, are correlated with an adult tendency toward violent "acting
out" (Ross 1986.444–49). Children may be trained directly in hostility, encouraged to give tit for tat (Chagnon 1983.114–15; Ember and Ember 1992),
although there are cases that combine a strict internal peaceability with extreme
external aggressiveness (Murphy 1957). Rites of passage link coming of age and
the assumption of warrior status (Fadiman 1982.63–75). Value systems will
conform to war, honoring the warrior and shaming those who will not fight
(Voget 1964). Social rewards of prestige, and even marriage partners, may flow
to the brave (Goldschmidt 1986.6–8). In many cultures, being a man means
going to war (Rosaldo 1983.144–46). As noted earlier, the addition of warrior
to the male role set has repercussions for gender relations[6] associated with ideologies of male supremacy and other male-centered values and institutions
(Divale and Harris 1976; Whiting 1965). It must be stressed, however, that gender relations among warring peoples vary considerably, linked to other factors,
such as the importance of intragender cooperation in critical labor (Ferguson
1988). The Iroquois, as warlike as they come, accorded substantial respect and
political power to women (Turney-High 1971.157).

In highly militarized medieval western Europe, military skills were taught in
rigid education "from the cradle" (Bachrach, personal communication). In
Warring States China, boys became men by donning a sword (Yates 29).
Achaemenid Persia started military education at age five, ritually marked the
passage to warrior status, and bestowed great honors on those who demonstrated bravery in battle (Briant 114–115). In archaic and classical Greece, the true
citizen was a farmer-soldier, with great emphasis on martial valor (Raaflaub
137). Sparta especially is famous for its extremely militarized child rearing (Nigel
1995). With military specialization, warrior classes develop an elaborate warrior
ethos, as in tenth-century Japan (Farris, personal communication). Writing provides an entirely new medium for valorization of war and warriors, as shown
here for Egypt (Gnirs 82, 84, 85–86). As written traditions evolve, they acquire
more complex perspectives, as in propagandist accounts reflecting Persian
dynastic struggles (Briant 113). War literatures become important sources of
information about military practice, as in the case of the Trojan war, and of
course become subject to all the inherent issues of textual interpretation.

What distinguishes murder from killing in war is that the latter is provided with social justification. Every polity at war has a pattern of beliefs that accomplishes this vital task. Beliefs involving witchcraft and revenge are often taken as hallmarks of savagery, but they can also be seen as expressions of extremely widespread psychological exercises that precede war, given form in beliefs that carry strong meanings and values (Ferguson 1992.223–25). They make killing moral, can be used to persuade others or oneself of the legitimacy of an attack, and bolster the resolve of men who face death. Witchcraft is invoked to blame others for problems afflicting a group, and the culprits are divined by specialists who invariably identify a source that is already known to be antagonistic, where bad blood already exists (Marwick 1970). Identified witches stand morally condemned, fit subjects for severe punishment or elimination. We all know that in war the enemy is often demonized—a witch accusation is a literal illustration of that principle. In a highly charged atmosphere, a public accusation of witchcraft may be tantamount to a declaration of war (Maybury-Lewis 1974.185).

Revenge is invoked to do two things. First, it means "they started it"—in one way or another the intended victims of an attack brought it on themselves. Second, it taps into emotional responses inculcated from childhood on. But revenge motivation is not the driving force it is often portrayed to be. Revenge-taking is rarely, if ever, automatic. When a true retaliatory strike occurs, it is most often for appreciable tactical reasons. Otherwise, reasons for revenge are constructed, overlooked, raised, dropped, or negotiated out of existence as circumstances dictate—yet every raid that does occur will somehow be justified as revenge. Taken all together, these "primitive" constructs provide a neat system for translating systemic pressures into personal motivations, for providing moral justification for the very antisocial activity of war, and powerful symbols for focusing and mobilizing opinion.[7] Beyond that, among warring people, the largest conceptual schema accommodates and encourages conflict. History and myth—often indistinguishable—project war through the immediate political past all the way to the dawn of humanity. Worldviews make war seem inherent in life (Ferguson 1992.224). Recent hermeneutic studies provide finely textured insights into how thoroughly war is woven through spiritual and cosmological beliefs (Viveiros de Castro 1992)—and vice versa (Lan 1985)—and the perceptions and dispositions those evoke. That is also true with ancient states such as the Inca (Bauer 1996).

In Egyptian political ideology, war was always seen as a response to enemy provocations (Gnirs 73–74). In Byzantium, it was important for the image of the state that it wreak punishment on outside troublemakers (Haldon 245). When Caesar led his army against Rome, setting off the civil war that ended in the empire, he claimed to be doing it in defense of the ancestral constitution of the Republic (Rosenstein 210). But to speak of political and moral justification for war in ancient and medieval states quickly leads us to organized religion.

It has long been understood that certain areas or aspects of human existence are strongly connected to religion: matters central to societal well-being, activities fraught with uncertainty and danger, problems in understanding pain, loss, and injustice. All apply dramatically to war, so it is entirely expectable that war should be drenched in religion, and that religion makes war right. Myth charters for war are reported here among Aztecs (Hassig 367–368) and Persians (Briant 114–115), and in Shinto beliefs (Farris 52). From Zhou to Qin China times, it was part of divine order for the state to make war, and conquest was legitimated by Heaven (Yates 12, 15, 30). Religions of Greece and Rome were thoroughly intertwined with war (Raaflaub, personal communication).

State ideologies often—not always—fuse military leadership, the sacred, and the right to rule. Ritually couched histories of war and corresponding dynastic claims were literally carved in stone by Mayan and other Mesoamerican elites (Webster 336–337). In the Egyptian cosmos, the king was divine, but legitimacy was demonstrated—in practice and in monumental art—by victory in war (Gnirs 76, 80, 83–84). Gods of Persia assigned the king the duty of protecting his subjects from outside enemies (Briant 111). The Yamato dynasty developed lineages that intertwined conquest and divinity (Farris 51), and Macedonian kings before Philip II were both war leaders and representatives to the gods (Hamilton 167–168). In late Western Rome and after, military leaders were representatives *of* god, and it is no surprise that a Christian just-war doctrine developed in a context of extraordinarily pervasive militarism (Bachrach 274–275). On the other hand, Hassig (368–369) sees religion as manipulated by Aztec elites and wonders how deeply these ideas penetrated in the general population. One might also question the depth of medieval Islamic commitment to holy war when it was waged by non-Muslims imported and converted for that purpose, and initiated by state officials who were often at odds with the clerics (Crone 322).

Religion goes right along into battle, although war is so thoroughly ritualized (Kennedy 1971.48) that it is sometimes hard to say what is religion (or magic) and what is not. Collective ceremonies precede, accompany, and follow war expeditions, both to bolster resolve and to mark off and so segregate violent ways from routine daily life (Chagnon 1983.181–86). The Shinto priests who traveled with invading forces fit in well with this pattern (Farris 51). Various supernatural means are used to foresee results—as with Greek oracles—and the spirits are usually quite canny. Shamans spy on the enemy and use their skills to weaken or confuse him (Turney-High 1971.109–110).[8] Something similar occurred in Old Kingdom Egypt (Gnirs 76). Shang armies were guided by consultation of oracle bones and accompanied by warring spirits. By the time of Confucius and Sun

Tzu, divination had faded before more practical considerations, but ancestral spirits still watched over expeditions (Yates 11, 14, 25). In some cultures, oaths of blood brotherhood are used to maintain alliances (Fadiman 1976.12–15). In Macedonia and early medieval western Europe, military men took oaths of loyalty to their sovereign (Hamilton 167; Bachrach 273, 289), as Tutmosis III took an oath to go in front of his army (Gnirs 85–86). War captives faced ritual sacrifice by Huron (Trigger 1987.73–75) as by Aztecs (Hassig 368–369) and Chinese (Yates n.97), not to mention the Assyrians (Saggs 1963.149–54). In many cultures, military success is thought to bring major spiritual benefits (Needham 1976). Certainly this has been so among Christians and Muslims.

This section has traced war and society connections within a polity from subsistence to divinity. It has attempted to establish that war is totally a product of its culture and that the existence of war is in turn a major factor shaping that culture. The next section makes a similar argument regarding the social space between war-making polities, which is anything but empty.

Interpolity Sociocultural Ramifications of War

Any polity exists within a broader field, interacting with other polities, each characterized by the manifold military connections outlined earlier in this chapter. Their juxtaposition gives character to this field. Dyadic relations between polities are the building blocks of a system that has its own emergent qualities, endemic warfare being a big one. Of course, what is intra- or inter- is not always clear, may vary by issue, and can rapidly shift as more extensive polities come and go. Nevertheless, it is useful to divide the two levels conceptually to focus attention on properties of larger systems, and to relate to various international relations approaches to war—although unlike much "realist" international relations theory (Levy n.d.), polities are not seen here as unitary, independent actors but as potentially divided congeries of people, dialectically interacting with the larger social system. Dimensions of systems will depend on the analyst's choice of analytic scale and time frame: from one defined locale to an expansive geographic region to a major hunk of the world system; from a point in time to a century to millennia.

Interpolity Infrastructure
Environmental variations pattern broad outlines of systemic conflict. Geographic circumscription (Carneiro 1970.733–36)—sharp ecological divides that restrict populations to one place—are important contributing factors to both war and political evolution. Fighting may involve clusters of peer polities (Tainter 1988.201; Price 1977), with equivalent subsistence systems (Morren 1984), or may include adversaries with different ecologies (Keeley 1996.132–36)—

although those may establish symbiotic relationships as well (Bamforth 1994.100). Groups with less secure provisions may raid those with better supplies (Cannon 1992.511–15); or relatively mobile groups from one niche may attack settled agriculturalists (Barfield 1994.164–66), a pattern that has been suggested as representing the origin of institutionalized warfare (O'Connell 1995.75).

The Nile Valley is a classic illustration of circumscription (Gnirs 73). Many cases in this volume illustrate peer-polity interactions, such as the Maya, with their unusually uniform ecology (Webster 337–338, 339–340), archaic Greek poleis (Raaflaub 131), and the Nile Valley during the First Intermediate Period (Gnirs 79). Chinese political history begins with wars between comparable centers, but the later, larger polities of the Western Zhou clashed with non-state peoples from other zones, most notably horsemen of the steppes (Yates 16, 18). Generally, state armies do less well against scattered, mobile, autonomous groupings than against more dense and centralized polities (Goldberg and Findlow 1984.376–78). When the Japanese adopted Chinese army styles, they were sorely tested by mounted barbarians who fought guerrilla-style (Farris 53). Seleucid Syria was harried by people of the mountains (Hamilton 179), pastoralists occupied large parts of the Byzantine Empire (Haldon 246), development of early Rome's flexible manipular legions was influenced by confrontations with southern tribesmen (Hamilton 184), and water-borne Vikings played havoc with medieval Europe (Bachrach 282). On the other hand, the mobility of surrounding barbarians did not always work in their favor. In medieval western Europe, it meant they could not effectively lay siege to fortified towns of warring *civitates* (Bachrach 277, 280).

Regional population characteristics may affect war, but relationships are complicated—nothing so simple as "more people, more war." Cross-cultural statistics have failed to establish any correlation between regional population density and intensity of warfare, although connections are apparent in particular cases (Keeley 1996.117–21). (It may well be that a relationship exists but is obscured by the failure of past statistical investigations to consider the war-generating impact of Western contact—see later discussion.) Theoretically, regional population-to-resource balances affect whether war embodies the politics of exclusion or aims to garner people (Price 1984). Empirically, war is often avoided or exited when local groups have the option of relocating to unoccupied lands (Ferguson 1989c.195–96). In some parts of Amazonia, New Guinea, and Polynesia, war seems to propel people outward from areas of high productivity and population growth, ultimately displacing some into ecologically marginal areas that act as population sinks (Ferguson 1989b.255–58; Morren 1984.179–80; Sahlins 1958.59). In areas where politically and militarily dominant urban zones experience higher mortality (Knauft 1987.97–105), a reverse movement might occur, either forcible importation of populations or a cycle of external invasion and takeover, perhaps as in Mesopotamia (Adams 1981.135). Population crashes associated with Western contact can lead to open and abundant lands that can, other conditions being right, make subsequent war unlikely, as in the remarkably peaceful Guyana region (Ferguson 1990a.242).

This volume suggests but does not establish connections between overall population density and war. The population explosion that followed the introduction of wet-rice agriculture and metal in Japan is accompanied by abundant osteological evidence of war (Farris 49). After the demographic collapse of Dark Age Greece, growing populations led to increasing territorial conflicts and war (Raaflaub 129–131, 134). Population growth in Mesoamerica was reflected in larger armies and more expansive wars (Hassig 363). The highly structured political universe encountered by New Kingdom Egypt (Gnirs 86) arose on the great populations of the eastern Mediterranean of the late Bronze Age. The Japanese case shows that when states experience sharp population losses, however, the result may be intensified violence aimed at securing exploitable workers (and secure taxes), not peace (Farris 60).

Population pressure exists only in relation to some specific environment. Anthropologists no longer see ecosystems as stable, and they look to change, both gradual and sudden, natural and anthropogenic (Balee 1998; Crumley 1994). Deterioration of a resource base as a source of war is best understood not in the impact on one group but on the larger system of groups. Simultaneous threats to different subsistence bases, and to the total societies that rest on them, can cause major disruption and forced migrations, which leads to massive conflict throughout the system. Thus the protracted desiccation in the two centuries bracketing A.D. 1250 witnessed population shifts and unprecedented warfare throughout much of North America (Ferguson 1997.341). Epidemics of introduced diseases can also alter regional power balances by hitting different populations differently, as with the destruction of the urban (versus nomadic) peoples of the Great Plains (Bamforth 1994.100). In this volume, too, ecological crises lead to massive war. The bloody southern Maya collapse was fueled by anthropogenic environmental degradation (Webster 335, 354). The Toltec empire fell when desiccation undermined their agricultural base and drove nomadic peoples across essential trade routes (Hassig 363–364). Early Rome was forced to contract when mountain people migrated in, probably pushed on by famine (Rosenstein 195). Of course, whatever combination of ecology, population, and climate might be involved, barbarian migrations have played a major role in ancient histories.

System infrastructure includes geography. In most situations, non-state or state, threats are geographically specific. This point may seem too obvious to mention, unless strikingly patterned as in Egypt (Gnirs 83, 89), but it is obviously important for those who live with war. System infrastructure also includes the space between groups and the ability to traverse it. Distance, ease of movement over terrain, and the ability to live off the land limit the kinds of attacks that can be mounted. Technology of movement plays a major role in determining what kind of wars will be fought. Mounted tribal warriors are famous the world over. Water transport can multiply striking distances, solve logistical problems, and enable much looting, as with the long canoes of the Pacific Northwest. Topography structures travel and trade routes, and their location and characteristics can be major features in regional war systems (Ferguson 1984b.296, 313). Roads increase range and rate of march (D'Altroy 1992.81–90). But beyond such scattered observations, anthropology has relatively little to say about the social geography of war.

By the time of Tsun Tzu, if not long before, Chinese tacticians fully appreciated the importance of terrain, hence the injunction to study maps (Yates 15–16). Philip V of Macedon was vanquished when his army fought on terrain more suited to Roman flexibility (Hamilton 184). Man-made features such as cities, roads, and fortifications are essential considerations in planning and executing any expedition, and the construction or maintenance of all of these for military purposes also illustrates how great an impact war can have *on* the environment (Bachrach 278, 290–291; Haldon 247; Yates 15–16). Most Mesoamerican army marches were constricted to short campaigns by topography and the lack of roads and wheeled vehicles, eliminating the possibility of siege or surprise. The ability of the Aztec empire to secure provisions from tributaries along main routes greatly expanded its range of military action (Hassig 376; Webster 338–339, 347–348). Variations in logistics need more comparative study, in history as well as in anthropology. Persian soldiers, for example, seem particularly trained for living off the land (Briant 115, 121). The importance of logistics is well illustrated by the logistical revolution of the Athenian navy. Supply by sea lifted the limitations of previous hoplite warfare, leading to more sieges and the ability to exercise control over widely scattered populations (Raaflaub 141–142). Something similar is observed for the Carolingian empire (Bachrach 290). Taken together, topography and logistics, if not theoretically "sexy," are important keys to victory on the battlefield.

The diffusion of military technology and accompanying techniques is a subject rarely observed by anthropologists, with the exception of firearms. An inferential case may be made that the spread of the bow and arrow in prehistoric North America was followed by a new form of more deadly warfare (Maschner 1997.277). Hassig's study of Mesoamerican warfare is unusual in discussing the relative effectiveness of weapons and changes over time (Hassig 1992). Differential access to important military technology has obvious implications, as noted earlier regarding guns. The introduction of such powerful weapons may lead to more war. So the Coast Salish of Vancouver Island became slavers to buy guns to defend themselves from other slave raiders (Ferguson 1984b.299–300), and South American "Jivaro" mass-produced shrunken heads once each head became worth a rifle (Ferguson 1990a.247). War practices also spread from group to group. Headhunting (Vayda 1969.218–20) and torture of prisoners (Knowles 1940.190–91) were adopted by those who were at first only victims of those practices. In situations of Western contact, new ways to do the work of war spread outward from states in a process dubbed "military trans-culturation" (Ferguson and Whitehead 1992a.26). These acquired formations and techniques became so integral to some groups' practice that they some-times were taken to be entirely indigenous (Fathauer 1954).

This volume illustrates several variations on diffusion. Western Zhou kings passed along military technology in ceremonialized exchange with allies and dependencies (Yates 17). The Eastern Roman state exercised a monopoly on the production and issue of weapons of war (Haldon 253). Markets for weaponry in Mesoamerica made anything available, but, as in diffusionist theory, an item was incorporated only if a people had the need and necessary social founda-tions to make it worthwhile (Hassig 367). Thus Western barbarians were able to construct the machines of siege warfare, but maintaining the thousands of troops to use them was generally beyond their capacity (Bachrach 277, 290). Briant (122–124) stresses a broader cultural compatibility between donor and receiver as a necessary prerequisite for the transfer of major institutional sys-tems, such as mechanisms of soldier recruitment and training. On the other hand, Muslim warriors readily adopted foreign innovations regardless of denouncements from religious scholars (Crone 311). However it occurs, major weapons systems do spread. Lamellar armor and later the crossbow passed from Korea to Japan (Farris 50, 54). Bronze Age China (Yates 11) and New Kingdom Egypt (Gnirs 87) illustrate one of the most dramatic military diffusions in his-tory, the spread of light chariots as mobile firing platforms after 2000 B.C (Moorey 1986).

The techno-organizational innovations discussed in the previous section also spread. First hoplite-style fighting, then Macedonian phalanxes with their eigh-teen-foot sarissas came to dominate political fields. The three Hellenistic king-doms all relied on a core army, which, if not Macedonian by blood, fought Macedonian-style (Hamilton 180). Perhaps the most general medium of military diffusion, noted again and again in this volume, is the development of rootless mercenaries who carry their way of fighting and often their weapons with them (Bachrach 285–286; Campbell 235–236; Haldon 258–259; Gnirs 90–91; Hamilton 180–183; Yates 26). Although mercenaries grade imperceptibly into other forms of enlistment, clearly there are major differences in how much states rely on profes-sional soldiers-for-hire. This is another area ripe for comparative study and gen-eralization. Altogether, the chapters in this volume suggest that the spread of technology and technique leads to spheres of military interaction, alternative military universes where foes meet for battle in distinctive and standardized ways. "Byzantine armies and Arab armies looked very much the same" (Haldon 245).

Interpolity Structure

Developing on interpolity infrastructure as just described, interpolity structure is the social universe, the patterned interactions between potentially war-making groups. Interpolity structure has various dimensions, presented here as economics, social organization, and politics, but in life, different dimensions combine into whole, complex relationships. Anthropology in the past has not appreciated the extent and strength of networks involving scattered indigenous people (Lightfoot and Martinez 1995), but now it must avoid swinging too far the other way. That some of the "simplest" people were bound into larger systems does not mean everyone was in a significant way (Martin 1997; Solway and Lee 1990), and the corrosive effects of Western contact could quickly destroy elaborate networks, creating isolation (Whitehead 1992.139). But it is probably safe to say that all *states* are bound into vital networks with neighboring and more distant polities (Mann 1986.1–32). The varying character and combination of ties create social constellations that provide the form and guide the process of military action.

External Economics   Intergroup economic organization involves trade and tribute. Anthropologists give far more attention to kinship than trade as a form of intergroup relation, but research on the Yanomami leads me to conclude that exchange of goods is stronger cement, without which even kin ties fade. Trade goods include both utilitarian and sumptuary goods—the latter playing an important role in the development of inequality (Schneider 1977.23). McNeil argues that up until the development of iron tools, trade remained of interest primarily to elites (McNeil n.d.). Yanomami middlemen illustrate the benefits of controlling trade in highly desired goods (Western manufactures), obtaining relative abundance for their own use, numerous labor-intensive local manufactures in exchange, brides and protracted bride service from other villages wanting to open channels of trade, political support from clients, and prestige on top of it all. Yanomami use force to preserve, break, or replace middleman control (Ferguson 1995b.345–48). Collective violence is very well suited to influence the movement of people through space, and efforts to improve one's position within regional trade systems are a common cause of war (Jablow 1994).

Efforts to protect or interdict trade appear frequently in this volume. The fact that Maya trade was confined primarily to elite goods (Webster 338) would not lessen the elite's efforts to acquire these markers of their status, as confirmed by the Shang elite's ritual dependence on prestige imports (Yates 14–15). Olmecs,

Toltecs, and Aztecs all had wars involving trade (Hassig 361–363), although this has not been demonstrated for the Maya (Webster 350). One of the principal assignments of Egyptian armies was protecting trade channels and expeditions (Gnirs 77–78, 81). Han emperor Wu expended enormous resources projecting force along trade routes (Yates 31–32). Imperial Rome constructed forts at key geographic points for trade (Campbell 224), a policy that was continued during medieval times (Bachrach 277; and see Hamilton 175–176). But forts do not work on water, and pirates preyed on shipping in tenth-century Japan (Farris 57).

Modalities of exchange are inherently social (Sahlins 1972.185–86) and reflect military considerations. Balanced trade is powered by mutual interest and is often opposed to war (Lévi-Strauss 1943). But mutual interest may not be strong enough for peace, and trade sometimes alternates with or exists within war (Keeley 1996.122). On Brazil's Upper Xingu River, trade based on artificial monopolies of goods anyone could make are the foundation of a remarkable system of regional peace among various ethnies (Gregor, 1990.111).[9] On the Pacific Northwest coast, intergroup sharing through redistributions at periodic gatherings is encouraged by a climate of war, as redistributors lose potential enemies and gain friends against outside adversaries. But in the same area, ritualized exchange between military superiors and subordinates can be "unbalanced"—goods from above are accorded more value in exchange because they come with attached status—as reciprocity verges into tribute (Ferguson 1983; Ferguson 1984b.287–88). With developing sociospatial power hierarchies, extraction of tribute may become the primary form of interpolity relations (Wolf 1987.141–44), and war to secure tribute may become a constitutive force actively transforming regional social relations (Reyna 1994a).

When Yates (17) notes the similarity of ceremonialized exchange between Western Zhou kings and local rulers to practices in Pacific cultures, it suggests something between trade and tribute. Certainly tribute is a major concern in ancient states. Tribute is strongly implicated as a major goal in Maya and Aztec warfare (Webster 350; Hassig 366). New Kingdom Egypt had tributaries in Africa and the Near East (Gnirs 84). Athens had to collect tribute to pay for its triremes (Raaflaub 143). Tenth- and eleventh-century tax wars in Japan (Farris 57) and the forcible appropriation of tax payments by Arab conquerors (Crone 311–312) make the point that what is tax and what is tribute may be a matter of degree and perspective.

External Social Organization Connections between non-state groups are given some permanence through the exchange of people in marriage. Intermarriage facilitates peaceable interactions (Brown 1978.167), although, as noted earlier, it is no guarantee of peace (Vayda 1960.120–22). Given deteriorating trade, marriage relationships can turn to especially bitter animosity, poisoned by feeling that contracted in-law obligations have not been fulfilled (Ferguson 1995b.288–89). As military decision making becomes more centralized and hierarchical, marriages of political importance increasingly are those that connect emerging regional elites (Ferguson 1984b.288–89). Intermarriage can be balanced or lopsided (women going in only one direction) depending on relative power, and as a form of connection can embody all the goodwill or tensions of the total relationship. Other social organizational unifiers already noted as applying within a group (e.g., lineages) also extend outward, sometimes as a continuum from family to regional network (Sahlins 1961), sometimes with status ranking of separate divisions (Chernela 1993.xi–xiii).

As noted in discussing internal structure, among Maya, Aztecs, and ancient Chinese and Egyptians, marriage ties united the elite, and these were as important between as within groups (Gnirs 89; Webster 340; Yates 11, 16; Hassig 1992a.93–95). At the other end of the spectrum, where military victory led to territorial incorporation, kinship took on a new role, as in Persia, the Macedonian kingdoms, and Roman and Byzantine Empires, where intermarriage of more-or-less permanent occupation forces with local peoples was an important means of integration (Briant 116; Hamilton 173; Campbell 223–224; Haldon 253, 258).

External Politics   Political issues take more space than the previous two discussions of external structure. War-society connections are extensive and involve a variety of external political relationships, some common to all societies, some associated primarily with states. This discussion will cover alliance and domination, hegemonic versus territorial incorporation, and political-military interactions at the fringes of state control.

Trade and intermarriage are common bases of political alliance, but it is such alliances themselves that provide the immediate structure of war. Alliance is not war's opposite but its accompaniment. It is in war that allies are needed, to provide assistance in combat, information, material support, refuge, and secure flanks. In this area, the Yanomami are probably typical (Ferguson 1995b). Although alliances are firmly structured by economic and social connections, there are always options. Actualizing potential alliances is one of the major military roles of leaders. Alliance building is a continuous process, always in need of reaffirmation or renegotiation. Skillful leadership requires considering the ramifications for alliance of every proposed action. The existing structure of alliances plays a key role in determining the initiation, spread, and cessation of hostilities, although war, of course, can tear apart old allies and make strange new ones.

Alliances vary in their durability. Among Yanomami, they shift with surprising rapidity. In some more densely populated areas of New Guinea, they tend to persist along with structured oppositions for years (Kaberry 1973.63–68). As alliances become more fixed and more the basis of organizing war and other political projects, autonomous local groups form into confederacies and sometimes tribes, although tribalization is always a matter of degree (Heider 1970.77–81). Theorists on the subject of tribe, although disagreeing on much else, concur that to the degree tribes are bounded and coordinated, it is a result of warfare with similar units (Fried 1967.164–66; Haas 1982.9).

Maya centers had long-term enemies and went to war in alliances, although how structured is debated (Webster 346–347). The expansion of Republican Rome depended on its allies, who provided half or more of its legions (Rosenstein 203). Yamato monarchs were first among equals in a confederacy of autonomous groups (Farris 51). By the age of Athens's glory, wars between individual poleis had given way to wars between alliances of poleis, and Athens's rise itself involved the transformation, in the face of far-flung wars, of a voluntary confederacy into a centralized empire (Raaflaub 144, 147). Thus alliance can grade into more fixed, hierarchical, and coercive political forms.

In some combinations, non-state peoples do conquer and exploit other non-state peoples, as mobile pastoralists have often done (Barfield 1993). But it is more simple dominance and extraction than incorporation. I argue that hegemony—military and political dominance—combined with some form of tribute is common among chiefdoms and may play an important role in the evolution of states (Ferguson 1994.104–5). But it is only with the development of a government that centralized administration of conquered peoples becomes a regular possibility. Hassig (374–375) discusses the difference between territorial conquest, where local rulers are replaced and occupying garrisons installed, and hegemony, where local rulers are left in place. This distinction had been elevated in theoretical importance by Luttwak (1976), who contrasted the expanding hegemony of Republican Rome—which developed via its regular call-up of allies' military forces (Rosenstein 198)—to the fort-building territorial consolidation of the later empire.

Although this often-useful distinction directs our attention to variations in political dominance, its theoretical significance is clouded by the very diversity of that variation. Among the Maya, with no standing armies to occupy anything, a hegemonic state is the *most* cohesive structure that most scholars imagine (Webster 346), but more consolidating conquests might be apparent with greater historical detail (Demarest 1996). Sparta reversed Rome's sequence, with territorial conquest and enslavement followed by hegemonic expansion of the Peloponnesian League. Hegemonic control remained the rule until the conquests of territorial empires in the fourth century, most decisively that of Philip II (Raaflaub 131–132), but even under Philip and Alexander, some hegemonic dominance remained (Hamilton 175). The Arab conquests—where military garrisons were inserted across a complex political landscape, and self-rule was allowed as long as taxes were paid (Crone 311–312)—would be hard to categorize as either territorial or hegemonic.

The territorial-hegemonic contrast may be too neat even for the type case of Rome (Mattingly 1992.42–43), and in many situations it is of limited utility. Virtually all early civilizations consisted of a number of basically similar centralized polities, city-states, or nearly such, exhibiting shifting degrees of independence or cohesion, and of equality or dominance.[10] Egypt has been cited as the only exception, being a territorial state (Yoffee 1995.299–302), but it was not so exceptional in predynastic times (Scarre and Fagan 1997.93–96) or during intermediate periods (Gnirs 79). Western Europe reverted to this form after the fall of Rome (Bachrach 279–280), and it can be seen underlying the complex Byzantine state (Haldon 241–243). City-state systems are characterized by alternating periods of consolidation and independence, and in agglutinating times, there is constant jockeying among potential regional centers. In such polycentric systems, there may be no clear division between hegemonic and territorial rule, as smaller, weaker polities closer to an emergent center undergo political assimilation (Vansina 1971.136, 145). At the peripheries of expanding states, some *combination* of direct and indirect control is the rule, in endless variations of central and local political agents (Ferguson and Whitehead 1992a.7, 11). Even within territorially consolidated states, as noted earlier, a weakening center may be matched by increasing local autonomy, to the point of independence (Bachrach 279–280; Farris 52–53; Haldon 244, 250; Yates 14, 16). In sum, the hegemonic-territorial distinction, although often descriptively useful and good for problematizing forms of military-backed control, seems inadequate for theoretically conceptualizing the variation that exists. We need better concepts.[11]

When state polities—territorial, hegemonic, whatever—abut on lands inhabited by non-state peoples, other dynamics ensue that feed back to affect military practice by state neighbors. Archaeological research on ancient states, inspired by Wallerstein's work on the modern world system, documents socioeconomic transformation of extensive regions around political centers (Champion 1989; Rowlands, Larsen, and Kristiansen 1987). World system theory, however, has suffered from neglect of the military interactions that accompany and often make possible economic penetration (Ferguson and Whitehead 1992a.4). There is ethnohistoric evidence that the military dimension of state interaction with non-state peoples produces equally momentous change (Ferguson and Whitehead 1992b). This is especially well documented for the unusually disruptive expansion of the West since 1500, but it is probably true—although not so extreme (Ferguson 1993)—for any situation where state-level systems arise, collapse, intrude, or retract. The interaction of polities of different scale, power, and complexity has major ramifications throughout system politics (Y. Ferguson 1991).

Whitehead and I call regions near to but not administered by states "tribal zones" because of the propensity for states to seek and/or create defined polities—tribes—out of the more acephalous and fluid political fields they commonly encounter (Ferguson and Whitehead 1992a.12–16). Tribes can evolve without states, but states make a lot of tribes, and most named tribes in the ethnographic record exist under the spell of states. Related processes create discrete ethnic groups, generating cultural categorizations along major contours of interaction with state agents (Hill 1996). These new social constructions go hand in hand with many other significant changes linked to state proximity, to transform and commonly *intensify* militarism among the non-state peoples. This is especially true for the expansion of the Eurocentric world system over the past five hundred years, which has contributed in Western culture to a misleadingly bloodthirsty image of "savages."

War by states with tribal peoples around their peripheries was noted earlier in this volume. Otherwise, there is little discussion of processes within those peripheries, although the gradual emergence of the Nubian kingdom of Kerma is noted south of Egypt's Middle Kingdom as well as the Hyksos kingdom in the north (Gnirs 81, 83), and the ethnogenesis of Clovis's Salian Franks is attributed to Roman policies of a century earlier (Bachrach 286). But tribalization and ethnogenesis are normal, and presumably occurred around these ancient and medieval states. Whether such state expansion led to intensified warfare *among* polities of their peripheries is a more open question, and one that is not addressed here at all. Increased fighting seems likely, however, since so many states encouraged the military prowess of peripheral peoples, institutionalizing them as units of "ethnic soldiers"—another normal accompaniment of state expansion (Ferguson and Whitehead 1992a.21–23).

Ethnic units within Mesoamerican armies are not explicitly discussed here, but they did exist (Hassig 1992b.49–52). Dominant polities regularly incorporated units from subordinate city-states that, although sharing language and customs, maintained different traditions of origins—an ethnic divide instantly recognized and used by the Spanish (Webster, personal communication). Western Zhou and Han mustered forces from numerous chiefdoms and tribes (Yates 17–18, 33–34). Ninth-century Japanese armies had ethnic units (Farris, personal communication). Egypt had Nubian troops from early on, and by the time of the Rammeside period, ethnic minorities settled within the kingdom dominated the military and eventually politics (Gnirs 77–78, 81, 87, 90–91). Thousands of Greek mercenaries were the main forces in Persia and elsewhere in the Hellenistic world, joined by units of Illyrians, Thracians, and Gauls (Hamilton 179–183). In the later Western Roman Empire, more and more of the army consisted of units of martial peoples from the periphery (Campbell 235), a practice that continued in medieval times (Bachrach 282, 285–286). Mid-eleventh-century Byzantium also relied heavily on ethnic soldiers (Haldon 246), in an area that had been transformed into an ethnic mosaic by the time of the Seleucids (Hamilton 178). The Arab conquests illustrate a pattern that

had become common in the world by then: the takeover of governmental apparatus by ethnically distinctive invaders. They also show how complex cultural
identity had become. Arabs lost much of their distinctive ethnic character,
while Islam provided a new basis of assimilation. Over time, armies were constructed of shifting mixes of outside peoples until settling, in the Mamluk institution, on enslaved and converted Turkish tribals (Crone 314, 318–319).

Briant (116–122) problematizes the way ethnic soldiers are integrated into
state armies, distinguishing autonomous native levies from ethnics fully integrated and trained as regular soldiers. Ethnic soldiers do come in many forms,
from units of independent allies under their own command, to largely "decul-
turated" lower classes disproportionately drafted into state armies (Enloe
1980), and it is impossible to draw a line between ethnic soldiers and mercenaries. Briant's view, that ethnically heterogeneous forces must be militarily
ineffective, and that the extensive native levies noted under Xerxes were more
symbolic than functional, would, if accurate, suggest a need to reevaluate the
countless situations where ethnic fighters have been reported. Clearly, this is an
important topic that requires more theoretical attention than it has received.

Superstructure

Interpolity aspects of war-related beliefs and dispositions appear in rules of
war. War has its conventions, shared expectations among opponents about how
the fighting will go (Keeley 1996.60–63). This is part of the general ritualization
of war (Kennedy 1971.48), although anthropology has sometimes exaggerated
the compelling character of these rules, which often go little beyond mutual
self-interest and are frequently violated as circumstances allow or dictate. Rules
may be especially apparent when hostilities involve opponents at different
degrees of social distance (Netting 1974.159–61). Pressure on both sides may
keep tactics to minimally damaging levels in temporary flare-ups against neighbors with continuing connections, while encouraging lethality against unrelat-
ed peoples (Meggitt 1977.16–43).

Contests between Maya nobles may have approached choreography, but they
still aimed at capture, public humiliation, and ritual sacrifice (Webster 345–347,
349–350). Aztecs also fought some highly ritualized combats in the flower wars,
which Hassig sees as an attritional strategy to grind down powerful but less pop-
ulous adversaries. Their full-scale assaults produced captives for ritual sacrifice,
up to (could it be true?) eighty thousand at one time when recalcitrant tributaries
needed to be intimidated (Hassig 369, 379–380). Early Chinese warfare was thoroughly ritualized but also produced thousands of sacrificial victims (Yates 14,
20–21), so no one should think that "ritualistic" means little bloodshed. Samurai
combat etiquette was so elaborate that their opening rituals sent the assembled
Mongol force (from a different military universe) into paroxysms of laughter

(Farris 64). Hoplite battle had a strong ritualistic aspect, making it a test of strength not designed to kill many, although it sometimes did (Raaflaub 133). In Warring States China, however, ritual faded before considerations of economics and terrain (Yates 25–30). New Kingdom Egypt expected a somewhat ritualistic initial campaign from a new king but otherwise practiced total war (Gnirs 74). The duels of champions that appear in Persia, on closer inspection, occur in the contexts of full combat between armies (Briant 111). Discussion of rules of war is notably absent in other cases, with the exception of medieval generals' sensible agreement not to destroy the material and resources base that everyone was fighting to control (Bachrach 289). Certainly all war has ritual and involves mutual understandings between adversaries, but ritual considerations appear to fade in contrast to practicalities after centuries of conquest warfare.

A few other aspects of interpolity superstructure are noted in this volume. The role of religion in forging the political and military unification of disparate local groups is well known, from twentieth-century Amazonia and Melanesia (Brown and Fernandez 1992; Worsley 1968.227) to rebellions in first-century Roman Africa (Mattingly 1992.35–38). Two millennial uprisings brought down the Han dynasty, thus opening the door to nomadic conquest (Yates 34). Religion also may accompany and encourage imperial expansion (Reyna 1994b), as "heathens" the world over learned about Christianity. If the Aztecs were not going to war to spread their religion, the fact that the god Huitzilopochtli demanded blood (Hassig 367–368) surely must have seemed significant to those captives whose hearts were ripped out. Islam, of course, welded autonomous tribal groups into a coordinated conquering force, for a while (Crone 309).

Polities exist within a cognized and moralized systemic map, affirming distinctions that reflect and influence military action (Whitehead 1992.133), as dramatically illustrated in varying perspectives on headhunting practices in Southeast Asia (Hoskins 1996). The Yanomami case reveals some of the more general dimensions of this mapping (Ferguson 1992.221–24). Status ranking of polities reflects many things besides war, but military superiority is one important basis for deference, and relative status strongly affects what behavior constitutes a politically serious insult. Grounds for revenge and suspicions of malevolent acts (witchcraft), keying into the symbolic and emotional complexes discussed earlier, ideologically demarcate political fields. Past injuries are interpreted according to *current* relationships, but actual history is a very real structuring force. A past war may leave little basis for communication, while a long-standing alliance may bear much stress before cracking. A history of violence contributes to expectations that violence will be used, which may become a self-fulfilling prophecy.

Such fine-grained, situation-specific mapping is not noted in cases presented here. What does appear in Chinese, Japanese, and Egyptian states is an ideological map of a civilization surrounded by barbarians, who deserved smiting (Farris 65–66; Gnirs 73–76; Yates 29–33). Persia had a similar self-image (Briant 107, 116), although hostile relations with barbarians are not specified. In medieval western Europe, it was the ability to lay siege that separated the civilized from the barbarians (Bachrach 277). Worldview also extends inward to conceptions of self, which in some cultures may only be fulfilled in violent opposition to foreign others (Viveiros de Castro 1992.1–4). There are at least echoes of this in some parts of the Persian kingdom (Briant 115). Mental images of political universes will exist in very different versions, reflecting different positions within the political system. These solidly grounded yet culturally constructed political maps frame decisions for military action. They are where materialist can meet symbolist perspectives as part of one analysis.

Another area where interpolity superstructure is important is in the dyadic psychodynamic process that leads up to war. Again, these fall below the resolution of chapters in this volume, but they seem to be general enough in principle so they may be expected to apply (Gluckman 1963; Coser 1956; Simmel 1964). Adversaries become more clearly defined and polarized. People in between are compelled to choose sides or withdraw from active roles. A developing rift colors all evaluations, until nothing those others do is good, everything gives more grounds for hostility and mistrust. It becomes "us" or "them," as extremely negative images of the enemy are generated and backed by peer pressure.

The Yanomami case, again, provides texture (Ferguson 1995b.11–12, 45–46). As relationships deteriorate, any aspect of the worsening interactions may stand for the whole. Thus, seemingly trivial slights can ignite violence because they symbolize all that has gone bad. Once war begins, the state of war includes an expectation of lethal violence from the enemy that will shape decisions and actions. Informational limitations are sharpened—the notorious fog of war—so that belligerents must make decisions based on misinformation and speculation. Prisoners' dilemmas encourage preemptive strikes. And if revenge is manipulated like history, while a group is actively taking casualties it certainly can motivate further attacks. But over time the will to war fades. The costs mount; people get tired of living in fear. If an initial consequence of war is to unify the group against an enemy, protracted war leads to internal division. Some start to seek a path to peace. Peace frequently comes through exit—one side leaves the field. But often a negotiated settlement is reached. This involves reactivation of latent crosscutting ties, sending protected emissaries, and diplomacy that, although little studied (Numelin 1950), shows many characteristics comparable to modern practice. There are specialized conventions for receiving emissaries and specialized language for diplomatic discussion that reduces the possibility of confrontation. Reestablishment of peace involves not just working out new ties of trade, marriage, and support but jointly reconstructing the history of relationships to defuse revenge, and jointly participating in rituals of solidarity.

Summary and Conclusions

Previous discussions separated intra- from interpolity connections between war in society, to call attention to the larger political fields that encompass any war-making group. In this conclusion, both will be merged for a unified presentation of infrastructural, structural, and superstructural connections between war and society in ancient and medieval states, as exemplified by cases described in this volume.

Agriculture is the foundation of state armies. Where soldiers must return to work the fields, war is seasonal and close to home. Sometimes these men are also drafted for other mass labor tasks. A Rubicon is crossed when the production system can sustain professional standing armies. Even professional soldiers, however, often are motivated by rewards of land, the possession of which may in turn obligate military service. Military force also brings land into cultivation as estates or via colonies of warriors. States place increased emphasis on land issues and territory, as borders firm up and are contested. In addition to land, capture of people to do both farm and other labor is a goal of many campaigns, sometimes the lifeblood of a regime. Broad ecological variation determines what basic types of societies will clash—peer polities rising on similar subsistence strategies, or radically different formations, adapted to differing niches. Hunting, riding, and other subsistence-related techniques can be put to important military use, and more mobile tribal peoples often force the ponderous armies of expanding states to adapt themselves to new fields of battle. If you can't lick them, have them join you, and imperial armies regularly incorporate units of ecologically specific adepts.

Major population growth over time is connected to increased territorial issues and war. Larger polities can have not only quantitative but also sometimes qualitative advantages over smaller polities in forces fielded and tactics employed. High population densities support more complex political systems, and that affects armies. Anthropogenic ecological degradation can lead to a population crash, which may intensify warfare as elites compete harder for whatever remains. Climatic fluctuations can shift ecological niches and impel migrations, leading to major military outbursts. The possibility has been suggested that war is the means by which people move from areas of positive to negative population growth. The impact of war itself on population levels is ambiguous. Although the armies that march across these pages sustain massive losses, war casualties seem to put little crimp in regional numbers. Yes, war destroys factors of production, limits the ability to exploit nature, and can feed into a process of demographic collapse, but on the other hand military need can stimulate production of food and babies.

Geography structures potential threats, allies, and trade routes. Terrain is often crucial in the course of campaigns. Transport technology, including roads, sets limits of campaigning, and good ships greatly expand military range and possibilities of siege. A developed system of fortifications affects what and how wars are fought. Advances in military technology are sometimes key to imperial expansion, although weapons become lethal only in use—in specific and trained labor of combat. Combat is men's work, and expectably that has an impact on gender relations. Spread of military technology, like all diffusion, requires an existing need and socioeconomic base supportive of the innovation. How diffusion occurs ranges from ritualized exchange, to markets, to government provisioning. Mercenaries become major carriers of military innovation. Where comparable military organizations face off, important advances in technique and technology will be adopted generally. Development of a navy stands out as a major watershed in military capacities, but at a major social and political cost, including reorganization of the collection of wealth.

Turning to structure, in what for want of a better term I will call "archaic" states (Maya, Shang, early Egypt), the kinship cement of affinity and descent provides some cohesion among elites, and transmits rights to property, rule, and status. Lineage organization may still be used to mobilize fighters. If blood and marriage can unify, they also structure fission in polycentric states, where claims to rule are routinely challenged by semiautonomous subordinates. But later states discount kinship for military accomplishment (within a tightly restricted group) as basis for rule, and shift to neighborhoods or institutions as bases for military drafts—although both bring along some back-home structure. Rome and perhaps Persia and Macedonia stand out for armies where unit cohesion was developed purely within the units. On the other hand, all three secured their conquests, in part, through soldier-marrying local communities.

In all cases, a critical dimension of social organization is stratification, which is geographically expressed in elite centers that eventually become urban. Most armies have some variation of elite and mass troops, with the elite on horse or chariot except in the New World. Complex social systems may have more than two layers of soldiers. Professionalization of any stratum of soldier, how well and how much each fights, is variable, and all that is connected to the position of their respective social classes. Success in battle is often a vehicle for upward mobility, a fact that provides a crucial incentive for soldiers in successfully expanding states. Armies are formal institutions with manifold connections to other institutions, and their relationship to ecclesiastical and civil administrative bureaucracies affects how militaristic a polity may seem.

In stratified economies, scarcity and how it is experienced vary by structural position, and that affects which scarcities become grounds for war. Tensions within a class structure may promote external military adventures. Different classes participate differently in the benefits of trade, but in general it is more attuned to elites than masses. Not surprisingly, trade is the basis of much warfare, in efforts to protect or tap into it. Trade can be converted through war or threat of war into tribute, and intermediate forms of unbalanced exchange are possible. Tribute is what sustains many systems of rule, although the line between tribute and tax may be ambiguous and contested. Taxation is a more secure and productive means of revenue, if the system can sustain the costs of such control; and intensified taxation—and the institutions of control that go along with it—may be necessary to pay for expanded military forces.

Regarding the political structure of decision making, some states' roots go back to (more) consensual forms—early Maya (perhaps), Dark Age Greece, tribal Arabs. But even with extremely centralized decision making, military policy usually (not always) involves conservative appraisal of circumstances. States have and use the power to compel subject-citizens to fight. The central government's ability to control independent military actions varies, from substantial autonomy to virtual elimination of locally controlled forces. Also highly variable is the manner in which armies act as internal police. The threats of war may compel a unity of purpose that, if sustained, allows those in power to extend and elaborate structures of control. War provides avenues for elite to vie with each other for wealth, power, and status—all interrelated, of course.

Internal politics thus plays a major role in shaping external policies; indeed, the boundary between the two may fluctuate. On the other hand, internal politics is conditioned by a structured external field of oppositions and alliances. Allies are crucial for success and war, and alliance making intensifies alongside war. Seen comparatively, using cases in this volume, alliance appears to be the end of a continuum that reaches to territorial conquest and incorporation. Alliances or somewhat more permanent confederacies tip from equality to hegemony, and from hegemony to empire, as hegemony grades into conquest and incorporation. In the other direction, regional autonomy can grow within territorial states to the point of independence. In sum, what often exists is a complex and fluid political field, involving varied political relations between varied types of polities. Strong dominance by a central power leads to regional and broader economic reorganizations, but that dominance depends largely on military force, and much of the restructuring is intended to meet specific military demands.

There are suggestions here (and strong evidence elsewhere) that most expanding states generate "tribal zone" effects of tribalization and ethnogenesis in areas beyond their administrative control. One standing question is whether ancient states had the effect of intensifying war and militarism among non-state people at the periphery. The cultivation of warlike ethnic soldiers suggests they did, to some degree. For their skills and martial attitude, the culturally distinctive fighters from imperial peripheries grew increasingly prominent in armies, to the point of taking them over. Ethnic soldiers grade into paid professional mercenaries. In the complex cultural tapestries of some of the later social worlds, after so many invasions, migrations, and administrations, every soldier was an ethnic.

Boys are raised for war, soldiering becomes part of adult male identity, and bravery is lauded. Political ideology and religion both provide moral justification for war, although there is significant variation in how tightly the two intertwine on this point. In many cases, religion refracts conquest into legitimacy. Religion is carried into war, preparing, guiding, and urging on combatants. Religion may impel imperial expansion, but it may also unite resistance to the same. There are always rules and rituals of combat, as sanguinary as they may be, but overt ritualisms seem to fade out over centuries of internecine war. Finally, a cognitive and moral mapping of the peoples of a social universe informs military thinking and action.

This chapter has presented a paradigm for the study of relationships between war and society, intended as an orienting framework for observation and theory, usable for comparison or in-depth case study. In closing, two general points can be made. First, at the start of this chapter, I asked whether a general model developed with reference to non-state people could apply to war-society relationships in ancient and medieval states. The fit has been variable. Authors here deal much more with politics of control, for instance, while anthropologists have paid greater attention to psychological dimensions of war. Nevertheless, this extended comparison has demonstrated extensive similarities—relationships between war and society are comparable for non-state and state-level societies. I cite this in support of a point I have argued for some time (Ferguson 1984a.26), but never with such extensive evidence, that the venerable distinction of "primitive" from "civilized" war obscures a fundamental similarity. War is war.

Second, this volume is about *war* and society. Recently anthropologists have begun exploring connections between *peace* and society (Gregor 1996; Howell and Willis 1989; Sponsel and Gregor 1994). There are non-state peoples with little or very limited war. While the great majority of ethnographically known societies practice war, often of an extremely intense character, archaeology strongly indicates that war did not become a regular practice until some time—often a very long time—after the transition to settled village life (Ferguson 1997). Moreover, a recent compilation of ethnographic cases where war is reported to be absent or mainly defensive indicates that peaceable peoples are not as rare as has been thought (Van der Dennen 1995.595–674). I doubt that there was any ancient or medieval state free of war. The idea is almost a contradiction in terms, with killing and taxing being the main thing many states did. But even states, like warring non-state peoples, vary in the frequency of warfare (Ember and Ember 1997). In an earlier work, I suggested that there may be alternative social trajectories, warlike or peaceable (Ferguson 1994.103). Of course a great many cases would not be easily pigeonholed, falling in the range between. But I suspect that protracted war or protracted peace contribute to their self-perpetuation. This chapter has shown how, in myriad ways, war reshapes society in its own image. A society in a system evolved for war is ready, even waiting, for war. Of course a bad thing can be pushed too far, as when a system of government is brought down by military defeat or the crushing burden of military expenses. But short of that, as these chapters show, in many cases war is so woven into the fabric of social life that a given polity could not survive without it. Often, war has been likened to an infectious disease. In some cases, it may be more apt to think of war as a societal addiction.

Notes

1. This paradigm, previously referred to as a synthetic or holistic model, is the subject of theoretical works that elaborate it in general terms (Ferguson 1990b) and discuss its theoretical underpinnings (1995a). In other articles, it is applied to the sometimes intense warfare of Venezuelan-Brazilian Yanomami in a situation of Western contact (1992), to the role of war in the process of sociocultural evolution (1994), and to anthropology's possible relevance for addressing the cold war of the late 1980s (1989a).

2. The absence of such histories of chronic war-making, and consequently the lack of adequate public finance instruments, is one reason for the weakness of postcolonial states in contemporary Africa (Herbst 1990).

3. In my own efforts to explain the actual occurrence of war in specific cultural and historical contexts, I apply the premise that war occurs when those who decide military policy believe war is in their material self-interest, considered from the perspective of their position within social and economic organization. This directs attention to the structure of decision making regarding war and peace: What kinds of people are involved, what are their interests in possible outcomes of potential conflicts, and in what ways are they able to influence direction of policy?

4. My own recent research on the history of the New York City police suggests that police forces need to be backed up by a military, but that men trained as soldiers make lousy cops.

5. Unlike many anthropologists, I (as in Ferguson 1995b.365–66; and see note 3) argue for the existence of a phylogenetically evolved, panhuman, cross-culturally similar motivation to maintain or improve material well-being. It is these interests as they apply collectively to decision makers that structure decisions for war. But these

interests can exist only within a specific culture milieu, just as any idea must be expressed in a particular language. Culture influences the conception of interests and dispositions to various kinds of action. Moreover, culture provides the moral framework for making needs and wants into rights and duties. Material interests are converted into high principles to mobilize public support and to avoid cognitive dissonance, which is why these concerns dominate participants' recollections and explanations of wars.

6. Enloe's (1995) discussion of war and genocide in contemporary Rwanda is a succinct and incisive presentation of the ways war can enter into gender relations (and see Sutton 1995).

7. Ferguson 1995b.353–54. In many ways, these constructs find parallels in the moralizing and antagonistic constructions of histories noted in many recent "ethnic conflicts."

8. Here I see a parallel to modern intelligence services, for which the term "spook" may be more appropriate than imagined.

9. "Ethnie" is a term recently come into use in anthropology. It designates a culturally distinctive group, without the implications associated with "ethnic group," which to most people indicates a subordinate grouping within a state system.

10. The concept of a "segmentary state" has been applied to several situations with multiple local polities linked as subordinates to some center (Southall 1988), as illustrated here regarding the Maya (Webster 341). This concept, however, emphasizes "ritual suzerainty" as the primary means of integration, where it may be more useful to consider perceived military superiority.

11. Another often useful distinction, that of territorial state versus empire, also becomes problematic under inspection. Sinopoli (1994.160) defines "empire as a territorially expansive and incorporative kind of state, involving relationships in which one state exercises control over other sociopolitical entities." Although huge expansions over previous systems are instantly recognizable as empires, at the other end there is no clear distinction separating empires from expansive local states.

Bibliography

Abler, Thomas S. 1992. "Beavers and Muskets: Iroquois Military Fortunes in the Face of European Colonization." In Ferguson and Whitehead 1992b.151–74.

Adams, D. 1983. "Why There Are so Few Women Warriors." *Behavior Science Research* 18, 196–212.

Adams, Robert McC. 1981. *Heartland of Cities: Surveys of Ancient Settlement and Land Use on the Central Floodplain of the Euphrates.* Chicago: University of Chicago Press.

Balée, William, ed. 1998. *Advances in Historical Ecology.* New York: Columbia University Press.

Bamforth, Douglas. 1994. "Indigenous People, Indigenous Violence: Precontact Warfare on the North American Plains." *Man* 29, 95–115.

Barfield, Thomas. 1993. *The Nomadic Alternative.* Englewood Cliffs, N.J.: Prentice-Hall.

———. 1994. "The Devil's Horsemen: Steppe Nomadic Warfare in Historical Perspective." In Reyna and Downs 1994.157–82.

Bauer, Brian S. 1996. "Legitimization of the State in Inca Myth and Ritual." *American Anthropologist* 98.2, 327–37.

Berndt, Ronald, and Peter Lawrence, eds. 1973. *Politics in New Guinea: Traditional and in the Context of Change, Some Anthropological Perspectives.* Seattle: University of Washington Press.

Billman, Brian R. 1997. "Population Pressure and the Origins of Warfare in the Moche Valley, Peru." In *Integrating Archaeological Demography: Multidisciplinary Approaches to Prehistoric Population,* edited by Richard Paine. Southern Illinois University Center for Archaeological Investigations, Occasional Paper No. 24. Carbondale, Ill.: Southern Illinois University.

Bonnemaison, Joel. 1994. *The Tree and the Canoe: History and Ethnography of Tanna.* Translated by Josee Penot-Demetry. Honolulu: University of Hawaii Press.

Brookfield, H. C., and Paula Brown. 1963. *Struggle for Land: Agricultural and Group Territories among the Chimbu of the New Guinea Highlands.* Melbourne: Oxford University Press.

Brown, Michael, and Eduardo Fernandez. 1992. "Tribe and State in a Frontier Mosaic: The Ashaninka of Eastern Peru." In Ferguson and Whitehead 1992b.175–97.

Brown, Paula. 1964. "Enemies and Affines." *Ethnology* 3, 335–56.

———. 1978. *Highland Peoples of New Guinea.* Cambridge: Cambridge University Press.

Cannon, Aubrey. 1992. "Conflict and Salmon on the Interior Plateau of British Columbia." In *A Complex Culture of the British Columbia Plateau,* edited by Brian Hayden, 506–24. Vancouver: University of British Columbia Press.

Carneiro, Robert. 1970. "A Theory of the Origin of the State." *Science* 169, 733–38.

Cartledge, Paul. 1981. "Spartan Wives: Liberation or Licence?" *Classical Quarterly* 31, 84–105.

Chagnon, Napoleon. 1974. *Studying the Yanomamo.* New York: Holt, Rinehart and Winston.

———.1983. *Yanomamo: The Fierce People.* New York: Holt, Rinehart and Winston.

Champion, T. C., ed. 1989. *Centre and Periphery: Comparative Studies in Archaeology.* London: Unwin Hyman.

Chang, Kwang-chih. 1986. *The Archaeology of Ancient China.* New Haven, Conn.: Yale University Press.

Chernela, Janet. 1993. *The Wanano Indians of the Brazilian Amazon: A Sense of Space.* Austin: University of Texas Press.

Cohen, Ronald. 1984. "Warfare and State Formation: Wars Make States and States Make Wars." In Ferguson 1984c.329–58.

Cooney, Mark. 1997. "From Warre to Tyranny: Lethal Conflict and the State." *American Sociological Review* 62, 316–338.

Coser, Lewis. 1956. *The Functions of Social Conflict.* New York: Free Press.

Crumley, Carole L., ed. 1994. *Historical Ecology: Cultural Knowledge and Changing Landscapes.* Santa Fe, N.M.: School of American Research Press.

Dalley, Stephanie. 1995. "Ancient Mesopotamian Military Organization." In *Civilizations of the Ancient Near East,* edited by Jack M. Sasson, Vol. 1, 413–22. New York: Scribner's.

D'Altroy, Terence N. 1992. *Provincial Power in the Inka Empire.* Washington, D.C.: Smithsonian Institution Press.

Demarest, Arthur A. 1996. "Closing Comment: The Maya State: Centralized or Segmentary." *Current Anthropology* 37, 821–24.

Divale, William, and Marvin Harris. 1976. "Population, Warfare, and the Male Supremacist Complex." *American Anthropologist* 78, 521–38.

Ekvall, Robert. 1961. "The Nomadic Pattern of Living among the Tibetans as Preparation for War." *American Anthropologist* 63, 1250–63.

Ember, Carol R., and Melvin Ember. 1992. "Resource Unpredictability, Mistrust, and War: A Cross-Cultural Study." *Journal of Conflict Resolution* 36, 242–62.

———. 1997. "Violence in the Ethnographic Record: Results of Cross-Cultural Research on War and Aggression." In Frayer and Martin 1997.1–20.

Ember, Melvin, and Carol Ember. 1971. "The Conditions Favoring Matrilocal versus Patrilocal Residence." *American Anthropologist* 73, 571–94.

Enloe, Cynthia. 1980. *Ethnic Soldiers: State Security in Divided Societies.* Athens, Ga.: University of Georgia Press.

———. 1995. "When Feminists Think about Rwanda." *Cultural Survival* 19.1, 26–29.

Fadiman, Jeffrey. 1976. *Mountain Warriors: The Pre-Colonial Meru of Mt. Kenya.* Papers in International Studies, Africa Series, No. 27. Athens, Ohio: Ohio University Center for International Studies.

———. 1982. *An Oral History of Tribal Warfare: The Meru of Mt. Kenya.* Athens, Ohio: Ohio University Press.

Fathauer, George. 1954. "The Structure and Causation of Mohave Warfare." *Southwestern Journal of Anthropology* 10, 97–118.

Feil, D. K. 1987. *The Evolution of Highland Papua New Guinea Societies.* Cambridge: Cambridge University Press.

Ferdon, Edwin N. 1981. *Early Tahiti: As the Explorers Saw It, 1767–1797.* Tucson: University of Arizona Press.

Ferguson, R. Brian. 1983. "Warfare and Redistributive Exchange on the Northwest Coast." In *The Development of Political Organization in Native North America: 1979 Proceedings of the American Ethnological Society,* edited by Elizabeth Tooker, 133–47. Washington, D.C.: American Ethnological Society.

———. 1984a. "Introduction: Studying War." In Ferguson 1984c.1–81.

———. 1984b. "A Re-examination of the Causes of Northwest Coast Warfare." In Ferguson 1984c.267–328.

———, ed. 1984c. *Warfare, Culture, and Environment.* Orlando, Fla.: Academic Press.

———. 1988. "War and the Sexes in Amazonia." In *Dialectics and Gender: Anthropological Approaches,* edited by Richard R. Randolph, David M. Schneider, and May N. Diaz, 136–54. Boulder, Colo.: Westview Press.

———. 1989a. "Anthropology and War: Theory, Politics, Ethics." In *The Anthropology of War and Peace: Perspectives on the Nuclear Age,* edited by David Pitt and Paul Turner, 141–59. South Hadley, Mass.: Bergin and Garvey.

———. 1989b. "Ecological Consequences of Amazonian Warfare." *Ethnology* 28, 249–64.

————. 1989c. "Game Wars? Ecology and Conflict in Amazonia." *Journal of Anthropological Research* 45, 179–206.

————. 1990a. "Blood of the Leviathan: Western Contact and Warfare in Amazonia." *American Ethnologist* 17.2, 237–57.

————. 1990b. "Explaining War." In Haas 1990.26–55.

————. 1992. "A Savage Encounter: Western Contact and the Yanomami War Complex." In Ferguson and Whitehead 1992b.199–227.

————. 1993. "When Worlds Collide: The Columbian Encounter in Global Perspective." *Human Peace* 10.1, 8–10.

————. 1994. "The General Consequences of War: An Amazonian Perspective." In Reyna and Downs 1994.85–111.

————. 1995a. "Infrastructural Determinism." In *Science, Materialism, and the Study of Culture,* edited by Martin F. Murphy and Maxine L. Margolis, 21–38. Gainesville: University of Florida Press.

————. 1995b. *Yanomami Warfare: A Political History.* Santa Fe, N.M.: School of American Research Press.

————. 1997. "Violence and War in Prehistory." In Frayer and Martin 1997.321–55.

Ferguson, R. Brian, and Neil L. Whitehead. 1992a. "The Violent Edge of Empire." In Ferguson and Whitehead 1992b.1–30.

———— , eds. 1992b. *War in the Tribal Zone: Expanding States and Indigenous Warfare.* Santa Fe, N.M.: School of American Research Press.

Ferguson, Yale H. 1991. "Chiefdoms to City States: The Greek Experience." In *Chiefdoms: Economy, Power, and Ideology,* edited by Timothy Earle, 169–92. Cambridge: Cambridge University Press.

Frayer, David W., and Debra L. Martin, eds. 1997. *Troubled Times: Violence and Warfare in the Past.* Langhorne, Pa.: Gordon and Breach.

Fried, Morton. 1967. *The Evolution of Political Society: An Essay in Political Anthropology.* New York: Random House.

Fukui, Katsuyoshi, and David Turton. 1979. "Introduction." In *Warfare among East African Herders,* edited by Katsuyoshi Fukui and David Turton, 1–13. Osaka: Senri Ethnological Studies, National Museum of Ethnology.

Gluckman, Max. 1963. "Gossip and Scandal." *Current Anthropology* 4, 307–16.

Goetze, Albrecht. 1963. "Warfare in Asia Minor." *Iraq* 25.2, 124–30.

Goldberg, Neil J., and Frank J. Findlow. 1984. "A Quantitative Analysis of Roman Military Aggression in Britain, circa A.D. 43–238." In Ferguson 1984c.359–85.

Goldschmidt, Walter. 1986. "Personal Motivation and Institutionalized Conflict." In *Peace and War: Cross-Cultural Perspectives,* edited by Mary LeCron Foster and Robert A. Rubenstein, 3–14. New Brunswick, N.J.: Transaction.

Golob, Ann. 1982. "The Upper Amazon in Historical Perspective." Ph.D. diss., City University of New York.

Gregor, Thomas. 1990. "Uneasy Peace: Intertribal Relations in Brazil's Upper Xingu." In Haas 1990.105–24.

———— , ed. 1996. *A Natural History of Peace.* Nashville, Tenn.: Vanderbilt University Press.

Gunawardana, R. A. L. H. 1992. "Conquest and Resistance: Pre-State and State Expansionism in Early Sri Lankan History." In Ferguson and Whitehead 1992b.61–82.

Gunther, Erna. 1972. *Indian Life on the Northwest Coast of North America: As Seen by the Early Explorers and Fur Traders during the Last Decades of the Eighteenth Century.* Chicago: University of Chicago Press.

Guy, J. J. 1981. "Production and Exchange in the Zulu Kingdom." In *Before and After Shaka: Papers in Nguni History,* edited by J. B. Peires, 33–48. Grahamstown, South Africa: Institute of Social and Economic Research, Rhodes University.

Haas, Jonathan. 1982. *The Evolution of the Prehistoric State.* New York: Columbia University Press.

————, ed. 1990. *The Anthropology of War.* New York: Cambridge University Press.

Harris, Marvin. 1974. *Cows, Pigs, Wars and Witches: The Riddles of Culture.* New York: Vintage.

Hassig, Ross. 1992a. "Aztec and Spanish Conquest in Mesoamerica." In Ferguson and Whitehead 1992b.83–102.

————. 1992b. *War and Society in Ancient Mesoamerica.* Berkeley and Los Angeles: University of California Press.

Heider, Karl G. 1970. *The Dugum Dani: A Papuan Culture in the Highlands of West New Guinea.* Chicago: Aldine.

————. 1979. *Grand Valley Dani: Peaceful Warriors.* New York: Holt, Rinehart, and Winston.

Herbst, Jeffrey. 1990. "War and the State in Africa." *International Security* 14.4, 117–39.

Hill, Jonathan D., ed. 1996. *History, Power, and Identity: Ethnogenesis in the Americas, 1492–1992.* Iowa City: University of Iowa Press.

Hoskins, Janet, ed. 1996. *Headhunting in the Social Imagination of Southeast Asia.* Stanford, Calif.: Stanford University Press.

Howell, Signe, and Roy Willis, eds. 1989. *Societies at Peace: Anthropological Perspectives.* London: Routledge.

Hulme, Peter, and Neil L. Whitehead, eds. 1992. *Wild Majesty: Encounters with Caribs from Columbus to the Present Day.* Oxford: Clarendon Press.

Jablow, Joseph. 1994. *The Cheyenne in Plains Indian Trade Relations, 1795–1840.* Lincoln: University of Nebraska Press.

Kaberry, Phyllis. 1973. "Political Organization among the Northern Abelam." In Berndt and Lawrence 1973.35–73.

Keeley, Lawrence H. 1996. *War before Civilization: The Myth of the Peaceful Savage.* New York: Oxford University Press.

Kelekna, Pita. 1994. "Farming, Feuding, and Female Status: The Achuar Case." In *Amazonian Indians: From Prehistory to the Present,* edited by Anna Roosevelt, 225–48. Tucson: University of Arizona Press.

Kelly, Raymond C. 1985. *The Nuer Conquest: The Structure and Development of an Expansionist System.* Ann Arbor: University of Michigan Press.

Kennedy, John. 1971. "Ritual and Intergroup Murder: Comments on War, Primitive and Modern." In *War and the Human Race,* edited by M. Walsh, 40–61. New York: Elsevier.

King, Victor. 1976. "Migration, Warfare, and Culture Contact in Borneo: A Critique of Ecological Analysis." *Oceania* 46, 306–27.

Kirch, Patrick V. 1997. "Microcosmic Histories: Island Perspectives on 'Global' Change." *American Anthropologist* 99.1, 30–42.

Knauft, Bruce M. 1987. "Divergence between Cultural Success and Reproductive Fitness in Preindustrial Cities." *Cultural Anthropology* 2.1, 94–114.

———. 1991. "Violence and Sociality in Human Evolution." *Current Anthropology* 32.4, 391–428.

Knowles, Nathaniel. 1940. "The Torture of Captives by the Indians of Eastern North America." *Proceedings of the American Philosophical Society* 82.2, 151–225.

Koch, Klaus-Friedrich. 1974a. "The Anthropology of Warfare." Addison-Wesley Modules in Anthropology, No. 52. Reading, Mass.: Addison-Wesley.

———. 1974b. *War and Peace in Jalemo: The Management of Conflict in Highland New Guinea.* Cambridge, Mass.: Harvard University Press.

Kracke, Waud. 1978. *Force and Persuasion: Leadership in an Amazonian Society.* Chicago: University of Chicago Press.

Kroeber, Clifton, and Bernard Fontana. 1986. *Massacre on the Gila: An Account of the Last Major Battle between American Indians, with Reflections on the Origin of War.* Tucson: University of Arizona Press.

Lambert, Patricia M. 1997. "Patterns of Violence in Prehistoric Hunter-Gatherer Societies of Coastal Southern California." In Frayer and Martin 1997.77–109.

Lan, David. 1985. *Guns and Rain: Guerrillas and Spirit Mediums in Zimbabwe.* Berkeley and Los Angeles: University of California Press.

Langness, L. L. 1973. "Bena Bena Political Organization." In Berndt and Lawrence 1973.298–316.

Law, Robin. 1992. "Warfare on the West African Slave Coast, 1650–1850." In Ferguson and Whitehead 1992b.103–26.

Lawrence, A.W. 1965. "Ancient Egyptian Fortifications." *Journal of Egyptian Archaeology* 51, 69–94.

Levy, Jack S. n.d. "The Study of War in Political Science." Paper presented at the Summary Conference, The Study of War Project, Cantigny, Ill., June 1997.

Lévi-Strauss, Claude. 1943. "Guerre et Commerce chez les Indiens de l'Amérique du Sud." *Renaissance* 1, 122–39.

Lightfoot, Kent G., and Antoinette Martinez. 1995. "Frontiers and Boundaries in Archaeological Perspective." *Annual Review of Anthropology* 24, 471–92.

Luttwak, Edward. 1976. *The Grand Strategy of the Roman Empire: From the First Century A.D. to the Third.* Baltimore, Md.: Johns Hopkins University Press.

Mair, Lucy. 1977. *Primitive Government: A Study of Traditional Political Systems in Eastern Africa.* Bloomington: Indiana University Press.

Mann, Michael. 1986. *The Sources of Social Power*, Vol. 1, *A History of Power from the Beginning to A.D. 1760.* Cambridge: Cambridge University Press.

Martin, Debra L. 1997. "Violence against Women in the La Plata Valley (A.D. 1000–1300)." In Frayer and Martin 1997.45–75.

Marwick, Max. 1970. "Witchcraft as a Social Strain-Gauge." In *Witchcraft and Sorcery,* edited by Max Marwick, 280–95. Harmondsworth, England: Penguin.

Maschner, Herbert D. G. 1997. "The Evolution of Northwest Coast Warfare." In Frayer and Martin 1997.267–302.

Mattingly, D. J. 1992. "War and Peace in Roman North Africa: Observations and Models of State-Tribe Interaction." In Ferguson and Whitehead 1992b.31–60.

Maybury-Lewis, David. 1974. *Akwe-Shavante Society.* New York: Oxford University Press.

McNeill, William H. n.d. "The Human Experience of War and Violence." Paper presented at the Summary Conference, The Study of War Project, Cantigny, Ill., June 1997.

Meggitt, Mervyn. 1977. *Blood Is Their Argument: Warfare among the Mae Enga Tribesmen of the New Guinea Highlands.* Palo Alto, Calif.: Mayfield.

Moore, John H. 1990. "The Reproductive Success of Cheyenne War Chiefs: A Contrary Case to Chagnon's Yanomamo." *Current Anthropology* 31, 322–30.

Moorey, P. R. S. 1986. "The Emergence of the Light, Horse-Drawn Chariot in the Near East c. 2000–1500 B.C." *World Archaeology* 18.2, 196–215.

Morren, George E. B. 1984. "Warfare on the Highland Fringe of New Guinea: The Case of the Mountain Ok." In Ferguson 1984c.169–207.

Morris, Donald R. 1965. *The Washing of the Spears: The Rise and Fall of the Zulu Nation.* New York: Simon and Schuster.

Murphy, Robert. 1957. "Intergroup Hostility and Social Cohesion." *American Anthropologist* 59, 1018–35.

Needham, Rodney. 1976. "Skulls and Causality." *Man* 11.1, 71–88.

Netting, Robert McC. 1974. "Kofyar Armed Conflict: Social Causes and Consequences." *Journal of Anthropological Research* 30.3, 139–63.

Nigel, Kenneth M. 1995. *The Gymnasium of Virtue: Education and Culture in Ancient Sparta.* Chapel Hill: University of North Carolina Press.

Nippel, Wilfried. 1995. *Public Order in Ancient Rome.* Cambridge: Cambridge University Press.

Numelin, Ragnar. 1950. *The Beginnings of Diplomacy: A Sociological Study of Intertribal and International Relations.* London: Oxford University Press.

O'Connell, Robert L. 1989. *Of Arms and Men: A History of War, Weapons, Aggression.* New York: Oxford University Press.

———. 1995. *Ride of the Second Horseman: The Birth and Death of War.* New York: Oxford University Press.

Otterbein, Keith. 1977. "Warfare: A Hitherto Unrecognized Critical Variable." *American Behavioral Scientist* 20, 693–710.

———. 1979. "Huron vs. Iroquois: A Case Study in Inter-Tribal Warfare." *Ethnohistory* 26.2, 141–52.

———. 1985. *The Evolution of War: A Cross-Cultural Study.* 2d ed. New Haven, Conn.: HRAF Press.

Pershits, Abraham. 1979. "Tribute Relations." In *Political Anthropology: The State of the Art,* edited by S. L. Seaton and H. Claessen, 149–56. New York: Mouton.

Postgate, J. N. 1974. *Taxation and Conscription in the Assyrian Empire.* Rome: Biblical Institute Press.

Price, Barbara J. 1977. "Shifts of Production and Organization: A Cluster Interaction Model." *Current Anthropology* 18, 209–34.

———. 1984. "Competition, Productive Intensification, and Ranked Society: Speculations from Evolutionary Theory." In Ferguson 1984c.209–40.

Rappaport, Roy A. 1968. *Pigs for the Ancestors: Ritual in the Ecology of a New Guinea People.* New Haven, Conn.: Yale University Press.

Reyna, S. P. 1994a. "A Mode of Domination Approach to Organized Violence." In Reyna and Downs 1994.29–65.

———. 1994b. "Predatory Accumulation and Religious Conflict in the Early 19th Century Chad Basin." In Reyna and Downs 1994.127–55.

——— , and R. E. Downs, ed. 1994. *Studying War: Anthropological Perspectives.* Langhorne, Pa.: Gordon and Breach.

Rosaldo, Michelle Z. 1983. "The Shame of Headhunters and the Autonomy of Self." *Ethos* 11.3, 135–51.

Ross, Marc Howard. 1986. "A Cross-Cultural Theory of Political Conflict and Violence." *Political Psychology* 7, 427–69.

Rowlands, Michael, Mogens Larsen, and Kristian Kristiansen, eds. 1987. *Centre and Periphery in the Ancient World.* Cambridge: Cambridge University Press.

Saggs, H. W. F. 1963. "Assyrian Warfare in the Sargonid Period." *Iraq* 25.2, 145–54.

Sahlins, Marshall. 1958. *Social Stratification in Polynesia.* Seattle: University of Washington Press.

———. 1961. "The Segmentary Lineage: An Organization of Predatory Expansion." *American Anthropologist* 63, 322–45.

———. 1972. *Stone Age Economics.* Chicago: Aldine.

Scarre, Christopher, and Brian Fagan. 1997. *Ancient Civilizations.* New York: Longman.

Schneider, Jane. 1977. "Was There a Pre-capitalist World System?" *Peasant Studies* 6, 20–29.

Sillitoe, Paul. 1977. "Land Shortage and War in New Guinea." *Ethnology* 16, 71–81.

———. 1978. "Big Men and War in New Guinea." *Man* 13, 252–71.

Simmel, Georg. 1964. *"Conflict" and "The Web of Group-Affiliations."* New York: Free Press.

Sinopoli, Carla M. 1994. "The Archaeology of Empires." *Annual Review of Anthropology* 23, 159–80.

Siskind, Janet. 1973. "Tropical Forest Hunters and the Economy of Sex." In *Peoples and Cultures of Native South America,* edited by Daniel R. Gross, 226–40. Garden City, N.Y.: Natural History Press.

Solway, Jacqueline S., and Richard B. Lee. 1990. "Foragers, Genuine or Spurious: Situating the Kalahari San in History." *Current Anthropology* 31, 109–46.

Southall, Aiden. 1988. "The Segmentary State in Africa and Asia." *Comparative Studies in History and Society* 30, 52–82.

Sponsel, Leslie E., and Thomas Gregor, eds. 1994. *The Anthropology of Peace and Nonviolence.* Boulder, Colo.: Lynne Rienner.

Starna, William A., and Ralph Watkins. 1991. "Northern Iroquoian Slavery." *Ethnohistory* 38.1, 34–57.

Sutton, Constance R., ed. 1995. *Feminism, Nationalism, and Militarism.* Arlington, Va.: American Anthropological Association.

Tacon, Paul, and Christopher Chippindale. 1994. "Australia's Ancient Warriors: Changing Depictions of Fighting in the Rock Art of Arnhem Land, N.T." *Cambridge Archaeological Journal* 4.2, 211–48.

Tainter, Joseph A. 1988. *The Collapse of Complex Societies.* Cambridge: Cambridge University Press.

Tilly, Charles, ed. 1975. *The Formation of National States in Western Europe.* Princeton, N.J.: Princeton University Press.

Trelease, Allen W. 1997. *Indian Affairs in Colonial New York: The Seventeenth Century.* Lincoln: University of Nebraska Press.

Trigger, Bruce G. 1987. *The Children of Aataentsic: A History of the Huron People to 1660.* Montreal: McGill University Press.

Turney-High, Harry H. 1971. *Primitive War: Its Practice and Concepts.* 2d ed. Columbia: University of South Carolina Press.

Van der Dennen, J. M. G. 1995. *The Origin of War.* 2 vols. Groningen: Origin Press.

Vansina, Jan. 1971. "A Traditional Legal System: The Kuba." In *Man in Adaptation: The Institutional Framework,* edited by Yehudi A. Cohen, 135–48. Chicago: Aldine.

Vayda, Andrew P. 1960. *Maori Warfare.* Polynesian Society, Maori Monographs, No. 2. Wellington, New Zealand: Polynesian Society.

———. 1961. "Expansion and Warfare among Swidden Agriculturalists." *American Anthropologist* 63, 346–58.

———. 1969. "The Study of the Causes of War, with Special Reference to Head-Hunting Raids in Borneo." *Ethnohistory* 16, 211–24.

Viveiros de Castro, Eduardo. 1992. *From the Enemy's Point of View: Humanity and Divinity in an Amazonian Society.* Translated by Catherine V. Howard. Chicago: University of Chicago Press.

Voget, Fred W. 1964. "Warfare and the Integration of Crow Culture." In *Explorations in Cultural Anthropology,* edited by Ward Goodenough, 483–509. New York: McGraw-Hill.

Warren, James. 1982. "Slavery and the Impact of External Trade: The Sulu Sultanate in the 19th Century." In *Philippine Social History: Global Trade and Local Transformations,* edited by Alfred McCoy and C. de Jesus, 414–44. Quezon City: Manila University Press.

Watson, G. R. 1969. *The Roman Soldier.* Ithaca, N.Y.: Cornell University Press.

Whitehead, Neil L. 1992. "Tribes Make States and States Make Tribes: Warfare and the Creation of Colonial Tribes and States in Northeastern South America." In Ferguson and Whitehead 1992b.127–50.

Whiting, Beatrice. 1965. "Sex Identity Conflict and Physical Violence: A Comparative Study." *American Anthropologist* 67, 123–40.

Wolf, Eric R. 1987. "Cycles of Violence: The Anthropology of War and Peace." In *Waymarks: The Notre Dame Inaugural Lectures in Anthropology,* edited by K. Moore, 127–50. Notre Dame, Ind.: University of Notre Dame.

Worsley, Peter. 1968. *The Trumpet Shall Sound: A Study of "Cargo" Cults in Melanesia.* New York: Schocken Books.

Yoffee, Norman. 1995. "Political Economy in Early Mesopotamian States." *Annual Review of Anthropology* 24, 281–311.

SIXTEEN

Epilogue

VICTOR DAVIS HANSON AND
BARRY S. STRAUSS

Introduction

This present volume is a welcome cross-cultural and historical study of warfare and society in the Near East, Europe, East Asia, and Mesoamerica, giving new meaning to the traditional European connotation of the "ancient" and "medieval" worlds. And while these chapters prove that notions like "Roman," "Chinese," or "Islamic" warfare are gross abstractions that can only inadequately capture changing military practice over hundreds of years, there is enough ethnic and cultural homogeneity present in each investigation to permit some rather large generalizations about the practice of war, and the place of soldiers in society throughout the world during the last four millennia of civilization.

Despite differences across time and space in these individual accounts, certain commonalities emerge—as we might expect in preindustrial societies where technology and industry in the modern sense were absent and agriculture and warfare were the usual callings of most of the population. In some way, the two occupations are always linked before the Industrial Revolution. Indeed, warfare's utter reliance on food production and farmers in our period of inquiry perhaps defines the very terms "ancient" and "medieval" in opposition to "modern," when capital, finance, and industrialization, not farming, now predicate the conditions, time, and participants of organized battle.

In all societies under study here, the rise of large armies and plentiful armaments that allowed extended campaigns arose from the creation of agricultural surpluses (Gnirs on the rise of irrigated agriculture in Egypt), which in turn permitted state formation, population growth, and the spread of bronze and iron metallurgy (Farris on the Yayoi period in Japan [300 B.C.–A.D. 300]). Often available food allows enormous numbers of combatants to be marshaled (e.g., the thirty-seven thousand infantry of Ramesside times), as battle casualties reach the many thousands (the twenty-seven thousand Japanese dead at the Paekch'on River [A.D. 663] in Korea). We often hear that peasants or farmers compose the majority of the military manpower of a state (Hassig on the Aztecs; Farris on medieval Japan; Raaflaub on classical Greece), and thus that war-making can paralyze a culture by draining away its agrarian workforce and leaving the countryside so unsettled as to prevent steady cultivation. Farris, for example, records the example of a near end to rice production in the Kanto province of A.D. 1027 due to predation and peasant flight; and Hassig points out that the Aztecs did not fight in the summer or early fall when soldiers were engaged in the harvest. Ultimately, early societies must either craft protocols to prevent agricultural damage (Raaflaub on the classical Greek city-states) or find manpower sources outside agriculture, permitting armies to be in the field without harming the productive capacity of the culture itself (Crone on Islamic soldiers; Raaflaub on Sparta; Rosenstein on the transition from republic to empire at Rome). Quite simply, armies composed of agrarians (Rosenstein on Republican Rome; Raaflaub on classical Greece; Bachrach on early medieval Europe) have innate checks on their military potential as warfare becomes more local and less imperial (Ferguson). It is no exaggeration to confess, then, that the historian of the early military must first see how a society is fed, before he can learn how it fights. The conditions of land tenure, the nature of rural settlement, the type of crops, and human adaptations to environment to produce food are inseparable from how an army is recruited, organized, maintained, and used.

A second constant in our wide-ranging investigations seems to be that warfare is pervasive in human society. Along with farming, most cultures of the past invested their human and material capital first in protection (fortifications and barriers) and offense (armaments, training, logistics, and manpower). Almost no culture studied reveals a pacifism of any sort or much conscious effort at avoiding or denying the necessity of formal war-making; even the purportedly peaceful and non-warlike Maya were in actuality obsessed with warfare and conquest (Webster on the Mesoamerican epigraphic and archaeological evidence). The chief question, then, is not whether ancient societies were warlike (the answer, it seems to us, is surely that they were) but rather to what degree fighting was subordinated to larger social and cultural concerns that might control its lethality. In many cultures, for example, warfare appears ritualistic, where tactics, strategy, armament, and killing technique are not entirely free to meet the exigencies of simply slaying the greatest number of foes in the most efficient manner but rather are subservient to larger questions of political and social control, hierarchy, and class.

Ancient and medieval states, in short, aspired to do far fewer things than modern states. Premodern societies had, to be sure, to secure the goodwill of heaven, and some attempted to make life better on earth by sponsoring economic improvements, such as canals, harbors, or marketplaces. The bulk of a state's energy, however, was spent on war and taxes. Taking care of the army—recruiting and training it, campaigning with it, and maintaining it—is one of the main things, and sometimes the only thing, premodern states did; so was paying for it. As Haldon says of the Byzantine Empire, to understand a premodern army is to go a long way toward understanding a premodern state and society.

Although premodern war was not total war in the sense that twentieth-century war can be, conflict was nonetheless "built into the fabric of warring societies" (Ferguson), shaped by and reshaping them in turn. Hence, the student of premodern war needs a "holistic perspective" (Ferguson). But what should the starting point be for such a perspective? Surely, the question of "What is war?"

Ritual and Nonritual

Without dipping into the never-ending debate on nature and culture, it can be said that as far back as the evidence goes, humans have shown themselves to be creatures who band together to compete over resources against other human groups; to have high intelligence, thriving on symbolic communication and abstraction; and to contain considerable capacity for killing each other and risking death. Enter war: organized violent competition over resources, involving substantial killing and the threat of death. Poised between life and death, war tends to invite religious reflection. War soon becomes "thoroughly ritualized," as Ferguson notes, a point most evident here in discussions of early Greek, Mayan, Aztec, and Japanese fighting. But war is not simply the threat or risk of death, nor simply competition, nor simply violence. War is ultimately the organization of men (sometimes, but rarely, women too) into fighting units (usually armies, sometimes navies). Hence, we cannot study war without studying society. By focusing on the social dimension of war, moreover, we tend to discount that part of war which is about death. As Crone puts it, we tend to study less the warrior than the soldier.

Not surprisingly, the chapters in this volume tend to see early war as a rational, pragmatic institution. Although several of the authors (Crone, Raaflaub, Hassig, Webster, Farris) note religious motivations for warfare, they tend almost always to see political or economic purposes behind them. Thus the emphasis in this volume is on the material causes of war—war for agricultural produce or territory or slaves or in pursuit of social mobility. Rightly so, but it needs to be underlined that in war premodern leaders and soldiers also sought symbolic capital. For example, the Aztec elites could not tolerate the thought of independent centers of power within their sphere of influence (Hassig). Roman Republican leaders coveted not only booty but also prestige in warfare, the latter to be translated into political power at home (Rosenstein). The Peloponnesian War did not begin because Sparta coveted Athens's wealth or because Athens wanted Spartan land; rather, Sparta feared the consequences of letting Athens dictate to Sparta's allies, and Athens feared the loss of prestige that would ensue from backing down before a Spartan ultimatum. As Donald Kagan points out, Thucydides was right—sometimes the cause of war turns out to be less greed than honor.[1]

Ask why war was so pervasive in antiquity and the Middle Ages; the answer is that it worked. One is reminded of Willy Sutton's famous rejoinder when asked why he robbed banks: "Because that's where the money is." In premodern times, when most wealth was agricultural and tangible, war was, as Aristotle reminds us, an efficient way to acquire resources—an "acquisitive art." What could not be acquired by diplomacy or threat would be taken by force. Remember, too, that the early battlefield was not a very lethal place, compared with its modern horrors. Victory, as long as the victors restrained their blood-lust—the thrust, by the way, of ancient and medieval antiwar writing, such as it was, was less to abolish war than to get warriors to keep hands off civilians—promised new land, treasure, and slaves, and prestige too. Warfare constituted adaptive behavior, to use the language of evolution.

It is thus true as a general rule that military expenditure should not always be equated with wasted investment or gratuitous killing; often mobilization and war-making can have profound and sometimes positive effects on the social fabric. Under the Principate, the Roman army served as a nexus for assimilation of different races and ethnicities, and provided a regular source of salaried pay and a guaranteed retirement stipend for recruits from the lower classes. In the middle Byzantine period of the tenth century, the need to ensure a reliable and plentiful source of army manpower resulted in greater concern for the economic well-being of the peasantry. Rosenstein demonstrates that in the initial centuries of Roman republican expansionism regular military service tended to give some leverage to the plebs, who provided critical manpower to the legions and thus were in a better position to broker privileges from aristocrats. Indeed, more cultures seem to suffer from overpopulation than from catastrophic military losses, and it is rare to see military preparation and wartime losses as the chief culprit for cultural decay, when set against resource depletion, overpopulation, or systems collapses due to overspecialization and the constant growth of nonproductive bureaucracies and castes.

It consequently proved difficult to knock martial ardor even out of defeated peoples. Take, for instance, the Jews, famous for their statelessness for the better part of two millennia. It has been argued that rabbinic Judaism, which grew up in the shadow of defeat and exile under the Romans, recoiled from war. Recent research, however, provides a reassessment.[2] The rabbis' position was not so much pacifism as prudence. Both the Jewish Revolt (A.D. 66–70) and the Bar-Kochba Revolt (A.D. 132–35) received strong rabbinic support. Afterward, when the impossibility of Jewish independence became clear, accommodationism came to mark much of rabbinic thought, both ancient and medieval. Yet, even so, there were other rabbis who rejected passivity. They celebrated their people's military past and argued for armed Jewish resistance against contemporary oppression when resistance proved possible. From time to time, late antique and medieval Jews did take up arms against their attackers, both in western Asia and in Europe, in the latter notably at the time of the First Crusade.

The classical Greeks, governed by assemblies of yeomen farmers, for a time centered war-making around the collision of hoplite phalanxes even though skirmishing, sea power, and cavalry brought enormous advantages to conflict, as Athens demonstrated to shocked conservatives in the fifth century B.C. (Raaflaub). The so-called flower wars (*xochiyaoyotl*) in imperial Mexico, in their initial phases, were not so much wars of conquest as demonstrations of strength, where Aztec prowess was showcased without deliberate efforts to kill or maim, or even to take captives for sacrifice. And the Maya of the seventh and eighth centuries A.D. often initiated campaigns by auspicious dates and astronomical events (see Webster on the so-called star-shell events) that were not always predicated on simple military efficacy. Even in Egypt of the New Kingdom, where we encounter a notion bordering on "total warfare," a ritualized campaign to Nubia, long conquered and colonized, seems to have been obligatory for every new king in order to cement his authority, demonstrate his responsibilities, and prove his ability to keep the world intact and defeat chaos (Gnirs).

Still, in such murky contexts it is often difficult to distinguish to what extent the gods were used to justify military exigency or were themselves engines of war-making. The medieval Japanese samurai, for example, recited their pedigrees to one another, dressed in elaborate garb, and engaged in combat to the death; the loser's head was both prize and proof of victory—a practice quite different from that of the nomadic Mongols, who laughed at such rites and preferred instead to attack in mass. In the East particularly, religious and military powers were blurred, and we hear of the "Divine Warriors" (Farris on the Yamato monarch in Japan) in the same manner that Pharaoh was God's representative on earth and properly the eternal warrior and rightful commander in chief of the armies. And the Arab invasions of the seventh century A.D. of the eastern Roman and Sasanid Empires seem to have been coordinated from a single locus, the religious center of Medina—all Muslims were soldiers, rather than merely soldiers being Muslims (Crone). Yet in contrast, in the West just as often the gods seem mere pretexts to more earthly concerns, not as motivations for invasion themselves. Even at Byzantium, where the notion of the emperor as God's appointed ruler and representative on earth was unusually enshrined, religion gradually gave way to military expediency, and by 800 the Byzantine army was reorganized, adept at technological innovation, and far less subject to religious control than its Muslim opponents (Haldon).

In no case did seemingly pacifistic religions such as Christianity or Buddhism inhibit the practice of arms. Haldon demonstrates, for example, just how entwined the Greek Orthodox Christian Church was in the entire fabric of Byzantine landowning and warfare without offering any formal hindrance to organized killing. No chapter of this book suggests that any culture crafted an all-encompassing belief system that at its heart deplored war, much less outlawed it. In most cases, the gods oversaw intramural wars, and in the case of foreign enemies, temples and shrines were often the first to burn as symbolic expression of the religious superiority of the victors. Yates points out that although the Confucian literati under the Han dynasty de-emphasized the role of war in Chinese society, military heroes nevertheless "were tolerated, or even considered necessary."

We do not wish to enter into the controversy of whether such rituals were simply ex post facto explications or met real material exigencies. Hassig has a good discussion on the role of religion in Aztec warfare and suggests plausibly enough that much more often there were real political and economic motives behind seemingly purely religious practices (see also Webster on the utilitarian, materialist functions behind much of the supposedly ritualistic and ideological basis of Mayan warfare). The massive human sacrifices by King Ahuitzotl in 1486 at the Great Temple of Tenochtitlán seemingly explain the Aztec need to take captives during battle, but in reality such mass killing may have been political spectacle, state terror to impress any would-be insurrectionists.

Certain constants also emerge from the study of war-making of the past that frame military ritual, particularly in areas that anthropologists would call "infrastructure"—those areas separate from the "structures" and "superstructures" that refer to larger notions of political and economic approaches to warmaking and the more cultural concerns of how peoples envision, describe, and experience organized killing. Obviously prime examples are geography and terrain that alter the human practice and experience of war. For instance, the majority of our case studies were cultures from temperate climates, well below the Arctic circle, and also rarely equatorial. The location of some of the larger military structures in our study (Rome, China, Persia) suggests that extreme cold and heat are obstacles to war, or at least impediments to the creation of large, aggressive armies bereft of technology that can be mobilized easily and maintained in the field. The warm climate of Egypt with its vast expanses of level ground made warfare a year-round enterprise characterized by the chariot (five thousand present at the battle of Qadesh alone) in a way that was impossible in, say, northern Asia or among mountainous terrain of the southern Balkans. Even in Mexico and Central America, whose equatorial climates limited war-making for much of the year, the Aztecs and Maya were able to fight for at most five months out of the year, almost exclusively from early December to late April during the dry season when farmers were not at harvest.

Natural resources, of course, also explain ritual fights and even larger trends in military specialization. The absence of readily available iron in early Japan, for example, may account for the absence of heavy infantry with effective body armor and edged weapons as an alternative to the small and ritualized samurai class. There were no horses in the pre-Columbian Americas, and Hassig emphasizes the Mesoamerican reliance on porters, where the difficult terrain of Central America and Mexico restricted both the range of the Aztecs' imperialism and their ability to move their large armies efficiently through their empire—intrinsic weaknesses when the Spanish arrived with more mobile forces, horses, and superior technology.

West and Non-West

Neither rituals nor geography and nature can explain away all differences of our armies under discussion. The most obvious gulf—visible as early as the fifth and fourth centuries B.C.—is the general divide between Western and non-Western warfare. We argue that Western societies tend to promote freedom more than non-Western societies, but this is not the place to discuss the point at length; here we speak primarily as military and social historians. In general the early societies of Greece and Rome take a differing approach to technology and seem more ready to welcome change and innovation, as part of an inevitable cycle of response and adaptation aimed at increasing military efficiency, quite unconcerned with religious or political ramifications. Their European cultural offspring inherit this notion of military dynamism, and thus are more likely to venture outside the West than to defend their territory from African, Asiatic, or American invasion. Roman imperialism, the Crusaders, Cortés, and English colonialist armies are all reflections of the innate aggressiveness and lethality of Western military practice, which sometimes alter—or end—the very societies they attack. Persia, Mexico, Japan, and Celtic Europe in Roman times are good examples of civilizations, castes, and tribes that were unprepared for the peculiar Western approach to military conquest.

Why this Western tendency to disconnect military innovation from religious or political audit? Most obviously, it is the decentralized nature of classical civilizations, which after the Mycenaean collapse tend to eschew palatial centralized economies and relegate religion away from politics—what Gnirs has called in the Egyptian context the "royal monopoly." Thus the presence of landowning citizens with constitutional prerogatives creates a strong body of militiamen who are accustomed in idiosyncratic and individualistic ways to find ways to slaughter the foe more efficiently as a mechanism to advance a shared consensus among their peers. Arms and armor, for example, are in control of the individual and widely held, unlike, say, the weaponry of Egypt or the New World stored under the royal seal or produced by regional temples (Gnirs, Hassig). At no time and place was the connection between landowning, soldiering, and citizenship closer than in archaic Greece and in the early and middle Roman Republics. Yet, even in other periods of Western history when government was more centralized, individual initiative among soldiers remained strong. Even at Byzantium, for example, individual soldiers provided their own weapons, usually purchased from local arms factories (Haldon). Bachrach similarly emphasizes the huge percentages of the late Roman civilian population who had access to their own weapons and formed local militias. People who own their arms and decide on when and where they fight are more open to the advantages of technological improvement.

Perhaps the notion of a free landholding citizenry also explains the peculiar Western tradition of heavy infantry who employ shock tactics that are designed to take and hold flatland. In no other culture under investigation were the horse and true cavalry as unimportant as in the classical states of Greece and the Roman Republic—often with dire consequences when such classical armies ventured into foreign theaters of operation. Horsemanship and skilled archers both represented the need for capital, required training and specialization, and were antithetical to the idea of a landowning yeomanry, who found their natural egalitarian identity as heavy infantry men in the phalanx or legion, fighting over their own land on their own initiative—in direct contrast to nomadic tribes and other cultures where permanent agriculture and private property were relatively rare.

For example, in Mesoamerica, China, Japan, or Africa, the notions of freedom and citizen do not seem to exist in the vocabulary, and there war serves a particular elite, caste, or ancestral tradition. Yates points out that under most dynastic governments in China the state claimed ownership of the greatest portion of the land. In Japan, samurai were used to chastise peasants to work the fields and pay taxes, and completely antithetical to the classical notion of farmers themselves deciding where and when and by whom warfare might be conducted. Early Asiatic war is confined more to particular castes, and often technology itself was limited by political or religious concerns. For example, in the second half of the ninth century A.D., the crossbow fell out of use in Japan, perhaps due to its potential deadliness against the samurai class. Warfare among the Aztecs was completely stratified, and the ancient Maya may have entrusted most of their war-making to small groups of elites. In general, it is a fair simplification to say that war in the Orient and often in the Muslim world was subject to ethical and religious restraints unknown in the West, protocols that tended to stagnate technological development and tactical flexibility even as they added a strong ethical or religious element to campaigning—in stark contrast to the wide-open dynamism of Western armies, whose sheer destructiveness in warfare frightened so many it encountered. There is an affinity across time and space among Alexander, Caesar, Cortés, and English colonialists in their savage mastery over non-Western adversaries.

Moreover, in the same manner as states with centralized and planned economies (Hassig on the Olmecs, Teotihuacán, Toltecs, and Aztecs; Briant on Persia; Yates on the Chinese) control economic production and land, so too they govern every aspect of tactics, armament, and technology, which allows them to field great armies but also ensures that such organizations are rigid, inflexible, and vulnerable to sudden outside stimulus, as attested by Mexico's defeat by Spanish invaders and the Mycenaean collapse under outside pressure, possibly in combination with other factors (in the thirteenth century B.C.). Bachrach, in contrast, points out that citizen-soldiers in early Europe diminished the need for a centralized bureaucratic government and assumed a great deal of freedom in deciding their own local issues of defense.

These wars across cultural divides, then, bring into sharp contrast radically different mentalities and technologies of warfare. Thus, while the Aztecs lacked bronze armor, such deficiencies mattered little when there were no iron offensive edged weapons or gunpowder present in the Americas. The appearance of the Spanish, and the integration of their firearms and horses into a combined Spanish-Tlaxcaltec force, made centuries of pre-Columbian military practice obsolete and completely outclassed Aztec armies of much greater size. On occasions such contacts—European armies in the Levant during the Crusades; the appearance of Western colonists in Asia, Africa, and the Orient; the repulse of the Persians' invasions of Greece; Alexander's trek to the Indus River; and Roman expansionism in the third through first century B.C.—reveal just how lethal and flexible Western military practice might be.

A vast gulf between East and West also emerges from the literature of war and illustrates the differing manner in which war is both represented and discussed by intellectuals. In China and Japan, literary genres arose that gave advice on war but were integrated with ideological and religious superstructures such as the Sun-Tzu. In Egypt, monumental records and court annals reflect elite ideology and were officially sanctioned depictions of war in language that indicated "how the world *should* be rather than how the world is"—in short, they represent early forms of what we might legitimately call "propaganda" (Gnirs). Individual historians and analysts are not free to see military practice as a dynamic science in and of itself—what the Romans called *res militares*—not subject to religious or political influence. Greek and Roman historiography and military writing (see Campbell on the Roman military handbooks), in contrast, are largely immune from both governmental and religious sanctions, and thus can serve as more practical and widely disseminated handbooks on how to improve military efficacy—knowledge available to any who choose to patronize the work of a particular author and who find his or her proposals in the marketplace of ideas worthy of experimentation or emulation.

Modern and Premodern

A central theme of this volume is the paradoxes and dilemmas of premodern government when it came to war. Neither demography nor technology matched the ambitions of a city-state for independence nor of an empire for universal rule nor of either state to keep outsiders out of the military. There were never enough original "good" soldiers—or their descendants—to go around, and force multipliers were few. To succeed, therefore, it was necessary to compromise on the crucial issue of recruitment: outsiders would have to become insiders. So Athenians had to admit resident aliens to their armies (in separate units) and to their warships, too, where allied mercenaries and occasionally slaves all rowed alongside the poorer Athenian citizens. Alexander not only recruited a corps of thirty thousand Iranians for his army, but in so doing he may have followed not a Macedonian but an Achaemenid practice: when in Persia do as the Persians do—and do it with Persians (Briant). Hellenistic Greco-Macedonian rulers had to admit Egyptians, Syrians, and Mesopotamians into the "Macedonian" phalanx (Hamilton), and soon the non-Greek-speaking soldiers were calling themselves Macedonians or Hellenes. Noncitizens served in separate units in the Roman imperial army (Campbell), which perhaps is best characterized as multicultural. To replace the original soldiers of their conquering host, who had "gone native" (that is, become assimilated and pacified), the early Arab rulers had to turn to, variously, Syrian Arabs who had not been part of the original armies, Persian-speaking Khurasani recruits, and Turks of non-Muslim and servile origin (Crone). They also used resettled captives—following in the footsteps of the pharaohs themselves (Crone, Gnirs). The Aztec elite had to admit commoners, including immigrants, to their military, often rewarding them with the equivalent of knighthoods (Hassig).

Nor could the premodern state govern a large area without local cooperation

(Crone), as the foregoing cases suggest. So while the distinction between hegemonic and territorial empire counts for something in the premodern world (Hassig), it means far less than when applied to modern times. For example, a hegemonic empire like that of Athens lacked the formal provinces of a territorial empire like that of the Achaemenids or Seleucids or Rome or Byzantium or the Abbasid empire and probably had proportionally fewer garrisons. Yet none of these territorial empires could impose uniformity on the periphery from the center. Each had to devolve power, to a greater or lesser extent, on local rulers, often of different ethnicity or language. In Japan, the Buddhist civilian court had to rely on the Shinto warrior-nobles to serve as district managers (Farris). It was generally easier to conquer territory than to govern it, although the prudent premodern leader, such as an Aztec, would go a step better and follow (if unwittingly) the Sun-Tzuian principle of cowing an enemy through the show of power rather than having actually to expend force (Hassig). Unruly and rebellious satraps of the frontiers were a constant irritant to the Great King at Persepolis (Briant).

A leitmotif of this volume is that armies are major formal institutions. Although they are shaped by society, they do not simply reflect it; rather, armies generate their own practices and values that reshape society in turn. Recruitment arrangements, therefore, like military organization more generally, entail political consequences. If the Athenians had manned their galleys exclusively with noncitizens, they might have gotten away with money payments. Because they used citizens as the core of their crews, however, and specifically because they relied on poor citizens, the elite had to pay a political price. They were forced to recognize the political power that Athenian protocols of freedom and equality demanded: hence, the navy made Athenian democracy into an ever-greater reality (Raaflaub). Alternatively, Arab government became more monarchical and less consensual once the descendants of the original conquering soldiers put down their warlike ways for civilian pursuits and ideologies and let others fight their battles for them (Crone). In the Byzantine Empire the army was the primary, perhaps the only, focus for expressing nonmetropolitan or provincial opinion (Haldon). Recruitment policies entail socioeconomic consequences as well. The military profession offered prosperity and social mobility in the Roman and Aztec Empires, as it did in Athens (Campbell, Hassig). The *kardakes* of Persia were a multiracial corps whose commonality as imperial infantry transcended Persian ideals of race (Briant).

Some of the case studies in this volume are of city-states (Archaic and classical Greece, Republican Rome, the Mayas, preimperial China), but most are of large kingdoms or empires. This pattern is partly coincidence (other premodern city-states might be considered, for example, Carthage or the cities of Sumer or the Levant or of medieval and Renaissance Italy or of West Africa) but not entirely coincidence. Although it was possible for premodern city-states to compete against empires and their large military resources, it was difficult. Success generally required that city-states pool resources in a federated league, and few city-states had the discipline to do that as well as or for as long as Republican Rome (Rosenstein). So it is no accident that so much of the history of premodern warfare is the history of kingdoms and empires. Yet, city-states were not without relative advantages. They tended to be more stable than empires because they were less dependent on fragile networks of tribute and on long-distance policing (Hassig). They were surely more cohesive, lacking the demographic luxury of larger political units to employ a low military participation ratio (following Andreski's term, here employed by Crone). And they lacked the scale of capital and labor to subsidize a bureaucratic elite that often siphoned off resources into nonproductive enterprises.

From these historical studies a few truisms emerge, many of them quite disturbing as we reach the end of another millennium of human history. The practice and intensity of warfare increase as state surpluses of human and material capital rise. In general, states that divorce war from particular aristocracies and religious bodies—Republican Rome and classical Greece—and are often pluralistic in nature, field more dynamic and better-led armies, and are far more successful in mobilizing the general population in the business of killing people. Rosenstein points out that by the beginning of the second century B.C., Rome was able to wage war simultaneously in Greece, the Near East, Spain, and northern Italy, mobilizing for foreign service nearly 50,000 legionaries out of an adult male citizen population of only 250,000. And by the time of the battle of Actium, Octavian and Antonius commanded sixty legions with about a quarter million men under arms. Constitutional governments—even under the Roman Principate many of the local political structures of the Republic survived—tend to form lethal armies of consensus and frown on reliance on specialized castes, making their "nation in arms" more, not less, successful forces of destruction. Even under Alexander's dynastic rule, the Macedonian army was still composed of "Foot Companions" and the "Companion Cavalry," both ostensibly egalitarian bodies, whose tough veterans saw themselves as military equals to the king himself, and with whom they could dine and speak freely (Hamilton). Such societies put few restrictions on technological innovation and generally reap the dividends of those efficiencies in military practices. Warfare, then, divorced from religious and cultural rites—classical Greek hoplite warfare seems to be the last expression of a Western society where larger social and cultural concerns restricted the free practice and evolution of warfare—seems more dynamic, free to follow economic laws of finance and to employ technology simply on the basis of its utility.

The logical evolution of these trends now coalesces in the military practice of the modern West. If other cultures within this study perhaps could teach

Western societies very little about the proper use of technology or tactics in fielding armies, their traditional subordination of war-making—however unattractive or exploitative the motives of such protocols may seem to modern sensibilities—to larger societal concerns seems the way of the future, or at least the only alternative to natural evolution of Western military practice whose logical conclusion will surely be to lead us to the abyss.

Conclusion

In modern times, the nation-state combines the military advantages of city-state and empire. It is large enough to control material resources on an imperial scale. Yet thanks to the modern technology of communications and policing, the nation-state is able to create citizen-armies almost as cohesive as those of an ancient republic. Because it takes advantage of trading networks that are maintained by international rather than imperial norms, the nation-state tends to be less fragile than an empire but wealthier than a city-state. The nation-state is flexible enough for kaleidoscopic diplomacy but durable enough for hegemony. So at its most successful, the modern European nation-state manipulated alliances with a suppleness that the Roman Republic might have envied. Since 1945, meanwhile, the United States has pulled off a virtuoso superpower performance recalling that of the Roman Empire, but only time will tell if the show will last as long as the two-hundred-year pax Romana from Augustus to Commodus.

Yet the deeper contrast between premodern times and our own day lies in the culture of warfare. Under premodern conditions, it was obvious that war was a rational, if violent, means to attain ends—that war was politics by other means. Everyone was an unwitting Clausewitzian in the ancient and medieval world. If modern times, by contrast, needed a Clausewitz (or a rediscovered Sun-Tzu) to explain the point of war, it is not because we moderns are more saintly than our ancestors. Rather, it is because war between capitalist states is self-defeating. The modern way of becoming wealthy, rooted in early modern notions of banking, scientific innovation, and the primacy of practicality over contemplation (hence of technology over theory), created the capitalism that began coming into its own in Clausewitz's day. Modern wealth is frequently too complex, too insidious, to be easily conquered by force of arms; bombing a bank is no way to acquire its products; a trader with a computer will always appear at the next intact phone line. Modern warfare, furthermore, is unprecedentedly lethal. Today, blackmail is more efficient than ever as a way to conquer wealth; war is correspondingly wasteful and expensive, as the cost of killing a human being in modern warfare is reaching astronomical levels even as the world's population explodes. So while there is much talk nowadays of the end of the nation-state, there is no talk about the end of the crime syndicate. On the contrary, mafias, drug lords, triad societies and *yakuza* are fast becoming part of the political science curriculum; they kill far more cheaply than national armies.

The nation-state and the *levée en masse* rose together at the end of the eighteenth century; two hundred years later, some say that they are headed for the elephant graveyard together. Nowadays, the leading industrial states are, on the one hand, divesting themselves of mass citizen armies for lean professional militaries (mercenariats?) while, on the other, chipping away at their sovereignty by joining international trading leagues in which bankers have as much say as politicians, peacekeeping forces more use than armored divisions. Globalization is in the air.

Which is not to say that the scourge of war has passed. As the evidence of premodern warfare shows, war is likely to continue forever. For one thing, even a high-tech economy depends on natural resources, which remain tempting prizes of war, as Iraq's invasion of Kuwait and its oil fields demonstrates. More important, many, if not most, people around the world continue to live, as it were, in a premodern condition. Left out of the prosperity of globalism, they are indifferent to the tut-tutting of the International Monetary Fund, and think nothing of going to war against their tribal, religious, or ideological enemies. Rwanda showed us how quickly and efficiently thousands can be killed in a "backward" state. A third point, and perhaps the most important of all, is that even prosperous people go to war to maintain their prestige. Neither the Aztecs nor the Athenians were poor, but they were bellicose. The former Yugoslavia was a relatively affluent state; so was Germany in 1914. The study of premodern warfare shows us how much we have progressed and how little, and how much the nature of man—vain, fearful, illogical—remains the same even as his culture transmogrifies. Fourth, as the planet's population is now measured in billions, not millions, the age-old quest to eat for one more day may, even in an era of high technology, return to haunt us. There is no reason to doubt hungry peoples will fight to take land and food from the weaker.

Finally, global government is a very old human ideal, almost as old as civilization itself; it dates back to Sargon of Akkad and his claim in the third millennium B.C. to be king of the four corners of the world. Yes, it is very old, but also very tenuous as well. The human tendency toward tribalism—competing for the resources of one's own group against others—has always stood in the way. From the Athenian Acropolis to the rock of Aornos, from the Roman Capitol to Masada, people have proven amazingly willing to die rather than permit the rule of another tribe. It is hard to imagine that changing.

Notes

1. Kagan 1995.
2. Biale 1986.

Bibliography

Biale, David. 1986. *Power and Powerlessness in Jewish History.* New York: Schocken.
Kagan, Donald. 1995. *On the Origins of War and the Preservation of Peace.* New York: Doubleday.

BERNARD S. BACHRACH is Professor of History at the University of Minnesota in Minneapolis, specializing in medieval social, political, and military history. His recent publications include *Fulk Nerra, the Neo-Roman Consul: A Political Biography of the Angevin Count, 987–1040* (1993) and *The Anatomy of a Little War: A Diplomatic and Military History of the Gundovald Affair, 568–586* (1994).

PIERRE BRIANT is Professor of Ancient History at the University of Toulouse, France. He is a specialist in the history of the Greek and Near Eastern Worlds in the first millennium B.C.E. His recent publications include *Histoire de l'Empire Perse* (1996) and *Alexander the Great* (1996).

BRIAN CAMPBELL is Reader in Ancient History at the Queen's University of Belfast, Northern Ireland, focusing on the military history of the Roman empire. Among his publications are *The Emperor and the Roman Army, 31 B.C.–A.D. 235* (1984) and *The Roman Army, 31 B.C.–A.D. 337: A Sourcebook* (1994).

PATRICIA CRONE is Professor at the School of Historical Studies, Institute for Advanced Study, Princeton. She is a specialist in early Islamic history. Her books include *Slaves on Horses: The Evolution of the Islamic Polity* (1980) and *God's Caliph: Religious Authority in the First Centuries of Islam* (1986, co-authored).

W. WAYNE FARRIS, a specialist in ancient and medieval Japanese History, is Professor of History at the University of Tennessee in Knoxville. His publications include *Population, Disease, and Land in Early Japan, 645–900* (1985) and *Heavenly Warriors: The Evolution of Japan's Military, 500–1300* (1992).

R. BRIAN FERGUSON is a historical anthropologist and Professor of Sociology and Anthropology at Rutgers University in Newark. Among other works, he co-edited a volume on *War in the Tribal Zone: Expanding States and Indigenous Warfare* (1992) and recently published *Yanomami Warfare: A Political History* (1995).

455

ANDREA M. GNIRS, a specialist in the social history of ancient Egypt, currently is a candidate for the "habilitation" degree at the University of Heidelberg in Germany. Her book on military and society in the New Egyptian Empire *(Militär und Gesellschaft: Ein Beitrag zur Sozialgeschichte des Neuen Reiches)* was published in 1996. She is preparing the publication of the tomb of Meri and Hunai in Thebes and working on a history of ancient Egyptian autobiographical writing.

JOHN HALDON is Professor of Byzantine History and Director of the Center for Byzantine, Ottoman and Modern Greek Studies at the University of Birmingham, England. His recent publications include *Byzantium in the Seventh Century: The Transformation of a Culture* (1990) and *State, Army and Society in Byzantium: Approaches to Military, Social and Administrative History, 6th–12th Centuries* (1995).

CHARLES D. HAMILTON is Professor of Ancient History and Classics at San Diego State University. He specializes in classical and Hellenistic Greek history and has published, among others, books on *Sparta's Bitter Victories: Politics and Diplomacy in the Corinthian War* (1979) and *Agesilaus and the Failure of Spartan Hegemony* (1991).

VICTOR DAVIS HANSON is a tree and vine farmer in California and Professor of Classics at the California State University in Fresno. His special interests lie in the history of society, agriculture, and warfare in ancient Greece and its meaning for our own time. Among his publications are *The Western Way of War: Infantry Battle in Classical Greece* (1989) and *The Other Greeks: The Family Farm and the Agrarian Roots of Western Civilization* (1995).

ROSS HASSIG is Professor of Anthropology and a specialist in Aztec history at the University of Oklahoma in Norman. His main publications include *Aztec Warfare: Imperial Expansion and Political Control* (1988) and *War and Society in Ancient Mesoamerica* (1992).

KURT RAAFLAUB is Professor of Classics and History at Brown University in Providence, Rhode Island, and Co-Director of the Center for Hellenic Studies in Washington, D.C. He is a specialist in ancient Greek and Roman history, and has published *The Discovery of Freedom* (1985, 2d ed. forthcoming) and co-edited, among other volumes, *Between Republic and Empire: Interpretations of Augustus and His Principate* (1990).

NATHAN ROSENSTEIN is Associate Professor of History at Ohio State University in Columbus, specializing in Roman republican and early imperial history. His *Imperatores Victi: Military Defeat and Aristocratic Competition in the Middle and Late Republic* was published in 1990. His current projects include a book on *War, Agriculture, and the Family in Mid-Republican Rome*.

BARRY S. STRAUSS is Professor of History and Classics and Director of the Peace Studies Program at Cornell University in Ithaca, New York. His interests focus on Greek and Hellenistic social and military history. His publications include *The Anatomy of Error: The Lessons of Ancient Military Disasters for Modern Strategists* (1990, co-authored) and *Fathers and Sons in Athens: Ideology and Society in the Era of the Peloponnesian War* (1993).

DAVID WEBSTER is Professor of Anthropology at Pennsylvania State University in University Park, specializing in early Mesoamerican archaeology and history. He published, among other works, *Defensive Earthworks at Becan, Campeche, Mexico* (1976) and co-authored *Out of the Past: An Introduction to Archaeology* (1993).

ROBIN D. S. YATES is Professor of History and East Asian Studies, Chair of the Department of East Asian Studies, and Director of the Center for East Asian Studies at McGill University in Montreal, Canada. His specialty is Chinese history, and his recent publications include *Science and Civilisation in China*, vol. 5 pt. 6 (*Missiles and Sieges*, 1994, co-authored) and *Five Lost Classics: Tao, Huang Lao and Yin-Yang in Han China* (1997).

Note: Frequently used words such as army, society, or warfare have not been indexed.

CPSIA information can be obtained at www.ICGtesting.com
Printed in the USA
BVOW02s1259180114

342069BV00002B/3/P

9 780674 006591